The Rule of Law in Action in Democratic Athens

The Rule of Law in Action in Democratic Athens

EDWARD M. HARRIS

OXFORD
UNIVERSITY PRESS

OXFORD
UNIVERSITY PRESS

Oxford University Press is a department of the University of Oxford.
It furthers the University's objective of excellence in research,
scholarship, and education by publishing worldwide.

Oxford New York
Auckland Cape Town Dar es Salaam Hong Kong Karachi
Kuala Lumpur Madrid Melbourne Mexico City Nairobi
New Delhi Shanghai Taipei Toronto

With offices in
Argentina Austria Brazil Chile Czech Republic France Greece
Guatemala Hungary Italy Japan Poland Portugal Singapore
South Korea Switzerland Thailand Turkey Ukraine Vietnam

Oxford is a registered trade mark of Oxford University Press
in the UK and certain other countries.

Published in the United States of America by
Oxford University Press
198 Madison Avenue, New York, NY 10016

Library of Congress Cataloging-in-Publication Data
Harris, Edward Monroe.
The rule of law in action in Democratic Athens. / Edward M. Harris.
pages cm.
Includes bibliographical references and index.
ISBN 978-0-19-989916-6 (hardcover)
1. Law—Greece—Athens—History—To 146 B.C. 2. Rule of law (Greek law)
3. Law, Greek. I. Title.
KL4115.A75H368 2013
347.38'505—dc23 2012036947

1 3 5 7 9 8 6 4 2

Printed in the United States of America
on acid-free paper

To the Memory of
Elias Psomas
(1938–2012)

Contents

Preface

THE ORIGINS OF this book go back to an essay on law and rhetoric I published almost two decades ago (Harris [1994b]). Since then, I have published several essays on the administration of justice in Classical Athens, some of which developed or modified the views advanced in that essay on law and rhetoric. A few years ago, I thought that it would be a good idea to revise these essays and publish them together in a book because all of them examine the rule of law in Classical Athens and provide an original approach to Athenian law. Chapter 1 is an extensively revised version of Harris (2007b); chapter 2 incorporates material from Harris (2005a); chapter 3 combines material from Harris (2006b) and Harris (forthcoming b); chapter 4 reproduces the text of Harris (2009/10a) with a few minor changes, chapters 5 and 6 draw on arguments presented in Harris (2000a) and Harris (2004b); chapter 7 is an extensively revised version of Harris (2007a) with new arguments; chapter 8 reproduces the text of Harris (forthcoming a); and chapter 9 includes some material from Harris (forthcoming c).

Many of these essays were presented as talks in several different countries. An earlier version of chapter 2 was delivered at *Symposion 2001* in Evanston, Illinois, and an early version of chapter 1 at *Symposion 2005* in Salerno, Italy. I would like to thank the organizers of these conferences, Robert Wallace, Michael Gagarin, and Eva Cantarella, for the invitations to speak. Earlier versions of other chapters were delivered at the Seminar for Legal History at New York University; the Institute of Classical Studies at London University; the Institut de droit romain (Université de Paris II); the Department of Classics and Ancient History at Durham University; the School of Archaeology, Classics, and Egyptology at the University of Liverpool; the Department of Classics at the University of Nottingham; the Department of Classics, Royal Holloway College, London; the Classical Association at its meeting in Durham (2011); the

Department of Law at the University of Milan; at the conference "The Eyesore of Aegina" on Aegina, Greece; at a conference on legal documents at the University of Trieste, Italy; and at the Department of Law at the University of Athens. A very early version of the final chapter was delivered as my Inaugural Address at Durham University in May 2007. I would like to thank all the institutions that invited me to speak for their kindness and generosity (especially the free meals).

Most of the manuscript was completed by early 2012. I have tried to consult all relevant works published before 2012, but I am sure that some items have escaped my notice.

I owe an enormous debt of thanks to Carlo Pelloso and Mirko Canevaro, who read the entire manuscript and offered much appreciated suggestions and encouragement. I am also grateful to David Lewis, who proofread the entire manuscript and checked the references, and to Vasia Psilakakou, who proofread chapters 1 and 9 and the bibliography. Peter Rhodes, Fred Naiden, and David Whitehead have read over earlier drafts of individual chapters and given helpful advice. A reader for Oxford University Press helped me correct minor errors and suggested ways of creating links between the chapters. I would also like to thank the excellent team at Oxford University Press (Stefan Vranka, Sarah Pirovitz, and India Gray) for their professional support in preparing the manuscript for publication.

Some may object to my practice of generally keeping the names of other scholars out of the text (except in the appendices) and referring to them in the footnotes. I have done this for two reasons. First, I think one should examine the views of other scholars and avoid personal attacks. Second, I believe scholars should concentrate on their own positive contributions to scholarship rather than on their criticisms of other individuals, which the general reader often finds tedious.

The transliteration of Greek names presents an insoluble problem. I generally use the forms of Greek names found in the Loeb translations but am not always consistent.

I owe a special debt of thanks to my wife Selene Psoma, who has given me loving support over the past four years when I was in the final stages of writing this book. Her patience and encouragement have meant a great deal. And our dog Brasidas has been a loyal companion.

I have dedicated this book to the memory of my father-in-law General Elias Psomas, who did not live to see its final publication. General Psomas joined the Greek armed forces as a young man and served as a pilot in the Greek Air Force. A talented leader, he rose to become Chief of Staff for the Greek Armed Forces in the 1980s. General Psomas was always a strong believer in democracy and the rule of law. He maintained these convictions during the dictatorship of the Greek Colonels from 1967 to 1974, often at the risk of imprisonment and torture. Selene and I miss him very much.

The Rule of Law in Action in Democratic Athens

Introduction

The hallmarks of a regime which flouts the rule of law are alas, all too familiar: the midnight knock on the door, the sudden disappearance, the show trial, the subjection of prisoners to genetic experiment, the confession extracted by torture, the gulag and concentration camp, the gas chamber, the practice of genocide or ethnic cleansing, the waging of aggressive war. The list is endless.

BINGHAM (2010) 9

THE RULE OF law was one of the most important cultural values in Athenian democracy. When delivering the funeral oration for the Athenian soldiers who fell at Lamia in 322 BCE, Hyperides (*Epitaphios* 25) declared: 'For men to be happy they must be ruled by the voice of law, not the threats of a man; free men must not be frightened by accusation, only by proof of guilt; and the safety of our citizens must not depend on men who flatter their masters and slander our citizens but on our confidence in the law' (trans. Cooper). In another funeral oration (this one probably not delivered), Lysias (2.19) praises the ancestors of the Athenians because 'they thought it characteristic of wild animals to gain power over each other through violence, but that men ought to define what is just by law, persuade each other with reason, and serve both these aims by submitting to the rule of law and being instructed by reason.'[1] Thucydides (2.37) attributes a similar idea to Pericles in the funeral oration he delivered in 430 BCE: 'In public life we do not violate the laws because we obey those in office at any time and the laws, especially those established to help those

1. All translations of Greek texts in this book are my own unless otherwise indicated. For the names of Greek authors and the titles of their works, I use the abbreviations found in H. G. Liddel and R. Scott, *A Greek-English Lexicon* (Oxford 1996). The only exception is the title of Aristotle's *Athenaion Politeia*, which I abbreviate *Ath. Pol.*

who are wronged.' In the Ephebic Oath, which the young men of Athens swore every year, each ephebe promises to obey the established laws, those magistrates who give prudent orders, and any laws that may be established prudently in the future.[2] The rule of law is also found in tragedy. When Creon invades Athenian territory with troops and attempts to seize Oedipus, Theseus comes to protect his suppliant and reminds Creon that he has come to a city that practices justice and does nothing without law (*k'aneu nomou*) (S. *OC* 913–14).[3]

The Athenians did not find the rule of law incompatible with the idea of popular sovereignty. In fact, they believed that the two ideals went hand in hand. Aeschines (3.6) asserts that when the Athenians obey the laws, the democracy remains safe. The same orator says that when the courts allow themselves to be distracted by irrelevant charges, the laws are neglected, and the democracy undermined (Aeschin. 1.179. Cf. 3.23 and D. 24.75–6). In his *Against Timocrates*, Demosthenes (24.215–6) goes so far as to claim that the power of Athens derived from its citizens' obedience to the laws:

> Although you should be angry with everyone who establishes shameful and wicked laws, you should be most angry with those who corrupt the laws that make our city weak or great. What are these laws? Those that punish wrongdoers and grant honors to the just. If all men were eager to do good for the community and ambitious to gain honors and awards for this, and if all were to refrain from criminal acts out of fear for the harm and penalties imposed on them, what prevents our city from being great? Does Athens not have more triremes than any Greek city? More hoplites? More cavalry? More revenue? More possessions? More harbors? What protects and preserves all these things? The laws. When the city obeys them, all these resources serve the common interest.

Isocrates (15.79) confidently affirms that the laws of Athens have been the source of many benefits not only for their city but also for the human race.

But did the Athenians have the same conception of the 'rule of law' as we have today? Or, by attributing the slogan the 'rule of law' to the Athenians, are we imposing an anachronistic modern idea on the ancient evidence? The

2. Rhodes and Osborne (2003) no. 88, lines 12–4.

3. Foxhall and Lewis (1996b) 7 claim that 'Law, for the Greeks, was a tool, not a master,' but this view is contradicted by passages like Hdt. 7.104.4.

only way to answer this question is to identify what modern scholars think are the basic features of the rule of law and to see whether the Athenian legal system under the democracy attempted to implement these features.[4] Even though legal theorists and political scientists differ on some points, most modern views about the rule of law share certain basic features.[5] One can divide modern attempts to define the term into 'thin definitions' and 'thick definitions.' 'Thin definitions' limit the term to the requirement of consistent application of fixed rules in adjudication and administration, equality before the law, and the accountability of officials. 'Thick definitions' are broader and include requirements to recognize basic human rights. Most writers nowadays adopt 'thick definitions,' though they may differ about which human rights deserve to be included in this definition.

The first feature agreed on by most writers is that the law should apply equally to all persons. In his list of the basic principles of the rule of law, Bingham includes the rule, 'The laws of the land should apply equally to all, save to the extent that objective differences justify differentiation.'[6] According to Dicey, the rule of law requires that 'no one is above the law and everyone is equal before the law regardless of social, economic, or political status.'[7] This principle is contained in an article in the *Déclaration des droits de l'homme* of 1789 ('Les hommes naissent et demeurent libres et égaux en droits'). There can be no question that the Athenians believed in this principle and followed it in their laws. According to Demosthenes (21.188), the Athenians enjoyed equality because of their laws (cf. D. 21.67). This principle was explicitly stated in the laws enacted in 403 BCE: 'It is not permitted to enact a law directed at an individual unless the same law applies to all Athenians.'[8] Even though this principle was not

4. Sealey (1982) 302 asserts that 'The Athenians achieved something more valuable and more fundamental than democracy. They achieved the rule of law.' Unfortunately, he never defines what he means by the 'rule of law,' does not examine modern discussions of the phrase, and does not compare modern views with ancient views of law.

5. Cohen (1995) 35 greatly exaggerates the differences among modern scholars about the rule of law and overlooks the areas of agreement.

6. Bingham (2010) 55–59.

7. Dicey (1885).

8. The law inserted into the text of And. 1.87 states that there can be an exception to this rule, 'if six thousand people vote,' but this document is a forgery—see Canevaro and Harris (2012) 117–8. The attempt of Hansen (1979) to find laws directed at an individual is not convincing. See Rhodes (1984). On the reply of Hansen (1985) to Rhodes see Canevaro and Harris (2012) 119, note 108.

explicitly stated until 403 BCE, it is implicit in the laws of Athens before that date. Several of the oldest laws in Athens, Draco's laws about homicide, begin with the words 'if anyone . . .' and make no distinction among different classes (D. 23.24, 38, 45, 60. Cf. *IG* i³ 104, lines 10, 27). A law dated to 485/4 contains several provisions that all begin with the same phrase 'if anyone . . .' (*IG* i³ 4, lines 6–8, 11–13, 15–6). There are many other examples from the fifth century, and one could add many examples from the fourth century.[9] This principle was not only implicit in the laws of Athens; it was recognized in literature and oratory. In a famous drinking song from the early fifth century, Harmodius and Aristogeiton are praised for killing the tyrant and making the Athenians 'equal before the law.'[10] In his Funeral Oration, Pericles boasts that 'in regard to disputes involving individuals all share equality (*to ison*) according to the laws (Th. 2.37.1. Cf. [Arist.] *Rhet. ad Alex.* 2.21.1424b15–6). In Euripides' *Suppliant Women* (433–4, 437. Cf. D. 51.11), Theseus, the ruler of Athens, tells the Herald from Thebes that 'when the laws are written, both the powerless and the wealthy have equal justice, and the lesser man with justice on his side prevails over the powerful man.' Equality before the law was obviously an Athenian ideal. It extended not only to all citizens but also to metics and foreigners as well.[11] In reality, metics and foreigners may have been at a disadvantage, but in principle they enjoyed equal access to the courts.[12]

Another key feature of the rule of law is that all officials are accountable for their actions.[13] This was certainly true for Classical Athens: all officials in Athens without exception were required to submit their accounts and their conduct was subject to judicial review (Aeschin. 3.12–27). Every official was required to submit his accounts to officials called the *logistai* who checked these accounts and received accusations of embezzlement and bribery. Anyone could also submit an accusation to officials

9. Fifth-century examples: *IG* i³ 10, 19–22; 19, lines 7–9; 34, lines 31–35; 41, lines 70–2; 58, lines 14–16; 63, lines 1–5; 78a, lines 7–8, 34–6, 57–9; 114, lines 12–3. Fourth-century examples: Harris (2006a) 46–7.

10. Ath. 15.695a–b.

11. Metics have access to justice at Athens: Whitehead (1977). For the rights of foreigners in Greek courts see Gauthier (1972).

12. Patterson (2000) argues that because metics did not have a network of family and friends, they would be at a disadvantage when pleading in court.

13. See for instance the definition of the rule of law formulated by the World Justice Project, http://www.worldjusticeproject.org: 'The government and its officials and agents are accountable under the law.'

called the *euthynoi* (Arist. *Ath. Pol.* 48.4–5). Miltiades was tried twice, shortly before the battle of Marathon and shortly after Marathon, and the second time fined heavily.[14] During the early years of the Peloponnesian War, Pericles exercised much power and influence, but he was still deposed from office and fined (Th. 2.65). As we will see in chapter 9, many more generals and politicians were put on trial in the following years. In the fourth century prosecutions and convictions of generals and politicians occurred with alarming frequency.[15] The Athenians and other Greeks recognized the principle that all magistrates should be accountable as early as the Archaic period: many laws from the Greek *poleis* from the sixth and early fifth centuries BCE contain penalties for officials who fail to perform their legal duties.[16]

A third basic feature of the rule of law is that the law be accessible to all. As Bingham states, 'the law must be accessible and so far as possible intelligible, clear and predictable.'[17] This has several aspects, but an important one is that all regulations are easy to read and to understand and are accessible.[18] The Athenians certainly endorsed this principle. In his speech *Against Leptines*, Demosthenes (20.93) says that the aim of the procedures for legislation is to ensure that 'opposing laws are repealed so that there is one law for each subject. This avoids confusion for private individuals, who would be at a disadvantage in comparison with people who are familiar with all the laws. The aim is to make points of law the same for all to read as well as simple and clear to understand.'[19] The Athenians put much effort into making the texts of laws accessible. The laws of Draco and Solon were

---

14. There is no reason to believe that the Areopagus controlled the *euthynai* procedure or had a general oversight of magistrates in this period. The three trials mentioned by Herodotus clearly took place before the Assembly or in a court (Hdt. 6.21.2; 104.4 [*dikasterion*]; 136.1). I plan to explore this topic elsewhere.

15. See Hansen (1975) 60.

16. See Harris (2006a) 18–21. For accountability of officials in Greek cities in the fifth century and later see Fröhlich (2004).

17. Cf. Fuller (1964) who says that two of the symptoms of the absence of the rule of law are failure to publicize or make known the rules of law and unclear or obscure legislation that is impossible to understand.

18. The discussion in this paragraph draws on the important essay of Sickinger (2004), which refutes Todd (1993) 55–8.

19. In this regard the Athenians appear to have anticipated the requirement of the World Justice Project, http://www.worldjusticeproject.org: 'The process by which the laws are enacted administered, and enforced is accessible, fair and efficient.'

written on *axones* and *kyrbeis*, which were probably made of wood, and were still in the center of Athens to consult in the late fifth century.[20] Laws pertaining to specific areas were posted next to the offices of the magistrates under whose jurisdiction they fell. Even though they were scattered in different offices, they were not difficult to find. In the fourth century, copies of all laws were kept in the Metroon, where anyone could consult them.[21] New procedures for legislation were enacted after 403 BCE, and one of the requirements was that copies of all proposals for new laws be displayed before the monument of the Eponymous Heroes in the center of the Agora (D. 20.94; 24.18).[22] Many laws were also on public display after being enacted: Athenian laws and decrees often contain publication formulae instructing officials to write them on large stone *stelai* and to place them in prominent places where all can read them.[23] For instance, the law of Nicophon (375/4) orders that its provisions be engraved on a stone stele and copies placed among the tables of bankers in the Agora and in the Piraeus in front of the stele of Poseidon (*SEG* 26:72, lines 44–7). Another law instructs the secretary of the Council to inscribe the law on a stele and place it in front of the Metroon, right in the center of Athens.[24] There is no reason to believe that these *stelai* were just symbolic monuments, which were intended only to impress but not to be read.[25] Several passages in court speeches indicate that litigants regularly consulted them when preparing their cases.[26]

When we examine the Judicial Oath in chapter 3, we will see that the Athenians also attempted to ensure that 'adjudicative procedures provided by the state should be fair.'[27] The accuser was required to present

---

20. On the *axones* and *kyrbeis* see Andrewes (1974a) and Stroud (1979) with the critique of Rhodes (1981) 131–35. Aristophanes refers to the *kyrbeis* in the *Birds* (1353–57). Davis (2011) argues that laws in Athens were first written on *kyrbeis*, then inscribed on *axones* during the revision of the laws starting in 410.

21. Lycurg. *Leocr.* 68 with Sickinger (1999) 149–52.

22. On the monument of the Eponymous Heroes see Shear (1970).

23. For these formulae see Liddel (2003). The decree of Teisamenus inserted into the text at And. 1.84 calls for laws to be inscribed on a wall, but this document is a forgery. See Canevaro and Harris (2012) 110–16.

24. Cf. the republication of Draco's law on Homicide—*IG* i^3 104, lines 4–10.

25. *Pace* Thomas (1989) 45–83. For an excellent critique of Thomas' primitivist approach see Pébarthe (2006).

26. See [D.] 47.71; [D.] 58.5–6.

27. Bingham (2010) 90–109.

his charges to the defendant and to provide him with all the evidence he planned to present in court. Judges swore not to be influenced by personal enmity or good will toward the litigants. Both accuser and defendant were given equal amounts of time to speak. The court consisted of judges selected at random to ensure impartiality.[28] In fact, in one notorious case we will study in chapter 6, the defendants were not given an adequate amount of time to address the charges, which led to the worst miscarriages of justice in Athenian history, a mistake the Athenians soon regretted. As we will see in chapter 9, there were weaknesses in the Athenian legal system, but these were rather the unforeseen consequences of measures that were, clearly, originally intended to ensure fairness in adjudication.

Another principle in modern conceptions of the rule of law is that there should be no punishment without law. For instance, according to Article 7 of the Treaty on European Union, 'no one shall be held guilty of any criminal offence on account of any act or omission which did not constitute an offence under national or international law at the time when it was committed.'[29] Article VII of the *Déclaration des droits de l'homme* of 1789 states 'Nul homme ne peut être accusé, arrêté, ni détenu que dans les cas déterminés par la Loi' ('No person can be accused, arrested, or detained except in the cases specified by the law'). Article VIII states 'nul ne peut être puni qu'en vertu d'une Loi établie et promulguée antérieurement au délit, et légalement appliquée ('no one can be punished except by virtue of a law enacted and promulgated prior to the commission of the offense and legally applied'). The principle that laws should not apply retroactively was recognized in Athenian law (D. 24.43). In fact, many Athenian laws contained a clause indicating that the statute was valid only 'in the future' (*to loipon*) or after a certain date (D. 24.43).[30] There was also a law that officials could not use an unwritten law (And. 1.87). This meant that an official could not punish someone for an offence not contained in a law passed by the Assembly (in the fifth century) or the Assembly and the *nomothetai* (in the fourth century) and recorded on a public document. Nor could someone bring a charge against a person unless he accused him of violating a specific law enacted by the Athenian people

28. For the methods of selecting judges see Arist. *Ath. Pol.* 63–69 with Rhodes (1981) 697–735.

29. Quoted in Bingham (2010) 73. Cf. Raz (1977) 198–99.

30. For the phrase *to loipon* in Athenian laws see Harris (2006a) 425–30.

(see chapter 3). There can be no question that the Athenians attempted to implement the basic features of the rule of law as they are understood today.[31]

On the other hand, one should not exaggerate the similarities between ancient and modern conceptions of the rule of law. Modern views are often based on a belief in universal human rights, which extend to all races, all social classes, and equally to women and men. For the Athenians the rule of law provided guarantees primarily to Athenian citizens. For instance, the rule against laws enacted for an individual requires only that laws be enacted for all Athenians (D. 23.86). The laws of Athens protected the rights of women. For instance, the law against outrage (*hybris*) explicitly includes women in its provisions (Aeschin. 1.15), and one speaker recalls a case in which the court sentenced a man to death for committing this crime against a woman (Din. 1.23). But women in general did not bring charges or conduct cases in court; they were represented by their husbands or male relatives. If a husband divorced his wife and refused to return her dowry or to provide maintenance, it was her male relatives who brought the charge. The laws of Athens guaranteed the freedom of citizens and metics by providing harsh punishments against those who tried to enslave them (Arist. *Ath. Pol.* 52.1), but these protections did not extend to those who were captured in war: the universal rule among the Greeks was that persons captured in battle belonged to the victors by right of conquest (Pl. *R.* 5.468a–b; Arist. *Pol.* 1.6.1255a6–7; X. *Cyr.* 7.5.73).

Another area in which the differences between the Athenian conception of the rule of law and modern conceptions are apparent is in regard to the use of torture. Over the centuries countries throughout the world have abolished the use of torture either to obtain evidence or as a punishment. France abolished torture in 1789, and the Eighth Amendment to the Constitution of the United States in the same year outlawed 'cruel and unusual punishments,' which included torture. According to Article 3 of the European Convention, 'no one shall be subjected to torture or to inhuman or degrading treatment or punishment.' In all these cases, the protection against torture extends to all human beings, not just to citizens.[32]

---

31. Cf. Cohen (1997) 33. Raz (1977) 199 adds the requirement that 'laws should be relatively stable.' For this ideal in Athenian law see D. 24.139–43. For attempts to ensure the stability of the laws by means of entrenchment clauses see Harris (2006a) 23–25.

32. For the abolition of torture see Bingham (2010) 14–7.

In democratic Athens, by contrast, only citizens were protected against torture (And. 1.43). Slaves and foreigners could be tortured.[33]

Some scholars have claimed that the Athenians had a 'rhetorical' approach to law because judges were dependent on the litigants for their knowledge of the laws, which could therefore be interpreted in very different ways.[34] This view collides with several objections. First, laws and decrees were passed at meetings of the Assembly, which all citizens could attend. As noted earlier, copies of new laws were posted at the statues of the Eponymous Heroes for all to read. One litigant tells the judges that they know the law because they enacted it (D. 42.18). Second, even though litigants quote from or paraphrase laws, it was the clerk who read out the text of laws and decrees to the court, not the litigant. What the judges heard from the clerk was the actual text, not an interpretation.[35] Third, the judges were not like modern jurors who may hear only one or two cases in a lifetime. Every year, six thousand judges were selected to serve for twelve months, during which they would hear dozens of cases. Unlike other offices in Athens in which one could serve only for a year, there was no prohibition against serving as a judge for several years in a row. To be sure, there was no formal training of judges, but repeated service on the courts would have given them a working knowledge of the law. This meant that the average judge was not dependent on a litigant for his knowledge of the law.[36] Fourth, if there had been a considerable amount of dispute about the meaning of laws, one would expect to find extensive discussion about the meaning of laws. However, most of the cases for which the extant speeches were written concern issues of fact, which reveals that, in the majority of cases, the accuser and defendant implicitly agreed about the meaning of the law under which the charge was brought.[37] Thus, there

---

33. For the torture of slaves see Thür (1977), Gagarin (1996), and Mirhady (2000). For the torture of a noncitizen see D. 18.132 with Harris (1995) 172. For the torture of noncitizens in homicide investigations see Bushala (1968).

34. Johnstone (1999); Wohl (2010) 2–4 and passim. In general, Wohl is interested mainly in rhetoric and pays little attention to legal procedures. For a trenchant critique of this book see Maffi (2009/10) 332–37.

35. Humphreys (2007) 156 ('Litigants quoted laws selectively and incompletely, subject to no control except the production of counter-quotations by the opposing side') both exaggerates and contradicts herself (cf. 152: 'Familiarity with Attic law was widespread owing to the jury system').

36. For the knowledge of Athenian judges see Harris (2010) 1–3.

37. See appendix 7.

is no reason to think that the Athenian view of the rule of law was largely 'rhetorical' and differed fundamentally from modern views.

The aim of this book is to study how the Athenians attempted to put the ideal of the rule of law into action and to understand the nature of litigation in its democratic context. Several recent books about the Athenian courts have concentrated mainly on Athenian social values, but they have paid less attention to the political ideal of the rule of law and to the procedures the Athenians followed to implement this ideal (e.g., Allen, Cohen, Christ, and Herman). This study moves beyond the study of rhetoric and ideology to examine how the law worked in action, both in the community as a whole and in the courts. One of the key themes is the importance of paying close attention to the precise features of legal procedures in order to understand how litigants behaved in daily life and made their arguments in court.

My approach is inspired by recent work in New Institutionalism, which stresses the role that rules and political procedures have in shaping the conduct of individuals in society. Writing in 1989 about work in political science in the previous four decades, March and Olsen found: 'From a behavioral point of view, formally organized political institutions have come to be portrayed simply as arenas within which political behavior, driven by more fundamental factors, occurs' (1). March and Olsen called for an approach that placed more emphasis on institutional analysis: 'Without denying the importance of both the social context of politics and the motives of individual actors, therefore, institutional analysis posits a more independent role for political institutions' (17). They note: 'Empirical observations seem to indicate that processes internal to political institutions, although possibly triggered by external events, affect the flow of history,' and 'political institutions define the framework within which politics takes place' (18). In contrast to some recent studies of the Athenian courts, which view them merely as arenas for social struggles among the elite or a place for negotiations between the elite and the masses, this book examines the legal rules and procedures that the Athenians created to implement their political ideals and their conception of justice. This book also demonstrates how the precise contours of those rules and procedures shaped the behavior and rhetoric of individuals both inside and outside of court. On the other hand, this study strives to avoid a simplistic functionalism. Even though the Athenians created these rules and procedures with specific goals in mind and tried to make these procedures suitable for achieving these goals, some of their decisions had unintended consequences, which we will study in the last chapter.[38] On the other hand, several handbooks of Athenian law (e.g., Lipsius, Harrison, MacDowell, and Todd) present the basic facts about Athenian laws in a static way without much attention to how they worked in practice. This study attempts to analyze how Athenian legal procedures worked (and in one case did not work) in daily life.

Though the main aim of the book is to enhance our understanding of the role of law in Athenian society, it also questions many basic assumptions about Athenian law in recent scholarship in North American and in the United Kingdom. These assumptions are (1) Athenian law was primarily concerned with procedure (e.g., Hansen, Gagarin, Osborne, Todd, Ober, and Cohen); (2) the main task of enforcement lay in the hands of private citizens (e.g., Osborne, Ober, Cohen, Hunter, and Christ); (3) the Athenians used the courts not to uphold the law but to pursue personal feuds (e.g., Cohen); and (4) the Athenian courts rendered ad hoc judgments and paid little attention to the letter of the law (e.g., Christ, Allen, and Lanni). As we will see, none of these assumptions are supported by a careful examination of the evidence.

The first chapter places the Athenian administration of justice in its broad political context. When analyzing the legal system of Classical Athens, one must first step back and ask, what kind of community was it? It makes a great deal of difference whether Classical Athens developed state institutions or not. Some scholars have claimed that Classical Athens was a 'stateless society' (e.g., Cartledge, Osborne, and Berent) in which social norms were enforced by self-help carried out by average citizens. As a result, social control often took the form of feuding (e.g., Cohen, Phillips). Chapter 1 shows that most policing was in the hands of magistrates acting in accordance with the laws and decrees of the Assembly. For instance, a study of all the extant decrees of the Assembly from the fifth century reveals that the Athenians entrusted the enforcement of regulations to officials. The literary sources from the fourth century present a similar picture. The Council of 500 and the Areopagus also played a major role in enforcing the law and detecting criminals. On the other hand, there were careful restrictions placed on the use of force by private citizens (*idiotai*), which was limited to a few exceptional circumstances. What made the enforcement of law democratic in Athens was not the widespread use of self-help by private citizens, but the restrictions placed on the use of force

38. For a functionalist approach see Ober (1989). For critiques of functionalism see March and Olsen (1989) 7–9.

by officials and the procedures enabling citizens to seek redress when officials misused their powers. A close study of the attempt of a trierarch to enforce an order of the Council illustrates how democratic accountability had a major influence on the ways officials went about their duties.

The second chapter takes a sociological approach and examines the ways individuals used litigation. Like many other Greek city-states, Athens allowed private citizens to bring public charges against individuals.[39] But how did citizens view this right? Did they see it as a public duty aimed at serving the community's interests by enforcing the law? Or did they consider it an opportunity to pursue feuds? Did Athenian social attitudes discourage aggressive behavior and the use of the courts to pursue vendettas? Or were the courts viewed as merely another arena for social competition? According to some scholars (in particular D. Cohen) Athenian society was an agonistic society, which encouraged aggressive male behavior and litigation initiated solely on the basis of private enmity (*echthra*). The aim of the legal system was therefore not to enforce the law but to channel feuding into an arena where conflicts could be regulated (but not necessarily resolved). This chapter starts with an analysis of recent work on Athenian social values (especially that of G. Herman), which shows that the Athenians valued co-operation and condemned aggressive behavior. The pursuit of private enmity was viewed as a threat to public order. The chapter goes beyond recent work to show that the Athenians enacted laws and created procedures to discourage frivolous lawsuits and to put these values into practice. Above all, the legal system was constructed in such a way as to discourage feuding.

The final section of the chapter shows how these rules and procedures influenced the ways individuals used the legal system. A careful analysis of several quarrels between Athenian citizens shows that there is no evidence for the use of the courts to pursue feuds. The kind of prolonged hostility between groups organized by kinship, vicinage, or clientage such as one finds, for instance, in medieval Icelandic and Norse epic, the classic examples of feuding societies, is absent from Athenian society. On the contrary, Athenian litigants often express their reluctance to go to court and claim that they have tried to avoid continuing disputes. The only evidence we have for feuding comes from sixth-century Athens, before the advent of strong centralized institutions and the dissolution of the power

39. On the volunteer prosecutor in other Greek city-states see Rubinstein (2003).

of wealthy families with their networks of relatives and dependents. After the reforms of Cleisthenes in the late sixth century, state institutions in Classical Athens were strong enough to prevent and discourage this type of behavior.

The second part of the study examines how the Athenians applied the law in their courts. The third chapter examines the Judicial Oath, which provides the best evidence for the way judges viewed their task. The Judicial Oath contained four basic pledges: (1) to vote according to the laws and decrees of the Athenian people, (2) to listen to both sides equally, (3) to vote with one's most just judgment, and (4) to vote only about the charges in the indictment. The third pledge has given rise to some debate. Some scholars have claimed that this clause gave judges the right to ignore the law and to vote in accordance with their own conscience (Lanni [2006], Christ [1998a]), but this view is not supported by an analysis of the extant speeches delivered in court. The clause is rarely mentioned in speeches and applied only in cases in which the laws did not give sufficient guidance. The next section of the chapter examines the fourth pledge in the oath, which has received very little attention from scholars. To understand this pledge, it is necessary to analyze the plaint (*engklema*) and its role in litigation, which recent work has also neglected. Every accuser who wished to initiate a charge had to present a plaint containing basic information, such as his full name, the name of the defendant, and the name of the action he was bringing. Most important, the accuser had to indicate how the defendant had violated the law and had to follow the terms of the statute when describing his illegal actions. The pledge to vote only about the charges made in the plaint meant that the judges could only consider whether the defendant had violated the law. This pledge thereby required the judges to disregard irrelevant issues such as public service and character unless they had a bearing on the legal charge in the plaint. This had a major effect on the arguments the litigants used in court and on how judges decided cases. Because litigants swore an oath to keep to the point, that is, to address only the charges in the plaint, they tend not to mention public service and their social background except when they are relevant to the legal charges. The Judicial Oath and the plaint, therefore, played an important role in making all Athenians equal before the law. The only stage of a trial in which one was allowed to place emphasis on public service was during the *timesis* phase of a public case (*graphe*). Some scholars have claimed that trials in Athens were social struggles in which litigants paid little attention to the law, but instead attempted to influence the court by advertising their credentials as powerful leaders (e.g., Ober [1989], Cohen [1995], Christ [1998]). The Judicial Oath and the plaint were designed to ensure that trials in court would ignore politics and concentrate on enforcing the law. In this way the Judicial Oath served to promote equality before the law, which was the democratic approach to law.

The fourth chapter examines the structure of Athenian laws and demonstrates that they are more concerned with substantive matters than with aspects of procedure. Many scholars in North America and the United Kingdom believe that Athenian law was mostly concerned with procedure, but an analysis of all the laws mentioned in the speeches of the Attic Orators and those preserved in inscriptions reveals the contrary. The only area in which there is a greater emphasis on procedure is in homicide law; in all other areas (public law, inheritance, commercial relations, and religion) there is an equal or greater emphasis on substantive matters (i.e., prescribing rights and duties in daily life). The Athenians did not therefore use their laws only to provide a way to get a dispute into court. The aim of legislation was to give orders about how to act in daily life and rules about how to resolve conflicts in the courts. The aim of law was to shape the behavior of everyone in society.

The fifth and sixth chapters examine the approach of litigants (chapter 5) and the courts (chapter 6) to law's 'open texture.' Although litigants could not ignore the law, they might attempt to stretch the meaning of the language in a statute to apply to cases not normally viewed as coming under the statute. These arguments reveal that litigants paid close attention to the precise wording of statutes and expected the courts to do likewise. On the other hand, when two litigants differed about the meaning of a statute or when an accuser attempted to interpret the law in a new and unusual way, the Athenian legal system did not give the official who received the charge the right to dismiss a case unless the plaint did not conform to the language of the law. The democratic approach to justice required that the courts, which had at least several hundred judges if not more, had the power to decide about how to interpret the law. This meant that the Athenian *dikastes* played the role of both judge and juror (or the role of a judge at a bench trial) in a modern court and decided questions of law and fact. Yet, even though litigants might attempt to stretch the meaning of the law, the judges tended to favor litigants who stuck to the traditional or literal meaning of the law. The judges did not view their role as lawgivers, who might create law by their decisions. Nor did they make ad hoc decisions. Their job was to serve as guardians of the laws passed by the people of Athens in the Assembly. This was the democratic conception of law.

The seventh chapter studies how the Athenians attempted to formulate ways of coping with law's 'open texture,' that is, the potential ambiguity of statutes: litigants often use precedents to justify an interpretation of statute or appeal to the intent of the lawgiver. Some scholars (Todd [1993], Lanni [2006]) have claimed that the Athenian courts were not interested in consistency and tended to judge cases on an ad hoc basis. True, litigants do not often cite previous cases in forensic oratory, but that is because most trials concerned questions of fact. On the other hand, when questions concerning the interpretation of statute arise, it is not unusual for litigants to appeal to precedents or to the intent of the lawgiver to support their legal arguments. In modern courts in common law jurisdictions, precedents are a way for judges to create law. In Classical Athens, on the other hand, litigants used precedents to show that their interpretation of the law was the traditional one, accepted by other citizens. In Athenian democracy, the right to enact laws was the power of the Assembly.

The eighth chapter examines to what extent the Athenian courts took other factors into account when judging cases. Some scholars have claimed that the Athenians took a *stricti iuris* approach to the law and did not take extenuating circumstances into account (Meyer-Laurin [1965], Lanni [2006]). The chapter begins with a careful reading of Aristotle's analysis of 'fairness' (*epieikeia*) in the *Nicomachean Ethics* and the *Rhetoric* and draws on an important essay by J. Brunschwig. Fairness was not a doctrine that attempted to undermine the authority of the law or placed the law of the city in opposition to the unwritten laws or the common law of mankind. Nor did the application of fairness introduce nonlegal factors into adjudication. Rather, fairness dealt with the problem of treating exceptions to the general rule contained in a specific written law. The rest of the chapter shows how litigants used arguments based on fairness and how the courts sometimes took extenuating circumstances into account. The chapter also provides insights into the relationship between Aristotle's *Rhetoric* and Athenian legal practice. It also sheds light on the meaning of the Judicial Oath. When the judges swore to decide according to the laws of Athens, they did not just consider the law under which the accuser had brought his case. They could also take into account general principles of justice implicit in the laws of Athens as a whole. In this way, they avoided a rigid positivist approach to law.

The ninth and final chapter looks at the breakdown of the rule of law during the Peloponnesian War and its impact on the Athenian military.

The chapter begins with Thucydides' observations about the change in Athenian politics after the death of Pericles. According to Thucydides, the leaders who came to power after 429 BCE competed with one another for power but neglected the interests of the state. One of their tactics was *diabole*, the use of the courts to bring false charges against their political opponents. This was a dangerous innovation in Athenian politics. To illustrate the difference between Cleon and previous Athenian politicians, the chapter examines the sources of political power in democratic Athens prior to 431 (military leadership, public largesse, foreign connections, and family support). What is striking is that before 431 leading politicians rarely (if ever) used the courts to attack their enemies and preferred to employ ostracism to send them into exile. This changed in the 420s when Cleon introduced new tactics and broke old taboos by prosecuting his enemies in court. He was able to take advantage of the weaknesses of the courts in public cases to intimidate generals and other opponents. Others imitated this radical approach after his death in 422 and drove talented generals like Alcibiades into exile. These attacks by politicians on generals culminated in the trial of the generals at Arginousai in 406, which was directly responsible for the crushing defeat at Aegospotamoi in 405 and led to the surrender of Athens in 404. Even though the Athenians attempted to achieve the rule of law, their failure to secure the rights of individuals against the will of the majority in times of tension and crisis and to protect generals against unscrupulous attacks by politicians contributed to the defeat and overthrow of the democracy. The chapter contributes to our understanding of the reasons *why* Athenian democracy was ultimately a failure. It also reveals the unintended consequences of certain features in Athenian legal procedures, which contained weaknesses revealed only in times of stress. Some writers in the fourth century thought that the flaws in democratic institutions were the source of Athens' problems. As the chapter shows, it was the problems inherent in the Athenian legal system that had a negative impact on the Athenian armed forces and helped bring about the defeat of democracy.

PART ONE

The Political and Social Contexts of Athenian Law

I

Was Athens a State or a Stateless Community?

THE POLITICAL CONTEXT OF ATHENIAN LAW

WHAT KIND OF community was Classical Athens? The Athenians themselves called their community a *polis,* a term that some modern scholars translate 'city-state.' This translation implies that the community of Athens was a state in the modern sense of the term. Is this translation justified? According to recent political theory, a community must possess three basic features to be called a state.[1] First, a state must have clearly marked geographical borders. Second, a state must have citizens, that is, a set of members who have the right to participate in its decision-making and enjoy certain rights that non-members (foreigners, resident aliens, etc.) do not. Third, there must be a distinction between private citizens and officials, who represent the interests of the state and have in the words of Max Weber 'a monopoly of legitimate physical violence within defined borders.'[2] The state must therefore have a set of officials who are authorized to use force to uphold the legal order.

There can be no question that the *polis* of Athens had a set of borders that were recognized by Athenians and foreigners alike. When King Archidamus of Sparta led an army of Peloponnesian allies in 431 BCE to begin war with Athens, he and his soldiers knew very well when they entered Athenian territory. Before entering Attica, the king sent a man named Melesippus to ask the Athenians if they were willing to yield to Spartan demands, but the Athenians refused to receive any herald while the Spartan army was in the field and told him to be outside their borders before

1. For the three features see Hansen (1998) 37–40 with references to recent works of political theory.

2. Weber (1972) 822.

the end of the day. The Athenians further said they would receive an embassy once the Spartans returned to their own territory.[3] Even though the two sides were enemies and disagreed about many issues, the Athenians and the Spartans had no difference of opinion about where Athenian territory began and where it ended. The Athenians also made a clear legal distinction between citizens (*politai*) and non-citizens, who were divided into metics and foreigners (*xenoi*).[4] Citizens were enrolled on deme registers as soon as they reached the age of eighteen and had the right to sit in the Council and Assembly, serve as judges in the law courts, hold one of many political offices, and own land in Attica.[5] Those who were metics and foreigners were not entitled to these privileges.

But did the representatives of the Athenian state have a monopoly of legitimate force? In recent years some have claimed that the ancient *polis* in general and Athens in particular was not a state but rather a stateless community because it did not meet this criterion.[6] One scholar has gone so far as to assert that in Classical Athens 'there was no equivalent to the authority of the state, no attempt to monopolize the use of force.'[7] Another believes that 'In Athens there was no such clear division between state and civil society . . . not even a conception of the state as distinct from the community of citizens. There was no state of Athens and Attica, only the Athenians.'[8] Because there was virtually no state, it is therefore believed that 'very often arguments were settled, violence quelled, and miscreants apprehended without the intervention of the authorities at all.'[9] In particular, 'the apprehension of criminals and other offenders . . . generally speaking . . . was left to the private initiative of individuals who caught or had knowledge of lawbreakers. An arrest is then a classic instance of self-help since it required the use of force.'[10] This leads to the conclusion that

3. Th. 2.12.1–2. Note also the boundaries (*horia*) mentioned at Th. 2.12.3. For the boundaries of Greek *poleis* see Rousset (1994).

4. For the status of metics see Whitehead (1977).

5. For the registration of citizens see Arist. *Ath. Pol.* 42.1–2 with Feyel (2009).

6. E.g. Manville (1994) 23: 'the polis was not a "state" in the modern sense of the word, but rather a unique kind of sociopolitical organization.' What he means by this term is not altogether clear.

7. Osborne (1985a) 7. Lintott (1982) 26 holds a similar view.

8. Wood (1996) 128.

9. Hunter (1994) 120.

10. Hunter (1994) 134.

'most of the major functions of policing Athens from investigations to prosecutions fell to citizens themselves'[11] and that 'policing was done by self-help and self-defense (that is, with the help of friends, neighbors, family).'[12] As a result, there existed at Athens nothing equivalent to the modern police force.[13] In a society such as this, one cannot therefore speak of 'the rule of law' because the Athenians had no officials whose duty it was to enforce the law. Private individuals brought their disputes into court to pursue feuds with their enemies, not to maintain public order. Indeed, the courts had little to do with substantive law and punishing lawbreakers but aimed only to distribute honor and status: 'the courts can be seen to be a publicly visible, non-violent, mechanism for determining the social position of the parties within the community.'[14]

This chapter challenges this primitivist view of the community of Athens and shows that in regard to the monopoly of force the *polis* of Athens qualified as a 'state' in the modern sense of the term.[15] First, it shows that the Athenians made a clear distinction between the public sphere and the private sphere and between officials (*archontes*), who had the primary responsibility for maintaining public order, and private citizens (*idiotai*). It was the duty of these officials to act in accordance with the laws, that is, those rules enacted by the deliberative bodies of the Athenian state, the Council and the Assembly. Second, it demonstrates that in laws and decrees passed by the Athenian Assembly the main responsibility for enforcing regulations was placed in the hands of public officials, not private individuals. Third, it studies the role of the Areopagus and the Council in investigating crime and arresting offenders. Fourth, it analyzes the

11. Hunter (1994) 149. Cf. Hunter (2000) 21.

12. Berent (2000) 261. Berent's position is endorsed by Cartledge (1999). Cf. Todd (1993) 79: 'The detection and prosecution of offenses at Athens remained at all times the responsibility of private individuals.'

13. E.g. Badian (1970) 851; Finley (1983) 18–20; Ober (1989) 300; Christ (1998b) 521; Fisher (1998) 77; Berent (2000) 260–61; Lanni (2006) 31. Todd (1993) 79 notes the Scythian archers 'performed some of the functions which we would associate with the police,' but asserts (without proof) that 'the role of the archers within the administration of justice was minimal.'

14. Osborne (2000) 76. Cf. Osborne (2000) 85–6: 'The concept of law (sc. at Athens) being primarily the regulation of relations between citizens rather than the control of human conduct.'

15. The findings of this chapter confirm in part the analysis of Hansen (1998) and Hansen (2002), studies that do not examine the evidence presented here.

laws about the use of force by private individuals and reveals that its use was restricted to a few exceptional circumstances, as it is in modern societies. This chapter looks only at the use of force and the imposition of fines to make arrests, to enforce compliance to the law, and to carry out legal judgments. The next chapter examines the role of private citizens to bring public actions to punish crimes. As we will see, even though the laws of Athens gave private individuals the right to prosecute criminals in court, they did not allow private citizens to use physical force in enforcing the law except in certain highly restricted circumstances. These officials might act on the basis of information given to them by private citizens (just as the police do in modern states), but the primary responsibility for day-to-day policing Athens lay mainly in the hands of public officials.

I

The Athenians made a careful distinction between the public and the private sphere.[16] In his Funeral Oration, Pericles contrasts Athenian conduct in private and public life. In private life the Athenians are easygoing and tolerant of others; they are not suspicious of their neighbors' activities and, when they pursue pleasure, do not grow angry or make them uncomfortable with frowning looks. In public life, however, they do not violate the law because they fear its penalties and obey those in office and the laws.[17] Private interests and the public good were not necessarily identical. When speaking to the Athenians during the plague of 430, Pericles draws a contrast between the two spheres; he describes how an individual may enjoy temporary good fortune while the community is being destroyed and how a person may experience private good fortune in a city that prospers.[18] Demosthenes (20.57) tells the court that there are different standards in public and private life; the city decides about a person's worth in

16. For the distinction between public and private and its implications see Hansen (1998) 86–91.

17. Th. 2.37.2–3. Pericles (Th. 2.37.1) also contrasts lawsuits, which concern disputes about individuals (*idia diaphora*) decided according to the laws, and magistrates, who are concerned with matters affecting the community (*koina*). For an analysis of the contrasts in this passage see Harris (2006a) 29–40.

18. Th. 2.60.2–4. Cf. Th. 2.44.3 where Pericles encourages parents who have lost sons in war to have more children; in private life new children will help them to forget the departed and at the same time prevent the city from losing manpower needed for public security.

a different way than a private individual does: 'In private life, each of us decides who is worthy to become his son-in-law or some other relation, and these questions are determined by certain laws and social attitudes. In public life, however, the people in the community decide who treats them well and protects their interests not on the basis of family or reputation but by their actions.' There are different principles for each sphere. In private life, one takes into account a person's family and social status when making decisions about marriage; these considerations do not apply in public life where service to the community is the only matter that counts.[19] According to Aeschines (1.30), the lawgiver thought that the man who did a bad job in running his private household would manage public affairs in the same way; it was impossible for the same person to be dishonest in private life but effective in public affairs.[20] In the legal system there was a strict distinction between private actions and public actions:

> There are two categories, men of Athens, into which the laws of all cities fall. One of these categories regulates our relations with one another, the way we conduct commercial exchanges, the rules we lay down about what must be done in the private sphere, in short, the way we live with one another. The other regulates the way each one should conduct the city's public affairs should he wish to be involved in politics and declare his concern for the city. The former kind of laws, those about private life, is mild and generous in the interests of the majority. The latter take the opposite approach for those in public affairs; they are firm and harsh to protect your interests.[21]

This distinction between the two spheres was also reflected in the penalties for defendants. In private suits, the successful plaintiff received an award of damages; in public suits a penalty was paid to the state (Isoc. 20.2).

19. In the Funeral Oration that Thucydides (2.37) attributes to Pericles, the Athenians are praised for granting honors to men not because of their membership in a class but on the basis of merit.

20. Compare Sophocles *Antigone* 661–62.

21. Compare the tripartite distinction among three kinds of legal dispute in an Athenian treaty with Selymbria dated to 408 (*IG* i³ 118, lines 22–25): those brought by private citizens against private citizens, those brought by private citizens against the community, and those brought by the community against private citizens.

In his speech *On the Crown*, Demosthenes (18.210) reminds the judges that one does not decide private cases and public cases in the same spirit. 'You, men of the court, must not judge private cases and public cases in the same frame of mind. You should decide about the legal matters of daily life in the light of private laws and actions, but matters of public policy in the light of the honors gained by your ancestors.'

To carry out the laws of the community, the Athenians appointed hundreds of magistrates and distinguished them from private individuals.[22] The contrast between officials and private individuals occurs in both literary texts and inscriptions. Lycurgus (*Leocr.* 79) divides the political structure of Athens into three parts: officials, judges, and private citizens. An Athenian treaty with Neapolis in Thrace dated to 410/09 promises protection for all the citizens of Neapolis against harm done either by officials or private citizens.[23] In the Charter of the Second Athenian League (378) the Athenians promise to release any property in the territory of their allies belonging to them, whether it be private (*idia*) or public (*demosia*), and forbids any Athenian to acquire or accept as security property in their territory either privately or publicly. It is also forbidden to move or put to the vote any proposal to overturn any part of the decree; this prohibition applies to every Athenian, either official (*archon*) or private individual (*idiotes*).[24] There was a hierarchical relationship between officials and private individuals: officials gave orders to private individuals, and private individuals pledged to obey them. In the Funeral Oration, Pericles praises the Athenians for their obedience to the authorities and to the laws (Th. 2.37.3). Every year the young men of Athens who became ephebes swore to heed the commands of those exercising power prudently.[25]

Special rules, which did not apply to private individuals, applied to officials. It was far worse to insult an official than a private individual.[26] If someone slandered a private individual, the victim could only bring a private action for damages; if he slandered a *thesmothetes*, one of the nine

22. For officials at Athens see Hansen (1980a) and Develin (1989). For the distinction between officials and private citizens (*idiotai*) see Rubinstein (1998).

23. *IG* i³ 101, lines 52–54.

24. *IG* ii² 43, lines 25-30, 35–41, 51–54.

25. Rhodes and Osborne (2003) no. 88: 11–12. This clause however gave citizens the right to disobey officials who were acting illegally. See Harris (2006a) 59–60.

26. [Arist.] *Problems* 952b28–32.

archons, he might lose his citizenship rights.[27] The reason for this difference is that 'the man who commits this crime (against an official) also insults the laws, your public crown, and the name of the city. The title of Thesmothete belongs to no individual, but to the city' (D. 21.32).When someone struck an archon, the penalty was the same; when he struck a private individual, all the victim could do was to bring a private suit.[28] Only officials had the right to administer public property.[29] When Meidias blocked and nailed up the entrances to the *skene* in the Theater of Dionysus, Demosthenes (21.17) exclaimed that it was outrageous for a private individual to treat public property in this way. To mark their special status and set them apart from ordinary citizens, officials wore crowns.[30] To make it clear which positions counted as magistracies as opposed to temporary appointments, the law went into considerable detail. Every position that was filled by election in the Assembly or by lot administered by the *thesmothetai* in the Theseum was included, as well as all who undertook any public business for more than thirty days or presided over a court (Aeschin. 3.13–14). Officials underwent a special scrutiny of their qualifications, which were different from the minimal qualifications required for citizenship.[31] After their term of office, they were required to submit their accounts to the *logistai* (public accountants). If anyone had a charge to make against them, he could bring it to the *euthynoi*.[32]

It was the duty of officials to follow the law. Each year the new members of the Council swore to perform their duties according to the laws (X. *Mem.* 1.1.18). The incoming archons swore a similar oath (Arist. *Ath. Pol.* 55.5). The stress in these oaths is on maintaining the rule of law, not promoting democratic ideology. When officials received honors for their performance of their duties, they were commended for carrying out their

27. D. 21.32. MacDowell (1990) 250 thinks the law only applied to the nine archons. There was another law about insulting officials in their office, which was punished with a fine (Lys. 9.6). For speculation about the relationship between these two laws see Todd (2007) 592–93.

28. D. 21.32 with MacDowell (1990) 250.

29. For public property in Athens see Lewis (1990).

30. Aeschin. 1.19; D. 21.33 with MacDowell (1990) 252.

31. For scrutiny of officials, see Aeschin. 3.15 and Arist. *Ath.Pol.* 55.2–5 with Feyel (2009). For the minimal qualifications for citizenship see Arist. *Ath. Pol.* 42.

32. For the procedure of the audit (*euthynai*) see Aeschin. 3.18–22; Arist. *Ath. Pol.* 48.3–5.

tasks 'according to the laws.'[33] The laws gave officials powers but also placed restrictions on their conduct that did not apply to private citizens. The official who had not yet submitted his accounts was not allowed to leave the country, dedicate property, make a votive offering, have himself adopted, or dispose of his property by will.[34] If officials did not carry out the laws they were required to uphold, they could be severely punished. The life of the private individual was relatively safe, but the life of the politician was more dangerous because he could face charges that could not be brought against private individuals.[35] Average citizens had the right to denounce to the Council any official who did not follow the laws. If the Council voted against the official, the matter was referred to the court for trial.[36] The Assembly took a vote about the conduct of officials once every *prytany*, that is, ten times a year; if the official did not win a vote of confidence, he was deposed and stood trial.[37]

The Athenians had a clear conception of the difference between the public realm, which included everything that affected the collective interests of the Athenians, and the private realm, which covered the personal concerns of individuals.[38] To serve the public interest, the community created officials, who represented the state and had special powers, and who were carefully distinguished from private citizens. The question now arises: which group had the primary responsibility for enforcing the law?

II

The best way to determine who enforced the law is to examine the actual statutes and decrees that laid down rules for all Athenian citizens and inhabitants of Attica. What one should not do is to draw broad conclusions

33. See, for example, *SEG* 35:64 (= Schwenk [1985] 49), line 14 (337/6) for a secretary of the *prytaneis*; *IG* ii² 330 + 445 (= Schwenk [1985] 18), lines 34–35 (335/4) for Hipparchs and Phylarchs; *Agora* 16:87, lines 6–7 (c. 325) for a *thesmothete*; *IG* ii² 1257, col. II.3, line 7 (324/3) for a *hieropoios*; *IG* ii² 514, lines 7–8 (end of fourth century) for members of the Council; *IG* ii² 1159, lines 13–14 (303/2) for a *sophronistes*; *IG* ii² 1194, lines 9–10 (c. 300) for a demarch.

34. Aeschin. 3.21.

35. D. 10.70.

36. For this form of *eisangelia* see Arist. *Ath. Pol.* 45.2; Antiphon 6.35.

37. Arist. *Ath. Pol.* 43.4; 61.2.

38. There was of course some public regulation of private life, but that does not invalidate the distinction. See Hansen (1998) 90–91.

from a handful of anecdotes found in a few orations.[39] Let us begin with the law of Nicophon on silver coinage, which was passed in 375/74.[40] The main official responsible for implementing the law is a public slave called the tester (*dokimastes*), who was to sit near the tables, that is, where the bankers conducted their business in the Agora, or in the Council when payments were made to the *polis* (lines 4–8). The tester is ordered to evaluate any coins given to him for examination. After testing them, he should return the genuine ones, but keep the counterfeit coins, cut them in two, and turn them over to the Mother of the Gods (lines 8-13). If the tester does not perform his duties, the convenors of the people are to give him fifty lashes (lines 13–16). In the event that someone refuses to accept silver coins approved by the tester, all his goods on display that day are to be confiscated, presumably by officials (lines 16–18). All charges (*phaseis*) about matters in the grain market are to be made to the grain-wardens (*sitophylakes*), all those about matters in the Agora and the rest of the city to the convenors of the people, and all those about matters in the port (*emporion*) to the overseers of the port (lines 18–23). The archons have the power to decide cases for amounts of less than ten drachmas. For larger sums, they must bring the case before the court (lines 18–26). If the offender is a slave, the officials only are instructed to give him fifty lashes (lines 30–32). If the various officials assigned to carry out the law do not perform their duties, a private citizen can report them to the Council, which has the power to impose a fine up to 500 drachmas and to remove the offender from office (lines 32–36). There will also be a tester in the Piraeus, but he too will be supervised by the Overseers of the Port (lines 36–44). In the final clause of the law, the secretary of the Council is instructed to destroy any decree that is contrary to Nicophon's law (lines 55–56).[41]

The primary responsibility for implementing and enforcing the law lies in the hands of a public slave, the tester, the convenors who supervise

---

39. For an analysis of the anecdotes on which Hunter (1994) 120–24 bases her view that private citizens did most of the policing in Athens see appendix 1.

40. For the text and commentary see Stroud (1974).

41. Note that this task is usually assigned to officials, not to *ho boulomenos* (the average citizen). See *IG* ii^2 43, lines 31–35 (Council); 116, lines 39–40 (treasurers). For a similar clause in *IG* ii^2 98, lines 9–12 where the name of a board of officials should probably be restored. One should note, however, that the Athenians under the democracy rarely instructed officials to destroy the texts of laws and decrees. See Bolmarcich (2007).

him, the grain-wardens, the secretary of the Council, and the Council, which supervises all these officials. Private individuals can provide information to these officials and receive rewards, but it is the officials who enforce the law by confiscating counterfeit coins and the goods of merchants who do not accept good coins. The officials alone have the power to impose fines and have slaves whipped. Private initiative plays a role only in reporting offenses to officials or to the Council, but private individuals may not use physical force to punish those who break the law. It is public officials who do most of the work of detecting counterfeit coins and carrying out the sanctions contained in the law.

One could also cite the duties of the ten *astynomoi*, who maintained order and enforced regulations for the entire city of Athens (Arist. *Ath. Pol.* 50.2).[42] One of their duties was to supervise the hiring of women who played the flute, harp, or lyre and keep their fees to no more than two drachmas. They kept watch on those who collected excrement or garbage to see that they did not dump anything too close to the city. They also enforced building regulations to stop construction that encroached on public roads or created drainage problems. Finally, they had a force of public slaves to pick up corpses found on the roads and remove them for burial. Another group of officials named the *agoranomoi* exercised an extensive jurisdiction over buying and selling in the marketplace (Arist. *Ath. Pol.* 51.1). There were ten *agoranomoi*; five stationed in the city and five in the Piraeus.[43] Their duties may have extended to regulating the price of commodities.[44]

Although Aristotle's *Constitution of the Athenians* lists the duties of the *agoranomoi* and the *astynomoi*, it does not indicate how they carried them out. More detailed information is found in an inscription containing a decree of the Assembly passed in the year 320 (*IG* ii^2 380). The decree transfers some of the duties of the *astynomoi* to the *agoranomoi* and instructs them how to carry out their duties. It thus gives some indication about how both boards of officials enforced the law. The Assembly orders the *agoranomoi* to keep the wide streets where the procession for Zeus the

42. For discussion and references to other evidence about their activities see Rhodes (1981) 573–74. Athens was not the only city where *astynomoi* had the responsibility for enforcing extensive municipal regulations. For Pergamum see *OGIS* 483 with Klaffenbach (1954).

43. For their duties see Rhodes (1981) 575–76.

44. See Bresson (2000) 151–208. For the duties of the *agoranomoi* in other *poleis* see Migeotte (2005).

Savior and Dionysus takes place clean and in good shape (lines 19–23). They have the power to force those who dump pots into the street to clean up their mess in any way they order (lines 25–8). The next clause deals with financial matters, then prohibits any dumping into the streets and singles out excrement in particular. The penalties are fifty lashes for slaves and most likely a fine for free persons (this part of the inscription is fragmentary). There is no provision at all for private initiative in this decree; the only ones with the power to enforce these regulations are officials. They may have acted on information provided by private citizens in the same way that the police in modern societies rely on tips or statements made by average citizens. But the task of implementing the decree's provisions is entrusted to officials and the power to impose fines on free men and physical punishment on slaves lies with them alone.

To supervise the use of weights and measures, the Athenians had five *metronomoi* in the city and five in the Piraeus (Arist. *Ath. Pol.* 51.2).[45] Aristotle's *Constitution of the Athenians* does not describe how they carried out their duties, but an inscription from the end of the second century BCE gives detailed regulations about the enforcement of standard weights and measures (*IG* ii^2 1013). It is unlikely that these regulations changed very much over time; many of its provisions therefore are probably tralatician with minor changes to take account of modifications in standards. The magistrates responsible for implementing this law are to make sample measures for wet and dry goods and weights and to compel all those who buy and sell to use them (lines 7–9). The law is comprehensive: it applies to sellers in the Agora, in workshops, in retail shops, in wine shops, and storehouses (line 9). Magistrates cannot make weights larger or smaller than these prescribed weights (lines 10–12). If the magistrates do not comply, they are to owe one thousand drachmas to Demeter and Kore (lines 12–13). Private citizens have the right to report the property of those officials who incur the fine (lines 13–14), but do not otherwise appear to play a role in enforcing the use of official weights and measures. The task of checking to see that everyone uses them is placed in the hands of officials (lines 14–15), and the Council has the job of making sure no one is using counterfeit weights and measures (lines 16–18). There follow detailed regulations about how to measure various items such as nuts and beans for sale (lines 18–27). If merchants do employ containers smaller than the

45. They may have been helped by an official called the *prometretes*. See Rhodes (1981) 577.

required size, the magistrate should sell the contents at public auction, deposit the price at the public bank, and destroy the container (lines 27–29). To keep the official weights and measures in permanent use, the law instructs a certain Diodorus, the son of Theophilus from the deme of Halieus, to hand them over to three public slaves stationed in various places. These slaves are to make them available to any magistrates who request them (lines 37–42). The final clause in the law makes those who commit offenses in regard to these weights and measures subject to the law about *kakourgoi* (criminals) (lines 56–58). It is not possible to tell whether this is the same law mentioned in the orators about *kakourgoi* (thieves, enslavers, and clothes–snatchers), which gave private citizens the right to arrest these offenders. What is significant is that the law instructs the Areopagus to mete out punishment to those who violate its provisions (lines 59–60). The significant point for the issue of enforcement is that the law issues almost all its commands to magistrates. Private initiative comes into play only when magistrates fail to carry out their duties and fail to collect fines.

The grain-wardens (*sitophylakes*) also played a major role in regulating activities in the marketplace (Arist. *Ath. Pol.* 51.3). Originally there were ten men selected by lot for this office, but the importance of their duties led the Athenians to increase their number to twenty in the city and fifteen in the Piraeus.[46] They had responsibility for overseeing the price of grain and bread (Arist. *Ath. Pol.* 51.3). Their duty was to make sure that grain was sold at a just price, that millers did not raise the price of flour too much over the price of grain, and that bread sellers did not raise the price of bread far above the price of flour. In the description of their duties the *Constitution of the Athenians* says nothing about private initiative playing a role in this area.

One might object that most of the evidence presented so far pertains to the marketplace, where the *polis* had a special interest in promoting order for the sake of trade. The task of maintaining order at festivals was also given to officials. Four supervisors (*epimeletai*) elected by the people and the *basileus*, one of the nine archons, were jointly responsible for overseeing the Eleusinian Mysteries (Arist. *Ath. Pol.* 57.1; Lys. 6.4). They had the power to levy fines on disorderly (*akosmountas*) initiates up to a certain

46. For the date of the increase see Rhodes (1981) 577. On the *sitophylakes* see Gauthier (1981).

amount.[47] For larger fines, they were required to make a charge in court. Private individuals played no role in keeping order; they might, however, report official misconduct to the *basileus*, who would then introduce the case to court.[48]

The task of enforcing rules about public sanctuaries was assigned to officials, not left in the hands of private citizens. An inscription from the early fifth century BCE lists several regulations concerning the Acropolis (*IG* i³ 4B), the main sanctuary of Athens, such as not lighting fires (line 6), not leaving dung from animals (line 11), and not to keep a house or make smoke (lines 13–15). For each infraction, the treasurers are empowered to levy a fine, three obols for the first two, one hundred drachmas for the last (lines 6–8, 11–3, 15–16). The treasurers are also required to open the doors of the *oikemata* (possibly treasuries) not fewer than three times a month (lines 18–21). If they fail to do so, the *prytanis* imposes a fine on them (lines 21–24). One might argue that this was an exceptional case because of the shrine's importance, but the responsibility for policing smaller temples outside of Athens was also entrusted to priests and other officials.[49] An inscription dated to the late fourth century found near the deme of Eupyridai at the foot of Aigaleos prohibits anyone from carrying away twigs, firewood, and leaves from the shrine (*IG* ii² 1362, lines 5–7). If a slave is caught chopping or taking away any of these forbidden items, the priest of the sanctuary is to give him fifty lashes and report his name and that of his master to the *basileus* and the Council (lines 7–13). If a free man is caught, the priest and the demarch are to impose a fine of fifty drachmas, report his name to the *basileus* and the Council (lines 14–17), and to act in accordance with a decree of the Council and Assembly (lines 17–18). There is no provision for private individuals to play a role.

The enforcement of regulations by officials is also found in the sphere of the family. For example, the eponymous archon was responsible for looking after orphans, heiresses, and pregnant widows (Arist. *Ath. Pol.* 56.7). He directly supervised the leasing of the estates of orphans and heiresses and made sure the lessees provided adequate security. Finally, he had the power to fine those who wronged them and could collect food from

47. Clinton (2005) no. 138, lines 29–38 with Clinton (1980) 280–81. This law is dated to the fourth century.

48. Clinton (2005) no. 138 with Clinton (1980).

49. For priests as public officials subject to official review (*euthynai*) see Aeschin. 3.18.

guardians who did not give it to their wards. In this case the protection of vulnerable women and children is not left in the hands of private citizens but assigned to a public official. The archon may have acted on information given by private citizens, but he was the one with the sole power to enforce the regulations.

One can also point to the regulations applying to schools listed by Aeschines (1.9–10). These rules are quite detailed and specify the times when boys can enter school, when they must leave, the number that can attend a school, the prescribed ages of students, and the qualifications for attendance. These rules extended to the supervision of slave-attendants given to the students (*paidogogoi*), the conduct of two festivals, the *Mouseia* in the schools and the *Hermaia* in the gymnasia, the kind of people whom the students could associate with, and the training of cyclical choruses. The task of enforcing these rules is not left to private initiative but assigned to an official.[50]

The examples we have examined so far pertain mostly to life in the city of Athens, but there were also many officials who maintained order in the countryside. Perhaps the best evidence for policing outside the city is a decree dated to 352/51 about the Sacred *Orgas*, which was located on the border between Attica and Megara and remote from the city.[51] The decree concerns the placing of boundary markers around the *Orgas* (lines 7–10, 69–73) and the issue of whether the *Orgas* should be cultivated (lines 23–53). The decree notes that the law entrusts the administration of the *Orgas* and other sacred matters to a series of public bodies and officials: those whom the law orders to look after the *Orgas* (lines 18), the Areopagus (lines 18–19), the general elected to protect the countryside (lines 19–20), the peripolarchs (lines 20–21), the demarchs (line 21), and the Council of 500 (lines 21–22). At the very end of this list, we find almost as an afterthought 'and any other Athenian who wishes' (line 22).

The document reveals two significant aspects about law enforcement in the countryside. First, the primary responsibility for protecting the *Orgas* and other religious matters is in the hands of numerous public officials. Private initiative is merely a supplement to the main work carried out by officials, a kind of default mechanism, which would be

50. Athens was not unusual in this regard. For the role of officials in enforcing regulations in the gymnasium see Gauthier and Hatzopoulos (1993).

51. *IG* ii^2 204. For discussion see Rhodes and Osborne (2003) 276–81.

necessary only in exceptional circumstances when officials were not able to perform their duties. Second, it shows that there were many authorities that policed the countryside. Although the Areopagus and the Council normally met in the city of Athens, there were many demarchs in the rural and coastal demes of Attica, and the peripolarch and the general for the countryside were assigned to areas outside the city.[52]

The peripolarch commanded the *peripoloi*, who manned garrisons throughout Attica and included foreign troops.[53] The general for the countryside is attested for the first time in this document; later in the fourth century he commanded the ephebes who patrolled the countryside during their second year of training.[54] Although the program for the ephebes was reformed in the 320s, this part of their training went back many decades: Aeschines (2.167) says that he served as *peripolos* when he was an ephebe around 372.[55] Although ephebes are often praised in decrees for obeying the laws or performing their duties prescribed by law,[56] these duties are never specified. Obviously most of their time was spent on military training and guarding the frontiers against foreign attacks. Yet there is no reason to rule out the role of ephebes and other soldiers in policing the countryside.[57] The decree about the Sacred *Orgas* shows that the duties of the peripolarch and the general assigned to protect the countryside extended beyond the military sphere. A decree dated to 268/67 from Rhamnous, located on the east coast of Attica, praises Epichares, who was first a cavalry commander, then the general assigned to the coast, for protecting the area both during the Chremonidean War and against pirates.[58] His actions were directed not only against the enemy but also against men from the city of Athens who had collaborated with pirates. He had these men, who were either citizens or foreign residents, arrested, interrogated,

52. For the location of demes see Traill (1975).

53. Th. 4.67.2; 8.92.2; X. *Poroi* 4.47, 52.

54. General for the countryside commands ephebes: Reinmuth (1971) no. 9.2: 10–12. Ephebes patrol countryside: Arist. *Ath. Pol.* 42.4.

55. For the date of Aeschines' birth (c. 390) see Harris (1988).

56. Reinmuth (1971) no. 2, lines 27–8, 56; no. 9.1, lines 6–9; 17.1, lines 5–6.

57. *Pace* Hunter (1994) 151–53.

58. Petrakos (1999) no. 3 (= *SEG* 24: 154). For the context see Knoepfler (1993). See also Couvenhes (1999), who lays more stress on the military function of the generals in the countryside than on their policing function.

and punished and thus fulfilled a policing function. Two other decrees from Rhamnous, one dated to 258/7, another to 248/7 praise generals elected to patrol the countryside for lending their assistance to the community and to private individuals, which suggest that their remit extended beyond military activity.[59]

There were 139 demes in Attica,[60] and each deme had several officials appointed either on a regular basis or for ad hoc assignments.[61] The most important official in the deme was the demarch, who was probably appointed by lot every year.[62] He had the power to summon the deme assembly and had the primary responsibility for carrying out its decisions.[63] Among his duties was collecting debts owed to the deme or its sanctuaries.[64] In a decree from the deme of Piraeus dated to around 350 BCE, the demarch is granted the power to impose fines on those who violate the rules about the Thesmophorion and to bring them to court.[65] Nothing in the decree suggests that this was somehow unusual, and there is no reason to doubt that demarchs in other demes held similar powers to maintain order.[66] The demarchs also played a role in collecting private debts. If a creditor needed to seize property from a defaulting debtor, he had to be accompanied by a demarch.[67]

59. Petrakos (1999) no. 8: 13–4; no. 10: 6–7.

60. For the number of demes see Whitehead (1986) 17–22.

61. For a list of officials attested in the demes see Whitehead (1986) 139–48.

62. For the method of appointment see Whitehead (1986) 115–16.

63. Whitehead (1986) 121–39.

64. D. 57.63.

65. *IG* ii^2 1177, lines 12–17. Note that the demarch helps the priest of Apollo to impose a fine in a document from the late fourth century: *IG* ii^2 1362, line 15.

66. Haussoullier (1884) 103. On the functions of the demarch see Osborne (1985a) 74–9. Hansen (1980a) 154, 173, followed by Whitehead (1986) 396, believes that demarchs did not hold an *arche*. But see Aeschin. 3.30 who lists those appointed by the demes to handle money, which would have included demarchs.

67. Ar. *Nub.* 37 with scholion *ad loc.*; Harp. s. v. *demarchos*; *An. Bekk.*242 16ff. with Harrison (1971) 189 with note 2. Whitehead (1986) 126–27 suggests that 'a demarch's role was restricted to debts incurred within his deme, and arose from a natural extension of the authority vested in him by his deme assembly to act against debtors to the deme as a whole' but admits that this is only 'a tentative hypothesis.' Hunter (1994) 142 questions the view of Haussoullier (1884) 104–6 that the demarch acted as a 'police civile' because no demarch is present 'at either of the two seizures of property described in Demosthenes 47.' Her objection carries no force. In the first seizure the trierarch was acting in an official capacity with

The demarchs also reported property to be confiscated to officials in Athens.[68] Officials who had the power to enforce the law were thus not confined to Athens: there were hundreds of demarchs and other officials throughout Attica responsible for policing. As early as the late sixth century BCE, there was an official on Salamis who was responsible for collecting fines from settlers who violated a ban against leasing their property on the island.[69]

When the Athenian army was stationed in the countryside or left Attica on campaign, the task of maintaining discipline in the army was the responsibility of the generals (Arist. *Ath. Pol.* 61.2).[70] They had the power to imprison,[71] 'to banish by proclamation,' which probably meant to dismiss them from the army, and to impose fines on disorderly soldiers.[72] Lysias (13.65) alludes to an incident when the general Lamachus executed a soldier caught sending messages to the enemy during the siege of Syracuse. In Demosthenes' speech *Against Conon* (54.4–5) Ariston recounts how the sons of Conon started to harass their slaves, then turned on him and his messmates. Instead of resorting to self-help, Ariston reported them to the general, who criticized their conduct. His warning did not put an end to their rowdiness: as soon as night fell, Conon's sons started another brawl. This time the general, the taxiarchs, and several soldiers intervened to quell the violence. Once again, the task of keeping order was in the hands of officials.[73] Trierarchs also had the power to arrest and imprison members of their crews who deserted.[74]

assistants and had no need for another official ([D.] 47.21–44). The second seizure is denounced as highly illegal because Theophemus enters without the owner's consent and hardly represents the norm ([D.] 47.45–66). Finally Hunter does not explore the implications of the decree about the *Orgas*.

68. See *IG* i³ 425, col. II, lines 23, 26–7, 30–31, 41, 44, and Walbank (1982).

69. *IG* i³ 1 (c. 510–500 BCE).

70. On the powers of generals in the field see Couvenhes (2005) 440–54. Note that Xenophon (*An.* 5.7.24–30) condemns the practice of soldiers taking the law into their own hands.

71. Cf. [D.] 50.51.

72. Arist. *Ath. Pol.* 61.2 states that the generals did not normally impose fines, but see Lys. 9.6–12; 15.5. On the disciplinary powers of generals see Hamel (1998a) 59–63.

73. On the public action for cowardice, which covered cases of desertion and leaving one's position in battle, see Harris (2004b) 256–57. For the composition of the court that tried these cases see Whitehead (2008) and Rhodes (2008b).

74. D. 51.8–9.

So far most of the evidence describes conditions in the fourth century for which there are more literary and epigraphical sources. But the evidence from the fifth century does not alter this picture.[75] When decrees of this period indicate who is to enforce a law, we rarely find the possibility of prosecution by private individuals; in general the enforcement of laws and decrees is assigned to officials. Especially noteworthy is the protection afforded to *proxenoi*; in decrees awarding this title, the responsibility for ensuring that those who are honored do not come to harm lies with the Council and other officials such as the generals (e.g., *IG* i³ 156, lines 1–9; 167, lines 12–7; 181, lines 7–9). A decree about Neapolis dated to 410/9 instructs the generals to protect the people of this community against injustice at the hands of private individuals and public officials (*IG* i³ 101, lines 52–53).

Some scholars claim that the Athenians never had an organization that resembled the police found in modern states.[76] From this they have concluded that the officials of the community lacked the coercive force to compel citizens and foreigners to obey their orders. This is misleading. First, as we have seen, Athenian officials had the power to levy fines. Those who did not pay fines became public debtors and incurred *atimia*, the loss of civic rights. The penalty for violating the terms of this *atimia* was harsh: Demosthenes (21.182) informs us that when Pyrrhus, one of the Eteobutadae, attempted to serve as a judge when owing money to the Treasury, he was denounced to a magistrate, put on trial, and executed.[77]

Officials were often accompanied by public slaves, who could be called upon to enforce their orders if someone refused to comply. Three passages in Aristophanes' comedies show that officials exercised a policing

75. See appendix 2.

76. See note 13.

77. For the procedure of *endeixis* of *atimoi* such as public debtors see [D.] 58.48–9; And 1.73 with Harrison (1971) 172–75. Here private initiative played a role, but the denunciation was made to an official, who carried out the arrest. Hansen (1976a) 13–17 claims that in *endeixis* the accuser made the arrest, but his argument rests on a questionable interpretation of D. 23.51, which instead appears to contrast *endeixis* with the arrest by a private citizen of a murderer who had returned from exile. Note that Demosthenes (23.31) explicitly states that the *thesmothetai* carried out the arrest of a murderer who returned from exile. None of the other passages he examines indicate who made the arrest. Moreover his view is unlikely; on this interpretation there would be almost no difference between *endeixis* and *apagoge* to the Eleven. On the latter procedure see section III of this chapter.

function as part of their duties and used Scythian archers to arrest citizens disobeying the law.[78] In *Acharnians* (54–8) the herald of the Assembly commands archers to arrest Amphitheus, who is disrupting public business. In *Lysistrata* (433–62) the *proboulos* tells archers to seize Lysistrata and other women. In *Women at the Thesmophoria* (930–34) the *prytanis*, acting on the orders of the Council, instructs the Scythian archer to tie the relative of Euripides to a plank and to guard him. If anyone comes near, he is to strike him with his whip.[79] This is not just comic fantasy; Demosthenes (21.179) reveals that the assessor (*paredros*) of an archon had a force of attendants (*hyperetai*) who could enforce his orders. The *astynomoi* had a force of public slaves who accompanied them and carried out their orders (Arist. *Ath. Pol.* 50.2). The trierarch who attempted to recover naval equipment from Theophemus took along a slave 'from the magistrates' ([D.] 47.35).[80] Androtion was helped by the Eleven in his efforts to collect arrears from the *eisphora*.[81]

Finally, an official might himself intervene to protect a private individual threatened with harm or to enforce a regulation. Demosthenes (21.36) refers to a *thesmothetes* who was struck while rescuing a female *aulos*-player from a drunken assailant.[82] In another passage Demosthenes (23.31) mentions how during a meeting of the Assembly the *thesmothetai* arrested a man who was exiled on a charge of murder. In *Acharnians* (723–26, 824–25) Aristophanes alludes to the use of whips by the *agoranomoi* to exclude banned individuals from entering the marketplace. When Meidias attempted to bring imported goods to Attica without paying duties, the *pentakostologoi* seized his cargo (D. 21.133). During the investigation

78. On the Scythian archers see the good treatment of Couvenhes (2012), who dates their introduction to after 458/7. Hunter (1994) 145–49 discusses these public slaves, but tries to downplay their importance. Hall (1989) claims that the average Athenian resented being manhandled by slaves, but see MacDowell (1995) 272–73.

79. The relative says that he is going to die, but the Council did not have the power to execute criminals without trial in this period. See Rhodes (1972) 179–207.

80. Cf. the public slave Opsigonos who accompanied the general Dicaeogenes in the dockyards. See *IG* ii^2 1631, lines 196–7, 380–82. On public slaves in Athens see Jacob (1979).

81. D. 22.49–55. Cf. D. 24.162, 197. Demosthenes paints a rather lurid picture of Androtion's activities, but cannot suppress the fact that the Assembly voted to have the Eleven help him to use force against defaulting debtors.

82. The scholion to the passage (121 Dilts) says that the *thesmothetai* were required to patrol at night to stop abductions, but MacDowell (1990) 255 may be right to consider this 'a false inference from this passage.'

about the parody of the Mysteries, the *prytaneis* made arrests and entered a house to seize slave women.[83]

It would thus be misleading to state that the ancient *polis* 'never developed a proper police system.'[84] It would be more accurate to say that in Classical Athens the functions of public administration and policing were not kept separate and assigned to different bodies but carried out by the same officials accompanied by public slaves. The officials who were responsible for conducting public business could inflict fines like modern policemen. They also had at their disposal the coercive power to compel compliance with their orders and might themselves use physical force against offenders. We should not think of Athenian officials as modern bureaucrats who sit behind desks and shuffle paper all day long. These officials did not issue orders to a police force, which arrested offenders, but did the policing themselves.

Even though officials had the power to impose fines, make arrests, and seize goods, they had to exercise this power with care. The eponymous archon was responsible for supervising the festival of the Dionysia and had two assessors (*paredroi*), who helped him to maintain order.[85] During the year 363/2 one of the assistants was trying to bar one of the spectators from taking his seat and laid his hand on him. At a meeting of the Assembly after the festival, a motion of censure (*probole*) was passed to condemn the assessor.[86] The man who introduced the motion had a very strong case: 'If I took a seat, man, and if I did not obey your orders as you said I did, what power does the law grant you even if you are the Archon himself? The power to order your assistants to bar him, not to beat me yourself. Suppose I do not obey even in this case: impose a fine, do everything except lay a hand on me. The laws have provided many remedies to prevent a person from suffering insulting abuse.'[87] In this case the official was not permitted to use physical violence. All he was allowed to do was to order his assistants to prevent the spectator from entering the theater or to issue a fine.

---

83. And. 1.64. Cf. And. 1.111: the *prytaneis* are instructed to bring Cephisius before the Council. This order may have authorized them to use force to ensure compliance. The arrests made at And. 1.13, 34 were presumably carried out by the *prytaneis*.

84. Thus Badian (1970).

85. Arist. *Ath Pol.* 56.1 with Rhodes (1981) 621–622.

86. On this procedure see Harris (2008) 79–81.

87. D. 21.179.

The restrictions on the power of officials to use physical force are best seen in the case of a trierarch who attempted to recover naval equipment from Theophemus during the Social War (357/56) and later brought a private suit for assault against him. Trierarchs were wealthy men appointed to serve as captains of triremes for a year and were required to make a contribution toward the ship's upkeep.[88] The state provided equipment, which each trierarch was required to return after each campaign. Sometime in the 360s, the Athenians ordered the fleet to sail, and several trierarchs were ordered to recover equipment from those who had failed to return it.[89] A law of Periander gave trierarchs the power to collect this from their predecessors, and a decree of the Council assigned defaulting trierarchs to their successors.[90] One trierarch was told to collect equipment from Demochares and Theophemus.[91] He started by confronting the two men and requesting that they comply, but they refused. His next step was to summon each one to trial and won a judgment against each.[92] Demochares returned the equipment in his possession, but Theophemus did not.[93] The trierarch then complained to the Council, which issued a decree instructing him to recover the equipment in any way possible.[94] This measure appears to have given him the power to distrain on Theophemus' property if he continued to disobey.[95]

---

88. On the duties of a trierarch see Gabrielsen (1994) 105–69.

89. [D.] 47.20. Rhodes (1972) 155 believes that this decree authorized confiscation of property from those who refused to surrender naval equipment or to sell equipment owned by private individuals, but this power was only granted by the decree of the Council after Theophemus disobeyed the court's decision (33).

90. [D.] 47.21. The supervisors of the dockyards probably drew up the list of defaulting trierarchs. See Rhodes (1972) 155.

91. [D.] 47.22.

92. [D.] 47.26–28. This trial would have taken place on the day after the summons. The law governing the procedure was first enacted in the late fifth century BCE: see Oliver (1935) 15–19; Rhodes (1972) 156–57.

93. [D.] 47.28–29.

94. [D.] 47.33. For examples of this clause in non-Athenian inscriptions see Rubinstein (2010).

95. Oliver (1935) 18–19, followed by Rhodes (1972) 157, believes that the trierarch proceeds against Theophemus as in a private suit and restores the phrase *καθάπερ παρὰ τô ἰδ[ιοτεῖ ὀφέλοντος . . .]* in lines 7–8 of *IG* i³ 236. This would indicate that a trierarch proceeded against someone like a private citizen, but the emendation is not compelling. The trierarch is a public official (Aeschin. 3.19), who is following the orders of the Council.

The trierarch then learned from Euergus where his brother Theophemus lived and went to the house.[96] He took a public slave with him. When a slave woman opened the door and said Theophemus was not at home, he asked her to look for him.[97] After Theophemus arrived, the trierarch once more asked for the equipment because the fleet was about to sail and showed him the decree of the Council. This demand was met with another refusal.[98] At this point the trierarch presented Theophemus with two alternatives, either to accompany him and go to the men in charge of sending out the fleet and the Council and tell them he was not responsible for the equipment, or to return it. If Theophemus refused to do either, the trierarch said he would seize his property as payment for what he owed. When Theophemus continued to disobey, the trierarch seized the slave woman, but Theophemus grabbed her to prevent him from dragging her away.[99] The trierarch and Theophemus clearly disagreed about what happened next. The trierarch claims that Theophemus struck him as he went to seize other property.[100] Theophemus claimed that the trierarch struck the first blow. It is difficult to tell who was lying. The trierarch went to the Council and revealed the marks of Theophemus' blows. The Council urged him to bring an action against Theophemus, and he was condemned to pay a fine of twenty-five drachmas.[101] But after the trierarch returned from the campaign, Theophemus brought a private action for assault against the trierarch and won a judgment.[102]

The story is worth recounting in detail because it shows the restraint expected of officials when carrying out the Council's orders. The account given by the trierarch is obviously only one side of the story, but his description of his actions should conform to the norms that the court expected an official to follow. Even though he is acting on their instructions,

96. [D.] 47.34–5.

97. [D.] 47.35.

98. [D.] 47.36.

99. [D.] 47.37–8.

100. [D.] 47.38.

101. [D.] 47.41–3. The trierarch presents evidence for all his assertions at 44. Theophemus appears to have finally complied at this point because the trierarch was able to sail with his ship. In his narrative of events, the trierarch omits this because he is trying to stress Theophemus' disobedience. See Rhodes (1972) 156, note 7.

102. [D.] 47.39, 45–8.

he proceeds step by step. First, he makes a request, then he brings a lawsuit. Second, he requests the equipment again and only goes to Theophemus' house after obtaining a decree of the Council. The decree only gives him the power to distrain on his property. Third, when Theophemus resists his attempt to seize the slave woman, he desists and looks for other property to seize.[103] To make sure that he would not meet Theophemus' wife once he enters the house, he goes to the trouble of finding out that he is not married.[104] The trierarch has the power to carry out the order of the Council, but this power is circumscribed and does not allow him to use physical force against Theophemus when he is not complying.

The trierarch's restraint illustrates an important principle about Athenian democracy, which is well expressed by Demosthenes (22.55): 'Indeed, if you wish to examine the difference between a free man and a slave, you will find this the greatest distinction: the bodies of slaves are subject to punishment for all their crimes, but free men can keep theirs safe from harm even in the worst disasters. In general, it is right to punish the latter by taking their property.'[105] This is the reason why Demosthenes criticizes Androtion so harshly: he alleges that he invaded private houses and hauled citizens off to prison when he was only empowered to confiscate their property (D. 22.51–53). It is therefore not surprising that the Areopagus, the Council, and public officials only resorted to arrest when there was a serious threat to the public safety. When the Areopagus arrested Antiphon, he was suspected of treason.[106] When the *thesmothetes* took hold of a man in the Assembly, he had been convicted for homicide, and his presence threatened to bring pollution on the city (D. 23.31). When the Council ordered arrests during the investigation of the mutilation of the Herms and the parody of the Mysteries, the Athenians feared that there was a plot to overthrow the democracy.[107] When some trierarchs were responsible

103. For slaves being seized from a defaulting debtor see [D.] 53.20. The prostitutes seized by Androtion were probably slaves owned by public debtors (D. 22.56).

104. It was considered shocking for an outsider to enter a house and come face to face with women who were not related to him. See Lys. 3.6; D. 21.79.

105. For the protection of citizens' bodies against physical violence in democracy, compare Aeschin. 1.5. For the different punishments given to slaves and free men see Hunter (1994) 155–62.

106. See D. 18.132–33 with the discussion in Part IV.

107. Note however the reluctance of the authorities to arrest Alcibiades when summoned to stand trial for his parody of the Mysteries. See Th. 6.61.

for a naval defeat in the 360s because they had hired replacements, Aristophon charged them with treason and passed a decree to have them arrested and put in prison (D. 51.8–9).

III

In section II it was shown that the main responsibility for enforcing the law lay in the hands of public officials, who could impose fines or arrest those who violated the law. Individual officials or boards of officials tended however to exercise a narrowly defined jurisdiction, often limited to one area such as the Agora, the port, a temple precinct, or a deme. The Council of 500 and the Areopagus, by contrast, held a broader jurisdiction and operated over a wider area. They also were responsible for policing major crimes, which were beyond the capability of small groups of officials.

The Council played a major role in policing public officials. The main procedure for reporting official misconduct was *eisangelia* to the Council.[108] In 420/19 a private citizen denounced four officials—Aristion, Philinus, Ampelinus, and the secretary to the *thesmothetai*—to the Council by *eisangelia* (Antiphon 6.35). The Council must have investigated the charges and sent the case to court. Despite the accused's attempts to thwart the prosecution, the citizen convicted all the defendants (Antiphon 6.38).

The Council also exercised wide jurisdiction over financial matters. It had the primary role in policing public debtors. A public slave working for the Council kept a record of all debts to the state listed in order of the dates when they were due. Those who defaulted might have their debts doubled. The Council had the power to collect these sums and to imprison those who refused to comply.[109] A decree of the Assembly from the fifth century appoints supervisors (*epistatai*) to manage the finances of the sanctuary at Eleusis and requires them to report to the Council (*IG* i^3 32, lines 14–17). The Council might also appoint a board of inquiry to investigate financial irregularities. When one of the *prytaneis* of the Council discovered in 419 BCE that several officials were committing crimes, he proposed that the Council launch an investigation into the matter (Antiphon 6.49).

---

108. On this procedure, which differed from the standard form of *eisangelia*, see Hansen (1975) 25–28, 112–20.

109. Arist. *Ath. Pol.* 48.1. Cf. And. 1.92–3.

The Council might investigate other charges and issue summons or order arrests. When Cephisius informed the *prytaneis* that Andocides was participating in the Mysteries when he did not have the right to do so, and the *basileus* also reported this to the *prytaneis*, the *prytaneis* issued a summons to Andocides and Cephisius ordering them to attend a meeting of the Council.[110] In 415 the Council appointed a committee to investigate charges about the mutilation of the Herms and the parody of the Mysteries (And. 1.14, 36). Their reports led to many arrests.[111] Sometime between 348 and 346, the Council investigated charges that Aristarchus had murdered Nicodemus; Demosthenes (21.116–17) says that Meidias attended the meeting and demanded that the Council go to his house and arrest him.[112]

During the Athenian Empire, the Council enforced many regulations about tribute. In the decree of Cleinias, the Council and officials in the allied cities and the overseers (*episkopoi*) are instructed to supervise the payment of tribute.[113] Each city is to record the amount of tribute paid on a sealed tablet, which is to be given to the Council to be read out. The *prytaneis* are then to hold an Assembly after the Dionysia and report to the Athenians which cities have paid and which have not. If any Athenian or citizen of any allied state commits an offense about the tribute, the charge is to be brought to the *prytaneis*, who are to report it to the Council so that the case can be tried in court. There are similar provisions about the sacrificial cows and the panoplies to be sent by the allied cities. The Standards Decree adds to the oath sworn by the members of the Council a promise to enforce the new measures about weights, measures, and coinage standards.[114]

The Areopagus exercised a general supervision over all residents of Attica and had the power to conduct investigations (*zetein*) and to make

110. And. 1.111. For the *basileus* reporting to the Council about violations of the rules about the first-fruits given to the shrine at Eleusis see *IG* i^3 78, lines 57–61.

111. And. 1.44–5. The arrests must have been carried out by the Eleven because those named were placed in prison.

112. According to Demosthenes (21.116), Meidias also insisted that the Council put Aristarchus to death, but the Council did not have this power. Cf. Rhodes (1972) 179–180 ('Demosthenes is representing Meidias' conduct as outrageous').

113. *IG* i^3 34. Meiggs and Lewis (1969) 119 dated the decree to 447 on the basis of letter forms, but see now Rhodes (2008a) for more recent views. Rhodes proposes 425/4.

114. For a text of the fragments based on autopsy see Schönhammer (1995).

reports of crimes (*apophaseis*).[115] The Assembly might order the Areopagus to investigate, or it might do so on its own initiative. These reports were presented to the Assembly, which then decided how to proceed. The Areopagus played a major role in detecting cases of treason. Dinarchus (1.63) states that Charinus was sentenced to exile for treason as a result of reports made by the Areopagus. In another case (Din. 1.58–60), the Assembly ordered the Council to investigate Polyeuctus of Cydantidae. After the Areopagus found that he was consorting with exiles, the Assembly elected prosecutors, and Polyeuctus was tried in court.[116]

The most famous case involving the Areopagus was the Harpalus affair. Harpalus was the treasurer for Alexander the Great. After Alexander's return from India, Harpalus was afraid that he would be punished and fled from Babylon in early 324 with five thousand talents of silver and six thousand mercenaries (D.S. 17.108.6). With thirty warships, he crossed the Aegean and arrived at Attica (Curtius 10.2.1). When he asked for permission to enter Athens, Demosthenes persuaded the Assembly to deny his request ([Plu.] *Mor.* 846a). After leaving his mercenaries at Taenarum in Laconia, he returned with some of his money and became a suppliant for Athenian help (D.S. 17.108.7).[117] This time his request was granted.[118]

Soon afterward envoys sent by Philoxenus, a Macedonian naval commander, arrived in Athens to demand the surrender of Harpalus. Demosthenes persuaded the Assembly not to hand over Harpalus but also wished to avoid causing offense to Alexander. He therefore proposed that Harpalus be taken into custody and that his money be placed on the Acropolis for

115. For the power to conduct investigations see Din. 1.50. Wallace (1989) 115–19 argues on the basis of Din. 1.62–3 that 'the *apophasis* procedure was introduced by a decree of Demosthenes probably in the early part of 343.' But see de Bruyn (1995) 117–18, who rightly notes that the passage has nothing to do with the introduction of the procedure, but concerns several decrees of Demosthenes aimed at applying the procedure. She attributes the procedure to Ephialtes, but her view is based on a dubious restoration in the text of *IG* i^3 102, 38–47. See Harris (1997). Wallace's view is also rejected by Rhodes (1995) 312–13. I plan to discuss the jurisdiction of the Areopagus in a forthcoming essay.

116. On these cases see chapter 8, section III.

117. For the procedure of supplication in the Assembly see Naiden (2006) 173–83.

118. I see no reason to follow Worthington (1992) 43–44, 315 in believing that Harpalus entered Athens by bribing Philocles in violation of the previous decree denying him entry. Worthington relies on Din. 3.2, but this passage probably refers to the earlier occasion when Harpalus came with his ships and mercenaries.

safekeeping (Hyp. *D.* 8–9, 12; Din.1.89).[119] Harpalus reported that the entire sum was 700 talents, but the amount was later discovered to be only 350 talents (Hyp. *D.* 9–10; [Plu.] *Mor.* 846B).[120] Harpalus was allowed to escape (Hyp. *D.* 12), collected the troops left at Taenarum, and fled to Crete where he was murdered (D.S. 17.108.7–8). Suspicion of bribery fell on Demosthenes and other politicians (D.S. 17.108.7–8). Demosthenes declared his innocence and proposed that the Areopagus investigate the matter (Hyp. *D.* 2; Din. 1.61). The Areopagus submitted its report six months later (Din. 1.45). This report listed the names of those who had taken money and the amounts they had received (Hyp. *D.* 5–6). Demosthenes and Aristogeiton were among those named (Din. 1.53). Ten prosecutors were appointed by the Assembly (Din. 2.6), and the accused were tried in court. What is significant here is that private initiative played no role at all in the detection and the prosecution of the crime. The investigation was undertaken at the suggestion of a politician, Demosthenes, but was carried out by the Areopagus on its own. The prosecutions of those reported by the Areopagus were brought by elected accusers, not by private individuals acting on their own initiative.

The Areopagus was not only involved in detecting major crimes against the community. More routine matters also fell within its competence. Dinarchus (1.56) alludes to two incidents in which the Areopagus reported minor infractions. In one case, the Areopagus fined one of its own members who had cheated a ferryman of his payment and reported him to the Assembly. In another case, it caught Conon fraudulently claiming a state payment worth five drachmas, hardly a large sum of money. The Areopagus also pried into the private lives of Athenians. When Phano, the wife of Theogenes, the *basileus*, participated in the Anthesteria, the Areopagus discovered that she was neither a virgin when she married her husband nor even a citizen ([D.] 59.79–81). Theogenes persuaded the Council that he was not aware of her true status and was forgiven, but it is clear that he could have been fined ([D.] 59.81–83).[121] The power of the Areopagus to examine the private lives of citizens is also attested in an anecdote of

119. Ambassadors also came from Antipater and Olympias to demand his surrender (D. S. 17.108.7). Worthington argues against the existence of these embassies, but see Blackwell (1999) 17–27.

120. On the figures see Whitehead (2000) 385.

121. On this incident see Kapparis (1999) 344–48.

Athenaeus (IV 168 a–b). When the philosophers Menedemus and Asclepiades were young, the Areopagus asked them how they could be in such good shape although they owned nothing and passed their time with other philosophers. The two youths produced a miller, who told the Council that every night they worked in his mill and received two drachmas. The Areopagus was so impressed that it gave them two hundred drachmas. This incident must date to the period 330–320.[122] This amusing story may have been invented, but its details ought to be authentic. There was a law against idleness (D. 57.32), and the wage paid to the two is comparable to the rate attested for unskilled labor in this period.[123] If the Areopagus could look into Theogenes' marriage, there is no reason to doubt that it also had the power to inquire into other aspects of the personal lives of metics and citizens.

Perhaps the best illustration of the limits of private initiative and the role of the Areopagus is found in the case of Antiphon (D. 18.132–33). Antiphon lost his citizenship through the *diapsephisis* procedure in 346. Several years later, between 343 and 340, Demosthenes seized him while 'hiding' and brought him before the Assembly, charging that he was a spy for Philip, the king of Macedon.[124] During the debate in the Assembly, Aeschines objected to the arrest on the grounds that Demosthenes had entered a private dwelling without a decree.[125] The Assembly sided with Aeschines and ordered Antiphon to be released. The decision in favor of Aeschines shows that it was illegal for an Athenian to enter a private house without a decree of the Council or Assembly, a significant restriction on the power to make arrests even in the case of traitors.

Antiphon's case did not end there. Demosthenes' charge aroused the suspicions of the Areopagus, which launched an investigation and arrested Antiphon shortly afterwards. This time Antiphon was tortured and evidently confessed because he was put to death. There is no need to believe that Antiphon's confession vindicated Demosthenes; confessions obtained under torture are notoriously unreliable as evidence.[126] What this incident

122. For the date see de Bruyn (1995) 135.

123. For wages in this period see Loomis (1998), esp. 104–120.

124. For the date see Harris (1995) 169–70.

125. For the legal grounds for Aeschines' objection see Harris (1995) 172.

126. Yunis (2001) 188 believes that the confession obtained by torture vindicated Demosthenes but see Harris (2005b) 216–17.

does show is the limits of private initiative in law enforcement and the key role of public bodies like the Areopagus.

Even though the powers of individual officials were limited, the Council and the Areopagus had a broad responsibility for policing all of Attica and for investigating major crimes. Because the average Athenian could rest assured that the Areopagus, the Council, and numerous officials were on duty to protect him and his family, he found no need to carry weapons (Th. 1.5.3–6.3). As a result, the Athenians lived in an atmosphere of peace and security and went about free from fear (Th. 3.37.2). Unlike other cities in Greece, there were no Athenian laws against carrying weapons in public, and Xenophon (*HG* 5.1.22) reveals that Athenians kept weapons in their houses to use in emergencies.[127] Had the responsibility for maintaining order and enforcing the law lain primarily in the hands of private individuals, they would have found it necessary to go about carrying their weapons. But the protection afforded by the state's officials made this unnecessary.

On the other hand, one should not exaggerate the effectiveness of the Council of 500, the Council of the Areopagus, and the numerous other officials in policing the city of Athens and the countryside of Attica. In a speech of Lysias (3.5–9, 11–19), the defendant describes two brawls in which he claims he was attacked. Even though the incidents took place in the center of Athens, the defendant does not mention any officials intervening to stop the violence. In another speech ([D.] 47.52–61), a plaintiff tells the court how his opponent Theophemus entered his house in the countryside and took his property without his consent (Theophemus claimed the plaintiff had not paid a legal judgment). His slaves called on a neighbor to help them, but there were clearly no officials in the immediate vicinity whom they could summon to assist them. When Conon and his son Ctesias assaulted Ariston at night near the Leokorion in the center of Athens, there appears to have been no official present to stop the violence (D. 54.7–9). Yet one should not conclude from these three incidents that there were no officials available to intervene or that policing was normally

127. For the provision of arms to citizens in the fourth and third centuries BCE see Couvenhes (2007). On the custom of carrying arms in early Greece and the end of this custom in the Classical period see van Wees (1998), who does not connect the change with the growth of the state but with changes in elite fashions. But see Th. 1.5.3–6.1 who connects carrying weapons with unsafe conditions and the threat of robbers and pirates. This implicitly connects the decline of the custom with safer conditions.

done by individuals. On the contrary, we have seen that there obviously were many officials who maintained public order. But one must bear in mind that even with patrol cars, radios, telephones, and the other benefits of modern technology, the police in contemporary states cannot be everywhere at once. The same was clearly true for officials in Attica. For this reason the laws of Athens had to allow private citizens to use self-help in certain circumstances.

IV

There were strict limits placed on the use of force by private citizens. Here it is necessary to make a distinction between the use of deadly force and the use of force to arrest or detain someone. As regards the use of deadly force there was a general rule that it was not permitted for anyone to kill either justly or unjustly.[128] This meant that even if a citizen caught someone breaking the law, one did not have the right to put him to death but was required to bring a legal charge against him in court.[129] Demosthenes (23.24–27) points out that in the laws about homicide and other laws there is always a procedure leading to a trial, which must be followed by anyone who wishes to punish the offender. The power to execute criminals was in the hands of the Eleven, who ran the prison (Arist. *Ath. Pol.* 52.1).[130] Even if a man was convicted of murder and fled abroad, it was illegal for a private individual to kill him (D. 23.44).

Citizens were allowed to use deadly force in only a few rare cases.[131] First, it was permitted for someone to kill a person caught with his wife, mother, sister, daughter, or concubine kept for the purpose of free children (Arist. *Ath. Pol.* 57.3; D. 23.53; Lys. 1.30). The law made no distinction between the person who had seduced the woman or the one who was using force but applied both to cases of seduction and those involving

128. Antiphon 3.2.9; 4.2.3. This was a general rule; the law about just homicide listed the permitted exceptions.

129. For the principle that no one could be put to death without trial see Lys. 19.7 with Carawan (1984). Cf. Hansen (2002) 33. For a similar rule in Arcadia see X. *HG* 7.4.38.

130. Arist. *Ath. Pol.* 52.1. Cf. Hansen (2002) 36–37. For modes of execution see Todd (2000a). For the prison see Hunter (1997). Athens was not unusual in placing the power to execute criminals exclusively in the hands of public officials. For Sicyon see X. *HG* 7.3.6.

131. For the cases tried at the Delphinion see MacDowell (1963) 70–81.

sexual violence.[132] The law limited this right to husbands and close male relatives and to cases in which the offender was caught in the act of making love.

The man who exercised this right to kill someone therefore did so at considerable risk. The man who killed a rapist or a seducer had to demonstrate that he had no motive for entrapping the victim and to prove that he actually discovered the man with his wife. When Euphiletus was on trial for killing Eratosthenes whom he caught with his wife, he had to show that he discovered his wife's affair by accident (Lys. 1.15–17). On the night that he killed Eratosthenes, he was careful to stress that he did not anticipate his arrival and was unprepared (Lys. 1.22–23, 39–40). As a result, he had to gather witnesses at the last minute. When he caught the victim in his house, he had to make sure that there were several people there who could testify to his account of the killing.[133] He also asserts that there was no previous quarrel between them so as to remove any suspicion that he plotted to entrap Eratosthenes (Lys. 1.4, 43–45). Had he not been able to establish these facts, Eratosthenes' relatives would have convinced the court that Euphiletus was guilty of deliberate homicide, which would have resulted in his death or permanent exile.

Second, it was permitted to kill someone who was attacking from an ambush.[134] One could not kill any person who attacked but only those who did so in very restricted circumstances. There were three main features of an ambush. First, the person who sets an ambush plans ahead and anticipates the arrival of his intended victim. Second, the person lying in ambush is concealed from view until he emerges from his hiding place and attempts to take advantage of surprise. Third, the person who attacks from ambush intends either to kill or to capture his intended victim. The law was clearly limited to the situation in which someone was attacked, could not retreat to safety or summon help, and was forced to strike back to prevent serious harm. The law did not permit retaliation in other circumstances. For instance, Demosthenes tells the story of Euaeon, who was struck in an insulting way by Boeotus at a party. Euaeon struck back

---

132. See Harris (2006a) 283–96; Hansen (2002) 32 mistakenly believes that only adulterers (his mistranslation of the term *moichos*) were subject to the law.

133. Lys. 1.23–24, 41, 46. Cf. 29 where the witnesses are called to testify.

134. D. 23.53 and Harpocration s.v. ἐν ὁδῷ καθελών with the discussion of Harris (2010) 132–33. MacDowell (1963) 75–76 does not discuss the meaning of the phrase.

with such force that he killed Boeotus. Demosthenes (21.73) observes that Euaeon could have restrained himself and went to the party on his own volition. Some of the judges at the trial felt sympathy for Euaeon, but the majority voted against him because the laws about just homicide did not permit the use of deadly violence in this case.[135]

Third, it was permitted to kill a person carrying off his property without justification provided that one did so immediately (*eutheos*).[136] The substantive provision was carefully worded to cover only those taking property without just cause. In other words, it did not apply to those who used deadly force against creditors distraining on property given as real security or against those who had won a court decision awarding them property. The law also required that the killing take place immediately, that is, during the commission of the robbery. An exception was made to the general rule against the use of deadly violence because if the victim waited to bring a lawsuit, the robber might escape with his property and leave Attica. If the robber was caught after the offense, however, the victim might arrest him if caught with the stolen goods but could not kill him (discussed later).

Fourth, if a man was convicted of homicide and sentenced to exile, then returned to Attica, one could kill him with impunity.[137]

Fifth, a private citizen could kill a tyrant or someone aiming at tyranny. There was a law attributed to Solon about killing tyrants, which appears to have been replaced by a decree of Demophantus soon after the overthrow of the Thirty in 403[138] and was renewed in slightly different terms in 336/35.[139] Needless to say, this provision applied only in highly unusual circumstances, and there is no evidence that anyone killed a person accused of aiming at tyranny in the years between the restoration of the democracy in 403 BCE and the oligarchy imposed in 322 BCE. In fact, when Alcibiades and others were charged with trying to set up a tyranny

135. For analysis of the verdict see Harris (1992) 78; Harris (2010) 133, 136.

136. D. 23.60; *IG* i³ 104, lines 37–38.

137. D. 23.28; *IG* i³ 104, lines 30–31 (restored).

138. For the law of Solon see And. 1.95. Lycurg. *Leocr.* 127 dates the decree of Demophantus after the Thirty. For discussion of the forged document found at Andocides 1.96 and the relationship between the law of Solon and the Decree of Demophantus see Canevaro and Harris (2012) 119–25.

139. *SEG* 12:87 = Schwenk (1985) 198 no. 6.

in 415 BCE, it was the Council that investigated the charge and interrogated suspects.[140]

These five cases reveal that private individuals could use deadly force in a few instances, which were exceptions to the general rule that the power to execute criminals was given to public officials.[141] In each case this right was carefully circumscribed. In two of these cases, private individuals were allowed to use force because it would have been unrealistic (or impossible) for them to summon an official to protect them. In this regard, the laws of Athens were not all that different from those of modern states, in which citizens are permitted to use violence for self-defense or to enforce property rights.[142]

Private individuals could use physical force to arrest (*apagoge*) only three types of offenders: enslavers (*andrapodistai*), thieves (*kleptai*), and a curious category called clothes-snatchers (*lopodutai*).[143] The distinction between the last two categories, thieves and clothes-snatchers, is probably between those who take another person's property stealthily and those who seize it openly. Even in this case one could not arrest the offender in any circumstances. The guilt of the offender had to be obvious (*ep'autophoro*), that is, the person who arrested him had to have strong evidence for his charge. In the case of the enslaver, he had to catch the offender in possession of someone who was clearly free. One could not seize someone who had made a free person into a slave at some time or another: one had to

140. Charge of aiming at tyranny: Th. 6.60. Council investigates: And. 1.15, 64.

141. *Pace* Christ (1998b) 521: 'Athenians engaged in a level of self-help that would shock most modern Westerners.' Hansen (2002) 33 does not examine in detail the evidence for the use of deadly force by private individuals but arrives at a conclusion similar to mine: 'in the Classical *polis* self-help was limited to a few defined offences. In all other matters self-help was a punishable offence as it is in modern states.'

142. If someone killed an Athenian in ignorance during a battle or killed someone in an athletic contest (Arist. *Ath. Pol.* 57.3; D. 23.53–55), he could not be convicted of murder. Here the law did not grant a right to use deadly force but recognized the validity of two kinds of excuses.

143. See Arist. *Ath. Pol.* 52.1 with Harris (2006a) 373–90. This procedure may have been extended to murderers, see Lys. 13.85–7 and Antiphon 5.8–10. Todd (2007) 124 tries to revive the suggestion of Paoli, followed by Cohen (1984) and (1991), 110–13 that *moichoi* (seducers) were subject to *apagoge* to the Eleven on the basis of Aeschines 1.90–92 and that this is the law cited by Euphiletus at Lys. 1.28. Neither argument is persuasive. First, Aeschin. 1.90–92 has nothing to do with *apagoge*, see Harris (2006a) 291–93; cf. Fisher (2001) 225–26. Second, Euphiletus needs to cite a law giving him the right to kill a seducer, but the law about *kakourgoi* only granted the right to arrest them and bring them to the Eleven. Carey (1995) 412 is thus correct to identify the law with that about *moichoi* cited at Lys. 1.49.

find the offender keeping the free person as a slave on his property. Dinarchus (1.23) alludes to two cases where Athenians were executed for this crime, but he also makes clear that in each case the offender was caught using the free victims as slaves: 'You put Menon the miller to death because he held a free boy from Pellene in his mill . . . You punished Euthymachus because he put a young girl from Olynthus in a brothel.' Neither defendant could deny his guilt since there was no question that the victim was a free person and that he was using this person as a slave, in the first case in a mill, which was considered onerous even for a slave, in the second case, in a brothel, where no respectable, free woman would work unless compelled.

In the case of the thief there were two special rules. First, there could be no arrest unless the value of the stolen item was at least fifty drachmas. Second, if the theft occurred at night, the victim could either kill or wound the thief during pursuit (D. 24.113). To arrest a thief or a clothes-snatcher, one had to catch the thief in highly incriminating circumstances, that is, either in the act or with the stolen object in his possession soon after the crime was committed. The clothes-snatcher presumably had to be seized during the actual assault or just after he took the clothes. One source ([D.] 45.81) indicates that the person who arrested a thief tied the stolen object to his back and brought him before the magistrate. We cannot tell whether this was a legal requirement or merely a means of proving that the offender's guilt was obvious. In any event, arrest by private individuals was highly restricted; the sources indicate that it was the exception and not the norm.

If one did not catch the thief with the stolen object, but suspected that someone had the stolen object in his house, one could not go ahead and enter the house simply because he thought he would discover the object. He had to conduct his search in accordance with the law. Aristophanes and Isaeus allude to the legally prescribed form of search (*phorazo*), which required that the person who claimed his property was in the house had to enter naked.[144] According to a scholion on Aristophanes, the purpose was to prevent people from taking something from the house without being detected or to stop them from maliciously (ὑπὸ ἔχθρας) planting the object they were looking for in the house to make the owner guilty of

144. Ar. *Nub.* 498–99; *Ran.* 1362–63; Is. 6.42.

theft.[145] In his *Laws* (954a), Plato sets forth the requirements for the search in some detail, and his rules are probably based on the Athenian procedure with some minor additions:

> If someone wishes to search for something in anyone's house, he must conduct his search in the following way: naked or with a small *chiton* without a belt after first swearing an oath by the legally prescribed goods that he expects to find [the stolen object]. Let him [the suspect] provide his house to be searched, both the sealed and unsealed items. If anyone does not give his house to be searched to someone who wishes to investigate, let the person who is prevented estimate the value of the object he is looking for and bring a private suit, and if he [the defendant] owes, let him pay damages double to the amount estimated.

Here we find strict regulation of a procedure carried out by a private individual to prevent its abuse as a means of personal vendetta.

Different rules applied to the use of physical force to arrest *moichoi*, those who seduced free women.[146] The man who caught the seducer could lock him up until he either paid compensation or made arrangements for payment.[147] Here too the Athenians placed careful restrictions on the use of force. In his speech *Against Neaera*, Apollodorus ([D.] 59.64–74) describes how his opponent Stephanus attempted to use this procedure against Epaenetus only to find that it backfired and almost landed him in serious trouble. At the time of her trial, Neaera was living with an Athenian politician named Stephanus. Apollodorus tells how Stephanus caught Epaenetus with Neaera's daughter and by threats induced him to make a promise to pay thirty mnai. Stephanus released him after Epaenetus named two respectable Athenians as his sureties for this sum ([D.] 59.65). Apollodorus claims that the entire incident was the result of a plot hatched by Stephanus and Neaera, but he provides no evidence for his allegation, which we are entitled to view with some skepticism. As soon as

145. For the similarity between this procedure and *quaestio cum lance et licio* in Roman law see Wyse (1904) 528–30.

146. Some scholars translate the term *moichos* as adulterer, but the word also applies to those who seduce unmarried women. See Kapparis (1999) 297 for a summary of the debate.

147. On this law see Kapparis (1999) 308–9.

Epaenetus was released, he brought a charge against Stephanus for wrongful imprisonment ([D.] 59.66). Here Apollodorus reminds the court that if someone claimed that he had been wrongfully held as a seducer, he could bring a charge against the man who detained him and, if he proved there was a plot against him, his sureties would win release from payment. If he did not convince the court, however, the defendant could do anything he wished to him provided he did not use a knife.[148] This statute once again reveals an awareness that self-help could easily be abused and that it was necessary to protect the victims of such abuse by providing them with legal remedies.

When Epaenetus made his charge before the *thesmothetai*, he admitted that he had had relations with the girl, but claimed that he was not a seducer ([D.] 59.67). He presented two arguments to support his point. His first argument was that the girl was not the daughter of Stephanus, but of Neaera, who was aware that he was having relations with the girl. He also pointed out that he had spent money on both mother and daughter and that they were under his care while he was in Athens. His probable reason for making this statement was to undercut Stephanus' claim to be the girl's *kyrios*, or protector. His second argument was that the law states that one cannot commit *moicheia* (seduction) with women who reside in a brothel or sell themselves openly in the marketplace, that is, work as prostitutes on the street ([D.] 59.67).[149] At this point Stephanus grew frightened because he was worried that he would be exposed as a brothel-keeper and an extortionist. He therefore agreed to submit the dispute to arbitration provided that Epaenetus withdrew his charge and the sureties were released from their obligation ([D.] 59.68).[150] Epaenetus agreed, and a settlement was worked out that required Epaenetus to contribute one thousand drachmas for the dowry of Neaera's daughter ([D.] 59.69–70). The entire incident reveals that the person who used self-help did so at some risk. He had to be certain that he had strong grounds for using physical force against his opponent and might be vulnerable to the charge that he had abused his power. In this case, Stephanus was forced to relinquish

148. For some suggestions about the reason for this limitation see Harris (2006a) 39; Todd (2007) 147–48.

149. On this law see Kapparis (1999) 311–13.

150. There was nothing illegal about withdrawing a public charge at this stage. See Harris (2006a) 405–22.

his claim to the payment of thirty mnai and accept a settlement for much less. He had also exposed himself to a charge of wrongful imprisonment, which could have brought serious penalties if he were convicted.

It is true that the successful plaintiff in a private suit could seize the property of a defendant who did not pay the money awarded him by the court.[151] Yet here too there were restrictions in place. First, the plaintiff could not enter the defendant's house without his permission. For instance, when Theophemus and two associates broke into the house of a defendant who owed him money from a legal judgment and carried off his property but was not present, his actions were considered highly illegal ([D.] 47.52–61. Cf. D. 37.45–6). Second, the plaintiff could not use force if the defendant resisted his attempt to take his belongings. After Demosthenes won his suit against Aphobus and the latter did not pay the money he owed, Demosthenes went to take possession of his land. When he arrived, Onetor claimed that the property belonged to him because Aphobus had given it to him as security for his daughter's dowry. When Aphobus divorced his wife and did not repay the dowry, Onetor took the property. Even though Demosthenes claimed that the dowry was never paid and that the divorce never took place, he did not use force to drive Onetor out of the property, but instead brought an ejectment suit (*dike exoules*) to gain possession (D. 30.8). The law may have granted the right to seize another person's property, but it did not allow anyone to use violence against a free person in such circumstances.[152] The only exception to this general rule was the right of the creditor to seize a debtor in order to take him into debt-bondage. This presumably occurred only when the debtor had no assets for the creditor to take and therefore had to pay his debt by working for the creditor.[153]

151. On this topic in general see Weiss (1923) 455–94. For Athens see Harrison (1971) 187–190.

152. Pelloso (2009/10) 130–31 fails to make a distinction between the use of self-help in seizing property and its use against free persons. This invalidates his objection to the analysis of Harris (2007b). Pelloso *per litteras* tells me that he now agrees with the revised version of my argument. As Weiss (1923) 461 notes, it is likely that the presence of the demarch may have been required for a creditor to seize property from a defaulting debtor ('Ferner dürfen wir vermuten, daß zur Aufschließung des Hauses Anwesenheit des Demarchen erforderlich war'). He cites the scholion to Ar. *Nub.* 37.

153. On debt-bondage see Harris (2006a) 249–70. Demosthenes (21.175–76) recalls that Evander of Thespiai won a maritime case against Menippus, a man from Caria, who did not pay him, and seized him during the Mysteries. Evander was censured for his offense against the festival, then brought to court by Menippus. The court decided that Evander should lose the right to collect the judgment awarded to him and to reimburse Menippus for expenses

The laws of Athens placed strict limits on the use of physical force by private individuals. The few cases in which physical force was permitted were clearly exceptions to the general rule that private individuals should not use violence and should entrust law enforcement to public officials who were under oath to follow the laws.[154] There does not appear to be a single overriding principle operating here. Some exceptions are granted in cases of a serious threat to public safety (killing a tyrant or murderer who has returned from exile); others are given for the protection of private property (killing and arresting thieves) or to maintain a family's honor (killing seducers and in cases of sexual violence).[155] In each case, however, the right was carefully ring-fenced, and procedures were enacted to prevent the abuse of this right, a clear sign that the Athenians were very reluctant to allow private individuals to enforce the law.[156]

To sum up. A study of the actual laws and decrees of the Athenians shows that officials and bodies like the Council of 500 and the Areopagus played the primary role in policing Athens. Far from entrusting private citizens with wide powers to employ self-help, the laws of Athens carefully circumscribed their right to use force. As Demosthenes says (21.221), the reason why every Athenian feels safe is because 'he knows in his own mind, is confident and trusts in our form of government that no one will drag him off or abuse him or beat him.' The average Athenian might sometimes rely on family, friends, or neighbors to protect him (Ar. *Nub.* 1322). In general, however, it was the state and its officials that made Athens and Attica a safe place to live.[157]

---

he incurred by staying in Athens to attend the trial. Demosthenes' brief description of the case does not allow us to determine whether the court punished Evander for using physical violence against Menippus or for using violence during the festival. The analysis of the incident by MacDowell (1990) 393–95 is undermined by his misunderstanding of the *probole* procedure, which was only a vote of censure and did include a trial in court. See Harris (2008) 79.

154. Private individuals had the right to punish slaves owned by other people whom they caught stealing their property: see Harris (2006a) 275–76. This however does not concern the use of force against free persons, which was permitted only in rare cases.

155. For the aims of the laws about seduction and sexual violence see Harris (2006a) 314–20.

156. *Pace* Christ (1998b).

157. Forsdyke (2008) 37 claims 'The Athenians, like other Greeks, participated simultaneously in two systems of justice–the official and the popular.' Forsdyke (2008) 6 further asserts that 'popular justice was not only frequently used alongside more "official" forms of punishment, but that the Greeks made more flexible use of the various modes of social

That is not to say that the Athenians had no concerns about official misconduct. But they clearly believed that it was better to place the administration of justice in the control of magistrates sworn to uphold impartially the laws and decrees of the Athenian people.[158] This was because the Athenians clearly understood the risks of leaving enforcement to the whim of private citizens who might abuse legal procedures to pursue personal feuds to the detriment of the public good. The measures that they took to discourage feuding and the effect they had on citizens' behavior are the subjects of the next chapter.[159]

---

control . . .' and that 'the classical Athenians (for example) showed no hesitation in punishing particular offenders through informal, yet highly public, forms of popular justice.' The evidence from the ancient sources does not support her argument. One of the most serious weaknesses of her argument is that she does not clearly define what she means by 'popular justice.' In some places this term appears to mean justice that is administered by large groups of private citizens outside the formal legal institutions of the *polis* and without the involvement of public officials. In other places she uses the term to refer to cases of self-help (on self-help see section IV of this chapter), in which an individual imposes punishment on a criminal, and in still other places to punishments imposed by the courts in which the offender is exposed to public ridicule (e.g., D. 24.114; [D.] 59.66). Each of these three categories is different and the latter two form part of the official legal system. Only the first—justice administered by large groups of private citizens without official authorization—qualifies as popular justice. There is very little evidence for this form of justice. For instance, Forsdyke claims that stoning to death was a form of popular justice, but the examples of stoning are rare: the stoning of Lycidas during the Persian Wars took place when the Athenians had fled Athens and was clearly exceptional (Hdt. 9.5.3). One should note, however, that Lycurgus (*Leocr.* 122) believes that this punishment was imposed by a formal decree. For stoning as a punishment imposed by an official see X. *HG* 1.2.13. On the other hand, Xenophon (*An.* 5.7.24–30) condemns execution of stoning by a crowd without a trial as a form of injustice. This passage, overlooked by Forsdyke, undermines much of her argument. I plan to deal with this topic in greater detail elsewhere.

158. For the requirement that officials perform their duties and enforce the law impartially see Rhodes and Osborne (2003) no. 58, lines 8–10; D. 23.96–7.

159. The conclusions of an earlier version of this essay, Harris (2007b), have been endorsed by Fuhrman (2012) 243: 'Edward Harris has argued that the power of public officials and the strength of formal law curtailed self-help, and I find his objections to Hunter's model convincing.'

2

Feuding or the Rule of Law?

AN ESSAY IN LEGAL SOCIOLOGY

ONE AREA IN which Athenian law provided much latitude for private initiative was in bringing public actions. A private action could only be brought by the person who had suffered an injustice at the hands of the defendant; a public action could be brought by any Athenian citizen and in some cases by a foreigner.[1] Modern legal systems generally entrust the prosecution of criminal cases to public officials, who are employees of the state and are elected or appointed to uphold the laws and to protect the public interest. Athens was far different in this regard: private individuals could bring public charges to court. What effect did this difference have on the nature of law enforcement? How did the private individuals who charged someone with a crime view their role? Did the Athenians possess an agonistic ethic and believe that the system permitted them to pursue their private enemies in court? Did the Athenian legal system give free rein to individuals who wished to use the courts to enhance their own prestige and to intimidate opponents so that litigation resembled a form of feuding? Or did the Athenians consider their primary responsibility the duty to uphold the law and to maintain public order? Did Athenian values discourage citizens from using the legal system to pursue conflicts? Did Athenian laws attempt to restrain litigiousness?

In the previous chapter, the Athenian legal system was placed in its political context. This chapter examines the social context of the law and falls into three parts. The first examines Athenian attitudes about the duties of private individuals and anger and enmity as motives for litigation. The second shows that the Athenians enacted several laws to discourage frivolous prosecution and lawsuits brought for the sole reason of harassing enemies and intimidating opponents. The third examines several quarrels

1. See Harrison (1971) 76–7.

between Athenian citizens and shows how social attitudes and public statutes worked to restrain litigiousness and resolve conflict. A study of the litigation conducted by several individuals illustrates the social reality of Athenian law.

I

Lycurgus, when prosecuting Leocrates for treason in 331 BCE, observes that there are three elements protecting the city's democracy and prosperity:

> First, the system of laws; second, the vote of the judges; and third the trial, which brings crimes under their control. It is the function of the law to indicate what must not be done, the task of the accuser to denounce those who are subject to the penalties set forth in the laws, and the duty of the judge to punish those whom both of these bring to his attention. (Lycurg. *Leocr.* 4)

According to Lycurgus, the function of the accuser in a public case was not to pursue his feud against a private enemy but to uphold the law:

> It is the duty of the just citizen therefore not to bring to public trial for the sake of private quarrels people who have done the city no wrong but to regard those who have broken the law as his own enemies and to view crimes that affect the community as providing public grounds for his enmity against them. (Lycurg. *Leocr.* 6)

Accusers in other cases view their role in similar terms.[2] One of Demosthenes' prosecutors in the Harpalus case says that it is the duty of the democratic politician to hate those who harm the city by their speeches or decrees. He goes on to criticize Demosthenes for failing to indict Demades for his numerous crimes against Athens (Din. 1.100–101). When Hyperides recalls his prosecutions of Aristophon, Diopeithes, and Philocrates, he says that he accused all of them because they were harming the city, not because of any personal enmity (Hyp. *Eux.* 28–30). Euthycles, when accusing Aristocrates of passing an illegal decree, asserts that he is not

2. Allen (2000b) believes that Lycurgus' view of the prosecutor's role was an innovation, but the passages quoted below show that it was the traditional view. See also Liddel (2007) 256–8 on prosecution as a public duty.

acting out of private enmity (D. 23.1). He brought his suit only because he saw the defendant and his associates harming the city's interests (D. 23.5. Cf. 190). A member of the Council speaking against Philon at his *dokimasia* declares that he is not pursuing any private hatred. Philon's crimes against the community are his reason for challenging his qualifications for office (Lys. 31.1–2). After Leodamas was rejected at his *dokimasia* to serve as archon in 382/1, a man named Euandrus was selected in his place. When a friend of Leodamas then challenged Euandrus at his *dokimasia*, he assured the court that he was not accusing Euandrus because Leodamas was his friend. His sole motive was to protect the citizens and city of Athens (Lys. 26.15).[3] Demosthenes, speaking in support of Apsephion's prosecution of Leptines' law, admits that he wishes to help Chabrias' son, who has been adversely affected by the law. He stresses however that his main reason for speaking is his conviction that the law's repeal would benefit the city. When charging Timocrates with passing an inexpedient law, Diodorus sets out the reasons for his prosecution: his aim is to defend the rights of all Athenians, which have been threatened by the passage of Timocrates' law (D. 24.1–3).[4]

The opposite of the public-spirited prosecutor was the sycophant.[5] The good prosecutor brought his case out of a sense of civic duty and expected no reward from the state (D. 21.28; 24.3. Cf. [D.] 53.2). The sycophant brought suits to extort money from defendants who would pay him in return for dropping the suit.[6] If their victims did not pay, they would bring their cases to trial (Hyp. *Lycurg.* 2). For the sycophant, public actions were an opportunity to gain cash ([D]. 59.43). The sycophant might also prosecute because someone hired him to harass an enemy (D. 21.103; 51.16; [D.] 59.43; Aeschin. 1.20). The honest prosecutor brought truthful charges about real crimes; the sycophant made false charges (Lys. 25.3; Aeschin. 2.5, 39, 183;

3. Compare Lys. 22.2–4 (the prosecutor states that he is accusing the grain-dealers to support the laws and gives no personal motive).

4. Diodorus admits that he has quarreled with Androtion, who he alleges has benefited from the law's provisions, but he mentions this conflict only to explain why he has become involved in litigation when normally he keeps to himself (D. 24.6).

5. On the sycophant in general see Harvey (1990), who demolishes the claim of Osborne (1990) that sycophants played a positive role in protecting democracy. Cf. MacDowell (2009) 304 note 40 ('Harvey convincingly refutes Osborne').

6. See for example And. 1.101, 105; Antiphon 5.79–80; D. 38.20. Todd (1993) 93, note 18 claims that such accusations of blackmail were rare and the examples mentioned in the sources 'the few exceptions.' But Harvey (1990) 111, note 27 lists thirty-four examples of the practice, which show that the practice was commonly associated with the sycophant.

D. 18.95).[7] His object was to slander his opponents (Aeschin. 2.145). The good citizen brings to trial only those who are guilty; the sycophant is always in court and harasses the innocent (D. 36.53–4; D. 38.3; Din. 2.12). The sycophant makes prosecuting his trade and earns his living from it (Ar. *Av.* 1422–35). The practice of sycophancy was considered so deleterious that the Athenians made it a crime and provided several procedures against sycophants: a public action, *eisangelia*, and the procedure of *probole* (Isoc. 15.314).

In recent years, however, it has become fashionable among certain scholars to claim that the Athenians were very litigious because they possessed an agonistic ethos and were obsessed with honor and status. As a result, litigants often used the courts not to enforce the law but to pursue feuds with personal enemies to enhance their power and prestige. Punishment for breaking the law was not the motive; accusers brought charges against opponents to wreak vengeance. Several passages from Aristotle would appear to lend support to this view:

> [It is more honorable] to take vengeance on enemies and not to be reconciled than to come to terms with them; for to retaliate is just, and the just is honorable, and not to be defeated is characteristic of a brave man. (Arist. *Rh.* 1.9.24.1367a24–5 trans. Kennedy)
>
> And revenge is pleasant; for it is painful to be unsuccessful, and it is pleasant to succeed. Now, those who are resentful are pained beyond measure when they fail to secure revenge, while the hope of it delights them. (Arist. *Rh.* 1.11.13.1370b13 trans. Kennedy)
>
> Human beings too then are distressed when angry, and take pleasure in retaliating; but people who fight from these motives are effective in fighting, not courageous, since they do not fight because of the fine, or as the correct prescription directs, but because of emotion (*pathos*). (Arist. *EN* 3.8.1117a7 trans. Rowe with one change)
>
> . . . putting up with being the target of abuse, and not intervening when those close to one are treated in that way, is slavish. (Arist. *EN* 4.5.1126a8–9 trans. Rowe)

In this agonistic society, enmity (*echthra*) played a greater role in court than legal issues. According to one scholar, 'Athenian judicial orations abound with references to enmity.' Enmity was 'a social state that carried

7. For other passages see Harvey (1990) 112, note 33.

with it particular consequences for the individuals, their friends and relations and the judges who heard the case' and 'might be made to appear the crucial issue in the interpretation and judgment of aggressive behavior.'[8] The courts did not act to enforce the law but rather acted as an arena where men might compete for honor and status. 'In this nominally egalitarian society in which neither titles nor offices fixed one's ranking, the question of settling relative standing was always open.' This created a situation where 'the courts were a natural arena for such contests and the rhetoric of enmity, envy, and invective was the primary instrument with which they were waged.'[9] As a result, 'speakers often sought to establish . . . that they were prosecuting because of genuine enmity.'[10] Litigants often 'advance enmity as a respectable motive for litigation,' and 'enmity and revenge are consistently portrayed as honorable.'[11] The key value for understanding litigation in democratic Athens was therefore the maxim 'help your friends and harm your enemies.'[12] Athenian society therefore glorified revenge: 'The attempt to retaliate upon an enemy being justified . . . successful retaliation was a joy, a failure a horror: a man might be respected for attempting revenge and denigrated for making no attempt.'[13] According to another scholar, 'Athenians shared with other Greeks the basic assumption that when a man suffered at the hands of another, he should pursue vengeance (*timoria*) in his own person not only to right the wrong, but also to defend his reputation.'[14]

This approach encounters several objections. First, the evidence from Aristotle is not as straightforward as it appears. In the *Nicomachean Ethics* and the *Rhetoric*, Aristotle is describing general aspects of human nature; he is not presenting an account of Athenian social values. Although Aristotle notes that many individuals desire vengeance, he also observes that people do not find vindictive individuals admirable. In the *Rhetoric* Aristotle says that '[we are friendly to] those who are pleasant to deal with and to pass

---

8. Cohen (1995) 70.

9. Cohen (1995) 82.

10. Cohen (1995) 72. For a similar view see Hansen (1991) 195.

11. Cohen (1995) 83.

12. See Blundell (1989) 24: 'Greek popular thought is pervaded by the assumption that one should help one's friends and harm one's enemies.'

13. Dover (1974) 182.

14. Christ (1998a) 161. For a similar view see Fisher (1998) 82–3.

the day with; such are those who are good-tempered and not contentious (*machetoi*) or quarrelsome; for all such are pugnacious and those always fighting clearly want the opposite' (Arist. *Rh.* 2.4.12.1381b trans. Kennedy). People tend to avoid those who tend to overreact to insults: 'And [people are friendly to] those not mindful of wrongs done to them nor inclined to cherish their grievances but who are easily appeased; for people think the attitude they suppose shown to others will also be shown to themselves. And [they are friendly to] those who do not say or want to know bad things about neighbors or friends but [look for] good things' (Arist. *Rh.* 2.4.17–18.1381b trans. Kennedy). In another passage in the *Rhetoric* Aristotle states that '[it is fair or reasonable] to remember the good things one has experienced rather than the bad and that it is fair or reasonable (*epieikes*) to put up with harm when one is wronged' (Arist. *Rh.* 1.13.18.1374b). In the *Nicomachean Ethics* Aristotle commends the reasonable man who does not insist on his full rights according to law (Arist. *EN* 5.10.1138a1–3). These works do not endorse the ethics of violent retaliation.

Second, when Athenian litigants spoke in court, they did not portray themselves as obsessed with revenge. The defendant in Lysias' speech *Against Simon* describes how after he was attacked, he went out of his way to avoid his assailant instead of striking back. The defendant and Simon were both in love with a boy named Theodotus. When Simon found out that Theodotus was staying in the defendant's house, he broke down the doors and invaded the women's quarters (Lys. 3.5–7). After being ejected by force, Simon found out where the defendant was dining and called him out into the street. When he emerged, Simon hit him, then when he defended himself, Simon retreated and threw stones at him (Lys. 3.8). Even after suffering this abuse, the defendant chose not to retaliate or even to bring a lawsuit against Simon, but he chose to move abroad to avoid further trouble (Lys. 3.9–10). Later, after his return to the Piraeus, the defendant went to see Theodotus at the house of Lysimachus and was attacked again by Simon and several of his friends, who tried to drag Theodotus away (Lys. 3.11–12). Once again the defendant retreated and tried to avoid Simon, but got into a fight with him when he tried to free Theodotus (Lys. 3.13–18). After each assault, the defendant did not attempt to retaliate. When he finally did attack him, it was not to take revenge but to free Theodotus.[15]

---

15. My analysis of this incident owes much to that of Herman (2006) 165–167. W. V. Harris (1997) claims that the defendant actually tries to excuse himself for not retaliating, but see Herman (2000).

The conduct of the defendant is that of the reasonable man described by Aristotle, who puts up with injustice rather than insisting on revenge.

A young man named Ariston acted in a similar way when assaulted by Ctesias, the son of Conon. The two young men were camped near Panactum in northern Attica when Ctesias and his companions started to insult the slaves of Ariston, beating and pouring excrement on them. Instead of striking back and starting a fight, Ariston and his messmates reported their conduct to the general, who criticized them for their disorderly behavior. His rebuke made no impression on Ctesias and his companions; that night they attacked Ariston, who was rescued by the general and several officers (D. 54.4–6). After his return to Athens, Ariston did not look for an opportunity to retaliate but did his best to keep away from Ctesias and his friends (D. 54.6). His restraint made no difference; Ctesias, his father Conon, and several others beat him until his lip was split and his eyes were swollen shut (D. 54.7–9). Like Simon's enemy, Ariston is the victim of drunken abuse but does not find it necessary to seek revenge or to bring a lawsuit. For him the correct response is to stay out of Ctesias' way.

Second, there is no reason to believe that the maxim 'help your friends and harm your enemies' was the golden rule of Greek morality. As G. Herman has observed, 'This conclusion is, to begin with, the result of an unsafe generalisation. It draws on a body of evidence self-servingly selected so as to exclude the many passages (from an equally wide range or sources) that recommend an entirely contrary, peaceful, conciliatory approach to friendship and enmity.'[16] For example, Cleoboulos of Lindos, one of the Seven Sages, advised that 'we should do a favor to a friend to bind him closer to us and to an enemy in order to make a friend of him' (D. L. 1.91). In a speech of Lysias (9.13–4), a speaker says that the powerful figure Sostratus has helped him to become well-known, but he has not taken advantage of his association with him 'either to avenge myself on an enemy or to serve a friend.' I think it is safe to assume his statement was not aimed at alienating the judges hearing his case. And there is Hesiod's advice to his brother to avoid the quarrels of the Agora. The man who does not have enough to eat cannot afford the luxury of strife. The man who has eaten his fill may indulge in disputes, but Hesiod urges his brother to settle their dispute and end their quarrel (Hesiod *WD* 27–36).

Some scholars who believe that Greek values demanded violent retaliation for all insults, both perceived and real, point to the plots of several

16. Herman (2000) 12.

Attic tragedies in which the main characters exact bloody revenge.[17] For example, Ajax in Sophocles' play feels humiliated when Menelaus and Agamemnon award Achilles' arms to Odysseus and attempts to kill all three of them but is driven mad by Athena and slaughters some cattle instead. But the play does not celebrate the joys of vengeance. In the prologue Athena shows Odysseus what Ajax, blinded by madness, intends to do to his enemies. When she asks him what he will do to Odysseus, Ajax replies he will tie him to a column and lash him until his back is red with blood (104–10). Athena asks him not to subject him to this treatment, but Ajax insists on meting out this revenge (111–113). Yet Odysseus does not feel any joy at the sight of his enemy driven mad by the goddess: 'I completely pity the wretched man,' he says, 'although he is my enemy, since he has fallen under the yoke of evil disaster' (121–23).[18] At the end of the play, Odysseus gives a speech that reveals both the limits of enmity and the existence of a higher standard of morality (1332–1345):

> Vindictiveness should not so govern you
> As to make you trample on justice. I too
> Found this man my enemy once, beyond the rest
> Of all my fellow soldiers, since the time
> I won Achilles' armor. Nevertheless,
> In spite of this enmity, I cannot wish
> To pay him with dishonor, or refuse
> To recognize in him the bravest man
> Of all that came to Troy, except Achilles.
> It would be wrong to do him injury;
> In acting so, you'd not be injuring him
> Rather the gods' laws. It's a foul thing to hurt
> A valiant man in death, though he was your enemy.

---

17. This is the theme of Burnett (1998).

18. Christ (2005) 144 states 'Odysseus does not so much reject the idea of doing harm to enemies as qualify it: one should not seek to harm an enemy when he is no longer a threat, namely, when is mad (121–26) or dead (1332–45); this gives considerable latitude for doing harm to sane and living enemies.' Christ appears not to have read the play carefully since he overlooks the fact that even after the death of Ajax his half-brother Teucer, wife Tecmessa, and son Eurysaces remain 'sane and living enemies' (to use Christ's phrase). Despite their *echthra*, Odysseus proposes to put an end to the conflict and prevails over the objections of Menelaus and Agamemnon, who wish to perpetuate the quarrel.

Finally, *echthra* does not figure as prominently in the forensic speeches of the Attic Orators as some scholars allege. The term *echthra* does occur in several forensic orations of Demosthenes, but it is entirely absent in the following speeches in the demosthenic corpus: 27, 28, 30, 31, 32, 34, 35, 38, 41, 42, 43, 44, 46, 47, 48, 50, 51, 52, 55, 56, or twenty out of forty-two. In 23 *Against Aristocrates* the accuser says he is not bringing his charge out of enmity (23.1) and asks the judges not to decide on the basis of *echthra* (23.97). In the third speech *Against Aphobus*, Demosthenes talks about witnesses who might be enemies of the defendant (D. 29.22–4), but does not use the term *echthra* to describe his relationship with him. In his first speech *Against Boeotus* (D. 39.11), Mantitheus only mentions the possibility of future enmity. In D. 44.99 the speaker says people who produce false affidavits are the enemies of all. In D. 45.65, 79 the speaker denounces someone as the common enemy of mankind and of the gods, not as his own foe. In most speeches delivered before Athenian courts, therefore, litigants do not refer to their opponents as their enemies.[19]

In fact, Demosthenes in his speech *On the Crown* in defense of Ctesiphon criticizes Aeschines for bringing his charge for no other reason than personal enmity (D. 18.12, 15).[20] He draws a contrast between insults made by enemies and the penalties provided by the laws (D. 18.123). Since Aeschines has brought his charge out of enmity, it is without substance (D. 18.143). According to Demosthenes, the good citizen is not motivated by personal enmity or anger (D. 18.278. Cf. D. 23.190), but Aeschines pursues his private enmity, the mark of the pusillanimous man (D. 18.278–9). If Aeschines were acting justly, he would not harm the public interest to satisfy his enmity (D. 18.293). In the speech *For the Soldier* the speaker criticizes Ctesicles and his fellow generals for conducting a vendetta

19. Cf. Rubinstein (2000) 179–80: 'Of the twenty-eight preserved prosecution speeches, fifteen do not cite personal enmity toward the defendant as a motive at all, while thirteen mention previous conflicts between prosecutors and defendants. However, of these thirteen only three prosecutors state that their feelings of hostility originate from their dealings with the defendants outside the political sphere. Of the remaining ten prosecutors, eight state explicitly that their previous conflicts with the defendants were firmly rooted in the political sphere (sometimes brought about by public actions initiated by the defendants against themselves), while two avoid specifying the nature of their hostile relationship altogether.' All this evidence undermines the analysis of echthra by Phillips (2008) 15–29.

20. On echthra as a motive in litigation see Kurihara (2003), whose general conclusions are anticipated to some extent by Harris (1999a) (= Harris [2006a] 405–22) and Harris (2005a), which was presented as a talk in 2001. The evidence presented in these essays refutes the arguments of Rhodes (1998).

against him: 'it is not right for any of our citizens to be registered as public debtors out of personal enmity' (Lys. 9.7. Cf. 15). The fact that enmity was their motive is used by the speaker as an argument to show that the charges against him are false.[21] These remarks reveal a deep suspicion of enmity as a motive for litigation.[22]

Even when accusers admit that they have a personal motive for bringing a public action, they still claim that their overriding concern is to serve the public good. After Meidias tried to destroy the costumes prepared for his chorus, then punched him at the Dionysia, Demosthenes first brought a *probole* against him in the Assembly, then prosecuted him in court on a public charge of aggravated assault (*hybris*). We will examine Demosthenes' quarrel with Meidias at length in the third section of this chapter. Although he had suffered directly from Meidias' abuse, Demosthenes claims that he brought the case because he decided to defend the rights of all citizens, which it was his duty to protect (D. 21.3). He does not aim to take revenge on Meidias but to shield other Athenians from his arrogance: 'Now the issue that is about to be debated and decided is whether or not someone should be allowed to do this sort of thing and to commit outrage with impunity against anyone whom he encounters. Therefore if any of you previously thought that this trial was about some private quarrel, let him now bear in mind that it is in the public interest for no one to be allowed to commit this sort of crime. Let him listen carefully because the matter affects the whole community' (D. 21.7–8).

There is no reason to believe that agonistic values ruled Athenian social life and that enmity provided the normal motivation for initiating legal action. In fact, the Athenians prided themselves on their reputation for being mild and generous.[23] Demosthenes praises the Athenians for their gentle character (21.184. Cf. Lys. 6.34) and reminds them that everything is kinder and gentler in a democracy (D. 22.51. Cf. Arist. *Ath. Pol.* 22.4). In other

21. Compare And. (1.117–23), who describes Callias' quarrel with him about the marriage of an *epikleros* to undermine the charges against him. See also Antiphon 4.1.4 and 4.2.1 for the connection between *echthra* and false charges.

22. There are a few speeches in which the prosecutor in a public case openly admits that the defendant is a personal enemy, but they appear to be exceptions to the general rule (e.g., [D.] 53.1–2). In two of these cases (Lys. 13; [D.] 58), the accuser says that he has brought the suit in obedience to his father's wishes. Even though Apollodorus had a personal reason to prosecute Neaera ([D.] 59.1–8), he does not mention this in his speech as *synegoros*, in which the stress is on Neaera's offense against the community.

23. On these qualities of the Athenians see de Romilly (1979) 97–112.

passages he says that the Athenians are famous for their mildness (D. 24.51, 170. Cf. Hyp. *D.* 25) and try to make their laws mild and moderate (D. 24.190).[24] Isocrates (10.37) attributes this Athenian quality to Theseus, who ruled lawfully and nobly and left traces of his mildness in contemporary institutions. According to Isocrates (15.20), the Athenians were recognized as the most merciful and gentle of all the Greeks (Arist. *Ath. Pol.* 22.4). Solon and Cleisthenes established a constitution hailed for its impartiality and mildness (Isoc. 7.20). In his Funeral Oration, Pericles describes life in Athens as tolerant and relaxed (Th. 2.37.2). Cleon says that Athenians normally went about free from fear and from plots against them (Th. 3.37.2). The laws and customs of Athens were known for their pity and forgiveness (D. 22.57. Cf. 24.171). The Athenians considered pity such an important quality that they established an Altar to Pity in the Agora, the very center of the city. Pausanias (1.17.1) knows of no other city in Greece that had an altar to pity. This may be an exaggeration, but Diodorus (13.22.7) reports that the Athenians were the first to establish such an altar.[25]

Far from promoting prolonged litigation and aggressive behavior, Athenian values discouraged men from using the courts to pursue feuds with each other. One litigant (D. 41.1) says it is better to accept a disadvantageous settlement than to go to court. Ariston, in the speech *Against Conon* (D. 54.24), says: 'If we chose not to bring an action under the laws concerning violence, that can reasonably be regarded as showing that we are not meddlesome (*apragmon*) and moderate (*metrios*), but not as showing him in any better light.' The metic Dareius, who brought an action against Dionysodorus for a debt, did not want to appear litigious (*philodikos*) (D. 56.14): 'We agreed to this, not because we were unaware of our rights under the contract, but because we thought we should accept a disadvantageous settlement in order not to be thought litigious (*philodikos*).'[26]

Rather than boasting about victories in court as a way of enhancing their prestige, litigants often seek to win the goodwill of the court by saying they have never been in court before. Aeschines (1.1) begins his speech

24. On this theme see Whitehead (2000) 437–8.

25. Thompson (1952) identifies the Altar of Pity with the Altar of the Twelve Gods, but see Gadbery (1992). The earliest reference to this altar is Apollodorus writing about 146 BCE. For the importance of pity in Athenian society see Sternberg (2006).

26. Cf. Lys. 10.2: 'Nor would I have proceeded against him if he had said anything else actionable about me, because I regard prosecution as not befitting a free man and as excessively *philodikos*.'

Against Timarchus: 'Never before have I brought a public charge against any man or given him trouble at his audit; no, I have in my opinion shown restraint in this regard.' A client of Isaeus (1.1) begins his speech by stating that he has never been in court even to listen to a case. Isocrates in his *Antidosis* (15.38) claims that 'no one has seen me in meeting places nor at preliminary hearings, nor in the courts, nor before the public arbitrators, but I have kept away from these things more completely than any other citizen.' The defendant in Lysias' speech *On the Property of Aristophanes* (19.55) says that although he lives near the Agora, he has never been seen around the courts. When prosecuting Timocrates, Diodorus says that it is unusual for him to get involved in litigation (D. 24.6). Aeschines (3.194) recalls how Aristophon was proud of winning seventy-five acquittals when tried on the charge of passing illegal decrees but finds his boasting misguided. More admirable in his opinion is Cephalus, who was never indicted once on this charge. For this reason plaintiffs and prosecutors often appear reluctant to bring cases and claim their opponents have forced them to go to court (cf. Is. 2.1). As G. Herman has rightly observed:

> The arguments put forward by the litigants show that they hoped, quite consistently, to enlist the dikasts' support by parading themselves not as vindictive, violent, explosive machos but as moderate citizens. This they did by imputing feuding characteristics to their opponents (hence the abundance of aggressive motives in the speeches) and gentle characteristics (self-restraint, meekness, a low-key sense of honour and a total lack of any explosive or aggressive disposition, for example) to themselves. In other words, they expected to sway their mass audiences by distancing themselves as much as possible from any suggestion that their actions might have been structured by feuding, violence, or vengeance. This must mean that feuding, violence and vengeance were behavioural patterns of which the dikasts, and hence the Athenian civic population in general, strongly disapproved.[27]

27. Herman (2000) 18. Christ (2005) claims that Athens was an agonistic society but only provides a list of contests to make his point. A list is not an argument. Later in the same essay he contradicts himself by stressing 'the conspicuous invocation of "quiet" or "cooperative" virtues in forensic oratory' and the fact that 'Athenian courts . . . might even reward those who sought to reduce rather than escalate conflict.' For a similar view see Christ (1998a) 160–92. If, according to Christ, agonistic values prevailed in Athens, why according to Christ did they have so little effect on the decisions of judges in court?

II

But were all these statements just rhetoric? When a litigant expressed his reluctance to go to court, was this merely a pose aimed at winning the court's sympathy? Or did the Athenians attempt to put the values expressed by these litigants into practice by enacting and enforcing measures to discourage frivolous litigation and the abuse of the legal system? There can be no question that the Athenians were not only aware of the problem of litigiousness but also tried to do something about the problem.[28] Social disapproval was not sufficient to discourage litigants from abusing the legal system. The Athenians expressed their convictions by enacting several practical measures against frivolous lawsuits.[29]

1. The Athenians recognized the principle of *res iudicata*, namely, the tenet that once a court has rendered its decision, that decision was binding and could not be altered or revisited (D. 20.147; D. 38.16; D. 40.39–43).[30] If the courts permitted litigants to bring the same issue to court again, it would have been impossible for the successful litigant to enforce his judgment or for the courts to resolve a single dispute. In the fifth century, when a litigant brought an action before a magistrate in a case that had already been decided, the defendant could bring a procedure called *diamartyria* before the magistrate, who would not allow the action to proceed if he found the objection valid.[31] In 403/2 Archinus introduced a law that created a new procedure called *paragraphe*.[32] Under this procedure, the defendant who claimed that the case had previously been adjudicated made his objection to the magistrate, who held a trial to decide this issue with the defendant speaking first, the plaintiff second.[33] If the court held for the defendant,

28. Herman (2006) succeeds in showing that the Athenian values discouraged aggressive behavior but does not study the laws aimed at discouraging litigants from using the courts to pursue personal feuds. Nor does Fisher (1998).

29. The account of measures against legal abuse found in Christ (1998a) 28–32 is incomplete and inaccurate.

30. This also held true for cases of homicide (Antiphon 5.87; 6.3).

31. See Isoc. 18.11–12; Lys. 23.13–14 with Harrison (1971) 124–5.

32. Steinwenter (1925) and Bonner and Smith (1930–38) 2: 78 believe that the procedure existed earlier than 403/2, but see Harrison (1971) 107.

33. Paoli (1933) believed that both the issue of the case's admissibility and the main issue were discussed and decided before the same court, but see Wolff (1966). For a summary of the debate see Harrison (1971) 106–24, who sides with Wolff.

the plea was barred; otherwise the case went forward. This principle was so important that the laws forbid those who had been convicted from supplicating the Assembly to have their verdict overturned (D. 24.52–53).[34]

2. The laws of Athens encouraged out-of-court settlements by recognizing such agreements as legally binding.[35] If a litigant brought a suit that had already been settled by private arbitration or by agreement, the defendant could bring a *paragraphe* action to stop the case from going forward.

3. For private cases there existed restrictions that required litigants to bring private actions within five years after the offense (D. 36.25–27; 38.17).[36]

4. The courts also required payment of fees called *prytaneia* by the plaintiff and defendant to discourage frivolous litigation in private cases. If the amount in dispute was more than one thousand drachmas, each litigant paid thirty drachmas each. If the amount was less than one thousand drachmas, but more than one hundred, each paid three drachmas. After the trial the loser reimbursed the winner for his fee.[37] In the case where someone claimed that a person being held as a slave was actually free but failed to prove his case, he had to pay the owner of the slave five hundred drachmas and in addition pay a fine of an equal amount to the treasury ([D.] 58.19–20). In many public cases, the accuser had to pay a fee called the *parastasis*, but the amount is unknown.[38]

5. Although Athenian law did not in most cases require those who brought a public suit to pay court fees, there was a serious penalty for bringing frivolous charges. If the prosecutor did not gain at least one-fifth of the votes, he lost his right to bring any public charges at all in the future and was subject to a fine of 1,000 drachmas.[39]

---

34. Pecorella Longo (2004) shows that the Assembly did have the power to overturn verdicts, but that this happened very rarely.

35. See Isocr. 18.11; D. 36.25; 37.1; 38.1 with Harrison (1971) 120. The law about arbitrators at D. 21.94 is not genuine—see MacDowell (1990) 317–8.

36. On statutes of limitations at Athens see Charles (1938). Wolff (1963) followed by Harrison (1971) 116–20, believed that there was a different rule for prescription in different procedures, but D. 36.25 refers to a single law about the matter. Wolff bases his argument on D. 33.47, but this is not a law about legal procedure but the period for which personal security, a contract, is valid. There was no statute of limitations, however, for homicide cases—see Lys. 13.83.

37. For the prytaneia, see Pollux 8.38 with Harrison (1971) 92–4.

38. See Arist. Ath. Pol. 59.3 with Rhodes (1981) 661–63.

39. For discussion of this penalty see Harris (1999) = Harris (2006a) 405–21. Wallace (2006) follows all my conclusions but claims that there was only a penalty of one thousand drachmas and no *atimia* when an accuser did not bring his case to court. This is contradicted by the Lexicon Cantabrigiense s.v. *prostimon* and D. 21.103. For a detailed refutation of Wallace's argument see Harris (2006b). MacDowell (2009) 295 misrepresents the evidence for the penalty.

6. There was also a penalty for litigants who lost private suits.[40] The earliest mention of this penalty occurs in a speech of Isocrates (18.11–12) delivered during the last years of the fifth century.[41] The speaker says that his opponent would have incurred a penalty of one-sixth (*epobolia*) if he had brought a private suit for false witness and did not gain one-fifth of the votes. A law of Archinus (Isoc. 18.2–3) imposed this penalty on either the accuser or the defendant who lost a *paragraphe* suit brought for violating the terms of the reconciliation agreement of 403. Several decades later Demosthenes brought a suit against his guardians and claimed that they had defrauded him of ten talents. In his speech *Against Aphobus*, he says that if he loses, he will have to pay his opponent one hundred minas, that is, one-sixth of the damages he claims, and will lose his citizen rights (D. 27.67).[42] Demosthenes does not say that he would pay this sum only if he failed to gain one-fifth of the votes, but he may be exaggerating the risk confronting him to gain the court's sympathy.[43] The loss of citizen rights would have lasted only until he paid the fine.[44] When Theophemus brought a private suit for assault (*aikeia*) against a trierarch who had tried to seize his property and won, the trierarch had to pay 1,100 drachmas as damages and 183 drachmas as *epobolia* ([D.] 47.64). In the previous cases, it was the unsuccessful plaintiff who paid the penalty, but in this case, it is the defendant who lost the case. Apollodorus admits that he too had to pay this penalty when he lost a *paragraphe* case to Phormion (D. 45.6). Aeschines (1.163) implies that the person who brought a suit for damages for failure to abide by the terms of a contract would have to pay the fine if he lost the case. Two litigants in mercantile cases, one a plaintiff, another a defendant

40. Pollux 8.47–8 says that the *epobolia* was also imposed in cases of *phasis*, a public suit, but there is no contemporary evidence that confirms his statement. For doubts see Whitehead (2002) 90, note 72. Wallace (2008) 98 claims that there is a provision for *epobolia* in a case of *phasis* found in the text of a law found at D. 43.71, but neither term is found in the text, which is of questionable authenticity.

41. MacDowell (1971) dates the speech to 401, and Whitehead (2002) to 403/2.

42. A scholion to Aeschin. 1.163 says that the penalty was paid to the public treasury, but the passage contains many errors and is not a reliable source of information. See MacDowell (2008) 89.

43. Wallace (2008) 97. Cf. Carey and Reid (1985) 208 ('it is probable that at 27.67 D. is using exaggerated language'). Note that Apollodorus ([D.] 53.1) says that he risks losing the right to bring public cases if fails to win his case against Nicostratus but does not mention that this penalty was only imposed when the accuser did not gain one-fifth of the votes. See Harris (2006a) 408.

44. MacDowell (2008) 90–91.

who has brought a *paragraphe*, say that if they lose the case and have to pay the one-sixth penalty, they will be thrown in prison (D. 56.4). This is probably a special provision that applied only in mercantile cases directed at traders who might leave Athens without paying.

The evidence appears to indicate that there was a general statute imposing a penalty of one-sixth of damages claimed in private suits on the litigant, plaintiff, or defendant.[45] The penalty was probably only incurred if the litigant did not gain at least one-fifth of the votes cast at the trial.[46] The intent of the penalty was clearly to discourage frivolous lawsuits and use of the courts for the sole purpose of harassing innocent people. It punished both the plaintiff who brought a private suit for damages without substance and the defendant who did not reach an out-of-court settlement with a plaintiff when he was clearly in the wrong.[47] At the same time, it prevented the person who lost a lawsuit from bringing another case until he paid the fine.

7. The aim of discouraging frivolous litigation is evident at the deme level in a decree of Myrrhinous about financial administration dated after 340.[48] The official appointed to manage the deme's finances is to undergo an audit of his activities before an elected board of ten men, who are to vote with a secret ballot. He cannot pass his audit unless a majority of this board votes that he should pass. If they vote against him, he has the right of appeal to all the members of the deme. If there are at least thirty demesmen present and they vote against him, however, he is to pay one-and-a-half times the amount assessed by the elected board, a measure providing a strong disincentive to pursuing a weak case.[49]

45. MacDowell (2008) 94 believes that there was a general statute while Wallace (2008) 97 asserts 'we have no good evidence for such a general procedural law.' The evidence of the lexica, however, supports MacDowell's view. See *An. Bekk.* 255.29f.; *Et. Mag.* 368.48ff.; Suda s.v. *epobolia*. In favor of MacDowell's view, one might also compare the penalty for frivolous prosecution in public cases, which was covered by a single statute for different types of procedures in public cases (see Theophrastus fr. 4b Szegedy-Maszak).

46. Harrison (1971) 185.

47. Despite their differences, both MacDowell (2008) and Wallace (2008) agree that the aim of the penalty was to discourage frivolous litigation. Cf. Harrison (1971) 184. This penalty and its implications for our understanding of Athenian attitudes to litigation are not discussed by Cohen (1995).

48. *IG* ii² 1183, lines 16–24 with Whitehead (1986) 119.

49. Note that the phratry of the Deceleans also discouraged frivolous appeals. The man who proposed a candidate for membership who was rejected paid a fine of one hundred drachmas. If he appealed and lost the case, he paid one thousand drachmas (*IG* ii² 1237, lines 20–22, 38–40).

8. The harshest penalties for losing a lawsuit were for those who appealed a deme's decision about citizenship. If someone presented himself as a candidate for Athenian citizenship to a deme and was rejected, he had the right to appeal the deme's decision to a court in Athens. If he won the case, the deme was compelled to accept him as a member and a citizen. If he lost, however, he was sold into slavery.[50] This penalty is so harsh that some scholars have argued that it only applied to slaves, but another procedure relating to citizenship supports the view that it applied to all applicants, free or slave.[51] In 346/5 the Athenians voted that the demes should examine their registers of citizens. Each deme voted on the membership of each citizen registered in the deme. If someone was rejected, he had the right to appeal his case to Athens, but if he lost, he was sold into slavery.[52] As one scholar notes, 'the Athenians tried by threatening heavy penalties to discourage frivolous litigation.'[53]

III

These measures reveal that the Athenians were serious about discouraging litigants from using the courts to pursue personal feuds by bringing cases without merit. But what effect did these laws have on the behavior of actual litigants? Were they successful in reducing the amount of litigation? Or did litigants merely pay lip service to the popular attitudes about litigiousness and attempt to flout the laws aimed at preventing it? Did the laws actually discourage litigants from pursuing feuds in court or did they have relatively little effect on their behavior? Is it therefore correct to conclude that 'much litigation should be viewed as feuding behavior'?[54] The best way to test this assertion is to examine the behavior of several individuals who were frequently involved in litigation.

Before examining their activities, however, it is necessary to examine the term 'feud.' Several historians and anthropologists have provided definitions

---

50. Arist. *Ath. Pol.* 42.1.

51. See Rhodes (1981) 501–2.

52. See Is. 12 *hyp.* [= D. H. *Isaeus* 16]; D. 57 *hyp.* MacDowell (2009) 288 doubts that the information of Libanius in the hypothesis to D. 57 is reliable, but he appears to be unaware of the hypothesis to Is. 12 and the similar punishment mentioned at Arist. *Ath. Pol.* 42.1, both of which show that his skepticism is unwarranted.

53. Rhodes (1981) 502.

54. Cohen (1995) 87.

of the term. Wallace-Hadrill offers a very broad and inclusive definition: 'We may call it first, the threat of hostility between kins, then, the state of hostility between them, and finally the satisfaction of their differences and a settlement on terms acceptable to both. The threat, the state and the settlement of that hostility constitute feud but do not necessarily mean bloodshed.'[55] Heusler came up with a similar definition, but added that feuds could involve lawsuits and arbitration instead of violence.[56] Drawing on the work of Black-Michaud and Nadel, W. I. Miller has drawn up a list of the basic features that characterize most feuds:[57]

1. Feud is a [hostile] relationship between two groups.
2. Unlike ad hoc revenge killing that can be an individual matter, feuding involves groups that can be recruited by any number of principles, among which kinship, vicinage, household, or clientage are most usual.
3. Unlike war, feud does not involve relatively large mobilizations, but only occasional musterings for limited purposes. Violence is controlled; casualties rarely reach double digits in any single encounter.
4. Feud involves collective liability. The target need not be the actual wrongdoer, nor, for that matter, need the vengeance-taker be the person most wronged.
5. A notion of exchange governs the process, a kind of my-turn/your-turn rhythm, with offensive and defensive positions alternating after each confrontation.
6. As a corollary to the preceding item, people keep score.
7. People who feud tend to believe that honor and affronts to it are the prime motivators of hostilities. Cross-culturally, there appears to be a correlation between the feud and a culture of honor.
8. Feud is governed by norms that limit the class of possible expiators and the appropriateness of responses. For instance, most feuding cultures recognize a rough rule of equivalence in riposte, the *lex talionis* being but one example.
9. There are culturally acceptable means for making temporary or permanent settlements of hostility.

---

55. Wallace-Hadrill (1962) 122.

56. Heusler (1911) 38.

57. Miller (1990) 180–81. Although Cohen (1995) draws on the works of Miller and Black-Michaud, he inexplicably does not mention their definitions of the term 'feud.'

A 'model' feud is found in *Njáls Saga*, an epic composed in Iceland in the late thirteenth century, which appears to recount events from 960 to 1020. Miller gives the following summary:

> Njal's wife Bergthora and Gunnar's wife Hallgerd exchanged insults at a feast. The next summer, when Njal and his sons and Gunnar were at the Allthing, Hallgerd sent a slave named Kol to kill a slave of Njal and Bergthora named Svart. After some prompting Kol sank his axe in Svart's head. Hallgerd then sent a messenger to the Allthing to inform Gunnar, who in turn went to Njal offering him self-judgment. Njal accepted the offer and immediately awarded himself twelve ounces of silver. Bergthora registered displeasure with the settlement and indicated that blood vengeance would also follow. To this end she engaged a man named Atli as a servant. The following summer at Allthing time, Bergthora sent Atli to kill Kol and sent a messenger to Njal to inform him of the killing. In a mirror image of the prior year's events, Gunnar accepted Njal's offer of self-judgment and awarded himself the same sum of twelve ounces. Njal paid over the same purse and silver that Gunnar gave him the year before. Gunnar, the saga tells us, recognized the money.[58]

The feud then continued for several years. Hallgerd then had Brynjolf, one of her kin, kill Atli, who was a freedman. Bergthora retaliated by having Thord, a freedman's son, kill Brynjolf. Hallgerd then arranged to have Sigmund, one of Gunnar's kin, kill Thord. Finally Bergthora had her son Skarphedin kill Sigmund. In this feud those on each side are linked by kinship or ties of dependence. It would therefore be a serious mistake to view a feud as any conflict that 'involves an institutionalized relationship of hostility between two individuals or groups.'[59] This description is so broad and vague that it could be applied to any prolonged conflict in any society.[60] What is significant for our purposes, however, is that there is a general consensus among historians and social scientists that feuding *always* involves hostility between groups.

---

58. Miller (1990) 183.

59. Cohen (1995) 88.

60. Phillips (2008) 15 uncritically follows Cohen (1995) and makes no attempt to respond to my objections in Harris (2005a).

The main evidence for the conflicts to be examined is found in the speeches of the Attic Orators. One must however approach this evidence with much caution.[61] Above all, one must avoid taking a positivist approach and accepting every statement about questions of fact made by a litigant as trustworthy.[62] Litigants in Athenian courts were not restrained by strict rules of evidence and might use lies, slander, or innuendo to attack an opponent. Even though the judges might shout when they thought the litigant overstepped the bounds of decency, the presiding magistrate did not stop a litigant from making unsubstantiated slanders. On the other hand, there were limits to what a litigant could get away with. He could not distort well-known recent public events without damaging his own credibility. One should therefore place more trust in accounts given soon after the event in question than to later accounts. Moreover, the court expected litigants to provide proof for their most important arguments either in the form of witness statements or documents.[63] Witnesses who lied could be prosecuted with a private action for false testimony, and the documents presented by a litigant were read aloud by the clerk, not the litigant. When evaluating an account given by a litigant, therefore, one should pay close attention to what evidence he provides.

Demosthenes' Quarrels with Aphobus and Meidias

Perhaps the most famous quarrels in Classical Athens are Demosthenes' conflicts with his guardian Aphobus and his rival Meidias. One scholar alleges that 'Demosthenes engaged for a significant portion of his adult

61. One should make a distinction between litigants' statements about common attitudes and statements about questions of fact. The former should be trustworthy (see Dover 1974), but the latter must be analyzed carefully in their contexts.

62. Cohen (1995), Ober (1989), MacDowell (1990), (2000), (2009), and Phillips (2008) tend to take a positivist approach to the evidence.

63. Todd (1990) believes that the main function of the witness in an Athenian court was to support the litigant and not to provide evidence. But if the evidence provided by a witness was not important, why did the litigants have to submit the testimony of witnesses in writing after 380 BCE? According to Humphreys (2007) the identity and status of the witness were more important than their statements about the facts, but this theory is undermined by the fact that litigants say little or nothing about the identity and status of witnesses when they introduce them. For good criticisms of Todd and Humphreys see Rubinstein (2005), especially 114: the function of the witness was 'to confirm specific "facts," which could be represented as relating more or less directly to the charge itself.'

life, in a series of feuding relationships.' These battles lasted 'for many years.'[64] Did these quarrels really last very long?

The basic facts of the conflict with the guardians are as follows: Demosthenes' father died when he was about eight, leaving him and his sister orphans and his mother a widow. The terms of his will appointed Aphobus, Therippides, and Demophon as guardians and granted them certain legacies (D. 27.13–15; 29.45). These men then mismanaged the estate for ten years until Demosthenes reached the age of majority at eighteen. At this point they turned over only a fraction of the original value of the estate, so Demosthenes brought an action against Aphobus to recover what he could. Before the suit came to trial, Thrasylochus challenged Demosthenes to an *antidosis* (D. 28.17). Demosthenes claims this was a ruse concocted by Aphobus to force him to exchange his property with Thrasylochus and thus drop his claims in regard to his father's estate. But Demosthenes parried this maneuver by accepting the liturgy despite the strain it placed on his resources. Demosthenes then won an award of ten talents against Aphobus. Aphobus tried to overturn the judgment by bringing a *dike pseudomartyrion* against one of Demosthenes' witnesses, but this suit failed (D. 29). As part of his effort to collect his award, Demosthenes attempted to seize a house and an estate belonging to Aphobus, but the latter claimed the property belonged to his father-in-law Onetor. His story was that he had pledged the property as security for the dowry of Onetor's daughter; now that they had divorced, Onetor had taken the security to recover the value of the dowry. Demosthenes argued that the dowry had never been paid and that the divorce was a sham (D. 30). We do not know the outcome of this suit, but Demosthenes was able to reclaim enough of his property to be in a position to undertake several liturgies in the following years.[65]

It has been claimed that 'Demosthenes' attempts to recover his patrimony indicate how initiating a single lawsuit can lead to many years of enmity and litigation, drawing in numerous other parties and involving matters totally unrelated to the initial case.'[66] To put it mildly, this is somewhat of an exaggeration. Demosthenes only brought one suit against Aphobus and one suit against Onetor. Aphobus brought one suit against

64. Cohen (1995) 101.

65. See Davies (1971) 135–36 (three more trierarchies between 360 and 352).

66. Cohen (1995) 101.

one of Demosthenes' witnesses, and Thrasylochus challenged Demosthenes to one *antidosis*, which never went to court because Demosthenes undertook the liturgy. Demosthenes (30.15–17) says he came of age and demanded the accounts for his property in the archonship of Polyzelus (367/6) and brought his action against Aphobus in the archonship of Timocrates (364/3). There is no reason to believe that the other cases occurred long after the original suit; all together they may not have taken longer than a year.

Far from showing how Athenians used the courts to pursue feuds, Demosthenes' disputes with his guardians show the limited range of options available to the person who wished to contest a judgment. Aphobus challenged the original decision Demosthenes won before the arbitrator, then attempted to fight the judgment rendered by the court by means of a *dike pseudomartyrion* (D. 29). When this too failed, he had run out of ways to overturn the judgment and tried to hide his assets to prevent Demosthenes from collecting the money awarded to him. By contrast, the modern lawyer has many more ways to challenge a court judgment or a judge's order. For instance, the *Rules Governing Civil Practice for the State of New Jersey* 4:49–2 provide:

> Except as otherwise provided by R. 1.:13–1 (clerical errors) a motion for rehearing or reconsideration seeking to alter or amend a judgment or order shall be served not later than 20 days after service of the judgment or order upon all parties by the party obtaining it. The motion shall state with specificity the basis on which it is made, including a statement of the matters or controlling decisions which counsel believes the court has overlooked or as to which it has erred.

This opens the door for a wide range of challenges based on a variety of procedural, substantive, and evidentiary grounds. In death penalty cases in the United States, the appeals process can drag on for years. There was nothing similar in Classical Athens.

Some scholars believe that Demosthenes' conflict with Meidias represented another stage in an ongoing feud. The only evidence linking Demosthenes' conflict with his guardians and that with Meidias is a passage from Demosthenes' speech *Against Meidias* delivered in 346 (D. 21.78–80). According to Demosthenes, Meidias and Thrasylochus broke into his house after the latter made his *antidosis* challenge.

There are two problems with this argument. First, one of the main characteristics of a feud is that it involves not individuals, but groups.[67] Demosthenes names several associates of Meidias who have helped him in the past or will plead for him at his trial, but none of these individuals figure in the earlier dispute with his guardians.[68] Second, the version of the dispute with Thrasylochus Demosthenes gave in 346 is rather different from the one he gave in 364/3, eighteen years earlier. In the first version, Demosthenes (28.17) says Thrasylochus challenged him to an *antidosis*, but Demosthenes barred him from his property because he wanted to obtain a *diadikasia*. But with his case against Aphobus about to go to trial, Demosthenes preferred to perform the liturgy instead of getting tied up in more litigation. In the later version, Demosthenes (21.78–80) changes his story considerably. Here Thrasylochus, now joined by Meidias, invades Demosthenes' property, tears off the doors of the rooms, uses foul language in front of his sister, and insults him and his mother. This is inconsistent with the earlier version in which Demosthenes says he kept Thrasylochus out of his property (*apekleisa*). Rather than accept the liturgy, Demosthenes pays his opponents twenty mnai, which they use to hire out the trierarchy. This directly contradicts the statement in his earlier speech that he performed the liturgy. The two versions are quite different and cannot be reconciled.[69] One should also note that although Demosthenes provides witnesses for many of Meidias' action in his speech of 346, he calls no witnesses to corroborate the later version of the incident. What is striking is Meidias' absence from the first version and that the second version adds violence and verbal abuse missing from the first. It is difficult to resist the conclusion that Demosthenes has deliberately altered important details in the later version, delivered eighteen years afterward, when the judges could not have remembered exactly what had happened, to make it suitable for inclusion in his *chronique scandaleuse* of

67. See Miller (1990) 180.

68. Demosthenes predicts that the following will support Meidias or have supported him in the past: Polyzelus (36–8), Euctemon (103, 139), Cratinus (132), Polyeuctus (139), Timocrates (139), Eubulus (206–7), Philippides (208, 215), Mnesarchides (208, 215), Diotimus (208), Neoptolemus (215), and Blepaeus (215).

69. I do not understand how MacDowell (1990) 297 can state: 'Although the two accounts . . . give different details, there is no inconsistency between them and no reason to regard either as inaccurate.' MacDowell (2008) 38–39 ignores all the arguments made in Harris (2005a) 238 and inexplicably asserts 'there is no inconsistency between them (i.e. the two accounts).'

Meidias' life. The only piece of evidence linking Demosthenes' quarrel with his guardians to that with Meidias turns out to be no evidence at all.[70]

Despite Demosthenes' allegations, his quarrel with Meidias appears to have begun in 348 and was resolved by the trial or settlement in 346. Early in 348 Demosthenes volunteered to serve as chorus producer for his tribe Pandionis at the Dionysia, which took place in Elaphebolion (March/April) (D. 21.13–14).[71] At this point Meidias set about sabotaging Demosthenes' attempt to win the prize for the competition. He bribed Demosthenes' trainer, tried to destroy the chorus' costumes, and blocked the entrances to stop the chorus from performing. On the day of the performance, he actually punched Demosthenes in the face in front of thousands of Athenians and foreigners (D. 21.15–18. Cf. Aeschin. 3.52). At a meeting of the Assembly after the Dionysia, Demosthenes used the procedure of *probole* to pass a vote of censure against Meidias for disrupting the festival (D. 21.1–2, 226).[72]

Demosthenes did not initiate further proceedings against Meidias after the *probole*, but Meidias continued to harass him. Demosthenes alleges that Meidias hired Euctemon to bring a charge of desertion against Demosthenes (D. 21.103). The penalty for conviction on this charge was loss of citizen rights, but Euctemon, after initiating his suit, did not bring the case to court and lost his right to bring public cases. There is no reason to doubt that Euctemon brought the charge, which was posted at the monument of the Eponymous Heroes, but Demosthenes provides no evidence proving that Meidias was behind the prosecution. Aeschines (2.148) reports that Nicodemus charged Demosthenes with the same crime, but Nicodemus was murdered. The relatives of Nicodemus charged Aristarchus, a friend of Demosthenes, with the murder, and Aristarchus fled into exile either before the trial or before the court pronounced its verdict (D. 21.116–22). Meidias appears to have accused Demosthenes of persuading Aristarchus to commit the murder (D. 21.114. Cf. Aeschin. 1.170–73) but could not convince the victim's relatives to bring a charge against him.[73]

70. This is decisive against the claim of Cohen that the quarrel lasted a long time.

71. This account of the quarrel between Demosthenes and Meidias relies on Harris (2008) 75–87, which corrects several aspects of MacDowell (1990) 1–13.

72. On the procedure of *probole* see Harris (2008) 79–81, 150–52.

73. On the murder of Aristarchus see MacDowell (1990) 328–30 and Fisher (2001) 316–20.

This accusation is probably the reason why Demosthenes brought a private charge of slander against Meidias (D. 21.83–92). The case was assigned to a public arbitrator named Strato, but Meidias tried to have the proceedings delayed with various excuses. On the day Strato was scheduled to give his decision, Demosthenes claims that Meidias failed to show up and therefore lost the case by default. The decision was overruled, however, when Meidias convicted Strato of misconduct before the other arbitrators. Strato then appealed their judgment to a court, which upheld the decision of the arbitrators. As a result of their verdict, Strato lost his rights as a citizen. Demosthenes tries to make Meidias the villain in the story, but Strato's conviction casts doubt on his version of events. Although Demosthenes (21.93) calls witnesses to support his account, he does not indicate what they said in their testimony. They may have testified only that the arbitrators and the court both convicted Strato. According to Demosthenes (21.111), Meidias also attacked Demosthenes at his *dokimasia* for the Council in the summer of 347, but it is hard to know how to evaluate this charge since no evidence is provided.[74]

In early 346 Demosthenes finally brought a charge of outrage (*hybris*) against Meidias. We do not know the outcome of the trial, but there are good reasons to believe that Meidias was convicted but sentenced to pay only a small fine.[75] Meidias certainly did not suffer any more serious punishment because he served as pylagoras to Delphi in 340 or 339 (Aeschin. 3.115). The conflict between Demosthenes and Meidias appears to have lasted only two years, from early 348 until early 346. It is certainly significant that when Aeschines alludes to Meidias' punch in a speech delivered in 330, he does not recount any further incidents in their quarrel. If there was a conflict between the two men that lasted after 346, one must ask why Aeschines, who dug up every piece of dirt he could against Demosthenes in 330, failed to exploit it to his opponent's detriment at the trial of Ctesiphon. One can hardly call this quarrel a 'feud.' It was not a conflict between two families: none of Demosthenes' relatives and none of Meidias' family was dragged into the conflict, which involved only these two men. Despite

74. MacDowell (1990) 10 suggests that Meidias brought up the murder of Nicodemus at the *dokimasia*.

75. According to Plutarch *Demosthenes* 12, Demosthenes came to a settlement with Meidias and did not bring the case to court. According to Aeschines (3.52), Demosthenes 'sold' the *probole* and the charge of *hybris* for thirty minas. Plutarch's statement is implausible, and it is difficult to know whether Aeschines is telling the truth and what he means by the expression 'sold.' For discussion see Harris (1989) and Harris (2008) 84–86.

Demosthenes' lurid account of Meidias' attacks, the two men battled only three times in court: the first time at the *probole* in the Assembly in 348, the second time at the arbitration before Strato sometime later, and the third time at Meidias' trial for outrage in early 346. Each time it was Demosthenes who initiated legal proceedings, not Meidias. Demosthenes claims that Meidias was behind Euctemon's prosecution but provides no evidence. He also alleges that he persuaded Aristarchus to kill Nicodemus, but no charges were ever brought. And Demosthenes' charge that Meidias attacked him at his *dokimasia* may be no more than slander. Demosthenes was a brilliant orator, but one should not believe everything that he says about his opponents. The statements found in his speeches are a weak foundation on which to build a theory about the existence of feuding in Athenian society.

The Conflict Between Demosthenes and Aeschines

The next conflict I will examine is the one between Aeschines and Demosthenes. The conflict began in 346 after the Second Embassy to Philip II. Aeschines and Demosthenes had major differences over foreign policy after the conclusion of the Peace of Philocrates. Aeschines encouraged Philip to intervene in Central Greece and free the Boeotian cities from Thebes; Demosthenes viewed this proposal as dangerous and irresponsible.[76] At Aeschines' *euthynai* for the Second Embassy, therefore, Demosthenes and Timarchus (not a family relation) brought a charge of violating the public trust while on an embassy and in particular accused Aeschines of taking bribes in return for acting against Athenian interests.[77] Later that same year, Aeschines struck back at Timarchus by charging that he was partially *atimos* because Timarchus had been a male prostitute and squandered his inheritance and thereby had no right to bring a public charge. Aeschines won this case, and Timarchus lost his citizen rights.[78] This victory appeared to keep Demosthenes at bay for a while; his opponent did not work up the courage to bring his suit to court until 343, when Philip's increasing power and influence caused the Athenians to doubt the wisdom of the Peace of Philocrates. Encouraged by the conviction of Philocrates himself, Demosthenes finally prosecuted Aeschines, but lost

76. On the Second Embassy to Philip see Harris (1995) 78–89 with the sources cited there.

77. See Harris (1995) 95–6 with the sources cited there.

78. For the prosecution see Harris (1995) 101–6 with the sources cited there.

by a narrow margin.[79] In the following years, Aeschines and Demosthenes continued to disagree about policy toward Philip, but Aeschines did not attempt to retaliate until 336, two years after the Athenian defeat at Chaeronea. Instead of attacking Demosthenes directly, however, he brought a *graphe paranomon* against Ctesiphon, who had passed an honorary decree for Aeschines' rival. It then took Aeschines six years before he felt confident enough to bring his case against Ctesiphon to trial.[80] The most likely explanation for the delay is that he was waiting to discover the outcome of Alexander's campaign against the Persian king.[81] The result was a complete fiasco: Aeschines failed to win one-fifth of the votes and thus lost his right to bring any public charges at all.[82] The ancient biographies of Aeschines give different accounts of his activities during his last years, but contemporaneous sources are notably silent about him after 330. If Aeschines had remained politically active, he would certainly have attacked Demosthenes during the Harpalus scandal in 324–23 as other prominent leaders did. His absence from all our accounts of that affair (Din. 1–3), when combined with the evidence of the ancient biographers, is strong evidence in favor of concluding that his defeat in 330 ended his political career. This demonstrates that the penalty for frivolous prosecutions was a harsh penalty and had devastating implications for a prosecutor's career.[83]

The conflict between Aeschines and Demosthenes is one of the longest in the annals of Athenian politics, yet it produced very little litigation. There was only one direct confrontation, the prosecution of Aeschines by Demosthenes in 343. Aeschines' other cases were against Demosthenes' political associates, Timarchus and Ctesiphon. There is no indication the conflict ever expanded to include other family members, relations, or dependents.[84] Even after Aeschines won acquittal in 343, he did not attempt

---

79. For Demosthenes' prosecution of Aeschines see Harris (1995) 116–18 with the sources cited there.

80. For the dates of the indictment and the trial see Wankel (1976) 13–37.

81. See Harris (1995) 141–2, 173–4.

82. Harris (1995) 148.

83. All of the prosecutors who incurred this penalty appear to have disappeared from political life: Tisis of Agryle (Hyp. *Eux.* 34), Euctemon (D. 21.103), Lycinus (Aeschin. 2.14; 3.62).

84. When Demosthenes arrested Antiphon as a spy, Aeschines objected to the arrest on legal grounds (D. 18.132–3); there is no indication Aeschines defended Antiphon because he was a relative or close friend. Demosthenes also arrested Anaxinus of Oreus and had him tortured (Aeschin. 3.223–5; D. 18.137). Aeschines' objections to the torture rested on legal grounds.

to escalate the conflict by bringing another public charge against Demosthenes. Quite the opposite; he attacked an ally of Demosthenes on a less serious charge. But what is most striking about this conflict is the conspicuous reluctance of the two men to bring their cases to court. Demosthenes waited three years between initiating his case at the *euthynai* in 346 and bringing it to trial in 343; Aeschines passed up the chance to prosecute Demosthenes after the disastrous defeat at Chaeronea, brought a charge against Ctesiphon in 336, then delayed for six years. Over sixteen years the two men faced each other in court only three times! The attitudes against litigiousness and the laws aimed at discouraging feuding in court appear to have acted as a strong deterrent for these two politicians.[85]

A Litigious Athenian: Apollodorus, the Son of Pasion

One of the most litigious Athenians was Apollodorus, the son of Pasion, who was born around 394.[86] In fact, one of his opponents rebuked him for prosecuting so many people (D. 36.53). His father, Pasion, had been a slave owned by two bankers, Archestratus and Antisthenes (D. 36.43), who later manumitted him (D. 36.48). By 394/3 he had become the owner of a bank (Isoc. 17.36), and he was later made an Athenian citizen as a reward for his generosity to the city ([D.] 59.2. Cf. D. 45.85). When Pasion died in 370/69 ([D.] 46.13), his property, which included the bank and a shield factory, was probably worth around seventy talents.[87] Apollodorus and his brother Pasicles inherited the property, which they held in common until Pasicles came of age in 362 when the property was divided, Apollodorus taking the shield factory, Pasicles the bank (D. 36.11).

Apollodorus' first lawsuits involved business relating to his father's bank. When Pasion was still alive, a man named Lycon from Heraclea deposited 1,640 drachmas in his bank and instructed him to pay it to Lycon's associate Cephisiades when he arrived in Athens. Archebiades of Lamptrai was to identify Cephisiades ([D.] 52.3–4, 6). After Lycon was killed during a trading voyage, Callippus, the *proxenos* of the people of Heraclea, came to the bank

85. The evidence of these three conflicts provides ample refutation to the claim of Christ (2005) 146 that the 'the pursuit of enemies—personal or political—through the legal process was a real possibility and probably a common phenomenon,' an assertion that rests on nothing more than his own *ipse dixit*. For criticism of Christ's general approach to the courts see Harris (2000b).

86. For his year of birth see D. 36.22; [D.] 46.13 with Trevett (1992) 19.

87. For the value of his estate see Trevett (1992) 27–31.

and asked if Lycon had deposited any money there. Pasion replied that he was holding his money but told Callippus he was instructed to pay it to Cephisiades ([D.] 52.5–6). Shortly afterward, Cephisiades came to the bank, and Phormio, who was managing the bank, paid him Lycon's money ([D.] 52.7). That should have been the end of the matter, but Callippus asked Pasion to pay him the money, and when Pasion refused, brought a suit against him for paying the money to Cephisiades without Callippus' consent ([D.] 52.8–14). Callippus then invited him to submit the matter to private arbitration by Lysitheides, but they could not agree on the terms ([D.] 52.14–16). After Pasion died, Cephisiades invited Apollodorus and his brother to submit the case to Lysitheides (probably in 369/8),[88] but Apollodorus insisted that Lysitheides be appointed by an official so that he would have a chance to appeal if he decided against him ([D.] 52.30). When Lysitheides gave judgment in favor of Callippus, Apollodorus appealed to the court ([D.] 52.31). There is no reason to think that Callippus brought his case out of any long-standing enmity.[89] Whatever the outcome of his case against Apollodorus, it did not lead to any subsequent hostility or litigation between their families, and Apollodorus never mentions Callippus or any of his relatives in any of his later speeches.

The next case involving his father's bank concerned several loans made to the general Timotheus. Pasion had made four loans to Timotheus: first, a loan of 1,351 drachmas given to Timotheus' treasurer Antimachus ([D.] 49.6–10); second, a loan of 1,000 drachmas borrowed to pay the crews of Boeotian ships ([D.] 49.15–17); third, a loan of one mina, 257 drachmas, and two silver bowls to entertain Jason and Alcetas ([D.] 49.22–4); and fourth, a loan of 1,750 drachmas to pay Philondas for the transport of some timber from Macedonia ([D.] 49.25–30). Pasion made these loans without security and witnesses, relying on his friendship with Timotheus and hoping that he would have plenty of money after fighting for the Persian king ([D.] 49.27). When Timotheus refused to pay, Apollodorus brought a suit against him in around 368.[90] There is no indication of any

88. For the date see Schaefer (1858) 136 followed by Trevett (1992) 31–21.

89. Cf. Trevett (1992) 126: 'there is nothing to suggest that his prosecution of Apollodoros was politically motivated. The dispute arose out of Pasion's activity as a banker, and Kallippos was apparently acting in his official capacity.'

90. For the date see Harris (2006a) 355–63 (= Harris [1988]). Trevett (1991) attempted to challenge my dating and defended the dating of Schaefer, but his arguments have been rejected by Rowe (2000) 288 note 37, and MacDowell (2009) 102–6 (who does not, however, take account of the events of Timotheus' generalship). Trevett's defense of Schaefer's dating is undermined by his failure to see that the loans were made from the bank, which passed into Pasicles' ownership when he reached the age of majority—see Harris (2006a) 363–64.

previous hostility between Pasion and Timotheus. According to Plutarch (*D.* 15.1), Apollodorus won his case and must have recovered his money. Apollodorus may have later prosecuted Timotheus for his conduct as general in Northern Greece (discussed later), but there is no reason to connect the two trials. Finally, there is no indication that Timotheus or any of his relatives ever tried to retaliate against Apollodorus or members of his family.

Around 366 or 364 Apollodorus became involved in a quarrel with his neighbor Nicostratus and his brother Arethusius.[91] Apollodorus and Nicostratus were close friends, and Nicostratus used to manage Apollodorus' affairs when the latter was abroad as a trierarch ([D.] 53.4–5). During one trip abroad, Nicostratus left Attica in pursuit of three runaway slaves and was captured and sold as a slave on Aegina ([D.] 53.6). Apollodorus sent Nicostratus' brother Deinon to rescue him and gave him 300 drachmas for the trip. On his return Nicostratus said he owed 26 minas for his release and asked Apollodorus to contribute ([D.] 53.7). Apollodorus borrowed a thousand drachmas on security and gave it to Nicostratus as a gift ([D.] 53.8–9). This was not enough to pay the full sum, and so Apollodorus raised the remaining amount by taking another secured loan. Nicostratus promised to repay this amount as soon as he could borrow money from his friends ([D.] 53.10–13).

At this point something went wrong, and Nicostratus turned against Apollodorus. First, Nicostratus told Apollodorus' relatives about the arguments Apollodorus would use against them in court, then had Lycidas the miller bring a case against Apollodorus without first serving a summons, entering the name of his brother as a witness to the summons on the plaint. After winning a judgment for 610 drachmas, Nicostratus entered Apollodorus' property and took items worth more than 20 minas ([D.] 53.14–16). Nicostratus later damaged Apollodorus' property and tried to lure Apollodorus into putting in chains or striking a young man so that he could indict him for outrage (*hybris*) ([D.] 53.14–16). Apollodorus claims to have acted with great restraint in response to these provocations, calling witnesses only to the damage done by the two brothers. When Apollodorus brought a public suit against Arethusius for falsely witnessing a summons and was about to bring the case to court, Nicostratus ambushed him. He would have thrown Apollodorus into a quarry had not some bystanders

91. For the date of the trial of Arethusius see Schaefer (1858) 143–47 followed by Trevett (1992) 32–33.

intervened and rescued him ([D.] 53.17). Apollodorus was not deterred by these threats and won his case against Arethusius, convincing the court to impose a penalty of one talent ([D.] 53.17–18). When Aresthusius did not pay the fine, Apollodorus reported to the Eleven two slaves belonging to him and brought the case to court ([D.] 53.19–28).

Several features of this quarrel are significant. First, Apollodorus and Nicostratus had been friends; there was no long-standing feud between their families. Second, Apollodorus claims that he demonstrated considerable self-restraint in the face of repeated attacks. It is difficult to know how much of his narrative was supported by testimony; he calls only one set of witnesses and does not specify what they testified about ([D.] 53.18–19). Naturally, he may omit some things he might have done to anger Nicostratus. Yet although we do not have the entire story, it is clear that the quarrel did not last very long, did not involve other members of their families, and produced very little litigation: only one private suit for damages and one public suit for falsely witnessing a summons. Finally, Apollodorus' later speeches never mention any subsequent troubles with the two brothers. This brief conflict hardly qualifies as a feud.

Apollodorus served as a trierarch in Northern Greece in the late 360s. Apollodorus was supposed to serve for only a year starting in late 362, but Polycles, the man appointed to succeed him, refused to take command of his trireme when Apollodorus' term of duty expired ([D.] 59.29–37). Apollodorus continued as trierarch for an extra five months. On his return to Athens, Apollodorus brought a suit against Polycles for the expenses he incurred during these five months. Nothing in the speech Apollodorus delivered against Polycles reveals that the two men had any relationship before their dispute over the trierarchy. The trial was not part of an ongoing feud; Apollodorus simply wanted his money back.[92]

One of Apollodorus' opponents accuses him of constantly bringing not only private suits, but also public suits and mentions prosecutions of Timomachus, Callippus, Menon, Autocles, and Timotheus (D. 36.53). All these cases appear to have been connected with Athenian campaigns in Northern Greece from 362 to 359 when Apollodorus was serving there as trierarch. Demosthenes (19.180) reports that Timomachus was punished for losing Thrace and Athenian strongholds there. According to Aeschines

92. Trevett (1992) 129–30: 'there is nothing in the speech to suggest that the two men were enemies, or even that they had known each other previously . . . There is no reason to suppose that he (i.e. Polycles) had acted out of personal animosity toward Apollodoros.'

(1.56), Timomachus' treasurer Hegesander was instrumental in his conviction, which suggests that he was also accused of embezzlement. Apollodorus may have also charged that Timomachus attempted to bring back Callistratus from exile ([D.] 50.46–52). Timomachus fled into exile before his trial (Hyp. *Eux.* 2). There is no evidence about the trial of Callippus (not to be identified with the *proxenos* of the Heracleans), but Apollodorus may have indicted Callippus for his illegal command to transport Callistratus ([D.] 50.43–52). We know nothing about Menon aside from the fact that he succeeded Autocles ([D.] 50.12). Demosthenes (23.104) reports that Autocles was tried for causing the downfall of Miltocythes around 361; Hyperides appears to have been involved in this trial, either as accuser or as supporting speaker (Hyp. frs. 55–65 [Jensen]). Timotheus was also serving in Northern Greece from 364 to 359, when he failed to capture Amphipolis.[93] Timotheus' activities during this campaign and his failure to capture Amphipolis probably served as the grounds for his prosecution. All the evidence about these trials suggests that Apollodorus undertook these prosecutions against generals who had failed to perform their duties.[94] There is no reason to believe that Apollodorus was pursuing a vendetta against any of them. Nor is there any indication that these men formed a group linked by the ties of kinship or friendship.[95] The sources certainly do not record any further litigation between Apollodorus and any of these men or their relations. It is more likely that Apollodorus' motive was to advance his political career by taking advantage of popular anger over Athenian defeats in Northern Greece.[96]

There is no evidence for Apollodorus' involvement in more litigation until around 350 when he charged Phormio with embezzling money when he leased Pasion's bank, which he and his brother jointly owned from 370/69 to 362/61.[97] Apollodorus gave up his share of the

93. Trevett (1992) 134 believes that Timotheus was not involved in the campaigns in Northern Greece in 362–60 but see Aeschin. *schol.* ad Aeschin. 2.31 with Harris (2006a) 355–63.

94. Trevett (1992) 136: 'The correct explanation of these prosecutions is surely to be found in the fact that all but one of the defendants had held positions of command while Apollodoros was serving as trierarch in 362–60.'

95. For an analysis of the political connections of these men see Trevett (1992) 135–36 ('he impeached men belonging to each of Sealey's three main political groups').

96. Trevett (1992) 137: 'an attempt by Apollodorus to exploit popular dissatisfaction with the conduct of the war to make a name for himself as a politician.'

97. For the dates see Harris (2006a) 359.

bank when his brother Pasicles came of age in 362/61, but Apollodorus did not bring his case against Phormio until around 350.[98] In response, Phormio brought a *paragraphe* against Apollodorus on the grounds that Apollodorus had granted Phormio a release (D. 36.23–5) and that the statute of limitations had expired (D. 36.26). Apollodorus lost the case, but retaliated against Stephanus, who had testified on behalf of Phormio (D. 45 and [D.] 46). We do not know the outcome of the case against Stephanus, but given the weakness of his case it is unlikely that Apollodorus won. The law about releases and the statute of limitations helped make sure this family quarrel did not continue to produce litigation.

Apollodorus found himself in court again in 348. This time he was a defendant, not a prosecutor. During that year Apollodorus was a member of the Council and passed a decree to have the surplus in the budget paid into the Military Fund. His motion was perfectly legal, but Stephanus, son of Antidorides, charged him with proposing an illegal decree ([D.] 59.3–6), possibly on the grounds that he was a public debtor, and won a conviction.[99] When the court decided on the penalty, the judges accepted Apollodorus' proposed sum of one talent. Stephanus may have also brought a charge of homicide against Apollodorus, which the court rejected when the alleged victim was produced in court ([D.] 59.9–10).[100] Apollodorus bided his time looking for a chance to strike back at Stephanus. Sometime after 343, he encouraged his brother-in-law Theomnestus to bring a public charge against Neaera, a former prostitute who was living with Stephanus, and accused her of usurping the rights of Athenian citizenship ([D.] 59.16–17).[101] Apollodorus acted as supporting speaker and delivered the main speech at the trial. Once again, we

98. For the date of the speech see Trevett (1992) 48.

99. I see no reason to believe that Apollodorus was working with Demosthenes to attack Eubulus' support for the Theoric Fund because it drained money from the military. First, there is no evidence that Demosthenes was hostile to the Theoric Fund. In fact, he ardently defends its value in the *Fourth Philippic* (D. 10.36–42) and later became the theoric commissioner. Second, Apollodorus' measure did not attack the Theoric Fund and affected only the payment of the surplus from the budget. Third, there is no reason to believe Demosthenes had any major policy differences with Eubulus before later 346. Fourth, Eubulus actually testified for Apollodorus in his case against Neaera, not against him ([D.] 59.48). For evidence and arguments see Harris (2006a) 121–40.

100. It is difficult to know how seriously one should take this story. The details invite skepticism and Theomnestus provides no evidence to corroborate it.

101. For the date see Kapparis (1999) 28.

have no evidence that would allow us to determine the trial's outcome, but the case does not appear to have been strong.[102]

During the thirty years between 370 and 340, Apollodorus was involved in at least fifteen trials, but none of these trials occurred as part of a long-term feud between Apollodorus' family and another family. Most of Apollodorus' opponents had no relationship to each other, and it is hard to detect any connection between these various trials. Apollodorus may have been a very quarrelsome fellow, but his conflicts with others do not appear to have generated all that much litigation. In most cases he faced his opponent in court only once or twice. Once he won or lost, the conflict came to an end. Apollodorus clearly sought revenge against Stephanus after his conviction for passing an illegal decree but had to wait over five years to find the right opportunity, but he could not attack Stephanus directly. His litigation certainly does not fit the pattern of feuding behavior.

Mantitheus' Quarrel with his Half-Brother Boeotus

The last conflict examined is the one between Mantitheus and Boeotus. Mantitheus was the son of Mantias (D. 39, 40). According to the plaintiff, Boeotus, who was not raised in his father's household, brought a suit against Mantias claiming he was his father and that he was treating his son in a terrible way and preventing him from becoming a citizen. The reason for the action was probably that Boeotus was approaching (or had reached) the age of majority and needed Mantias to acknowledge paternity so that he could prove he had two Athenian parents and was thus entitled to citizenship. Mantitheus claims disingenuously that his father was reluctant to go to court because he was afraid someone he had offended during his political career would try to retaliate against him (D. 39.3). Naturally, he passes over in silence the possibility that he did not want to go to court because he knew the facts were against him. Instead, he tried to resolve the dispute out of court by challenging Boeotus' mother, Plangon, to swear an oath that Boeotus was not his son. The plaintiff claims she had agreed to deny on oath his paternity in exchange for a sum of money. When the parties met to make the challenge, Plangon double-crossed Mantias and swore that Boeotus was in fact his son (D. 39.4; 40.11).

102. Apollodorus reveals the weakness in his case when he admits that Stephanus will show that Phano, who Apollodorus claims is the daughter of Neaera, is actually the child of another woman, who was in fact an Athenian.

This outcome gave Mantias little choice but to enroll Boeotus as a member of his phratry (D. 40.11), but he died before he could enroll Boeotus as a member of his deme (D. 39.5). As a result, Boeotus had himself enrolled in the deme but under the name Mantitheus (D. 39.5). The plaintiff provides no evidence to prove the existence of any agreement between Plangon and his father to prove his allegations about the oath, and the story is clearly designed to undermine her credibility. The witnesses he calls testify only about the way he and his brothers were enrolled (D. 39.6). His wording is slightly vague, but seems to indicate they corroborated his statement that Boeotus was enrolled under this name in the phratry, but under the name Mantitheus in the deme.

Since Boeotus and his brother were enrolled in their father's phratry, Mantias must have recognized them as his *gnesioi* (legitimate) sons, which enabled them each to gain one-third of their father's estate. Mantitheus claims that he agreed to let them have two-thirds of the estate, which was (by now) all his own (D. 39.6). What is significant, however, is the way Mantitheus chooses to portray himself: he expects the court to approve his decision not to contest the inheritance in court.[103] Not long after, however, Mantitheus demanded that Boeotus and Pamphilus hand over his mother's dowry (D. 40.6–7). When they refused, he brought an action against them (D. 40.3, 18). This appears to have occurred in 358.[104] Not to be outdone, Boeotus and his brother Pamphilus also claimed that their mother had been given a dowry of 100 mnai for her marriage to Mantitheus (D. 40.19). The case went before an arbitrator named Solon, who died before he could give judgment (D. 40.16). Mantitheus won his suit for the dowry against Boeotus when it was heard by the arbitrator, and Boeotus did not appeal the judgment (D. 40.17). When his own suit against Mantitheus came before the arbitrator, Boeotus failed to show up, so the arbitrator ruled against him (D. 40.17). In this case too Boeotus chose not to take the case before the popular court (D. 40.3, 31). His only way of evading the judgment was to argue that the plaint should have listed Mantitheus, his real name, as the defendant, not Boeotus. This led to another trial, which occurred about eleven years after the death of Mantitheus (D. 40.18).

To prevent him from using this ruse again, Mantitheus brought a private action for damages against Boeotus. This case was referred to a private

103. For an analysis of the case and the reason why it failed see 223–25.

104. For the chronology see MacDowell (2008) 72.

arbitrator who ruled against Boeotus when he failed to show up (D. 39.37). Boeotus then succeeded in having the arbitrator's judgment set aside (D. 39.38). The case went to the arbitrator again. This time Mantitheus appears to have lost the case, then appealed the decision to one of the regular courts. The case probably came to trial in 348/7.[105] After Mantitheus lost this case, he brought another action for his mother's dowry, this time against his half-brother under the name of Mantitheus (D. 40.18). We do not know the outcome of this case, which appears to have taken place in 347.[106]

Several aspects of this conflict are significant. First, once Mantitheus yielded to the claims made by his half-brothers to their father's estate, he did not attempt to challenge the basic division of the inheritance during the rest of the conflict. Although the conflict continued, the solution to this dispute remained untouched. Here the principle of *res iudicata* held firm. Second, several of the actors in this family drama avoided going to court at important points. When Boeotus threatened to bring an action against his father Mantias, the latter agreed to resolve the issue by an oath challenge. When this did not turn out as he hoped, he abided by the result and did not pursue the matter in court. Later, after Boeotus lost his two suits before the arbitrator, he did not elect to appeal the judgments to a court. Moreover, each brother attempts to portray himself as a reluctant litigant. Mantitheus claims his brother has forced him to go to court (D. 40.2), while Boeotus asserts he is not someone who likes to make trouble (*apragmon*) or to go to trial (*ou philodikos*). Third, these events took place over the course of more than eleven years between 362 and 347 (D. 40.18).[107] During this time there were the following disputes: (1) The *dike blabes* brought by Mantitheus against Boeotus before the arbitrator; (2) the appeal to the popular court brought by Mantitheus; (3) the suit for the recovery of his mother's dowry brought by Mantitheus brought before the arbitrator; (4) the suit brought by Boeotus to recover his mother's dowry brought before the arbitrator; (5) the suit to recover his mother's dowry brought by Mantitheus against Boeotus under the name Mantitheus before the popular court; (6) a possible charge of intentional wounding

105. For the date see Carey and Reid (1985) 160, and MacDowell (2008) 74.

106. For the date see MacDowell (2008) 75. Mantitheus claims that Boeotus prosecuted him before the Areopagus for deliberate wounding but lost the case (D. 40.32–3) and made other charges against him (D. 40.36–7), but provides no evidence to support these allegations.

107. For the chronology see MacDowell (2008) 72–75.

brought before the Areopagus by Boeotus against Mantitheus (D. 40.32); and (7) a suit to recover a debt allegedly paid to Mantias by the people of Mytilene brought by Boeotus against Mantitheus (D. 40.36). That makes a total of seven cases heard before an arbitrator or a court, just one week of litigation, during more than eleven years. Fourth, this conflict does not appear to have escalated as often happens with feuds. After Boeotus brought a serious charge against his brother, Mantitheus did not retaliate by bringing an equally serious charge. And the conflict did not expand to draw in other kin and friends; it occurred within a family, not between two families. In short, this conflict did not produce all that much litigation, and several times the participants chose not to pursue every legal option at their disposal. It certainly does not resemble the feuding behavior one finds in medieval Iceland—or between the Montagues and Capulets in Shakepeare's *Romeo and Juliet*.[108] In this case Athenian values and legal measures worked together to ensure that disputes, once settled, were not continued and that conflict was kept at a peaceful and acceptable level.

Alcmeonids and Peisistratids

The only conflict in Athenian history that resembles feuding behavior is the long-standing struggle between the Alcmeonids and the Peisistratids. The conflict began in the early sixth century when Attica was divided into three regions, each held by a powerful family. The Alcmeonids controlled the plain, the supporters of Lycurgus the shore, and the Peisistratids the Upland region (Hdt. 1.59.3).[109] The Alcmeonids appear to have been a large group linked by kinship: Herodotus (5.72.1. Cf. Arist. *Ath. Pol.* 20.3) reports that when Cleomenes drove them out, they numbered seven hundred households. Peisistratus won the first round of the feud around 561/0 BCE by seizing the Acropolis with a band of club-bearers and gaining political power (Hdt. 1.59.4–6; Arist. *Ath. Pol.* 14.1–2).[110] The Alcmeonids and the supporters of Lycurgus retaliated by driving him out, probably around 560 BCE (Hdt. 1.60.1; Arist. *Ath. Pol.* 14.3). Peisistratus then entered into an alliance with Megacles, the leader of Alcmeonids, and married his

108. I owe this point to Lin Foxhall.

109. Arist. *Ath. Pol.* 13.4 (cf. Arist. *Pol.* 1305a23–4; Plu. *Sol.* 13.1–2; 29.1) associates each group with a different political philosophy, but this is probably anachronistic. See Rhodes (1981) 185–6. For the regional basis of politics in early Athens see Sealey (1960).

110. For the chronology of the tyranny see Rhodes (1981) 194–99.

daughter around 556. This enabled him to gain power a second time (Hdt. 1.60.2–61.1; Arist. *Ath. Pol.* 14.4). The alliance ended when Peisistratus insulted his wife by not having sexual relations with her 'in the normal way' (*ou kata nomon*). As a result, relations with Megacles broke down, and Peisistratus was driven into exile a second time shortly afterward (Hdt. 1.61.2; Arist. *Ath. Pol.* 15.1). Peisistratus then gathered allies and money from Thebes, Argos, Eretria, and Lygdamis of Naxos (Hdt. 1.61.3–4; Arist. *Ath. Pol.* 15.2). Setting out from Eretria, Peisistratus landed at Marathon and defeated an Athenian army at Pallene around 546 BCE (Hdt. 1.62.1–63.2; Arist. *Ath. Pol.* 15.3). Peisistratus died in 528/7 and handed power to his son Hippias (Arist. *Ath. Pol.* 17.1). In 514/3 Hipparchus, the brother of Hippias, was assassinated by Harmodius and Aristogeiton, who were put to death, but neither killer was associated with the Alcmeonids (Arist. *Ath. Pol.* 18.1–6).

The Alcmeonids appear to have fled Athens when Peisistratus seized power for the third time (Hdt. 1.64.3; 6.123.1).[111] They tried to set up a base at Leipsydrion, but the Peisistratids besieged them and forced them to withdraw (Hdt. 5.62.2; Arist. *Ath. Pol.* 19.3). The Alcmeonids then convinced the priestess at Delphi to urge the Spartan king Cleomenes to overthrow Hippias (Hdt. 5.63). In 511/10 BCE Cleomenes invaded Attica and surrounded Hippias on the Acropolis. After capturing the sons of the Peisistratids, Cleomenes allowed Hippias and his relatives to withdraw (Hdt. 5.64–5). Hippias left Attica with his family and went to the court of Artaphernes at Sardis where he defamed the Athenians and urged the satrap to place Athens under his control and that of the Persian king. When the Athenians sent messengers to protest, Artaphernes insisted that they reinstate Hippias, but the Athenians refused (Hdt. 5.96.1–2). Several years later, in 490, Darius sent Mardonius to invade Attica and set up Hippias as tyrant again, but the Athenians defeated the Persians at Marathon (Hdt. 6.102, 107–17). Had the Persians won and the Peisistratids returned to power, Hippias would no doubt have taken his revenge against the Alcmeonids. In 488/7 the Athenians ostracized Hipparchus, the son of Charmus, a relative of the Peisistratids (Arist. *Ath. Pol.* 22.4), and in 486/5 more friends of the tyrants were ostracized (Arist. *Ath. Pol.* 22.6).[112] It is

---

111. *SEG* 10:352, line 4 is a fragment of an archon list containing a name which could be restored as Cleisthenes as the archon for 545/4, which would call into question the narrative of Herodotus. But the restoration is questionable—see Dillon (2006).

112. For the identity of the ostracized see Rhodes (1981) 276.

possible that the Alcmeonids may have supported this move, but some of their members also fell victim to ostracism (Arist. *Ath. Pol.* 22.5–6).

This conflict fulfills several of the criteria used to identify feuding behavior. First, the conflict took place between two large groups linked by kinship. Second, the conflict lasted for many years, from about 560 BCE down to the 490s BCE. Third, the conflict followed a certain rhythm, with retaliation followed by retaliation over several decades. The significant point is that this kind of conflict between two large kinship groups has no parallel in the Classical period. The obvious reason for this is that the reforms of Cleisthenes broke up the power bases in the countryside of these two large families. By these reforms, the Athenians divided all of Attica into 139 demes under the control of demarchs elected by the local population.[113] To prevent these demes from coalescing into groups, the demes from each region were divided among trittyes assigned to ten tribes. This fragmented political power in countryside and made it impossible for any one family to dominate a region. As Aristotle says in his *Politics* (6.2.11.1319b19–27), the creation of the new tribes made sure that all citizens would be connected with each other as much as possible and previous associations would be dissolved. Cleisthenes' reforms therefore destroyed the social basis for feuding behavior.

Another development that discouraged feuding behavior was the creation of numerous magistracies with the power to enforce the law. As we saw in the previous chapter, the growth of the state reduced the scope for self-help and placed all residents of Attica under the protection of officials who monopolized the use of legitimate force. The average citizen, therefore, no longer had to rely on powerful families for his safety. The formal justice of the law courts replaced the informal justice of the vendetta.

113. For the reforms of Cleisthenes see Arist. *Ath. Pol.* 21.1–6 with Rhodes (1981) 248–60. For the division of Attica into tribes, trittyes, and demes see Traill (1975).

PART TWO

Applying the Law

3

The Judicial Oath

EVERY YEAR THE six thousand men who were selected to serve as judges swore an oath to cast their votes in accordance with the laws and decrees of the Athenian people.[1] Judges swore by Zeus, Apollo, and Demeter and prayed that they would prosper if they abided by their oath but called down destruction on themselves and their families were they to violate their oath.[2] According to Pollux (8.122) and Harpocration (s.v. *Ardettos*) the judges swore the oath near the Ilissus River in the deme of Ardettus, which was named after an Attic hero. In the speeches delivered before Athenian courts, litigants often refer to the oath and clearly expect the judges to abide by it.[3] Aeschines mentions the oath in all three of his speeches: twice in *Against Timarchus*, twice in *On the False Embassy*, and seven times in *Against Ctesiphon*. All three of the preserved speeches of Dinarchus invoke the oath. Even though Hyperides' speeches are preserved only in fragments, one can find references to the oath in four of his five court speeches. Andocides refers to it four times in *On the Mysteries*, Lycurgus four times in *Against Leocrates*, and Antiphon three times in *On the Murder of Herodes*.[4] Demosthenes quotes from the oath or paraphrases its terms very

1. The text of the Judicial Oath found at D. 24.149–51 is a forgery. Even though it contains some of the clauses in the oath, it omits others and is not reliable evidence. See Fraenkel (1878), followed by Drerup (1898) 256–64. There is no reason to accept the view of Lipsius (1905–15) 153, followed by Bonner and Smith (1930–38) II: 154–5, that the document contains sections of the oath from different periods. Johnstone (1999) and Thür (2007) treat this document as if it were reliable and appear to be unaware of Fraenkel's work.

2. Note that the document at D. 24.149–51 has the judges swear by Zeus, Poseidon, and Demeter, an indication that it is a forgery.

3. For a list of the passages in which the oath is mentioned either in general or in part see appendix 3.

4. The judicial oath is not mentioned in speeches before the Areopagus and the other courts for homicide: Antiphon 1, Antiphon 6, Lysias 1, and Lysias 3. But the members of these courts appear to have abided by the same standards as the regular courts. See section II. One should bear in mind that the members of the Areopagus had taken an oath to abide by the law when they were archons—see Arist. *Ath. Pol.* 55.5.

frequently in his speeches involving public cases. In *On the Crown*, he reminds the judges of its promises five times, in *On the False Embassy* eight times, in *Against Leptines* five times, in *Against Meidias* seven times, in *Against Androtion* six times, in *Against Aristocrates* four times, in *Against Timocrates* nine times, and in *Against Eubulides* four times. *Against Theocrines*, a speech in the Demosthenic corpus but not written by Demosthenes, contains six references to the oath. The private speeches of Demosthenes allude to the oath less frequently, but roughly two-thirds mention it at least once. Seven of the twelve speeches of Isaeus, all delivered in private cases involving family and inheritance, also allude to its provisions.[5]

The Judicial Oath contained four main pledges:

1. To vote in accordance with the laws and decrees of the Athenian people (e.g., Aeschin. 3.6; Antiphon 5.8; D. 20.118).
2. To listen to both the accuser(s) and defendant(s) equally (Aeschin. 2.1; D. 18.2; Isoc. 15.21. Cf. Lucian *Cal.* 8).
3. To vote or judge (*dikasein*) with one's most just judgment (*dikaiotate gnome*) about matters for which there are no laws and without favor or hostility (e.g., D. 23.96; 57.63).
4. To vote about matters pertaining to the charge (Aeschin. 1.154; D. 45.50. Cf. Aeschin. 1.170).[6]

The first pledge is clear and straightforward: the judges are to follow the laws when casting their votes for or against the defendant. As we will see in chapter 8, the meaning of this pledge is not quite so straightforward as it appears, but we must postpone that discussion for the moment. The second pledge seems equally clear: it bound the judges to pay attention to the arguments of both sides and thereby maintain their impartiality. At first glance the third pledge seems to bind the judges to vote honestly, that is, without allowing their hatred or friendship for the litigants to influence their decision and only in cases where the laws do not give clear guidance. Some scholars, however, have interpreted the third clause to mean that

5. For a list of quotations and allusions to the Judicial Oath see appendix 3. The speeches of Lysias mention the oath less frequently, but this is because several of them were delivered before the Areopagus and Delphinium, at procedures involving the Treasury or at proceedings for the *dokimasia* of officials.

6. After the Amnesty of 403, there was a clause requiring the judges to respect the Amnesty added to the oath—see And. 1.91.

the judges could dispense with the law when making their decisions as long as they consulted their consciences about what they considered just.[7] The fourth pledge has attracted relatively little attention, yet as we will see, it is closely connected to the second pledge and is key for our understanding of Athenian legal procedure.

Part I of this book examined the broader political and social contexts of Athenian law and studied the officials who enforced the laws and the motives of the accusers who initiated legal proceedings. Part II turns to the way the courts applied the law; the Judicial Oath is key for our understanding of the way Athenian judges approached their task.[8] The first section of this chapter looks at the second and third pledges contained in the oath and their relationship to one another. Some scholars have argued that the pledge to follow the laws was not binding and that litigants only cite the laws as evidence, not as a guide to the way judges should decide a case.[9] According to these scholars, this was because the Athenians did not attempt to achieve the rule of law. As a result, they assert (mostly without evidence) that Athenian judges paid more attention to extra-legal considerations than they did to the laws. The courts were thus not 'guardians of the laws' (D. 24.36) but arenas for political ambition or feuding.[10]

The second section takes a close look at the fourth pledge, which bound the judges to vote only about the charges listed in the indictment. To understand this part of the oath, it is necessary to study the contents and the function of the indictment (*engklema*), a document whose importance recent works have tended to neglect. The indictment required the accuser to prove that the defendant had broken the law and to pay no attention to matters such as social status and public service. It also obligated the defendant to reply to the legal charges brought by the accuser and to show that he had not violated the law. In this way, it required litigants to 'keep to the point' and not to introduce irrelevant issues such as public service. The indictment therefore served to ensure that the judges would act as 'guardians of the laws' (D. 24.36).

---

7. E. g., Too (2008) 107 ('the dicasts voted to uphold the democracy, to vote according to their conscience, and to give prosecuting and defending parties a fair hearing'); Lanni (2006) 72.

8. Some recent works completely ignore the Judicial Oath. For instance, the glossary in Cartledge, Millett, and Todd (1990) 232 has an entry under Oath, but does not mention the Judicial Oath. Todd (1993) 54–5 has a single page on the oath.

9. For this view see Todd (1993) 60. For good criticism of this approach see Carey (1996) 34, note 8.

10. The most extreme proponents of this view are Ober (1989) and Cohen (1995).

I

As we have seen, the first clause of the oath required the judges to vote according to the laws and decrees of the Assembly and Council and the third clause to vote according to their most just judgment. The first clause is the most frequently cited part of the oath. By contrast, the orators rarely quote or refer to the third clause. When they quote or paraphrase it, they appear to interpret it in two different ways. In his *Against Leptines*, Demosthenes (20.118) says: 'As for matters where there are no laws, you have sworn to follow your most honest judgment.' In *Against Boeotus* (D. 39.39–40), there is a similar version. But in *Against Aristocrates* (D. 23.96–7), this pledge appears to have a different meaning: 'They have sworn to judge with their most just judgment, but the decision made by their judgment depends on what they hear. Now when they cast a vote in accordance with this, they are righteous. For everyone who casts his vote neither through enmity nor through favor nor any other unjust reason against their judgment, is righteous [i.e., upholds his oath].' In *Against Eubulides* (D. 57.63), we find the same view of this pledge: 'They have erased from the oath the pledge to vote according to one's most just judgment, not out of favor or enmity.'[11]

One might therefore infer that the oath only contained the words 'I will vote [or judge] with my most fair judgment' and argue that the actual text of the oath did not contain these phrases and that they are only the interpretations invented by litigants.[12] This argument faces two obstacles. First, Pollux (8.122) explicitly states that the phrase 'about issues for which there are no laws' was in the oath. Second, there are several parallels for this phrase in oaths from other Greek communities. The closest parallel comes from the Gymnasiarchal Law from Beroia dated to the second century BCE.[13] Every year the man elected to serve as gymnasiarch was required to swear: 'I will perform the office of gymnasiarch according to the law about the gymnasiarch and regarding all matters not written in the law I will [perform the office] using my own judgment as best I can following the rules of justice and morality (*hosiotata kai dikaiotata*), neither doing favors for a friend nor harming an enemy in violation of justice' (lines A 26–30).[14] Like the Judicial Oath in Athens, the gymnasiarch promises to obey the

11. Plato *Apology* 35c appears to allude to this part of the oath.

12. Thus, Mirhady (2007).

13. For the date see Gauthier and Hatzopoulos (1993) 35–41.

14. For the text see Gauthier and Hatzopoulos (1993) 18.

law and to use his best judgment only in cases where the law gives no guidance. He also pledges to act impartially, without special regard for friends or enemies. The wording is slightly different from the oath in Athens, but the terms of both oaths correspond very closely.

There is another parallel in an inscription from Eresos dated to the reign of Alexander the Great.[15] The inscription records a decree from Eresos establishing procedures for the trial of tyrants in accordance with a *diagraphe* of Alexander. The decree instructs the judges in the case to swear: 'I shall judge the case, as far as it lies within the laws, according to the laws, and in other regards industriously, as well and as justly as possible' (lines 9–17 trans. Rhodes). Here a distinction is also made between cases where the laws provide guidance and other kinds of cases, those presumably where the laws do not give answers about how to decide.[16] Another parallel can be found in a decree recording a treaty between Temnos and Clazomenai dated to the early second century BCE: 'Let the following be the oath: I will judge cases for the people of Temnos and the people of Clazomenai and the metics and the rest of those dwelling in those cities who have lawsuits according to the treaty (*synthekai*), but about matters that have not been written in the treaty, with my most just judgment (*gnome dikaiotate*).'[17] Here the term 'treaty' (*synthekai*) has been substituted for 'laws,' but the general phrasing and ideas are the same. These parallels show that there is no reason to doubt that the phrases 'about issues for which there are no laws' and 'without hatred or favor' were in the oath sworn by Athenian judges.

In his *Rhetoric* Aristotle appears to allude to this part of the Judicial Oath in his discussion of the judges' pledge to 'vote with one's best judgment.' It might be tempting to rely on Aristotle's analysis of the phrase in his *Rhetoric* for an understanding of this part of the Judicial Oath, but that temptation should be resisted. Aristotle's *Rhetoric* tends to mingle theory with observations about contemporary practice; its discussion of forensic rhetoric in chapters 13–15 of Book I does outline some arguments similar to those found in the court speeches of the orators (see chapter 8). But many of the arguments presented there never occur in these speeches.[18]

---

15. Rhodes and Osborne (2003) no. 83 iii, lines 9–17.

16. A similar distinction has been restored in the judicial oath found in an Amphictyonic law—*IG* ii² 1126, lines 2–3.

17. *SEG* 29:1130*bis*, lines 28–30 (= Herrmann *MDA [I]* 29 [1979] 249–71).

18. Cf. Carey (1996) 46: 'the advice of Aristotle and Anaximenes should come with a health warning, that use of the argument proposed could seriously damage a litigant's chances of success.'

Aristotle's discussion needs to be placed in context. Aristotle (*Rh.* 1.15.1375a5–b12) advises the potential litigant in two potential cases: one where the written law does not favor one's case and another where it does. For the first possibility he suggests eight possible arguments. The first is, 'If the written law is contrary to our case one must use the common law and arguments based on fairness (*epieikeia*) because they are more just; that to judge according to one's best judgment is to follow the written laws not completely (*pantelos*).' As we will see in chapter 8, *epieikeia* is not a separate source of justice that is at odds with the written law. *Epieikeia* comes into play only when a rigid application of the written law would produce an unjust result by not taking into account issues like intent or extenuating circumstances. Arguments based on *epieikeia* are not aimed at overthrowing the authority of the law but at dealing with unusual cases and with exceptions to general rules. Moreover, the arguments that employ *epieikeia* are often based on general principles implicit in the written laws. Furthermore, one never finds an appeal to the 'common law' in opposition to the written laws of Athens in Attic forensic oratory. When orators refer to a general rule that most Greeks follow, this rule is always in accord with the laws of Athens. For instance, Euphiletus, a client of Lysias, opens his defense against a charge of murder by telling the court that the laws of all the Greek cities provide harsh punishments for seducers (Lys. 1.1–2). A client of Isaeus tells the court that the rule allowing men to adopt an heir is found not only throughout Greece but also among the barbarians (Is. 2.24. Cf. Isoc. 19.50).

The second argument is that fairness (*to epieikes*) always remains and never alters nor does the common law (for it is in accordance with nature) but written laws often change. This argument is also never found in court speeches. As we will see later, the Athenians believed that their laws went back to Draco and Solon and had not changed for over two centuries.[19]

The third argument is that 'the just is something true and advantageous, but what appears to be just may not be; thus, the written law may not be; for it does not perform the function of law' (trans. Kennedy). This argument appears to go closely with the next one: 'the judge is like one who tests silver insofar as he distinguishes counterfeit and true justice'

19. Aristotle quotes here the famous lines of Antigone from Sophocles' play, but Antigone opposes the unwritten laws of the gods not with the written laws of the city but rather with the order of a ruler. See Harris (2006a) 61–80, esp. 74–6. Carey (1996) 40 mistakenly calls Creon's order a *psephisma*, a word that never occurs in the play.

(trans. Kennedy). In Athenian courts litigants never argue that the judges should disregard a law because it appears to be just but in reality is not. On the contrary, litigants always praise the law as advantageous and just (D. 20.93, 98, 153; 21.9, 48–50; 24.24, 34, 43, 59; Is. 6.49).[20]

The fourth argument is that it is the task of the better man to follow and abide by the unwritten laws rather than the written laws. In the only two passages in the orators where the unwritten laws are mentioned, however, one finds a very different view of the relationship between the written and unwritten laws. In his *On the Crown* Demosthenes (18.274–5) discusses three levels of culpability: doing wrong willingly (*hekon*), doing wrong unwillingly, and lack of success where there is no wrongdoing or mistake. Demosthenes continues by observing that these distinctions are found not only in the laws, but also in the unwritten laws set down by nature (for the distinction between willing and unwilling actions see also D. 21.41–6). In *Against Aristocrates*, Demosthenes (23.70) claims that Aristocrates' decree violates both the written and unwritten laws. Thus when Demosthenes mentions the unwritten laws in an argument, he sees no conflict between the two kinds of laws.[21] Indeed, his view of their relationship with the written laws is exactly the opposite of Aristotle's view in this passage of the *Rhetoric*.

The fifth argument is that if a law is contrary to a well-esteemed law or is self-contradictory (for example, in some cases one law provides that all agreements are binding, but another forbids one to make agreements contrary to the law), the written law should not be followed. This argument is also never found in court speeches. As we will see in the arguments made regarding the laws about announcing the award of crowns in the Theater of Dionysus, both Aeschines and Demosthenes cite two laws, which one might think contradict each other, but they never say this (see chapter 6). Instead, Aeschines (3.37–9) observes that the laws of Athens could not contain two contradictory statutes because there was a procedure to eliminate such contradictions. In his reply, Demosthenes also does not think

20. Cf. Carey (1996) 44: 'It is not uncommon for citation of the law to be accompanied by praise of the law.'

21. For the relationship between the unwritten and written laws of the *polis* see Harris (2006a) 53–57: the unwritten laws of the gods are the principles of justice on which the laws of the city are based. One should distinguish between this type of unwritten laws and the unwritten laws that are informal rules of conduct enforced by moral disapproval (e.g., Th. 2.37.2). Cf. Carey (1996) 40 ('the two categories are seen as governing different areas of conduct').

that the two laws contradict each other; he simply interprets them in a different way.[22] The only kinds of speeches in which one litigant claims that one law stands in contradiction to another are those delivered in cases against inexpedient laws (D. 20, 24). But this is not the type of case that Aristotle has in mind. Aristotle is providing arguments to dissuade the court from applying a law to convict a defendant. In a case against an inexpedient law, an accuser attempts to prove that an existing law is opposed to other statutes and should be repealed.

The sixth argument is that if a law is ambiguous, so that one can twist it and see to which interpretation justice or advantage lends itself, one should then use that one.[23] Yet it never happens that any litigant states that a law is ambiguous.[24] On the contrary, the Athenians believed that their laws were easy to understand and that the meaning of their laws was clear (D. 20.93). If a word or phrase in a law could be interpreted in different ways, litigants do not say that the meaning of the law was ambiguous because this would undermine the authority of the law. As we will see in chapter 6, there was a law forbidding the award of crowns to an *arche*, a term that can be translated 'official' or 'term of office.' At the trial of Ctesiphon in 330, Aeschines (3.11) adopted the first interpretation of the term, Demosthenes the latter (18.119). Neither litigant recognizes the possibility that the term could be ambiguous but argues as if his own interpretation of the statute is based on the natural or standard meaning of the key term. To prove this, Demosthenes then cites precedents to support his view (see chapter 7). So when there is an ambiguity in the law, litigants do not say that the judges must apply their own best judgment (as Aristotle advises). Instead, they cite precedents or the intent of the lawgiver as it is found in written statutes to show that their interpretation of the law is preferable.

The seventh argument is that if the circumstances in which the law was established no longer obtain, one should try to make this clear and use this argument to combat the law. Nowhere in any extant judicial speech does a litigant say that the judges should ignore a law because it is

22. On this general point see the excellent essay of Sickinger (2008).

23. Carey (1996) 38 believes that 'the scope for exploitation of internal inconsistency within a law . . . was considerably limited by the procedural orientation of Greek laws,' but this rests on an untenable assumption about the procedural orientation of Greek laws. See the next chapter.

24. In fact, the word used by Aristotle in this passage to describe an ambiguous law (*amphibolos*) never occurs in all the speeches of the Attic Orators.

obsolete. The attitude toward old laws found in the speeches is quite the opposite: speakers often praise old laws either because they were established by a venerable lawgiver like Draco or Solon (e.g., D. 20.90, 93, 158; 22.25, 30–31) or because they have stood the test of time and have proven their value (D. 20.8). The view of Antiphon (6.2. Cf. 5.14; Isoc. 15.82) is characteristic: 'Everyone would agree in praising the laws governing these matters as the finest and most righteous of laws. They are the oldest established laws and have always remained the same, which is the best sign of well enacted laws for time and experience teach people the faults in things' (trans. Gagarin). Once more, Aristotle's analysis cannot be used as a guide to the rhetorical strategies employed in Athenian courts.[25]

One should not, therefore, use Aristotle's discussion in the *Rhetoric* of the arguments to be used against the authority of the law as evidence that the clause in the Judicial Oath instructing the judges to vote according to their most just judgment allowed them to ignore the law.[26] As the wording of the oath makes clear, its pledges bound judges to vote in accordance with the laws and decrees of the Athenian people. Judges were to rely on their most just judgment alone in cases where there were no laws pertaining to the issue being debated. This was clearly a default clause to be used only in exceptional cases.

Yet, how often did litigants believe that it was necessary to resort to this default clause? Were there so many gaps in the Athenian law code that judges often had no choice but to rely on their own judgment? Some scholars assume that Athenian laws were so riddled with contradictions and ambiguities that they provided inadequate guidance, making it necessary for judges to make up their minds on general considerations of justice.[27] This assumption is contradicted by the evidence of the extant court speeches: in the roughly one hundred orations written for delivery in court, this default clause in the oath is mentioned only twice. This stands in marked contrast to the pledge binding judges to vote in accordance with the laws and decrees of the Athenian people, which is quoted, paraphrased, or alluded to over fifty times.

---

25. Anaximenes *Rhet.* 1443a20ff. has a similar set of arguments which also have no parallels in forensic oratory at Athens. See Carey (1996) 38–9.

26. Cf. Carey (1996) 39: 'the advice on means of counteracting appeal to the law by the opponent is difficult to square with what actually happened in the courts.'

27. E.g., Christ (1998a) 195–6. The view that the laws of Athens contained many contradictions has been decisively refuted by Sickinger (2008).

The passages where the clause is found deserve scrutiny. The first occurs in Demosthenes' speech *Against Leptines* (20.118–9). Just before mentioning this clause, Demosthenes reminds the judges about the first clause: 'You have come here having sworn to judge in accordance with the laws, not those of the Spartans or the Thebans, nor even those that your earliest ancestors followed, but those under which they received the exemptions that this man here is taking away through his law.' Up to this point, in fact, Demosthenes has built his case against Leptines' law in part on its procedural violations of the existing statutes. In particular, he discusses the law that requires anyone wishing to propose a new law first to repeal any opposing statutes (D. 20.92). He charges Leptines with having violated this law by failing to repeal the law making all awards granted by the people irrevocable before enacting his own law abolishing the exemptions (D. 20.95–7). Demosthenes (20.118–19) then continues:

> As for matters where there are no laws, you have sworn to follow your most honest judgment. Apply this kind of judgment to the entire law. Is it not then right to give honors to your benefactors? It is right. What next? Is it not right to allow people to keep what someone once has given them? It is right. Then do this in order to abide by your oath, and show your anger if anyone claims that your ancestors acted differently. If anyone should cite examples of cases where those men did not grant an honor to someone after receiving an important benefit, you should consider them dishonest and uncouth, dishonest because they tell lies about your ancestors and misrepresent them as ungrateful, uncouth because they are unaware that even if that was the way things were, it is their duty to deny it rather than to repeat it.

In this passage Demosthenes does not ask the judges to rely only on their most just judgment. He uses this clause to introduce another argument based on general considerations of justice in addition to (and not as a substitute for) arguments based on the written laws.

The clause is used in a similar way in the other passage in Demosthenes' speech *Against Boeotus* I (39.39–40). The accuser is a man named Mantitheus who has brought a suit against his half-brother Boeotus for using his name.[28] He claims that if Boeotus continues to use the name Mantitheus, it

28. For an analysis of the legal issue in the speech see below 223–25.

will cause him enormous hardship. In the final part of his speech, Mantitheus challenges Boeotus to find a law that gives children power over their names. To anticipate his reply, he reminds the court that the law gives parents the power to give their children names and also to erase these names and disinherit them if they wish. Here he says that the judges 'have sworn to vote with their most just judgment so that if there is no law laid down about the topic, even in this case, they would rightly cast their vote for him.' He next asks the judges if any of them have given his child two names or if those without children will do so. 'No, of course,' he replies for them. If in their opinion this is right for their children, then it is right (*hosion*) for them to decide this way in his case. In the final words of the speech, Mantitheus concludes that the judges should vote for him on the grounds that such a decision is in accordance with their most just judgment, the laws, and their oath. Thus Mantitheus does not invoke this part of the oath because he has no laws to support his case and must resort to the judges' most just judgment alone. Nor does he use this clause to undermine the validity of the existing laws. Like Demosthenes in *Against Leptines*, Mantitheus uses this part of the oath to introduce a supplementary argument in addition to his arguments based on the written laws. One should not therefore use this clause of the Judicial Oath as an argument that the laws of Athens were full of gaps and that as a result judges relied on their own judgment.[29]

Nor should one claim that the laws and justice represented two different standards, with the latter superior to the former, and that the clause about using one's most just judgment gave judges the right to follow their judgment if they believed that justice was in conflict with the laws.[30] As noted, this would place the two clauses of the oath in opposition to each

29. As, for example, does Harrison (1971) 48: 'The general tenor of the oath suggests that the juror [*sic*] is to vote according to his conscience; there would certainly have been many cases not completely or not at all covered by law or decree.' Harrison does not examine the passages where the default clause is cited and provides no evidence whatsoever to support his sweeping statement. For a similar view see Ruschenbusch (1957), who claims that there were gaps in Athenian law, but most of the evidence discussed pertains to the alleged lack of clarity of Athenian statutes, a very different issue. For a similar view see Wohl (2010) 31. Todd (1993) 54–5 only discusses the clause of the oath about voting according to the laws and decrees, but claims that litigants often 'call on their hearer to bring in a verdict on the basis of more general considerations of justice, in circumstances where (we may suspect) the letter of the law is against them.' To support this sweeping statement, Todd does not cite a single ancient source.

30. For the view that law and justice represented two different standards see Christ (1998a) 195: 'While law was in a certain uncontroversial sense a standard (*kanon*: Lycurg. 1.18–9; cf. Aeschin. 3.199–200) of the courts, jurors [*sic*] determined how and whether to enforce the laws on the basis of a more fundamental standard—namely their sense of "what is just" (*ta diakaia*).' The passages cited later in this chapter decisively refute Christ's assumption that the Athenians believed that their laws and justice were two different standards.

other. Second, as we have seen, this clause is never used this way. Third, there is no reason to think that litigants and judges thought that the laws and justice represented two different standards. In fact, litigants use the terms law and justice as virtual synonyms and never view the two as in conflict. The following passages illustrate the point:

Aeschines 3.199–200: 'For *justice* is not left undefined, but has been defined in your *laws*. As in carpentry when we would like to know what is straight and what is not, we set the ruler, which we use as a standard, next to it, so in public actions against illegal proposals there is available as a ruler of *justice* this tablet with the decree proposed and the *laws* written next to it.'

Antiphon 5.7: 'For you it is *just* and in accordance with your oath, for you swore to judge the case according to the *laws*.'

Isaeus 2.47: 'Remember the law and the oath that you have sworn and what has been said about the case and cast a vote that is *just*, true to your oath, and in conformity to the *laws*.'

Isaeus 4.31: 'Remember the *laws* and the oaths that you swore, and also the testimony that we have provided and cast a *just* vote.'

Isaeus 6.65: 'If you order him to prove the allegation made in his claim, you will cast a righteous vote in accordance with the *laws*, and *justice* will be done for these men.'

Isaeus 8.46: 'Remember, therefore, the oaths that you swore when serving as judges and the arguments that we have made and the *laws* and cast a vote as *justice* requires.'

Isaeus 9.35: 'Therefore lend me your support, and if Cleon is more talented at speaking than I am, do not let this talent, which is without *law* and *justice*, prevail, but make yourselves arbitrators of the entire case.'

Isaeus 11.18: 'Those who were judging the case considered *justice* and their oaths very important with the result that they voted for me because my case was in accordance with the *laws*.'

Isaeus 11.35: 'This is what is most *just*; this is also what the *laws* command.'

Lysias 9.19: 'Their action was completely in accordance with the *laws* and fairness (*eikos*), and they clearly committed no injustice, but paid most attention to what is *just*.'

Lysias 14.22: 'So that if *justice* is not on their side, and they demand that you do them a favor, you must bear in mind that they are telling you to violate your oath and disobey the *laws*.'

Lysias 14.42: 'Have they not acted contrary to *justice* and *law* both toward other people in public and in their personal relations?'

Lysias 14.47: 'Read the *laws*, the oaths, and the charge to the judges. Let them keep these in mind and give a *just* verdict.'

Demosthenes 43.34: 'Whoever of these two you think speaks more *justly* and more in conformity with the *laws*, it is clear that you will take his side.'

Demosthenes 43.52: 'This is what the *law* states, and this is what is *just*.'

Demosthenes 43.60: 'But if Theopompus has died, the *laws* have not died, nor has *justice* died, nor have the judges who decide the case.'

Demosthenes 43.84: 'Defend the laws and take care of the dead so that their house does not become abandoned. By doing this you will cast a *just* vote, one that is in conformity with the *laws* and in your interests.'

Demosthenes 46.28: 'I implore and beg all of you, men of the court, to defend me and to punish those who so readily give false testimony for your own sake, for mine, for *justice*, and for the *laws*.'

Aristotle *Constitution of the Athenians* 55.5: Oath of the Archons: 'They swear that they will rule *justly* and *according to the laws* and not accept gifts on account of their office.'

Note that in many of these passages, the litigant explicitly states that a just vote is one cast according to the laws.[31] Significant also is the placement of these phrases: they are often the last words in a speech. They thus are found in a very prominent place, which amply demonstrates how much stress litigants placed on the equivalence of law and justice. What these litigants wanted the judges to bear in mind as they decided how to vote was that they had sworn an oath and that oath required them

31. Note that the word *dikaia* does not refer to the 'issues of fact' as opposed to legal questions (*pace* Mirhady [2007]).

to vote in accordance with the laws, not just in a way that seemed right to them.

The message of the Judicial Oath is clear: it bound the judges to vote in accordance with the laws. It is therefore not surprising that when orators mention or allude to the oath, they also mention the laws.[32] On the other hand, the importance of the clause 'I will vote with my most fair judgment in cases where there are no laws' should not be exaggerated or taken out of context. Above all, it did not grant the judges the right to ignore the law if they considered it wrong. What is most striking (and most ignored by some scholars) is how rarely this clause is invoked and how it is used in the two passages where it is found. And in no extant speech delivered in an Athenian court does a litigant rely solely on this clause and ignore the pledge to vote in accordance with the laws.

II

The fourth clause of the Judicial Oath required the judges to vote only about the charges made in the indictment (Aeschin. 1.159; D. 45.50). This means that if an accuser charged a defendant with theft, the court should only consider the question, did the defendant steal the item mentioned in the indictment? This requirement implicitly instructed the judges to disregard matters that were not relevant to the main charge. If a defendant were accused of taking bribes and betraying Athenian interests, the court should not decide, is he a good citizen? but rather, did he take money in return for helping the enemy? Linked to this clause in the Judicial Oath was an oath sworn by the litigant not 'to speak outside the subject' (*exo tou pragmatos*).[33] Litigants in homicide cases swore a similar oath that they would only address the charge of murder and disregard all other issues.[34] This meant that the accuser should confine his arguments to proving the charges in the indictment and that the defendant should devote his speech to disproving them.

---

32. E.g., D. 19.134, 239, 297; 21.177, 211; 22.45; 23.101; 27.68; 39.41; Is. 2.47; 8.46.

33. For this oath sworn by litigants in private cases see Arist. *Ath. Pol.* 67.1. There appears to have been a similar oath for those in public cases because litigants in public cases often mention the need to 'keep to the point.' Cf. Rhodes (2004) 137.

34. Antiphon 5.11. This evidence is decisive against the view of Lanni (2006) 75–114 that the homicide courts had a stricter standard of relevance—see Harris (2009/10b) 327–28.

But what did the indictment contain? How did it shape the arguments made by the litigants in court? Despite its importance in Athenian legal procedure, the main handbooks on Athenian law pay little attention to the plaint.[35] Several recent essays have discussed the plaint but only examine some of the evidence and do not provide an extensive analysis of its role in Athenian legal procedure.[36]

When an Athenian citizen or other resident of Attica initiated a private or public suit, he began by issuing a summons to the defendant to appear before a magistrate on a certain day.[37] On this day he submitted a written document to the magistrate, which recorded his name, the name of the defendant, the type of action he was initiating, and the charges against the defendant.[38] This might be called an *engklema* (D. 32.2, 4, 27; 34.16) or *graphe* (D. 18.18).[39] If the defendant denied the charges, he submitted a written statement to that effect called an *antigraphe* (Lys. 22; D. 45.46; Hyp. *Eux.* 31; Pollux 8.58). Each litigant swore an oath that the statements

35. Beauchet (1897) contains no general discussion of the plaint. Lipsius (1905–15) 815–24 mentions only the plaints found at D. 37.22, 25, 26, 28, 29; 45.46 D. H. *Din.* 3; Plu. *Alc.* 22; D. L. 2.40 and does not discuss many of the passages examined in this chapter. The index to his work contains no entry for the term *engklema*. Harrison (1971) 91–2 mentions only those plaints cited by Lipsius and contains no extensive discussion of their contents and role in litigation. MacDowell (1978) 150–1, 201, 239 gives translations of the plaints at D. 37.22, D. H. *Din.* 3, and D. L. 2.40 but states only that 'the prosecutor or claimant gave the magistrate a statement of his charge or claim' and that by the time of Demosthenes it was submitted in writing. Todd (1993) 126 mentions only the possibility that the magistrate might not accept the indictment but has nothing about the indictment's form and contents or its role in litigation. Gagarin (2008) 112–3 discusses only the plaints cited by Harrison and has nothing to add to his discussion. Pébarthe (2006) 315–43, whose discussion of the written documents used in litigation is superior to that of Gagarin, has only three pages on the *engklema*, *phasis*, and *paragraphe*.

36. Faraguna (2006) discusses only the plaints mentioned by Lipsius and Harrison and the document at [Plu.] *Mor.* 833e–834b (I am skeptical about the authenticity of this document). Bertrand (2002) and Thür (2007) only discuss some of the evidence and provide little analysis of the document's role.

37. For the methods of initiating legal procedures see Lipsius (1905–15) 804–28.

38. Calhoun (1919) 190 believes that 'in the time of the earlier orators complaints were still made orally and were written down by the court officials, and that the practice of handing them in in writing was introduced in the fourth century, probably not long before the commencement of Demosthenes' career.'

39. *Engklema* appears to be the term used mainly in private actions, but it is used for the plaint in a public charge at Lys. 9.8 and Pl. *Ap.* 24b–c. In the procedure of *phasis* the plaint was called the *phasis*—see [D.] 58.7. In a *paragraphe* procedure the plaint was called the *paragraphe*—see D. 34.16. In the *eisangelia* procedure the plaint could be called the *eisangelia*—see Lycurg. *Leocr.* 137; Hyp. *Lycurg.* 3, 12; *Eux.* 29–32. In the *apographe* procedure the plaint was called the *apographe*—see Lys. 9.3. See Lipsius (1905–15) 817 with note 48.

in his document were true, and the document could therefore also be called an *antomosia* (Is. 3.6; 5.2; Lys. 23.13; Pl. *Ap.* 19b; Harpocration *s.v.* ἀντωμοσία; Pollux 8.55).[40] If the magistrate accepted the case, he posted a copy of the plaint before the statues of the Eponymous Heroes in the Agora (D. 21.103).[41] Before the trial began, the secretary of the court read the plaint to the judges (Aeschin. 1.2). At the end of his speech the accuser might read out the plaint (Hyp. *Phil.* 13; *Eux.* 40) or remind the court of the main charges (D. 19.333; 23.215–18). After the trial, the verdict was written on the plaint, which was kept on file in the Metroon or in the office of a magistrate.[42]

The basic form of the plaint contained the name of the accuser, the name of the defendant, and the name of the offense. A good example is the plaint submitted by Apollodorus in his case against Stephanus: 'Apollodorus, the son of Pasion, from the deme of Acharnai, [brings a charge] of false testimony against Stephanus, the son of Menecles, from the deme of Acharnai. Penalty: one talent' (D. 45.46). The version Demosthenes (21.103) gives of the plaint written by Euctemon follows the same pattern: 'Euctemon from the deme of Lousia has brought a charge of desertion against Demosthenes from the deme of Paiania.'[43] The names of the accuser and the defendant are followed by the patronymic and the name of their demes (Demosthenes is probably abbreviating Euctemon's plaint by omitting the patronymics). Demosthenes (21.87) says that the names of

---

40. On this term see Wyse (1904) 294. Cf. Harrison (1971) 99.

41. Demosthenes (21.103) says that Euctemon brought a charge, which was displayed, then did not attend the *anakrisis*, which would indicate that the magistrate posted the charge before the *anakrisis*, not after. *Pace* Faraguna (2006) 205, note 34 ('dopo l'*anakrisis* una copia dell'atto di accusa veniva esposta dal magistrato'). Cf. Isoc. 15.237; [D.] 58.7–8. On the monument of the Eponymous Heroes see Shear (1970).

42. Lanni (2004) 164 and Gagarin (2008) 195 do not think that verdicts were recorded and kept on file, but see Harris (forthcoming b).

43. The accuser in a public case apparently did not have to decide about what penalty he was going to propose at the *timesis* phase of the trial until after the court voted about the guilt of the defendant. This would explain why Demosthenes in his speech *Against Meidias* mentions several possible penalties for the defendant. See Harris (1989) 125–26. This would also explain why Euctemon's plaint did not contain a penalty. See, however, [D.] 58.43 (Theocrines adds a penalty of ten talents in a *graphe paranomon*), Aeschin. 1.14 (Lycinus writes one hundred talents as penalty), Arist. *Ath. Pol.* 48.4 (the accuser at the *euthynai* writes the penalty), and the comic version of a plaint found at Aristophanes *Vesp.* 894–97. See also the law about archives from Paros, which required the accuser in a public suit against those who tampered with public documents to write the amount of the penalty in the plaint (*SEG* 33: 679, lines 27–32).

the *kleteres*, the witnesses to the summons, were also written on the plaint (cf. [D.] 53.14).[44]

This information was important for the magistrate who received the charge for several reasons. The first was to establish the full identity of each party for all subsequent stages of the procedure. If the defendant lost the case and had to pay damages, the record of the trial would clearly indicate who had to pay. If the defendant were condemned to pay a fine or lose some political rights, the *praktores* collecting fines would know whom to record as a public debtor.[45] The second was to determine the status of the two parties; if both were citizens, the magistrate would send the case to one of the regular courts, but if one party was a metic, he would have to refer the case to the Polemarch and the *prostates* of the metic might become involved. If the defendant were a slave, the magistrate would have to make sure that his master would represent him in court. Lysias' speech *Against Pancleon* illustrates the importance of establishing the status of the defendant. The accuser recounts how he summoned Pancleon before the Polemarch because he assumed he was a metic. (Lys. 23.2). When he replied that he was a Plataean and belonged to deme of Decelea, the accuser summoned him before the court of the tribe Hippothontis (Lys. 23.3). The fact that he was careful to select the right jurisdiction reveals that he obviously expected the magistrate to reject the charge if it was not brought in the right venue.

Third, the magistrate had to know the precise nature of the charge so that he could be sure that the accuser was initiating a procedure contained in one of the laws. All magistrates in Athens were forbidden to follow any unwritten law, that is, a law that was not found in the written law code of Athens (And. 1.86).[46] If a magistrate accepted a charge that did not follow one of the legal procedures in the law code, he would violate this rule and be subject to prosecution at his *euthynai* (Arist. *Ath. Pol.* 48.4). The Athenian magistrate did not issue an edict indicating what kinds of charges he

---

44. Lipsius (1905–15) 805 thought that this was not necessary because the names of these witnesses are not found on the plaints in the passages cited in note 6, but there is no reason to believe that these documents are complete.

45. For the *praktores* see Antiphon 6.49; *IG* i^3 59 (c. 430 BCE), fr. e, lines 47–8; *IG* ii^2 45 (378/7), line 7; *Agora* 15: 56A, line 34.

46. Note that several passages state explicitly that an action was brought in accordance with a specific procedure provided by law—see, for example, [D.] 59.66; D. 24.32, 34–8; 32.1; 33.2–3; 35.3.

would accept. He was not like a Roman magistrate who could make procedural innovations by applying standard procedure to new kinds of offenses or modify the traditional formulae; he could only accept charges in accordance with a particular law. Fourth, the plaint would enable the magistrate to make sure that the accuser had brought his charge in the correct jurisdiction. If the accuser had brought his charge before the wrong magistrate, the latter would reject the charge and could indicate to the accuser another magistrate to whom he should submit his case. This also served to protect the magistrate by helping him avoid accepting cases that lay outside his jurisdiction.

Fifth, in private cases, the magistrate, the public arbitrator, and the court had to know the exact amount of damages the plaintiff was requesting. The public arbitrator and the court needed to know so that it could determine whether the losses suffered by the plaintiff were roughly equivalent to the damages he requested. For instance, Demosthenes, when arguing his case against his guardians, had not only to prove that they had embezzled a large amount of his inheritance but also to show the exact amount that they had taken (D. 27.4–46). Sixth, if the plaintiff lost the case, the court had to know how much he had requested to determine the amount of the *epobolia*, a fine of one-sixth the amount he had requested.[47] Seventh, if the defendant were to charge the accuser with making a false summons (*graphe pseudokleteias*), it was necessary to know the names of the alleged witnesses to the summons so that they could be invited to testify.[48] For all these reasons, it was crucial to have a written record of all this information.

But the plaint contained much more information than these basic facts. The accuser also had to indicate the illegal actions performed by the defendant. He could not just assert that the defendant had broken the law; he had to show what the defendant had done to violate the law. When describing the actions of the defendant, the accuser also had to follow the language of the statute under which he had initiated his procedure.[49] In

47. On the *epobolia* see MacDowell (2008).

48. On the *graphe pseudokleteias* see [D.] 53.14–8.

49. Yunis (2005) 197, note 13 claims that 'there was no mechanism for the court to be apprised of the relevant law' and that the '*dikastai* were entirely dependent on the litigants for being informed of whatever law, if any, the *litigants* deemed relevant,' but the form and contents of the plaint shows that this is not true. In his brief and superficial discussion of the judicial oath, Yunis does not mention the fourth clause, which is decisive against his argument. Yunis also claims that any information about the law was 'potentially inaccurate and deceptive' but fails to note that it was the clerk who read out laws and decrees at the trial, not the litigants.

343 Hyperides brought a charge of treason against Philocrates using the procedure of *eisangelia*. This law applied to three types of offenses: (1) attempts to overthrow the democracy, (2) treason (betraying [*prodo*] the city, its ships, land or naval forces), and (3) speaking, as a public orator (*rhetor*) against the best interests of the Athenian people while accepting money (*chremata lambanon*) (Hyp. *Eux.* 7–8).[50] When he wrote his indictment, Hyperides (*Eux.* 29–30) followed the wording of the third offense very carefully.

> The impeachment that I drew up was just and in accordance with the law, referring to him as 'an orator giving counsel against the best interests of the people and receiving money and gifts from those working against them.' Even so I was not satisfied to bring in the impeachment before I had added underneath: 'These proposals he made against the best interests of the people, because he had taken bribes.' And I wrote his decree underneath. And again I added: 'These further proposals he made against the best interests of the people, because he had taken bribes.' And I wrote the decree alongside. Indeed this statement is written down five or six times because I thought that the trial and the judgment should be just.

Hyperides included the three key terms 'public speaker' (*rhetora*), 'not in the best interests of the Athenian people' (*ta arista to demo Athenaion*), and 'taking money' (*chremata lambanon, chremata labon*) not just once but several times.[51] He also included texts of the decrees Philocrates had proposed when he committed these offenses. The complete document must have been rather long. The charges in the *eisangelia* brought by Polyeuctus against Euxenippus contained the same terms from the statute: 'speaking against the best interests of the people of Athens and taking money and gifts from those acting against the Athenian people' (Hyp. *Eux.* 39). After Lycurgus drew up his indictment against Leocrates using the same procedure, several people approached him and asked why he did not include the charge that Leocrates had 'betrayed' his father's statue dedicated in the temple of Zeus the Savior. Even though Lycurgus did not include this charge, it contained the key word 'betrayed'

50. For discussion of the terms of the law in this passage see Whitehead (2000) 186–88.

51. Cf. Whitehead (2000) 236: Hyperides 'had taken care there to echo the words and phrases of the impeachment law itself.'

(*prodedokenai*) from the statute about *eisangelia*. When Lycurgus initiated the same procedure against Lycophron for seducing the wife of Charippus, he included in his plaint a statement of her relatives that during her wedding Lycophron followed her and tried to persuade her to avoid having sexual relations with Charippus (Hyp. *Lycurg.* 3, 12). He also wrote that Lycophron was making many women grow old unmarried or to live illegally with men who were unsuitable for them. Even though his use of this procedure was highly unusual, Lycurgus still followed the language of the statute by stating that these actions undermined the democracy by violating the laws (Hyp. *Lycurg.* 12: *kataluein ton demon parabainonta tous nomous*).[52]

When Epaenetus brought an accusation before the *thesmothetai* against Stephanus for wrongfully holding him as a seducer, he wrote a detailed justification of charges and quoted the relevant laws. The term *moichos*, which I have translated as 'seducer,' refers to someone who has illicit sexual relations with a woman, usually the wife of another man or an unmarried daughter living under the protection of a male relative.[53] Epaenetus began by citing the law that allowed him to bring this kind of public suit.[54] He then admitted that he had had sexual relations with the daughter of Neaera, but denied that he had seduced her in violation of the law. Next he presented his main arguments. First, she was not the daughter of Stephanus, but of Neaera. Second, Neaera knew that her daughter was having sexual relations with him. Third, he cited the law that did not permit anyone who has sexual relations with prostitutes to be taken as a seducer and argued that the house of Stephanus was a house of prostitution. Epaenetus closely follows the law that mandates the procedure he is following, presents the main facts he promises to prove, and adduces the law about prostitutes he will use to support his case.[55] His plaint was clearly

---

52. A fragment from one of Lycurgus' speeches against Lycophron (fr. 63 Conomis) indicates that the accuser's argument was that breaking the law was equivalent to overthrowing the democracy because the laws protected the democracy. See Whitehead (2000) 129.

53. See Kapparis (1999) 297–8 for discussion with reference to earlier scholarship.

54. Kapparis (1999) 308–13 does not discuss the nature of the plaint brought by Epaenetus.

55. To prove his statements about Epaenetus' plaint, Apollodorus does not have secretary read the plaint but calls the sureties and arbitrators who brought about a settlement ([D.] 59.70, 72). The plaint was evidently not kept in the archives because Epaenetus withdrew his charge before the case came to court ([D.] 59.68–9). On withdrawing charges before the *anakrisis*, see Harris (2006a) 405–22.

very long and detailed.[56] The plaint that Meletus brought against Socrates for impiety appears to have been shorter but still contained the main charges and facts alleged against the philosopher. Meletus alleged that Socrates was guilty because (1) he corrupted the youth, (2) he did not believe in the gods that the community of Athens recognized, and (3) he introduced new gods (Pl. *Ap.* 24b6–c3. Cf. Pl. *Euthyphr.* 3b).[57] By forcing accusers to frame their accusations in the language of the statute, the plaint compelled them to prove that the defendant had broken a specific law. It would therefore be a mistake to claim that the law only served as evidence at an Athenian trial; the plaint ensured that the court would focus on the issue, did the defendant violate the law under which he has been charged?[58]

In a public suit against an illegal decree, the plaint not only stated the charge against the proposer of the decree but also listed the laws that the decree contravened (Aeschin. 3.200) and the specific clauses of the decree that were illegal.[59] When Diodorus accused Aristocrates of proposing an illegal decree for Charidemus, he included in the plaint all the laws Aristocrates had violated: (1) the law about the Areopagus, (2) the law about convicted murderers, (3) the law about bringing convicted murderers to the Thesmothetai, (4) the law about just homicide, (5) the law requiring trials for all accused of murder, (6) the law about taking hostages, (7) the law about laws being the same for all individuals, and (8) the law requiring

56. The charges mentioned by Demosthenes (19.8) in his prosecution of Aeschines were probably listed in a similarly long plaint: (1) Aeschines made no true report, (2) prevented the people from hearing the truth from Demosthenes, (3) his proposals were not in the interests of Athens, (4) Aeschines did not obey the instructions in the decree about the embassy, (5) Aeschines wasted time during which the city lost opportunities, and (6) Aeschines accepted gifts and payments. Demosthenes repeats several of these charges at 278–9.

57. Aeschin. 1.173 indicates that the Athenians believed that the judges convicted Socrates because they thought he was guilty of the first charge (Socrates corrupted Critias). I am skeptical about the authenticity of the denunciation of Alcibiades brought by Thessalus (Plu. *Alc.* 22.4. Cf. 19.2–3), but the authenticity of this document is not assured. For a defense of its authenticity see, Prandi (1992) 281–84, Stadter (1989) LXIX–LXXI, and Pelling (2000) 27.

58. The evidence of the plaint is decisive against the view that Athenian courts viewed that law as only another type of evidence similar to witness statements or other documents. For this view see Todd (1993) 59–60, followed uncritically by Scafuro (1997) 53, and Kästle (2012) 204–5. The role of the plaint also undermines the view of de Brauw (2001–2) that litigants only cite laws to show their law-abiding character.

59. Cf. [D.] 58.46: if Theocrines had brought a *graphe paranomon*, he would have added the laws violated by the defendant in his indictment.

that no decree take precedence over a law (D. 23.215–18. Cf. D. 23.51). Demosthenes (18.56) says that Aeschines' indictment of Ctesiphon singled out three clauses in his decree of honors as contrary to the laws: (1) that Demosthenes always speaks and acts for the public benefit, (2) that Demosthenes should receive a crown, and (3) that the award of the crown should be announced in the Theater of Dionysus.[60] When Diodorus charged Androtion with proposing an illegal decree of honors for the Council, he included in his plaint the laws that he claimed Androtion had violated (D. 22.34). These included the law requiring that all decrees of the Assembly receive prior approval from the Council (D. 22.5–7), the law forbidding honors for members of the Council who have not had triremes built (D. 22.8), and the law forbidding prostitutes and public debtors to propose motions in the Assembly (D. 22.21–24, 33–4).[61]

The plaint in a private suit also included a description of the main facts the plaintiff had to prove and followed the language of the relevant statute. Dionysius of Halicarnassus (*Din.* 3) gives the text of a plaint brought by Dinarchus against Proxenus: 'Dinarchus, the son of Sostratus, a Corinthian, [brings a case of] damage against Proxenus. Proxenus harmed (*eblapse*) me by receiving into his house in the country when I had fled from Athens and returned to Chalcis, two hundred and eighty-five gold staters, which I had sent from Chalcis with Proxenos' knowledge and which I had when I came to his house, and silver items worth not less than twenty mnai. He plotted against these.' As in the plaints brought in public cases, the charges contain the key word from the statute (*eblapse*) and specify the facts the accuser seeks to prove. The law about damage also contained different penalties for damage caused willingly, for which there was double compensation, and damage caused involuntarily, for which there was simple compensation (D. 21.43). This is probably the reason why Dinarchus added the phrase to show that Proxenus had acted willingly, which would have entitled Dinarchus to double compensation. When Apollodorus brought his charge of false testimony (*pseudomartyrion*) against Stephanus, he stated in his plaint: 'Stephanus

60. Aeschines' charges: Aeschin. 2.9–31 (Ctesiphon's decree awarded a crown to an official who had not yet passed his *euthynai*), 32–48 (the decree provided for an announcement of the crown in the theater of Dionysus), 49–170 (the decree contains false statements).

61. The plaint in charges against inexpedient laws may also have contained texts of the laws violated by the new laws, but the two preserved speeches delivered in cases brought on this procedure, Demosthenes' *Against Leptines* and *Against Timocrates*, do not discuss the plaint.

gave false testimony against me (*ta pseude mou katemartyrese*) by testifying to the written statements contained in the document' and added a copy of Stephanus' testimony (D. 45.9–11, 46).

The plaint that Pantaenetus brought against Nicobulus also contains many details about the defendant's actions.[62] First, it states that Nicobulus made a plot against him and his property and that Nicobulus instructed his slave to carry out the plot. Second, Nicobulus placed his slave in his mining works and forbade him to continue working in them (D. 37.25). The third charge appears to have been related to the slaves of Pantaenetus. The summary of Nicobulus does not allow us to determine the nature of the fourth charge (D. 37.28), but the fifth charge was that Nicobulus had violated the contract, probably by seizing the mining works (D. 37.29). At the end of the plaint were several additional charges including assault, outrage, violence, and offenses against heiresses (D. 37.32–3), but Nicobulus does not specify what actions Pantaenetus accused him of committing. Later in the speech, however, Nicobulus reveals that Pantaenetus charged him with entering his house and going into the rooms of his daughters (D. 37.45). In his plaint in a maritime suit, Zenothemis stated that he had made a loan to Hegestratus on the security of a cargo and that after Hegestratus was lost at sea Demo misappropriated the cargo (D. 32.2, 4).[63] As in the plaints for public charges, those for private charges also contained the main facts the accuser intended to prove.

The plaint in a suit for damages might contain a detailed list of sums. Demosthenes says that his plaint against Aphobus began: 'Demothenes makes the following charges against Aphobus: Aphobus holds money belonging to me, which he received as guardian, eighty mnai, which he

62. The inserted document cited at D. 37.22 and 29 must be forgeries because the statements they contain are not consistent with the information found in the speech. First, the document uses the first person singular, but other examples of plaints use only the third person (D. 21.103; Ar. *Vesp.* 894–97). Second, the narrative states that Evergus seized the mining works of Pantaenetus and caused him to become a public debtor. This implies that Pantaenetus became a public debtor because he could not operate his mining works and earn the money needed to make his payments to the state. Pantaenetus also claimed that Evergus and Nicobulus violated their agreement by seizing his mining works (D. 37.6). The document at 22, however, states that Pantaenetus became a state debtor because Nicobulus' slave seized the money his slave was taking to make the payment for the mine. The document at 29 states that Nicobulus violated the agreement by selling the mining works and the slave, but this is at odds with the statement at D. 37.6. This casts doubt on the other inserted documents at D. 37.25, 26 and 28.

63. Cf. the charges in the plaint summarized and read out at D. 34.16.

received as the dowry of my mother according to the will of my father' (D. 29.31). He then listed all the items he claimed, 'specifying the source of each, the exact amount, and the person from whom Aphobus received it' (D. 29.30). These items included (1) money from the sale of slaves for his mother's dowry (D. 27.13–17), (2) money owed from the failure to return the dowry (D. 27.17), (3) thirty mnai raised from the revenue of workshop and the sale of slaves (D. 27.18–22), (4) money from thirty slaves given as security for a loan (D. 27.24–29), (5) value of iron and ivory from the workshop (D. 27.30–33), and (6) cash left with guardians and its accrued interest (D. 27.33–39). Demosthenes was also careful to mention that Aphobus received this money in his capacity as guardian (*epitropes*), using the key word in the statute governing the procedure he had selected. Once again, the plaint must have been very long.

The counter-plea might contain the basic facts the defendant intended to prove. In his reply to the charges of Apollodorus, Stephanus replied that his testimony was true (D. 45.46). When the half-brother of Astyphilus brought his case against Cleon, he not only claimed the estate of Astyphilus but also outlined his main arguments and the facts he intended to prove: first, Astyphilus did not adopt Cleon's son; second, Astyphilus did not leave his property to anyone; third, Astyphilus did not make a will; and fourth, he, the half-brother, has the best claim on the property of Astyphilus (Is. 9.1).

Even though Athenian law contained nothing like the prescribed phrases of the Roman formulary system, one should not exaggerate the difference between the two systems.[64] When the accuser drew up his plaint he had to follow the language of the statute.[65] If the plaint did not contain the key words of the relevant statute, the magistrate who received the charge might compel the accuser to add them. When Dionysius used the procedure of *apagoge* to the Eleven against Agoratus, he charged him with killing his father. For one to use this procedure, however, one had to apprehend the defendant *ep' autophoro*, that is, in circumstances that made his guilt obvious.[66] To make the plaint Dionysius submitted conform to the

---

64. Tendency to exaggerate the differences between Athenian law and Roman law: Gagarin (2008) 217–18.

65. Note that the *diamartyria*, which was equivalent to the plaint submitted in other cases, submitted by Leochares against the claim of Leostratus to the estate of Archiades followed the terms of the law—D. 44.46 (*onton auto paidon gnesion kai kyrios kata ton thesmon*).

66. For the procedure and the meaning of the term *ep' autophoro* see Harris (2006a) 373–90. The term is mistranslated as 'in the act' by Wohl (2010) 220, which undermines her analysis of Lysias' speech *Against Agoratus*.

language of the statute, the Eleven insisted that he add the key term *ep'autophoro* to the charge (Lys. 13.85–87).

One of the reasons for requiring the accuser to write the specific charges he intended to prove at the trial was to ensure procedural fairness for the defendant. The defendant needed to know not only the kind of action the accuser was bringing but to know also what the accuser claimed that he had done. This would allow him to prepare a detailed reply to each one of the charges. T. Bingham rightly stresses the importance of informing the defendants about charges against them for achieving the rule of law:

> The fair trial of a civil action is now held to require the parties to reveal their respective cases and almost all material relevant to them before the trial even begins. The point of the law is that litigation should be conducted with the 'cards face up on the table.' This is achieved, first, by requiring the claimant to set out in writing in some detail the grounds on which he claims. He cannot appear at trial and present a case different from that which he has advanced in writing. The defendant in turn must set out in some detail in writing the ground on which he resists the claim. He cannot simply deny the claim and leave the claimant and the judge wondering what his defence is. Nor can he appear at trial and advance a defence different from that indicated. Thus the line of battle should be drawn with some precision before the first shot is fired in court.[67]

The use of the plaint in Athenian law helped to prevent the nightmare scenario confronting Joseph K. in Kafka's *The Trial*:

> It followed from this that all court documents, and above all the indictment, were not available to the accused or to his defense, and so there was no means of knowing in general, or at least in particular, how the first submission should address the charges, since only by accident could it contain material bearing on the case. Only later could effective and pertinent submission of evidence be prepared, once the separate charges, and the grounds for these charges,

67. Bingham (2010) 101.

> emerged more clearly, or could be inferred, during the examination of the defendant. Under these conditions the defense is of course in a difficult and most unfavorable position.[68]

The accuser was also required to provide at the *anakrisis* all the evidence he planned to present at the trial.[69] This evidence was then placed in a container called an *echinos*; the accuser could not present at the trial any evidence of documents not placed in the *echinos*. On the other hand, the reply of the defendant would also let the accuser know how he planned to reply to his charges.[70]

Of course, there was always the possibility that at the trial the accuser might make charges that were not contained in the indictment. Hyperides (*Eux.* 32) describes how this tactic might put the defendant in a difficult position: if the defendant were to reply to charges not contained in the indictment, the court might reprimand him for discussing irrelevant matters, but if he were to neglect them, the court might assume they were true. Several defendants complain about this tactic. A soldier accused of slandering generals claims that instead of concentrating on the charges in the plaint his opponents are slandering the defendant's character (Lys. 9.1–3). When defending Ctesiphon, Demosthenes (18.9) criticizes Aeschines for using this tactic: 'because he has spent the larger part of his speech on other topics and told very many lies about me, I think that it is necessary and correct to say a few words about these charges so that none of you be misled by irrelevant arguments and listen to my just points about the indictment in a hostile spirit.' Aeschines, when prosecuting Timarchus, complained that Demosthenes would attempt to distract the judges from the charges by talking about the recent peace with Philip and other irrelevant matters (Aeschin. 1.166–70). In the speech *Against Androtion*, the accuser Diodorus complains that the defendant is skilled in rhetoric and that he will deceive the judges and make them forget about their oath (D. 22.4).[71] Nicobulus claims that Pantaenetus won his suit against

68. Kafka (2008) 86–7.

69. See Thür (2007).

70. On the anticipation of arguments see Dorjahn (1935), who may underestimate the amount of information obtained through the plaint and at the *anakrisis*.

71. Cf. D. 21.208, 211 where Demosthenes predicts some wealthy trierarchs will ask the judges to acquit Meidias as a favor to them and to pay no attention to their oath. Cf. D. 23.95, 219 for attempts to distract the judges.

Evergus by presenting at the trial charges not included in the plaint. Because Evergus could not prepare a defense against these charges in advance, he lost his case (D. 37.45–8).

Hyperides exaggerates the problem because there was a safeguard protecting the defendant. As we have seen, in their oath Athenian judges swore to vote only about the charges in the indictment (D. 45.50).[72] This meant that when casting their votes, the judges should consider only the facts that the accuser promised to prove and disregard all statements that did not bear directly on these charges (*exo tou pragmatos*). In fact, Hyperides (*Eux.* 35–6) reports that Lysander charged Epicrates of Pallene with digging his mine inside the limits of another man's mine and tried to sway their decision by promising to bring in three hundred talents for the city's budget.[73] 'The judges paid no attention to the accuser's promises but followed what justice required: they determined that the mine was inside its own boundaries and by that same vote made their property secure and confirmed the rest of their period for working the mine.' The accuser's promise did not sway the judges; they paid attention to the law and the facts of the case. When they saw that the defendant's actions did not violate the law and that he was not guilty of the charge of encroaching on another's mine, he was acquitted. As one defendant tells the court, the task of the accuser is not to discuss the defendant's character but to prove the charges in the indictment (Lys. 9.1).

Another way of distracting the judges from the charges in the plaint was for the defendant to boast about his public service. Lysias (12.38) claims that some defendants make no attempt to answer the charges against them but 'show that they are good soldiers, or have captured many ships from the enemy, or have made cities that were hostile into your friends.' Several passages however show that the courts normally ignored such statements because they were strictly irrelevant to the charges contained in the plaint.[74] Aeschines (3.195) says that the court that tried Thrasybulus on a charge of proposing an illegal decree did not take into account

72. This clause is mentioned or alluded to many times in forensic oratory: Aeschin. 1.154, 170; D. 22.4, 43, 45; 24.189; 30.9; 32.13; 37.17; Is. 6.51–2; Lycurg. *Leocr.* 11–13.

73. For the nature of the charge see Whitehead (2000) 248–9 with references to earlier literature.

74. *Pace* Lanni (2006) 46–64, who does not discuss the plaint and its role in litigation. Lanni does not discuss any of the passages mentioned in this paragraph, which directly contradict her view that the courts took public service into account when determining guilt.

his role in restoring the democracy but convicted him because he was guilty as charged. When Aristophon charged Timotheus with bribery, the court paid no attention to his victories and conquests but convicted him on the charge Aristophon brought: 'You did not allow public services like these to influence the trial or the oath that you obeyed while casting your votes, but you fined him one hundred talents because Aristophon said he received money from the Chians and Rhodians' (Din. 1.14). According to Demosthenes (21.143–47), the court did not allow the achievements of Alcibiades and his ancestors to affect their decision, but sent him into exile for violating the law.[75] When Epicrates was accused of bribery and other offenses in the Assembly, Demosthenes (19.277) tells us that his service in restoring the democracy did not help him to win acquittal. Nor did they take the diplomatic successes of Callias into account when they convicted him of bribery (D. 19.273). In the speech *Against Timocrates* (D. 24.133–34), the accuser mentions several politicians who had distinguished careers but were convicted and punished despite their public service:

> After the archonship of Eucleides, as you judges all remember, first Thrasybulus of Collytos was twice placed in prison and put on trial both times in the Assembly. Yet this man was one of the men of Phyle and the Piraeus.[76] Next Philepsius of Lamptrai, then Agyrrhius of Kollytus, a fine man and a democrat who had many times demonstrated his loyalty to you the people. Yet this man still thought that the laws must apply equally to him just as to the weak. He spent many years in that place until he paid the money belonging to the city he was judged to have taken.

The written plaint and the litigant's oath to stick to the point obviously played an important role here. The plaint and the oath compelled the defendant to reply to the specific charges against him and discouraged him from introducing irrelevant material. The plaint also served to keep the judges focused on their duty to punish those who had violated the law.[77]

---

75. Demosthenes alters some of the details to make Alcibiades' case resemble that of Meidias, but that does not alter his point that the courts paid no attention to public service.

76. That is, he was one of the democrats who overthrew the Thirty.

77. Note Antiphon 5.11—the judges are to consider only whether the defendant committed the crime. Rhodes (2004) observes that Athenian litigants generally keep to the point, but he does not discuss the role of the plaint, which showed the judges what was relevant and what was not. Rhodes' judgment about what is relevant in a given speech is therefore often arbitrary.

When the orators mention the social status of a defendant, they normally indicate that the courts were not influenced by it. For instance, Demosthenes recalls the trial and execution of a man named Pyrrhus, who was a member of Eteobutadae, a famous *genos* (D. 21.182).[78] Despite his high social standing, he was harshly punished. Ariston recalls the case of a man who was condemned for murder even though he belonged to the family from whom the priestess of Athena Polias was selected (D. 54.25). Despite his high social status, Pyrrhus 'was denounced for serving as judge when he owed money to the Treasury; some of you thought that he must be put to death, and after being convicted in your court, he was executed. And yet he tried to receive his payment because of poverty, not to commit abuse.' The judges might have taken either of two factors, his social status or his poverty, into account, but they looked only at his actions.[79] Litigants in homicide cases also swore an oath to address only the charges made in the indictment (Antiphon 6.9). As one defendant says, this oath compelled the accuser to address only the issue, did the defendant commit the murder with which he has been charged? No matter how many other crimes he has committed, the court can convict him only on the specific charge brought by the accuser. Conversely, no matter how many good deeds the defendant has done, they will not gain him an acquittal if he is guilty (Antiphon 5.11).

This would explain why Athenian litigants rarely mention public service unless it is directly relevant to the legal charge. For instance, when Lysias charged Eratosthenes with responsibility for his brother's death, the defendant's participation in the regime of the Thirty was pertinent to the case (Lys. 12). When Alcibiades was charged with desertion from the army, his alleged failure to perform military service was the main legal charge (Lys. 14, 15). When Demosthenes charged Aeschines with treason during the negotiations about the Peace of Philocrates, the legal charges concerned his service as an Athenian ambassador (D. 19; Aeschin. 2). One of Aeschines' charges against Ctesiphon's decree was that it contained false statements about Demosthenes' services to Athens, which made it necessary for both the accuser and the defendant's supporting speaker to examine his political career (Aeschin. 3; D. 18). In speeches delivered in

78. On this *genos* see Parker (1996) 290–93.

79. See also D. 54.25 where the Areopagus convicted a man and sentenced him to exile for deliberate homicide despite the fact that he was the father of the priestess of Brauron. For the nature of the charge see Harris (2006a) 397–8.

cases about an official's qualifications for office (*dokimasia*), the court needed to know if the candidate was a citizen and whether he had performed his military service (Arist. *Ath. Pol.* 55.3; Lys. 16.12–18).[80]

Some litigants cite their public service to demonstrate their good character, but they do not argue that they should win their case simply because they have helped the community. Their argument is rather that their public service is evidence of their good character, which shows that they are unlikely to have committed the offense with which they have been charged. Several litigants who are accused of treason discuss their liturgies or military service to show that they are patriotic and therefore innocent of the charges (Aeschin. 2.167–71). Agoratus claims that he helped to kill Phrynichus and joined the men of Phyle to restore the democracy to prove that he did not collaborate with the Thirty (Lys. 13.70–79).

In a few cases litigants mention their public service to gain the goodwill of the court (And. 1.141, 144–45, 147–9), but no litigant ever admits guilt and then argues that his public service entitles him to an acquittal.[81] In fact, Ariston, when prosecuting Conon on a charge of assault, ends his speech by telling the court that he could mention his liturgies, but they are not relevant to his charges (D. 54.44). Lycurgus (*Leocr.* 139–40) insists that no one who has performed liturgies can ask the court to acquit a traitor as a favor to himself (Cf. D. 36.39–42). One speaker complains that some men who were guilty have been acquitted because of public services, but implies that the practice is dangerous, an abuse of the legal system (Lys. 30.1. Cf. Lys. 12.38–40). Another speaker predicts that his opponents will ask to be given what they do not deserve because they have performed liturgies; he counters this argument by saying that only those who perform liturgies and do not bring false charges are entitled to gratitude (D. 38.25–26). When prosecuting Meidias, Demosthenes insists that his

80. On the *dokimasia* of officials at Athens see Feyel (2009) 148–97. Cf. Rhodes (2004) 142: '*dokimasiai*' are cases 'where general passages on a man's character may be considered relevant.'

81. Davies (1981) 92–96 greatly exaggerates the appeals to 'forensic *charis*' in the speeches of the orators (he cites only four passages and does not discuss the passages such as D. 54.44 indicating that public service is irrelevant). Davies (1981) 95 claims that 'the appeal to *charis* runs through the entire corpus of Athenian private forensic oratory.' In point of fact, public service is not even mentioned in many speeches delivered in private cases (e.g., Antiphon 1, Lys. 3, 4, 5, 8, Is. 1, 3, 8, 9, 10; D. 30, 31, 32, 33, 35, 37, 41, 43, 48, 55, 56). When it is mentioned, it is generally relevant to the legal charge. As appendix 8 reveals, there are relatively few appeals to forensic *charis* in both private and public speeches.

liturgies should not influence the court's verdict and allow him to escape punishment (D. 21.225. Cf. 169–70).[82]

Although the public service or social status of a defendant was not considered relevant when assessing guilt or innocence, there was a different standard of relevance in the second part of a public case.[83] In his speech *Against Meidias,* Demosthenes (21.151) makes it clear that it was permissible to mention liturgies during the second phase of the trial when the penalty was assessed (*timesis*). Demosthenes imagines a friend advising him not to pursue his case against Meidias because of his wealth. He admits that the court will probably convict Meidias because he is clearly guilty of *hybris,* but at the second part of the trial Meidias will boast about his public service and convince the court to give him a light penalty. 'He has been convicted, and the vote was against him. What penalty do you expect the court to assess for him? Don't you see that he is rich and will mention his trierarchies and liturgies? Watch out lest he asks for lenient treatment with these tactics and has a good laugh at your expense when he pays a fine that is smaller than the amount he is offering to give you.' The imaginary friend does not say that such conduct is illegal or immoral. Nor does Demosthenes object to such a tactic. Instead he argues that Meidias' public services are not that impressive and therefore should not count in his favor (D. 21.152–68). In other words Demosthenes appears to consider it acceptable for a defendant to ask the court to take liturgies and military service into account during the second part of the trial.[84]

In his speech *Against Ctesiphon,* Aeschines (3.197–200) also indicates that there was a different standard of relevance in each part of a trial on a public charge. In a public trial the day is divided into three parts: the first is for the accuser, the laws, and the democracy; the second for the

82. Cohen (1995) 190–1 ('the issue which Demosthenes principally addresses is whether or not that act clearly violating the statute should or should not be punishable, based on consideration of a whole variety of other factors concerning the defendants and their relations to each other and to the community [including who had provided the most benefits to the city]') seriously misrepresents Demosthenes' arguments.

83. Rhodes (2004) does not discuss the different standards of relevance in the two parts of a public trial.

84. Demosthenes probably deals with the question in his speech delivered at the first part of the trial in order to anticipate Meidias' arguments in the second part of the trial. Because Meidias' record of service appears to have been impressive, Demosthenes probably thought that the relatively short amount of time allotted to him for discussion of the penalty at the *timesis* phase would not be enough for an adequate response. He therefore decided to devote part of his first speech to the topic.

defendant and those who speak to the point (*eis auto to pragma*), that is, supporting speakers who address the charge in the indictment; and the third for the assessment of the penalty and to measure the extent of the judges' anger. 'To measure the extent of the judges' anger' means that if the offense is greater and stirs more anger, the penalty will be more severe; if the offense is less serious and stirs less anger, the penalty will be less severe. At this point Aeschines introduces a contrast between those who speak to the point and a person 'who asks for a vote.' The implicit contrast suggests that the person who 'asks for a vote' is one who does not speak to the point and address the legal issue but asks for a vote in gratitude for their public service or a sign of respect for their power and influence. Aeschines does not criticize a speaker for making such an appeal at this stage in the trial. But the person who 'asks for a vote' for these reasons during the first phase of the trial is in effect asking the judges to betray their oaths, the laws, and the democracy. Aeschines says that it is immoral to make such a request or to grant it when the judges are considering the guilt of the defendant. He then goes one step further and argues that there is no need for supporting speakers at all during the first part of the trial because here the decision is guided solely by the laws. This proposal is clearly aimed at Demosthenes, who, he claims, is the type of supporting speaker who employs sophistry. As a result, the judges should not listen to him if he addresses the court during the first part of the trial.

Some of Aeschines' argument in this passage is tendentious, designed to undermine his opponent's credibility before he has a chance to reply to the charges against Ctesiphon. In actuality, Demosthenes does address the main points in the indictment against Ctesiphon; though there is room for debate about his defense of his political career, his interpretation of the laws about crowns is based on a more straightforward reading of the statutes and supported by numerous precedents. What is significant is that Aeschines makes a clear distinction between the types of arguments that are appropriate at each part of the trial. In the first part of the trial a supporting speaker should keep to the point; during the assessment of the penalty a speaker can 'ask for a vote' and use arguments that would be inappropriate during the first part of the trial.

These different standards of relevance at a public trial explain the behavior of Eubulus at the trials of Hegesilaos and Thrasybulus. During his prosecution of Aeschines in 343 for misconduct as ambassador to Philip, Demosthenes (19.290) was concerned that Eubulus would use his prestige to influence the judges and tried to discourage him from speaking for his opponent. He therefore reminds Eubulus how when Hegesilaos and Thrasybulus called on him during the first phase of their trials (*protes psephou*), he did not respond.[85] Then during the assessment of the penalty (*timema*) he did step forward (*anabas*), which was obviously a show of support and was in contrast to his earlier refusal. Demosthenes adds that Eubulus still did not say anything at this point and asked the judges to forgive him.[86] Eubulus acted differently at each stage of the trial because he did not think his intervention was appropriate at the first stage of the trial. He was not in court to plead the case for the defendants, but to lend moral support for a relative and a friend. He therefore did not consider it right to come forward during the first part of the trial when the judges were deciding whether the defendant had broken the law or not. During the second phase by contrast it was expected of him to say something in support of his relative and friend and to try to influence the court. When he was unable to say anything (Demosthenes does not give the reason), he failed to perform his duty as relative and friend and therefore asked to be forgiven. After all, one only asks for pardon when one cannot do what is expected or required.

The only example of a speech that purports to have been delivered at the *timesis* phase is found in the second part of Plato's *Apology of Socrates* (35c–38c). It is impossible to determine how closely the text of this speech reproduces what Socrates said in court at his trial in 399, but it should contain the kind of arguments one would expect to find in a forensic speech. Indeed, the first part of the *Apology* adheres to many of the conventions of forensic oratory even when Socrates subverts or critiques them. For instance, Socrates prefaces his speech with a standard *captatio benevolentiae*, attempting to gain the court's sympathy by portraying himself at a disadvantage. Toward the end of his first speech he alludes to the well-known practice of bringing one's family into court even if he declines to follow it. In general, Socrates attempts to 'stick to the point' by addressing the main charges in the indictment (19a–b). The earlier charges against him, which might prejudice the court's opinion, are dealt with at 19c–24b. Meletus' charges are refuted at 24b–34b. At the end of this section Socrates

85. MacDowell (2000) 331 rightly argues that Demosthenes refers to two trials, not one trial of two men.

86. Neither MacDowell (2000) 332 nor Paulsen (1999) 272–3 analyzes the reasons for Eubulus' behavior.

produces witnesses to refute one of the main charges and to prove that he does not corrupt the youth (32c–34b). He mentions his military service only as part of an analogy: he obeyed the order of the Delphic oracle just as he obeyed the orders of his commanders in battle (28e–29a).

In his second speech, however, Socrates discusses the benefits he has conferred on each Athenian individually in his private life. In his first speech he denied that he corrupted the youth. Here he switches from the negative to the positive: he talks not about his guilt or innocence but about his worth (*axian*) and his claim to be considered a benefactor. Had he been a normal citizen, he would have spoken about his public service, his military offices, and his liturgies at this point. Thus topics that Socrates did not consider relevant in his first speech come to the fore when the court was deciding which penalty to choose.

An anecdote from Aeschines' speech *Against Timarchus* confirms this analysis. Aeschines (1.113) recalls Timarchus' conviction for theft of public funds. Timarchus had been elected inspector of mercenary troops in Eretria and on his return to Athens was put on trial for embezzling money entrusted to him along with two other inspectors. At the first part of his trial, Timarchus did not speak about the charges in the indictment, but admitted his guilt and immediately supplicated the court about the penalty. What he said was therefore not relevant at this part of the trial (*ou peri tou pragmatos*).[87] As a result, it was not taken into consideration by the court, and Timarchus was convicted just like the other two inspectors who did not confess. The fact that he confessed his crime set him apart from his colleagues, but since his confession had nothing to do with the question of guilt or innocence, it made no difference, and all three received the same verdict. His confession did however make a difference at the assessment stage: those who denied their guilt were fined a talent apiece, whereas Timarchus was fined thirty *mnai*, half that amount. The incident reveals how the two different standards worked in practice. Timarchus and other litigants might attempt to sway the court with irrelevant arguments during the first part of the trial, but if the judges obeyed their oath, they would ignore extraneous considerations and examine just

87. The phrase *ou peri tou pragmatos* clearly alludes to the litigant's promise to speak to the point and the judges' duty to pay attention only to matters relevant to the charge brought by the accuser. Carey (2000) 62 translates the sentence 'He did not address his defense to the question of fact' but this misses the allusion to the requirement to speak 'to the point.' The translation of Fisher (2001) 97 is closer to the required sense: 'he made no defense on the charge.'

the relevant issues.[88] Like the other cases examined in the beginning of this section, Aeschines' explanation shows that even in cases involving politicians, the court did not make its decision about innocence and guilt on political grounds. One should also recall the trial of the general Miltiades. Xanthippus accused Miltiades of 'deceit' and asked for the death penalty. Miltiades appeared for the trial but could not defend himself because his thigh was infected. His friends spoke on his behalf and reminded the Athenians about his victory at Marathon and his capture of Lemnos. His achievements did not cause the Athenians to acquit him of the charges but only to reduce his punishment from execution to a fine of fifty talents (Hdt. 6.136.1–3).

The only speeches that contain extensive discussion of the defendant's public service that is not directly relevant to the legal charge are those delivered at trials arising from the Harpalus affair.[89] This is because the procedure followed in these trials was an unusual one.[90] The legal proceedings began when the Assembly ordered the Areopagus to investigate charges that several politicians held money they received from Harpalus (Hyp. *D.* 2; Din. 1.61). After six months, the Areopagus reported the names of those who received money, among whom were Demosthenes and Aristogeiton (Hyp. *Dem* 5–6; Din. 1.53). The Assembly then elected prosecutors to accuse those mentioned in the report (Din. 2.6), but as one of the prosecutors states, the purpose of the trial was not to determine guilt, but to decide about the penalty (Din. 1.3, 18, 84 [the Areopagus has found Demosthenes guilty], 105; 2.20). This made these trials more like the *timesis* phase of a public trial. For this reason, they take the defendant's career

88. Fisher (2001) 253 refers to Timarchus' strategy as 'plea-bargaining,' but this misunderstands the nature of the Athenian legal system. Plea-bargaining is only possible in a system where a permanent public prosecutor has the power to bargain with defendants on behalf of the state and offer them a reduced sentence in exchange for a plea of guilty, which avoids a trial. Because the Athenian legal system had no permanent public prosecutor with such power, plea-bargaining was not possible. Fisher also claims, 'There is likely to be no little evasion and distortion in this account' but does not specify what the distortion might be. Yet because the trial involved a public figure, its outcome must have been common knowledge. And the explanation of the different standards of relevance must have appeared plausible to the judges Aeschines was addressing as the evidence analyzed in the rest of this section reveals.

89. For mentions of public service in these speeches see appendix 8.

90. For a more detailed analysis of the incidents see 46–7. Rhodes (2004) 149 rightly notes that Dinarchus' speech *Against Demosthenes* 'strays "outside the issue" more than most' but does not see how it resembles the *timesis* phase of a public trial, which explains its unusual features.

into account. For instance, one of Demosthenes' accusers gives a review of his career, including his cowardice at Chaeronea, his embassies to Thebes, his failure to support the revolt of Thebes in 335, his role in the Peace of Philocrates, his role in politics during the reign of Alexander, his corruption during the reform of the trierarchy, and the bribes he received for proposing honors (Din. 1.12–13, 16, 18–21, 28–29, 32–36, 41–5). None of these is directly relevant to the charge of receiving money from Harpalus, but the accuser urges the court to take them into consideration when determining the penalty.

III

The Judicial Oath is the best evidence available for the way the judges in Athenian courts viewed their task. The oath made them swear to uphold several of the basic principles of the rule of law. First, it contained a pledge to decide cases according to the laws and not to use their own discretion. Second, it compelled them to be fair and impartial; they could not allow their personal feelings toward the litigants to interfere with their decisions. Third, they did not have the right to question the authority of the law and to use their own opinion. The judges were authorized to use their own most fair judgment only about issues in which the laws did not give clear guidance, but, as we have seen, this rarely (if ever) happened. Fourth, the oath bound them to implement equality before the law, one of the key elements of the rule of law and democratic ideology (Th. 2.37.1; Eur. *Suppl.* 429–37). When deciding about the guilt of the defendant, the judges could only examine what he had done, not who he was. The requirement to submit a plaint when initiating legal action compelled the accuser to specify what law the defendant had violated and which of his actions violated the law. By requiring that the judges pay attention only to the charges in the plaint, the oath compelled them to treat all men as equal before the law and to disregard irrelevant issues like public service. This prevented trials at Athens from degenerating into contests about who spent more money on liturgies, passed more decrees in the Assembly, or won more battles.[91] Several litigants do discuss these topics, but only when they are

91. By claiming that the courts took public service into account, scholars like Ober (1989), Christ (1998a), Cohen (1995), and Lanni (2006) present a very antidemocratic view of the Athenian courts.

relevant to the legal issue before the court. The rules about the plaint therefore had a profound impact on the way litigants acted in court. By helping to ensure that all would be equal before the law, the plaint and the Judicial Oath also protected the poor against intimidation by the rich. This is one of the main themes of Demosthenes' speech *Against Meidias*. Finally, the plaint helped the judges to concentrate on their main task, which was to judge according to the laws of the Athenian people. The pledges to judge according to the laws and to vote only about the charges in the plaint were therefore closely connected.

The plaint served to define the issue about which the judges were to vote and thereby simplified their task, but it still left room for considerable debate about how to apply the law. For instance, an accuser might charge in his plaint that the defendant had committed treason and list the actions that he considered treasonous. On the other hand, the defendant might admit that he had committed the actions described in the plaint but argue that they did not constitute treason. This might lead to a debate about the meaning of the term 'treason' and how to define it. The question of how to apply the general rules contained in the laws to particular situations might as a result be not all that straightforward because the law contained what legal theorists have called 'open texture.' Chapters 5 and 6 examine this problem and study how litigants attempted to exploit the law's open texture.

Another possibility was that a defendant might admit that he had committed the acts that the accuser charged were violations of the law but argue that the court ought to take other considerations into account when reaching its decision. Even though prior public service was not considered relevant to the question of guilt, the defendant might point to his lack of wrongful intent, his ignorance of key facts, the presence of duress, or other extenuating factors. These arguments were an appeal to fairness (*epieikeia*), that is, to other principles implicit in the laws that might take precedence over the law followed by the accuser. Chapter 8 addresses this issue. In most cases, the application of the law was a simple matter of deductive reasoning once the facts were established. Yet one should not assume that it was always a straightforward task.

4

What Are the Laws of Athens About?

SUBSTANCE AND PROCEDURE IN ATHENIAN STATUTES

LAWS IN ALL societies generally contain five basic features. First, they are enforced by a political authority recognized by the community.[1] For instance, the responsibility for enforcing the laws of Athens lay primarily in the hands of the courts and public officials, who are often named in laws (see chapter 1). Second, laws have general application. A law is a rule that regulates the conduct of large categories of persons. Laws are not enacted for individuals. In Classical Athens, many laws begin with the words 'If anyone . . .' which indicates that they applied to all citizens or to all those in Athenian territory.[2] In fact, there was a law forbidding a law pertaining to a single man (*nomos ep'andri*).[3] Third, laws enumerate rights and duties. In the words of Cicero (*De Legibus* 1.18), laws order what must be done and forbid what must not be done (*lex est ratio summa insita in natura, quae iubet ea quae facienda sunt, prohibetque contraria*). The law may grant the right to make a contract, impose the duty to pay taxes, or forbid individuals from stealing property belonging to others.[4] These rules concern either the rights or the duties of private individuals in their relationships with each other (private law) or the rights and duties of the individual toward the community (public law) (D. 24.192–93). This is the substantive side of

1. For the basic features of law see Pospisil (1971) 44–78, who lists four characteristics. I have added procedure to his list. For law as a set of rules enforced by a sovereign see Hart (1961) 49–76.

2. For examples see Harris (2006a) 46–47.

3. See D. 23.86, 218; 24.18, 59, 116, 188; [D.] 46.2.

4. Ober (1989) 10 and Jones (1956) 151 have claimed that the Athenians of the Classical period did not have a conception of rights; Dover (1974) thinks that the Athenians would not have understood the modern conception of rights. See, however, Cohen (1997) and Miller (1995) 87–139.

law. Fourth, a law must provide a procedure to be followed against those who violate the laws. This part of the law gives instructions to private individuals and public officials who wish to enforce rights and duties and tells them how to set the mechanism of the state in motion. The procedural side of law provides rules about how to get a case into court and how to proceed with it once it comes before a judge or other official. The rules for initiating a lawsuit, serving a summons, securing a court date, presenting documents to the court, summoning and questioning witnesses, selecting judges or jurors, challenging testimony or authenticity of documents, and imposing a sentence all belong to the procedural part of law. Fifth, the law must provide a sanction. The private individual must receive compensation for any damage or loss he suffers; the community must impose a penalty for any offense against the public interest as a punishment and to deter others from committing the same offense (Isocr. 20.2).

In the previous chapter we saw that the Judicial Oath required judges to follow the law in rendering their verdicts and that the plaint compelled the accuser to prove that the defendant had violated a specific law. But what were these laws about? This chapter examines the content of Athenian laws and their substantive and procedural aspects. The difference between these two aspects has been well described by the modern jurist Salmond:

> Substantive law is concerned with the ends which the administration of justice seeks; procedural law deals with the means and instruments by which those ends are to be attained. The latter regulates the conduct and relations of courts and litigants in respect of the litigation itself; the former determines their conduct and relations in respect of the matters litigated. Procedural law is concerned with affairs inside the courts of justice; substantive law with matters in the world outside.[5]

Substantive and procedural provisions are often clearly distinguished in separate clauses of Athenian laws.[6] For instance, Aeschines (1.28–32) discusses a law about public speakers which orders that if someone speaks

5. Salmond (1913) 438, quoted by Gagarin (1986) 72.

6. Several passages in the orators make a clear distinction between substance and procedure by contrasting the offense committed by the defendant and the method by which the accuser has brought his charge to court. See D. 21.25–28; 22.25–29.

in the Assembly after beating his father or mother, failing to provide them support, not performing military service, throwing away his shield, acting as prostitute, or squandering his patrimony, anyone can initiate the procedure called the 'scrutiny of public speakers' (*dokimasia rhetoron*).[7] The law of Nicophon about silver coinage prescribes several duties to various officials (*SEG* 26:72, lines 13–32), then states that if they do not perform these duties any Athenian who wishes may initiate the procedure of *eisangelia* to the Council (*SEG* 26:72, lines 32–34). Like some Athenian laws (but, as we will see, far from the majority), these statutes are expressed in the casuistic form of a conditional sentence. The protasis names the substantive offense (speaking in the Assembly after committing one of the actions listed in the statute or not performing one's legally prescribed duties), and the apodosis names a procedure.[8] This is not the only form of an Athenian law. As we will see, other laws simply give commands. For example, the law on agreements states 'All those transactions to which each party agrees willingly are binding' (D. 56.2). The law about the proclamation of crowns provides that the award of a crown may be announced in the Theater of Dionysus if the Assembly so votes (D. 18.121; Aeschin. 3.32–35). A law about inheritance states that all legitimate sons should inherit equal shares (Is. 6.25). Another law about inheritance grants the testator the right to dispose of his property as he wishes (Is. 10.2). In several laws preserved in inscriptions one finds orders to officials expressed by verbs in the imperative mood (e.g., *SEG* 47:96, lines 36, 41, 44, 47–8, 49–50, 52, 53) or in the future indicative tense (e.g., *SEG* 47:96, lines 9, 10–11, 12–3, 14, 15–6, 20, 21–2, 24–25, 27, 29–30, 32, 33). One can call this the prescriptive form.[9]

Some scholars have claimed that Athenian law was mostly about procedure and paid little attention to substantive issues. One scholar asserts that 'our sources show that the Athenians took much more interest in procedural law than in substantive law' and that 'Athenian laws dealt more with procedure and less with the subject matter which brought about the employment of the procedure prescribed.'[10] The same scholar claims that 'in the speeches the emphasis on procedural law is so predominant that even scholars stressing the importance of substantive law are forced to

7. On this procedure see MacDowell (2005).

8. For the analysis of this type of law see Carey (1998) 99.

9. I have taken the terms 'casuistic' and 'prescriptive' from Carey (1998).

10. Hansen (1975) 10 and 14. Cf. Hansen (1975) 21: 'the Athenians took much more interest in procedural than in substantive law.'

base their account on procedural distinctions.'[11] In his opinion, 'Laws in a modern society are organized according to content; in Athens they were organized according to procedure, i.e. according to which magistrate was responsible for their administration. Nowadays we distinguish constitutional law, administrative law, criminal law, and so on; in Athens they distinguished the Council's laws, the archon's laws, the king archon's laws, and so on.'[12] Two other scholars assert, 'In Athens, so far as we can tell, procedural law held both a chronological and logical priority . . . Procedures came first, and a substantive right could only exist where there was a procedure available to create that right.'[13] One of these scholars believes that 'the priority of procedure over substance is characteristic of those societies in which legal theory remains latent: where there are no jurists, law is formulated only to fit situations, and the primary concern is to enable a case to be heard, rather than to promote the autonomous development of legal doctrines.'[14] A recent collection of essays about Ancient Greek law reflects this general approach,[15] and several scholars in Anglo-Saxon countries have endorsed this view of Athenian law.[16] Though several scholars

11. Hansen (1980b) 94. Hansen continues by stating that 'I do not know of any historian who has ventured to rearrange the sources according to substantive law and to write one chapter on *katalysis tou demou*, one on *prodosia*, one on *klope*, etc.' Two years before, however, D. M. MacDowell (1978) had organized his account of Athenian law mainly by substantive categories. The titles of chapters 5 through 12 are: Personal Status, the Family, Death, Assault and Abuse, Property, Life in the Community, Treason, and Religion. Harrison (1968) also organized his account by substantive categories in the first volume of his work, and so did Beauchet (1897). Several years after Hansen wrote this, D. Cohen published a book entitled *Theft in Athenian Law*.

12. Hansen (1991) 165. Hansen bases this view on a law inserted into the text of D. 24.20–3, but this law is a later forgery and its contents are unreliable as evidence. See Canevaro (forthcoming).

13. Todd and Millett (1990) 5. They go on to suggest that 'a general textbook on Athenian law should give priority to legal procedure rather than to substantive law.' Note that Hart (1961) 89–96 takes exactly the opposite approach: he calls rules about obligations 'primary' and places procedure among the 'secondary' rules.

14. Todd (1993) 65.

15. Todd (2005) 98 writing about Gagarin and Cohen (2005): 'the priority given to legal procedure over substantive law in this volume.'

16. See, for example, Ober (2000) 541 and 545 ('the procedural emphasis of Athenian law'), Foxhall and Lewis (1996b) 3 ('legal debate and laws in Greek cities centre almost exclusively on procedure rather than substance'), Scafuro (1997) 7–9 with note 18, and Lanni (2006) 87 ('One of the most distinctive features of the Athenian legal system is its focus on procedural rather than substantive law'). Cf. Hunt (2010) 228. Carey (1998) 101 draws attention to the substantive features of many Athenian laws but in general endorses the view of Hansen and Todd: 'It may be that the majority of Athenian legislation was procedural in emphasis, but even if we accept this assumption (and I am inclined to), we are left with a substantial number of laws which are substantive in orientation.' Carey bases this conclusion on an analysis of only twenty-eight laws. This chapter studies over three hundred laws.

have dissented from this view, there has not yet been an extensive study of the issue.[17]

The question whether procedural or substantive matters held priority in Athenian law might appear, at first glance, to be a mere quibble over terminology. One might ask, What difference does it make for our understanding of Athenian law? The answer to the question is crucial for two reasons. First, it affects our view of the role played by law in Athenian democracy. If laws were concerned mainly with procedure, then the aim of the legal system was simply to resolve disputes among individuals. On this view, the Athenians courts did not attempt to enforce substantive norms (which hardly existed), but to regulate conflict among individuals and direct competition into socially acceptable channels.[18] One scholar asserts that the Athenian courts did not enforce substantive norms but rendered ad hoc judgments.[19] An extreme version of this approach alleges that the Athenian courts served primarily as an arena for struggles among the wealthy for power and prestige.[20] This is a minimalist (or primitivist) view of the legal system, which holds that the aim of an Athenian statute was limited to getting a dispute into court.[21] On the other hand, if laws provided clear and numerous substantive norms, that is, orders setting out rights and duties, our view of the legal system changes radically. Laws no longer restrict their aim to providing rules for procedure in court but extend their sphere to all aspects of life in the community. They prescribe the duties of citizens and officials, provide regulations about economic life, establish rules about marriage and inheritance, restrict or outlaw the use of violence, and contain orders about religious

---

17. Rhodes (1979) 106 notes that 'the standard form for a law dealing with an offence and the procedure available against offenders' begins with the substantive offence, not the procedure' but does not really address the issue concerning the contents of Athenian laws. In what follows I use definitions of the terms 'substance' and 'procedure' in the way Carey and others use them. I agree with Carey that in the casuistic form of a law, the substantive part is found in the protasis, the procedural in the apodosis. One cannot therefore claim that my conclusions differ from those of the scholars I criticize because we adopt different definitions of these terms.

18. For this view of the Athenian legal system see Osborne (1985b) 52: 'much of the work of the Athenian courts was at the level of regulating conflict.'

19. This is the general approach of Lanni (2006). For a critique of Lanni's approach see Harris (2009/10b).

20. For this approach see Ober (1989) and Cohen (1995).

21. This is the view of Todd (1993) 65 ('Where procedure matters most is in getting a case to court.').

rites and festivals. The role of the court as the guardian of the laws (D. 24.36; Din. 3.16) is to enforce substantive norms that shape the conduct of individuals in daily life.

Second, the answer to the question makes a difference about how we read the court speeches of the Attic Orators. If the laws did not attempt to provide clear rules about rights and duties nor clear guidance about how to resolve disputes on the basis of substantive rules, then a trial might become a contest of strength between the reputations of two individuals. In this kind of struggle any statement was relevant, and litigants could say whatever they wanted to persuade the court to take their side. Speeches in court would not differ at all from arguments presented in other places and might degenerate into exchanges of insults.[22] On the other hand, if the laws provided clear guidance and the role of the court was to enforce substantive norms, we should then expect accusers to concentrate on proving the charge brought according to the law (D. 45.50). For his part, the defendant would attempt to prove either that he did not commit the illegal action or that his conduct did not violate the law. On this approach, the rhetoric and arguments of speeches in court would differ significantly from those of speeches given in other contexts such as the Assembly.

The issue of substance versus procedure in Athenian laws is complex and should be approached from several different angles.

1. The organization and conceptualization of Athenian laws: When the orators discuss several statutes or groups of statutes, how are they organized, by substantive content or by procedure? When an orator refers to a law, does he mention the procedural or substantive aspect?
2. The content of Athenian laws in the Attic Orators: Do the clauses of Athenian laws mentioned in the Attic Orators address mainly procedural or substantive matters?
3. The content of Athenian laws preserved in inscriptions: Do these laws address mainly procedural or substantive matters?
4. Definitions in Athenian laws. Some writers have argued that the alleged failure of Athenian laws to define key terms indicates a lack of interest in substantive issues. Is this assumption correct?

22. For court speeches as mere exchanges of insults see D. Cohen (1995) 79–81.

I

The Organization of Athenian Laws

There are several passages in the Attic Orators where litigants discuss the rationale or the organization of Athenian laws. In a speech written for a case of *eisangelia*, Hyperides (*Eux.* 5–6) says that the laws are enacted to deal with different offenses, then proceeds to list the offense and the magistrate responsible for each one.[23]

> This is the reason why you have enacted separate laws about each and every crime that occurs in our state. Someone commits impiety regarding religious matters: there are public actions for impiety before the *basileus*. Someone treats his parents badly: the archon takes his seat for this kind of case. Someone proposes an illegal decree in the state: the *thesmothetai* meet. One does something that deserves immediate arrest: the office of the Eleven has been established. In similar fashion also for other crimes you have set up laws and courts suitable for each offense.

The basic idea expressed in this passage is that laws are grouped by substantive categories, and actions are assigned to magistrates on the basis of their jurisdiction over certain areas defined in substantive terms. The *basileus* is responsible for religious matters; the eponymous archon looks after family matters; and the *thesmothetai* accept cases about illegal decrees. In two cases procedures are mentioned (public actions for impiety and arrest [*apagoge*]), but in each case the emphasis is on the offense, not the procedure, as the determining factor in the jurisdiction of officials. There is a similar passage in the speech *Against Lacritus* (D. 35.47–48):

> But, men of the court, where are we to get justice in commercial contracts? Before what official or at what time? Before the Eleven? But they bring into court burglars and thieves and other criminals who are charged with capital offenses. Before the Archon? But it is for heiresses, and orphans, and parents that the Archon is appointed to care. Then before the *basileus*? But we are not gymnasiarchs, nor

23. For discussion see Whitehead (2000) 184–86.

> are we indicting anyone for impiety. Or will the Polemarch bring the case to court? Yes, for deserting a patron or for not having a patron. Well then, the generals are left. But they appoint trierarchs; they bring no mercantile suits to court. (Trans. adapted from A. T. Murray)

In this passage too the jurisdiction of different officials is determined by the nature of the substantive offense; there is almost no mention of judicial procedures.[24]

In his speech *Against Timarchus*, Aeschines (1.7–8) begins his case with a discussion of the laws about various age-groups and about politicians (*rhetores*): 'First, they [the lawgivers] enacted laws about the good character of our children and explicitly indicated what activities a free boy must pursue and how he should be raised, then second about young men, then about the other age-groups, not only about private individuals, but also about politicians.' His discussion of the laws (Aeschin. 1.9–30) follows this basic arrangement. This passage does not mention a single legal procedure; the principle of organization is based on substantive matters.

The litigant Ariston describes how the laws of Athens are designed to prevent the escalation of violence (D. 54. 17–19):

> As for me, I am amazed if there has ever been found in your court a reason or excuse for someone to avoid punishment when convicted of insolent abuse or assault. The laws take quite the opposite approach and have provided compelling incentives so that offenses do not escalate. For example . . . there are private actions for slander; indeed, they say that these exist so that men may not go from insulting to striking each other. Next, there are private actions for assault, and I hear that these actions are there so that no one, when he finds himself in the weaker position, strikes back with a stone or something like this, but waits for the punishment provided in the law. Next, there are public suits for wounding so that those who are wounded do not go on to murder. The slightest offense, that of slander, in my opinion, is covered with a view to preventing the last and most serious, murder, from occurring and so that offenses not escalate gradually from insults to blows, from blows to wounds, and

24. Cf. Is. 11.32–5, which also assigns the jurisdiction of different officials according to the substantive issue to be decided.

> from wounds to killing. No, there is a punishment for each of these offenses so that the decision is not left to the anger or whim of whoever happens to be involved.

Ariston mentions several different types of procedures and kinds of offenses, but the charges are arranged in ascending order of gravity, from slander (*kakegoria*) to murder (*phonos*). The order is determined by the nature of the substantive offense, starting with the least harmful and ending with the most serious. The entire orientation of this description of Athenian statutes about violence is toward substantive matters.[25]

In this regard the laws of Athens were similar to the laws of Gortyn, which were also grouped by substantive topics (*IC* IV 72). A recent study of the organization of the Great Code of Gortyn has noted that those who inscribed it were careful to divide it into clearly marked sections. They indicate each new section by asyndeton, in almost all cases preceded by a *vacat* of one or two spaces.[26] Each of these sections concerns one substantive issue such as sexual violence, divorce, separation of spouses, children of divorced women, inheritance and division of an estate, marriage and remarriage of the heiress, and adoption (see appendix 4). Only two sections are primarily concerned with procedural issues: section 1 on seizure of persons before trial, and section 31 on the duties of judges. It has recently been observed that one can also 'identify sections of closely related legislation.' The first group of laws 'consists of the four laws on sexual assaults' (sections 2–5). Another group contains 'six laws related to estate settlement due to divorce or the death of one of the spouses' (sections 6 and 7). A third has two laws on the exposure of children. There is also a group of laws about inheritance and the heiress (sections 21 through 24).[27] When there are connections between sections, therefore, the link is based on a similarity between the substantive issues treated in each section. None of the sections are linked by procedural matters: the code does not describe a certain procedure, then list the various cases which can be

25. The only passage that appears to suggest that the emphasis in Athenian laws lies on the procedural aspect is D. 22.25–9, on which Osborne (1985b) relies heavily for his view of Athenian law. This passage is however tendentious and its analysis misleading because it gives the false impression that several different procedures existed for each offense and that there were no significant substantive differences between procedures. See Carey (2004) and more briefly Harris (2008) 179–81.

26. Gagarin (1982).

27. Kristensen (2004).

brought to court through this procedure. In terms of the general organization of the collection, the orientation is toward substantive matters.

The laws of Gortyn and Athens were not unusual in this regard. When Aristotle (*Pol.* 2.12.10.1274b) discusses the laws Philolaus enacted for Thebes, he singles out those about bearing children, which are called the laws of adoption, a substantive category. According to Aristotle (*Pol.* 2.8.4.1267b), Hippodamas of Miletus believed that there should be only three categories of laws, corresponding to the main sources of actions: *hybris*, damage, and homicide. He also proposed that elected officials address three main areas: public matters, matters concerning aliens, and matters concerning orphans. His proposal may have been utopian, but his method of organizing statutes by substantive category was obviously traditional.

In fact, when Athenian litigants in court refer to a law or a set of laws, they describe the law according to the name of the substantive offense, the type of offender, or the category of individuals to whom the substantive part of the law applies.[28] Not one of the laws in the following list is named after a procedure.

1. Law about wrongdoers (*peri ton klepton kai lopodyton ho nomos*)—Antiphon 5.9.
2. Laws about thieves (*hoi de nomoi . . . ton klepton*)—Aeschin. 1.113.
3. Law about damage (*ho tes blabes nomos*)—D. 21.35.
4. Law about assault (*ho* [sc. *nomos*] *tes aikias*)—D. 21.35.
5. Law about the holy month (*hieron nomon . . . peri tes hieromenias*)—D. 21.35.
6. Law about gifts to officials (*ton peri ton doron nomon*)—D. 21.107–8.
7. Law about the Dionysia and about the Mysteries (*ho nomos tode to peri ton Dionysion ho peri ton mysterion*)—D. 21.175.
8. Law about *hybris*—Aeschin. 1.15; D. 21.46, 48.

28. Hansen (1991) claims that the document at D. 24.20–23 shows that the Athenians grouped their laws by procedure, but this argument is vulnerable to two objections. First, the document groups laws by the institutions and officials of the Athenian *polis* (the Council, public laws, the nine archons, other magistrates), not by procedures. Second, the document is a forgery: its contents do not agree with the accounts of *nomothesia* found at D. 20.89–93 and D. 24.19, 24–26, and its language does not conform to that of contemporaneous documents. See Canevaro (forthcoming). Rhodes (1979) 107 accepts the evidence in this document but does not conclude from this passage that Athenian laws were organized according to procedure.

9. Law about pandering (*ton* [sc. *nomon*] *tes proagogeias*)—Aeschin. 1.14.
10. Laws about order in the Assembly (*nomoi peri eukosmias*)—Aeschin. 1.22, 34.
11. Law about presidency of a tribe (*ton . . . peri tes proedrias ton phylon nomon*)—Aeschin. 1.34.
12. Laws about homicide (*hoi phonikoi* [sc. *nomoi*])—D. 21.43.
13. Laws about the good conduct of women (*peri tes ton gynaikon eukosmias*)— Aeschin. 1.183.
14. Laws about blood-relatives and gifts to them (*hoi nomoi ou monon oi peri ton genon alla kai hoi peri ton doseon tois sungenesi*)—Is. 4.16.
15. Law about mining (*ton metallikon nomon*)—D. 37.35.
16. Laws on traders (*tous emporikous nomous*)—D. 35.3.
17. Law on wills (*ho peri diathekon nomos*)—Hyp. *Ath.* 17.
18. Law about trierarchs (*ton peri trierarchon nomon*)—Dinarchus 1.42.
19. Law about exemptions from the trierarchy (*ton peri ton trierarchion*)—D. 20.27.
20. Law about slander (*peri tes kakegorias nomon*)—Isoc. 20.3.
21. Law about idleness (*peri tes argias nomos*)—D. 57.32.
22. Dionysiac law (*ton Dionysiakon nomon*)—Aeschin. 3.36 (law relates to proclamation of crowns in the Theater of Dionysus).
23. Law about prostitution (*tou tes hetaireseos nomou*)—Aeschin. 1.160; D. 22.21.
24. Law about dowry (*ton tes proikos nomon*)—D. 40.19.
25. Law about officials subject to audit (*ton ton hypeuthynon nomon*)—Aeschin. 3.205.
26. Law about announcement of crowns (*ton peri ton kerygmaton* [sc. *nomon*])—Aeschin. 3.205.
27. Laws about orphans (*nomous . . . peri ton orphanon*)—Lys. 32.23.
28. Law about mistreatment of parents (*tou peri kakoseos nomou*)—Is. 8.32.
29. Law about the one-twelfth of grain from the islands (*nomos peri tes dodekates tou sitou ton neson*)—Stroud (1998).
30. Law of Chaeremonides on first-fruits (*ton Chairemonido no*[*mon peri te*]*s aparches*)—*IG* ii^2 140, lines 8–9.
31. Draco's law about homicide (*ton Drakontos nomon tom peri to phonou*)—*IG* i^3 104, line 5.

There are a *nomos eisangeltikos* (Hyp. *Eux.* 3) and a statute of limitations about bringing private cases (D. 36.26), but these appear to be rare exceptions. Even though all these laws contained a procedural element, the significant point is that when a litigant refers to a law, he stresses the substantive aspect. This is not just a matter of preference on the part of litigants: the last three laws come from official documents.

When litigants speak about groups of laws, therefore, they arrange them in substantive terms. When litigants and official documents give a name to a law, they designate it by its substantive content. But what about the content of individual laws? Were they oriented more toward procedures or toward substantive issues?

II

Substance and Procedure in the Attic Orators

The speeches of the Attic Orators refer to many laws. In some cases the litigants quote verbatim from the law while more frequently they give a paraphrase or summary. These quotes, paraphrases, and summaries ought to be reliable because they often precede or follow the reading of the law by the clerk. If the litigant misrepresented the contents of the law, his dishonesty would have been immediately apparent. Besides, if litigants tended to distort the contents of laws, one would expect to discover inconsistencies when two different orators summarize the same law or when the same orator summarizes the same law in different speeches. But that is not the case.[29] For instance, Aeschines and Demosthenes both refer to three laws in the speeches they delivered at the trial of Ctesiphon in 330: the law requiring magistrates to undergo an audit of their activities (Aeschin. 3.17–22; D. 18.111–18), the law about crowns for magistrates (Aeschin. 3.11, 31; D. 18.111–18), and the law about the announcement of crowns in the theater (Aeschin. 3.35–6; D. 18.120–22). Although they differ about the interpretation of these laws (see chapter 6), they do not differ about their basic terms.[30] When Demosthenes and Aeschines refer to the decree of the Council passed in Munichion of 346, their statements about this document do not contradict each other.[31]

---

29. For this general point with more references to the evidence see Canevaro and Harris (2012) 99–100.

30. For an analysis of the legal arguments in these speeches see 225–33.

31. D. 19.161; Aeschin. 2.91, 98, 103 with Harris (1995) 79.

On the other hand, most of the documents inserted into some of the speeches of the Attic Orators are forgeries and are not reliable evidence.[32] For instance, the prescripts of the decrees found in Demosthenes' *On the Crown* contain the names of archons who are not attested in the fourth century BCE and contain other features that are inconsistent with the epigraphical evidence for the period.[33] Scholars have recognized that the laws inserted into Aeschines' *Against Timarchus* are not genuine documents.[34] D. M. MacDowell has analyzed the witness statements in Demosthenes' *Against Meidias* and has shown that they have post-Classical linguistic forms.[35] Similar problems exist with the texts of three laws in the same speech, which reveal them to be forgeries.[36] A recent essay has shown that the five documents inserted into the text of Andocides' *On the Mysteries* 76–98 are also forgeries.[37] These documents require a complete study.[38] For the moment, however, it is best not to rely on the evidence they contain.

The main advantage of studying the quotations and paraphrases of the law provided by the orators is that they offer a broad cross-section of legal issues. Antiphon's speeches were delivered in cases of homicide; those of Isaeus are concerned with inheritance; Lysias and Demosthenes wrote speeches for a wide variety of cases, both public and private. Some were delivered by accusers, others by defendants, and still others by supporting speakers. As a whole, they provide varied samples over a period of roughly a century. Appendix 5 contains a complete list of all the laws (and some decrees) mentioned by the Attic Orators. For each law there is a description

32. The last general study of the documents inserted into the speeches of the Attic Orators is Drerup (1898), who showed that many are forgeries. Carey (1998) bases much of his argument on laws found in inserted documents (sixteen out of twenty-eight laws studied), several of which have now been shown to be forgeries; the authenticity of many others has been questioned. On the law inserted at D. 21.47 see Harris (1992) 77–78 and Harris (2008) 103–4. On the law inserted at D. 21.8 see Harris (1992) 76–77 and Harris (2008) 89–90. On the laws inserted at D. 24.20–23 and at D. 24.33, see Canevaro (forthcoming).

33. See Schläpfer (1939). Cf. Wankel (1976) 79–82.

34. See Drerup (1898) 305–8; Fisher (2000) 68, 138–40, 145, 164, 183, 204–5, 206.

35. On the witness statements at D. 21.22, 82, 93, 107, 121, and 168, see MacDowell (1990) 245–6, 302, 316, 333, 343–4; MacDowell (1990) 317–18 also rejects the authenticity of the law at D. 21.94.

36. On the laws at D. 21.8, 10, and 47 see note 32.

37. See Canevaro and Harris (2012).

38. Mirko Canevaro and I are now working on such a study. The first volume on the laws and decrees in the public speeches of the demosthenic corpus is by Canevaro (with a chapter by myself) and is now forthcoming.

of its main provisions and an analysis of its substantive and/or procedural content. In what follows, the findings from this study of the evidence are presented in roughly chronological order, starting with Antiphon, the earliest orator whose forensic speeches have been preserved.

The three speeches of Antiphon (c. 480–411) were delivered in cases of homicide: the first in a case of deliberate homicide, the second through the procedure of *apagoge* of *kakourgoi*, and the third for a case of unwilling homicide.[39] There are no laws cited in the first speech (*Against the Stepmother*); in the other two speeches the defendants cite or mention ten laws. One concerns punishment, one concerns a substantive matter, one addresses issues of substance and procedure, but seven deal exclusively with procedure. The obvious reason for the greater emphasis on procedure in Antiphon's speeches is that they were delivered in cases of homicide. The substantive rules in homicide law were few and relatively simple. There were four basic categories of homicide: deliberate, unwilling, planning a homicide (*bouleusis*), and just homicide.[40] The serious nature of the offense, which was thought to create pollution, led to the creation of more complex and elaborate procedures to set it apart from other private actions.[41] As a result, the laws about homicide are very different from Athenian laws about other matters, and one should not take these laws as characteristic of the system as a whole.

There are thirty-two speeches preserved in the manuscripts attributed to Lysias and long extracts from two other speeches quoted by Dionysius of Halicarnassus, but three of these thirty-four were not written for trials in court. There are very few laws cited in these speeches. This is partly due to the nature of the cases for which the speeches were written. Four were written for the scrutiny of officials before the Council (16, 25, 26, 31), at *euthynai* (27, 30), in special proceedings before the Treasury (17, 18, 19) or before the Council (24). All these cases concerned issues of fact (qualifications for office, conduct in office, ownership of property, and personal income and disability). This is also true for many of the other speeches in

39. I exclude the *Tetralogies* because their authorship is disputed and because they appear to be rhetorical exercises not intended for delivery in court. On these speeches see Sealey (1984) with the references to earlier treatments. For the nature of the charges in *Against the Stepmother* and *On the Chorister* see Harris (2006a) 391–404.

40. Gagarin (1990) attempts to deny that there was a charge of plotting a homicide (*bouleusis phonou*) but see Harris (2006a) 400–4.

41. For the role of pollution in shaping the procedures for homicide see Harris (2010) 126–30.

the Lysianic corpus.[42] There are only eighteen laws cited or discussed in these speeches, but the summaries of four disclose little information or only mention penalties. Out of the remaining fourteen, eight are concerned exclusively with substantive matters, and two with procedural issues. The two laws that contain both substantive and procedural aspects are primarily concerned with substantive matters (Lys. 1.30–33; 14.5). In his valuable new edition of Lysias, Carey collects 513 fragments attributed to the author, but few contain paraphrases or quotations from laws. Two fragments mention laws about procedure, and two contain laws with substantive rules. In one fragment the death penalty for *hybris* is mentioned. In the Lysianic corpus, therefore, the laws cited and discussed have more to do with substance than procedure.

Four speeches of Andocides (c. 440–c. 385) have been preserved, but two are not genuine, and one was delivered to the Council.[43] The remaining speech was delivered at a trial on a charge of impiety in 400/399. Andocides in this speech cites or mentions sixteen laws or decrees with general provisions, but one of these is probably an ad hoc invention.[44] Of the fifteen remaining laws, four deal with substance and procedure, seven with substantive matters, and five with procedural matters. Four of the laws that appear to deal exclusively with substantive matters were enforced by special procedures (*graphe paranomon* and the *graphe* against inexpedient laws), which Andocides does not mention because he does not find them relevant to his argument. The laws in Andocides therefore contain both substantive and procedural features. In some substance is more prominent; in others procedure comes to the fore.

Six forensic speeches attributed to Isocrates (436–338) are extant, but one was delivered before a court on Aegina. Three of the remaining speeches do not cite or paraphrase any laws. There is one law mentioned in *Against Callimachus* (Isoc. 18.2) about bringing a *paragraphe*, which concerns legal procedure, and another mentioned in *Against Lochites* (Isoc. 20.3) about the penalty in a private suit for slander, which concerns punishment.

42. For the issues in the speeches in the Lysianic corpus see Harris (2006b) 368–69.

43. On the authenticity of *On the Peace* see Harris (2000b); on the authenticity of *Against Alcibiades* see Edwards (1995) 131–36, 208–11, and Cobetto Ghiggia (1995).

44. The law at And. 1.107 is probably an ad hoc invention designed to create a fictitious precedent for the amnesty of 403. Note that Andocides does not have the text of the law read out.

There are eleven speeches of Isaeus (c. 420–c. 340) preserved in manuscripts, and a large portion of another found in Dionysius of Halicarnassus' essay *On Isaeus* (17). All were written for cases about inheritance. There are twenty-nine laws referred to in these twelve speeches. Four of these are mentioned twice, reducing the total to twenty-five. Of these, eighteen provide substantive rules with no mention of a procedure. Most of these pertain to rights of inheritance and indicate who may and who may not inherit. Only five give rules about procedure, in most cases how to lay claim to an estate. One law has both substantive and procedural aspects, and another is rather vague. The laws cited by Isaeus' clients are therefore more concerned with substance than procedure. It is also worth noting that all four laws mentioned twice or more deal with substantive matters, which means that it is likely these kinds of laws were more often considered relevant to the issue before the court.

There are three speeches written and delivered by Aeschines (c. 390–322?). The first was delivered in a case brought under the procedure *dokimasia rhetoron* in late 346,[45] the second in response to a charge of treason brought in regard to *euthynai* in 343/2, and the third a prosecution in a *graphe paranomon* brought in 330. Aeschines mentions, paraphrases, or quotes thirty-eight laws. The overwhelming majority of these contain substantive rules: twenty-nine are concerned primarily or exclusively with substantive matters, and five with both substantive and procedural matters. In two cases, the only provision mentioned concerns the penalty, or the law is only named without its contents discussed. Only two laws cited by Aeschines (1.79; 2.87) are mainly concerned with procedural matters.

The speeches of Hyperides (389/8–322) were written for different types of trials and give us a smaller but more varied sample. Two were for *eisangeliai* (*For Lycophron, Against Euxenippus*),[46] one in a dispute about a contract (*Against Athenogenes*),[47] one in a special prosecution arising from the Harpalus affair (*Against Demosthenes*),[48] and one in a *graphe paranomon* (*Against Philippides*).[49] There are extensive fragments of two more

45. For the procedure see MacDowell (2005).

46. For the charges see Whitehead (2000) 82–4, 157–58.

47. For the charge see Whitehead (2000) 267–69.

48. For the charge see Whitehead (2000) 359–61.

49. For the charge see Whitehead (2000) 31–32.

speeches, *Against Timandrus* and *Against Diondas*.[50] The first was delivered in a case involving an orphan, the second in a prosecution of an illegal decree.[51] The speakers mention twelve laws, but only two are primarily concerned with procedure (Hyp. *Lycurg.*, fr. 3; *Against Diondas* p. 8, lines 3–5 [Carey et al.]); nine give substantive rules and do not mention procedures (Hyp. *Phil.* 3; *Ath.* 13, 14, 15, 16, 17, 33; Hyperides *Against Timandrus* 138r, lines 3–11 [Tchernetska et al.]; Hyperides *Against Timandrus* 138v, lines 17–21 [Tchernetska et al.]). One concerns mostly substantive matters, only mentioning the name of the procedure (Hyp. *Eux.* 7–8), one deals with both procedural and substantive matters (Hyp. *Ath.* 29, 33), and one mentions a penalty for bribes (Hyp. *D.* 24) but no procedure. The final one concerns the *proedroi* and most likely prescribes their duties in the Assembly, a substantive issue (Hyp. *Phil.* 4). That makes nine concerned mainly or exclusively with substantive matters, one primarily with procedure, one with both, and one naming a penalty. Once more, the emphasis is on substance, not procedure.

There is only one completely preserved speech attributed to Lycurgus (c. 390–c. 325/4). This speech mentions three laws. One concerns substantive matters and mentions a penalty but no procedure (*Leocr.* 27); one gives a substantive rule but does not mention a procedure (*Leocr.* 102); and one concerns both substance and procedure (*Leocr.* 120). The fragments of Lycurgus appear to contain no summaries or paraphrases of laws.

The demosthenic corpus contains forty-two forensic orations, but two (25 and 26) are generally recognized to be later forgeries.[52] Most of these speeches are attributed to Demosthenes (384–322), but several were written by Apollodorus (c. 394– after 343) or other orators.[53] Demosthenes' speeches can be roughly divided into the public speeches (18–24, 52, 57–59) and the private speeches (27–51, 53–56). In the public speeches, there are one hundred thirteen laws mentioned or discussed. In eleven cases the litigant does not discuss the contents of the law or mentions only the penalties. A large majority of these laws, fifty-seven, are however

50. For the texts see Tchernetska et al. (2007) and Carey et al. (2008).

51. The charge in *Against Diondas* is a *dike epitropes* or an *eisangelia kakoseos orphanou*. For discussion and references to other discussions see Whitehead (2009) 138–48.

52. On the authenticity of D. 25 and 26 see Sealey (1993) 237–39 with references to earlier discussions.

53. Trevett (1992) 50–77 attributes speeches 46, 49, 50, 52, 53 59, and possibly 47 to Apollodorus.

primarily or exclusively concerned with substantive matters. For several of these laws we know that there was a procedural component, but the litigants who cite these laws evidently did not find this part relevant to their cases. In fourteen cases the laws concern both substantive and procedural issues. In only thirty-one cases is the law primarily or exclusively concerned with procedural matters. Some laws are mentioned twice, but this does not alter the basic picture: there is more concern with substance than with procedure. The private speeches contain references to about fifty-nine different laws (several laws are mentioned two or three times). There are twenty-eight primarily concerned with substantive matters, and an equal number concerned with procedural issues; three contain both substantive and procedural aspects. Here there is some selective quotation: the litigants often quote or mention just the substantive part of the law even though other sources indicate there was a procedural aspect to the law (e.g., the law about theft mentioned at D. 29.36). The reason for the higher percentage of procedural rules in Demosthenes' private speeches is probably because several were delivered at trials for *paragraphe*, which concerned procedural violations (D. 32–38).

The three preserved speeches of Dinarchus (361/0– after 292/1) were delivered at special trials about the bribery of officials arising out of an investigation of the Harpalus affair by the Areopagus.[54] As we saw in the previous chapter, the prosecutors say that the issue for the court to decide was not the guilt of the defendants (which was proved by the reports of the Areopagus) but the penalty (Din. 1.105; 2.20). These speeches therefore resemble those given at the *timesis* phase of a *graphe* and contain few references to laws. It should come as no surprise that the speakers concentrate on the penalties provided in three of the nine laws found in these speeches (one of these is mentioned twice:—Din. 1.60 and 2.17). One law is only mentioned by name without any discussion (Din. 1.42). Out of the four remaining laws, two are concerned with substantive issues (Din. 1.71; 2.24; 3.4), one with procedural matters (Din. 1.71), and one with both substance and procedure (Din. 3.4).

A partial explanation for the larger number of substantive rules is the fact that in some cases several substantive rules could be enforced by a single procedure. Take, for example, the *graphe paranomon*: this one procedure was used against decrees that violated the laws regulating honors

54. On these speeches see Worthington (1992).

to officials (Aeschin. 3.11, 36), laws about announcing honors in the theater and elsewhere (Aeschin. 3.32–5), laws about honors for the Council (D. 22.8), the law prohibiting public debtors from proposing decrees (D. 22.21–24; 59.6), and the law requiring that all decrees receive the prior approval of the Council (D. 22.5–7). There were also several laws about succession that could be enforced through the procedure of *diadikasia* in inheritance cases; this would explain why the laws mentioned in the speeches of Isaeus are more concerned with substantive matters. There were also a number of rules about qualifications for office that were enforced through the *dokimasia* procedure.[55] Many laws specified various duties for different officials (e.g., *IG* i^3 52, lines 15–32 for the Treasurers of the Other Gods), but all these rules could be enforced by *eisangelia* to the Council during the official's term of office or by the *euthynai* procedure after their term of office.[56]

The evidence about laws in the speeches of the Attic Orators may also contain a bias in favor of substantive matters. After all, laws about procedure are aimed in part at getting a case into court: these provide rules about bringing an action, assigning the case to the right court, appointing days for the preliminary hearing (*anakrisis*) and the trial, and selecting judges. Or they provided rules about what was to happen after the trial: how to enforce judgment, how to collect fines, or impose punishment. When the case was before the court, these rules were not relevant; the main issue was whether the defendant had violated the substantive portion of the law. Yet this too is significant: even though litigants in court paid more attention to the substantive part of the law than to procedure, this reveals that they found the former more important for their arguments than the latter. This emphasis on substantive law in the orations also indicates that the litigants expected the judges to base their decisions primarily on substantive rules rather than on procedural rules. Yet even if we were to correct for this bias resulting from selective quotation, there is generally more concern with substantive matters than with procedure in the laws cited and discussed in forensic oratory.

55. On this procedure see now Feyel (2009) 148–97.

56. On *eisangelia* to the Council see Arist. *Ath. Pol.* 45.2, Antiphon 6.35 with *SEG* 27:72, lines 32–4. On *euthynai* see Arist. *Ath. Pol.* 54.2, which states that one can bring charges of theft of public funds, accepting gifts, and misdemeanor (*adikiou*) through this procedure.

One should also note that the emphasis on substance or procedure varies from one area to another.[57] The speeches of Antiphon give the impression that there was a greater emphasis on procedure in homicide law.[58] The public speeches in the demosthenic corpus and the speeches of Aeschines, all delivered in public cases, and the public speeches of Hyperides reveal that in public law the rules about substantive matters were more numerous. The same appears to hold true for marriage and inheritance, which are the subject of Isaeus' speeches. On the other hand, in the private speeches of the demosthenic corpus one finds that both substantive and procedural rules are relevant to the case. In general, however, there tend to be a larger number of rules about substantive issues, and in several cases where a statute contains both substantive and procedural elements, the stress is on the former.

III

Substance and Procedure in Laws and Decrees Found in Inscriptions

The problem of selective quotation or paraphrase does not arise with the laws preserved in inscriptions. These laws are far fewer in number, but they nicely complement the evidence from the orators, who often give only excerpts from the laws. Nine of these laws have survived, of which seven have been fully published, one has been partially published, and another awaits publication.[59] The regulations for the Mysteries at Eleusis found in a fragmentary inscription dated to the fourth century are probably also a law.[60] The content of these laws varies: two concern coinage, one contains a contract for rebuilding city walls, one legislates about two

57. The conclusions of this part are similar to the tentative observation made by Carey (1998) 107: 'I think one can see a trend toward the definition of rights and obligations in specific areas: property law, especially the transfer of property, and family law, two areas which converge in the case of inheritance; religion; constitutional law.'

58. Cf. Carey (1998) 108: 'the laws on homicide . . . are procedural in emphasis.'

59. The unpublished law about the mint (Agora Inv. 7495) appears to contain orders for different officials but does not name any legal procedure. I would like to thank Molly Richardson for allowing me to see her proposed text of this inscription. The law of Lycurgus about offerings dated to 334 (*IG* ii^2 333) is very fragmentary. For recent discussion see Lambert (2005) 137–44. Hansen (1981–82) argues that *IG* ii^2 412 is a fragment of a law, but not enough remains of the inscription to allow a definitive answer.

60. Clinton (2008) 116.

taxes on grain, one deals with tyranny, and five issue rules about religious festivals and sanctuaries. There are very few legal procedures mentioned in these statutes, and most of the clauses take the prescriptive form.

The law of Agyrrhius dated to 374/73 concerns two taxes on grain: the first a tax of one-twelfth collected in Lemnos, Imbros, and Scyros; the second a tax of one-fiftieth on grain imported into Attica.[61] The main clauses of the law give orders to various parties, those who purchase the right to collect the tax, the *polis*, and a board of ten elected by the Assembly. These orders are expressed in prescriptive form by verbs in the future indicative (lines 9, 10–11, 12–3, 14, 15–6, 20, 21–2, 24–25, 27, 29–30, 32, 33), infinitives (lines 42–43, 56, 59, 60), or imperatives (lines 36, 41, 44, 47–8, 49–50, 52, 53). None of the clauses conform to the casuistic form of a conditional sentence with the offense named in the protasis, the procedure in the apodosis. The first major clause of the law states that the purchaser will transport grain to the Piraeus and place it in the Aiakeion (lines 10–15). The *polis* will provide a roof and doors for the building and will weigh the grain within thirty days of delivery (lines 15–19). The city will not charge for use of the space and will weigh the grain in a certain manner (lines 19–27). The purchaser will make no advance payment, but will pay certain fees for the contract (lines 27–29). The purchaser will provide sureties (lines 29–31). The city will collect payment from any or all in the *symmory*, that is, joint and several liability (lines 33–36). The Assembly is to elect ten men to supervise the grain and sell it in the Agora at a time not before Maimakterion and at a price set by the Assembly (lines 36–51). This board of ten is to provide an account of the money earned by the sale and give the money to the Military Fund (lines 51–55).[62] There is not one legal procedure such as *graphe, phasis, apagoge, endeixis*, or *ephegesis* named in the law. All the clauses give substantive rules, mostly in the form of orders to officials and political bodies.

A similar emphasis on substantive provisions is found in the law on first-fruits for Eleusis dated to 353/2 (*IG* ii² 140).[63] The law modifies an

---

61. For the text and commentary see Stroud (1998). For discussion see Harris (1999b). Jakab (2007) and Hansen (2009) believe that the law concerns contracts for the transport of grain, but their arguments are not convincing. See Faraguna (2007). Stroud, followed by many scholars, believes that the *dodekate* (tax of one-twelfth) was a tax on grain grown in the islands, but see Harris (1999) 270–72 and Rubel (2009) 340–41 ('scheint mir die Interpretation von Harris . . . immer noch am plausibelsten zu sein.').

62. For the meaning of lines 55–61 see Harris (1999b) 269–70.

63. For a recent text see Clinton (2005) no. 142. For commentary see Clinton (2008) 133–35.

earlier law of Chaeremonides (lines 8–10) and grants the Assembly the power to determine how best to collect the first-fruits for the two goddesses (lines 10–13). The law delegates to the Council the tasks of implementing the Assembly's decisions and conducting the rituals (lines 13–25). After the first-fruits have been collected, the Council is to conduct sacrifices (lines 25–31). The final section of the law contains orders to the secretary of the Council to have the law inscribed (lines 31–38). Here too there is no mention of any legal procedure.

The famous Law against Tyranny dated to 336 is a very different type of statute but also does not name any legal procedure in its three major clauses.[64] Although the first clause of the law takes the form of a conditional sentence with the protasis listing the crimes of setting up a tyranny and overthrowing the democracy, the apodosis says nothing about a legal procedure but grants the person who kills anyone committing these crimes the status of ritual purity, in other words, an exemption from prosecution and from exclusion from rituals and temples (lines 7–11). The second clause forbids members of the Areopagus to ascend the Areopagus, sit together in their meeting place, or conduct business (lines 11–16). The third clause is another conditional sentence, but once again no legal procedure is mentioned in the apodosis, which contains only the penalty of loss of citizen rights and confiscation of property for those members of the Areopagus who violate the prohibition in the previous clause (lines 16–22).[65] Once again the law takes up substantive matters by imposing rules on the members of the Areopagus. The law does not mention any legal procedures.

The law of Nicophon on silver coinage dated to 375/4 contains more about legal procedure than these three laws, but more than half the text gives orders to various officials.[66] The first clause of the law is a general provision ordering that Attic silver coinage made of actual silver and carrying the public stamp is to be accepted (i.e., as legal tender) (lines 2–3). The next sentences list the duties of the *dokimastes*, or tester of coins, a public slave supervised by the Council (lines 4–16). These duties are expressed by a series of verbs in the imperative (line 6: *dokimazeto*;

64. For a text based on autopsy see Schwenk (1985) 33–46.

65. The final clause of the law orders the secretary of the Council to have the law inscribed on two *stelai* (lines 22–29).

66. For the text and commentary see Stroud (1974).

line 10: *apodidoto*; and line 11: *diakopteto*). The final sentence in this section orders that if the tester does not perform his duties, the convenors of the people are to give him fifty lashes (lines 13–16). This sentence takes the casuistic form, but there is no mention of a legal procedure. The next twenty-one lines (lines 16–36) do provide detailed procedural rules about what to do when someone refuses to accept coin approved by the *dokimastes*. The law states where individuals are to bring a *phasis* (lines 18–23),[67] who can impose fines (lines 23–26), the duties of the *thesmothetai* (lines 26–28), rewards to those who bring the *phasis* (lines 28–29), punishment for slaves who violate the laws (lines 30–32), and *eisangelia* to the Council for those officials who do not follow the law (lines 32–36).[68] The rest of the law orders the Council to have another tester in the Piraeus and the overseers of the market to ensure that he carries out his tasks (lines 36–44). The final clauses of the law gives instructions for publication (lines 44–49), payment for the tester (lines 49–55), and the demolition of any opposing legislation (lines 55–56). Despite the amount of space devoted to procedural matters, most of the law, thirty-three out of fifty-five lines, grants powers and imposes duties on various officials and therefore pertains to substantive matters.

The law about the rebuilding of the walls of Eetionia and Mounichia dated to 337/6 (*IG* ii^2 334) is over 110 lines long and divided into two parts, the first 46 lines about legal matters, the part starting at line 47 giving the building specifications. The latter part is very well preserved, but the first half is heavily damaged on both sides. Despite the damage it is possible to discern the subject matter of the clauses in this section. The architects paid by the state are to hand over designs to the *prytaneis* and secretary, who are to display them in the Council house (lines 6–8). The Council is to select or approve the designs (lines 9–12). Next follow provisions about payment for work, the source of the funds, and dates of payments (*katabolai*) (lines 15–27). The *proedroi* must hold meetings about the work or face a fine (line 28). Supervisors are to be elected to oversee the contractors and their wages (lines 28–31). These supervisors are to preside over a court hearing cases about contracts (lines 31–32). There are penalties for contractors who do not complete work and a provision for hearing their cases in court (lines 32–36). The Council is required to hold meetings

67. On the procedure of *phasis* see MacDowell (1991) and Wallace (2003).

68. For *eisangelia* to the Council see Arist. *Ath. Pol.* 45.2; Antiphon 6.35 with *SEG* 27:72.

about the construction (lines 36–38). Payments are to be made to the Council and supervisors for construction of walls for dedications (lines 38–40). A procedure is set forth for submitting designs for the harbor (lines 40–42). Officials are to be appointed to supervise the work and the method of payment (lines 42–45). All the clauses in this part of the law give orders to officials or to the Council (lines 6–32, 36–46). Only six lines appear to concern the legal procedures for enforcing contracts (lines 31–36).

Two fragments of a stele found in the Agora contain a law proposed by Aristonicus and a decree of the Assembly about the Lesser Panathenaea, both of which have been dated to around 335.[69] The aim of the law is to ensure that the sacrifice to Athena at the Lesser Panathenaea is as beautiful as possible and that the *hieropoioi* gain as much income as possible (lines A5–7). The *poletai* are instructed to let out the Nea to the highest bidder, to accept guarantors for the leases (lines A7–11), and to sell the right to collect the tax of one-fiftieth (lines A11–13). The *prytaneis* are to hold a meeting of the Council for these contracts (lines A13–17). The rest of the law is very fragmentary. The decree that follows contains orders for the *hieropoioi* (lines B8–31). The *hieropoioi* are to punish with the legally prescribed fines those who do not obey them (lines B31–35). There is no indication that these officials must bring the offenders to court, and there are no legal procedures named in the law and in the decree.

A law about the shrine of Artemis Brauronia dated to the fourth or third century BCE contains instructions to various officials—the *exetastai* of the Council and the Treasurers of the Other Gods (lines 9–15), the architect for the sanctuaries (lines 15–19), the *poletai* (lines 19–20), and the *apodektai* (lines 20–22).[70] There may however be rules about legal procedures in the unpublished part of the law.

The fragments of a set of regulations about the Eleusinian Mysteries dated to the middle of the fourth century BCE are probably a law.[71] The prescript of the measure has not been preserved, but the preserved portions appear to fulfill the criteria for a *nomos* because the regulations

69. For the text see *IG* ii^2 334 with Lewis (1959) (= Lewis [1997] 252–62).

70. For the text see Themelis (2002) (= *SEG* 52:104). One should note however that Themelis has published only twenty-five of the forty-seven lines in the inscription.

71. For the text see Clinton (2005) no. 138.

contain general provisions to be applied over a long period.[72] Clinton has well summarized the contents of the law:

> The announcement of the Mysteries and the selection and sending of *spondophoroi* to the other Greek cities (A.1–13), the limits and nature of the Sacred Truce surrounding the festival (lines 14–17), the behavior of the cities toward the *spondophoroi* and the report of the latter on their mission (lines 20–26), regulations concerning *myesis* (lines 27–29), the appointment of the *epimeletai*, their duties and those of the *basileus* in managing the festival (lines 29–38), the duties of the exegetes before the festival (lines 38–40), an unclear selection by lot (lines 41–42), and (after a long lacuna) regulations pertaining to the initiates (B.*h*,*a*), and the general responsibilities of the *epistatai* (B.*a*.23–24).[73]

In other words, most of the regulations concern the conduct of officials. There are, however, several clauses in the standard casuistic form with an offense described in the protasis and a legal procedure in the apodosis. In lines 11–13 there appears to be a conditional clause (line 11) followed by mention of the *thesmothetai* (line 12) and possibly a penalty (line 13: *ophei[lein . . .*). In lines 27–29 there is a conditional clause concerning the person who knows that he is not a member of the Eumolpidai or Kerykes but who nonetheless performs *myesis* and the person who introduces someone seeking initiation to such a nonmember with a reference to the legal procedure of *phasis* (line 28), which can be initiated by any Athenian citizen, in the apodosis. Stumpf has proposed that the next clause (lines 28–29) provides a legal action against the *basileus* who does not perform his duty.[74] In lines 36–38 there is a conditional clause about the failure of the *basileus* to impose fines on the disorderly and the mention of a penalty in the apodosis (line 37).[75] Lines 40–41 appear to contain a similar formula with the protasis concerning elected officials who do not perform their duty (line A40) and the apodosis providing a legal procedure (line A41).

72. See Clinton (2008) 116 with Hansen (1979) 32–35.

73. Clinton (2008) 117.

74. Stumpf (1988) 223–26.

75. For discussion of the phrase (line 37) see Stumpf (1988) 226–28 and Clinton (2008) 121–22.

The same kind of formula may be present in lines 44–5. The *thesmothetai* are mentioned at line A46, the Heliaea at line A49, the procedure of *timesis* in a public action at line Ba12, and *euthynai* at Ba24. The rest of the regulations, however, provide orders to various officials about their duties.

In the fifth century, there was no formal distinction between laws (*nomoi*) and decrees (*psephismata*).[76] Honors for individuals, ad hoc measures passed for a specific situation, and general rules intended to apply to all residing in Attica or to large groups for a long period of time were all called decrees (*psephismata*). Very few of the measures preserved in inscriptions dated to the fifth century fall into the last category, but those that do tend to confirm the conclusions drawn on the basis of the laws dated to the fourth century BCE.

The late fifth-century decree about first-fruits for the sanctuary at Eleusis starts with the general provision that the Athenians should give first-fruits to the two gods, then gives the percentages of wheat and barley to be collected (*IG* i^3 78, lines 4–8).[77] The next two clauses give orders to officials: the demarchs are to collect first-fruits and give them to the *hieropoioi* (lines 8–10), and the *hieropoioi* are to build silos to store the wheat and barley (lines 10–14). The following clause orders the allies to provide first-fruits (lines 14–18) and gives instructions about how they are to be informed (lines 24–26, 30–36). If the *hieropoioi* do not obey these orders, they are subject to a fine of one thousand drachmas each (lines 18–21). This clause gives only the penalty but does not indicate the legal procedure to be employed against these officials. The *hieropoioi* are also to make a record of the amounts they collect (lines 26–30). In the next clauses there follow orders about what sacrifices are to be made (lines 36–44). The first part of the decree ends by stating that those who do not wrong the Athenians, their city, and the two gods will enjoy good and plentiful harvests (lines 43–45).

The second part of the decree contains a rider proposed by Lampon, who is probably to be identified with the famous seer (lines 47–61). This section gives more orders to officials: the secretary of the Council is to supervise the inscribing of two copies of the decree and their placement in the shrine at Eleusis and on the Acropolis (lines 49–51. Cf. lines 52–3); the *poletai* are to hire out the task of making the stele (line 51); the *kolakretai*

76. See Hansen (1978).

77. For detailed discussion see Cavanaugh (1996).

are to provide the money (lines 51–52); the next archon is to intercalate an extra month of Hekatombaion (lines 52–3); the *basileus* is to mark out a border around the Pelargikon (lines 54–55). In the future no altar should be placed in the Pelargikon without the approval of the Council and Assembly, nor any stones quarried, nor any earth or stones removed (lines 55–7). There then follows a clause in the standard casuistic form, the only one in the entire decree: if anyone violates these orders, he is to pay a fine of five hundred drachmas and the *basileus* is to report the violation to the Council (57–59). This is the only place in the entire decree that mentions a legal procedure (*eisangelia*).[78] The decree ends with an order to Lampon to draft a proposal to submit to the Council in the ninth *prytany* and another to the Council to introduce this proposal to the Assembly (lines 59–61). Almost every clause in the decree gives orders to various officials and provides substantive rules about religious matters. There are only two lines concerning legal procedure.

A measure proposed by Cleinias and dated either to the 440s or to the 420s provides general rules about the collection of tribute (*IG* i³ 34).[79] The first clause places responsibility for collecting tribute in the hands of the Council, officials in the cities, and overseers (lines 5–11). The next clause concerns the identification seals (*symbola*) that will prevent those who transport the tribute from committing theft and fraud (lines 11–18). The *prytaneis* are to call a meeting of the Assembly after the Dionysia for the Hellanotamiai to report about the payment of tribute (lines 18–22). The Athenians are to elect and send four men to present receipts to those cities which have paid and to ask for payment from those cities which have not (lines 22–31). Up to this point there is no mention of legal procedure. The next clause, however, takes the casuistic form with the protasis containing the offense (doing wrong in regard to the collection of tribute) and a legal procedure in the apodosis (lines 31–35). The *prytaneis* are instructed to bring the charge before the Council or face a fine (lines 35–37). After the Council makes a decision, the *prytaneis* are to bring the case before a popular court (lines 37–41). A similar procedure is provided against those who interfere with the transport of the cow or panoply (lines 41–43). The remaining lines of the decree (lines 47–77) are very fragmentary but

78. This form of *eisangelia* appears to be the same one mentioned at Arist. *Ath. Pol.* 45.2.

79. Lewis assigned a date of 448/7 in *IG* i³ 34, but Mattingly (1966), now followed by Rhodes (2008a) 503, argues for a date in the 420s.

appear to contain some terms denoting legal procedures (line 67: *graphen*; line 70: *esagonton*; line 72: *menyseos*). Although the decree does give rules about legal procedures, two-thirds of the extant portion gives orders to various officials and political bodies.

There is another decree about tribute passed by Cleonymus, which is dated to 426/25 (*IG* i³ 68). This inscription is very fragmentary, but it is possible to determine the main topics covered by its provisions. The decree calls for the cities to elect officials responsible for collecting the tribute (lines 8–9). As in the Cleinias decree, the *prytaneis* are to convene a meeting of the Assembly for the Hellanotamiae to report about the tribute (lines 10–16). The Assembly is to elect five men to demand payment from defaulting cities, and the Hellanotamiae are to record payments and amounts owing (lines 16–21). There is a special provision for Thera and Samos (lines 21–25). Next is an order to place a copy of the decree on the Acropolis and a rider about convening a meeting of the Assembly on the next day (lines 25–30). There follows another decree, which discusses legal procedures (lines 37–51). Supervisors are to be elected to oversee cases about the tribute (lines 38–41). There is a clause in the casuistic form (lines 43–47) with the protasis containing the offense (conspiring to prevent the implementation of the decree or the collection of tribute) and an apodosis mentioning a legal procedure (line 45: *graphesthai*), then instructions for bringing the case to court, and the penalty imposed by the court (lines 43–47). But these rules about procedure take up only about one-quarter of the decree; the rest contains substantive rules for officials.

The only decree from the fifth century that deals primarily with legal procedures is the treaty with Phaselis (*IG* i³ 10).[80] The main provision states that if any cause for legal action arises at Athens with a citizen of Phaselis, the case is to be brought in the court of the Polemarch (lines 6–11). The sense of the next clause is unclear, but it also concerns legal procedure (lines 11–14). If any other official accepts a case against a citizen of Phaselis, his judgment is null and void (lines 15–19). If anyone violates this decree, he is to owe one thousand drachmas to Athena (lines 19–22). One might argue however that the decree has more to do with jurisdiction than with legal procedure. The clauses state where an action should be brought and who should decide the case rather than prescribe rules to be followed when hearing the case.

80. For discussion with references to earlier literature see Meiggs and Lewis (1969) 66–69.

This survey of the laws preserved in inscriptions confirms and strengthens the conclusion reached in section II from a study of the laws mentioned by the Attic Orators: most Athenian laws are concerned with substantive matters, not with indicating a legal procedure to be followed in a given situation.[81] In stylistic terms this means that most of the laws give orders with sentences containing main verbs in the imperative mood, in the indicative future tense, or in infinitives dependent on a main verb 'The *nomothetai* have decided that . . .' or 'the Assembly has decided that . . .' There are relatively few clauses in the casuistic form.[82] As in the case of many of the laws found in the orators, it is clear that one legal procedure is used to prosecute violations of several different substantive rules. For instance, in the law of Nicophon about silver coinage and in the fifth-century law about first-fruits for the shrine at Eleusis, officials are given several responsibilities, then threatened with the single procedure of *eisangelia* to the Council if they do not perform their duties.

IV

Definitions of Key Terms in Athenian Laws and Decrees

Another argument used to show that Athenian laws placed little emphasis on substantive matters is the alleged absence of definitions for offenses. One scholar claims, 'The purpose of a statute phrased in this form (i.e. the casuistic form) is not so much to define theft or adultery, but to indicate a form of action which may (not 'must') be taken against a thief or adulterer [*sic*].'[83] The same scholar alleges that 'Athenian statutes were notoriously vague in their use of terms.'[84] Other scholars have also asserted that the

81. One should note however that the laws preserved in inscriptions concern mostly public law. The findings in this section confirm the conclusion reached in section II that substantive rules are far more numerous in laws about public administration than procedural rules.

82. Rhodes (1979) 106 is therefore misleading when he asserts: 'the standard form for a law dealing with an offence and the procedure available against offenders seems to have been: ἐάν τις (ἀδίκημα τι ἀδικῇ), τούτων εἶναι γραφὰς πρὸς τοὺς θεσμοθέτας or εἰσαγγελίαν εἰς τὴν βουλήν or other form of procedure.' Rhodes bases this general statement on a mere five examples. Cf. Gagarin (2008) 210–11, who considers the law about *hybris* typical.

83. Todd (1993) 66–7.

84. Todd (2000b) 26. Cf. Todd (2000b) 29: 'the linguistic obscurity of some Athenian laws' and Hansen (1975) 10: 'the substantive rules concerning offences, obligations, property, etc. are vague and often obscure.' Cf. MacDowell (1978) 61.

typical Athenian statute names a substantive offense without giving a definition.[85]

The question we need to pose is whether the Athenians recognized the need in certain cases to define key terms in their statutes and did litigants use these definitions to help clarify issues and resolve disputes about the meaning of statutes. Yes, they did. Take, for instance, the law about *kakourgoi*. This law covers a broad category of offenders, but does not leave the term undefined. On the contrary, several sources reveal that only three types of offenders were subject to this law: thieves (*kleptai*), clothes-snatchers (*lopodytai*), and enslavers (*andrapodistai*) (Antiphon 5.9; Arist. *Ath. Pol.* 52.1; Lys. 10.7–10; D. 24.113; D. 54.24; Isoc. 15.90).[86] These are offenders who could be caught in highly incriminating circumstances (*ep'autophoro*), that is, in possession of the *corpus delicti* even after the commission of their offense.[87]

The law on the procedure of *eisangelia* (often translated as 'impeachment') covers major threats to public safety. Despite its wide application, Hyperides (*Eux.* 8) shows that the law is careful to list the specific activities subject to the procedure of *eisangelia*: attempting to overthrow the democracy, which includes meeting anywhere for this purpose or forming a political club; treason (*prodosia*), which includes betraying the city, ships, land or naval force; and bribery, which means not giving one's best advice to the Athenian people because one has received gifts (*dora*). Hyperides continues by observing that the last offense applies only to public speakers (*rhetores*).[88] Two defendants accused under the procedure based their cases on a close reading of this statute. The man who defended Euxenippus argued that he was innocent because he was not a public speaker, then gives a persuasive definition of the term (Hyp. *Eux.* 8).[89]

---

85. See, for example, Cohen (1995) 152, 190, Gagarin (2008) 210–11, and Lanni (2006) 67–68.

86. Some scholars have argued that seducers (*moichoi*) were also classified as *kakourgoi* but see Harris (2006a) 291–93 and Fisher (2001) 224–26.

87. On the meaning of the term *ep'autophoro* see Harris (2006a) 373–90. Gagarin (2008) 211–12 seriously distorts my arguments and misrepresents my main conclusion. The argument of Gagarin (2003) that *kakourgoi* were 'career criminals' is not supported by the evidence.

88. For discussion of the passage see Whitehead (2000). Rhodes (1979) 107–8 believes that the procedure also covered unnamed offenses but see Hansen (1980b) 92–93. If the law contained a general clause allowing for prosecution of any serious crime under this procedure, Lycurgus would certainly have mentioned it in his prosecution of Leocrates.

89. For analysis of the speaker's argument see 189–92.

Leocrates was accused under the terms of this law and is reported to have claimed that his actions did not fit the precise terms of the statute (*Against Leocrates* 68). His accuser Lycurgus retorted that they did, but he has to stretch the meaning of key terms to make his case (*Against Leocrates* 8–9).[90] What is important for our topic is that the law contained a detailed list of the actions that fell under the general rubric of major crimes against the state and attempted to define offenses by giving a list of specific actions.

Athenian law had four main categories of homicide, which were tried in three different courts: intentional homicide (*phonos ek pronoias*) (D. 23.22; Arist *Ath. Pol.* 57.3), homicide against the killer's will (*akousios phonos*) (Arist. *Ath. Pol.* 57.3; D. 23.71), plotting or attempted homicide (*bouleusis phonou*) (Arist. *Ath. Pol.* 57.3), and just homicide (*phonos dikaios*) (Arist. *Ath. Pol.* 57.3; D. 23.74). Although there might be some ambiguity about the exact limits of the first three categories in some cases, the basic outlines of each offense were clear enough and required no elaboration.[91] The last, just homicide or homicide according to the laws, however, was far too broad and vague to be left undefined. One of the aims of the Athenian legal system was to restrain violence and to encourage the peaceful resolution of disputes. For this reason the Athenians tightly circumscribed the use of self-help and restricted it to a few ring-fenced areas. As we saw in chapter 1, the law on just homicide therefore was limited to a handful of situations:

1. If someone against his will killed a contestant in an athletic event (Arist. *Ath. Pol.* 57.3; D. 23.53).
2. If someone killed a person caught with his wife, mother, sister, daughter, or concubine kept for the purpose of free children (Arist. *Ath. Pol.* 57.3; D. 23.53; Lys. 1.30).
3. If someone kills an Athenian in ignorance during battle (Arist. *Ath. Pol.* 57.3; D. 23.53).
4. If someone kills a person attacking him from an ambush (D. 23.53 with Harpocration s.v. *en hodo*).[92]

---

90. For the legal arguments in this speech see 233–40.

91. For the potential ambiguity and the different interpretations of the phrase *phonos ek pronoias* see 182–89.

92. On the meaning of the phrase see 51–2.

5. If someone kills a person carrying off without justification his property or leading away his livestock as long as he does so immediately (D. 23.60).
6. If someone kills a person aiming at tyranny (*SEG* 12:87, lines 7–11).

There is a law about officials discussed by Aeschines (3.14, 28–9) at length in his speech *Against Ctesiphon*. Here Aeschines predicts that Demosthenes will argue that Ctesiphon's decree to crown him does not violate the law forbidding the award of crowns to officials who have not yet passed their audit (*euthynai*) because Demosthenes was not an official at the time. According to Aeschines, Demosthenes plans to base his argument on a close reading of the law, which, he claims, applies only to those appointed by the *thesmothetai* or elected by the Assembly. Demosthenes, on the other hand, held a commission (*epimeleia*) or public service (*diakonia*). Aeschines demolishes his argument by reading from the law, which defines the term 'elective offices' with the phrase 'those which the Assembly elects' and specifically names 'superintendents of public works' and adds 'all who have charge of any business of the state for more than thirty days, and all who preside over a court.' Once again the lawgiver had not neglected to clarify his meaning by defining key terms, and a litigant appeals to the definition set forth in the law to refute his opponent's argument.

In 405, after the defeat at Aegospotamoi, the Athenians passed the decree of Patrocleides recalling those who had lost their civic rights (And. 1.73–76).[93] This was another broad category of persons covering many classes subject to different penalties. Patrocleides felt it necessary to spell out which groups he intended to include in this amnesty. What is remarkable is the length and organization of the list: three general categories (state-debtors, those who have lost civic rights but retained property, and those who have lost some but not all civic rights), then twenty-one subcategories (see appendix 5)! Patrocleides was not just trying to be specific but also giving an exhaustive list. This explicitly excluded exiles (And. 1.80).

Contained in this list are those convicted of military offenses, and this is another area where the law broke down a general category into several smaller categories. There was a general law about military offenses that provided public indictments for cowardice (Aeschin. 3.175) and covered several specific offenses: not reporting for duty when called up (*astrateia*)

93. The document at And. 1.77–79 is a later forgery and the information contained in it unreliable. See Canevaro and Harris (2012) 100–10.

(Lys. 14.6–7; [D.] 59.27; D. 39.16); leaving one's post in battle (*lipotaxion*) (Lys. 14.5); deserting the fleet (And. 1.74); and throwing away one's shield (And. 1.74).[94] The meaning of the second term (*lipotaxion*) was clarified by the law's wording: it applied to those who went toward the back out of cowardice while others were fighting (Lys. 14.5). This clause supplies several key details about the meaning of the law and the circumstances in which the statute would apply.

In 378 the Athenians created a new league of allies to defend the freedom and autonomy of the Greeks (*IG* ii² 43). As recent experience has shown, the terms freedom and autonomy can be very elastic; rival groups or competing nations are quite capable of defining 'freedom' in different ways to suit their interests or to justify the invasion of foreign countries. One of the most notorious examples of persuasive definition in Thucydides history comes from the speech of Brasidas to the people of Acanthus in 424 in which he tells them that he may have to liberate them against their will (Th. 4.87.4). When the Athenians drew up the charter of their league in 378, they spelled out what they meant by freedom (lines 19–20): (1) cities could conduct their affairs according to the constitution of their choice (lines 20–21); (2) not be forced to accept a garrison or official (that is, from Athens) (lines 21–23); and (3) not pay tribute (line 23). Those who concluded the treaty with the Athenians would regain possession of land held by Athenians in public or private ownership (lines 25–31). In the future, it would be illegal for any Athenian, either publicly or privately, to purchase or receive as security any land or building in the territory of the allies (lines 35–44). Freedom is thus not an empty slogan in this charter. The Aristotle who proposed the decree was not the philosopher, yet he still knew that he had to start with an axiomatic definition of the potentially ambiguous term 'freedom.'

Some definitions of key terms can be very precise. The laws about inheritance allowed *gnesioi* children to inherit property and denied this right to those who were *nothoi*. According to Hyperides (*Ath.* 16), the law did not leave the term *gnesioi* without clarification but defined it as 'those who are born from betrothed women.' The decree about first-fruits for Eleusis gives a clear definition of the key term 'first-fruit': 'the Athenians are to offer first-fruits . . . for barley not less than one-sixth of a *medimnos* per one hundred *medimnoi*, for wheat one-twelfth per one hundred *medimnoi*'

94. For discussion of this offense see 217–22.

(*IG* i³ 78, lines 4–7). The law of Agyrrhius about two taxes on grain defines the term *meris* ('share') as 'five hundred *medimnoi*, one hundred of wheat, four hundred of barley' (*SEG* 47:96, lines 8–10) and the term *symmoria* as a group of six men who are responsible for a share of 3,000 *medimnoi* (*SEG* 47:96, lines 31–33). The law about slander prohibited the use of certain forbidden terms (*aporrheta*) and appears to have given a list of these terms: murderer (Lys. 10.6: *androphonos*); father-beater and mother-beater (Lys. 10. 8: *patroloias* and *metroloias*); and throwing away one's shield (Lys. 10.9).[95] A defendant on a charge of slander appears to have based his defense on the fact that he did not use any of the specific terms listed in the statute (Lys. 10.6).

Athenian laws could also spell out in great detail the specific duties of officials. The decree of Callias establishing the Treasurers of the Other Gods (*IG* i³ 52, lines 15–32), dated to the late fifth century, goes far beyond merely saying that the treasurers are responsible for administering the funds of the other gods and carefully defines their duties:

> Those selected are to serve as treasurers on the Acropolis in the Opisthodomos [administering] the funds of the gods capably and piously, and they are to share the opening and closing and sealing of the entrances of the Opisthodomos with the Treasurers of Athena. [As they receive the treasures] from the present treasurers and the superintendents and the Hieropoioi in the temples, who now have charge of them, they shall count them and weigh them in front of the Council on the Akropolis, and then the treasurers selected by lot shall take them over from the current officials and shall record on one stele the whole of the treasure, both according to the individual gods, how much belongs to each of them, and the entire sum, with silver and [gold] separately. In future, records shall be inscribed by successive Treasurers on a stele. They shall draw up accounts [showing] the balance of monies [they receive], and the revenue of the gods and whatever is spent throughout the year, [and shall submit them] to the *Logistai*, and the Treasurers shall submit to the scrutiny [at the expiration of their term of office]. From the [Great] Panathenaia to [Great] Panathenaia they shall draw up their accounts, in the same way as Athena's Treasurers. The *stelai* on

95. For discussion of the law see Todd (2007) 631–35.

which they shall inscribe the treasures of the gods shall be set up on the Akropolis by the Treasurers. When repayment has been made to the gods of the money, [the Athenians] shall apply what remains of the money to the dockyards and the walls. (Trans. adapted from Fornara)

It is hard to find any 'linguistic obscurity' in these rules. The method of election, the type of financial records, and the term of office are set forth with considerable precision. The decree even specifies who can open and close the doors of the Opisthodomos.

On the other hand, many of the laws and decrees examined in this chapter do not define procedural terms. The decree of Cleonymus does not define the term 'bring a public charge' (*IG* ^{3} 68, line 49). The law of Nicophon on coinage does not define the terms 'show' (*phainein*) or 'bring an impeachment' (*eisangelleto*) (*SEG* 26:72, lines 18, 32). The law about public speakers does not define the term *dokimasia* (Aeschin. 1.28–32). The law about *hybris* does not define the term *graphe* (Aeschin. 1.15; D. 21.46). If one is going to argue that the failure of a law to define a key term betrays a lack of interest in a topic, one would have to argue by the same token that the lack of definitions for procedural terms shows that Athenian laws reveal little interest in procedural issues. No legal system can provide exhaustive definitions of legal terms, and the attempt to do so is often counterproductive, if not ridiculous. For instance, Ordinance 75—1994, codified as Article 711 of the Codified Ordinances of the city of Erie, Pennsylvania, in the United States provides a definition of the term 'buttocks' that runs to 328 words. If the Athenians had tried to provide similar definitions for all key terms in their statutes, they would have had to use every stone in Attica to publish their laws for public display.

Even though Athenian statutes often do not provide definitions of key terms, they do in some cases reveal an attempt to clarify the meaning of key substantive terms to avoid potential ambiguities.[96] The Athenians aimed to make their laws clear and easy to understand for everyone. This way the average citizen would not be at a disadvantage when up against a speaker who had more experience than he did (D. 20.93). This was obviously an ideal that the Athenians could never attain. But the ideal did have an influence on the way they formulated their statutes and inspired them

96. On the problems posed by the 'open texture' of law see chapters 5 and 6.

in many cases to spell out in some detail the precise meaning of important substantive terms.

V

Athenian Laws and Everyday Behavior

We have now seen that Athenian laws were NOT primarily concerned with procedure; the aim of an Athenian statute was not merely to get a dispute between two people into court. The laws do more than lay down procedural rules governing conduct in court. Athenian laws provide substantive norms for citizens to follow in daily life. In fact, Athenian laws about procedure were far fewer and much simpler than the rules for procedure in Roman law of the Later Republic or Early Empire. Athenian law contained nothing similar to the complex rules of the formulary system (Gaius *Institutes* 4.32–68), to the difference between the *vindicatio* and the *condictio* (Gaius *Institutes* 4.1–5), and to possessory interdicts (Gaius *Institutes* 4.143–55).

The Athenians considered the courts to be the guardians of the law (D. 24.36; Din. 3.16), and this meant that their purpose was to punish those who violated substantive norms. The litigants therefore believed that the strict enforcement of the law would influence life outside the courtroom. Aeschines (1.192) predicts that the conviction of Timarchus will lead to an improvement in public morality.[97] When Demosthenes charged Meidias with *hybris*, he told the judges that the punishment of the defendant would bring benefits for all of them. It would teach others to act with more restraint and thus make the lives of the judges and everyone else more secure (D. 21.227. Cf. Antiphon 2.3.11). In a speech written to be delivered against the politician Androtion, the prosecutor says: 'You should impose a penalty today for all his crimes and provide an example for others so they will show greater restraint' (D. 22.68. Cf. Isoc. 20.18). A prosecutor who accuses Timocrates of proposing an inexpedient law

97. Rubinstein (2007) confuses this kind of argument with an argument from precedent, but this kind of argument fulfils a different function. Precedents are used to show that a court has decided to interpret a statute in a certain way as a way of persuading another court to adopt the same interpretation or to show that a certain way of interpreting the law is the standard view. Aeschines on the other hand is encouraging the court to enforce the law so that it will have its deterrent force on potential offenders. Precedents, on the other hand, have an influence on other courts. Rubinstein (2007) 362, note 5 gives examples of this kind of argument.

tells the court: 'For these crimes, if you act wisely, men of Athens, he will be punished and receive the punishment he deserves so that he becomes an example to deter others from enacting such laws' (D. 21.101). Litigants in two commercial cases claim that their victory in court will bring tangible economic benefits to everyone in Attica. If the court enforces the law and orders defaulting borrowers to pay, this will increase business in the *emporion* and result in more trade, more goods, and lower prices (D. 34.50–52; 56.48). In a case involving military discipline, a supporting speaker, or *synegoros*, says that if the court convicts the defendant, the Athenian army will gain respect from its allies and enemies (Lys. 14.14). An accuser who charged that Nicomachus had stolen public funds warns the judges: 'The people who would like to steal public funds are paying close attention to the outcome of Nicomachus' trial. If you acquit him, men of the court, you will render them immune from punishment. If, on the other hand, you find him guilty and give him the harshest sentence, by that verdict alone you will punish the defendant and make others more honest' (Lys. 30.24). Apollodorus urges the court to condemn Neaera so that others will be more careful and respect the gods and the city ([D.] 59.77). At the end of his speech in a case of assault, Ariston says that if the court acquits Conon there will be more violent crime; if it convicts, there will be less (D. 54.43).

The Athenian courts did not give ad hoc judgments or consider only the status of the two litigants when judging a trial.[98] Because the laws of Athens contained many substantive rules designed to shape the conduct of citizens and others resident in Attica, the Athenians believed that the strict enforcement of the laws would influence the way people behaved in daily life.[99] As J. Raz has observed, 'This is the basic intuition from which the doctrine of the rule of law derives: the law must be capable of guiding the behavior of its subjects.'[100] The Athenians certainly believed that their laws met this criterion.

98. *Pace* Lanni (2006).

99. The evidence presented in this essay decisively refutes the assertion of Osborne (2000) 85–6: 'the concern of law (sc. at Athens) being primarily the regulation of relations between citizens, rather than the control of human conduct.' Cf. Osborne (1985b) passim. Gagarin (1986) argues that early Greek law was more concerned with procedure than with substance. David Lewis and I plan to challenge this view in a forthcoming essay.

100. Raz (1977) 198.

5

Open Texture in Athenian Law

THE APPROACH OF THE LITIGANTS

AFTER PHILIP II defeated the coalition of Greek states at Chaeronea in 338 BCE, there was panic in Athens. Everyone in Athens thought that Philip would invade Attica within a matter of days. The Assembly passed several emergency measures: women and children were to be brought in from the countryside and placed inside the city walls; the generals were to assign citizens and metics to guard duty.[1] Hyperides went so far to propose that all slaves in Attica be set free to fight alongside the citizens of Athens. During this time an Athenian citizen named Leocrates left the city and sailed away to Rhodes. After leaving Rhodes, he decided not to return to Athens and took up residence in Megara where he lived as a metic for six years and worked as a merchant in the grain trade (Lycurg. *Leocr.* 21–27, 58).

In 331 Leocrates left Megara and returned to Athens. Shortly after his return, the politician Lycurgus charged him with treason (*prodosia*), using the special procedure of *eisangelia* (Lycurg. *Leocr.* 5). Even though Leocrates had had no contact with the enemy, Lycurgus accused him of betraying his country to Philip because he left Athens in a time of military crisis. When others were reporting for duty, Leocrates ran away. At his trial Leocrates and his supporters denied that his voyage to Rhodes was an act of treason: he had not been summoned for duty, and his intent in sailing to Rhodes was to engage in trade, not to help the enemy (55). Lycurgus replied that his desertion was a serious threat to public safety: had everyone else behaved like Leocrates, Attica would now be a wasteland (66).

The disagreement between Lycurgus and Leocrates about whether a voyage to Rhodes during an emergency was an act of treason provides a good illustration of law's open texture. In his *The Concept of Law* H. L. A. Hart observes that the law must refer to broad classes of persons or classes

1. On these measures see Engels (2008) 99–114.

of acts, things, or circumstances. The operation of the law therefore depends on the 'capacity to recognize particular acts, things and circumstances as instances of the general classification which the law makes.'[2] In most cases, this is not a difficult process. From time to time, however, one encounters 'fact-situations . . . which possess only some of the features of the plain cases but others which they lack.'[3] For instance, in the case of Leocrates, Lycurgus argues that his voyage to Rhodes was an act of treason because he left his country when it was threatened by the enemy and did not try to defend it. Leocrates, on the other hand, denies that it was an act of treason because he lacked the intent to help the enemy and because his actions did not cause any direct harm for Athens.

One might try to avoid this problem by formulating detailed definitions of key terms that would clarify how they were to be applied in any given situation. In the last chapter, we saw that in certain cases Athenian laws did attempt to define key terms or to specify detailed categories. For instance, the decree of Patrocleides did not leave the term 'disenfranchised' undefined but listed the specific categories included under this general term (And. 1.73–76). The law about *kakourgoi* (wrongdoers) specified three categories of offenders who could be accused under this law.[4] Yet, as Hart rightly notes, it is impossible to find a rule 'so detailed that the question whether it applied or not to a particular case was always settled in advance and never involved, at the point of actual application, a fresh choice between open alternatives.'[5] The legislator simply cannot know in advance all the different kinds of situations that will occur in the future ('ignorance of fact'). Or one might attempt to eliminate the problem by formulating canons of interpretation. As Hart observes, however, this approach would lead to similar problems because such canons would likewise be general rules, which one would also have to apply to particular cases of interpretation.[6] In hard cases, where it is not clear how to apply

2. Hart (1961) 121.

3. Hart (1961) 123.

4. See Harris (2006a) 291–93.

5. Hart (1961) 125.

6. Hart (1961) 123. R. Dworkin appears to be more optimistic about such an approach. In addition to written statutes, Dworkin believes there are rules of interpretation implicit in the law, which can help to determine which of two interpretations is the better one. For Dworkin's 'interpretative concepts' see Dworkin (1986) 45–86. For a criticism of this approach see Posner (1990) 21–26, 197–203.

the general rule to a specific situation, Hart believes 'all that the person called upon to answer can do is to consider (as does one who makes use of a precedent) whether the present case resembles the plain case "sufficiently" in "relevant" respects.'[7]

One extreme approach to the issue of the open texture of the law is formalism, which 'seeks to disguise and to minimize the need for such choice once the general rule has been laid down.' In this 'heaven of concepts' a rule has the same meaning in all situations. The other extreme is an approach that regards all rules as 'perennially open or revisable.' Hart criticizes this approach because it pays 'too little respect to such limits as legislative language, despite its open texture, does after all provide.' In his opinion, most legal systems tend to compromise between two needs: first, there is the need for clear rules that everyone can apply to his or her conduct, and second, the recognition that there will arise disputes about the law that only an individual can resolve.[8]

Hart's analysis of open texture is perceptive, but his main observation is not entirely original. The view that the law must provide general rules goes back to Plato and Aristotle. In the *Statesman* (295a) Plato compares legislators to trainers who 'cannot do their work in detail and issue special commands adapted to the condition of each member of the group. When they lay down rules for physical welfare, they find it necessary to give bulk instructions having regard to the general benefit of the average pupil.' In a similar way, the legislator 'who has to give orders to whole communities of human beings in matters of justice and mutual contractual obligation will never be able in the laws he prescribes for the whole group to give every individual his due with absolute accuracy.' Instead the legislator will make 'the law for the generality of his subjects under average circumstances. Thus he will legislate for all individual citizens, but it will be by what may be called a "bulk" method rather than an individual treatment.'[9]

Aristotle (*Politics* 1292a33) also notes that the laws should deal with all general matters, but that magistrates would deal with particular circumstances (*kath' hekasta*). This was necessary 'because of the difficulty of making a general rule to cover all cases' (*Politics* 1282b2). In particular, Aristotle (*Ath. Pol.* 9.2) noted that the laws of Athens were often unclear,

7. Hart (1961) 123.

8. Hart (1961) 126–7.

9. Cf. Theophrastus in *Digest* 1.3.3. 'Laws should be drawn up, as Theophrastus said, for the most common situations, not for the exceptional.'

leaving the power of decision for any given case in the hands of the court. Some argued that the lawgiver Solon did this deliberately to unfetter the judges' power of the judges to decide cases. But Aristotle rightly dismisses this view and argues that the alleged lack of clarity results from the difficulty of 'defining (*perilabein*) what is best (*to beltiston*) in general terms (*katholou*).'[10]

Aware of the open texture of law, Aristotle (*Rhetoric* 1373b–74a) realizes that one of the crucial tasks facing a litigant was to define clearly the nature of the wrongdoing his case involved:

> Since people often admit having done an action and yet do not admit to the specific terms of the indictment. Or the crime with which it deals—for example, they confess to having 'taken' something but not to have 'stolen' it or to have struck the first blow but not to have committed *hybris* or to have stolen something but not to have committed 'sacrilege' ([claiming] what they took from a temple did not belong to the god) or to have trespassed but not on state property or to have had conversations with the enemy but not to have committed treason—for this reason [in speaking, we] should give definitions of these things: What is theft? What is *hybris* (outrage)? What is *moicheia* (seduction)? In so doing, if we wish to show that some legal term applies or does not, we will be able to make clear what is a just verdict.

Despite Aristotle's discussion of the importance of definitions in forensic oratory, recent scholars have paid little attention to the issue of open texture in Athenian law.[11] Scholars who take a formalist approach find little scope for an analysis of open texture in Athenian law.[12] These scholars argue that Athenian litigants based their cases on the actual wording of the laws and do not appeal to general principles of equity. Meinecke points

---

10. Cf. Rhodes (1981) 162: 'There is no need to suppose that Solon was intentionally ambiguous (on this point A. P. is eminently sensible): the accusation probably arose in the late fifth century, when the Athenians' addiction to litigation was notorious, and experience had shown that there were difficult cases not adequately covered by Solon's laws.' Cf. Arist. *Ath. Pol.* 35.2 (the Thirty abolished laws giving rise to disputes about their application).

11. Osborne (1985b) uses the term 'open texture' but confuses it with procedural flexibility. Ober (1989) 144–5, who appears not to have read Hart, repeats Osborne's mistake. I pointed this out in Harris (1994b) 149, and my criticism was endorsed by Carey (2004) 112, 132 note 2.

12. Wolff (1963) 87ff.; Meyer-Laurin (1965); Meinecke (1971). Cf. E. Wolf (1956) 167, 343ff., 361ff.

to Demosthenes' list of requirements for the correct kind of law, which includes the need to be 'written in terms that are simple and easy for all to understand, not in a way so that it is possible for one man to think says this, another that' (D. 24.68).[13] He might have also pointed to statements made by Aeschines (3.199) and Lycurgus (*Leocr.* 9), both of whom compare the law to a ruler, which one can use to measure a person's conduct with almost scientific precision and accurately determine whether it is just or unjust. Since the laws provided clear guidance, all that the accuser had to do was to demonstrate that the action of the defendant fits the offense specified in the relevant law.[14] The duty of the court was to enforce the commands found in the laws. As we saw in chapter 3, the oath sworn by the men who sat on the courts bound them to vote 'in accordance with the laws and decrees of the Athenian people.'[15]

This view has much to recommend it, but it tends to underestimate the amount of open texture contained in Athenian laws.[16] Demosthenes' requirements for the right kind of law are the description of an ideal; there is no need to assume that the actual laws of Athens always lived up to this ideal. Indeed, Aristotle in the *Constitution of the Athenians* (9.2) noted that the laws of Solon were often not simply nor clearly written, a situation that gave rise to many disputes, which the court had to decide. Wolff and others point out that the Athenian legal system, unlike the Roman legal system, contained no experts who could develop the law through interpretation of statutes. This is not completely accurate since it ignores the role of the

13. Meinecke (1971) 354–5.

14. See Meinecke (1971) 280: 'Der Redner bemühte sich vielmehr, der archaisch-steifen Denkweise der Athenischen Dikasten entsprechend, den Tatbestand derart darzustellen, daß er lückenlos under das seiner Partei genehme Gesetz zu subsumieren war, sodaß die Richter mit ihrem Gewissen vereinbaren konnten, die seinem Mandanten nich genehmen Gesetze für unanwendbar zu halten.' Cf. Wolff (1968) 18–19.

15. Meyer-Laurin (1965) 36. Johnstone (1999) 22 with note 4, misrepresents my position by implying it is virtually similar to that of Meyer-Laurin. He pays no attention to my remarks about open texture in Harris (1994a) 137–40. Though I find much of Meyer-Laurin's analysis of individual cases persuasive, I reject his general conclusions in Harris (2004a).

16. Hillgruber (1988) 105–20 briefly discusses the nature of legal interpretation in Athenian law. Hillgruber makes valuable points but does not discuss the open texture of law. As a result, he comes close to regarding most interpretations of law in the orators as misinterpretations (e.g., on p. 116: 'Die Gesetzinterpretationen der Redner haben ihren Ursprung in der Sophistik, sie sind ein Teil der sophistischen Bemühungen, *τὸν ἥττον λόγον κρείττω ποιεῖν*'). He also underestimates the potential ambiguity of Athenian statutes and the possibility that arguments about the law may stem from honest disagreements about the meaning of various laws.

exegetai and the expertise of the Areopagus.[17] Yet, even if it were, that would not mean that litigants did not have to deal with the problem of interpreting potentially ambiguous or vaguely worded statutes. In Aristophanes' *Clouds* (1178–1200), Pheidippides, who has just returned from Socrates' Thinkery, shows his father how the law about bringing a summons on the last day of the month can be interpreted in two ways. The argument presented by Pheidippides is meant as a joke, but it reveals that Aristophanes and his audience were familiar with the open texture of law and knew that statutes might be ambiguously worded and could be interpreted in different ways.[18] And Aristotle would not have advised potential litigants to pay careful attention to the definition of key terms if the meaning of all terms in every statute was always clear and unambiguous. By the same token, the inevitable presence of open texture in many statutes meant that the courts had sometimes to decide between litigants, who were basing their cases on different interpretations of the same statute.[19]

Those who have criticized the formalist approach of Wolff and Meyer-Laurin often point to the absence of definitions for key terms in Athenian statutes.[20] If the Athenians were really interested in substantive issues, they would have surely have provided definitions. As a result, litigants might arbitrarily adopt any definition of an offense they wished, and the courts might follow one interpretation of the law on one day, another on the next day.[21] There are several general objections one can bring against this approach to the Athenian legal system. As we saw in the last chapter, it is not true that Athenian laws in general do not provide definitions of offenses. We found that many statutes attempt to define key terms or provide very specific rules for officials to follow. True, there are some important statutes that do not

17. For consultation of the *exegetai* for their legal expertise, see Plato *Euthyphro* 4c8; D. 47.68–70. The Athenian legal system differed from the Roman not only because the former contained no experts while the latter did, but also because the Athenian system contained nothing like *ius respondendi*, which made the views of the *iuris prudentes* a source of law. See Harris (1991). For the *ius respondendi* see *Digest* 1.2.2.48–9 and for the *responsa* of the *iuris prudentes* after the time of Augusuts as a source of law see Gaius *Inst.* 1.7 with Crook (1967) 26 with references to the debate about these passages.

18. Cf. Hillgruber (1988) 115–16.

19. Meinecke (1971) 280 appears to think that a litigant who did not have the law on his side would try to distract the court with irrelevant matters. He does not consider the possibility that two litigants could propose different interpretations of the same law.

20. For example, Todd (1993) 65–67.

21. This is the main argument of Lanni (2006).

provide definitions such as the law on *hybris* (outrage) or the law on impiety (*asebeia*),[22] but this cannot be used as evidence that the Athenian legal system in general did not take an interest in substantive matters or that the courts did not consider substantive issues when deciding disputes.[23] For instance, the American Constitution states that Congress can impeach the president if he commits 'high crimes and misdemeanors,' but does not define these terms nor even give examples of what actions might fit this description. Yet no one would argue that when the Senate voted whether to impeach President Clinton, it did not consider whether his misconduct with Monica Lewinsky fit the description 'high crimes and misdemeanors.' Nor do the laws of the United States provide a definition of the term 'executive privilege.' Once again, no one would argue that the Supreme Court did not consider the substantive issue of whether President Nixon had a right to refuse to hand over tapes relating to the Watergate scandal on the grounds of 'executive privilege.' And many of the judge-made rules in the law of the United States contain general and elastic terms like 'good faith,' 'reasonable,' and 'relevant.' Likewise in Athens, we will find that even in cases where the law does provide a definition or other explanation, the litigants sometimes base their case on interpretation of statute.[24] When they argue for an interpretation of the law, they pay careful attention to the wording of the law. Furthermore, they assume that the wording of the statute provides guidance as to how the court should decide the case. As Hart says, 'legislative language, despite its open texture, does after all provide' some limits to judicial interpretation.

In this chapter, I examine several speeches where there is a dispute about the meaning of the law and study how litigants approached the issues posed by the open texture of the law. How closely did they adhere to the precise language of the statute? To what extent did they attempt to take advantage of the law's open texture?[25] Before we approach the evidence,

22. For the law on *hybris* see D. 21.46.

23. On the problem of definitions in modern law, see Katz (1987) 88–96.

24. One might object by pointing out that the American courts often use precedents to determine the meaning of a statute whereas Athenian courts did not. Even though Athenian law did not have a doctrine of binding precedent, litigants in court often appeal to precedents when presenting interpretations of the law. See chapter 7.

25. My approach is close to that of Biscardi (1999) 90: 'Pour ma part, je me propose de démontrer que peut-être la vérité se trouve à mi-chemin.' Cf. Hillgruber (1988) 119: 'Die Athener sind offentsichlich bei der Lösung juristischer Probleme sehr flexibel gewesen, da sie sich an kein juristisches Prinzip der Billigkeit—insofern die Hauptthese von Meyer-Laurin zutreffend—noch an ein starres Gesetzprinzip.'

however, there is an important point to bear in mind. Athenian legal procedure involved basically three stages. The first stage was the summons, where the accuser invited the defendant to appear before a magistrate on a given day.[26] When they met together, the magistrate appointed a day for the *anakrisis*, or preliminary hearing. At the hearing, the magistrate took the names, patronymics, and residences of each litigant and heard the main charge and the evidence (see chapter 3). The magistrate had the right to reject the case at this point or to insist that the accuser modify his plaint to fit the terms of the statute under which it was brought (e.g., Lys. 10.10; 13.86; Is. 10.2).[27] If the magistrate accepted the case, he assigned it to a court for trial or, if it was a private suit, to an arbitrator (*diaitetes*). The trial was thus the third stage in the procedure. During the *anakrisis*, the defendant also had the right to bring a *paragraphe*, that is, a motion to dismiss the case on the grounds it was not admissible.[28] We do not know if the magistrate had the right to accept or reject a *paragraphe*, but this motion led to a trial where the defendant spoke first and argued that the case was not admissible, while the accuser argued that it was. If the court voted for the defendant, that was the end of the matter. We do not know what happened if the court voted for the accuser; either he won his case or the case went forward. This means that there were two stages in the procedure where the interpretation of statute might come into play. The first was at the *anakrisis*, where the magistrate had to decide whether he should accept the charge. At this stage the defendant also had to decide whether he would bring a *paragraphe*. The second was at the trial where the litigants appealed to the court. Even though we have very little evidence for what happened at the *anakrisis* (we have no speeches that were delivered at the *anakrisis*), we can get an idea of what kinds of cases magistrates were willing to accept because the cases that went to court must have passed the basic test of admissibility.

I

Athenian law contained three basic categories of homicide (Arist. *Ath. Pol.* 57.3): *phonos ek pronoias*, which was tried at the Areopagus, *phonos akousios* (involuntary homicide) tried at the Palladion, and *phonos dikaios* or *kata*

26. On the summons see Harrison (1971) 85–94.

27. On the *anakrisis* see Harrison (1971) 94–105.

28. On the *paragraphe* see Harrison (1971) 106–24.

tous nomous (just homicide or homicide in accordance with the laws) at the Delphinion. The Palladion also tried cases of *bouleusis phonou* (plotting homicide), which was roughly equivalent to attempted homicide.[29] The range of offenses covered by the first kind of homicide has been the subject of disagreement among scholars. Several writers translate the term *ek pronoias* as 'premeditated homicide' or 'with malice aforethought,' while others translate it as 'intentional homicide.'[30] The best way to resolve this debate over the meaning of the term is to examine the passages in Greek prose where the phrase occurs and find which meaning fits best in each context. What one should not do is to assume that the Athenian category is equivalent to a category in a modern law code or determine the meaning of *ek pronoias* on the basis of a superficial linguistic similarity.[31]

The word *pronoia* is found in over 150 passages in the surviving literature of the fifth and fourth centuries BCE. The word is normally used in the sense of foresight, that is, the ability to see the future consequences of present actions. For instance, Thucydides (2.65.6) speaks of Pericles' ability to foresee what would happen during the war with Sparta. To take another example, when he was struck by Meidias, Demosthenes (21.76) says that he used so much *pronoia* about causing irreparable damage that he did not strike back. Here the noun does not refer to any planning or prior intent on Demosthenes' part, since he had no way of knowing that Meidias would strike him in the theater at the Dionysia. He acted with *pronoia* because he considered the potential future consequences of a violent reaction. His *pronoia* concerned the irreparable damage that might have occurred as a result of striking back. The word *pronoia* is thus unlike the noun *boule*, which refers to a plan formed in the past, that is, before one acts. When one acts with *pronoia*, by contrast, one looks into the future and considers the consequences of one's actions. Thus when writers say that a person 'has *pronoia*' or 'had *pronoia*,' this person acted in a way that

29. On attempted homicide in Athenian law see Harris (2006a) 400–404.

30. Carawan (1998) 235–8 translates the term 'with malice aforethought'; Stroud (1968) and Wallace (1989) 125 translate the term as 'premeditated homicide,' while MacDowell (1963) translates it as 'intentional homicide.' None of these authors provide a philological analysis of the term *ek pronoias*.

31. For instance, Loomis (1972) assumes that *phonos ek pronoias* is premeditated homicide, but then after a study of several passages about trials for murder discovers that this translation does not fit the context. He would have done better to begin without making any assumption about the meaning of the term. On the essay of Pepe (2009/10) see the criticisms in Pelloso (2012).

showed he was aware of the possible results of his actions. When Aristocrates drew up his decree for Charidemus, he had *pronoia* that it would remain in force and not be repealed or changed in the future (D. 23.62).[32] An action done with *pronoia* is not planned in advance and contrasted with a spontaneous action; on the contrary, it is an action done on purpose as opposed to one that happens 'by chance' and with contemplation of future consequences (Antiphon 5.6, Xen. *HG* 7.5.8; Hdt. 3.121).

The expression *ek pronoias* is relatively rare. It is found in fewer than twenty passages, only a handful of which indicate the circumstances of the action in enough detail to help determine its meaning. Perhaps the most helpful passage comes from the story of Artemisia at the battle of Salamis told by Herodotus (8.87.2–3). During the battle Artemisia's ship was being pursued by an Athenian trireme and was unable to get away since its path of escape was blocked by a friendly ship. Instead of stopping or attempting to change course, Artemisia rammed the friendly ship. Xerxes, who was observing the battle from afar, thought she rammed a Greek ship and praised her for her valor. Herodotus adds that is uncertain whether Artemisia did hit the other trireme *ek pronoias* or happened to collide 'by chance.' The contrast is between an action undertaken on purpose and one that is a product of happenstance, not between planned and unplanned action. There can be no question of premeditation since Artemisia found herself in an unexpected predicament and acted on the spur of the moment.

Another passage in Herodotus (1.159) points in the same direction. Aristodicus had received Pactyes as a suppliant when he had fled from the Persians. When the Persians demanded his surrender, Aristodicus went to Branchidai to consult the god there about what to do. To his astonishment, the god instructed him to surrender Pactyes. Aristodicus then went around the temple removing all the swallows and other birds nesting there. At this point the god indignantly asked why he was removing his suppliants. Aristodicus replied by pointing out the god's hypocrisy: how could the god object to Pactyes removing suppliants when he commanded Aristodicus to surrender Pactyes? Once more *ek pronoias* must mean 'on purpose.' The act of removing the birds is not planned ahead of time; Aristodicus clearly did not expect to receive the initial response from the god and undertook his action after he received an unexpected response to

32. Compare D. 20.88 where we find the phrase 'we have *pronoia*' followed by a *hopos* clause containing verbs in the future tense.

his inquiry. Note that an action taken *ek pronoias* looks forward to another action taken in the future. The removal of the birds is done for the purpose of eliciting the god's objection so he can point out his hypocrisy.[33]

In a passage from Aeschines (3.178) there is a different kind of contrast, this time between *ek pronoias* and *ex ethous*—'from custom' or 'by habit.' Aeschines is discussing how Athenians in the past were sparing about conferring honors; they thought that a reputation for virtue in and of itself used to be considered sufficient. In the degenerate present, however, the Athenians confer honors 'as a matter of habit, but not deliberately.' An action done with thought is contrasted with one done without thinking about the consequences.

This examination of passages where the term is used shows that *phonos ek pronoias* must be 'intentional homicide' or 'homicide committed on purpose.'[34] Yet the question then arises, 'what kind of intention?' Did the accuser have to prove that the defendant intended to kill his victim or merely that the action which brought about the death of the victim was intentional? The decisions reported in two actual cases seem to point in different directions. Aristotle (*Magna Moralia* 1188b30–37) reports: 'They say that a woman gave a potion to someone to drink, and then the man died from the potion, and the woman was put at trial at the Areopagus. When she appeared there, they acquitted her for no other reason than because [she did] not [do it] intentionally. For she gave it out of love but she failed to achieve her goal. For this reason it did not seem to be willing since she gave it as a potion and not with the intention that the man die.' The significant point about the decision of the Areopagus is that these judges appear to have interpreted the term *phonos ek pronoias* to mean 'with the intention that the victim die' as a result of the defendant's action.[35] In other words, the Areopagus required the accuser to show that the

33. The expression is used in a similar way at Aristophanes *Eq.* 848–57. In this passage the sausage-seller accuses the Paphlagonian slave—a thinly disguised Cleon—of plotting against the Athenian people. He draws attention to the shields captured at Pylos which Cleon had given as a dedication. The sausage-seller observes that the handles were left on the shields when they were dedicated and triumphantly declares that this was done *ek pronoias*—on purpose. If Cleon is ever ostracized, the sausage-seller says, Cleon's cronies will arm themselves with these shields and stage a coup d'état to prevent his banishment. The act of leaving the handles on the shields is done with a purpose—looking forward to a future action—enabling Cleon's cronies to start a revolution.

34. Cf. Pelloso (2012).

35. Note that Aristotle glosses the phrase *ek pronoias* with the word *dianoia* with a future infinitive.

defendant intended not just to harm, but to kill the victim. In this case, the defendant (or the person who spoke for her) convinced the court that her intention was to make the victim fall in love (or stay in love) with her and not to kill him. Though one might have argued that giving a love potion was an attempt to harm, the Areopagus found her innocent since she did not intend to kill her victim.

Another case points in a different direction. In his speech *Against Meidias*, Demosthenes (21.71–76) recounts the murder of a man named Boeotus by an acquaintance called Euaeon.[36] Both men were at a party attended by several friends, when Boeotus became drunk and hit Euaeon in an insulting way. Euaeon felt humiliated and immediately struck back with such violence that he killed Boeotus. The case must have come before the Areopagus because the relatives of the victim could charge with Euaeon causing death by a deliberate blow. Besides, the case does not fit any of the categories listed under the rubric 'just homicide' or 'homicide according to the laws,' which were tried elsewhere.[37] Demosthenes (21.75) says that the court voted narrowly to convict Euaeon and infers the reason for their decision. In his opinion, the majority who voted against Euaeon considered that he had struck back in such a way as to cause the death of his victim. The court decided to convict him even though it was clear that he was only attempting to retaliate for the humiliation he had suffered. The court did not expect the accuser to prove that Euaeon intended to kill his victim. It was enough for him to show only that Euaeon wanted to hurt Boeotus, which was beyond question. Euaeon had struck back intentionally, and his deliberate action had caused death: that was enough to merit conviction.

Needless to say, an accuser or a defendant would choose the interpretation of the term *phonos ek pronoias* that tended to favor his case. An accuser might have a hard time proving that a defendant actually intended to kill his victim. Even if the defendant used a weapon, it might be difficult to determine whether he meant to kill or merely to wound. By contrast, it would be much easier to demonstrate that the defendant wanted to harm the victim. All one would have to show was that the defendant had hostile

---

36. MacDowell (1990) 292–3 believes the trial involved a case of self-defense and was tried at the Delphinion, but Demosthenes' narrative does not indicate that Euaeon had to use deadly force to avoid serious physical harm. In fact, he says Euaeon could have restrained himself and won the approval of those present. For an analysis of the case see Harris (1992). 78. My analysis of the word has been endorsed by Pelloso (2012) 215.

37. For these categories see MacDowell (1963) 70–81.

intent and was acting in a way that was likely to cause harm. The defendant, however, would naturally want to make his opponent's task as difficult as possible and would ask the court to require that the accuser show that he aimed to kill the victim, not just harm him.[38]

The author of the *Tetralogies* attributed to Antiphon was aware of the potential ambiguity and realized that an accuser and a defendant might adopt different interpretations of the term.[39] The *Third Tetralogy* deals with a case of *phonos ek pronoias* that is roughly similar to the murder of Boeotus by Euaeon. Just as in the case described by Demosthenes, both the victim and the defendant were attending a party. The victim got drunk and struck the defendant in an insulting way. The defendant retaliated by striking back, but hit the victim so hard that he caused serious injury. Here the case in the *Third Tetralogy* differs from the case recounted by Demosthenes: the victim did not die immediately but several days later after receiving treatment from a doctor (Antiphon 4.2.4). The *Tetralogy* follows Athenian procedure in giving two speeches to the accuser and two to the defendant, but in this case the defendant voluntarily went into exile after the first pair of speeches and allowed a relative to make the second speech for him (Antiphon 4.4.1. Cf. Antiphon 5.13; D. 23.69).

In his first speech, the accuser states that the defendant became drunk and hit and choked the victim until he died (Antiphon 4.1.6). In reply, the defendant draws attention to extenuating circumstances and presents several arguments to deny his guilt (Antiphon 4.2). In his second speech to the court, the accuser notes that the defendant admits that he struck the victim with blows that caused his death (Antiphon 4.3.2) and finds it paradoxical that he claims that he has not murdered the victim. His phrasing is significant: he implies that all that it is necessary to prove is that the defendant struck deliberately and that his blows caused death. Later in his

38. Note how the defendant in a case of *trauma ek pronoias* claims that his accuser must prove not that he intended to wound but actually intended to kill (Lys. 3.41). The defendant claims that this is the way previous courts have interpreted the law and argues that otherwise those involved in brawls would be sent into exile (Lys. 3.42–3). His opponent apparently relied on the fact that he was carrying a potsherd, which indicated his intention to wound (Lys. 3.28), and may have argued that all he needed to do was to show that the defendant intended to wound. Cf. Phillips (2007).

39. On the authorship of the *Tetralogies*, see Gagarin (1997) 8–9 with references to earlier opinions. The question of authorship does not affect my argument here. Gagarin (1997) 160–73 contains no analysis of the legal issue about the meaning of *ek pronoias* in this case and mistakenly believes that it is a case of self-defense. Wohl (2010) 145–54 repeats this mistake, which undermines her analysis of Antiphon's *Third Tetralogy*.

speech he makes this point explicit: 'if our hands accomplish for each of us what we intend . . . the man who struck with deadly force was responsible for the death. For the man died from actions which that man did intentionally' (Antiphon 4.3.4). In his opinion, he does not have to prove the defendant intended to kill; it is sufficient for him to show that the act which caused death was intentional (*dianoetheis*).

The relative of the defendant who took up his case after he left for exile followed a different interpretation of the term. He admits that 'if the man who struck the first blow intended to strike and not to kill, while the man who struck back intended to kill, the latter would have been the one who aimed to cause death' (Antiphon 4.4.4). In other words, if the accuser can prove that the defendant intended to kill, then he is guilty of *phonos ek pronoias*. But this is not the case: 'now, as it is, the man who struck back failed to achieve his aim when intending to strike and not to kill.'[40] This defense is similar to the one used to secure the acquittal of the woman tried at the Areopagus for poisoning: just as she claimed to give the potion for love, not intending that the victim die, the speaker in the *Third Tetralogy* asserts that his relative struck with the intent only to hit the victim, not to kill him. In each case, therefore, the defendant was not guilty since there was no intent to kill. The speaker concludes that the defendant was only the person responsible for the blow (Antiphon 4.4.5). The speaker then goes a step further and claims that because the defendant was responding to a provocation, he was acting against his will (*akousios*) and cannot be held responsible for the results of his action. He stresses again that his motive was to avenge an injury (Antiphon 4.4.5). The death was the result of a mistake, namely, his failure to achieve his aim of merely striking a blow, an error that occurred when he was acting under compulsion.[41] In the next section, the speaker shifts his ground slightly but sticks to his point that the defendant did not intend to kill (Antiphon 4.4.6). Here he claims the defendant was seeking to avoid harm and to thrust the victim away. Instead of trying to kill, the defendant merely wished to escape from the assailant.

40. Here and elsewhere Gagarin in Gagarin and MacDowell (1998) 46 translates the participle *amunomenos* 'defending himself' or 'in self-defense' but the verb does not imply the agent is defending himself but is striking back in retaliation. See for instance Th. 1.96.1 where the ostensible aim of the Delian League is 'to retaliate for what the cities suffered by ravaging the King's land.' Here the Greeks are not defending themselves but going on the offensive to avenge the damage done by the Persians.

41. Compare the defense offered for the woman who gave the love potion.

In the statutes about homicide in his *Laws* (865a–874e), Plato attempted to remove these ambiguities. To deal with cases of provocation such as the one in the *Third Tetralogy*, Plato adds two categories of homicide not found in Athenian law (*Laws* 866d–867e). First, there is the case where someone acts in anger and retaliates immediately without planning ahead to kill, then feels repentance. Second, there is the man who is insulted and becomes angry, then later kills with the intent to kill and feels no remorse. The latter resembles the person who kills willingly, while the former is like the person who kills unwillingly. Plato therefore imposes a harsher penalty on the latter and a milder one on the former. If a man kills a free person with his own hand, in anger, and without prior planning, he will go into exile for two years. On the other hand, if a man kills in anger and kills 'after planning'—that is, planning to kill—he will go into exile for three years.[42] Thus Plato distinguishes between a case where the defendant kills without intending to and a case where the defendant aims to kill and achieves his aim. Because the latter is a more serious offense, it receives a harsher penalty.

The law of homicide provides a good example of the open texture of Athenian law. The expression *ek pronoias* in the Athenian category of *phonos ek pronoias* contained an ambiguity, which made it possible to interpret the law in two ways. The *Third Tetralogy* shows how an accuser and a defendant might interpret the phrase in different ways, each one suited to the needs of his case.[43] This ambiguity and the potential problems it might cause did not go unremarked: in the *Laws* Plato created two additional categories of homicide and specified the nature of the intent required in each category as a way of removing the ambiguity and solving the problem.

II

The law about the procedure of *eisangelia* dealt with major offenses against public security and made several types of offenders subject to its provisions.[44] One clause of the law covered those who tried to overthrow the

42. In his discussion of *phonos ek pronoias* Plato (*Laws* 869e–870d) does not mention the problem of the killer's intention. By listing the possible motives for this category of homicide, however, he helps to clarify the ambiguity about the term.

43. The Sophists may have played a role in the analysis of law's open texture. Note how in Aristophanes' *Clouds* (1185–1200) Pheidippides, who receives a sophistic education, claims to find an ambiguity in the laws about delivering a summons and exploits it to help his father's case.

44. For the terms of the law on *eisangelia* see Hansen (1975) 12–20.

Athenian people or who held a meeting or formed a group for that purpose (Hyp. *Eux.* 7–8). Another clause applied to those who betrayed a city, or ships, or an army, or fleet (Hyp. *Eux.* 8). The law also made it possible to prosecute the person who 'says things as a public speaker (*rhetor*) not in the best interests of the Athenian people and takes money for doing so.' This clause did not apply to all citizens but only to the 'public speaker.' The law does not define the term 'public speaker,' but the Athenians in the fourth century made a general distinction between 'public speakers' (*rhetores*) and 'private citizens' (*idiotai*). In general, private citizens were those who were not active in politics.[45] *Rhetores* were obviously included those who regularly spoke in the Council and Assembly and proposed decrees. But how much public speaking did one need to do to qualify as a public speaker? Was one speech in the Council or Assembly enough to make one a public speaker? Or did one have to propose a decree? And was passing one decree enough to earn one the title of public speaker?

A thorough study of the term *rhetor* concludes that the term *rhetor* had both a narrow and a broad sense.[46] In a more narrow sense '*rhetor* denotes a citizen who moves a *psephisma* in the *ecclesia* or in the *boule* or a *nomos* before the *nomothetai* or brings a public action before the *dikasteria*. In a wider sense a *rhetor* is a speaker addressing the *ecclesia* or the *boule* (either supporting or opposing a *psephisma* moved by another *rhetor*) or a *synegoros* addressing the court (either for the prosecution or the defense).' In fact, the law regulating the examination of public speakers (*dokimasia rhetoron*) allows for prosecution in the case where 'someone speaks in the Assembly' (Aeschin. 1.28). This would appear to cover anyone who makes a speech in the Assembly, not just those who propose decrees—*rhetores* in both senses.

The meaning of the term *rhetor* may seem like a trivial point, a matter of quibbling over words, but it became a matter of life or death when Polyeuctus prosecuted Euxenippus by *eisangelia* sometime between 330 and 324.[47] The main facts of the case were not in dispute. After Philip of Macedon restored the territory of Oropus to the Athenians, the land was divided into five parcels and distributed to pairs of Attic tribes (Hyp. *Eux.* 16).[48] There then arose a dispute about a hill given to the tribes Acamantis

45. On the *idiotes* see Rubinstein (1998).

46. Hansen (1983) 39–40.

47. For the date of the speech see Whitehead (2000) 155–57.

48. This took place either in 338 or in 335. See Whitehead (2000) 207.

and Hippothontis. Before the division, fifty border commissioners had marked out the hill as the property of the god Amphiaraos (Hyp. *Eux.* 16). To resolve the dispute, the Assembly instructed Euxenippus and two other men to pass the night in the temple of Amphiaraos. That night Euxenippus fell asleep and had a dream, which he reported to the Assembly (Hyp. *Eux.* 14). Hyperides does not say what Euxenippus told the Assembly; all he says is that Polyeuctus proposed a motion to restore the land to Amphiaraos (Hyp. *Eux.* 16) and that the remaining eight tribes make payments to Acamantis and Hippothontis by way of compensation for their loss (Hyp. *Eux.* 17).[49] An unknown accuser prosecuted Polyeuctus for proposing an illegal motion and won a conviction.[50] Polyeuctus had to pay a small fine, then brought his case against Euxenippus (Hyp. *Eux.* 18).

When he drew up his indictment, Polyeuctus followed the language of the statute about *eisangelia*: he accused Euxenippus of 'speaking against the best interests of the people of Athens while taking money and gifts from men who were acting against the people of Athens' (Hyp. *Eux.* 39). By using the procedure of *eisangelia*, Polyeuctus had in effect placed Euxenippus in the category of *rhetores* (Hyp. *Eux.* 30). Despite Hyperides' protests, this was not unjustified since someone who had spoken in the Assembly was on the broad interpretation of the term *rhetor* subject to *eisangelia*. But Hyperides insists that the law does not apply to Euxenippus. He observes that the law only applies to those who are *rhetores*, then adopts the narrower definition of this term as those who propose decrees (Hyp. *Eux.* 8). On this definition, Euxenippus is not a *rhetor*, but a private citizen (*idiotes*), a point which Hyperides repeats several times. Polyeuctus should not prosecute private citizens (Hyp. *Eux.* 27); Hyperides himself has prosecuted only generals and public speakers (Hyp. *Eux.* 28). Although Euxenippus is a private citizen, Hyperides argues that Polyeuctus treats him as if he were a public speaker (Hyp. *Eux.* 30). If Euxenippus had made a false report about the god's wishes and did not propose a decree, *eisangelia* was the wrong procedure to use against him: one should have instead sent to Delphi to find out what the god really thought (Hyp. *Eux.* 15).

It has been observed that the trial of Euxenippus illustrates the 'clash between . . . two uses of the term rhetor.' In the broad sense, *rhetor* 'occurs in *nomoi* and signifies any citizen who addresses his fellow citizens in the

49. For the various possible relationships between Euxenippus' report and the proposal of Polyeuctus see Whitehead (2000) 201–3.

50. There is no need to think that Euxenippus was the accuser. See Whitehead (2000) 202.

assemblies.' But 'in the much narrower sense' the term *rhetor* is 'a citizen who addresses his fellow-citizens habitually, sometimes even professionally' and is distinguished from 'the citizen who only once or at intervals performs the part of *ho boulomenos* is described as an *idiotes*.'[51] Hyperides (*Eux.* 3, 9–10, 30) claims that the prosecutor had drawn up an illegal indictment, but Hyperides' charge is plausible only if we accept his definition of the term *rhetor*. What is more likely is that Polyeuctus followed the broader interpretation of the term, one that was implicit in the law about the scrutiny of public speakers. Here again we find a law that contains a potentially ambiguous term, which can be interpreted in at least two ways. Not surprisingly, opposing litigants might base their arguments on varying definitions of the same term. When composing his speech, Hyperides clearly paid careful attention to the substantive provisions about the law on *eisangelia*. Despite Hyperides' allegations, it is likely that his opponent did the same.

III

The next case to be examined concerns the law of succession. In Athens there were three main laws about inheritance. The first was that if there are *gnesioi* sons or daughters, the estate goes to these as 'universal successors,' or *kleronomoi*, and there is no need for a will (Is. 6.28; 8.34). The *gnesioi* are the offspring of a formal marriage, which is concluded by an agreement called an *engye* or solemn pledge between the husband and the bride's father or guardian. This kind of marriage often included a dowry given to the husband, but a dowry was not legally required for the marriage to take effect.[52] This kind of union was contrasted with one with a *pallake* (concubine), where there was no solemn pledge. The offspring of this kind of marriage were classified as *nothoi* (often translated as bastards, but this is misleading), who have no right to inherit, though they could receive gifts out of the inheritance.[53] Second, if there are no *gnesioi* children, the estate goes to the nearest relative in a fixed order but not including *nothoi* (Is. 11.2). Third, the testator can draw up a will to adopt a

51. Hansen (1983) 48. Hansen thinks however that the clash occurs as a result of a 'gap between the constitution and the way it works.' I would view the debate between the competing definitions as another example of open texture in Athenian law.

52. See Biscardi (1999) 1–22.

53. On *nothoi* at Athens see Vérilhac and Vial (1998) 53–60.

son in the event he has no *gnesioi* sons. This person can then take the will to a magistrate and lay claim to the estate. This step was not necessary for *gnesioi* sons, who could simply take over their father's assets upon his death without applying to the courts.[54]

The inheritance case I want to examine concerns the estate of Cleonymus (Isaeus 1). Although we have only the speech given by the plaintiff, there appears to have been general agreement about the basic facts of the case. The plaintiff and his brother were orphans and placed under the guardianship of their uncle Deinias (9). For some reason or other, Cleonymus was angry with Deinias and did not want his property to fall into his hands. Cleonymus therefore drew up a will that gave his estate to other relatives and deposited the will in the public archive. The speaker is rather vague about several details, but Cleonymus must have had no *gnesioi* children and may have used his will to adopt posthumously some relative to serve as his *kleronomos*, a relative who would not have inherited under the normal rules of succession. After Deinias died, Cleonymus brought the plaintiff and his brother into his house, raised them at his own expense, and saved them from their creditors (12). Shortly before his own death, Cleonymus wished to alter his will and told a man named Poseidippus to summon the *astynomos*, a magistrate in charge of the archive. When Poseidippus failed to follow his instructions, Cleonymus repeated his request, but died before the magistrate could arrive. The plaintiff provides witnesses for the quarrel between Cleonymus and Deinias and to prove that Cleonymus asked Poseidippus to summon the magistrate. There was naturally some dispute about Cleonymus' aim in asking the magistrate to come. The plaintiff argues that he intended to annul his will, while the defendants claim he merely wanted to confirm the existing provisions. Despite their disagreement here, the plaintiff does not dispute the existence, authenticity, or contents of the will. The plaintiff asks the court to declare the will invalid and to award the estate to him and his brother according to the law that grants control of the estate to the nearest relative when there are no *gnesioi* sons or daughters.

One scholar harshly criticized the speaker's arguments: 'All the skill of a practical advocate cannot disguise the weakness of their case. No attempt is made to dispute the meaning or authenticity of the instrument.'[55]

54. On adoption in general see Rubinstein (1993) and Ghiggia (1999). Rubinstein does not believe it was necessary for the testator to adopt a son in order to make him his *kleronomos*.

55. Wyse (1904) 177.

He believed the clear intent of Cleonymus was to leave his property to the speaker's adversaries—he made a will, deposited it with the city's magistrates, and did not alter the will for a long time. During his last illness he sent for the will, but the speaker cannot prove that Cleonymus' intent was to annul the will. Opponents present the plausible argument that his aim was to straighten out details, not to revoke it. This scholar thinks that the speaker relies on two arguments: first, that he and his brother are the closest relatives and, second, that 'Cleonymus had a greater affection for them than for their adversaries.' Both arguments ignore the right of the testator to adopt a son and make him the *kleronomos* of his estate.

This misrepresents the speaker's argument. There are two parts to the speaker's case: first, the law grants the estate of the deceased to the nearest relative, and, second, Cleonymus' will is invalid. The first argument is designed to establish the speaker's claim, the second to refute their adversaries' claim. Both claims are based on the law—the first is on the law of succession, which ranks the claims of relatives in the event there are no *gnesioi* children. The second claim is also based on the law—the law that granted the testator the right to make a will also contained a clause that declared such a will invalid if the testator was either sick, deranged, under the influence of drugs, obeying a woman, senile, locked up in prison, or under some duress.[56] Like many Athenian statutes, the legislator does not use one broad term, then provide a general definition. Instead, he gives a number of specific categories. The problem with this approach is that it is often not clear whether the categories listed are intended to be exhaustive. Are they merely examples given to illustrate the general category of acts to which the law applies, or are they a complete list of the kinds of acts subject to the law? If the latter, we must assume that any acts that do not fall into one of these specific categories are outside the law's provision. Some litigants take the former approach and claim that the law declared invalid those who were not in their right mind. For instance, a client of Demosthenes (46.16) states that the law that a man does not have the right to give away his property even when he does not have children, if he is not in his right mind (*me eu phronei*). A client of Isaeus (6.9) says there is a law common for all that permits a man to dispose of his property: first, if he

---

56. For the law see Hyp. *Ath.* 17 with Whitehead (2000) 313; D. 48.56; Is. 6.9. Cf. Meyer-Laurin (1965) 20–22 with references to earlier literature. Note also Rubinstein (1993) 76 ('alluding to the clause in the Solonic law on wills which required that the testator be of sound mind when making his dispositions').

has no male *gnesioi* children; second, if he does not make the will when insane (*maneis*) or senile or not in his right mind (*paranoon*); and, third, for any of the other reasons found in the law.

The plaintiff also uses the law about invalid wills in his alternative argument (18–21). He asks the court to consider the possibility that his adversaries are right in claiming that Cleonymus actually intended to confirm his will. If their version of events is correct, he argues that they are accusing Cleonymus of the greatest insanity (19: *paranoian . . . megisten*). What greater madness (*mania*), he continues, could there be than to make a will that deprived his nephews, for whom he had shown great affection, of any share in his property (20)? What man in his right mind (*eu phronon*) could have acted this way (20. Cf. 21: *paraphronon*)? Note how closely the plaintiff keeps to the wording of the law while at the same time expanding the meaning of madness (*mania*) to cover any senseless act. Further on in the speech he tries to show Cleonymus had fallen out with the plaintiff's opponents (30–33) and repeats his charge that they are accusing the deceased of madness (34: *manian kategorousi*) by claiming in his will that he set those whom he detested ahead of those with who he enjoyed good relations.

In another part of his speech, the plaintiff bases himself on the broad interpretation of the law (41–43). He reminds the court how judges often decide in favor of the closest relatives against those who make their claim on the basis of a will. But he does not pretend that they do this on the grounds of equity, an unwritten principle that the nearest relative ought to inherit.[57] The reasons why they vote this way are, first, that wills are often forged and, second, that testators do not make correct decisions. This is a rather generous interpretation of the law, one that stretches the meaning of *mania* beyond its normal limits or attempts to formulate a general standard on the basis of the specific situations listed in the law. What the litigant does not do is ask the court to rule against the letter of the law. Nor does he appeal to general grounds of equity that take precedence over the law. He asks the court to reject a will that was not just and proceeds to remind the judges that Cleonymus was not in his right mind, but angry and not making correct decisions when he drew it up. The court should therefore not confirm what he did in anger rather than his true intention. At the end of the speech (50), he emphasizes that even if the judges accept the defendants' version of events, they will pronounce Cleonymus out of

57. Cf. Meyer-Laurin (1965) 21: 'Dann hätte das Argument schon darum nichts mit Billigkeit zu tun.'

his mind (*paranoian*); if they accept his version, it is clear that Cleonymus deliberated well (*orthos bebouleusthai*) when he wished to annul his will.

We do not know the outcome of the trial, but we can safely assume that the magistrate who accepted the case found the litigant's claim legally admissible. Even though the plaintiff relies on a very broad interpretation of the word *mania* (madness), the magistrates did not see fit to reject the case for that reason. Furthermore, his opponents did not think they had grounds for bringing a *paragraphe* against the charge. When it came to deciding whether to accept cases, therefore, magistrates were willing to let an accuser bring a case that relied on a remarkably broad interpretation of statute.

IV

Athenian law granted the right of inheritance to relatives according to a strict order.[58] First came descendants with legitimate sons and their children, followed by daughters and their children (Is. 7.20). Next came collaterals, with brothers and their children (that is, nephews and nieces of the deceased) taking precedence over sisters and their children. The most remote degree that the law recognized was 'the sons of cousins' (Is. 11.1–2; D. 43.51), but there was some dispute about the meaning of this term. As we will see, it could mean second cousins, that is, those related through a common great-grandfather, or cousins once removed, that is, the children of first cousins (those related through a common grandfather).

When Theopompus made a claim for the estate of Hagnias, he followed the first interpretation of the statute.[59] The great-grandfather of Hagnias (whom I will call Hagnias II) was Bouselos. Bouselos had four sons, Hagnias I, Eubulides I, Stratius I and Habron. Hagnias I had a son, Polemon, and a daughter, Phylomache I. Eubulides I had two sons, Callistratus and Philagrus, who was married to Phylomache I. Stratius I had two sons, Phanostratus and Charidemus. Charidemus had two sons, Stratocles and Theopompus. Habron had two sons and a daughter, who was married to Theopompus. Hagnias II was the son of Polemon and the grandson of Hagnias I. Because Polemon, the father of Hagnias II, and Charidemus, the father of Theopompus, were cousins, Hagnias II and

58. For the law of succession see Harrison (1968) 13–49.

59. For a defense of this interpretation of the statute see Miles (1950) and Thompson (1976) 4–6.

Theopompus were sons of cousins, that is, second cousins. This is exactly the way Theopompus makes his claim. He starts by citing the law: if there are no sons, brothers, or nephews on the father's side, or sisters and their children on the father's side, the law 'gives the right of inheritance to the third degree, that is, the cousins on the father's side including their children' (Is. 11.2). He then states that he falls within the third degree: 'Hagnias, Eubulides, Stratocles, Stratius, the brother of Hagnias' mother, and I, gentlemen, are all the children of cousins, our fathers having been cousins, the children of brothers by the same father' (Is. 11.8).

After the death of Theopompus, his son Makartetus had the right to inherit his property (D. 43.26). At this point Sositheus claimed Hagnias' estate on behalf of his son Eubulides III, a descendant of Hagnias' aunt, Phylomache. Phylomache had a son Eubulides II, who had a daughter, also named Phylomache. Phylomache married Sositheus, and they had a son Eubulides III, who was later adopted by his grandfather Eubulides II (D. 43.14–15, 81). Because Euboulides II was the cousin of Hagnias II, the adoption made Eubulides III the son of the cousin of Hagnias II. On this basis his father Sositheus argued that the estate should belong to Eubulides III: 'this boy here belongs to one of the categories mentioned in the law, and up to which the law permits that the right of inheritance should extend because he is the child of the first cousin of Hagnias because his father Eubulides was the cousin of Hagnias, to whom the estate belongs' (D. 43.27). Sositheus clearly interprets the law to include only first cousins once removed. For this reason he denies that Theopompus had a right to the estate 'because he belonged to another branch of the family,' that is, he was the descendant of Stratius, not Hagnias I (D. 43.27–8. Cf. 52, 60–1, 65). Eubulides II, the adoptive father of Eubulides III, and Hagnias shared a common grandfather Hagnias I. Theopompus, on the other hand, did not share a common grandfather with Hagnias II and therefore lay outside the categories contained in the law. Sositheus thereby clearly rejects Theopompus' interpretation of the term 'children of cousins.'

Both Theopompus and Sositheus based their cases on the actual wording of the statute. Before beginning his speech Theopompus has the laws about inheritance read out and bases his claim on its actual wording (Is. 11.1–3). Sositheus also has the law read out and claims that it supports his case (D. 43.50, 52).[60] Neither speaker appeals to considerations of fairness or asks

60. Cf. Meinecke (1971) 295: 'Die Analyse ergibt jedenfalls, daß der Redner bemüht war, seinen Sachverhalt genauestens unter den Wortlaut des Gesetzes zu subsumieren.'

the court to ignore the law.[61] Each litigant, however, interprets the key term 'children of cousins' in a different way.[62] Unfortunately we do not know how the court voted in response to Sositheus' claim for Eubulides.[63]

V

Our next example comes from the law of contract. Although the Athenians developed rudimentary local and regional markets in many commodities and carried on an extensive overseas trade, they came nowhere near to developing anything that resembled the range and complexity of the regulations for sale formulated during the Classical period of Roman law.[64] Athenian law appears to have contained a few simple provisions—the courts promised to enforce agreements willingly entered into by the parties, distinguished among various forms of contracts, and appeared to understand the basic differences between various contracts.[65] In agreements concerning sale, the Athenians held that the seller had a duty to warrant title (*bebaioun*).[66] There was also a law about the sale of slaves that provided a warranty against latent defects (Hyp. *Ath.* 15) and a law against fraud in the marketplace (Hyp. *Ath.* 14). Finally, there were provisions designed to ensure the accuracy of weights and measures (e.g., *IG* ii^2 1013—see 31–32). In short, nothing very elaborate, just a few simple provisions designed to meet the needs of a small and simple market economy.[67]

---

61. *Pace* Thompson (1976) 64: 'Sositheus shows his determination to make the issue one of morality and not one of law.'

62. Cf. MacDowell (1978) 107: 'The truth is that "as far as cousins" is an ambiguous phrase. The fact that Theopompos and Sositheos could propound different interpretations, each with some hope of convincing a jury that his interpretation was right, indicates that its meaning was obscure to the Athenians as to us, and each interpretation had some plausibility.' Cf. Todd (2008) 58.

63. *Pace* Broadbent (1968) 62 and Thompson (1976) 106–7, I see no reason to believe that the inscription from Oropos about the ephebes of Leontis in the year 324/3 containing the name Hagnias, son of Makartetus of Oion proves that Makartetus won the case.

64. The standard work on sale in Athenian law remains Pringsheim (1950).

65. For an implicit awareness of the different incidents of leases and loans see Harris (2006a) 228–31. The Athenians use the general terms for security *apotiman, apotimema* to apply to security deposit in lease, but not language of sale, whereas in loans, they use both kinds of terms.

66. On warranty of sale see Pringsheim (1950) 472–97.

67. On market regulations in general see Stanley (1976).

The case to be analyzed is the dispute between Epicrates and Athenogenes known from a speech of Hyperides preserved in a fragmentary papyrus. The beginning and the end of the speech are missing, and there are gaps in the rest of the papyrus,[68] but most of the narration and the legal arguments presented by Epicrates remain. The preserved portion of the narrative reveals that Epicrates had fallen in love with a young boy, who worked in a perfume shop with his father Midas and his brother, all of whom were slaves owned by Athenogenes, who was a metic. Epicrates wanted to contribute money to purchase the freedom of the three slaves (Hyp. *Ath.* 4). At first, it appears that Athenogenes quarreled with Epicrates and refused to go along, but thanks to the intervention of a former *hetaera* turned madam named Antigona the two men were reconciled (4–5).[69] Athenogenes then proposed that Epicrates buy the three slaves outright and liberate them himself. This way they would owe Epicrates gratitude for their freedom, not Athenogenes. He might have implied that if he were to liberate them, he would remain their *prostates*, and they would owe him their loyalty, not Epicrates. In the interests of full disclosure, Athenogenes warns Epicrates that this arrangement would make him liable for all the debts incurred by the slaves (6–7). This is in accord with the general principle in all slave societies that the debts and assets of the slave automatically become the debts and assets of the master.[70] Alternatively Epicrates was in effect buying the perfume shop, which included the slaves and the items in the shop.[71] This would have included any debts made on the security of the shop. Roman law had regulations limiting the liability of masters for their slaves' debts, but we know of no similar rules in Athenian law, a point that is relevant to this dispute.[72] To

68. For discussion of what is missing at the beginning see Whitehead (2000) 279.

69. On the name Antigona see Whitehead (2000) 283.

70. For this principle see D. 53.20.

71. At Hyp. *Ath.* 6 it is clear that Epicrates was buying all the items in the shop because Athenogenes says that these items exceeded the value of the debts. The phrase *ti allo katetheto tis epi to myropoleion* appears to imply that the debts were secured by the perfume shop and its contents. The translation of Whitehead (2000) 292 'any other routine sums deposited in the perfumery by its clientele' makes no sense. The translation of Burtt (1954) 435 'any other sums which customers have invested in the perfumery' is closer to the actual meaning. For the preposition *epi* with the meaning 'on the security of' see for example D. 37.4; [D.] 56.6. For discussion of the issue whether the debts accompanied the slaves or the perfume shop see Maffi (2008) and Talamanca (2008).

72. For the peculium of slaves in Roman law see Buckland (1908) 187–238.

reassure Epicrates, Athenogenes claimed the property of the slaves in the shop was enough to cover the various debts. Epicrates says he bought the slaves and formally agreed to accept their debts on the assumption they were small but claims he was distracted when the written agreement was read to him (Hyp. *Ath.* 8). The written agreement was then deposited with Lysicles of Leuconoe, Epicrates paid the agreed sum, and the sale took place (we would say the property was conveyed) (Hyp. *Ath.* 8–9). Soon afterward, creditors began to appear and continued to come forward for three months until the debts claimed amounted to five talents (Hyp. *Ath.* 9). Epicrates grew alarmed and summoned friends and relatives to study the agreement. A close reading revealed the names of two creditors, Pancalus and Polycles, and next to their names small debts owed to them, which were covered by the value of the materials in the shop. There was also a clause—the ancient equivalent of fine print—that provided for payment of 'any debt that Midas owes to anyone.' There was also listed one *eranos* loan, for which three more payments remained (Hyp. *Ath.* 10–11).[73] When Epicrates confronted Athenogenes in public, the latter denied any knowledge of the other debts and claimed that the document for the agreement covered these debts (Hyp. *Ath.* 12). To prove his statements, Epicrates has the agreement read to the court, but does not provide witnesses who were present when Athenogenes stated the remaining debts were small and certainly less than the value of the assets in the perfume shop.[74]

When the case went to court, both parties based their claims on the law. Athenogenes cited the law that 'whatever agreements one man makes with another are binding' (Hyp. *Ath.* 13). Actually the complete version of the law included the word 'willing' but Epicrates omits this word and does not attempt to argue that he entered into the agreement against his will.[75] The reason for this is probably that he could not deny that he was under no duress when he agreed to the terms of the sale—Plato in the *Laws* 920d interprets this law to apply to cases where one of the parties is 'forced by unjust compulsion,' which suggests violence or the threat of violence,

73. These must be payments on the *eranos* loan, as Whitehead (2000) 301, following Lipsius (1905–15) 73, note 204, observes.

74. This is crucial for Epicrates' case, but is not noted by the commentators, e.g., Whitehead (2000) 304.

75. For the text of the law with the word 'willingly' see D. 56.2. For other passages containing the law see D. 42.2; [D.] 47.77.

which was not the case with Athenogenes and Epicrates. If this is correct, it would explain why he chooses to rely on another law that declares unjust contracts are not binding (13: *ta de me tounantion apagoreuei me kyria einai*).[76] It would therefore be wrong to assume that Epicrates asks the court to lay aside the law or appeals to considerations of equity that supersede the written law.

The question immediately arises, what is an unjust agreement? Here this specific law gave no answer. To determine the meaning of this phrase, Epicrates attempts to interpret the statute by examining other laws to discover general principles implicit in the law that can be used to determine the meaning of the statute. In other words, he seeks to discover the intent of the lawgiver in this one law from what he has written in other laws.[77] This approach might strike us as dubious; we would object that different laws are written by different legislators, each of whom may have had a different intent. But the Athenians believed that all their laws were the product of one legislator. In fact, Epicrates, like other Athenian litigants, speaks of 'the legislator' when he mentions the law about marriage (16), whom he later identifies as Solon (21). To discover the meaning of any one law, the litigant could therefore look to the other laws enacted by 'the' lawgiver. In fact, Aristotle in the *Constitution of the Athenians* (9.2) explicitly states that one ought to search for the meaning of a law not from what takes place now (*ek ton nun ginomenon*), that is, the way it may have been applied by present-day courts, but from

76. Whitehead (2000) 306, following Harrison (1971) 53, believes that the 'essence of the argument here is of course an appeal to the spirit, not the letter of the law in question.' But the passage makes clear that this phrase is from a law, albeit a different one. See Burtt (1954) 439: 'the law forbids that they be binding.' For these two different laws see Aristotle *Rh.*1375b9–11 (*οἷον ἐνίοτε ὁ μὲν κελεύει κύρια εἶναι ἅττ' ἂν συνθῶνται, ὁ δ' ἀπαγορεύει μὴ συντίθεσθαι παρὰ τὸν νόμον*), a passage overlooked by Harrison and Whitehead. This law is similar to the law about agreements among members of an association quoted at *Digest* 47.22.4: *ὅτι τούτων διαθῶνται πρὸς ἀλλήλους, κύριον εἶναι, ἐὰν μὴ ἀπαγορεύσῃ δημόσια γράμματα* (= Ruschenbusch [1966] F 76A). The authenticity of this law has been doubted by Arnaoutoglou (2003) 44–57 who dates this law to the Roman era, but see Ismard (2010) 44–57, who considers it Solonian. *Pace* Harrison and Whitehead, Epicrates relies on the precise wording of the law, and there is no appeal to the spirit of the law. See Meyer-Laurin (1965) 17 and Meinecke (1971) 349, note 17 ('keine Berufung zur Billigkeit'), both overlooked by Whitehead. The attempt of Phillips (2009) 93–97 to reconstruct the law about contracts is undermined by his failure to understand that litigants often quote only the parts of a statute that are relevant to their case. Just because one passage omits a certain phrase in a law does not mean that the phrase was not in the law. The arguments of Phillips are followed uncritically by Kästle (2012) 193–4, whose analysis of the speech is questionable.

77. After I wrote this, I discovered that Johnstone (1999) 27–30 makes a similar point.

the rest of his constitution (*ek tes alles politeias*), that is, from his other laws.[78]

To discover the meaning of the law about contracts, Epicrates turns first to a law that requires everyone to refrain from lies in the marketplace (14).[79] He then alleges that Athenogenes lied to him because he did not declare all the debts and list the names of the creditors. The problem with this argument is that the agreement made no statement about the total number and size of the debts. Athenogenes listed some debts, and the two parties agreed that Epicrates would be liable for any other debts Midas might have contracted. This means Athenogenes admitted the possibility other debts might exist without saying anything about them. Epicrates alleges that Athenogenes said the other debts were small and covered by the assets in the shop, but provides no witnesses to prove Athenogenes actually made such a statement. The statement certainly could not be found in the written agreement. Epicrates seems to stretch the meaning of 'refrain from falsehood' to cover the deliberate failure to provide relevant information. This would require Epicrates to prove that Athenogenes knew about the other debts. Epicrates appears to have been aware of this requirement since he later does address this very issue (Hyp. *Ath.* 19–20).

But the law about refraining from lies does not mention contracts nor the effect a lie would have on the validity of an agreement. To show that a falsehood would render an agreement null and void, he discusses two other laws (Hyp. *Ath.* 14–16). The first law Epicrates cites concerns the sale of slaves. This law required someone selling a slave to declare in advance any disease the slave might have. If he does not, the buyer has the right to return the slave and demand back his payment, in other words, cancel the transaction, the Athenian equivalent of *restitutio in integrum* in Roman law. Epicrates constructs an *a fortiori* argument from this law: if the law permits the buyer to cancel the sale if a slave has a disease, how is Athenogenes not liable for the injustices he plotted? Epicrates attempts to

78. Christ (1998a) 196 arbitrarily claims that when litigants appeal to the intent of the lawgiver, 'they are not engaging in a search into legislative history but attempting to show how their interpretations of laws are consistent with community norms' but provides no evidence to prove his point. Christ's view is undermined by the fact that litigants cite other laws to infer the intent of the lawgiver and never refer to informal norms of the community when making such arguments.

79. This law is also mentioned at D. 20.9 and at Harpocration s.v. *kata tên agoran apseudein*. The enforcement of this law appears to have fallen under the jurisdiction of the *agoranomoi*—see Arist. *Ath. Pol.* 51.1 with Rhodes (1981) 575–76.

argue by analogy from an existing statute: if the law cancels a sale where there is a hidden disease that occurs by chance, it should also declare invalid a transaction where the seller has deliberately plotted to defraud the buyer. In both cases, the item sold contains some hidden quality that renders it less valuable than it might appear. In the case of the slave, this quality comes about by chance, that is, through no action of the seller. *A fortiori*, when the hidden quality is the result of a deliberate action by the seller, the sale should also be cancelled. What Epicrates does is devise a general warranty against latent defects from the particular statute about the sale of slaves, then applies this general rule to argue for his view of what constitutes a just contract. In other words, to interpret the law about contracts, Epicrates looks for a principle inherent in another law and uses this to discover the meaning of the law about contracts.

The second law Epicrates brings forward to show that a falsehood invalidates a contract is the law about the status of children of a woman married by a solemn pledge (Hyp. *Ath.* 16). As noted earlier, the law states that the children of a woman who is married in this way are legitimate (*gnesioi*), those who are entitled to inherit their father's estate. Epicrates points out that if a man pledges a woman who he falsely claims is his daughter, the agreement is not valid. Epicrates does not develop his argument in detail, but once again implicitly argues by analogy. In the case of marriage, the man who gives away the bride to the husband cannot misrepresent her relationship to him. If she is not his daughter, he has no right to give her in marriage and the agreement is invalid. Epicrates seems to argue that Athenogenes has misrepresented the debts of his slaves, so the court should declare his contract invalid. Epicrates may be working toward the Roman idea that *error in substantia* cancels a contract of sale. Such an error occurred when the parties are agreed about the physical identity of the object sold but are mistaken about some essential characteristic.[80] But there was no such rule in Athenian law. As a result, Epicrates had to argue that this rule was implicit in the law about just contracts, find the rule in the law about solemn marriage to support his interpretation, and argue by analogy.

Epicrates next looks at the law about wills that we have already studied (see section III of this chapter). Epicrates notes the law declares invalid a will made under the influence of a woman and says that he made his agreement under the influence of Athenogenes' mistress Antigona (Hyp. *Ath.* 18). As he does with the other laws, Epicrates claims to find a general rule about

80. On *error in substantia* see Buckland (1963) 418–19.

contracts in a law about one type of agreement (wills) and applies it to another type of agreement (sale).[81] Given his assumption that the laws of Athens are the creation of a single lawgiver, this is a reasonable way to discover the meaning of a statute that contains a potentially ambiguous term.

After building his case, Epicrates anticipates the objection that Athenogenes may honestly not have known about the other debts. Epicrates handles this objection in two ways (19–22). First, he argues that it is unlikely that Athenogenes did not know about the debts since he was an experienced tradesman. His father and grandfather had been in this line of business, and he himself spent every day in the market, owned three shops, and received accounts every month. Second, he says that even if Athenogenes did not know about the debts, he would still be liable for any debts incurred while he owned the slaves (20–21). To support his point, Epicrates cites the law of Solon that made the master liable for the penalties and wrongs incurred by slaves.[82] The law appears to cover any damages committed by a slave whom the master has given to someone else to work on their property.[83] Epicrates says this is only just since the master also benefits from any profit the slave makes. The wording of the law indicates that it applies only to delicts, not contracts, but Epicrates talks as if the law covered debts as well. The problem with the argument is that Epicrates has explicitly agreed to assume the debts of the slaves he bought.

Epicrates concludes his legal arguments by citing another law that he attributes to Solon (Hyp. *Ath.* 22). This law stated that decrees of the Assembly do not take precedence over the laws. The Athenians made a distinction between statutes called *nomoi* that were passed by a cumbersome process known as *nomothesia* and measures called *psephismata* that were passed by the Assembly at one of its meetings. Solon's law granted priority to the former and made it possible to indict the proposer of an illegal decree on a charge called a *graphe paranomon*. If the proposer was convicted, the decree was rescinded. Epicrates argues that if laws are superior to decrees passed by the entire Assembly, *a fortiori* agreements concluded between two private individuals do not have greater validity than the laws.[84]

---

81. Whitehead (2000) 313 calls the law a 'quasi-precedent' but the concept of precedent, which refers to previous judgments made by the courts, does not apply here.

82. On the text see Whitehead (2000) 324 who prefers to read *ἀ[δική]ματα*.

83. This is similar to the law at Plato *Laws* 936c–d and a law of Gortyn (*IC* IV 72, col. vii, lines 10–15).

84. Cf. Whitehead (2000) 323.

It is unclear how this argument relates to the previous ones. Epicrates may have included it merely for rhetorical purposes to overcome the judges' natural reluctance to declare a fixed agreement invalid.

Epicrates' arguments are some of the most sophisticated attempts to exploit the open texture of Athenian law. His method of interpretation is eminently democratic; it assumes that the average citizen is capable of finding the meaning of a statute on his own with only the guidance of other statutes. In point of fact, the speech was written for him by a professional speechwriter, but to maintain democratic appearances, Epicrates claims he looked at all these laws by himself (Hyp. *Ath.* 13).[85] Although Epicrates may exploit the open texture of the law, he is no cynic: he does not draw attention to the potential ambiguity of the law, then boldly assert its wording can be stretched to cover any situation he wishes. He implicitly recognizes the need to justify his reading of the law by finding principles inherent in other statutes and using them to guide his interpretation of the law about just contracts. We do not have the reply Athenogenes made to his legal arguments, but Epicrates' speech indicates he expected him to base his defense on a straightforward reading of the law that enforced agreements willingly accepted. Unfortunately, we do not know how the court viewed their respective arguments or how it ruled on the case. Yet once again, it is clear that the magistrate who accepted the case did not find Epicrates' case without legal merit. And Athenogenes did not think he had grounds for bringing a *paragraphe*.

VI

In his *Laws* Plato attempts to provide a law code for the utopian city of Magnesia that is so comprehensive that it will contain no gaps (Plato *Laws* 820). He sets down rules for all aspects of life in the community: public administration, marriage, education, sports, sexual conduct, agriculture, murder and violence, religion, property, inheritance, and a host of other topics. Many of these laws are based on Athenian statutes, but Plato often changes the laws of his native city.[86] As in the case of murder examined in

85. Cf. Whitehead (2000) 307: 'Demosth. 54.17 is a comparable instance of an inexperienced plaintiff, who needs to account for his sudden jurisprudential expertise, being made to say this sort of thing by his *logographos*.'

86. For valuable studies of the relationship between the laws of Athens and the laws of Magnesia see Morrow (1960) and Piérart (2008). Neither of these scholars discuss Plato's attempt to reduce the open texture of Athenian statutes.

section I, he creates a more detailed set of rules with several additional categories to replace the simpler classification found in Athenian law. What is interesting for the topic of this chapter is that Plato implicitly recognizes that several Athenian statutes contained ambiguities and tries to reduce the amount of open texture in the statutes of Magnesia by providing more detailed definitions of key terms. Plato's view of the difference between his approach and the standard practice of legislation in his day is evident in a remark he makes when discussing rules about fraud in the marketplace. Plato (916d–e) criticizes *hoi polloi*, the majority of mankind, for believing that lying and deceit are acceptable as long as they are done *en kairo*—on the right occasion, or in the right circumstances—but leaving these circumstances undefined (*aoristos*). In his view, it is not permissible for the lawgiver to leave this matter undefined. On the contrary, he must clarify the upper and the lower limits. In other words, it is not enough for a lawgiver to lay down a general rule and then allow litigants and judges to decide what circumstances permit exceptional considerations to override the rule. The lawgiver must indicate precisely where the exceptions lie and what effect they will have on the application of the rule. When discussing penalties, Plato advises the lawgiver to give clear guidance to the judge (934c). In public cases, Athenian law gave the court the power to impose whatever fine or punishment the court deemed appropriate after listening to arguments made by both sides. But Plato says that the lawgiver should act like painter and give a sketch of the actions covered by the law and thus help the judge find the appropriate penalty for an offender.

One can see how the method works in the law of sale concerning latent defects. As we have just seen in the discussion of Hyperides' *Against Athenogenes* (15), the Athenians had a law about the sale of slaves, which required: 'When anyone sells a slave, he must state in advance any ailment the slave has; should he fail to do so, there is a procedure for return (*anagoge*).'[87] The law does not specify what kinds of illnesses nor envisage the possibility that the slave may have a disease that the master cannot discern. Nor is a time limit set down. The regulations formulated by Plato (*Laws* 916a–b) are much more detailed: he lays down different rules depending on whether the seller or the buyer are skilled workers such as doctors and trainers and thus should be able to recognize diseases. He imposes a time limit on the right of return, which makes sense since it would be unlikely that a disease noticed long after the purchase originated

87. On the *anagoge* procedure see Wyse (1904) 436–37.

before the purchase and was thus the fault of the seller. He also makes a separate rule for epilepsy, which of course might not show up as soon as other diseases. Finally, he creates a special rule for the slave who has committed murder and is thus polluted. We may find this an odd sort of defect, but since the Greeks believed that pollution could cause disease or misfortune, this provision makes good sense.[88] Instead of creating a general rule and leaving it to the courts to determine how to deal with unusual circumstances, Plato sets forth time limits and deals with exceptional cases.

Another area where Plato is more specific and detailed than Athenian law is in regard to impiety. As far as we can tell, the crime of impiety was not defined in Athenian law, though the Athenians obviously had some idea of what the term meant and what kinds of actions normally fell under the description 'impious.'[89] For instance, as we saw in chapter 3, when Meletus brought his charge of *asebeia* against Socrates, he listed three charges: (1) introducing new gods (Pl. *Ap.* 24b–c), (2) not believing in the gods (Pl. *Ap.* 27a), and (3) corrupting the young (Pl. *Ap.* 24c). In his reply to these charges, Socrates implicitly accepts Meletus' view that these actions did constitute *asebeia* because he does not challenge his accuser on this legal point, but he seeks rather to show that the charges are false on factual grounds. In the *Laws* (885b), Plato does not leave the concept undefined. Instead he lists three specific types of *asebeia*: (1) not believing in the existence of the gods, (2) believing that the gods exist, but do not pay attention to human beings, and (3) believing that the gods are easily influenced and led astray by sacrifices and prayers. Where Athenian law left the term undefined, Plato lists several specific categories of *asebeia* to clarify meaning of the term and remove potential ambiguities.[90]

Plato's most extensive reform of Athenian law is found in the rules about homicide.[91] In section I, we saw how there existed a potential ambiguity in

---

88. On pollution in homicide law see Harris (2010) 126–29. I plan to return to this topic in the future.

89. For some interesting comments on the notion of *asebeia* see Cohen (1991) 203–17. Cohen recognizes that the Athenians shared a basic understanding of the term even though the Athenian legal system did not provide a definition that judges could use to decide hard cases. For an attempt to find a legal definition of the term see Rudhardt (1960).

90. On the relationship between the common understanding of *asebeia* and Plato's conception see Cohen (1991) 216: 'Hasn't Plato just systematized the traditional notion of *asebeia* and fitted it into his larger political theoretical framework?'

91. The most detailed analysis of the treatment of homicide in the *Laws* is Saunders (1991a) 217–57. Cf. Saunders (1991b). Saunders is mostly interested in the penalties for the different types of homicide and not in the general classification and description of the offense.

the term *phonos ek pronoias* and how Plato created two new categories of homicide to deal with special circumstances involving provocation, which were hard to classify according to the rough and ready categories of Athenian law.

In regard to the second category of homicide, *phonos akousios*, or 'involuntary homicide,' there was an issue about the extent to which someone could be held responsible for a death caused by his own actions. In Athenian law, one could be held responsible for murder not only when one caused death by direct physical violence, but also for causing death indirectly, for instance, by giving an order to kill someone. But if one committed an action that set off a chain of events that resulted in the death of another person, to what extent could this person be held responsible? For instance, if someone was responsible for a choral competition and for training the boys for the performance, but then one of the boys died after drinking a potion given by someone else to improve his voice, could he be held responsible for involuntary homicide (*phonos akousios*)? One could argue that by placing the boy under the supervision of another person, who administered the potion, the chorus-producer had 'caused' his death and was guilty of murder. This is in fact the argument made by an accuser in an Athenian court (Antiphon 6.11–14).

Plato attempts to resolve this issue by limiting the extent to which someone could be held responsible for a death caused by his own actions but against his will. Plato does not allow a charge of unwilling homicide to be brought whenever someone's actions set off a chain of events that eventually leads to the death of another person. The law applies only when death comes about by the direct physical causality of the defendant (*Laws* 865b): 'And if one man kills another by his own hand, but unwillingly, whether it be by his own unarmed body, or by a tool or a weapon, or by giving a drink or solid food, or by application of heat or cold [lit. fire or winter], or by deprivation of air, either with his own body or through other bodies, in every case let him be considered to be one who has killed with his own and let him pay the following penalties.' In other words, the defendant's action cannot be a remote cause of death, but must be a proximate cause. Here again Plato is specifying the circumstances covered by the statute and attempting to remove potential ambiguities of the category of involuntary homicide in Athenian law.

Athenian law contained a general statute about cowardice, which provided a procedure and a penalty for several offenses relating to military discipline. We will take a closer look at this law in the next section; the only clause relevant here is the one concerning throwing away one's shield. The law about cowardice made this an offense punished with the loss of citizen rights but did not provide a definition of the term. In the *Laws* (943d–944c) Plato observes that one must distinguish between cases in which one is forced to abandon one's weapons and cases in which it is shameful to throw them away. He recalls the example of Patroclus, who lost his weapons to Hector, but was no coward (*Iliad* 16.791–817; 17.125; 18.78–85). One can also lose one's weapons when thrown from a height, in a storm at sea, when caught in a torrent, or in many other circumstances. One should therefore make a distinction between 'abandoning' one's shield (*rhipsaspis*) and 'losing' one's shield (*apoboleus hoplon*). When one loses one's shield because of circumstances beyond one's control, it is not the same as deliberately throwing it away (Plato *Laws* 944c). The person who deserves punishment is the one who 'finds the enemy at his heels and instead of turning round and striking back with the weapons he has, deliberately let them drop or throws them away, preferring a coward's life of shame to the glorious and blessed death of a hero' (trans. adapted from Saunders). Where Athenian law left the phrase 'throws away one's shield' undefined, Plato describes the specific circumstances that the judge must take into account when deciding cases, thereby reducing the open texture of the law.

VII

In the next chapter, we will look at more arguments in which litigants attempt to exploit the law's open texture, but we can draw a few tentative conclusions at this point. First, it should be clear that when addressing the court, litigants based their arguments on a close reading of the law. In chapter 3, we saw that the accuser had to follow the language of the law when drawing up his plaint and that Athenian judges had to decide only about the charges brought in the plaint. This meant that the accuser had to prove that the defendant had violated the law under which he brought his case and that the defendant had to prove that he had not broken the law. The arguments studied in this chapter demonstrate how the plaint compelled litigants to base their cases on a careful reading of the relevant law. A detailed analysis of several arguments also confirms the conclusions of chapter 4: when constructing their arguments, litigants pay more attention to the substantive aspect of the law than to the procedural. To this extent, the formalist approach of Wolff, Meyer-Laurin, and Meinecke is correct. We should not, therefore, draw the wrong conclusion from the absence of definitions in some Athenian statutes. In all the cases we have examined, the litigants pay careful attention to substantive issues and questions about the interpretation of law; they would only have done so if they thought that the substantive aspect of law was important for their cases.

Second, the task of applying the general rules contained in the laws was not always simple and straightforward. Even though the Athenians attempted to formulate their statutes in clear and unambiguous terms, they could not provide detailed definitions of all words in a statute and often used general terms, which might give rise to dispute in particular cases. On the other hand, one should not exaggerate the amount of open texture in Athenian law. As one can see in appendix 7, most of the cases in the speeches of the Attic Orators concern questions of fact, not questions of law. This means that in the majority of cases, both the accuser and the defendant implicitly agreed on the meaning of the key terms of the statute under which the case was brought and disputed only the facts. Yet, at the same time, one should not underestimate the amount of open texture in Athenian statutes. In this respect, the formalist approach does not do justice to the sophistication of Athenian speechwriters, who knew how to exploit the potential ambiguities in statutes to strengthen their clients' cases.

The findings of this chapter also shed an interesting light on the way the Athenian legal system worked in practice and how political institutions shaped the nature of litigation in Classical Athens. In chapter 3 we saw that magistrates did not accept a plaint submitted by an accuser unless it contained the key terms of the statute under which the case was initiated. From the cases examined in this chapter and the next, one can see that Athenian magistrates appear to have been willing to accept cases that relied on unusual interpretations of statutes that pressed against the edges of open texture. Or perhaps we should say they were afraid to reject cases as long as they met the minimum requirement that the charge employed the language of the statute on which it was based. This may have been because they knew they would have to submit to a process of review after they left office.[92] At this review a disgruntled litigant who had his case dismissed might lodge a charge against them for failure to do their duty. For this reason, the magistrates who received the accuser's plaint and presided at the *anakrisis* confined themselves mainly to procedural matters, such as taking

92. This point was made to me by Stephen Todd and Chris Carey. For the principle that all magistrates must undergo review see Aeschin. 3.17–22. For harsh punishments of officials who did not perform their duties see Isaeus 4.28.

the names of the litigants, ascertaining their status, and determining the nature of the dispute. This enabled them to fulfill their main task, namely, deciding which court would hear their case. For instance, if the charge were deliberate homicide, the case would go to the Areopagus, but if the victim were a foreigner, it would go to the Palladion (Arist. *Ath. Pol.* 57.3). If the plaintiff brought a private charge, the case would go before an arbitrator. The magistrate at the *anakrisis* did not evaluate the merits of the case as far as we can tell or deliver summary judgment if he thought the alleged facts did not meet the threshold criteria for conviction. This is in keeping with the Athenian reluctance to place major decisions in the hands of magistrates when it was possible to refer them to larger bodies, which were less susceptible to corruption. This practice went all the way back to Solon, who granted all Athenian citizens the right to have their cases judged by a court of their peers (Arist. *Ath.Pol.* 9.1), and who attempted to prevent the concentration of power in the hands of a single person.[93]

Perhaps the best evidence for what happened when an official received a charge and conducted the *anakrisis* is found in Aeschylus' *Eumenides*. When both the Erinyes and Orestes come before Athena, she first asks the accusers who they are (408), and the Erinyes give their name, their parent, their place of residence (416–17), and their status (419, 421). They then give the charge (425). Athena then asks if there were any mitigating circumstances (426), and the Erinyes deny there were (427). Here Athena attempts to determine what kind of homicide the defendant is charged with just as the *basileus* attempted to determine whether the accusation was deliberate homicide (*phonos ek pronoias*), involuntary homicide (*phonos akousios*), or just homicide (*phonos dikaios*) so he could assign the case to the right court (Arist. *Ath. Pol.* 57.2–3). The Erinyes ask her to demand Orestes swear an oath he did not do it, but she refuses to decide how to try the case until after hearing from the defendant (428–32). After getting all the information she needs from the accusers, she turns to the defendant and asks him for the same information (436–37) and for his version of the facts. Orestes prefaces his answer by assuring Athena he is not polluted (445–53), which is equivalent to saying he is innocent.[94] Orestes complies by giving his place of residence and his father's name (455–56), then presents his case (456–67), and asks her to judge it (468). Like the *basileus,* Athena does not presume to

93. On the aims of Solon and the early Greek lawgivers see Harris (2006a) 3–28.

94. For innocence and purity as equivalent see Hewitt (1910).

judge the dispute (470–72) or even require the Furies to make a prima facie case by asking for witnesses or other evidence. She simply takes the names of the plaintiff and defendant, hears the nature of the charge, and assigns the case to the appropriate court (480–90). This meant all the plaintiff or prosecutor had to do at the *anakrisis* was to select the charge and procedure he wished to follow and draw up his plaint in the correct terms. He did not have to make a prima facie case for conviction.

In a similar fashion, the defendant did not initiate a *paragraphe* because the plaintiff's case did not fit the substantive requirements of procedure he had chosen. The *paragraphe* was designed to deal with purely procedural matters like the status of the suit, whether it qualified as a maritime suit (D. 32, 33, 34, 35), whether the defendant was an Athenian citizen (Lys. 23), or whether the dispute had already been settled by a release (D. 36, 37, 38), or was brought after the stipulated period of time (D. 36).[95] The result of these features of the Athenian system of justice was that it was easy for plaintiffs and prosecutors to get their case to court provided they could find an offense and a procedure that arguably covered the actions committed by the defendant. Because crucial legal issues were not addressed by the magistrate at the *anakrisis* or subject to the *paragraphe* procedure, they fell into the hands of the arbitrators (in private cases) or the courts (in public cases) that tried the cases. These features of the system also meant that magistrates did not have the power to deliver summary judgments and throw out frivolous suits before they reached the courts. Nor did defendants have the right to lodge a demurrer and ask the judge to reject the case because it did not fit the parameters of the offense as the courts understood them. The Athenian reluctance to trust magistrates with this authority must have contributed to increasing the case load of the courts. One should therefore not argue that the volume of litigation was the result of an agonistic ethos or a culture of feuding; it was in part the consequence of the way the Athenians constructed their legal system, which reflected their distrust of magistrates and their fear of bribery. This provides further confirmation of the arguments in chapter 2: the best way to explain the nature of litigation in Athens is not to examine attitudes in isolation, but to study how the Athenians put their values into practice in their legal procedures and how these procedures shaped the conduct of individuals.

95. I share the view of Wolff (1966) 136–46 about the rationale for the *paragraphe* procedure and its relationship to the *anakrisis*. I plan to return to the legal issues in D. 32–35 in a forthcoming essay.

6

Open Texture in Athenian Law

THE RESPONSE OF THE COURTS

IN THE PREVIOUS chapter we saw that litigants paid close attention to the letter of the law but also might try to take advantage of the law's open texture. In the cases we studied, the accuser might interpret the law in one way, the defendant in another. But how did the courts respond to these arguments? In most of the cases examined in the last chapter, we do not know the court's verdict. In this chapter we will examine six cases for which we know or can infer how the court decided; the final trial occurred in the Assembly. In each of these cases, the court had to choose between a litigant who based his arguments on a more straightforward reading of the law and one who adopted a new or unusual reading of the statute. In two of these cases, the accusers go so far as to ask the judges to act as legislators, that is, to apply the law in a new way (Lys. 14.4; Lycurg. *Leocr.* 9). Did the courts tend to stick with the standard way of interpreting the law, or did they often attempt to extend laws to include new categories of offenders?[1] Or did they decide cases in an ad hoc manner without any consistent pattern?

I

The Athenians had three laws about real security that protected the rights of the creditor to property he acquired as a result of a debtor's default.[2] One law granted full rights of ownership to the creditor who accepted some property, either movable or immovable, as security for a loan or other obligation and

1. Johnstone (1999) 21–45, shows how litigants attempted to interpret the laws of Athens, but does not study how the courts responded to their interpretations. None of these cases are discussed by Meinecke (1971), who concentrates on private cases.

2. On these laws see Harris (2006a) 234–38.

took possession of this property in lieu of repayment of the principal (Is. 10.24).[3] A second law protected the creditor who acquired a security against any claims made by the debtor and his heirs (D. 41.7–10).[4] A third law provided the lender with an action against the borrower if he defaulted and refused to turn over goods pledged as security (Is. 6.31; D. 56.3, 38, 40, 45). But when did the creditor have the right to seize the security? Did he have to wait until the debtor failed to repay the principal? Or could he distrain after the debtor missed an interest payment? That depended on the way one interpreted the relationship between the creditor and the debtor in regard to the security during the life of the loan. In a loan agreement, the security is pledged to ensure repayment of the principal, not the payment of interest. In favor of this view of the arrangement is the fact that the value of the security was set in relationship to the amount of the loan, not to the amount of interest to be paid.[5] And when a creditor distrained on a security, it was not to recover interest that was owed to him, but the principal. For instance, when the merchant Parmeno borrowed forty mnai on the security of his ship and failed to repay the loan, his creditors threatened to seize his ship to recover the principal (D. 33.6). After Parmeno repaid these creditors by borrowing from two other lenders, the new creditors drew up an agreement that transferred ownership of Parmeno's ship and slaves until the principal of the loan was repaid (D. 33.8).

But there was another way of viewing the relationship between the lender and his creditors in regard to the security. When Nicobulus and Evergus made a loan of 105 mnai to the borrower Pantaenetus on the security of thirty slaves and a workshop in the mining district of Maroneia, they called the resulting arrangement between the parties a 'lease (*misthosis*) with a release at a fixed time' (D. 37.4–6).[6] They viewed the pledge of security as a sale that made them the owners of the slaves and workshop. Because they were the owners, the borrower Pantaenetus was therefore in a position similar to that of a lessee. Like the lessee who made regular payments of rent for use of the property, the lender made regular payments of interest for the loan. This view of the relationship brought one significant advantage to the creditors. If one took the standard view that

3. See Wyse (1904) 668–9.

4. On this law see Harris (2006a) 234–7.

5. For securities worth twice the amount of the loan see D. 34.6; 35.18; 37.4, 31.

6. For an analysis of their view of the agreement see Harris (2006a) 192.

security in a loan was pledged to assure repayment of the principal, a creditor would not be permitted to seize the security until the borrower failed to repay the principal at some fixed date. But in a lease, the lessee who does not make a payment of rent must leave the leased property immediately, a principle that was well recognized in Athenian law.[7] Thus, if a loan on security was like a lease, the security like a leased property, and the borrower like a lessee, the borrower would have to vacate the property pledged as security as soon as he missed a payment of interest.

These different views of the arrangement led to a dispute between the creditor Evergus and his borrower Pantaenetus. Soon after the agreement (mentioned earlier) that Evergus and Nicobulus drew up with Pantaenetus was concluded, Nicobulus set off on a voyage to Pontus while Evergus remained in Athens. Sometime later Nicobulus returned to discover that trouble had erupted during his absence. Not surprisingly, there were two versions of what had taken place. Pantaenetus claimed that Evergus had used force to eject him from the workshop contrary to the terms of the agreement. Prevented from carrying on his business, Pantaenetus was unable to make payments on the mine he had leased from the state and became a public debtor (D. 37.6). Evergus' account was somewhat different. He assured Nicobulus that he had seized the workshop only after Pantaenetus had failed to make several interest payments and denied the accusation that he had used force when taking over the workshop (D. 37.7). The trouble did not end there. After Evergus took possession, Pantaenetus went away and returned with another set of creditors who said the workshop had also been hypothecated to them. We should not be skeptical about the existence of this other loan; although Mnesicles, who had introduced the two lenders to Pantaenetus and acted as guarantor, derided the claims of the other creditors, Nicobulus and Evergus dealt with them in the subsequent negotiations as if their declaration was trustworthy (13–15).[8]

Even if we accept Evergus' version of what happened, it is clear that he and Pantaenetus had different views about the legal implications of their contract. Evergus considered himself in the position of a lessor, who was entitled to evict his lessee Pantaenetus once the latter missed a few payments. Pantaenetus did not share his view of the matter; he obviously considered himself the owner of the security, which entitled him to pledge

7. See *IG* ii[2] 2496, lines 17–20; 2499, lines 30–33; 2501, lines 15–20.

8. For the negotiations with these other creditors see Harris (2006a) 193–98.

his workshop and slaves as security for another loan from a second set of creditors (D. 37.13–15).[9] Since Evergus was not the owner and thus not in a position comparable to that of a lessor, Pantaenetus, therefore, did not think Evergus had the right to evict him from the workshop after he fell behind on his payment of interest. He may not have kept up with his payments, but the date for repayment of the principal had not arrived.[10] Until he failed to repay the principal, he believed that Evergus could not take over the security and claim the workshop as his own. When the dispute came to trial, the court sided with Pantaenetus and awarded him a payment of damages (D. 37.8). His partner Nicobulus claims that Evergus was the victim of malicious suit, but even if we accept Nicobulus' version of events, the court had good reason to decide in Pantaenetus' favor. By voting for Pantaenetus, the court decided to follow the more straightforward interpretation of the agreement between the creditor and the borrower about the security. Because the security was pledged to ensure repayment of the loan, Evergus should have waited to take over the workshop until Pantaenetus defaulted on the principal. By deciding against Evergus, the court rejected his view of the loan on security as a lease, a less straightforward interpretation of the agreement.[11] Although the Athenians had laws about real security, these laws did not clear up all questions about the subject. In this case, however, the court, when confronted with two differing views of an agreement, sided with the litigant who based his arguments on a more straightforward understanding of the contract.

---

9. Earlier I believed that there was a difference of opinion about the ownership of the security, with lenders believing that it belonged to them, borrowers thinking they retained ownership, see Harris (1988) (= Harris [2006a] 163–206). I now realize that the use of the language of sale by creditors is misleading; it only expresses their right to the security in the event of default, not an actual conveyance. In fact, Nicobulus clearly distinguishes the 'sale' of the slaves and workshop to himself and Evergus from an actual sale (D. 37.50: *kathapax*) later in the speech. Despite using the language of sale, he also deals with the second set of creditors as if their claims to the security are valid. Had he believed the pledge of security was an actual sale, he would not have done so. The creditor therefore had only a lien on the security and did not obtain ownership until he distrained on the property. Real security in Athenian law was therefore similar to the accessory contract of *hypotheke* in Roman law. See Harris (2012). Pelloso (2008) independently came to the same conclusion.

10. It is no accident that when describing the agreement, Nicobulus does not specify the due date for repayment of the principal (D. 37.5).

11. The court may have also favored an interpretation of the agreement that tended to favor the borrower because the average Athenian who was a member of the court was more likely to be a borrower than a lender. Nicobulus in fact alludes to the hostility toward lenders and claims that he is not typical of this group (D. 37.52–5).

II

The Athenians had one main law concerning military discipline, which punished various forms of cowardice (*deilia*). The law contained several provisions, each of which dealt with a specific offense under the general rubric of 'cowardice.'[12] In this way it was similar to the law on *eisangelia*, which enumerated several kinds of crime under the general heading of treason (*prodosia*). Two offenses included in the law on cowardice were 'leaving one's position' (*lipotaxion*) and desertion or 'leaving the army' (*lipostration*). In regard to the first offense, the law provided for a public action in the case where 'someone leaves his position [and goes] to the rear because of cowardice when others are fighting' (Lys. 14.5).[13] This provision needs to be understood in the context of hoplite tactics. Before battle, every hoplite was assigned a position in line by his commanding officer (Plato *Ap.* 28e; D. 15.32). It was absolutely necessary that a hoplite remain in his position: the strength of the formation depended on strict discipline and required that each soldier stand in place next to his comrade to present a continuous line of shields to the enemy. In fact, every year each ephebe swore in his oath of loyalty that 'I will not leave my companion in line in whatever place I will be stationed.'[14] If the line broke, the enemy would be able to attack from the side and the rear. One should also bear in mind that the hoplite shield was only large enough to cover the soldier's left side. He therefore relied on the man to his right to keep his shield in place to protect his unprotected side (Th. 5.71; E. *HF* 190–94). The part of the law covering this offense is carefully worded and pays careful attention to three substantive issues. First, it only applies to conduct during battle when the duty of maintaining one's position was

12. Note how Aeschines (3.175) mentions several types of offenses, then states that one can prosecute them all with the *graphe deilias*. Cf. Ar. *Ach.* 1129; *Eq.* 368. Hamel (1998b) shows that *lipotaxion* and *astrateia* are different offenses but does not understand the structure of the law about *deilia*. She appears to assume that the two were separate offenses, which were the subject of different laws, not two forms of cowardice that were listed in the general law about cowardice. Note that after discussing the two offenses, Lysias (14.4–5) has only one law read out and then says (14.6) that the law covers both offenses. If there were two separate offenses contained in two separate statutes, it is impossible to make sense of the prosecution of Alcibiades because an accuser could only use one procedure at a time against a defendant.

13. The speaker then paraphrases this part of the law in the following section where he says it applies to all those who 'move toward the back when there is a battle.'

14. Note how Lycurgus (*Leocr.* 77) considers leaving one's companion equivalent to deserting one's post. There is an allusion to this phrase of the Ephebic Oath in Soph. *Ant.* 671–2.

crucial. Second, it only punishes those who retreat; there was no reason to punish a man for moving forward since this would have brought him closer to the enemy, not farther away. Although the best thing to do was to remain in place, the Greeks did not find moving forward worth punishing. For instance, Herodotus (9.71.2–3) says that in his opinion Aristodemus was the best soldier who fought on the Greek side at Plataea even though he left his position. During a meeting shortly after the battle, however, the Spartans agreed that Aristodemus fought well but was not as distinguished as several other soldiers. Their reason was that Aristodemus acted like a madman and rushed forward leaving his position. This shows that it was not considered cowardly to leave one's post provided that one did so to advance toward the enemy, but the man who did so was not as good a soldier as the man who stayed at his post. Third, the law punishes only those who retreat for reasons of cowardice. This leaves open the possibility that a soldier might move back for other reasons such as to change formation under orders or to assist a weak position under attack. One might try to interpret the notion of a soldier's *taxis*, or 'post,' more broadly, but the wording of the law indicates that the law took it in a narrower sense.[15] The second main offense was *astrateia*, and the law shows that this was the failure to show up for duty when summoned and to serve on a campaign (Lys. 14.6–7).[16] Other offenses covered by the law were desertion from the fleet (*anaumachiou*) and throwing away one's shield.[17]

In around 395, an Athenian named Archestratides brought a charge of 'cowardice' against Alcibiades, the son of the famous general of the same name.[18] The speech of Archestratides has not survived but the corpus Lysiacum preserves two speeches delivered by speakers (*synegoroi*) who

15. For instance, Lycurgus (*Leocr.* 77) accused a man who had left Athens during the crisis after the defeat at Chaeronea of deserting his post. Cf. Aeschin. 3.159.

16. For *astrateia* as failure to go on campaign see [D.] 59.27; D. 39.16. In the next section, however, the charge is given as *lipotaxiou*. *Lipotaxion* appears to have had a narrow sense in the law about cowardice ('leaving one's position in line during battle') and a general sense (desertion from the army).

17. And. 1.74. For desertion from the fleet see also Suidas s.v. *anaumachiou*.

18. For the date of the speech see Carey (1989) 141. For the charge see Lys. 14.11, which shows the court will vote whether he is guilty of cowardice. The court appears to have included only those who had served in the army (Lys. 14.5, 14–15), but they are bound by the terms of the Judicial Oath just like other judges (Lys. 14.40). Cf. Bertrand (2001) 17–18. On the composition of the court see the debate between Whitehead (2008) and Rhodes (2008b).

supported the accuser. Although the speeches of Alcibiades and his supporters have not been preserved, it is possible to recover the main, basic facts of the case, on which both sides implicitly agree. First, neither of the speakers who supported the accuser claim that Alcibiades did not join the expedition or that he left it before its return to Athens. The first speaker says that Alcibiades was enrolled in the infantry but chose to serve in the cavalry (Lys. 14.7–8, 11). The second speaker agrees with the first but is slightly more precise: he states that the generals placed Alcibiades among the mounted archers although he was initially assigned to the infantry (Lys. 15.6, 11). What is also striking is that neither speaker accuses Alcibiades of deserting his post in battle. When the first speaker notes that their opponents will draw attention to the fact that the army did not fight a battle, he does not contradict them but argues that the law applies anyway (Lys. 14.5). This much is clear: Alcibiades was enrolled in the infantry, departed with the army, and was transferred to the mounted archers. Thus Alcibiades did not leave the army, and the army never fought a battle during its campaign.[19]

The accusers claim that Alcibiades violated the law in three ways (Lys. 14.6–7).[20] First, he is guilty of desertion (*astrateia*) because he did not serve on the campaign as a hoplite although he had been enrolled as one (cf. Lys. 15.11). Second, he is guilty of leaving his post (*lipotaxion*) because he did not allow himself to be assigned a position in the army (i.e., he transferred to the mounted archers). Third, he is guilty of cowardice in general since he chose to serve in the cavalry and did not share the danger of serving as a hoplite. For the first charge, the accusers are narrowing the term 'army' (*stratia*) in the second provision of the law to include only the infantry, not the entire expedition as a whole, both cavalry and infantry. By leaving the hoplites, or army, on foot, they argue, he has left the army. As Carey has noted, 'Only by a linguistic trick can the relevant clause of the law, which by *peze stratia* [foot army] meant the land army as distinct from the fleet, be stretched to fit his conduct.'[21] For the second charge, the accusers are

19. If Carey (1989) 141 is right to identify the Athenian expedition with the one described by Xenophon *HG* 3.5.25, this would confirm the assertion of Alcibiades' supporters.

20. The two supporting speakers probably summarize the main points against Alcibiades, which were developed in greater detail by Archestratides, who was the actual accuser. On the relationship between supporting speakers and the main accuser in public suits see Rubinstein (2000) 131–47.

21. Carey (1989) 145.

clearly stretching the term *taxis* to apply to a broader range of actions than those explicitly covered in the statute. The law covers only those who leave their post and move back because of cowardice. The accusers concentrate on the term *taxis*, or assigned place, and generalize from it: they claim that anyone who leaves the position assigned to him by law is guilty of deserting one's post (*lipotaxion*). But Alcibiades took the position in the mounted archers that was assigned to him and did not leave his position during battle nor move to the rear during battle out of cowardice.

The first speaker admits that he is interpreting the law in a new and unusual way when he urges the court to act as lawgivers (Lys. 14.4). He says that the judges should realize that the way they decide the case now will be the way the community applies the law in the future. This implies that in the past the courts had not applied the law to the kinds of offenses Alcibiades committed. If they convict him in this case, they would therefore be expanding the law to cover a wider range of actions than it had before.

The two speakers give some hints about the arguments their opponents planned to use. First, they would point out that the provision in the law about leaving one's post did not apply because no battle was fought (Lys. 14.5). Even if one applied this provision in the broader way to apply to any position a soldier was assigned to, one could not argue that Alcibiades was disobedient since he had taken the position in the mounted archers assigned to him by the generals (Lys. 15.6.). Significant also is the fact that the generals intended to testify for Alcibiades (Lys. 15.1–4). It is hard to tell who testified for the accusers because all that has survived are the orations delivered by two supporting speakers. But equally significant is the fact that neither speaker attempts to undermine the witnesses' statements by accusing them of lying. The second speaker claims that the generals in their capacity as magistrates have a duty to remain impartial, but he does not attack the veracity of their testimony (Lys. 15.3–4). If Alcibiades had in fact been disobedient, the generals would no doubt have sided with the accuser. To counter their argument, the second speaker claims that they did not have the right to transfer Alcibiades from the infantry to the counted archers, but he cites no law that forbade them to (Lys. 15.6, 12). The second speaker appears to assume that Alcibiades was assigned to a place in the infantry by law, which the generals did not have the right to alter, and that it was the magistrates of Athens who assigned a soldier his post (D. 15.32; Pl. *Ap.* 28e). This makes sense: the laws could not order how the generals were to conduct a campaign. If generals could make decisions about how to draw troops up for battle, they must have in the same way been able to move soldiers from one kind of unit to another as the need arose.

The case against Alcibiades relies on a strained reading of the law about cowardice (*deilia*). Both sides implicitly agree that the army did not fight a battle so the first provision of the law about leaving one's post did not apply. The accusers also do not deny that Alcibiades served on the campaign, did not leave the army, and joined the mounted archers following the orders of his commanding officers so he was not guilty of leaving the expedition. He may have technically violated the provision about serving in the cavalry without passing a scrutiny (Lys. 14.8–9), but we do not know if this law also applied to mounted archers. Besides, there were extenuating circumstances: Alcibiades served in this group on the orders of his commanding officers, not by his own choice.

Although no source reports the court's verdict, it is possible to determine the outcome of the trial. A trial resulting from a charge of cowardice was an *agon atimetos*: the penalty was fixed by statute so there was no assessment of the penalty (*timesis*) following the court's first vote on the guilt of the defendant (Lys. 14.9).[22] The penalty was severe: the man convicted of cowardice suffered total disenfranchisement with the complete loss of all rights as a citizen (D. 15.32. Cf. [D.] 59.27 and D. 21.103).[23] Aeschines (3.176) says that the person guilty of this offense was banned from the sacred area of the Agora and could not participate in public rituals. If someone no longer qualified as a citizen, his children and grandchildren could not become citizens.[24] But Alcibiades appears to have had a daughter who was a citizen and a grandson, who was also named Alcibiades.[25] This would have been impossible if Alcibiades had been convicted for cowardice. Because the case against him was very weak, it is not surprising that Alcibiades must have been acquitted.[26]

22. Cf. Harrison (1971) 82.

23. According to And. 1.74 the person convicted on a charge of cowardice retained his property, but Lys. 14.9 may imply that the penalty included confiscation of property. See Carey (1989) 155.

24. Arist. *Ath. Pol.* 42.1.

25. For the daughter, see *IG* ii^2 7400; for her husband, see *IG* ii^2 6746 with 7400; for the grandson, see *IG* ii^2 6719. Cf. Davies (1971) 21–22.

26. Cf. Carey (1989) 145: 'the case against Alcibiades is not strong.'

If this analysis is correct, the case against Alcibiades conforms to the pattern noted in the previous chapter. On the one hand, the magistrate who received the accusation, presided at the *anakrisis*, and assigned the case to a court for trial was willing to accept a case that relied on a novel interpretation of the law. On the other, the court, by contrast, was unwilling to convict a defendant on charges based on an unusual reading of the law's provisions.

III

The speech of Lysias (9) *On Behalf of the Soldier* was delivered by a soldier named Polyaenus, who had been accused of slandering a general. Polyaenus recounts how the generals enrolled him for military duty even though he had recently served in the army (4).[27] When he objected to one of the generals, the general did not grant his request and insulted him. Polyaenus says he kept quiet, then went to consult with another citizen (5). He then discovered that the generals intended to arrest him (5). This conversation with the citizen took place at Philius' bank (6). The generals heard about the conversation and decided to impose a fine on him for slandering them (*loidoroimi*. Cf. 16: *zemiosantes men ten archen loidorounta*). Polyaenus reminds the court that the law only forbids slandering magistrates at their offices (6: *ean tis archen en to synedrio*. Cf. 10).[28] The generals did not attempt to collect the fine, then at the end of their term of office recorded the debt on a record they handed over to some treasurers.[29] These officials asked the generals about their grounds for imposing the fine. When they learned what had happened, they tried to persuade them to change their mind, then when that failed, they judged the fine null and void (7: *akyron*. Cf. 12). Despite this decision, Polyaenus was later prosecuted by an *apographe* procedure (21) since his opponents claimed he still owed the fine and had not paid it.

---

27. For a helpful discussion of the speech see MacDowell (1994), Dreher (1994), and Todd (2007) 581–93, 604–24.

28. It is difficult to determine the relationship of this law to the one mentioned at D. 21.32–33, which punished with total *atimia* the crimes of insulting and striking a magistrate (cf. Arist. *Prob.* 952b28–32). It may be that the law mentioned at Lys. 9.6 gave an official the power to impose a fine, while the one mentioned by Demosthenes created a public charge, for which the penalty was *atimia*. Or both provisions may have come from the same law (compare the law at Arist. *Ath. Pol.* 56.7: *epiballein e eisagein eis to dikasterion*).

29. MacDowell (1994) 161–2 identifies these treasurers with the *praktores*, and Dreher (1994) 167 accepts the identification.

The decision of the treasurers was not the verdict of a court, but it did aim to resolve a legal dispute (note the use of the verb *ekrinan*) arising from an interpretation of the law. The generals clearly took a broad interpretation of the law and applied it to someone who criticized their conduct. They may have argued that the aim of the law was to encourage respect for magistrates and to punish disrespect. Polyaenus relies on a narrow interpretation and keeps close to the actual wording of the law. For Polyaenus the aim of the law may have been to enable officials to carry on their duties without interference but not to discourage criticism.[30] Whatever the reasons for their differing interpretations, the significant point is that the treasurers sided with Polyaenus' reading of the law. In other words, these officials, when confronted with two different interpretations of the law, chose to adhere to a literal reading of its language and resisted an attempt to broaden the application of the law to anyone who criticized officials no matter where.

IV

For the next case, Mantitheus' suit against Boeotus (D. 39), we know not only the decision of the arbitrator but can also infer the verdict of the court. The dispute arose between two half-brothers, Mantitheus and Boeotus, both the sons of a man named Mantias. We have examined the long-term quarrel between the two men in chapter 2; the only matter that concerns us here is the legal issue in their first confrontation in court. It is necessary to recall the background of the case. Boeotus did not grow up in his father's household; he lived with his mother, Plangon. When he reached the age of majority, he needed to have his father acknowledge paternity so he could be registered in a phratry and on the list of citizens in his deme (2). Mantias was reluctant to comply but was finally forced to register Boeotus in his phratry under that name (3–4). Mantias died before he could register him in his deme, so Boeotus took the initiative and had himself registered under the name of Mantitheus (5). Mantitheus naturally resented this and brought an action against his half-brother. When the case came before the arbitrator, Boeotus provided witnesses to prove that Mantias had performed his *dekate* (tenth-day) ceremony after his birth and given him the name of his grandfather Mantitheus (22). Since he claimed to be the elder son, he was entitled to the name of their paternal grandfather (27).

30. For *parrhesia* at Athens including the right to criticize officials see D. 22.31.

The charge Mantitheus brought appears to have been a suit for damages (*dike blabes*).[31] In two places he accuses Boeotus of causing him harm (5: *blaptei,* 13: *blaptetai.* Cf. 18: *blaben*). In his second case against Boeotus (D. 40.35), Mantitheus says he brought the action not to get money from him but so that he would use the name Boeotus if the court decided Mantitheus was suffering terribly and enduring great harm (*blaptesthai*). Even though he says that his aim was not to receive money, Mantitheus obviously hoped the court would award him a payment of damages and thereby discourage Boeotus from using his name again in the future. Normally the terms *blabe* and *blaptein* apply to physical damage to some material object (e.g., D. 55.12, 20, 28), but the courts might award a payment for damages to a litigant who proved that a defendant's actions had caused him to incur expenses without doing any physical damage. For instance, Menippus, a man from Caria, lost a suit to Euandrus, a citizen of Thespiai. When Euandrus could not find Menippus to collect the amount awarded by the court, he grabbed a hold of him during the celebration of Mysteries, when it was illegal for creditors to seize debtors (D. 21.176). After initiating his action by *probole,* Menippus brought a private action for damages (*tas blabas*). The court compelled Euandrus to forfeit his earlier award and granted Menippus a payment of damages for the expenses he incurred for having to remain in Athens for the legal proceedings.[32]

In this case, however, Mantitheus extends the terms to cover acts that simply cause some annoyance or might cause inconvenience in the future. Mantitheus describes the potential confusion in public affairs that might arise from two men bearing the same name (7–12). For instance, the archon might not know whom to summon to court, the generals whom to call up for duty, assign to a symmory, or select as a trierarch. If the name Mantitheus, son of Mantias, from the deme of Thorikos, was selected for office, who would serve (10)? Or the two men might collude to increase the chances of one to gain an office filled by lot (12). Mantitheus then turns to situations that might cause him harm. He notes that Boeotus associates with Menecles and others who bring many public cases. If Boeotus were to use his name, then lose a case and owe a fine to the Treasury, Mantitheus might be considered responsible for paying (14). Mantitheus describes several other hypothetical problems the shared name might

31. Cf. Carey and Reid (1985) 166.

32. For this case see Harris (2008) 80.

create (15–18). But Mantitheus provides evidence for only two actual events in which Boeotus caused him some irritation, once when his half-brother was a defendant in a public case and another time when Boeotus disputed his right to an office to which the people had elected him (19). Mantitheus claims that the first incident damaged his reputation and implies that the second caused him some annoyance. Mantitheus does not show that the actions of his half-brother caused him to lose money or otherwise diminished the value of his assets.

It should come as no surprise that Mantitheus lost his case before the arbitrator (22) and appears to have been no more successful before the court.[33] The effort of Mantitheus to stretch the meaning of the term 'harm' to cover actions that merely caused some annoyance was a clever attempt to exploit the open texture of the law, but obviously went far beyond the standard meaning of the term. As in the previous cases, both the arbitrator and the court voted against a litigant who attempted to broaden the application of a law beyond its normal limits.

V

Aeschines' speech *Against Ctesiphon* (Aeschin. 3) contains some of the most detailed legal arguments in all of Attic oratory. The dispute began in 336 when Ctesiphon proposed a decree of honors for Aeschines' rival Demosthenes. Aeschines immediately brought a charge of proposing an illegal decree (*graphe paranomon*) against Ctesiphon, but the case did not come to trial until 330.[34] Aeschines makes three main charges against Ctesiphon's decree: (1) It violated the law about the award of honors to magistrates who had not passed their *euthynai* (Aeschin. 3.9–31); (2) it violated the law about the announcement of awards in the Assembly (Aeschin. 3.32–48); and (3) it contained false statements (Aeschin. 3.49). The third charge dealt mainly with issues of fact, but the first two involve interpretation of law. Both ancient and modern scholars believe that Aeschines, who lost the case by a wide margin, had stronger legal arguments.[35] Quintilian

33. See *IG* ii^2 1622, lines 435–6 with Carey and Reid (1985) 167–68. One might add that if Mantitheus had won the case, he would certainly have said so when he referred to it in his later speech against Boeotus ([D.] 40.35).

34. For an analysis of the reasons why Aeschines delayed bringing his case until 330 see Harris (1995) 138–42.

35. For Aeschines' defeat see [Plu.] *Mor.* 840d; Plutarch *Demosthenes* 24.1.

(7.1.2) thought Aeschines began with a discussion of the law because that was his strong point (*a iure quo videbatur potentior coeperit*).[36] The author of the most detailed study of the legal arguments in the case concluded 'the better reasoning is that of Aeschines.'[37] Since Demosthenes was *hypeuthynos* in the legal sense in 336, when the crown was proposed, Gwatkin claims that Ctesiphon's proposal was illegal and that he should have been convicted. Another scholar believes that 'Aeschines had the actual wording of the laws on his side' (*Aischines hatte den Wortlaut der Gesetze auf seiner Seite*) and that the outcome of the trial hinged on political factors.[38]

These scholars appear to assume that Aeschines must have had the stronger legal arguments because he spends so much time discussing the law, whereas Demosthenes devotes little space to legal issues.[39] None of these scholars considers the possibility that the laws cited by each litigant were potentially ambiguous and capable of different interpretations. There is also the possibility that Aeschines had to analyze the laws at considerable length because he was arguing for a new and unusual reading of their contents, whereas Demosthenes was relying on the customary interpretation of their provisions, which did not require elaborate argument.

Let us begin with Aeschines' first charge against Ctesiphon. Aeschines (3.9–10) says that the law forbidding the award of crowns to magistrates subject to audit was passed because of the dishonesty of corrupt magistrates. These magistrates, knowing they would not pass the examination of their pilfered accounts at their *euthynai*, conspired with friendly speakers in the Assembly to have decrees of praise passed for them during their terms of office. Thus, if they were subsequently prosecuted after their accounts were examined, the members of the court would be reluctant to convict them and thereby condemn men whose conduct in office had already received commendation from the Athenian people. Aeschines (3.11–12) notes that Ctesiphon could have avoided breaking the law by calling for the award to be granted to Demosthenes after he had successfully passed his

36. Cf. D. 18. Hyp. 2.

37. Gwatkin (1957).

38. Meyer-Laurin (1965) 32. Wankel (1976) 17 also believed that Aeschines had the stronger legal case.

39. One must bear in mind that Demosthenes spoke only as a *synegoros*. It is therefore possible that Ctesiphon himself may have spoken first and carried the main burden of the legal argument (cf. Lysias 14.3, where it is clear that the previous speaker Archestratides dealt with the laws and produced witnesses).

euthynai but failed to do so. Aeschines disapproves of the practice of inserting such a clause in decrees of praise but admits it was common at the time, and contemporaneous inscriptions show that his statement is correct. We will return to these inscriptions later.[40]

That would appear to be the end of the matter. But one must look at the precise wording of the law. Aeschines first gives the provision of the law at 3.11 where he says it explicitly forbids the crowning of those subject to audit (*tous hypeuthynous me stephanoun*). At 3.26 he paraphrases the provisions of the law with similar language: 'If someone is subject to audit for one office, even a very small one, the lawgiver does not allow the crowning of that man before he undergoes his audit.' What is rather suspicious is that Aeschines does not have the actual text of the law read out by the court clerk until 3.30–31, where he gives a slightly different version of the law: 'another law forbids the crowning of an *arche*' (*heteros d'apagoreuei nomos archen hypeuthynon me stephanoun*). The versions of the law he presents at 3.11 and 3.26 are not verbatim quotes but paraphrases, which interpret the key term *arche* as meaning 'magistrate.' This is a possible interpretation of the term,[41] but it is not the only one: the term could also mean 'term of office.'[42] These different interpretations of the term may seem minor, but they have major implications for the meaning and application of the law. If we adopt Aeschines' interpretation, the law banned all decrees of praise for a magistrate who had not yet passed his *euthynai*. If we adopt the other interpretation, the law only made it illegal to award a crown for a term of office, that is, for the performance of duties attached

40. Aeschines (3.13–15) predicts that his opponents will claim Demosthenes was not technically a magistrate when Ctesiphon proposed his decree and refutes the argument by proving that Demosthenes' office of *teichopoios* was indeed a magistracy. Despite Aeschines' prediction, Demosthenes does not appear to have used this argument in his speech, but Ctesiphon may have dealt with the matter in his speech—see the previous note.

41. For *arche* with the meaning of 'magistrate' see D. 39.9; Lys. 9.6.

42. For this meaning of the term see for instance Lys. 9.6; Arist. *Ath. Pol.* 56.2; Aeschin. 3.11. MacDowell (2009) 388 note 20 objects that 'a crown was not given to an office and ἀρχή must have the sense of holder of an office "magistrate."' MacDowell failed to note, however, that Demosthenes (18.117), when discussing the law, uses the term in precisely this sense and that there were different types of decrees of honors; his objection is therefore groundless. MacDowell read only my analysis in Harris (1994b) 141–48 but not that in Harris (2000a) 59–67 and did not attempt to address my other arguments about the interpretation of the law. If one believes that the term *arche* must refer to a magistrate, one could still interpret the law in two ways. It could forbid the award of a crown either for anyone *while serving* as magistrate or for a magistrate for his performance of duties *as a magistrate*. Aeschines adopts the first interpretation, Demosthenes the second.

to an office before this magistrate passed his audit for that term of office. This means that the law did not prohibit a person who held an office from receiving a crown before undergoing his audit, but only a crown awarded for his performance in that office. In other words, a magistrate still *hypeuthynos* (subject to audit) might still be able to receive a crown for some remarkable achievement, for a generous donation of money, or for earlier public service.

What kind of decree of praise had Ctesiphon proposed? Suspiciously enough, Aeschines never has Ctesiphon's decree read out during his discussion of the laws about crowns but only quotes a few phrases from it later in the speech (3.49–50). These phrases appear to indicate that Ctesiphon's decree was a general commendation, for Demosthenes is praised for his merit (*arete*) and virtue (*andragathias*) and for continually (*diatelei*) saying and doing what is best for the people (cf. 237).[43] The only other place where Aeschines refers to the actual contents of the decree is toward the end of the speech (3.236–37). Here he says that Demosthenes was praised for having trenches dug around the walls of Athens. Aeschines recalls how this work resulted in tearing up the public burial grounds, which would place Demosthenes' supervision of the work in late 338, a year before his election to the post supervising the construction of walls (*teichopoios*).[44] This is one of several 'good deeds' (*euergesiai*) listed in the decree. Demosthenes (18.113–14) in his reply also quotes the phrase 'constantly does and says what is best for the people' and adds that he was praised for donating a sum of money toward the building of fortifications.

These passages reveal that Ctesiphon's decree was not a decree of praise for Demosthenes' performance of his duties as *teichopoios* or as administrator of the Theoric Fund, a post he held simultaneously (Aeschin. 3.24). Ctesiphon's decree must have been similar to the one that Euchares moved for Callias of Sphettus in 270/69 or the one Laches passed for Demochares in 271/70.[45] It was an award for a long record of public service and a general commendation for his consistent devotion to city's welfare.

This makes it possible to make sense of Demosthenes' reply to Aeschines' first charge against Ctesiphon. Demosthenes (18.113) rightly draws attention to the fact that he was praised not for any of the actions for

43. This verb is often found in honorary decrees for those who have performed long-term service for the Athenians. See for example *IG* ii^2 346, line 15; 422, lines 4–5.

44. See Lycurg. *Leocr.* 44.

45. For Euchares' decree see Shear (1978). For Laches' decree see [Plu.] *Moralia* 851d–f.

which he was subject to audit (*hypeuthynos*), but on the grounds that he had donated money (*epedoka*).[46] Demosthenes draws attention to the very issue Aeschines ignores, namely, the nature of the praise contained in the decree. Demosthenes stresses the fact that he was not praised for his performance of his duties supervising construction of the walls or as administrator of the Theoric Fund. Demosthenes (18.117) sums up his argument briefly and forcefully: 'I made a contribution (*epedoka*). I am praised for that reason. I am not subject to audit (*hypeuthynos*) for what I gave. I was a magistrate. I underwent an audit (*euthynas*) for my term of office (*arches*), not for what I contributed (*epedoka*).' Because Ctesiphon's decree did not praise a term of office, it is therefore not subject to the provisions of the law on which Aeschines relies. If Aeschines thought Demosthenes had committed an injustice during his term of office, Aeschines should have accused Demosthenes before the *logistai* at his audit after his term of office. To provide evidence for his argument, Demosthenes, unlike Aeschines, has Ctesiphon's decree read out (18.118).[47] Demosthenes' brevity does not mask a rhetorical bluff. His argument is terse because it bears directly on the legal issue at stake, which is more than we can say for the long-winded Aeschines.

To sum up so far. Aeschines adopts a broad interpretation of the statute about the awarding of crowns and construes it as forbidding any award to a magistrate currently holding office. Demosthenes takes a narrower interpretation of the statute and holds that it only applies to decrees of praise for the performance of the duties of an office, not to other types of commendation.

Several pieces of evidence indicate that Demosthenes' interpretation was the way the courts normally understood the implications of the law. First, Demosthenes himself adduces the examples of Nausicles, Diotimus, Charidemus, and Neoptolemus, all of whom received the honor of a crown during their terms of office for acts of generosity (D. 18.114). Demosthenes is not fabricating evidence, for he has the decrees praising these men read out by the clerk (D. 18.115). These decrees do not show that the Athenians ignored the law about crowns. Rather they prove that Demosthenes' interpretation of the law was the customary one and had been followed many times before. More evidence comes from the speech *On the Trierarchic*

---

46. For decrees of praise for contributions see Migeotte (1992) passim.

47. The document inserted in the text at 118 is a forgery. See Wankel (1976) 632.

Crown (D. 51). The trierarch who delivers the speech addresses the Council and informs its members that shortly before he had received a crown for being the first to launch his trireme (D. 51.4). Since he claims that after this he was the first to have his trireme fully equipped (D. 51.1), he must have received the first crown while he was serving as trierarch, that is, while he was still subject to audit.[48] Like Nausicles and the others, the trierarch had received a crown for some remarkable achievement during his term of office.

Next there are several decrees that call for the award of a crown and contain the clause that the award not be conferred until after the honorand submits his accounts at this audit. All the decrees that contain this clause are motions praising one or more magistrates for their performance of their official duties, not for single achievements or long-term service to the community.[49] On the other hand, decrees of praise for long-term service do not contain this clause, which would indicate that they were not subject to the law Aeschines bases his case on.[50]

Finally, if the Athenians followed Aeschines' interpretation of the law, it would have been impossible for a general like Lycurgus, who served in an office supervising Athenian finances for twelve straight years, to receive any crowns during this time. Yet, we knew that he received many crowns while he held this office.[51]

Our analysis so far reveals that there were two possible ways of interpreting the law about awards to magistrates, a broader one proposed by Aeschines and a narrower one followed by Demosthenes. All the available evidence about how the law was applied shows that the Athenians shared Demosthenes' interpretation of its provisions.

The second law Aeschines claims Ctesiphon violated is one that provides that a crown awarded by the Council can receive an announcement in the Council, a crown awarded by the Assembly in the Assembly, and 'nowhere else' (3.32–4). Aeschines lays great stress on this last phrase. In his opinion, the law implicitly forbids the announcement of a crown in the Theater of Dionysus. He then acknowledges that there is another law about crowns, which he calls the Dionysiac law (3.36). This law permits

48. For trierarchs being subject to *euthynai* see Aeschin. 3.19.

49. *IG* ii² 223 (343/42), 330 (336/35), 338 (333/32), 354 (328/27), 410 (c. 330), 415 (330/29), 672 (279/78), 780 (249/48 or 248/47); *Agora* XV (328/7) 49; *SEG* 43:26 (315/14).

50. For examples of this kind of decree see note 45.

51. [Plu.] *Mor.* 852b.

the announcement of crowns in the theater if the Assembly votes to allow it. Aeschines predicts (accurately in this case) that his opponents will rely on this law but asserts that it is not relevant to Ctesiphon's decree. But he argues that this law could not contradict the one he relies on since the procedures for reviewing the laws make this impossible (3.37–40). Aeschines then describes the circumstances that led to the enactment of the law about the Dionysia: so many proclamations were made without approval from the Assembly that people grew angry and the announcements disrupted the dramatic performances. The lawgiver then enacted a law about those who are awarded crowns not by the Assembly, but by tribe or deme and about manumissions and foreign crowns. The law forbids that these be announced in the theater (Aeschin. 3.44). Aeschines then says that the previous law applies to crowns awarded by the Council and the Assembly (which can only be announced in those venues), but that this laws forbids those crowned by demes and tribes to be proclaimed in the theater. On the other hand, the law does permit the announcement of a crown. Since this second law cannot apply to crowns awarded by the Assembly, Aeschines infers that the law must apply only to crowns awarded by demes or foreign communities (Aeschin. 3.45).

To support his interpretation, Aeschines (3.41–3) recalls the circumstances that gave rise to the law. Although he provides no evidence for his account of the background to the law, his method of argument is significant. Aeschines places the creation of the law in its historical context and attempts to discern the intent of the law by describing the abuse it was created to correct. As further support for his view, Aeschines (3.46) then appeals to another law. This law requires that any crown announced in the theater must be dedicated to Athena. Aeschines infers that this cannot apply to crowns awarded by the Assembly: why would the people award a crown only to demand that the honorand surrender it soon afterward? Such a stingy regulation would be unworthy of the Athenian people. On the other hand, the Athenians rightly insisted that a crown awarded by a foreign community and announced in the theater should be given to Athena. The aim of this practice was to make the honorand more grateful to the Athenian people for granting the announcement than to the foreign community for the crown (Aeschin. 3.47).

Aeschines may be deliberately misunderstanding the complex economy of public honors. The Athenians understood the need to reward their benefactors, but they were also concerned that such honors might lead those honored to consider themselves superior to the city and its laws.

Thus when the Athenians conferred honors on a citizen, they often required that this individual at the same time make a display of his loyalty to the city and its laws. By requiring that the crown be dedicated to Athena, the city was not taking away the honor it granted, but merely asking the honorand to display his loyalty to Athens by dedicating the symbol of that honor to their divine protectress. What is significant for our topic is the way Aeschines argues for his interpretation of the two laws about announcing crowns. He argues that each law applies to a different type of crown and justifies his interpretation by appealing to the intent of the law. He attempts to reconstruct the intent of the law first by placing the law in its historical context, then by examining another law, and finally by an appeal to the 'Athenian character.' The final argument is similar to an argument found in Demosthenes' speech *Against Leptines* (20.11–14), where he argues that it is contrary to the character of the Athenian people to take away an award once it has been given.

But is Aeschines' argument that the law only permits the announcement of foreign crowns correct? We need to return to his paraphrase: Aeschines says that the law applied to crowns awarded by tribe or deme, to manumissions and to crowns awarded by foreign communities. He then says that the law forbade the proclamation of a crown by the tribe or deme and (here he quotes from the law) 'or by anyone else.' But this must include the award of foreign crowns too. If one applies the prohibition to crowns awarded by tribes and demes, one must also apply it to crowns awarded by foreign communities. In fact, in describing the reasons for passing the law, Aeschines says that it was caused by the announcement of crowns awarded by tribes, demes, and foreign communities without the Assembly's approval (Aeschin. 3.41–2). If the problem was caused by all kinds of announcements made in the theater without the Assembly's approval, the solution should have been to require the Assembly's approval for any type of crown.[52]

Demosthenes (18.120–21) replies to Aeschines' second argument by having the clerk read out the relevant law and quotes from it: 'except when the Assembly or Council so votes. Let them [i.e., their honors] be announced.' From this phrase and from Aeschines' paraphrase, it appears

52. This interpretation of the law is supported by an inscription dated to the end of the fourth century enacted by the deme of Eleusis, which calls for the demarch to announce a crown given by the deme to Smikythion at the Dionysia during the tragedies (*IG* ii^2 1193, lines 13–17). I have modified my argument about Aeschines' interpretation of the law as the result of conversations with Mirko Canevaro.

that the law created two categories: crowns awarded by the Council and Assembly and those awarded by other groups. For the first category, it provided that these crowns would always be announced in the theater without need for further approval. In the case of the latter, it was not enough for the group to vote that crowns be announced in the theater. Here the additional approval of the Assembly was required. Demosthenes thus interprets the second law as creating an exception to the provisions of the first. Although he claims that thousands have received this honor in the past, he provides no evidence to support the assertion, but there is no need to doubt him since several inscriptions show he is correct.[53] Once again, Demosthenes relies on a more straightforward reading of the law, one that the Athenians had consistently followed.

If the court had voted for Aeschines, it would be difficult to know which of his three arguments the judges had found convincing. If that had happened, the court might have rejected two of the charges, but have decided that the remaining one was strong enough to justify conviction. But since the court sided with Demosthenes and rejected Aeschines' case by a large margin, we are safe in concluding that the judges did not find any of Aeschines' arguments persuasive. Their verdict in the case falls into the pattern we noted in the previous cases: the courts appear to have been unwilling to side with litigants who based their cases on novel and unusual interpretations of the law and preferred to stick to the standard meaning of legal provisions.

VI

The next case to be examined is Lycurgus' prosecution of Leocrates for treason in 331.[54] Lycurgus was a leading politician at the time and held a powerful position supervising Athenian finances.[55] Lycurgus brought a charge of treason (*prodosia*) against Leocrates and used a procedure called *eisangelia*,

53. See Gwatkin (1957) 138, note 57.

54. For the date of the speech (331 BCE) see Lycurg. *Leocr.* 45 (in the eighth year after Chaeronea, that is, seven years after August 338. The phrase is mistranslated by Burtt in his Loeb translation). See Harris in Worthington, Cooper, and Harris (2001) 159, note 1, endorsed by Whitehead (2006) 132, note 2. Engels (2008) 113 is misleading when he claims that Aeschines (3.252) dates the speech to 330. All that Aeschines says is that the acquittal of Leocrates had occurred recently, which could have meant anything from a few weeks ago to several months or a year. The expression is far too vague to support Engel's view. The information given about the length of his residence in Megara (58: six years; 145: more than five or six years), ignored by Engels, also points to the earlier date of 331.

55. For Lycurgus and his administration see Faraguna (1992).

which was available only for the most serious crimes.[56] The law about *eisangelia* did not provide a definition of what constituted a 'serious crime' but listed various offenses under three main rubrics: subversion of the democracy, treason, and making speeches against the public interest in return for gifts.[57] According to Hyperides (*Eux.* 8), one could employ this procedure 'if anyone overthrows the democracy of the Athenians . . . or conspires for the overthrow of the democracy or forms a group of conspirators (*hetairikon*), or if someone betrays some city or ship or infantry or naval force, or when a public speaker does not give the best advice while accepting money.' Information derived from Theophrastus' *Laws* preserved in Pollux and the *Lexicon Cantabrigiense* lists similar types of offenses as subject to *eisangelia*. Under treasonable activities, Pollux (8.52) includes 'those who go to the enemy without being sent, or betray a fort, or a military force or ships.' The *Lexicon* gives a slightly different list: 'if anyone betrays some territory or ships or an infantry force or if anyone goes to the enemy or changes residence (to live) with them or serves in the army with them or accepts gifts.'[58]

Whatever the specific offenses, the statute obviously attempted to cover treasonable acts in general, but did so by listing various kinds of treasonable activities instead of offering a comprehensive definition of treason. Thus the law attempts to provide some guidance about the type of actions the lawgiver had in mind when he provided this special procedure against treason. The problem with this sort of list is that the lawgiver does not make clear whether he intended the specific actions listed to form a comprehensive list or to provide representative examples of treasonous actions. If the former, this meant that one could not bring a case against someone or win a conviction unless his action fit one of the activities named in the statute. If the latter, all one had to do was to claim that the defendant had committed treason and leave it to the court to decide whether the action deserved punishment.[59]

56. Engels (2008) 112 claims that Lycurgus brought the charge before the Assembly, but none of the passages he cites (1, 5, 29–30, 34, 55, 137) mentions the Assembly.

57. Engels (2008) 111–12 contains no detailed discussion of the contents of the law about *eisangelia*. He also does not make a clear distinction between *eisangelia* to the Council and *eisangelia* to the court, which were separate procedures for different offenses. On the meaning of the term *rhetor* in the law see 191–92.

58. For the relationships among the three sources with good discussion see Hansen (1975) 12–14.

59. Rhodes (1979) 107–8 believes that the procedure also covered unnamed offenses but see Hansen (1980b) 92–93. Engels (2008) 118 claims that Lycurgus takes advantage of such a clause, but the text makes it clear that the law does not specifically cover the actions committed by Leocrates. Engels appears unaware of Hansen's refutation of Rhodes' views.

This problem arose at the trial for the murder of Herodes for homicide (Antiphon 5). The relatives of Herodes did not use the standard action for homicide, the *dike phonou*, against the defendant, but employed the procedure of *apagoge*, which was available against a special class of 'wrongdoers' (*kakourgoi*). Instead of leaving this general term unclear, the law attempted to define it by listing three groups that were subject to the procedure: thieves, 'clothes-stealers,' and enslavers (Arist. *Ath. Pol.* 52.1).[60] The defendant claims that their use of the procedure is illegal since murder does not fall into one of these categories; his opponents claim that he is subject to the procedure because murder is a 'serious wrong' (Antiphon 5.10: *mega kakourgema*).[61] The defendant thinks the list of wrongdoers listed in the law was intended to be exhaustive; his opponents argue that his offense fell under the general category of 'serious wrongs' covered by the law.

Like the law about *eisangelia* with treason, the law about *apagoge* to the Eleven attempted to define a general term. But the 'solution' may have created more problems than it solved. Instead of trying to express the precise meaning of the word, the lawgiver simply gave examples, which provide some, but not complete, guidance about how to use the term.[62] The lawgiver is similar to several of Socrates' interlocutors, who, when asked to explain the meaning of a term, give a set of examples.[63] When Socrates asks Theaetetus what knowledge is, he replies 'Knowledge is the subjects one can learn from Theodorus—geometry and all the sciences you mentioned just now, and then the skills of the cobbler and other craftsmen.' Socrates makes fun of Theaetetus for giving him several things when he asked for one. This is like being asked what clay is and answering that it is potter's clay, and oven-maker's clay, and brick-maker's clay. Such an answer does not help us to understand the term (Pl. *Tht.* 146c–147b). Theaetetus does a better job with the terms 'square number' and 'oblong number,' for which he can give a simple formula (Pl. *Tht.* 147e–148d). Euthyphro has similar difficulty with the term 'holy' (Pl. *Euthphr.* 5d–6b), and Meno has the same trouble with 'virtue' and 'shape' (Pl. *Meno* 71d–75b). In each case

---

60. For the rationale behind grouping these felons together see Harris (2006a) 385–88.

61. Cf. Gagarin (1997) 179–182.

62. Cf. Engels (2008) 149: 'athenische Gesetze üblicherweise einen justiziablen Tatbestand wie die *prodosia* (Verrat) nich allgemein definierten, sondern exemplarish einzelne Handlungsweisen aufführten, die als Verrat galten.'

63. This is also true for the term 'just homicide'—see D. 23.53–61; Arist. *Ath. Pol.* 57.3. For the categories see 50–53 and 168–69.

Socrates complains that the examples do not show him the one quality or set of qualities all the examples have in common. Because the Athenian lawgiver was no Socrates, his only attempt to clarify key terms was to offer a list, but this did little to make the court's decision any easier in the case of Leocrates.

The facts of the case of Leocrates were not in dispute. After their disastrous defeat at Chaeronea in 338, the Athenians expected the victorious Philip to invade Attica at any moment. The Assembly voted to bring all women and children inside the walls of Athens and instructed the generals to assign any Athenian or foreigner resident in Athens to guard the city (16).[64] During the crisis, Leocrates left Athens and sailed to the island of Rhodes. Lycurgus claims that Leocrates left Athens with the intention of moving away permanently since he took the belongings he had and his mistress (17). A later portion of the narrative reveals that Leocrates left slaves behind in Athens and did not sell his house until sometime later, thereby casting doubt on this claim (21–23). After arriving in Rhodes, Leocrates told people about the situation in Athens (18). Witnesses testified at the trial that Leocrates left Athens during the war and reported news about Athens in Rhodes. Another witness, Phyrcinus, had accused Leocrates in the Assembly of 'harming the one-fiftieth tax,' which was a tax on imports and exports (19). His charge was probably that by spreading news about the crisis, Leocrates discouraged merchants from bringing their cargoes to Athens, which would have reduced the amount of tax Phyrcinus could have collected. One should not place too much weight on the testimony of Phyrcinus, who had invested in the contract for collecting the tax and must have lost money during the crisis when imports were scared away. With an obvious motive to find a scapegoat, Phyrcinus had a reason to exaggerate the impact Leocrates' news had on merchants in Rhodes. But the other witnesses do not appear to have had a similar bias. Besides, Lycurgus appears to have assumed that his opponents would not deny his journey to Rhodes and expected them to base their case on other grounds.[65]

After leaving Rhodes, Leocrates went to Megara, where he took up residence (21). From there he asked his brother-in-law to buy his house and slaves, settle his debts, and send the remaining money to him. Leocrates then invested this money to buy grain in Epirus and to ship it to Leucas,

64. On the measures taken after Chaeronea see Engels (1993) 99–114.

65. Lycurgus also challenged Leocrates to turn over his slaves for questioning under torture, but Leocrates declined the request—Lycurg *Leocr.* 28–36.

and thence to Corinth. Lycurgus called witnesses to prove the sale took place, but provides no evidence about his trading in grain (23–4).[66] After living in Megara for six years, he returned to Athens in 331 and was indicted by Lycurgus for treason.[67]

Lycurgus bases his case on the law, but admits that he is asking the court to innovate by applying it to an action that was not listed in the law. The lawgiver formulated the law for a general category designated by a single word, treason (9), then listed several offenses in the law under this general category. Lycurgus argues that the offense of Leocrates falls under the general category, though it does not fit one of the specific examples listed in the law (9). Since Leocrates' offense is far worse than any of the specific offenses listed in the law, it should be subject to the same penalties. Lycurgus does not devote much space to discussing the meaning of 'treason' until he deals with the objections he predicts his opponents will bring. To support his interpretation of the law, he appeals to several precedents; we will examine them in the next chapter.

A little over one-third of the way through his speech, Lycurgus declares he has proven his case and turns to meet possible objections. The main line of defense he predicts his adversaries will take is that Leocrates sailed as a merchant, not to flee Athens (55–8).[68] The argument is significant for it reveals that to convict on a charge of treason a prosecutor could not only look at the defendant's actions but must also prove that he had the intent to betray the city. What Lycurgus does not say is that the Athenians desperately needed large supplies of grain in 338 to withstand the long siege they anticipated from the Macedonian army. Leocrates could easily have alleged he intended to sail to Rhodes to buy grain and ship it back to Athens, then changed his mind after he heard that peace was concluded.

Lycurgus tries to refute this objection on the grounds of lack of intent in three ways. First he draws attention to the manner in which Leocrates left the city, not openly by the harbor, but through a small gate in a surreptitious fashion. Second, he left with his mistress and her slave attendants.

---

66. On the suggestion of Tritle (1999) that Lycurgus charged Leocrates with treason for his close relations with the Macedonian Antipater see Engels (2008) 130.

67. Engels (2008) 132 believes that the narrative about Leocrates' residence in Megara (25–27) has nothing to do with the legal charge, but the details are important for supporting Lycurgus' arguments about Leocrates' motives in leaving Athens.

68. Durrbach (1956) 51, note 1 and Malcovati (1966) 97, note 1 claimed that the *emporoi* enjoyed an exemption from military duty in the same way as toll collectors, archons, and members of the Council did, but see Engels (2008) 145, note 104.

Merchants, on the other hand, normally took only their own personal slave attendant (55). Finally, Lycurgus asks why Leocrates then spent five years working as a merchant in Megara. He contrasts Leocrates, who aimed at increasing his wealth, with other Athenians, who thought only about preserving what they had (56–7). The most useful thing Leocrates could have done was to report for duty—what more valuable cargo could he have brought to the city? Lycurgus passes over the city's need for grain at the time and attacks his story as implausible since Leocrates had never sailed as a merchant before but had made money from slaves working as smiths (58).[69] But his reply to these objections does yield to his adversaries on one point: Lycurgus implicitly acknowledges that is not enough to prove that Leocrates left Athens during a crisis. He must also prove that he intended to harm the city.

The potential objection and Lycurgus' reply show that both sides expected the court to take Leocrates' intention for leaving Athens into consideration. This was not an unreasonable expectation. Dinarchus (1.58) recalls a case where the Assembly had ordered the Areopagus to investigate whether Polyeuctus of Cydantidai had met with exiles in Megara. After the Areopagus reported that he had, the Assembly elected prosecutors, and the case came to court. Polyeuctus admitted that he had gone to Megara to meet his stepfather Nicophanes. The court acquitted him for the reason that there was nothing unusual or dangerous about speaking to a stepfather who had fallen on hard times and trying to help him after he had been driven into exile. The court clearly examined Polyeuctus' intent and concluded that his aim was not to help the enemy but to assist a poor relative. Since he did not intend to harm Athens, the court did not convict him of treason. Although the law did not provide a definition of treason (as opposed to a list of examples), the courts clearly understood that the *Tatbestand* of the offense required the intent to harm Athenian interests; simply communicating with the enemy (*dieilechthai men tois polemiois*) was not treason (*ou prodounai*).

The next argument Lycurgus (*Leocr.* 59–62) anticipates is that Leocrates may say he was not responsible for the dockyards, gates, or camps. This argument relies on the standard use of the terms 'treason' (*prodosia*) and 'betray' (*prodidonai*). In most of the cases where the terms are found, the traitor betrays the city by opening gates in the defenses or allowing the

69. Leocrates' decision to sell his slaves who worked as smiths (22, 58) may have been caused by the drop in demand for weapons after peace was concluded with Philip.

enemy to gain control of the dockyards or a camp in a similar way. For instance, Dinarchus (3.8–10) calls Philocles a traitor and says the he is the sort of person who will sell strategic parts of the city, betray triremes and their ship-sheds, sell Munychia, make signals to the enemy, and reveal secrets, or betray the army and the fleet. In fact, the law about *eisangelia* appears to envisage precisely these kinds of treasonous actions. Thus this objection relies heavily on a close reading of the law and assumes that any treasonous action not enumerated in the law is not subject to its provisions. If the defendant did not place, or attempt to place, some strategic point in the hands of the enemy, the law does not apply. Lycurgus interprets treason more broadly as any one simply abandoning the country or not taking up a position to defend it.

The third objection Lycurgus expects to hear is that the action of one man would not have done any serious harm to the city (63–7). The point of this objection is that Leocrates' departure did not place the city in jeopardy in the same way that opening a gate to the enemy would have. The absence of a single person would not have made any difference to the city's survival. Lycurgus will have none of this: he appeals to the ancient lawgivers, who did not vary penalties according to the harm done, but assigned the death penalty for many offenses great and small. They considered one factor alone: what would the impact be on other people if the crime grew more widespread? As in the case of Epicrates versus Athenogenes, Lycurgus justifies his interpretation of the statute by appealing to the intent of the lawgiver and uses one statute to justify his interpretation of another. He then draws a parallel to a man who walked into the Metroon and erased one law, then sought refuge in the excuse that the loss of one law would not do great damage.

A further objection is that the act of leaving Attica is not in itself treason (68–74). After all, the Athenians deserted Attica and went to Salamis in 480, then defeated the Persian invaders and helped to liberate Greece. Lycurgus ridicules this argument and denies that the Athenians abandoned Attica during the Persian Wars; they merely changed place as part of their plan to face the danger confronting them. Once again, Lycurgus expects his opponents to raise the question of motive and to stress that the act of leaving is not sufficient grounds for conviction. Lycurgus also recognizes the need to prove Leocrates' intent: he contrasts the aim of the Athenians in 480, which was a strategic withdrawal to place themselves in a better position to attack, with Leocrates' aim, which was to avoid danger altogether.

Lycurgus' own view of treason is closely linked to his view of citizenship. In his opinion, every citizen must do all in his power to defend his country. Although Leocrates may not have received an order from an official to perform a specific duty, Lycurgus maintains that all citizens have an implicit duty to remain in Attica during a crisis and take part in her defense. His main evidence for this view is the Ephebic Oath, which he claims all citizens swore.

> I shall not disgrace my sacred weapons nor shall I desert my comrade at my side, wherever I stand in the line. I shall fight in defense of things sacred and holy and shall hand down to my descendants a fatherland that is not smaller but larger and stronger to the best of my ability and with the help of all, and I shall obey those who on any occasion are governing prudently and [I will obey] the established laws and any that may be established prudently in the future. If anyone tries to destroy them, I shall resist to the best of my ability and with the help of all, and I shall honor the ancestral sacred rites.[70]

Lycurgus' argument depends heavily on these promises (77–78):

> Gentlemen, this is certainly a fine and sacred oath. All of Leocrates' actions have violated it. Indeed how could a man be more sacrilegious or more of a traitor to his country? How could anyone disgrace his arms more than by refusing to take them up and repel the enemy? How has the man who has failed to report for duty not abandoned his comrade and his post? How has the man who did not face danger defended what is holy and sacred? With what greater treason could he have abandoned the country? For his part, the country was deserted and left in the hands of the enemy. Well, then, won't you put to death this man who is guilty of every crime?

For Lycurgus any failure to live up to the duties of the oath constitutes treason and deserves serious punishment.

According to Aeschines (3.252), Leocrates escaped conviction by one vote.[71] It was in Aeschines' interest to exaggerate the closeness of the vote,

---

70. For the text see Rhodes and Osborne (2003) 440.

71. Sullivan (2002) attempts to interpret Aeschines' words as implying that Leocrates was convicted but escaped the death penalty but see Bianchi (2002) for the correct interpretation of his words.

but speaking only a year after the trial, he could not have misrepresented the outcome. If the Athenian trial was an *agon* (contest) where two Athenians competed to prove who was the better citizen and thus deserved to win regardless of the merits of his case, Lycurgus should have won hands down. He was one of the most powerful politicians in Athens at the time and had an impressive record of public service. He had secured the conviction of Lysicles, one of the generals who lost the battle of Chaeronea and persuaded the court to put him to death. He increased Athenian revenues and kept the fleet strong.[72] Leocrates, by contrast, had been living in Megara as a resident alien for five or six years and had no public service to boast about. But Lycurgus lost, and Leocrates went free. If the court paid close attention to the legal issues of the case, it is easier to make sense of the verdict. Lycurgus was obviously stretching the meaning of the term *prodosia* (treason) beyond its normally accepted sense. Although he succeeded in convincing almost half of the judges (who may have been swayed—or intimidated—by his prestige), the majority reasonably rejected his attempt to press the limits of the law's open texture. The plain language of the statute did provide some guidance. Because the facts of the case did not fit one of the situations enumerated in the law, the court sided with the defendant. We cannot know what weighed most heavily on the minds of the judges. But it is unreasonable to assume that the arguments Lycurgus feared his adversaries might make did not influence their decision.[73]

VII

There was a law in Athens that no one could be put to death without a trial (*akriton apokteinein*).[74] In a case against some grain-dealers, the accuser recalls how some members of the Council wished to put the defendants to death immediately. He objected to this because it was against the law to put anyone to death without a trial (Lys. 22.2). When prosecuting Aristocrates for an illegal decree, the prosecutor argues that the decree violates the law because it would result in those accused of murder being put to death without a trial (D. 23.27, 36). The Athenians extended this principle to their relations with their allies in the fifth century BCE. In their treaty with Chalcis,

72. For Lycurgus' achievements see [Plu.] *Mor.* 852b.

73. Allen (2000b) does not analyze the arguments of Leocrates' supporters nor analyze the problems involved with the law on *eisangelia* in her study of the case.

74. On this law see Carawan (1984). Putting citizens to death without a trial was one of the greatest crimes of the Thirty: Aeschin. 2.77; 3.235; Isoc. 7.67; 20.11.

the Athenians promised not to put any Chalcidians to death or to confiscate their property without first presenting a summons and granting a trial (*IG* i^3 40, lines 8–10).[75] Like some Athenian statutes, this law appears not to have defined what a trial was, but in most cases this would not have posed a problem because most Athenians had a common understanding of the basic features of a trial: the defendant should be summoned to appear before a magistrate, the accuser should present his charges according to a procedure provided by law and in written form, the accuser and the defendant should be given an equal amount of time to speak and to present evidence, and the case should be decided by judges who had sworn an oath and who voted by secret ballot. Although the law also did not define what the term 'without a trial' meant, the laws of Athens required that litigants and officials follow specific procedures set forth in different statutes.[76]

But the precise definition of what constituted a trial became a matter of controversy in 406 after the battle of Arginousai. We will study the political context of the trial more closely in chapter 9; the only aspect of the trial examined here is the legal issue. Six of the generals who participated in the battle returned to Athens and made a report to the Council stating that they could not recover men whose ships were wrecked because of a storm (X. *HG* 1.7.1–3). Timocrates then passed a motion that they be tried in the Assembly. At a meeting of the Assembly, Theramenes demanded that the generals be held accountable for the men lost (X. *HG* 1.7.4). The generals 'briefly' defended their actions but were not given the time to speak allotted by law (X. *HG* 1.7.5). This must mean that they were not allowed to speak for the length of time normally allotted to defendants in a public trial, which may have been up to three hours each. They almost persuaded the Assembly of their innocence, but the discussion was postponed to another meeting because it was late. The Council was instructed to draw up a decree about how the men were to be tried (X. *HG* 1.7.6–7). At a subsequent meeting of the Assembly, Callixeinus introduced a motion, which he had passed in the Council. According to this decree, the people were to cast votes by secret ballot, each tribe separately about the guilt of the generals. If they were guilty, they were to be handed over to the Eleven for execution, and their

75. The right to a trial did not automatically apply to foreigners—see Lys. 6.54. Cf. D. 18.133 (Antiphon who had lost his citizenship is tortured and put to death, apparently without a trial).

76. One litigant says that those who are convicted after the court has learned the facts are not condemned 'without a trial' but only those who are slandered by their enemies in matters about which the court has no knowledge (Lys. 27.8), but this may be a persuasive definition.

property confiscated. The reason why they should proceed to a vote about their guilt was that the accusers and the generals had already had an opportunity to present their cases at the previous meeting of the Assembly (X. *HG* 1.7.9–10). Euryptolemus attempted to serve a summons to Callixeinus on the grounds that he had made an illegal proposal, but he was forced to back down by threats and the motion was put to a vote (X. *HG* 1.7.12–16).

In the debate about the motion, Euryptolemus proposed an alternative motion from the floor, which would have granted the defendants their right to a trial either under the law of Cannonus or the law about temple-robbers and traitors: 'let them be tried according to that law (whichever one you choose), each one separately, with the day divided into three parts, one during which you must gather and vote whether they are guilty or not, another during which the accusation is made and another during which the defense is made' (X. *HG* 1.7.20–23). Euryptolemus was, therefore, asking the Athenians to grant each defendant his right to a normal trial (cf. Aeschin. 3.197–98). Otherwise, the Athenians would put the generals to death without a trial (*akritous*) in violation of the law (*para ton nomon*) (X. *HG* 1.7.24–5). Callixeinus and Euryptolemus clearly understood the law forbidding execution without trial in different ways. Callixeinus thought that the generals had been given their chance to defend themselves at the previous meeting; Euryptolemus did not because each defendant had not been given the normal amount of time to defend himself. When the vote was taken, Callixeinus' motion was ultimately approved, and the vote about the generals followed. They were condemned and put to death.

Soon afterward, the Athenians understood that they had made a serious mistake in not following the normally accepted meaning of the statute. For twisting the meaning of the law, the Athenians attempted to put Callixeinus and his associates on trial, but he escaped from prison. When he returned to Athens in 403, everybody hated him, and he died of starvation (X. *HG* 1.7.35). In this case the Athenians realized too late that there were limits to exploiting the law's open texture. They knew that it was best to stick to the standard interpretation of the law.

VIII

The findings of this chapter provide further support for the conclusions reached in the previous chapter. First, the litigants in the speeches studied in both chapters pay close attention to the exact wording of the law. Because the charges in the plaint had to conform to the language of the relevant statute and because the litigants had to address the charges, they also had to structure their arguments in terms of the language of the statute. Second, some litigants attempted to stretch the meaning of key terms and to take advantage of the law's open texture. The officials accepted the plaints of the accusers who interpreted the law in new and unusual ways; they did not reject a plaint because the charges did not adhere to the standard interpretation of the relevant statute but left the decision in the hands of public arbitrators and judges. Third, when judges were confronted by two different interpretations of the same statute they tended to accept the traditional interpretation of its wording and to reject new or unusual readings of the law.[77] They were reluctant to follow clever and ingenious interpretations of the law not because they were suspicious of legal expertise, but because they distrusted intellectuals and those trained in rhetoric. In the next chapter, we will see how litigants used precedents to convince judges that they were following the traditional interpretation of a statute.

The conclusions of this chapter also help us understand how the judges viewed their role in the broader context of Athenian democracy. In two of the speeches studied in this chapter, the accuser asks the judges to act as lawgivers (*nomothetai*), that is, to apply the law in a new way so that it covers actions that had not previously been punished (Lys. 14.4; Lycurg. *Leocr.* 9). As we have seen, the courts in both cases rejected the accusers' invitations to act as lawgivers. Their oath obligated them to decide cases in accordance with the laws and decrees of the Athenian people; it did not grant them the power to legislate. In the fifth century, the constitution of the Athenians placed that power in the hands of the Assembly, in the fourth century, in the hands of the Assembly and the *nomothetai*.[78] This was the democratic approach: decisions about general rules regulating the public and private affairs of those resident in Attica should be made by the citizens of Athens voting in the Assembly, where all male citizens had the right to vote.[79] To have a court, which might have had as few as two or

77. Cf. Todd (1996) 121: when it came to laws 'a text was to be read according to its natural and contemporary meaning.'

78. Even though the *nomothetai* gave final approval to the laws in the fourth century, it was the Assembly that initiated all laws and submitted them to the *nomothetai*. Their authority derived from the citizens of Athens, which is why they were called the laws of the Athenians (not the laws of the *nomothetai*). See Hansen (1979).

79. For this general principle see Th. 2.37.1 with Harris (2006a) 29–40. On the other hand, it would be anachronistic to read into Athenian practice the modern doctrine of 'judicial restraint' when interpreting the law.

three hundred judges, enact legislation for all Athenians was not democratic but oligarchic. The best way to respect the authority of the Assembly, therefore, was to read the laws the Athenians enacted in the most straightforward way possible. Democratic ideology and the absence of any doctrine of binding precedent, therefore, inhibited the development of 'judge-made law,' which the Athenians would have viewed as oligarchic.

7

Did the Athenian Courts Attempt to Achieve Consistency?

THE USE OF PRECEDENTS IN FORENSIC ORATORY

MOST LEGAL SCHOLARS would agree that one of the main requirements for achieving the rule of law is that the courts should maintain consistency and predictability by judging like cases alike.[1] This means that the courts should not apply one rule in a certain case and another rule in a similar case or use discretion instead of consistent rules.[2] One of the ways to achieve consistency is to ensure that the laws do not contradict each other and do not contain inconsistent rules. The Athenians certainly valued consistency in their legislation. When Nicomachus served as one of the *anagrapheis* selected to revise the laws of Athens, an accuser criticized him for providing litigants with conflicting statutes in the same cases (Lys. 30.3). Another litigant complains that the existence of two contradictory laws would make it impossible for the judges to uphold their oath: 'Imagine if there should be two laws contradicting each other, and two litigants should appear before you in court about some private or public matter, with each one demanding to win his case without citing the same law. It would certainly be impossible for the judges to vote for both litigants. How could they? Nor could they vote for either litigant and abide by their oath for their verdict would go against the opposing law, which was equally valid' (D. 24.35).

Throughout the Classical period, the Athenians attempted to maintain consistency in their laws.[3] In the fifth century, the Athenians established

1. See, for instance, Rawls (1971) 235–41. See also Fuller (1964) who states that the lack of consistent rules or laws, which leads to ad hoc or inconsistent adjudication, and contradictions in the law are two signs of the absence of the rule of law.

2. See for example Bingham (2010) 48–54.

3. On this topic see Sickinger (2008) with examples from other Greek *poleis*.

a public action against illegal proposals, which was aimed in part at preventing politicians from introducing measures violating existing legislation. When Callixeinus proposed that the Assembly vote about the guilt of six generals accused of not recovering bodies after the battle of Arginousai, Euryptolemus attempted to stop his motion by charging that it violated the laws forbidding execution without trial (X. *HG* 1.7.9–12). After the restoration of the democracy in 403, a distinction was made between laws (*nomoi*) and decrees (*psephismata*), and a special new procedure was created to enact laws.[4] It was illegal to propose a law contradicting existing legislation. If someone attempted to introduce such a law, there was a public action against inexpedient laws (D. 24.32, 34). When enacting a new law, the proposer had first to rescind any laws that might contradict it by following this procedure (D. 20.93, 96; 24.32–36). The law of Nicophon enacted in 375/4 instructs the secretary of the Council to destroy all decrees that contradict its provisions (*SEG* 26:72, lines 55–56). By the middle of the fourth century, the Athenians also instituted an annual review of legislation. Every year the *thesmothetai* examined the laws to see if there were laws that contradicted each other or were invalid or if there was more than one law on a given topic. If the *thesmothetai* found any such laws, they posted them in the Agora before the statues of the Eponymous Heroes, and the *prytaneis* held a meeting of the Assembly to determine which laws were to be removed and which were to be retained (Aeschin. 3.39).

In the last two chapters, we have seen that even though two litigants would base their cases on the same law or set of laws, there was no guarantee that they would interpret the law in the same way. The Assembly and the *nomothetai* certainly showed a concern for consistency when passing legislation, but did the courts have the same concern for consistency when it came to applying the law? When it was possible to interpret the law in two or more different ways, did the courts apply the law one way in one case and another way in a different case? Or did they adopt an ad hoc approach?

In common law jurisdictions, the primary way of maintaining consistency in the application of the law is through the doctrine that precedents are binding. If there is a controversy about the meaning of a statute, each party will attempt to find previous decisions where the courts chose to follow a certain interpretation of law, one that each hopes favors his or her

4. On the procedures for *nomothesia*, Canevaro (forthcoming) supersedes all previous work.

client. Judges and courts are obliged to follow these precedents, and any judgment that does not follow them is subject to appeal to a higher court. To enforce these precedents, courts in the United States, Canada, and the United Kingdom keep extensive written records of previous decisions, which normally contain the reasons for a decision.

In Classical Athens during the fourth century, litigants could consult written copies of the laws kept in the Metroon and in the offices of various magistrates. As we saw in chapter 3, however, the records of court decisions were rather laconic by modern standards, containing only the names of the plaintiff or accuser and defendant, the nature of the charge, the main facts of the case, the verdict, and if a public charge, the penalty.[5] If the case dealt with a controversial legal issue, the record did not state the reasons why the court decided in the way it did.[6] And certainly in a system where the trials were heard by hundred of judges, it would have been difficult if not impossible to write down the collective opinion of the court in any given case.

One scholar has recently argued that the Athenians did not have the written documents needed to achieve consistency in the application of the law.[7] She has rightly drawn attention to the sparse documentation for cases kept in the Metroon and contrasted it unfavorably with the extensive records kept in modern legal systems. She also believes that the orators rarely discuss previous cases in the way modern lawyers analyze precedents. For instance, she claims that the orators do not generally search for the *ratio dicendi* of the verdict they cite and do not discuss adverse precedents to show that they do not apply to the case before the court. From this she concludes that the Athenian courts did not pursue legal consistency as a goal since they lacked the written records that would have enabled them to do so. In this respect the Athenian courts did not attempt to achieve the rule of law but rendered justice on an ad hoc basis.[8]

---

5. Lanni (2004) 164 claims that 'it is highly probable that verdicts were not regularly recorded in the Metroon or elsewhere' but see chapter 3, section II.

6. The only records that give the reason for a decision are the naval records, which sometimes state that a defendant was acquitted on the charge of losing equipment because a storm prevented him and decrees passed about judicial proceedings in the Assembly (D. 19.276–9). See 299–300.

7. Lanni (2004). Wohl (2010) 31–2 claims that the 'jurors in any given case followed or set precedents only in a figurative sense,' but it is not clear what she means by 'in a figurative sense.' Wohl discusses none of the uses of precedent studied in this essay. On the topic of precedents she cites Lanni (2004) but appears to be unaware of Harris (2006b).

8. This assumption recurs like a leitmotif throughout Lanni (2006).

This view of precedents in Athenian courts is vulnerable to several objections. First, the use of the statistical method is misleading; the alleged rarity of precedents in the modern sense is an illusion. Second, the list of passages where orators appeal to precedents is incomplete.[9] Third, this view underestimates the oral and written resources available to help the courts achieve consistency in their decisions. These objections seriously undermine her general conclusion that the Athenian courts judged cases on an ad hoc basis.

This chapter shows that the Athenian courts were far more concerned with consistency than this scholar assumes. Although we find relatively few instances where previous cases are cited as precedents in the modern sense of the term, this is because relatively few of the cases for which the preserved speeches were written involve disputes about the meaning of the law.[10] In cases where a legal issue does arise, however, the orators often do appeal to precedents.[11] Although the orators often rely on the public memory rather than documents, they are careful to refer to cases that the judges would know either because they were recent causes célèbres or cases that had previously come before them. When a case was not recent, an orator would try to produce a written document to support his argument. Furthermore, when a litigant knows that his opponent will appeal to precedents in support of his case, he does not ignore them but argues that they are not relevant to the case under consideration by the court. He would not have done so unless he had been worried that the court would be influenced by arguments based on precedent. Furthermore, in actions against illegal decrees (*graphai paranomon*) there were written copies of

---

9. Lanni (2004) 168, note 5 did not make her own list of precedents but relies on a list from an unpublished paper of Rubinstein delivered at the American Philological Association.

10. For a list of the issues in Athenian court speeches see appendix 7. Dorjahn (1928) 377–378 claims that the cases cited by Athenian litigants 'are scarcely comparable to the modern practice of defining and establishing a law by court decision.' But his reason for this view is that in modern American courts 'only the decisions of a judge establish a legal precedent' whereas 'there were no judges in ancient Athens and all trials were by jury.' This argument rests on a mistranslation of the Greek word *dikastes* as 'juror.' The noun *dikastes* is formed from the verb *dikazein* (to judge) and therefore means one who judges, i.e., decides both the legal and the factual issues in a case. See Harris (1994b) 136–137. In Athenian law there was no division of functions between a judge, who decided questions of law, and a jury, which decided questions of fact. The Athenian *dikastes* combined both roles and was therefore like a modern judge at a bench trial, where the defendant gives up the right to a trial by jury.

11. This evidence presented in this chapter shows that the assertion of Foxhall and Lewis (1996b) 6 that 'Though laws are often cited in forensic speeches, precedents are not' is untenable.

previous decrees whose legality had been questioned but then upheld or had been passed without challenge. These could serve as precedents when a decree was challenged and were cited in *graphe paranomon* cases.[12] One must also bear in mind that the use of precedent is not the only way to achieve consistency: a litigant can also appeal to the intent of the lawgiver and argue that his own interpretation of the law is consistent with the principles found in other statutes. In several cases orators draw on the written copies of the laws to show that their reading of the law is correct. Finally, the evidence that we do have for verdicts in cases where the courts had to make a decision on a legal issue suggests that the Athenian legal system was more concerned about achieving consistency than several modern scholars have assumed.

I

The orators often mention previous cases, but only some of these are cited as precedents to help decide a legal question. At times, earlier cases are presented as evidence to support statements of fact. For instance, one speaker calls as witnesses some men from Decelea who had brought cases against Pancleon before the Polemarch and won convictions (Lys. 23.4). The speaker mentions these cases to prove that Pancleon is not a Plataean and a citizen, as he claims, but a freedman. Another speaker has witnesses testify that his father brought a suit against Erasistratus for a debt owed to his father (the speaker's grandfather) and obtained a judgment against him (Lys. 17.3). Here the litigant's object is to show that Eraton, who succeeded to Erasistratus' estate and inherited his debts, now owes him money. Demosthenes describes in some detail a public arbitration for a case he brought against Meidias not to make a legal point but to denounce his opponent's cruelty and dishonesty (D. 21.83–101). Finally, Apollodorus describes a decision made by the Areopagus to prove that Neaera's daughter was not an Athenian ([D.] 59.79–84).[13]

Orators might also refer to previous cases in which the court had imposed a harsh punishment (usually death). The speaker's aim in these passages has nothing to do with the legal issue but is rather to overcome

12. Cf. Faraguna (2006) 206.

13. Cf. Lys. 13.65–66 where the speaker mentions that Agoratus' three brothers were executed to show that he comes from a bad family.

the court's natural reluctance to put someone to death (e.g., D. 21.182; 24.138; Lys. 12.36; 22.16). The reasoning is usually 'others have put dangerous criminals to death so therefore you should too because the defendant is clearly guilty of a serious crime.'[14] Demosthenes (22.51, 57) tells us that the Athenians prided themselves on their reputation for mildness; if they were going to punish someone with great severity, they therefore needed to be reassured that they were doing nothing unusual or extreme. Accusers will also describe cases where the court voted to impose a severe penalty on men who had performed many public services or enjoyed high status as a way of arguing that liturgies and social prestige should not stand in the way of conviction and punishment (D. 21.178, 182; 34.50; Din. 1.14; Aeschin. 3.195). Here the speaker is urging the judges to pay more attention to their oath to uphold the laws of Athens than to the prior achievements of the defendant.[15]

The scholar who claims that the Athenian courts made ad hoc judgments does, however, admit that in eight passages orators cite previous cases as true precedents and these passages show 'an attempt at the application of the *ratio dicendi* derived from an earlier case. This demonstrates that Athenian litigants could construct an argument by analogy.'[16] But she

14. Several of the cases listed in Rubinstein (2007) 367 fall into this category and are not precedents used as evidence to support the interpretation of a specific law: D. 19.180, 280; D. 21.143–7; 24.138; Aeschin. 3.252; Lycurg. *Leocr.* 112–5, 117–8; Din. 1.23. Other cases listed by Rubinstein are also not legal precedents *stricto sensu*: Antiphon 5.69–70. (cases cited to illustrate the point that one should not put someone to death without clear evidence); Lys. 6.54 (a Megarian put on trial for impiety to show how pious the Athenians are); 12.36 (an a fortiori argument: you put generals to death although they had an excuse so therefore you should punish Eratosthenes who has no excuse); Lys. 27.4 (the speaker criticizes the court for inconsistency!).

15. Lanni (2004) 161–163 recognizes that these are not true precedents but claims that 'these passages seem to reflect rather than rectify the general tendency of Athenian litigants to mix the social context of a particular case with legal arguments.' *Pace* Lanni the speakers in these passages tell the judges that their oath compels them to pay no attention to the social position of the defendant. Rubinstein (2007) 367, note 14 makes the mistake of calling these cases precedents. See chapter 3, section II.

16. Lanni's eight passages are D. 21.72–76; 175–184; 19.273ff.; Lys. 6.17; 13.56; Din. 2.25; Aeschin. 1.86–88; Isoc. 18.22; Lycurg. *Leocr.* 52. D. 21.72–76 is not relevant since Demosthenes is contrasting his own conduct, not that of the defendant Meidias, with the way Euaeon reacted when he was punched by Boeotus. Rubinstein (2007) 367, note 14 also makes the mistake of calling this case a precedent. Aeschin. 1.86–88 has more to do with a question of evidence than a legal issue (can one convict in the absence of the testimony of witnesses?). The banishment of Arthmius mentioned at Din. 2.24–25 is not used as a precedent to resolve a legal point nor are the two cases alluded to at Aeschin. 3.252. The latter two trials serve to show that Demosthenes is asking to be praised for actions for which one man was executed and another almost put to death (cf. Aeschin. 3.258).

claims that such arguments are uncommon and attributes their 'relative rarity' to the 'general Athenian reservations about overly legalistic arguments.' She finds the 'sophisticated use of previous decisions' in just two speeches, Demosthenes' *Against Meidias* (21.69–73, 175–178) and Lycurgus' *Against Leocrates* (52), but she calls these examples 'exceptional.'

But how often would a litigant normally find it necessary to cite precedents to persuade the court to follow one interpretation of the law as opposed to another? One should bear in mind that a speaker only needed to adduce precedents when there was a crucial legal issue to be decided. On the other hand, if both litigants implicitly agreed on the meaning of the law and disagreed only about the facts, there would be no reason to present legal arguments that relied on precedents. So the relative absence of precedents need not mean that the Athenians found them 'legalistic'; it may only indicate that they rarely found that kind of argument relevant to the case. Even in modern legal systems, lawyers do not cite precedents in most routine cases, which tend to be dominated by questions of fact, not legal issues.[17] For instance, almost all the speeches of Isaeus concern issues of fact, and previous cases are never cited to resolve a legal issue. The same is true for most of the private speeches in the demosthenic corpus.[18]

Let us take the thirty-three speeches in the Lysianic corpus. Two of these orations were not delivered in court (2 and 8), one is a summary of the preceding speech (11), and two speeches concern a single case (14 and 15). That leaves us with thirty speeches about twenty-nine cases. Yet, out of these twenty-nine cases, twenty-six primarily involve questions of fact (see appendix 8). In three of these cases legal issues surface briefly: there is a short discussion of the meaning of the law on deliberate wounding at Lysias 3.40–43, an answer to a legal point made by the defendant at Lysias 13.55–57, and an argument about the legal implications of remaining neutral at Lysias 31.27. The legal issue predominates in only three cases (Lys. 9, 10, 14/15). Therefore in the vast majority of cases in the Lysianic corpus an argument based on precedent would have been out of place.

What is striking is that in four of the six cases where legal issues arise, the speaker refers to precedents to support his interpretation of

17. Rubinstein (2007) does not link the use of precedent to the type of issue in a speech and thus cannot explain why precedents occur in some speeches and not in others.

18. See appendix 7 for the issues in Isaeus, the private speeches of the demosthenic corpus, and Lysias.

the law. At Lysias 3.40–43 the defendant discusses the nature of the intent required to prove a charge of deliberate homicide and claims that the accuser must show that there was intent to kill, not just to wound.[19] He backs up his interpretation by claiming 'you have decided this way many times in the past on the matter of intention' (43).[20] In other words he appeals to the precedents created by the Areopagus. He does not have to call witnesses or present documents to prove that the Areopagus ruled this way before because he is addressing the members of that Council, who, of course, were fully aware of their own previous decisions.

The legal issue in Lysias' *Against Agoratus* is somewhat more complex. Agoratus is charged with having denounced the speaker's father Dionysodorus for treason (Lys. 13.23–35). As a result of his statement, Dionysodorus and several others were tried and put to death (Lys. 13.36–42). The speaker has accused Agoratus of murder since he was responsible, in his opinion, for the death of these men and has used the procedure of *apagoge* to the Eleven to bring him to court. The case turns partly on questions of fact: the speaker claims that Agoratus could have left Athens without denouncing anyone, but Agoratus was evidently prepared to argue that his denunciation was obtained under duress (Lys. 13.23–30). But according to the speaker, Agoratus also intended to argue that he was not 'clearly' responsible for killing Dionysodorus since he did not directly cause his death. The speaker counters this defense by arguing that all those who cause the death of another person are guilty of killing (Lys. 13.85–87). This might appear to be an unusual interpretation of 'to kill,' but it is not unparalleled in Athenian law.[21] The significant point for this chapter is that the speaker presents a case that supports his interpretation of the law. He recalls how Menestratus, who had been denounced by Agoratus, denounced others in return for his freedom. After the overthrow of the Thirty, Menestratus was charged with murder, convicted, and executed

19. The speaker appears to equate the charge of deliberate wounding with that of attempted homicide, but this is unlikely since we know there was a separate action for 'planning a homicide' (*bouleusis phonou*). See Harris (2006a) 400–4. It is more likely that the speaker is inventing a persuasive (and unusual) definition of the term to increase the burden of proof on the accuser.

20. Rubinstein (2007) 367, note 14 does not list this passage as an example of argument from precedent.

21. See Harris (2006a) 396–98.

(Lys. 13.55–57). The precedent here is directly relevant to the legal issue in the case.[22]

Against Philon (Lys. 31) is another speech where a legal issue is briefly discussed. This speech was delivered in a *dokimasia* before the Council of 500. Before someone who had been selected by lot to serve as an archon could assume office, he had to have his qualifications checked. The Council asked a series of questions to determine whether he was an Athenian citizen, observed certain religious rites, treated his parents well, belonged to the right property class, and had served on military campaigns (Arist. *Ath. Pol.* 55.3). If anyone had an objection to him serving in office, that person could then bring an accusation (Arist. *Ath. Pol.* 55.4). An accuser at Philon's *dokimasia* charged that the candidate went to Oropus after the overthrow of the democracy in 404, failed to support the democrats in their efforts to oust the Thirty Tyrants in 404/3 and thus should be disqualified (Lys. 31.8–16). The speaker anticipates that Philon will reply that he broke no law by remaining in Oropus during the Civil War and should therefore not be barred (Lys. 31.27).[23] The accuser attempts to refute this argument by contending that his actions were equivalent to desertion and treason (Lys. 31.28–29, 31). At the end of the speech, the accuser appeals to precedent by asking the members of the Council to apply to Philon the same standard that was used in each of their own cases (Lys. 31.34). The *dokimasia* was not strictly speaking a trial that determined guilt and imposed a penalty, but an administrative procedure. Yet, even here, the speaker finds it appropriate to refer to previous decisions and to ask the members of the Council to follow the standard set in those cases.

In one of the cases where legal issues are more prominent, the speaker appeals to the decision of a board of officials as a precedent. In *For the Soldier* (Lys. 9) the defendant has been accused of breaking the law by slandering officials.[24] In his reply he relies on the letter of the law, which he says applies only to slander uttered in the official's office, not to criticisms

22. Lanni (2004) 168, note 5 includes this in her list of precedents but does not analyze its direct relevance to the legal issue in the case. There is also a brief discussion of a legal point at 88–90, but the speaker does not use any evidence to support his view of the reconciliation agreement of 403.

23. There was an old law requiring everyone to take a side during a period of civil war (Arist. *Ath. Pol.* 8.5), but Carey (1989) 198–200 is probably right to conclude that it had fallen out of use by 400 BCE.

24. On the case in general see MacDowell (1994) and Dreher 1994; Todd (2007) 604–23.

made outside their office (6); the generals who claim he slandered them apparently interpreted the law more broadly. To support his view of the law, the defendant points to the decision of clerks in the Treasury, who ruled that the fine imposed by the generals was null and void.[25] This is a ruling made by an official, not a court's verdict, but the defendant still uses the decision as a kind of precedent in support of his argument that the fine was illegal.

In the other two cases where legal issues predominate, the litigants appear to have had no precedents to support their arguments about the meaning of the law. In one case, the litigant virtually admits as much by asking the court to act as legislators by applying the law to a new category of offenders (Lys. 14.4). In the other, the speaker appeals to the intent of the lawgiver, a type of argument that I examine later (Lys. 10). But it is perhaps no coincidence that the courts found the first case weak.

A survey of the cases in the corpus Lysiacum therefore shows that when legal issues did arise, litigants regularly employed arguments from precedent. And when litigants faced legal issues and did not have precedents, the courts found their cases weak. We should now turn to examine three other cases, two from the demosthenic corpus and another by Lycurgus, where accusers use precedents to show that the pattern found in the speeches attributed to Lysias is not uncharacteristic.

In his speech *Against Meidias* Demosthenes brings a public charge of aggravated assault (*graphe hybreos*) against his opponent for interfering with his preparations for his chorus and mainly for punching him in the head during the competition at the Dionysia (D. 21.13–18).[26] The charge of *hybris* was a serious one, and Demosthenes contends that Meidias' offense was so heinous that he deserves the death penalty (D. 21.70, 118) or at least a heavy fine (D. 21.152, 211–212). The burden of Demosthenes' case is to prove that a mere punch on the head is actually a serious crime, and his accusation might appear at first glance to rely on an unusually broad interpretation of the term *hybris*.[27] To support his argument that Meidias' punch did fall into the category of actions covered by the law, Demosthenes

---

25. It is not clear what evidence the speaker provides at this point since there appears to be a lacuna in the text, but most editors assume that witnesses were called in the missing passage.

26. For the charge in *Against Meidias* see Harris (2008) 79–81.

27. On the term *hybris* see MacDowell (1976). For good criticisms of the approach of Fisher (1992) see MacDowell (1990) 19–20 and especially Cairns (1996).

(21.175–182) adduces several precedents and analyzes them to bring out their similarities to his own case. He recalls three similar cases in which the accuser initiated proceedings by bringing a *probole* in the Assembly, and after the Assembly voted against the defendant, then brought a case in court. Demosthenes is careful to select cases that have followed the same procedure that he did; he too had begun by making his charge with a *probole*, and after receiving a favorable vote in the Assembly, brought a case in court (as mentioned, a *graphe hybreos*). In other words, Demosthenes chooses three cases that were broadly similar to his in procedural terms.

Demosthenes does not start with a case from the distant past, which the judges might not know or only vaguely recollect. He begins with the most recent case, which would have been familiar to the court. He also deliberately selects a case that involves physical force so that it resembles his case against Meidias. The first case involves two foreigners, Evander of Thespiai and Menippus from Caria (D. 21.175–177). Evander had won a judgment in a maritime suit against Menippus, but had not been able to collect the money awarded to him. He finally caught up with Menippus during the Eleusinian Mysteries and seized him. Grabbing hold of defaulting debtors was perfectly legal at other times, but there was a law that banned the practice during the Dionysia and the Mysteries.[28] Menippus therefore brought a *probole* against Evander in the Assembly, which passed a vote of censure against Evander. Menippus could have left it at that but decided to press his advantage by bringing an action in court against his opponent. Demosthenes does not specify what kind of case Menippus brought, but it must have been a private action (probably a *dike blabes*, an action for damages) since the court cancelled the award made to Evander and granted him a payment of damages (*blabas*) for the expenses he incurred by remaining in Athens for the trial. Demosthenes' description of the verdict indicates that Menippus did not bring a public action after initiating proceedings in the Assembly; in that case the penalty would not have been paid to Menippus but to the public. In fact, Demosthenes (21.177) says that it was a private case (*ex idiou pragmatos*).[29] This creates problems for Demosthenes since he himself brought a public suit against Meidias after the vote in the Assembly. But Demosthenes still tries to

---

28. For the law see D. 21.10.

29. The case is misunderstood by Harrison (1971) 64, MacDowell (1990) 395, Rowe (1995) 57–8, Rubinstein (2000) 209, 42, and Scafuro (2004) 123–24. See Harris (2008) 80.

make Menippus' case similar to his by claiming that the court wanted to put Evander to death and relented only at the request of the accuser. Demosthenes' interpretation of the court's attitude must be speculative and is unlikely to be correct: Athenian courts never had a choice between imposing the death penalty (possible only in public suits) and awarding a payment of damages to the accuser (applicable only in private suits). What is important for our purposes, however, is that Demosthenes knows that for a precedent to be convincing it must resemble the present case as closely as possible. Since the case is not as similar to his as he would like it to be, Demosthenes adds a detail to make it look more similar than it actually was.

Demosthenes then compares the two cases. Menippus' case involved a private matter and did not contain any aggravating factors such as *hybris*. In both cases the defendant used physical force against the accuser. In his case, however, Meidias had no justification for attacking him (i.e., Demosthenes did not owe Meidias money), but did it solely to insult him. Despite the absence of aggravating factors, the court still voted to grant a settlement to Menippus. Demosthenes does not give the exact amount but gives the impression that it was large. One suspects that he avoids giving a precise figure because the amount was not all that great. Since Meidias' crime was much worse (D. 21.181), a fortiori he deserves a more serious punishment. Demosthenes' presentation and analysis of the precedent may shade the truth to some extent, but he clearly realizes that for his precedent to be persuasive its basic features must correspond as closely as possible to the present case in both procedural and substantive terms.

Demosthenes' next case is more similar to his in one regard but not as similar in another regard. The second case concerns a man who was serving as assessor to his son Charicleides, who held the position of archon and was highly regarded (D. 21.178–179). The assessor found someone who had taken the wrong seat in the theater and laid a hand on him as he escorted him out. The man who was struck brought a *probole* against the assessor, and the Assembly voted to censure him. During his speech in the Assembly, the accuser argued that the assessor should have punished him with a fine if he took the wrong seat and ignored the assessor's order to leave. He should have had his assistants remove him, not have touched him with his hand. Demosthenes naturally stresses the fact that the assessor used physical force in the same way Meidias did. He then argues that this use of force constituted *hybris*, the same charge that Demosthenes brought against Meidias. Demosthenes takes the Assembly's vote as an endorsement of the speaker's broad interpretation of the term *hybris*, which is here applied to a case where an official merely laid hands on a spectator. The similarity ends at this point since the victim did not live long enough to take his case to court.

Demosthenes' strongest precedent is his third case, and one suspects that he keeps his best case for last (D. 21.180). The defendant in this case was a man named Ctesicles. During a procession at a religious festival, Ctesicles got drunk and hit one of his enemies with a whip that he was carrying. Either his victim or someone else brought a *probole* against him in the Assembly for committing an offense against the festival. A separate charge was then brought against Ctesicles in court, and he was condemned to death. The charge must have been the *graphe hybreos* since Demosthenes says that the court decided that he had committed *hybris* despite his attempt to present an excuse. This precedent is much closer to his case than the other two. First, Ctesicles hit his victim during a religious festival; Meidias punched Demosthenes during the Dionysia. Second, Ctesicles struck a personal enemy; Demosthenes was a personal enemy of Meidias. Third, Ctesicles was judged to have struck with intent to humiliate; Meidias allegedly hit Demosthenes as a way of insulting him. The only difference is minor: Ctesicles used a whip while Meidias used his fist. Striking someone with a whip was the way one treated slaves, which is why Ctesicles was accused of treating free men like slaves. Yet, one could also beat slaves, so the type of violence employed in each case was similar. Ctesicles, however, claimed that he struck his victim because he was drunk and that the event took place during a procession.[30] The procession was probably part of the Dionysia, and one should bear in mind that Dionysus was the god of wine. Since one of the best ways to worship him was to drink, his festivals could be raucous affairs. Ctesicles may have argued that he had only entered into the spirit of the Dionysia and that he meant no harm. Evidently the court did not accept his excuse and sentenced him to death. Thus Demosthenes has chosen a precedent that is quite close to his case. The one difference tends to work in his favor: while Ctesicles was drunk, Meidias had no such excuse and therefore is all the more guilty.

Demosthenes has artfully arranged these three precedents in ascending order of relevance to his own case. In each case he examines the differences between the precedents and his own suit against Meidias and

---

30. One should not use this passage as evidence that drunkenness was exculpatory. See Harris (2006a) 301–3.

their implications. At the conclusion of this tricolon crescendo, Demosthenes (21.181) draws out the meaning of the three cases and their bearing on his charges against Meidias. The reasoning may not be sophisticated by modern standards, but the Athenian legal system was much simpler than ours and the issues in most cases not as complex. What is striking is that Demosthenes has taken some effort to show that his case against Meidias is similar to previous cases. He would not have taken this effort unless he thought that the court had some concern about consistency in the application of the law.

Demosthenes used several precedents when prosecuting Aeschines for treason in 343. Aeschines, Demosthenes, and eight others had been elected to serve as Athenian ambassadors to Philip, the king of Macedon in 346.[31] During their first visit to Philip, they negotiated the terms of a peace treaty, which was ratified by the Assembly in Athens on 19 Elaphebolion of that year.[32] They were then re-elected to serve on another embassy whose task was to administer the oath for the treaty to Philip. During this embassy the two men had a serious disagreement about Athenian policy, and on their return to Athens, Demosthenes brought a charge against Aeschines when he presented his accounts (*euthynai*) for his service as ambassador.[33] As we saw in chapter 4, laws about officials might specify their duties with some precision, but in other cases these duties were not set forth in detail. Demosthenes notes that all the law he is following says is that officials should not accept gifts and cause harm to the city, but the law does not specify what form that harm would take (D. 19.7). In the case of ambassadors, Demosthenes says that there was a general understanding that they should be responsible for their reports, for their advice, for the instructions given to them by the Assembly, for paying attention to 'times,' and for carrying out their duties honestly, that is, without accepting gifts (*adorodoketos*) (D. 19.4). He clearly used this list when

31. See Harris (1995) 50–62.

32. Harris (1995) 63–77.

33. For these events see Harris (1995) 78–95. The procedure for the *euthynai* fell into two parts: at the first the official presented his account to the *logistai* (Arist. *Ath. Pol.* 54.2), at the second the *euthynoi* could receive accusations against the official (Arist. *Ath. Pol.* 48.4–5). Demosthenes probably charged Aeschines at the second part—see MacDowell (2000) 19–20. MacDowell believes 'it does not appear . . . that the prosecution in the non-financial part of *euthynai* had necessarily to prove that the defendant had transgressed any particular law,' but see D. 19.7 which clearly alludes to a law against accepting gifts (cf. Aeschin. 3.232 alluding to a *graphe doron*).

drawing up his indictment, which appears to have included the charges: Aeschines 'made no true report and prevented the people from hearing the truth from me, and that all his recommendations were the opposite of what was advantageous, and that he carried out none of your instructions on the embassy, and that he wasted the time in which the city lost opportunities for many important actions, and that for all these he accepted bribes and payments along with Philocrates' (D. 19.8 trans. MacDowell).

In the absence of any law specifying the duties of ambassadors, Demosthenes (19.277–79) cites a decree passed to condemn Epicrates and other ambassadors for their part in negotiating the Peace of Antalcidas in 387.[34] The decree gives the grounds of the punishment, and Demosthenes quotes from it and compares them with his accusations against Aeschines:

> Just consider. 'Since they conducted the embassy contrary to their instructions,' it says; that's the first of the charges. But didn't these men act contrary to their instructions? Didn't the decree say 'for the Athenians and the allies of the Athenians,' and yet these men excluded the Phocians from the treaty? Didn't the decree say 'to administer them to the officials in the cities,' yet these men administered them to the people Philip sent to them? Didn't the decree say 'not to meet Philip alone anywhere,' and yet these men never stopped doing private business with him? 'And some of them were proved to have been making an untrue report in the Council.' These men were proved to have done so in the Assembly too—and by whom? This is the clear point: by the facts themselves, for surely everything turned out just the opposite to their report. So did these men. 'And telling lies against our allies and accepting gifts.' Well, for 'telling lies' substitute destroying them completely, and that is surely much worse than telling lies. But as for accepting gifts, if they denied it, it would remain to prove it, but since they admitted it, they should surely have been arrested. (trans. MacDowell with some changes)

The passage deserves to be quoted in full to show how Demosthenes reads each of the charges from the decree and carefully compares them with his

34. The negotiations should be identified with those for the Peace of Antalcidas. See Bruce (1966) and Hamilton (1979) 233–9. Keen (1995), followed by MacDowell (2000) 323, is not convincing.

charges against Aeschines. Where the law was vague, this precedent is very specific about the kind of harm ambassadors can do to the community. Demosthenes uses this precedent to justify his argument for the death penalty: just as Epicrates and his colleagues were condemned to death, so too should the court vote to execute Aeschines. This is in fact the third precedent Demosthenes cites in this passage; he also mentions a decree declaring Arthmius of Zelea an outlaw (D. 19.271–72) and the fine imposed on Callias for accepting gifts when negotiating with the Great King (D. 19.273–75). But neither of these precedents is as close to his case against Aeschines as the verdict against Epicrates. Arthmius was a foreigner and condemned for attempting to give money to the Athenians; Callias was sentenced only to a fine and negotiated a treaty that no one could fault. On the other hand, Epicrates accepted gifts for negotiating a treaty that allegedly harmed Athenian interests. The pattern in discussing precedents is similar to the one we observed in *Against Meidias*: Demosthenes starts with two cases that are not closely similar and ends with one that is closer to the present case. What is also significant is that Demosthenes (19.276) presents written documents in support of his use of these precedents.

Another case where the legal issue is paramount is Lycurgus' prosecution of Leocrates.[35] Lycurgus brought his charge by the process of *eisangelia*, which could be used against those who had committed acts of treason (*prodosia*). Like some Athenian statutes, the law about *eisangelia* did not define the term 'treason' but listed various offenses under three main rubrics: subversion of the democracy, betraying the city, and making speeches against the public interest. For instance, according to Hyperides (*Eux.* 8), one could employ this procedure 'if anyone overthrows the democracy of the Athenians, or conspires for the overthrow of the democracy or forms a group of conspirators (*hetairikon*), or if someone betrays some city or ship or infantry or naval force, or when a public speaker does not give the best advice while accepting money.'

As we saw in the last chapter, the facts of Leocrates' case were simple and not in dispute. During the crisis after the Athenian defeat at Chaeronea in 338, Leocrates left Athens and sailed to Rhodes (Lycurg. *Leocr.* 17). There he told people about the situation in Athens (18). After leaving Rhodes, Leocrates went to Megara, where he lived as a metic (resident

35. For an analysis of the legal issue in the case see 233–41.

alien) (21). From there he asked his brother-in-law to buy his house and slaves, settle his debts, and send him the remaining money so he could buy grain in Epirus and ship it to Leucas and thence to Corinth (23–24). After living in Megara for six years he moved back to Athens, where he was greeted upon his return by Lycurgus' indictment for treason. While Leocrates' supporters claimed that he left Athens to go abroad as a merchant, Lycurgus alleges that his true motive was desertion and that his dereliction of duty is equivalent to treason (55–58).

Lycurgus bases his case on the law but admits that he is asking the court to innovate by applying the procedure to an action not listed as one of the offenses in the law (*Leocr.* 9). The novelty of his approach is evident in his request that the judges act as lawgivers (*nomothetas*). The author of the law devised the procedure of *eisangelia* for a general category designated by a single word, treason (9), then listed several offenses in the law under the general category. Lycurgus argues that Leocrates' offense falls under the general category, though it does not fit one of the specific examples listed in the law. Yet, despite his admission that he is asking the court to extend the law to cover a new class of offender, Lycurgus still attempts to find precedents for his bold new interpretation of the law.

In one passage Lycurgus refers to three different precedents (Lycurg. *Leocr.* 52–54). First, he recalls how during the crisis after Chaeronea, the Areopagus arrested and put to death men who were deserting Attica. Second, he alludes to his conviction of Autolycus for sending his wife and children abroad at the time. Third, he reminds the court that the Assembly also voted then to make those who fled the country guilty of treason. From a legal point of view, each of these precedents is slightly different. In the first Lycurgus refers not to a trial but to arrests and executions carried out by the Areopagus under a grant of special powers after Chaeronea. In the third he cites a decree of the Assembly. Only the second concerns the verdict at a trial. But the three precedents mentioned do show that the Athenians considered leaving Attica in an emergency equivalent to treason and that several people had been punished for it. Later on in the speech, Lycurgus reaches back into Athenian history to find precedents. Most of them are far-fetched: Lycurgus mentions men who defended Phrynichus after his death (112–115), the member of the Council who proposed that the Athenians on Salamis accept the Persian offer of an alliance (122), and the condemnation of Hipparchus (117). But one is much closer to Leocrates' case. This is the decree that the Athenians passed after the Spartans occupied Decelea in 413 making it a crime to move to that town. Those who were caught returning from Decelea were subject to arrest and immediate execution (120–121). Lycurgus then uses an a fortiori argument to make his point: 'Well, then, this was the way they punished men who moved from one part of Attica to another; will you not put to death the man who left the city and country, fled to Rhodes in time of war, and betrayed the people?' Of course, the parallel is not all that strong: this decree was aimed at men who went to a town held by the enemy while Leocrates left not to join the Macedonians, but to go to Rhodes. Significant, however, is the fact that he does not rely on the judges' memory but produces the text of the decree to corroborate his account of a decision made in the distant past.

If an orator knew that his opponent was going to cite precedents in support of his case, he might try to anticipate his argument by showing that these precedents were not strictly relevant. We find a good example of such an attempt to dismiss an opponent's precedents in the speech Dinarchus wrote for one of the accusers at Demosthenes' trial in 323.[36] When Demosthenes was suspected of taking money from Harpalus during his visit to Athens in 324, the politician tried to clear his name by proposing that the Areopagus investigate the charge (Hyp. *D.* col. 2; Din. 1.61). Six months later the Areopagus presented its report, which stated that Demosthenes and several others had received various amounts of money from Harpalus (Din. 1.45; Hyp. *D.* cols. 5–6). Ten accusers were then elected to prosecute the men listed in the report of the Areopagus (Din. 2.6).

In a speech written by Dinarchus, one of the accusers predicts that Demosthenes will mention four cases where the Areopagus reported that men had broken the law, but none of the men reported had been convicted in court (Din. 1.54). The accuser could simply have argued that the precedents made no difference because Demosthenes was guilty and that was that. But that is not the approach that he takes. Instead he examines each case to demonstrate that it is not similar to Demosthenes' case. The first three cases he refers to briefly (Din. 1.56). In the first a member of the Areopagus did not pay a ferryman his fare and was fined by the Areopagus and reported to the Assembly. In the second the Areopagus reported someone who claimed a payment of five drachmas under the name of someone who did not show up. In the third case another member of this council tried to sell the 'Areopagite share.' The Areopagus expelled the offender from its ranks and reported him to the Assembly. All three men

36. Lanni (2004) 168, note 5 does not include these cases in her list of precedents.

were tried and acquitted. The accuser argues that the reason why they were acquitted is not that they were innocent, but that the penalty proposed in each case was considered too harsh for the nature of the offence (Din. 1.57). The accused does not simply present the cases but also searches for the rationale behind the decision by a process of inductive reasoning.

The accuser discusses the next case at greater length (Din. 1.58–59). Here the Assembly ordered the Areopagus to inquire whether Polyeuctus of Cydantidae was meeting with exiles in Megara. After the Areopagus confirmed that he was doing this, accusers were chosen, and Polyeuctus was tried in court. The procedure was probably *eisangelia*, and the charge was treason for meeting with those conspiring to overthrow the democracy. Polyeuctus admitted that he was going to Megara but he was going to see Nicophanes, who was married to his mother. The court decided there was nothing wrong with helping his father-in-law during a difficult period. In other words, the court decided that Polyeuctus may have been meeting with an enemy of Athens (Nicophanes had obviously been convicted of a crime since he was in exile), but he lacked the intent to commit treason. The accuser says that the court did not decide that the report of the Areopagus was false. Quite the opposite, he claims that it reported the truth. But the circumstances surrounding his actions made it clear that Polyeuctus was not guilty of a crime.[37] We will examine these cases more closely in the next chapter.

The accuser then compares these cases with that of Demosthenes (Din. 1.59–60). First, the accuser argues that in each case no one disputed the veracity of the Areopagus' report so there is no reason to doubt its report about Demosthenes. Second, the actions committed by the defendants in these precedents are not comparable with the crimes of Demosthenes. Their offenses were minor and did not deserve severe penalties; Demosthenes took money to attack the interests of his own country. The accuser notes that for other offenses the penalty is twice the amount of the damage, but for bribery it is either death or ten times the amount of the bribe (Din. 1.60). Once again, we find a close analysis of the similarities and differences between the precedents adduced and the present case. When the differences are too great or the principles applied in the decision are not the same, the speaker concludes that the precedents are not persuasive and should not influence the court's decision. This is not

37. For discussion of this case as an example of *epieikeia* see 293–95.

the only place where an orator argues that precedents adduced by his opponent are not relevant: we find a similar close analysis of adverse precedents in Demosthenes' speech *Against Meidias* (21.36–41). Such arguments reveal that the speaker assumes that these precedents would have a powerful influence on the court's decision. It is no wonder then that Anaximenes, when giving advice to speakers in court, recommends that they appeal to precedents ([Arist.] *Rhetorica ad Alexandrum* 1422b20).

But how reliable are the accounts given of previous cases that we find in the orators? One scholar is skeptical: 'We cannot accurately assess the depth and the extent of judges' knowledge of previous cases, but the volume of litigation over many decades and the relatively short lifespan of the average Athenian make it most unlikely that many judges would have an accurate impression of many earlier cases.' To justify her skepticism this scholar then refers to Thucydides 1.20 and calls it the '*locus classicus* for the unreliability of Athenian historical memory.'[38] Unfortunately, she neglects to mention that Thucydides was writing at the very end of the fifth century and in this passage is discussing what contemporary Athenians remembered about the assassination of Hipparchus in 514 BCE. By contrast, the orators, when citing precedents, tend to refer to cases that were recent and well known. For instance, Lycurgus, speaking in 331, refers to cases and decrees from 338. When he mentions events from the distant past at 112–122, he is careful to provide written evidence in the form of decrees to back his statements.[39] When the man who accused Agoratus cited the case of Menestratus, this trial had taken place within the past few years (Lys. 13.55–57). When discussing the *probole* cases that serve as his precedents, Demosthenes starts with the most recent case (D. 21.175–182).

One should also bear in mind that many of these cases came to the attention of the Assembly before they went to court. This means that they were known to virtually everyone in Athens. The *probole* cases discussed by Demosthenes were initiated in the Assembly and concerned offenses that took place during festivals attended by everyone in Athens. The cases that the accuser in Dinarchus' speech *Against Demosthenes* (Din. 1.55–60) discusses must have been public knowledge since they were reported to the Assembly by an *apophasis* of the Areopagus. Other cases will have attracted attention because they were causes célèbres and involved heavy fines or the

38. Lanni (2004) 169, note 21.

39. The authenticity of these decrees is another question—see Habicht (1961) 22–3.

death penalty. And if the cases were private matters settled out of court, a litigant like Meidias could have the parties testify about them before the court (D. 21.36–41). In two of the cases in Lysias (Lys. 3.43; 31.34) where the litigant appeals to precedents, he uses examples drawn from the judges' and councilors' experience. In none of these cases have we any reason to doubt that the judges were not reasonably familiar with the basic facts in each case and with the actual verdicts. Speakers could be selective about what they included in their account of an incident or alter small details (as Demosthenes obviously tried to do in the case of Evander). But they could not invent important events or change the basic facts about well-known actions without jeopardizing their credibility in front of the court. Athens was not a large nation-state with a tremendous volume of legal business where few people could keep up with what happened in court and where only a small number participated in trials. It was a direct democracy where all male citizens could attend the Assembly and hundreds often sat as judges in the courts. It was also a small community where word of mouth about important events like major trials spread quickly. Thucydides may criticize Athenian misconceptions about events long past, but he also has Pericles state in his Funeral Oration that in their democracy even those who are busy with work are still well informed about public business (Th. 2.40.2).

II

In most of the passages examined so far, the speakers do not rely on documents to argue that their interpretation of the law is the standard one. But one should not underestimate the amount of written material that could be used to help the courts achieve consistency in their decisions. In *graphe paranomon* cases there were written copies of previous decrees whose legality had been questioned but then upheld or had been passed without challenge. These decrees could serve as precedents when a later similar decree was challenged. And arguments from precedent are not the only way that courts can achieve consistency; litigants and judges can also appeal to the intent of the lawgiver.[40] By this method the courts maintain

40. Lanni (2004) 168, note 2 is aware of this fact: she knows that the legal systems of France and Austria do not follow the doctrine of binding precedent (one could add Denmark) and that in Germany only the decisions of the Federal Constitutional court are binding. But she tends to downplay its implications for our understanding of the Athenian legal system because she wishes to believe that 'comparisons with the common law are more fruitful than with the civil law.' But her reason for this belief is a strange one: she claims that the latter 'is

consistency by basing all interpretation on the aims of the person who created the law. One often finds this kind of argument in the Attic Orators, and in most instances the litigant supports his argument with written copies of other laws.

The best illustration of the way previous decrees could be used as precedents in a legal argument is found in Demosthenes' speech *On the Crown*. As we saw in the previous chapter, Aeschines and Demosthenes differ about the meaning of two laws about the award of crowns. The first charge was based on a law that Aeschines (3.31) quotes and has read out by the clerk: 'another law forbids the crowning of an *arche* that is still subject to *euthynai*,' in other words, when the magistrate has not yet passed his audit after his term of office. The key term in the statute is *arche*, which can have two meanings. It can mean 'magistrate,' which is the way Aeschines (Aeschin. 3.11, 26. Cf. D. 39.9; Lys. 9.6) interprets it. It can also mean term of office (e.g. Arist. *Ath. Pol.* 56.2; Aeschin. 3.11), which is the way Demosthenes implicitly interprets the term. As we saw in the previous chapter, if one takes Aeschines' interpretation, the law banned all decrees of praise for a magistrate who had not yet passed his audit conducted after his term of office. Yet if we follow the other interpretation, the law only made it illegal to award a crown for a term of office, that is, for the performance of duties attached to an office, before the magistrate passed his audit for that term of office. If the latter is the correct interpretation, the law bans only one type of decree of commendation prior to the audit but did not forbid other types of praise for a magistrate while in office, such as a crown for a remarkable achievement, for a generous donation of money, or for a lifetime of public service.

Which interpretation of the law was the generally accepted one? In his speech for Ctesiphon, Demosthenes does not simply argue that his reading of the law is the more logical or straightforward interpretation of the law and leave it at that. He proves that his way of interpreting the law is the standard way of reading it by having the clerk read out several decrees that awarded crowns for Nausicles, Diotimus, Charidemus, and Neoptolemus (D. 18.114).[41] All these decrees were passed when these

predicated upon an academic legal tradition and professional expertise among judges and practitioners.' Does she mean to imply that there is no 'academic legal tradition and professional expertise among judges and practitioners' in the common law?

41. Rubinstein (2007) 367, note 14 misses these precedents. On the use of decrees as written precedents in *graphai paranomon* cases see also Faraguna (2006) 206.

politicians held office, and none was challenged by a *graphe paranomon*. In other words, Demosthenes cites precedents for his interpretation of the law about crowns to show that Ctesiphon's proposal did not violate the law. The evidence for these precedents came in the form of written documents kept on file in the Metroon. Demosthenes (18.223–224) also recalls that on two earlier occasions, a decree of praise that was exactly similar to that of Ctesiphon was proposed for him and was then indicted on a *graphe paranomon*. In each case the proposer was acquitted. That makes not one, but six precedents in Demosthenes' favor.[42] And the evidence for every one came in the form of written documents kept in the Metroon.

Demosthenes also cites precedents to support his interpretation of the law when replying to Aeschines' second charge. Aeschines (3.32–47) here relies on the law that made it illegal to announce an award of honors in any place other than the Council or Assembly. Demosthenes (18.120–121), however, cites another law that allowed honors to be announced in the Theater of Dionysus as long as the Assembly voted to order it. For Demosthenes this law provided for an exception to the general rule stated in the general law about announcing the award of a crown. Demosthenes points out that many people have in the past had their awards announced in the Theater of Dionysus. Here again Demosthenes cites precedents to support his interpretation of the statute. True, Demosthenes does not have any of these decrees read out, but there was no need: the members of the court had all attended the festival of Dionysus and knew what kinds of announcements were made in the theater.[43] What is important for our purpose is that there did exist written documents that showed there were ample precedents for Demosthenes' interpretation of the law.

Another *graphe paranomon* case where one of the litigants, we are told, would cite written records of decrees is the case against Androtion, which Demosthenes composed for the politician Diodorus (D. 22).[44] Androtion had proposed that honors be awarded to the Council for its performance during its term of office. Diodorus brought a *graphe paranomon* on three grounds: (1) The law forbade the Council to ask for an award if it had not had triremes built during its term of office, and the Council had not

42. These precedents are not discussed in Lanni (2004).

43. There is no reason to doubt the existence of these decrees—see Gwatkin (1957) 138, note 57.

44. On this speech see Harris (2008) 166–70.

had triremes built; (2) the Assembly was not allowed to ratify a proposal without a *probouleuma*, and this proposal lacked a *probouleuma*; and (3) Androtion was a male prostitute and thus ineligible to make a proposal in the Assembly. Unlike the trial of Ctesiphon, we only have the speech delivered by the prosecutor here, but Diodorus does inform us that Androtion intended to cite other decrees that are similar to his and were passed by the Assembly without challenge (D. 22.6). Since Androtion's speech has not survived, we do not know if he actually had these decrees read out, but it is nonetheless clear that such decrees did exist and could be used as precedents. What is also interesting is that Diodorus anticipates this argument by claiming that these precedents are irrelevant since they violated the law. What one should pay attention to, he claims, is not these decrees, but the law itself. Of course, his argument assumes that the law cannot be interpreted in another way. But it also reveals that the Athenians did not consider precedents binding, only persuasive.

A third *graphe paranomon* case in which one of the litigants intended to use earlier decrees as precedents to support his case is found in Demosthenes' speech *Against Aristocrates*. The accuser charges that Aristocrates has proposed an illegal decree for Charidemus. This decree provided that 'If someone kills Charidemus, he is subject to arrest (*agogimos*) from the territory of the allies' (D. 23.16). The accuser charges that this gives anyone at all the right to punish Charidemus' killer without bringing him to trial (D. 23.18–85). As several scholars have noted, this is a strained reading of the decree; all the term 'subject to arrest' (*agogimos*) implied was that the killer was subject to extradition so that he could stand trial in Athens.[45] It should therefore come as no surprise that Aristocrates intended to present several similar decrees passed for other people (D. 23.95, 99). The accuser's attempt to anticipate this objection is interesting (D. 23.96–99). He argues that just because a decree has been approved and gone into effect does not mean that it is not illegal. Even if it had been attacked as illegal but not overturned, this still does not stop it from being illegal because those who brought the *graphai paranomon* might have been bribed or been incompetent speakers. He does not imply that the judges would have violated their oath in this case; they are not at fault because they depend on the speeches of the litigants to make their decision. As long as they vote without enmity or favor toward either litigant, they

45. On this provision and its meaning in Aristocrates' decree see Lonis (1988b).

remain true to their oath. This argument is similar to the one presented by Diodorus in *Against Androtion*, but the speaker in *Against Aristocrates* provides a rationale for disregarding precedents: the courts can be misled by dishonest speakers. The speaker does not say that the courts should not pursue consistency as a goal; his argument is that the decisions of the courts are not a reliable way to achieve consistency because they may be erroneous.

The use of precedents is not the only way to achieve consistency. One can also appeal to the intent of the lawgiver. For instance, in civil law countries, such as France, Germany, and Austria, previous decisions do not have the force of law.[46] In Denmark, precedents are only persuasive, not binding. In this regard the legal system of Classical Athens was closer to those of these civil law countries than it was to common law countries. To determine the intent of 'the lawgiver' (a fictitious figure to some extent, but a fiction that the Athenians believed in), a litigant would cite another law and elicit a general principle from this specific law by a process of inductive reasoning. This principle would then be used to justify the litigant's interpretation of the law that was directly relevant to his case. The best example of this is found in Hyperides' speech *Against Athenogenes*. As we saw in chapter 5, Athenogenes based his case on the law that made all agreements that one made willingly with another person binding (Hyp. *Ath.* 13). Epicrates however draws attention to the fact that the law also states that unjust agreements are not binding. Because the law does not define the term unjust in this context, Epicrates examines other laws for guidance about how to interpret this term. In the arguments that follow, Epicrates cites a law forbidding lying in the marketplace (14), a law about latent defects in the sale of slaves (15), a law about the status of children in a marriage by solemn pledge (16), the law about wills (17), and a law making masters liable for the damages caused by their slaves (21–22). None of these laws is directly relevant to his case, but Epicrates finds a principle implicit in each law, then applies that principle to his own case.

There are two points to be made here. First, Epicrates, when dealing with a problem of legal interpretation, refers to written texts, which he has the clerk read out. Second, Epicrates uses these written texts to interpret the law about agreements made willingly in a way that is consistent with the perceived intent of other laws about contracts. One can find similar

46. See Lanni (2004) 168, note 2.

kinds of arguments employed by Demosthenes in his *Against Leptines* (D. 20.95–96) and by Aeschines in his *Against Timarchus* (Aeschin. 1.9–27). In all these speeches, the litigants aim to convince the court that their interpretation of the law is consistent with the rest of the Athenian law code and the evidence they draw on is the written texts of the laws.

III

So far we have found that litigants in Athenian courts, when confronted with a legal issue, often appeal to precedents to show that their reading of the law is the generally accepted one. Although in most cases they rely not on documents but on public memory, they are careful to refer to recent or well-known trials. In several cases litigants do cite precedents contained in written documents. Finally, litigants also cite the written texts of other laws to show that their interpretation of statute is consistent with the intent of the lawgiver. From this evidence it should be clear that litigants expected the courts to apply the law consistently and that they expected that oral knowledge and written records would be thought sufficient to help the courts pursue this goal. But to what extent did the courts actually achieve consistency? Is there any information that would enable us to determine whether the Athenian courts did make their decisions in a consistent way? It is not easy to find evidence that would allow us to answer this question since our sources are not as informative as we would like. In many cases we do not even know the verdicts rendered in the cases where the speeches of Lysias and Demosthenes were delivered.[47] On the other hand, the speeches of the Attic Orators often do refer to the verdicts in other cases, but they rarely tell us very much about the issues involved in these cases.

There is, however, one set of trials where we know the verdicts rendered in similar cases. These are the *graphai paranomon* cases brought against men who proposed honors for Demosthenes. In his speech *On the Crown* Demosthenes (18.223–224) reports that Hyperides and Demomeles proposed exactly the same kind of honors for him as Ctesiphon proposed and also had their decrees challenged by *graphai paranomon*. In each

47. The speeches of Aeschines form an exception since we know the outcome of each of the trials at which his speeches were delivered: in 346 he convicted Timarchus (D. 19.2, 257, 284–285, 287); in 343 he was acquitted when prosecuted by Demosthenes (Aeschin. 2 hypoth.); and in 330 he failed to convict Ctesiphon (see next note).

case the outcome was the same; both Hyperides and Demomeles were acquitted. We also know that Ctesiphon was also acquitted for proposing a decree that was exactly similar to those put forward by Hyperides and Demomeles.[48] In each case the charge was the same, in each case the decree was the same, and in each case the verdict was the same.

There are also four cases where the accuser asks the court to act as 'lawgivers' (*nomothetai*) and to apply the law in a new way (Lys. 14, D. 56, Lycurg. *Leocr.*, D. 39). As the arguments contained in these speeches make clear, each accuser is asking the court to apply the law in a new way that is without any precedent. In three of these four cases, we know the verdict. The first case is Lysias 14, *Against Alcibiades*, where the accuser charges the defendant with violating the law that required soldiers not to leave their position (*taxis*) because he served in the cavalry when he had been called up to serve in the infantry. As we saw in chapter 6, this was an unusual reading of the law, which normally applied only to those who left their assigned position in the line during a battle. Had he been convicted, he would have lost all citizen rights and been unable to contract a marriage and pass on citizenship to his descendants. Since we know that his descendants were Athenian citizens, it is clear that he was not convicted. In this case, the court, when asked to apply the law in a way that was without precedent, rejected the accuser's charge.

The second case is the *eisangelia* that Lycurgus brought against Leocrates for treason. As we noted in our discussion earlier, Lycurgus was asking the court to extend the law about *eisangelia* to cover an offense that was not included among those specifically listed in the law. He therefore asks the judges to act as 'legislators' by applying the law in a new way (*Leocr.* 9). Aeschines (3.252) says that Leocrates was acquitted, albeit by a narrow margin.

The third case is the one that Mantitheus brought against his half-brother Boeotus for damages (Demosthenes 39). As we saw in the previous chapter, the *dike blabes* was normally brought when the defendant was charged with causing physical damage to an object owned by the plaintiff or performing a wrongful action, such as a breach of contract that caused loss to the plaintiff. But Mantitheus brought his action because his half-brother was using the same name, which he claimed might cause him inconvenience, if not serious trouble, in the future. Mantitheus virtually

48. For the verdict see Harris (1995) 148 with note 61.

admits that he is asking the court to innovate when he asks the court to apply the law in a new way (D. 39.40). Here again the plaintiff wants the court to apply the law in a way that is not consistent with previous decisions; here too the plaintiff appears to have lost his case.[49] In all these three cases, the accusers did not have precedents to support their interpretation of the law; in each case the court rejected the charge.[50]

This examination of arguments based on precedents has shown that litigants believed that the courts should be dedicated to achieving consistency in their application of the law.[51] There is, therefore, no reason to believe that the Athenian courts made ad hoc judgments. We have also discovered that we should not underestimate the knowledge of the average Athenian about earlier trials gained by personal experience and oral tradition and from the written records available for past decisions. And the little evidence that we do have suggests that they were able to achieve some consistency in the way they interpreted the law. Of course, they did not reach the goal of perfect consistency in all decisions. But then again, no legal system ever does. The important point is that the Athenians were concerned about consistency and had the oral and written resources to enable them to pursue this aim. The attempt to judge cases according to consistent rules is one of the hallmarks of the rule of law.[52]

---

49. See Carey and Reid (1985) 167–8.

50. One might also add D. 19.232 where an accuser asks the court to enact a law by its verdict. It is not clear how Demosthenes is proposing a legal innovation here, but it is worth noting that he lost his case. Rubinstein (2007) 366 discusses this type of argument but does not see how rare it is and that accusers who use this argument are not successful in convincing the court.

51. One should bear in mind that even though litigants could use precedents to show that their interpretation of a statute was the conventional one, the courts did not use precedents to create new rules. As we saw in chapter 6, the Athenians would have considered this practice antidemocratic. Cf. Harris (2006a) 287, note 12.

52. Bingham (2010) 48–54.

8

How Strictly Did the Athenian Courts Apply the Law?

THE ROLE OF *EPIEIKEIA*

DURING THE FINAL years of the Peloponnesian War, the Athenians led by Alcibiades laid siege to Byzantium, an ally of Sparta. The Athenians surrounded the city with siege works and made repeated attacks. Clearchus, the Spartan commander, had a force consisting of *perioikoi*, freed helots, a contingent of Boeotians led by Helixus, and a contingent of Megarians led by Coeratadas. Clearchus, believing that none of the Byzantines would betray the city, left the troops under the command of Helixus and Coeratadas and went to the Persian satrap Pharnabazus to raise money. During his absence, five men of Byzantium betrayed the city to the Athenians. One of these, Anaxilaus, was later arrested and put on trial in Sparta. Anaxilaus did not deny what he had done but based his defense on three arguments. First, he said that he was a Byzantine, not a Spartan. This meant that his main loyalty was to his native city, not to his allies. Second, Clearchus was giving all the available food to the troops under his command and as a result women and children were dying of hunger. Third, his intent in betraying the city to the Athenians was to prevent his fellow citizens from starving, not to gain money through bribery nor out of hatred for the Spartans.[1]

A strict application of the law would have required that the court sentence Anaxilaus to death, but he was acquitted. The Spartans who judged the case accepted his arguments that the case was exceptional because of the unusual circumstances. The Spartan commander had neglected the interests of his Byzantine allies by refusing them food and had forced Anaxilaus to take action. His motive was honorable: he wished to save the lives of his fellow citizens and did not act out of greed or enmity toward

1. X. *HG* 1.3.14–19.

the Spartans. As a citizen of Byzantium, he should be judged by what he had done for his community, not for the Spartans.

At the trial of Anaxilaus, the Spartan judges decided not to follow the strict letter of the law and took extenuating circumstances into account. How rigorously did the Athenian courts apply the law? Did they also take unusual circumstances into account in the same way as the Spartans who acquitted Anaxilaus? Or did they apply the law strictly and pay no attention to the excuses that a defendant might present to prove his innocence? In his *Nicomachean Ethics* and *Rhetoric* Aristotle says that there is a form of justice called *epieikeia* (fairness), which is contrary to the written law. Did this form of justice allow judges to take extenuating circumstances into account? Scholars have been divided about the meaning of *epieikeia* and its role in Athenian courts. Some have asserted that *epieikeia* was a doctrine that allowed the courts to consider a broad range of considerations and even to ignore the law completely.[2] One scholar has compared it with the doctrine of 'jury nullification' in Anglo-American law.[3] Others have denied that *epieikeia* played any role in the courts' decisions, which were based on a strict application of the law.[4] On this view Aristotle's ideas about *epieikeia* were an innovation that had nothing to do with contemporary legal practice.

This chapter begins with an analysis of Aristotle's discussion of *epieikeia*. A careful study of the term shows that *epieikeia* is not an appeal to a higher standard of justice above the written law but applies only in unusual circumstances that could not have been anticipated by the legislator who had to formulate a general rule. When a litigant used an argument based on *epieikeia*, he was not asking the court to reject the written law but

---

2. Vinogradoff (1922) 65–69, esp. 68: 'the range of considerations of justice was very large, and was not really restricted to cases where there were no laws.' Jones (1956) 64ff. takes a similar position. Todd (1993) 54–55 asserts that the Athenian courts took into account factors that had nothing to do with the laws, but cites no evidence to support this general statement. He does not provide any analysis of Aristotle's discussion of *epieikeia*.

3. Allen (2000a) 177–78.

4. The most extensive defense of this position is Meyer-Laurin (1965), who is followed by Meinecke (1971). I endorsed Meyer-Laurin's position in Harris (1994b) 140, then expressed reservations about it in Harris (2000a) 30–32, and rejected it in Harris (2004a). Lanni (2006) 50–51 takes a position similar to that of Meyer-Laurin ('the popular courts did not formally recognize' extenuating circumstances) but does not cite his work. Nor does she examine Aristotle's analysis of *epieikeia*. Engels (2008) 119, note 52 believes that 'Gegen ein strict "gesetzpositivistisches" Verständnis des athenischen Rechtswesen sprach sich schon Meyer-Laurin 1965' but has clearly not read Meyer-Laurin carefully. Like Wolff, Meyer-Laurin in fact argues in favor of a positivist approach.

was demonstrating that his case was an exception to the general rule contained in a statute and that in his specific case other *legal* considerations should take precedence. An argument from *epieikeia* was not an appeal to extra-legal considerations but to a general principle of justice implicit in the written laws. The second part of the chapter examines several passages in which litigants in Athenian courts use the arguments that Aristotle gives as examples of arguments from *epieikeia.* The final part of the chapter studies several cases in which Athenian judges acquitted defendants for reasons of *epieikeia.*

I

Aristotle discusses *epieikeia* in two passages. It is best to start with the discussion in Book 5 of the *Nicomachean Ethics,* where the analysis of *epieikeia* forms part of a general discussion of justice. The focus of Book 5 is very broad and covers legal, political, and moral aspects of justice. Although Aristotle provides a general analysis of this virtue, he realizes that the way justice is understood may vary from one context to another. For instance, Aristotle (*EN* 5.3.1130b–31a) observes that there are different types of justice and makes a distinction between distributive justice (*dianemetikon*) and rectificatory justice (*diorthootikon*). The former allocates respect, money, and other items among the members of a political community (*politeia*) and comes into play when the Assembly distributes awards for public service. The latter regulates interactions between individuals (*en tois sunallagmasi*) and operates in the law courts. Distributive justice allocates goods to a person for some virtue. This kind of justice is achieved by the correct geometrical proportion: the person who is better receives a greater share than the one who is not as good (Arist. *EN* 5.4.1131b27–30). Rectificatory justice, on the other hand, treats both parties, accuser and defendant, on an equal level and considers only the wrong done by the latter to the former. It does not take the defendant's general moral character into account (Arist. *EN* 5.4.1132a: *nomoi*). One cannot therefore argue that Aristotle's discussion concerns only the moral virtue of justice in individuals.[5] The discussion examines justice in all contexts, including legal.

5. *Pace* Meyer-Laurin (1965) 50: 'Während der moderne Begriffe "Billigkeit" mit der Rechtsprechung verbunden ist, steht die aristotelische *epieikeia* im Zusammenhang mit dem ἐπιεικὴς ἄνθρωπος von dem der Philosoph ergründen will, ob er sich durch Nachgiebigkeit nicht Unrecht zufüge.'

The analysis of *epieikeia* in the *Nicomachean Ethics* (5.10.1137a–38a) falls into two sections: the lengthier section examines *epieikeia* as a corrective of the law, while the shorter one considers the man who possesses the virtue of *epieikeia*.[6] In legal matters, *epieikeia* is a form of justice that is not justice according to the law but a correction (*epanorthoma*) of the law. Here Aristotle makes a distinction between two types of justice, one that is broader (general principles of justice), and another that is narrower (justice according to a strict reading of the law). The reason why *epieikeia* is necessary in certain cases is that the laws provide general rules and cannot take into account all possible situations.[7] The fault lies not with the legislator or with the law, but with the nature of the task (*pragma*), that is, the difficulty of formulating a general rule to be applied in many different situations. If the law does not provide specific rules for dealing with exceptional cases, it is necessary to 'correct them by taking into consideration what the legislator himself would have added to the law had he known about the situation.' Aristotle is discussing exceptions in particular cases to a general rule. *Epieikeia* is not a way of arguing that a law should not be applied because it is unjust. It only comes into play in those cases where the law is deficient (*elleiphthen*) because it is formulated in general terms. He reinforces this point in the next phrase where he states that there are 'situations when one must formulate a decree (*psephisma*), which can be adapted to fit events in reality.' While laws are formulated for all persons or for broad categories of persons and apply permanently, decrees address a particular situation or grant honors or privileges to a particular person.[8] By analogy, one appeals to *epieikeia* only in particular and exceptional circumstances.

Aristotle does not say that *epieikeia* comes into play because of gaps in the law. A judge does not apply *epieikeia* because there is no relevant law containing a rule about the type of case he must decide. As Brunschwig,

---

6. Georgiadis (1987) 165–66 finds a certain lack of connection between the two sections. Brunschwig (1996) 135 counters that both sections are linked by a common interest in the judge who exercises equity. But Aristotle says that the equitable man is one who does not demand everything that he is entitled to by law: this is not the conduct of a judge who decides a case, but that of a litigant who can decide whether to bring a case to trial or to settle out of court. The connection between the two types of *epieikeia* is that both consist in mitigating the full rigor of the law: the judge decides not to apply the law in a rigid way, which results in reducing or exempting the defendant from punishment, and the accuser chooses not to insist on the full extent of his rights by refraining from legal action. In each case *epieikeia* operates for the benefit of the defendant.

7. Here Aristotle appears to have in mind Plato's discussion in the *Statesman* (*Pol.* 295a).

8. For the distinction between laws and decrees see Hansen (1978).

drawing on the work of Shiner, observes, 'The cases where it is legitimate to make an appeal to equity are not, according to Aristotle, the cases where there is no existing written legal code concerning the type of act; they are the cases where there exists a perfectly applicable law, but where a mechanical or blind application of it would result in a verdict which would be too severe according to the moral intuitions of the judge and those of the society in which he works.'[9] This is confirmed by Aristotle's analysis of the term in the *Rhetoric* (Arist. *Rh.* 1.13.13.1374a), where he gives the example of the man who strikes someone while wearing a metal ring. In this case there is a law, probably one requiring a more severe punishment for assault with a metal object, but the blind application of the law would result in a punishment that would appear unfair because the assailant was not using the ring as a weapon. *Epieikeia* does not therefore attempt to fill gaps in the law; it relates to the way laws are applied in particular situations, especially ones that merit special treatment as exceptions to the general rule.[10]

Nor is there any reason to see in *epieikeia* an appeal to extra-legal considerations or an argument for ignoring the law altogether. When one recognizes the need to treat exceptional cases in a different way, this in no way undermines the authority of the law. As Brunschwig states, 'Aristotelian *epieikeia* . . . does not seem to be a suspension, without principle and unregulated, of legal rules, nor simply a foray "hors du domaine du droit."'[11] When one appeals to *epieikeia*, one does not ignore the intent of the lawgiver but tries to imagine what he would have done had he known about the situation. And the only way to determine what the lawgiver would have done is to examine his legislation as a whole or to interpret his meaning in specific statutes. It would therefore be a mistake to believe that *epieikeia* bears any similarity to the modern doctrine of jury nullification, which holds that jurors have the right to ignore a law that they consider unjust.[12]

9. Brunschwig (1996) 139, drawing on Shiner (1987) 182–83.

10. Cf. Brunschwig (1996) 139: 'Strictly speaking, the law does not manifest "gaps," but "deficiencies" in the etymological sense of the word, i.e. it falls short.'

11. Brunschwig (1996) 140. Even though Wohl (2010) 109, note 74 appears to be unaware of the essays by Brunschwig and myself on *epieikeia*, she grasps the basic point: 'Equity's correction involves more precise application of general rules and does not look beyond the bounds of law.' The view of Todd (1993) 54–5 that *epeikeia* consists of appeals to extra-legal considerations is untenable.

12. *Pace* Allen (2000a) 177–79. Such a doctrine can only arise in a legal system that makes a strict distinction between the judge who decides questions of law and jurors who normally decide questions of fact and take instructions about legal matters from the judge. This distinction did not exist in Classical Athens where the *dikastai* were judges of fact and law.

Finally, one should note that Aristotle does not introduce the unwritten laws, divine law, or the concept of natural law in this section. The absence of these concepts is significant because it means that one cannot interpret *epieikeia* as an appeal to a higher standard of justice, which transcends (and possibly contradicts) the written law. When one argues from *epieikeia*, one examines the intention of the lawgiver and what he would have added to the law had he known about the particular case. To discover the intention of the lawgiver, one must interpret his laws, not search for a principle lying outside his legislation. Moreover, the Athenians and other Greeks saw no conflict or opposition between the unwritten laws, the laws of the gods, and the law of nature, on the one hand, and the laws of the city on the other. On the contrary, the former supplied the basic principles that provided the foundation for the written laws. According to Heraclitus (fr. 253 Kirk-Raven; 114 Diels-Kranz), 'all laws of men are nourished by one law, the divine law.' Xenophon (*Mem.* 4.4.19) lists three unwritten laws: honor the gods, respect one's parents, and repay a benefit. The written laws of Athens contained many provisions aimed at upholding all three of these general precepts. Plato (*Laws* 793a–b) compares the unwritten laws to 'the bonds of every constitution, joining all laws laid down in writing and those to be laid down in the future.' In the speech *Against Aristocrates* Demosthenes (23.70) says that the defendant has offended against the written and unwritten laws, implying that both kinds of laws contain similar rules. In another speech Demosthenes (18.274–75) observes that men draw a distinction among three types of actions: unjust actions deliberately committed, culpable errors (*hamartiai*), and accidents for which men are not held responsible. He adds, 'This principle will be obvious not only in the laws, but nature herself has marked out these distinctions in the unwritten laws and human habits.'[13]

Aristotle also discusses the term *epieikeia* in the *Rhetoric* (1.13.13–19. 1374a–b). Unlike his analysis in the *Nicomachean Ethics*, chapters 9–15 in Book 1 of the *Rhetoric* are addressed to the advocate who is pleading a case in court and form part of his general discussion of forensic rhetoric.[14]

13. For the relationship between the unwritten laws (or laws of the gods) and the laws of the *polis* see Harris (2006a) 51–57.

14. Brunschwig (1996) 141–42: 'the reader is clearly an orator, and, more precisely, in the chapters in which equity is discussed, a court orator . . . the point of view distinctive of the *Rhetoric*: the lawyer's interest is in presenting the innocence of his client as a fact which he can confidently state.'

Whereas the analysis of *epieikeia* in the *Nicomachean Ethics* is very general, the *Rhetoric* provides several specific examples of arguments from *epieikeia* to be used in court. At the start of chapter 13, Aristotle makes several distinctions. First, he divides laws into two main categories, particular and general. The first are those that each community lays down for itself and can be further subdivided into written and unwritten. The second are laws based on nature. These laws do not necessarily clash with the laws of a particular community; they embody universal notions of right and wrong. The term 'common law' is also found in Demosthenes (23.61), who states that the right to strike back against someone who is stealing property is found not only in the written laws but also in the common law (i.e., of mankind). Aristotle then quotes a passage from Sophocles' *Antigone* (456–57), in which the 'unwritten laws' are described as those that 'live not just now and yesterday but always, and no one knows from whence they came into being.' The unwritten laws cited by Antigone in this passage are thus identical to the law of nature or the law common to all mankind. They are not the same as the unwritten laws of the individual city.

Aristotle clarifies his point when he resumes his discussion of the written and unwritten laws of the city later in the chapter after discussing the difference between public and private law (Arist. *Rh.* 1.13.3–8.1373b) and the importance of defining the nature of legal offenses (Arist. *Rh.* 1.13.9–10.1373b). The first kind are those designated in the written laws, the second are those that are 'unwritten,' that is, actions that are considered just or unjust but are not prescribed or forbidden in the written laws. This group of unwritten just and unjust actions is then subdivided into two groups. The first are those resulting from an excess of virtue or vice and receive praise or blame, dishonor, honors, or rewards. What Aristotle has in mind here are the kinds of actions not discussed in the written laws, but which receive a community's approval or disapproval. Aristotle gives the positive examples of gratitude to a benefactor, requiting good with good, and helping one's friends. One might add conduct like outstanding public service or voluntary contributions of money to the community (*epidosis*).[15] The laws do not require such behavior, but the community praises such actions and often expresses its admiration by praise, say, in the form of honorary decrees, honors in the form of election to public office, or in the form of rewards and exemptions from public

15. On the institution of the *epidosis* in the Greek cities see Migeotte (1992).

duties and of other privileges. On the other hand, the laws do not explicitly order one to help one's neighbors in need or to repay a favor, and there are no formal penalties for not fulfilling these obligations. In this case the community may express its disapproval by giving the person a bad reputation. Individuals may convey their attitude by shunning his company. These unwritten kinds of just and unjust actions are those contained in the unwritten laws mentioned by Pericles in his Funeral Oration (Th. 2.37), which bring 'acknowledged shame' (*homologoumenen aischunen*) on those who break them. What is crucial for the understanding of *epieikeia* is that these kinds of unwritten just and unjust actions and unwritten laws have nothing to do with the unwritten laws, which are often equated with the laws of the gods or the laws of nature.[16] The unwritten laws mentioned by Pericles are social attitudes that regulate conduct in an informal manner. The unwritten laws discussed in Xenophon's *Memorabilia*, in Demosthenes' *On the Crown*, and in Sophocles' *Antigone* are very different: they are transcendent norms that provide the basic principles of justice on which the formal written laws of the city are based. There is therefore no reason to believe that Aristotle in the *Rhetoric* places his analysis of *epieikeia* within the broader context of natural or divine law.

The second kind of just and unjust actions arise from what is omitted (*elleimma*) in the specific written law. The language here appears to recall the description of *epieikeia* in the *Nicomachean Ethics* (5.10.6.1137b26–7) as a correction of the written law (*epanorthoma nomou*) where it is deficient because it speaks in general terms (*elleipei dia to katholou*). The next phrase also recalls the discussion of the *Nicomachean Ethics*: *epieikeia* is a form of justice but it is contrary to the written law. The need for *epieikeia* arises for the same reason in both discussions of the term: the lawgiver must make a general rule. In the *Rhetoric*, however, Aristotle says that the lawgiver may omit something from the written law willingly or unwillingly, a distinction not found in the *Nicomachean Ethics*. The legislator makes an involuntary omission when he does not foresee some possible exception to the general rule. He makes a voluntary omission when he realizes that he must make a general rule to cover most, but not all, possible cases. Yet in both discussions, Aristotle locates the need for *epieikeia* in the same place, the area where the general rule contained in a written law must be applied to a particular case.

16. See Carey (1996) 35 and Harris (2006a) 54, note 41.

To illustrate his point, Aristotle gives an example of how *epieikeia* works in practice. If one were drafting a law about wounding, one could not specify precisely the size and type of iron instrument that someone might use to wound his victim. Aristotle's discussion here is brief and vague, but he appears to assume that a charge of wounding differed from a charge of assault and battery insofar as the former charge could only be brought if the offender carried a metal object, normally a weapon, while the latter charge did not require this aggravating circumstance.[17] Aristotle then mentions the case of a man who attempts to strike or strikes while wearing a ring. Since the ring qualifies as a metal object, the defendant would be guilty of wounding, not just assault and battery, which would presumably result in a harsher penalty. In Aristotle's view, this is a case for *epieikeia*. Again Aristotle's discussion is rather brief, but his point appears to be that the legislator intended to punish assailants who strike with a weapon with a more severe penalty and thus formulated a general rule applying to those who strike with a metal object. The person who strikes with his fists does not intend to do as much harm as someone who strikes with a weapon and is thus less culpable. But he did not consider that some metal objects, such as a ring, do not reveal an intent to wound more harshly. The general rule is too crude and does not fit the intent of the lawgiver in each possible situation. If one were to appeal to *epieikeia* in a case like this, one would not be asking for the court to ignore or bypass the written law. One would be arguing that a strict application of the law in this specific case alone would result in a decision that would be contrary to the legislator's intent. In other words, the advocate would ask the court to do what the legislator would have done had he know about this particular case.

In the following section, Aristotle gives several examples of arguments from *epieikeia*. He makes his famous distinction among the trio of terms misfortune (*atychemata*), errors (*hamartemata*), and vicious acts (*adikemata*) that do not deserve the same penalty (Arist. *Rh.* 1.13.15–16.1374b). A misfortune is an action that occurs contrary to one's expectation (*paraloga*) and not through moral vice (*me apo ponerias*). An error does not occur contrary to expectation but also not because of any moral vice. Errors would appear to encompass cases of negligence in which one did not intend for harm to occur but could have foreseen the possibility that it

17. Cf. Lys. 3.28: to prove a charge of wounding (*trauma*), the accuser must show that the defendant carried a weapon. Cf. Carey (2004) 119.

might occur and taken measures to prevent it. Wrongful acts are those that occur not contrary to expectation and through evil intent. For instance, when one aims a firearm at someone and pulls the trigger, which causes a serious wound or death, the agent intends to do harm and the resulting harm is not something that one could not have foreseen. In fact, as we have seen earlier, Demosthenes (18.274–75) makes a similar distinction in *On the Crown* and observes that the distinction is made both in the unwritten laws and in the written laws. For instance, the laws of Athens made a distinction among three types of homicide, deliberate (*ek pronoias*), against one's will, and just homicide or homicide according to the laws, the first two of which incurred different penalties, and the third no punishment at all. The first category covered those cases in which the defendant intended to cause harm, and the second appears to have covered cases of negligence. The best example of the latter is the case *On the Chorister*, in which a man is accused of causing the death of a young boy by having him drink a potion intended to improve his voice (Antiphon 6).[18] The defendant did not wish to bring about the death of the victim, but the accusers hold him responsible because they charge he could have acted with greater caution. The category of just homicide covered many different kinds of cases but included those in which the defendant was not held responsible because he acted out of ignorance (D. 23.55) or under compulsion (D. 23.60), in other words, in circumstances he could not have foreseen. The law about damage also made a distinction between damage caused willingly and that caused unwillingly and imposed a greater penalty on the former, a smaller on the latter (D. 21.43). The principles that Aristotle includes under the category of *epieikeia* are therefore principles that are implicit in the laws of Athens.

Aristotle continues his illustration of arguments based on *epieikeia* with the adage that it is fair to pardon 'human qualities,' which presumably means human shortcomings, that is, those faults inherent in common human nature. Here Aristotle appears to be discussing *epieikeia* as a moral virtue, but the next examples indicate that *epieikeia* can also be viewed as a principle of legal interpretation: it is fair (*epieikes*) to consider not the law but the legislator, not the letter of the law but the intention (*dianoias*) of the lawgiver, not the action but the moral intent (*proairesin*). The following two examples are somewhat vague (to consider not the part but the whole;

18. For the nature of the charge in this case see Harris (2006a) 391–404.

not what a man is now but what he has always been). These could apply to the judge deciding a case or to a private individual making moral decisions. The remaining examples of *epieikeia* relate to moral conduct: to remember good treatment rather than bad, benefits received rather than those given,[19] to put up with unjust treatment, and to prefer to go to arbitration rather than to court.[20]

The need for *epieikeia* arises as a result of 'law's open texture.' As Hart has noted, 'human legislators can have no . . . knowledge of all the possible combinations of circumstances which the future may bring. This inability to anticipate brings with it a relative indeterminacy of aim.'[21] Hart gives the example of the standard of due care in cases of negligence such as the duty to stop, look, and listen where one expects there to be oncoming traffic at a stop sign. The aim of this standard is 'to ensure (1) that precautions will be taken which will avert substantial harm, yet (2) that the precautions are such that the burden of proper precautions does not involve too great a sacrifice of other respectable interests.' Yet if one is driving a man who is bleeding to death to the hospital, the normal amount of caution may result in the victim not arriving at the hospital in time. In other words, 'one cannot *ab initio* foresee what combinations of circumstances will arise nor foresee what interests will have to be sacrificed or to what extent, if precaution against harm is to be taken.'[22] Or one might have a general rule that one cannot drive a vehicle in the park. This rule is obviously designed to maintain peace and quiet in the park so that those using the park can relax and not worry about traffic. The person who framed such a rule might not have thought about a motor-driven toy automobile that a child might bring into the park for his or her own amusement. If an official were to find a child with such a vehicle, he or she would have to decide 'whether some degree of peace in the park is to be sacrificed to, or defended against, those children whose pleasure or interest it is to use these things.'[23] In this case, one has to choose between two competing

19. For this idea see D. 18.269.

20. To explain the final example, Aristotle says that the arbitrator looks at what is fair whereas the judge looks at the law. This dichotomy is simplistic however because the rest of Aristotle's analysis shows that the judge can also exercise *epieikeia*.

21. Hart (1961) 125. One should distinguish 'indeterminacy of aim' from 'ignorance of fact,' which was discussed in chapters 5 and 6.

22. Hart (1961) 129.

23. Hart (1961) 125–26.

interests, each of which is legitimate. Hart frames his analysis in slightly different terms from those of Aristotle. Where Hart speaks of competing interests, Aristotle draws a contrast between the written law and a broader sense of justice based on general principles implicit in the laws. Yet both writers are analyzing the same aspect of law's open texture. Like Aristotle, Hart identifies the inability of the legislator to foresee all possible circumstances as the source of the problem.

A close study of Aristotle's analysis of *epieikeia* shows that the term applies to a kind of justice that takes account of exceptions to the general rules laid down in the law. When these exceptions occur, the judge should look to the intent of the lawgiver, the intent of the defendant, extenuating circumstances, and other such matters. On the other hand, *epieikeia* is not an appeal to extra-legal factors or to a higher standard of justice that transcends the written law. The application of *epieikeia* does not undermine the authority of the law.

Do the kinds of arguments that Aristotle lists as examples of *epieikeia* in this passage occur in speeches delivered before Athenian courts? As we have seen in chapters 5 and 6, several speakers appeal to the intent of the lawgiver. But what about the other arguments he lists in the *Rhetoric*? Do defendants use pleas of necessity, duress, or ignorance to prove that they are innocent? Is Aristotle inventing new types of arguments, or is he describing some of the kinds of arguments speakers actually used in court?

II

The orators certainly believed that the Athenian legal system reserved a place for *epieikeia*. In his Funeral Oration, Gorgias (fr. 6 Diels-Kranz) says that the Athenians do not follow 'harsh justice' (*authade dikaion*) but 'a mild sense of fairness' (*to praon epieikes*). This phrase comes from a funeral oration, which was composed as a sophistic exercise, so one might argue that the statement is not relevant to contemporaneous legal practice. Demosthenes (21.90), however, states in a speech written for delivery in court that defendants were normally entitled to *epieikeia*.[24]

24. Meyer-Laurin (1965) contains no discussion of this key passage, which directly contradicts his main thesis. Isocrates (7.33) claims that in the good old days when the Areopagus had more power those who judged civil cases (*symbolaion*) did not use *epieikeia* but obeyed the laws. This implies that contemporary courts did use *epieikeia*.

Several passages in the Attic Orators show that arguments from *epieikeia* were sometimes made in court. In *Against Androtion,* the accuser expects the defendant to use a plea of necessity in reply to one of the charges. Demosthenes wrote the speech for a politician named Diodorus, who spoke in support of Euctemon, who had brought a charge of proposing an illegal decree of honors for the members of the Council in 356/5 against Androtion.[25] One of the charges in the indictment was that the Council had not had triremes built and the decree therefore violated the law forbidding honors to members of the Council who had not had triremes constructed during their term of office (D. 22.8). Diodorus says he has heard that Androtion plans to argue that the reason why the triremes were not built was not the fault of the Council: the treasurer in charge of the board responsible for constructing triremes ran off with two-and-a-half talents (D. 22.17). This was their misfortune or bad luck (*atychema*), not something for which they could be blamed. The accuser uses the same word for misfortune that Aristotle uses in the *Rhetoric* (1.13.16.1374b) when discussing *epieikeia*: one should distinguish mistakes and misfortunes from injustices, which are done with evil intent (*mochtheria*). A misfortune is something that one cannot foresee and therefore deserves pardon. Androtion was clearly going to argue that the Council could not have foreseen that the treasurer would embezzle the funds entrusted to him; the Council had suffered a misfortune, not committed an offense.[26]

Diodorus rejects Androtion's argument for several reasons (D. 22.18–20). First, he argues for the strict application of the law: if the law forbids honors for members of the Council who have not had triremes built, it is not right for them to receive honors when they have not been built, even if Androtion can show it is someone else's fault. Second, he points to grounds of public utility: if the court allows excuses in this case, future members of the Council will look for excuses rather than having triremes built. Third, he argues that the Council was responsible for the failure to build triremes because they elected the treasurer in the first place. In other words, the accuser does not object to the defendant's appeal to *epieikeia*; he argues rather that the circumstances do not justify a plea of necessity and that the admission of such an excuse as this one would have

25. For the date and background to the speech see Harris (2008) 166–70.

26. Meyer-Laurin (1965) does not discuss this passage, which also contradicts his main thesis.

damaging consequences in the future. The members of the Council should have investigated the treasurer's character, taken steps to investigate his background, or supervised his conduct more carefully. They may not have deliberately chosen a corrupt official or shared in the money he embezzled, but they should have been aware that officials can be dishonest. In this regard they were negligent by not evaluating his character before appointing him and by not keeping an eye on him once in office. They were therefore responsible for the fact that no triremes were built during their term of office. On the other hand, Diodorus does not question the basic principle that a defendant cannot be held responsible for events beyond his control or those that he could not foresee.

A plaintiff in a private case concerning a maritime loan also expects his opponent to use a plea of necessity. Dareius and Pamphilus made a loan of 3,000 drachmas to Parmeniscus and Dionysodorus on the security of their ship (D. 56.3, 6). The terms of the contract required that the ship sail from Athens to Egypt and then return to Athens (D. 56.6, 36). If the loan was not repaid or the security turned over to the lenders, the borrowers were to pay double the amount of the loan (D. 56.20, 27, 38–40). At the trial Dareius claims that Parmeniscus sailed to Egypt and bought a cargo of grain. At the time he left, the price of grain at Athens was high, but when a large shipment arriving from Sicily caused prices to fall, Dionysodorus sent a messenger to meet Parmeniscus at Rhodes, where he knew he would stop on his return journey, to tell him about the drop in price at Athens (D. 56. 8–9). When Parmeniscus received the news, he decided to sell the grain in Rhodes where the price was higher (D. 56.10). Dareius learned what Parmeniscus had done and confronted Dionysodorus (D. 56.11–12). When attempts to settle the dispute out of court came to naught, Dareius brought a private suit against Dionysodorus (D. 56.13–18).

In his speech to the court, Dareius predicts that Dionysodorus will base his defense on several arguments.[27] The first is that the ship was 'wrecked' (*ragenai*) on its return voyage from Egypt and for this reason Parmeniscus was forced (*anagkasthenai*) to put in at Rhodes and to unload

---

27. Meyer-Laurin (1965) 12–14 denies that Dareius says that Dionysodorus will make a plea of necessity. Meyer-Laurin claims that the accuser predicts the defendant will base his case on an interpretation of a key clause in the contract. Meyer-Laurin does not see that Dareius says that Dionysodorus will make two different arguments, one based on a plea of necessity, the other based on an interpretation of the contract. In Harris (1988) (= Harris [2006a] 187–88) I endorsed Meyer-Laurin's analysis of the speech. I have now changed my mind.

his cargo there. To prove this, he says that he leased some ships at Rhodes and transported some of his cargo from there on these ships (D. 56.21). Dareius adds that Dionysodorus will also make two other arguments: first, that other lenders were willing to accept payment of interest only for the journey to Rhodes (D. 56.22), and, second, that the contract stipulated that the borrowers were obligated to repay the loans only if the ship arrived safely at Athens (D. 56.22). Dareius makes several replies to these arguments, but it is the reply to his first argument which interests us. Dareius does not argue that the court should not consider a plea of necessity but claims that Parmeniscus acted willingly and not under compulsion (D. 56.42: *hekontes kai ouk ex anagkes*). Dareius admits that the damage done to the ship was an accident that occurred against Parmeniscus' will (*akousion symptoma*). But the accident did not prevent him from fulfilling the terms of the contract because he was able to repair (*epanorthoumenoi*) the damage resulting from the accident and make his ship seaworthy again. In other words, Dareius implicitly accepts the principle that a plea of necessity is a valid argument in court. He rejects his opponent's argument on the grounds that the unforeseen circumstances did not compel him to violate the contract.

In *Against Eratosthenes* Lysias charges one of the former members of the Thirty with causing the death of his brother Polemarchus. He recounts how Eratosthenes came to their house and arrested his brother, who was then led to prison and forced to drink hemlock. The speech reports the questions Lysias posed to Eratosthenes (Lys. 12.24–5). He starts by asking him if he arrested Polemarchus. He admits that he did but claims that he did so only out of fear (*dedios*) about the orders of those in power. He then asks him if he spoke about him and his brother in the Council chamber. This time Eratosthenes says that he opposed the arrest. Finally, Lysias asks him if what happened to his brother was just or unjust. Eratosthenes replies that it was unjust.

Lysias rejects this plea of duress. First, he argues that Eratosthenes' actions were inconsistent: he spoke against the death penalty for Polemarchus but then arrested him and placed him in prison, which led to his death. Second, he argues that it is implausible that Eratosthenes acted under orders: the Thirty would never have entrusted the task of arresting Polemarchus to someone who had spoken against his execution (Lys. 12.27). Second, Eratosthenes was a member of the Thirty and thus was responsible for the orders that were given to him. He did not receive orders from some higher authority (Lys. 12.29). Third, he could have allowed

Polemarchus to escape and told the Thirty that he had not met him or seen him without fear of being caught in an act of disobedience (Lys. 12.30–32). Lysias implicitly accepts the principle that someone acting under duress would deserve pardon. His argument is rather that there was no duress in this case because Eratosthenes could have failed to carry out the order and avoided punishment.

A speaker in another Lysianic speech also uses a plea of duress to defend his father, Polystratus (Lys. 20.14). Polystratus had been appointed registrar (*katalogeus*) during the reign of the Four Hundred during 411 and was one of those responsible for drawing up the list of the Five Thousand. His son defends Polystratus in two ways. First, he claims that he enrolled nine thousand instead of five thousand and thus acted in a democratic manner by increasing the number of citizens (Lys. 12.13). He also uses a plea of duress. At first Polystratus refused to take the oath or to draw up the list. Polystratus did so only after the oligarchs forced him by the threat of fines and punishments (Lys. 12.14). The speaker would never have employed this argument unless he expected the court to take it seriously.[28]

In his speech *Against Meidias* Demosthenes (21.13–18) starts to prove his charge of *hybris* by recounting what his opponent did to him: how he broke into the house of the goldsmith and tried to destroy the costumes for his chorus, how he tried to corrupt the chorus trainer, and how he punched him at the Dionysia.[29] Demosthenes (21.36–41) predicts Meidias, in an attempt to show that what he did not was not all that serious, will point to two other cases in which men who received insulting blows did not bring their assailants to court. One man struck an archon, a public official, when the latter was protecting a female musician, and another named Polyzelus struck a *proedros*, another public official. Demosthenes observes that there are significant differences between what these two men did and what Meidias did. The first man had three excuses (*prophaseis*): drunkenness, passion, and ignorance because the event took place at night.[30] Polyzelus acted in anger and on the spur of the moment, not out of deliberate intent to insult a personal enemy. Meidias had none of these excuses: he acted intentionally and in broad daylight. In other words,

---

28. For other cases in which defendants use the orders of magistrates as an excuse see Harris (2006a) 68–69.

29. MacDowell (1990) believes that the speech was delivered in an action for *probole* but see Harris (2008) 79–81 (*graphe hybreos*).

30. On drunkenness as an excuse see Harris (2006a) 300–3.

Meidias cannot claim that he was acting in ignorance or without deliberate intent (D. 21.38). Demosthenes (21.41. Cf. 42) denies that Meidias has any legitimate excuse such as a sudden fit of anger because his repeated acts of hostility amply demonstrate that he intended to insult his victim. Demosthenes does not say that a defendant has no right to present excuses for his conduct. His point is that the judges must find Meidias guilty because he has no excuse for what he did. Yet he implicitly admits that had Meidias had one of these excuses, he would have deserved lenient treatment.

Socrates, in his *Apology* (25c–26a), appeals to the principle that ignorance provides an excuse and clearly expects the court to follow it when making its decision. Meletus has accused him of corrupting the youth. Socrates asks Meletus if evil men do harm to those who associate with them while good people benefit their companions; Meletus agrees. He next asks if anyone prefers to be harmed by his associates rather than benefited. Meletus again agrees that nobody does. Socrates then says that Meletus has in effect accused him of ignorance (*amathian*) for if he makes his associates worse, and his corrupt associates do him harm, he is actually bringing harm on himself, something which no one would do knowingly and willingly. But if Socrates corrupts the youth unwillingly out of ignorance, the law does not allow Meletus to bring him to court for mistakes committed against his will. Socrates does not cite the text of a particular law, and legal historians would be hard put to identify a specific law explicitly stating this principle. Socrates must be appealing to a generally recognized principle which is implicit in the laws and which judges can apply in any given situation. This passage in turn brings us back to Aristotle's discussion of *epieikeia* where he makes a tripartite distinction among three types of acts and states that actions involving unwilling actions are cases for compassion (*Rh.* 1.13.16.1374b).

The most famous example of a plea of *force majeure* in Attic oratory occurs in Demosthenes' *On the Crown*. When Aeschines indicted Ctesiphon for proposing an illegal decree of praise for Demosthenes, he charged that Ctesiphon had made a false statement when he asserted that Demosthenes 'always does and says what is best for the Athenian people' (Aeschin. 3.49–50). To prove this charge, he divides Demosthenes' political career into four periods and argues that in each period Demosthenes was dishonest and that his policies harmed Athens. Aeschines (3.106–58) lays particular emphasis on Demosthenes' actions before the battle of Chaeronea. He denies that Demosthenes deserves any credit for the alliance with Thebes (Aeschin. 3.137–144), charges him with seizing complete control and bypassing democratic procedures (Aeschin. 3.145–7), and, most serious, accuses him of having prevented the Athenians from making peace with Philip when the king was ready to negotiate (Aeschin. 3.148–51). His words and actions were therefore directly responsible for the Athenian defeat.

In reply to these charges, Demosthenes presents several arguments. First, he recalls the events of 338 to show that he was primarily responsible for the alliance with Thebes (D. 18.169–80, 188–91, 211–18). Second, he insists that even if the Athenians had known that they were about to be defeated, the honorable course of action was to resist Philip's attempt to enslave the Greeks (D. 18.199–209). Third, even after the defeat, the Athenians continued to trust Demosthenes' good judgment by following his advice and electing him to a position in control of the food supply (D. 18.248–50). Fourth, Aeschines never offered any advice that was better than his own (D. 18.273). Fifth, he was not in command of the army and thus cannot be held responsible for the military defeat at Chaeronea (D. 18.247).

These are not the only arguments Demosthenes uses. He also asserts that the ultimate success or failure of his policy lay not in his hands but those of the gods (D. 18.192–93). Demosthenes took every precaution that he possibly could imagine or implement. He compares himself to a shipowner who, after doing everything possible to ensure the ship's safety, encounters a storm and is then accused of causing a shipwreck (D. 18.194–95). The defeat at Chaeronea, like the storm, was something beyond his control, and he is therefore innocent. Demosthenes' argument resembles the one Dareius predicts Dionysodorus would use at his trial, namely that one cannot be blamed for damages caused by natural events. Later in the speech, Demosthenes makes the same tripartite distinction among three types of actions: willing injustice, harm caused against one's will, and the failure to achieve one's aim through no wrongdoing or negligence (D. 18.274). This distinction is not only found in the laws but also in nature itself. Because the rout at Chaeronea occurred through no fault of his own but because of circumstances beyond his control, Demosthenes is innocent.

As these examples make abundantly clear, the kinds of arguments that Aristotle considers to be examples of *epieikeia* can be found in the speeches of the Attic Orators. The next question is, how did the courts respond to these arguments?

III

In most cases we do not know the outcome of the trials at which speeches of the Attic Orators were delivered. Even when we do know how the court voted, there is no evidence that gives the reason for their decision. These speeches, however, often contain brief accounts of trials and explain why the judges in these cases decided to convict or acquit. The speaker does not indicate how he discovered the *ratio dicendi* for the decision, but there is no reason to doubt that he could have spoken with the judges after a trial and discussed why they voted as they did. After all, Athenian judges were not like jurors in the United Kingdom, who are barred by statute from discussing the case they heard. On the other hand, if the analysis of a court decision by a litigant is only speculation, his analysis must have appeared plausible to the judges who heard the case. A litigant is unlikely to have described the reasons for a court's decision in a way that did not appear plausible to his audience.

In the speech *Against Demosthenes* Dinarchus (1.55–7) discusses three cases where the court acquitted a defendant although he was technically guilty of the charge brought against him. The first case concerns a member of the Areopagus, who somehow deprived a ferryman of his fee. The Areopagus imposed a fine on him (*zemiosasa*) and reported him to the Assembly. In the second case, someone asked for the payment of five drachmas in the name of someone who was not present. The Areopagus caught him and reported the offense to the Assembly. The payment was made from the Theoric Fund.[31] In the third case, someone sold the 'allotment (*merida*) of the Areopagus.' No other source mentions this allotment so the precise nature of his offense is unclear, but Dinarchus states that it was against the laws.[32] The Areopagus fined (*zemiosas*') the offender and expelled him from its ranks, then reported him to the Assembly. In each case, the court then acquitted the defendant. Dinarchus' brief description

31. See Hyp. *D.* 26 with Whitehead (2000) 441. Some have identified the offender with Conon of Paeania mentioned by Hyperides. Conon however was sentenced to a fine of a talent whereas the offender mentioned by Dinarchus was acquitted. See Whitehead (2000) 442 and Worthington (1992) 220–21.

32. L.-S.-J. s.v. *meris* says that it was a portion of sacrificial meat given to members of the Areopagus. See *IG* ii^2 334, lines 10–11; 1187, lines 20–21; 1214, lines 12–13. I owe these references to Fred Naiden. *Pace* Worthington (1992) 220, who thinks it is 'a meat allowance for the Areopagites, the equivalent of a modern-day sustenance allowance for those on official business.'

of each case leaves much uncertain. In the first case, the member of the court did not make an agreed payment. The fine would appear to have been a sufficient punishment, but the Areopagus reported his crime to the Assembly as if it merited additional punishment. In the second case, we know that it was illegal to collect payment from the Theoric Fund for someone who was abroad.[33] Why this deserved to be brought before the Assembly is left unclear. Equally frustrating is Dinarchus' silence about the charge made in court and the precise penalty. Dinarchus' analysis of the reasons for the decision to acquit implies, however, that the penalties were rather harsh. All that Dinarchus says is that the Athenians paid more attention to sympathy than to justice and did not convict the offenders.

Although Dinarchus omits key details, he does give the reason why the Assembly or court decided the way it did: they considered the punishment greater than the wrongful action of the accused. The reason why the courts or Assembly did not convict was because a conviction would have violated the principle that the punishment must fit the seriousness of the crime. The Athenians were certainly familiar with the general legal principle that the punishment should be proportional to the offense. For instance, the law about damage imposed a payment of double the amount if the damage was done willingly, but only for the simple amount if done against the defendant's will. The punishment for homicide committed intentionally was greater than that for homicide committed unwillingly (D. 21.42–5). In other words, when the courts decided to acquit these defendants, they did not take into account extra-legal considerations such as public service; Dinarchus certainly does not mention this as a reason for their decision. The court was faced with a choice between applying the law in a rigid and inflexible way or applying a general legal principle implicit in the laws and opted for the latter. One could even argue that the judges 'did what the legislator would have done if he had known about the situation.'

Dinarchus (1.58–9) is more informative about the next case he discusses. Here Dinarchus gives the name of the defendant Polyeuctus of Cydantidae and says the Assembly ordered the Areopagus to report whether Polyeuctus was meeting with exiles in Megara. The Areopagus investigated and reported to the Assembly that Polyeuctus was indeed meeting with exiles. The Assembly elected public prosecutors and the case against Polyeutus went to court, but the defendant was acquitted. At

33. See Harpocration *s.v. theorika*.

the trial Polyeuctus admitted that he did go to Megara to see Nicophanes who was an exile (*apesteremeno tes patridos*), but who also happened to be married to his mother.

The charge against Polyeuctus is most likely to have been treason and the procedure *eisangelia*.[34] The law about *eisangelia* provides for the prosecution of anyone who 'meets anywhere for the purpose of overthrowing the people' (Hyp. *Eux.* 8). In a passage later in the same speech Dinarchus (1.94) recalls how Demosthenes charged Callimedon with meeting exiles in Megara for the overthrow of the people (*sunienai . . . phygasin epi katalysei tou demou*), then withdrew the charge in the *eisangelia*. That similar terms were used to describe the offense of Polyeuctus and that of Callimedon indicates that they were charged with the same crime.[35]

Dinarchus does not say why Nicophanes was in exile, but the penalty was a serious one and strongly suggests that whatever his actual offense it was one that threatened public security. Because Nicophanes was regarded as dangerous, any attempt to speak with him and help him might be construed as an attempt to overthrow the democracy. But the courts did not look only at Polyeuctus' actions; they also considered his intent in meeting with Nicophanes. The court decided that although Nicophanes was an exile and thus a criminal, Polyeuctus helped him not for the purpose of overthrowing the democracy but for personal reasons. Nicophanes was married to his mother, and Polyeuctus was helping his stepfather not as a co-conspirator but as a relative who had fallen on hard times.[36] One might argue that his actions fit the criteria of treason in the law of *eisangelia*, but he lacked the necessary intent. For this reason, the court decided to be forgiving (Din. 1.59: *syngnomes*). If this analysis is correct, the court's approach to the case fits one of Aristotle's examples of *epieikeia*: in the *Rhetoric* (1.13.17.1374b) Aristotle says that the person who uses fairness looks

34. Carawan (1985) 132 believes that the charge was for deserting the state during the emergency after Chaeronea but see Worthington (1992) 222. Wallace (1989) 113 does not discuss the trial of Polyeuctus in detail but follows Hansen (1975) 30, 39–40 and considers it a case of *apophasis*, not an *eisangelia*. The term *apophasis* applies, however, only to the report given by the Areopagus. The trial in court that followed was an *eisangelia* (*pace* Hansen [1975] 39 'the whole procedure from the indictment until the passing of the sentence').

35. Hansen (1975) 111 considers the case of Callimedon an *eisangelia* (no. 129) but does not see the similarities with the case of Polyeuctus. Worthington (1992) 222 does not discuss the procedure but assumes the charge was treason.

36. Worthington (1992) 222–23 and Hansen (1975) 111 do not discuss the reasons for the acquittal.

not at the action but at the moral intent (*proairesin*).[37] The court did not look outside the law to find this principle but followed a rule that was implicit in several laws, which considered not only the actions of the defendant but also his intent (D. 21.42–45).

Dinarchus portrays the Areopagus as a body that applies the law very strictly and contrasts its methods with the more indulgent approach of the regular courts. In his speech *Against Neaera*, however, Apollodorus recalls an incident in which the Areopagus took a more lenient approach. According to Apollodorus, his opponent Stephanus gave the daughter of Neaera in marriage to the *basileus* Theogenes ([D.] 59.78–84).[38] The wife of this official had the duty of administering the oath to the Venerable Priestesses. There was a law that required the wife of the *basileus* to be an Athenian by birth and a virgin at the time of her marriage ([D.] 59.75); the daughter of Neaera was allegedly neither. Apollodorus reminds the court about the Areopagus' interest in religious matters and recalls how its members launched an investigation into Neaera's background ([D.] 59.80–81: *ezetei, zemiouses*). Upon discovering the truth, the Areopagus wished to impose on Theogenes the highest fine it was allowed to ([D.] 59.80: *ezemiou*). When Theogenes learned about these deliberations, he went to the Areopagus and supplicated them for pardon on the grounds that he did not know she was the daughter of Neaera and that Stephanus had deceived him into thinking she was his own daughter.[39] His mistaken appointment of Stephanus as his assessor he blamed on his lack of experience and his good nature (*akakian*). To prove his sincerity, he promised to divorce the daughter of Neaera without further delay ([D.] 59.82). This promise made an impression on the Areopagus, which took pity on Theogenes for two reasons: first, his naiveté (*akakian*), and, second, the fact that Stephanus had deceived him (*exepatesthai, exapatethenti*) ([D.] 59.83).

Strictly speaking, Theogenes was guilty of breaking the law about the wife of the *basileus*. The daughter of Neaera was neither an Athenian nor a virgin when she married Theogenes when he was *basileus*. But the court of the Areopagus chose not to impose a fine on Theogenes. As in the previous case, the court of the Areopagus considered Theogenes' intention:

---

37. Aristotle *Rh.* 1.13.9.1374a alludes to just this kind of case ('when a man admits he talked with enemies [*dieilechthai men tois polemiois*] but did not commit treason [*all' ou prodounai*]').

38. For commentary see Carey (1992) 126–27 and Kapparis (1999) 344–53.

39. On this supplication see Naiden (2006) 151–52.

he did not knowingly break the law. He married the daughter of Neaera because he trusted Stephanus as a friend and was a bit naive. The Areopagus also accepted Theogenes' excuse that Stephanus had deceived him. There is no indication that the law about the wife of the *basileus* contained a clause indicating what to do when this official unknowingly married a woman who was not an Athenian and a virgin.

The principle that someone should not be held guilty when he broke the law through ignorance was, however, recognized in two other laws concerning religious activities and in Draco's law about homicide.[40] The first comes from an inscription dated to around 485/4 containing rules about conduct on the Acropolis (*IG* i^3 4). The inscription is fragmentary but lists a series of offenses that the treasurers can punish with a fine of up to three obols (lines 7–8, 12). The lacunose state of the inscription makes it difficult to know exactly what these offenses are, but two clauses state that the treasurers can inflict this fine only 'if anyone knowingly (*eidos*) does any of these things' (lines 6–7, 9–10). These clauses implicitly exempt those who perform these forbidden actions without knowing they are illegal.

The second comes from fourth-century law about the Eleusinian Mysteries.[41] The law concerns initiation into the Eleusinian Mysteries and contains a clause that begins: 'If anyone conducts an initiation knowing (*eidos*) that he is not a member of the Eumolpidai or Kerykes . . . anyone who wishes can initiate a *phasis* and the king Archon must bring the case to the Heliaea' (lines 27–29).[42] Here again the law recognizes that someone who breaks the law unknowingly cannot be held guilty of wrongdoing. The law about just homicide also contains a clause that

40. Carey (1992) 127–28. Kapparis (1999) 147 speculates that 'the reasons (i.e. of the Areopagus) were probably personal.' It is not clear what he means by this; Apollodorus certainly does not suggest that the Areopagus acted for this reason. Kapparis does see that the reason why they let Theogenes off was that they believed he did not know about the first marriage, but does not discuss the legal rationale for their decision.

41. For the text see Clinton (2005) no. 138. For the *editio princeps* see Clinton (1980).

42. Clinton (1980) 278 rightly wonders: 'It may seem odd that someone might not *know* that he was not a member of the Eumolpidai or Kerykes.' But he remarks: 'We do not know how well the membership lists of these gene were maintained, or how strictly participation in a formal (as opposed to the simple fact of descent) was necessary for membership.' If one became a member of a *genos* at an early age and was not informed by one's parents, it is possible that one might not know. Clinton then points to the case of Valerius Mamertinus who 'believed that he was a member of the Kerykes, even though he was not, and the genos actually elected him Dadouchos; but he was removed from the priesthood when a legal challenge proved that he was not a member of the genos.' See Oliver (1970) 4.

absolves one kind of killing done in ignorance. Demosthenes (23.55) quotes the beginning of one clause from this law: 'if [sc. anyone kills] during war in ignorance (*agnoesas*),' then notes that the man who kills in these circumstances 'is clean,' that is, innocent and therefore free of religious pollution.[43] He then gives the rationale for this rule: 'if I have destroyed a man thinking that he was one of the enemy, it is not right for me to stand trial but [it is right for me] to receive forgiveness.' In each of these three rules, the law implicitly recognizes that the person who commits an act in ignorance does not deserve punishment. In fact, one accuser states that it was generally understood that one should grant pardon to those who unwillingly (*akontes*) break the law because of their lack of experience (*apragmosynen*) ([D.] 58.24). When deciding not to punish Theogenes, therefore, the Areopagus followed a general principle implicit in the laws of Athens.

Almost half the judges at the trial of Euaeon took extenuating circumstances into account and wanted to acquit the defendant (D. 21.71–76). Euaeon killed Boeotus at a party because of a single punch Boeotus had given him. What made Euaeon angry was not the blow itself but the humiliation (*atimia*) it brought. Demosthenes then reminds the court how the actions, voice, and posture of an assailant can transform a single blow into a display of arrogance that degrades the victim to the point where he finds it difficult to control himself (D. 21.72). Demosthenes next describes the circumstances surrounding Euaeon's action: he was struck by a friend, who was drunk, in front of six or seven other friends. These men would have praised him if he had restrained himself. Euaeon was also attending a dinner at his own choice (D. 21.73).

When the case came to trial, the court decided to convict Euaeon by one vote. The charge must have been deliberate murder (*phonos ek pronoias*).[44] Half the court voted to convict him not because he retaliated but because he struck in such a way that he killed Boeotus. In other words, this half of the court did not let the fact that Euaeon did not initiate the violence but merely struck back influence their judgment. In their opinion he caused the death of his victim and did so as the result of a deliberate

43. For the equivalence of the terms *katharos* and *anaitios* see Harris (2010) 133–34.

44. MacDowell (1990) 292–93 believes that the trial was a case of just homicide (*dikaios phonos*), but this is impossible because Boeotus did not attack Euaeon with the intent to kill. See Harris (1992) 78 and Harris (2010) 136.

action (*ek pronoias*), that is, an act aimed at harming the victim. These judges therefore decided to apply the law strictly and paid no attention to the surrounding circumstances.

It is the opinion of the other half of the judges that interests us. These judges did find the surrounding circumstances relevant and 'granted to the victim of physical humiliation this excess amount of retaliation (*hyperbolen tes timorias*).' The reason for their votes was not based on some vague sense of 'what was just' but on basic principles implicit in the laws of Athens. The law of Athens implicitly granted the victim of a blow permission to strike back. In the private action for assault (*aikeia*), the plaintiff must prove that in the case of a brawl it was the defendant who started the unjust blows ([D.] 47.45–7). This clearly implied that the person who did not start the fight, but merely struck back, could not be found guilty of the charge. On the other hand, the law did not state how much the victim might retaliate. The law on just homicide also allowed the victim of ambush (*en locho*) to kill his assailant[45] and to kill someone who was stealing his property provided he retaliated immediately (D. 23.61). Here the law allows retaliation against someone who was taking property. The judges who voted to acquit thus granted to Euaeon the same amount of retaliation granted in these two other cases. Thus these judges did not go outside the law to find a principle to apply to Euaeon's case; they used a rule implicit in other statutes. They evidently reasoned that the humiliation Euaeon suffered was so serious that it justified the greater amount of retaliation. Their willingness to look not only at the illegal action by itself (the blow that caused death) but also at the surrounding circumstances recalls one of the examples of *epieikeia* given by Aristotle (*Rh.* 1.13.18.1374b), namely, that one should look not at the part (i.e., of a situation) but at the whole.

Athenian judges may have taken extenuating circumstances into account at the trial of the general Anytus (D. S. 13.64.5–7). In 410 or 409/8 the Spartans sent an expedition against Pylos, which was held by a Messenian garrison.[46] As soon as they heard about the attack, the Athenians sent Anytus as a general with thirty ships to support the Messenians. Anytus departed on his mission but was unable to reach Pylos because of storms and returned to Athens. The Messenian garrison could not continue to fight

45. For this law see Harris (2010) 132–3, 140–42.

46. For the date of the incident see Rhodes (1981) 344.

without support and evacuated Pylos under a truce.[47] The people were so angry, that he was accused of treason and brought to trial. The court, however, acquitted him. This led to charges of bribery, but that explanation for the verdict is highly improbable: the Athenian courts had many measures that made bribery virtually impossible.[48] It is more likely that the court took extenuating circumstances into account and recognized that the storm had indeed prevented him from carrying out his mission.

This explanation is to some extent speculative, but we know from official records that in other cases the Athenian courts acquitted defendants for this reason. Every year the Athenians appointed trierarchs to serve as captains of their triremes. Each trierarch had the duty to return the ship in good repair to the dockyards of the fleet.[49] The supervisors (*epimeletai*) of the fleet in conjunction with a tester (*dokimastes*) inspected the triremes when returned, classified them as in good shape or not, and reported their findings to the Council.[50] If there was damage to the ship or it was lost, the trierarch could be held financially responsible, and the case was heard before a court, which might impose a penalty of double the value of what was lost.[51] The trierarch could present an excuse (*skepsis*) and claim that the loss or damage was caused by a storm. If the court accepted his excuse, the trierarch was exonerated.[52] One entry in the records of the supervisors for the year 325/4 states that the trierarchs Euthydicus, the son of Antiphanes of Phegai, and Diphilus, the son of Diopeithes of Sounion, presented such an excuse and were acquitted (*IG* ii[2] 1629, lines 771–80). One should recall that when the Athenian Assembly voted to condemn the generals at Arginousae to death after they were prevented by a storm from rescuing shipwrecked sailors, the Athenians later regarded the decision as very

47. Cf. X. *HG* 1.2.18.

48. Cf. Arist. *Ath. Pol.* 27.5. The case of Anytus must have been heard by at least five hundred, or possibly one or two thousand, judges. Even if Anytus had been able to approach them before the trial, he would have had to pay a fortune to buy enough votes for acquittal.

49. For the duties of trierarchs see Gabrielsen (1994) 105–69.

50. For the role of the Council in supervising the fleet see Arist. *Ath. Pol.* 46.1 with Rhodes (1972) 115–22, 153–58.

51. For references see Rhodes (1972) 154, note 2.

52. *IG* ii[2] 1629, lines 746–49, 796–99; 1631, lines 115–20, 140–43, 148–52.

unjust and started legal proceedings against the men who convinced the Assembly to condemn them.[53]

All these cases show that when a defendant or a trierarch presented an excuse, the court might acquit him for this reason. When Demosthenes (21.90) says that defendants were entitled to 'fairness' and Gorgias (fr. 6 Diels-Kranz) praises the Athenians for their 'mild sense of fairness,' they were accurately describing an important aspect of the way the Athenian courts made their decisions.

IV

The findings of this chapter shed light both on Aristotle's analysis of *epieikeia* and on the way the Athenian courts enforced the law. First, it is now clear that in his discussion of *epieikeia* Aristotle is not introducing a new concept into the field of Athenian law. Aristotle was familiar with the kinds of arguments that litigants presented to the Athenian courts and knew that defendants sometimes offered several types of excuses to argue for their innocence. In chapter 3 we found that the arguments Aristotle suggests that one should use when the law was not on one's side are not the kinds of arguments that Athenian litigants used in court. In his discussion of *epieikeia*, however, Aristotle's analysis draws on the rhetorical strategies that we have encountered in several court speeches. What these two chapters show is that one must be careful when using Aristotle's *Rhetoric* as a source for attitudes to law in Athenian courts. As is often the case in Aristotle's work, some parts of the *Rhetoric* are theoretical or prescriptive while others are more descriptive of contemporaneous realities. Aristotle's discussion of the reasons for ignoring the law probably draws on an intellectual tradition of ideas about the law going back to the Sophists. Aristotle's analysis of *epieikeia*, by contrast, is an attempt to discover the rationale behind an accepted practice in the Athenian courts. Both accusers and defendants accepted the basic principle that the judges might consider excuses when making their decision. Because litigants are not philosophers giving a lecture to a group of students or colleagues, they do not stop to explain or justify the use of *epieikeia*. Nor did they need to do so because everyone in the courts, both litigants and judges, accepted the

---

53. For the failure to rescue the sailors because of a storm see X. *HG* 1.6.35. For the trial and death sentence see X. *HG* 1.7.1–34. For the later attitude of the Athenians see X. *HG* 1.7.35.

principle that excuses might be valid in certain cases. Aristotle's contribution is to explain the reasons why one needs to have recourse to *epieikeia* and relates it to the philosophical issue of the relationship between the general and the particular, a topic already explored by Plato (*Statesman* 295a) in the context of legislation. Here, as elsewhere in his ethical works, Aristotle supplies a theoretical justification for some customary views (*endoxa*).

This analysis also provides us with a more nuanced understanding of the Judicial Oath. As we saw in chapter 3, the oath bound the judges to vote 'according to the laws and decrees of the Athenian people.' As is evident in many of the cases we have examined, the oath did not order the judges to take into consideration only the law that that accuser in his plaint claims the defendant has violated. For example, if one accused someone of committing outrage (*hybris*) or theft (*klope*), the oath did not restrict the judges to applying only the clauses found in the law on outrage or the law about theft when reaching their decision. The plural 'laws and decrees' in the phrase 'according to the laws and decrees of the Athenian people' is significant. When a court judged a case of outrage or theft, it would, of course, pay attention to the laws on these topics, but it could also consider general principles of justice implicit in all the laws taken as a whole.[54] In other words, the oath implicitly gave litigants and judges the freedom to choose between a strict application of the relevant law and a more flexible approach that took extenuating circumstances and other factors into consideration.[55] The oath therefore allowed room for more creative interpretations aimed at achieving the general aims of the laws as a whole.

---

54. *Pace* Mirhady (1990) 398 there is thus no reason to believe that *epieikeia* introduced extra-legal considerations into trials.

55. Cf. Saunders (2001) 77–8 who perceptively notes that the Attic Orators 'take enormous care to give the impression that the equity arguments they present demonstrate something which *is* part of or integral to the existing substantive law itself, rather than a departure from it . . . But the fact that they were not presented in this guise betokens to my mind that the Athenians could easily become uncomfortable with the concept. A deep reverence for the law, which the orators harp on, no doubt rightly up to a point, makes equity arguments look suspect, as generating positions extra to, and therefore different from, and therefore even contrary to, the law.'

PART THREE

The Breakdown of the Rule of Law

9

Cleon and the Defeat of Athens

ACCORDING TO THUCYDIDES, something went seriously wrong in Athenian politics after the death of Pericles. During his lifetime Pericles advised the Athenians to follow a defensive policy, to maintain the strength of their fleet and to avoid extending their power and endangering the city by taking risks. His successors ignored his good advice. Driven by ambition for their reputations and greed for their own profit, they pursued policies that when successful brought individuals glory and benefits, but when unsuccessful damaged the city's position (Th. 2.65.7). Thucydides attributes Athenian success prior to 429 to Pericles' intelligence, honesty, frankness, and what we might call today his 'leadership skills' (Th. 2.65.5, 8). In Thucydides' opinion, it was his moral and intellectual qualities, not the institutions of Athenian democracy, which kept Athens powerful during these years (Th. 2.65.9).

His successors fell far beneath his level. They competed with one another for political supremacy and indulged the people's pleasures (Th. 2.65.10). This led to many mistakes, especially the defeat in Sicily. Thucydides pins the blame for this debacle more on those who sent the expedition than on errors regarding strategy. It was their strife that blunted the force of the expedition and led to political chaos at home (Th. 2.65.11). Speaking before the Assembly in Sparta after his exile from Athens, Alcibiades makes a similar criticism of Athenian leaders in his day. He states that his family had always opposed tyranny and always championed the cause of the people. He gives two reasons for supporting the democracy. First, that is was a form of government opposed to tyranny,[1] and second, that it was the prevailing form of government in his community (Th. 6.89.4). He blames his current troubles on those who have misled the people

1. For his ancestors' opposition to tyranny see Hdt. 6.121, 123; Isocr. 16.25–6. As Debnar (2001) 205–6 notes, this view of democracy is designed to appeal to the Spartans, who had a reputation for opposing tyranny (Hdt. 5.92.1–2).

(Th. 6.89.5) and then calls democracy a type of government that is generally agreed to be insane (Th. 6.89.6: *homologoumenes anoias*). Here Alcibiades appears to be making a distinction between the political system of Athens which his ancestors defended because it was the best protection against tyranny and the present situation of political indiscipline (*akolasias*), in which contemporary leaders have led the 'mob' into corrupt practices (*ponerotata*).[2] It is impossible to know to what extent Thucydides reproduces Alcibiades' actual words and arguments, but the view is similar: something had changed in Athenian politics in recent years.

According to Thucydides, the tactics these politicians used were 'slanders against individuals' or 'attacks on personal character' (Th. 2.65.11: *tas idias diabolas*). This phrase has not attracted the attention of modern commentators on Thucydides, but it is crucial for our understanding of Thucydides' analysis of the reasons for Athens' defeat.[3] The word is common in forensic oratory and often has the meaning 'malicious prosecution.' For instance, Aeschines (2.145) distinguishes between report (*pheme*) and slander (*diabole*), the former reflecting common knowledge, the latter associated with malicious prosecutions (*sykophantia*).[4] Demosthenes (18.7, 11) uses the term *diabole* to refer to the charges Aeschines has brought against Demosthenes' political activity in his prosecution of Ctesiphon. Later in the same speech, Demosthenes (18.225) accuses Aeschines of mixing up the dates and attributing false motives to old decrees, all for the purpose of slandering (*diaballein*) him. Theomnestus says that Stephanus' prosecution of Apollodorus and his use of false witnesses were done to slander him (*epi diabole*) ([D.] 59.5). Euxitheus calls the allegations made about his mother to prove that he is not a citizen mere 'slanders' (*diabolas*) (D. 57.36). In a suit about a mining business, Nicobulus calls the dishonest charges made by Pantaenetus against

2. Hornblower (2008) 513 does not observe the parallel between Thucydides' criticism and Alcibiades' criticism. Dover in Gomme, Andrewes, and Dover (1970) 362 also does not see the link between the two passages.

3. Gomme (1945–56) I: 195 perceptively sees here 'a reference to the attack on Alcibiades for the mutilation of the Hermai and the profanation of the Mysteries; but not only to this' but does not follow up on this insight and does not explore the meaning of the term *diabolas*. Cf. Rhodes (1988) 245. Rusten (1989) 213 and Hornblower (1991) 348 make no comment on the word. Mann (2007) believes that the change in Athenian politics occurs after 420; he does not discuss Cleon's innovations in using the courts to prosecute political enemies. On the meaning of the term *diabole* see Rizzo and Vox (1978).

4. For other passages in Aeschines in which *diabole* is linked to prosecution see Aeschin. 1.126, 152; 2.10, 11; 3.223.

Evergus 'slander' (D. 37.47). A soldier who was charged with insulting a general claims that the charges against him are just 'slander' (Lys. 9.1. Cf. 3). Another defendant recalls unjust verdicts made on the basis of false testimony and reminds the court that slander (*diabole*) is the worst thing in the world (Lys. 19.5. Cf. 3).[5]

When Thucydides analyzes the civil strife at Corcyra in 427 BCE, he stresses the destructive role of prosecutions brought for political reasons. The problems began when some Corcyreans who had been captured by the Corinthians were released and allowed to return home on the condition that they would attempt to bring their city over to the Corinthians (Th. 3.70.1). When they failed to convince the Assembly to change its policy, the former prisoners brought Peithias, the leader of the pro-Athenian party, into court on a charge of enslaving the city to the Athenians. After being acquitted, Peithias counter-attacked by convicting the city's five wealthiest men of cutting vine-poles in the sanctuaries of Zeus and Alcinous. When they could not pay the fine, the convicted men went to the temples to supplicate, requesting to be allowed to pay in installments (Th. 3.70.2–5).[6] When Peithias persuaded the Council to apply the full rigor of the law, the convicted men gathered supporters, invaded the Council with daggers, and killed sixty men including Peithias (Th. 3.70.6). This was the first step in the cycle of violence that ultimately led to civil war. In fact, Thucydides singles out the use of unjust prosecutions against political enemies as one of the characteristics of civil war. It was this pursuit of revenge without any respect for justice and the common good that led to the breakdown of the rule of law (Th. 3.82.6, 8). This pattern of events was not confined to Corcyra, but spread to the entire Greek world (Th. 3.83.1).

In these two passages, therefore, Thucydides links malicious prosecutions with the outbreak of civil strife and implies that there was not only a shift in political culture but also a change in political tactics. He nowhere implies that Pericles used the courts to eliminate his enemies and to advance his political career and nowhere associates him with 'slanders' of his opponents. We find a similar view of the change in Athenian politics in Isocrates' *On the Peace* (8.124–28. Cf. 15.230–6). During the period of Pericles' leadership, Athens was well governed, but after his death the

5. The word *diabole* is frequently used in Lysias in regard to legal charges: Lys. 9.18–19; 13.17; 14.31; 16.1; 19.34, 53; 25.5–6, 24; 27.8.

6. On this type of supplication see Naiden (2006) 132.

sycophants, those who made a profession out of bringing lawsuits, took over and convinced the Athenians to extend their power overseas.[7]

This chapter attempts to fill in the details of the development that Thucydides and Isocrates only hint at in their analyses of Athens' defeat. Whereas Thucydides analyzes the change in moral terms and sees a decline in ethical standards, this chapter places the change in an institutional context. The change in behavior should be linked to the strain of a long war dragging on inconclusively for years, which gave rise to political tensions that in turn put a strain on the judicial system and exposed its weaknesses. The first section briefly reviews the traditional methods of gaining power and influence in Classical Athens. The second section shows how a change in political culture occurred in the 420s. Before this decade politicians used ostracism to attack their enemies.[8] This changed after 430, when some politicians exploited the weaknesses of the Athenian courts to eliminate their opponents. The leading practitioner of these new tactics was Cleon, who according to Thucydides was notorious for his 'slanders' (Th. 5.16.1: *diabolas*).[9] Cleon and others took advantage of the weaknesses of the Athenian courts to attack their opponents. The third section shows how Cleon attempted to drag the tactics he used in the courts into the Assembly during the debate about the punishment of Mytilene. The fourth section traces the use of these tactics by other politicians after Cleon's death and the disastrous impact they had on Athenian military leadership.

I

To understand the precise nature of the change in Athenian political culture in the 420s, we need to review briefly the traditional methods of acquiring and maintaining political power in the period before the Peloponnesian

7. For a similar view see Arist. *Ath. Pol.* 28.1: when Pericles was leader of the people, political matters (*ta kata ten politeian*) were in good shape, but after his death became much worse. For Cleon as the catalyst of change see Arist. *Ath. Pol.* 28.3.

8. *Pace* Hornblower (1991) 340 ('Th. here implies, surely wrongly, that there was a radical difference between the style and methods of Pericles and those of his successors'), and 346 ('in most respects it is hard to see what was so "new" or different about Pericles' successors, especially if they are compared not with Pericles the senior statesman but with Pericles the pushing politician of the 460s and 450s').

9. Aristophanes also uses the verb *diaballein* in connection with Cleon. See *Ach.* 380, 502; *Eq.* 63–64, 288, 486–7.

War. Even though Athens had a form of democracy in which all major decisions were made in the Assembly by majority vote, the Athenians still required leaders to make proposals, to implement the Assembly's decrees, and command its armed forces. These leaders won power and influence in three main ways: through military leadership, distribution of largesse, and family connections.[10]

The first was by military leadership. Almost all the major politicians in the period between 508 and 430 were elected as generals (*strategoi*). Themistocles won his prestige by masterminding the naval victory at Salamis (Hdt. 8.57–63, 75–82). Cimon may have begun his career by forcing Pausanias to yield control of Byzantium in 478/77 (Plu. *Cim.* 6.5–6; Th. 1.95.1–96.1). In 477/76 he took Eion from the Persians and drove the Thracians out of the area around the Strymon (Plu. *Cim.* 7.1–2; Th. 1.98.1; schol. Aeschin. 2.31 (Dilts). Cf. Her. 7.107).[11] Shortly afterward, he captured Scyros (Plu. *Cim.* 8.3–4; Th. 1.98.2). Later he brought Phaselis into the Athenian alliance (Plu. *Cim.* 12.3–4. Cf. *IG* i^3 10) and around 468 decisively defeated the Persian fleet at Eurymedon, then won a victory on land (Th. 1.101.1; Plu. *Cim.* 12.4–6).[12] Cimon put down the revolt of Thasos and took control of the island's gold mines on the Thracian coast (Plu. *Cim.* 14.2; Th. 100.2–101.3; *schol.* Aeschin. 2.31). The Athenians later sent Cimon to help the Spartans put down the revolt of the Helots (Plu. *Cim.* 16.8–17.1; Th. 1.102.1–3). After his ostracism and exile, Cimon led an expedition to Cyprus where he died around 450–49 (Plu. *Cim.* 18.1–9.1; Th. 1.112.2–4; D. S. 12.3–4).[13]

Pericles' father Xanthippus commanded the Athenian forces at Mycale in 479 (Plu. *Per.* 3.2; Hdt. 7.33; 8.131; 9.96–101; D. S. 11.34.2). Around 455 Pericles commanded an expedition to the Corinthian gulf (Th. 1.111.2; D. S. 11.85, 88.1–2; Plu. *Per.* 19.2–3). Pericles put down the revolt of Euboea around 446 (Th. 1.114.3; Plu. *Per.* 22.1; D. S. 12.7, 22) and the revolt of Samos between 440 and 439 (Th. 1.115.2–117.3; D. S. 12.27–28).[14] Around 447 he led an expedition to the Chersonnese (Plu. *Per.* 19.1; *IG* i^3 1162,

10. My analysis shares some common points with Mann (2007) 45–190, who, however, sees more continuity with the Archaic period than I would. Mann believes the sources of power lie with friendship, noble birth (*eugeneia*), wealth, and education.

11. For the date see Badian (1993) 86–7, 99.

12. See Badian (1993) 8–9.

13. For the date see Gomme (1945–56) 1: 329, 396; Badian (1993) 103.

14. For the date see Gomme (1945–56) 1: 356.

lines 1, 45).[15] Between 438 and 432 he commanded an expedition to the Black Sea (Plu. *Per.* 20.1; *IG* i^2 1180, line 25).[16] During the first year of the Peloponnesian War he led an invasion of the Megarid (Th. 2.31.1; Plu. *Per.* 34.2). Pericles' associate Hagnon also had a distinguished military career (Plu. *Per.* 32.4). He was a general at Samos in 440/39 (Th. 1.117.2), founded the colony at Amphipolis in 437/6 (Th. 4.102.2–3; *schol. ad* Aeschin. 2.31), and served as general in 431/0 (Th. 2.58; 6.31.2) and 429/8 (Th. 2.95.3). His military service no doubt helped him to be chosen as one of the peace commissioners in 421 (Th. 5.19.2, 24.1) and *proboulos* in 413 (Lys. 12.65).

Nicias also exercised influence through his position as general. In 427 he captured the island of Minoa and blocked the harbor of Megara (Th. 3.51; Plu. *Nic.* 6.4). In 425 Nicias and two others led an attack on Corinthian territory (Th. 4.42–5; Plu. *Nic.* 6.4) and in the following year took the island of Cythera and established a garrison there (Th. 4.53–4; Plu. *Nic.* 6.4). In 423 Nicias and Nicostratus retook Mende, which had revolted and joined Brasidas, and began the siege of Scione, which had also revolted (Th. 4.129–32). In 417/6 he was assigned to lead forces against the Chalcidians of Thrace and Amphipolis, but the expedition was aborted (Th. 5.83.4). In 415 he was elected one of the three generals for the expedition to Sicily and served there until his surrender and execution in 412 (Th. 6.8.2–7.86 passim).

Alcibiades served as a soldier at Potidaea (Plu. *Alc.* 7.3) and at Delium (Plu. *Alc.* 7.4; Pl. *Symp.* 221a). He was appointed one of the generals for the Sicilian expedition (Th. 6.8.2–7) and commanded forces there until his arrest and flight to Argos and later Sparta (Th. 6.61). After his return to favor, he was elected general (Th. 8.82; Plu. *Alc.* 26.3), commanded Athenian forces in Ionia (Th. 8.88; Plu. *Alc.* 26.6–7), and negotiated with Tissaphernes for Persian support (Th. 8.108.1). In 409 he captured Cyzicus (X. *HG* 1.1.10–20; Plu. *Alc.* 28.3–6) and the following year took Byzantium (X. *HG* 1.3.21–23). In modern democracies there is a strict separation between the civil and military spheres, but in Athens generals were chosen by election, a political process (Arist. *Ath. Pol.* 44.4). They were also subject to the same political control at *euthynai* (rendering accounts) as other politicians.[17] Finally, they could be tried for their military conduct in

15. For the date and discussion see Meiggs (1972) 159–61.

16. For the date see Stadter (1989) 216–17.

17. On the *euthynai* of generals see Hamel (1998a) 126–30.

the regular courts like other citizens. This has larger implications that I shall explore later.

To get elected general, one had to purchase golden opinions of oneself by performing liturgies and other public duties and by distributing largesse.[18] In some cases this might be a more important qualification than military talent. Xenophon (*Mem.* 3.4.1–3) recalls how Socrates once met a man named Nicomachides, who had been a candidate for general but lost the election to a merchant named Antisthenes. Nicomachides complained that unlike himself Antisthenes had not served in the infantry and had won no distinction in the cavalry. But Socrates pointed out that he had gained many victories as a producer of choruses and that his desire to win was certainly a desirable quality in a general. Socrates is probably using his notorious irony here, but his observation is valuable. Spending money was an important means of winning the popularity needed to win elections. Cimon was renowned for his generosity both in performing liturgies and in helping the members of his deme (Arist. *Ath. Pol.* 27.3; Plu. *Cim.* 10.1–2. Cf. Theopompus *FGrH* 115 F 135). One of the earliest known facts about Pericles is that he produced the tragic trilogy of Aeschylus that included the *Persians* and won first prize (*IG* ii^2 2318, lines 9–11). Plutarch (*Nic.* 3.2, 4–6) reports that Nicias outdid all his predecessors and contemporaries with his benefactions. He sent choirs to Delos, won many choral victories, and dedicated tripods to celebrate these triumphs in the precinct of Dionysus.[19] Alcibiades was no different from his rival Nicias in this regard: he paid for a boys' dithyramb before 415 ([And.] 4.20–21; D. 21.147; Plu. *Alc.* 16.5), an *epidosis* (Plu. *Alc.* 10.1),[20] and a trierarchy to Sicily in 415.[21] Alcibiades also kept horses for Panhellenic competitions at Nemea (Plu. *Alc.* 16.7; Athenaeus 12.534d; Paus. 1.22.7) and Delphi (Athenaeus12.534d). He entered seven chariots in the Olympic games and won first, second, and fourth prizes (Th. 6.16.2; Athenaeus 1.3e).[22] The Athenians did not find such displays of wealth contrary to democratic values. They believed in equality before the law, but did not find inequalities in wealth a threat

18. On the role of wealth and largesse in Athenian politics see Davies (1981) 88–132.

19. For other evidence for his liturgies see Davies (1971) 403–4.

20. Cf. Migeotte (1992) 10–11.

21. See Th. 6.61.6 with Davies (1971) 20.

22. Alcibiades may have also won the chariot race at the Great Panathenaea of 418—see Amyx (1958) 183–4.

to political stability provided that the privileged were willing to spend large sums on supporting the military and on public entertainment.[23]

Another way to get ahead in Athenian politics was to contract marriages with women from prominent families. In the 480s there was a 'great dynastic coalescence' among the important families of the Alcmeonids, the relatives of Cimon, and the Kerykes: Cimon married Isodike, the daughter of Euryptolemus, an Alcmeonid,[24] Cimon's sister may have been married to Thucydides of Alopeke,[25] and Cimon married his sister Elpinike to Callias, a member of the Kerykes (Plu. *Cim.* 4.8).[26] As Davies observes, 'from the 450's to the 420's the families of Perikles, Teisandros, Kallias, Kleinias, Glaukon, and Andokides conglobulated themselves into a virtual Whig aristocracy with the marriages of Xanthippos (II), Glaukon (II), and Leogoras (II) to the daughters of Teisandros (II), of Hipponikos (II) to Perikles' ex-wife, of Kallias (III) to the daughter of Glaukon (II), and of Alkibiades (III) to Hipparete (I).'[27]

All politicians tend to acquire enemies, who can pose obstacles to their ambitions and may need to be removed. Before the Peloponnesian War the preferred way of getting one's enemies out of the way was to use ostracism.[28] This procedure appears to have been instituted in the early years of the democracy and was originally designed to remove potential tyrants. In fact, the first few victims were men like Hipparchus, son of Charmus, who was a relative of the tyrants, and Megacles, who was thought to be one of their friends. But the procedure soon started to be used by leading politicians to get rid of their rivals. Themistocles appears to have pioneered this tactic by sending his enemy Aristides into exile in 483.[29] Themistocles'

---

23. For attitudes toward liturgies and the gratitude of the people see Fisher (2003).

24. For the marriage see Plu. *Cim.* 16.1. For Euryptolemus' family connections see Davies (1971) 376–7.

25. Davies (1971) 232.

26. For discussion see Davies (1971) 303.

27. Davies (1981) 119. On the importance of marriage ties for politicians see also Connor (1971) 15–8. Connor (1971) 35–87 attempts to argue that political friendship was an important way for politicians to build a power base, but most of the evidence he cites are anecdotes from Plutarch's *Lives.*

28. Connor (1971) 79–84 discusses only the ostracism of Hyperbolus and does not analyze its use by other politicians.

29. On the ostracism of Aristides see Hdt. 8.79.1 with Brenne (2001) 114–18 and Brenne in Siewert (2002) 193–204.

enemies later turned the weapon against him and had him ostracized around 470.[30] Pericles used the tactic against his opponents Cimon and Thucydides the son of Melesias.[31] Alcibiades and Nicias employed it against Hyperbolus.[32]

What is striking is that all these politicians refrained from using the courts to prosecute their enemies.[33] In fact, there were hardly any trials involving politicians before the Peloponnesian War. Herodotus (6.21) alludes to a trial of the tragic poet Phrynichus around 493 and two trials of Miltiades, one before 490 and another in 489 (Hdt. 6.104, 136.3). There is evidence for one trial of Cimon in 463, but it comes from later sources, Aristotle's *Constitution of the Athenians* (27.1) and Plutarch's *Lives*.[34] Most important for our purposes, it did not result in a conviction. Finally, there is evidence for a trial of Themistocles around 470, but the sources mentioning it invite skepticism. Aristotle's *Constitution of the Athenians* (25.3) states that Themistocles was about to be accused before the Areopagus around 462 and gives this as his motive for attacking that court. The problem with this is that Themistocles was ostracized around 470 and never returned to Athens.[35] Plutarch (*Them.* 23.1) and Craterus (*FGrH* 342 F 11) mention a prosecution of Themistocles, but it is suspicious that Thucydides (1.135.1–138.2) does not mention any trial.[36] Equally striking is that, to my knowledge, no ancient source records a trial of a general between 460 and 430. For most of the fifth century there seems to have existed a gentlemen's agreement not to use the courts against opponents but to resort to the gentler option of ostracism. These were also the years of Athens' greatest power and success.

---

30. On the ostracism of Themistocles see Th. 1.135.2–3, Pl. *Grg.* 516d, D. 23.204–5, Plu. *Them.* 21.5 and D. S. 11.55.1–3 with Brenne in Siewert (2002) 247–57.

31. On the ostracism of Cimon see Pl. *Grg.* 516d with Brenne (2001) 193–95 and Scheidel in Siewert (2002) 350–57. On the ostracism of Thucydides the son of Melesias see Theopompus *FGrH* 115 F 88 with Scheidel in Siewert (2002) 373–87.

32. On the ostracism of Hyperbolus see Rhodes (1994a).

33. Some late sources mention prosecutions of Pericles' associates, but their reliability is suspect. See Plu. *Per.* 31.2–32.6 with Stadter (1989) 284–305.

34. Plu. *Cim.* 14.3–4 and *Per.* 10.4. Note that when his enemies wished to drive him out in 462, they used ostracism.

35. Rhodes (1981) 320 follows Wilamowitz-Moellendorf (1893) I.140–42 in rejecting the story as a 'fable.'

36. For sources and discussion see Frost (1980) 196–99. Plutarch (*Them.* 24.4) mentions a prosecution of Epicrates by Cimon reported by Stesimbrotus, but expresses skepticism by noting that Stesimbrotus contradicts himself.

II

The situation changed after the beginning of the Peloponnesian War, when politicians started to use the courts to eliminate or intimidate their enemies. The first sign of the change was the trial of Pericles in 430/29. Thucydides (2.65.3) reports that he was removed from office, put on trial and fined. Plutarch (*Per.* 32.3–4, 35.4) says the fine was between fifteen and fifty talents; Diodorus (12.45.4) puts it at eighty talents.[37] A fragment of Androtion (*FGrH* 324 F 8) reports that Phormio was found guilty and fined a sum of one hundred mnai, probably in 429/8. According to Plutarch (*Arist.* 26.3; *Nic.* 6.1), Paches was accused at his *euthynai* and killed himself with his sword in court. The sensational story of his death invites skepticism, but there is no reason to doubt that the prosecution took place.[38] The trial is probably dated shortly after Paches' successful campaign against Mytilene in 428/7 (Th. 3.18, 25–36, 49–50). The atmosphere had grown so dangerous that after his defeat by the Aetolians in 426, Demosthenes decided to remain in Naupactus 'because he was afraid of the Athenians because of what happened' (Th. 3.98.5). He was reluctant to return to Athens because he obviously feared prosecution. By contrast, there is no evidence that any Athenian general failed to return to Athens after a defeat in the years 480 to 431. Two years later, in early 424, Thucydides (4.65.3) says that Sophocles, Pythodorus and Eurymedon were prosecuted when they returned from their campaign in Sicily. Pythodorus and Sophocles were punished with exile while Eurymedon received a fine.[39] In his comment on their trials, Thucydides (4.65.4) clearly implies the verdicts were unfair and based on unreasonable expectations. Finally, Thucydides (5.26.5) himself writes that he was in exile for twenty years. Scholars have plausibly linked his exile with his failure to prevent Brasidas from taking Amphipolis in the winter of 424/23.[40] Marcellinus' *Life of Thucydides* (26, 46, 55) says that he was tried by Cleon for treason, but this is probably guesswork. Thucydides either returned to Athens and was sentenced to exile or, like

37. For recent treatments see Ostwald (1986) 191–94, and Roberts (1982) 31–2, 59–60 and 204, note 20.

38. See Westlake (1975) who argues that Paches was prosecuted for letting the Spartan fleet under Alcidas escape.

39. Hamel (1998a) 144 believes that Pythodorus and Sophocles may have fled before the trial and been sentenced to death *in absentia*, but Thucydides' makes it clear that the court sentenced them to exile (*ezemiosan*).

40. See for example Hamel (1998a) 144; Hansen (1975) 74.

the general Demosthenes, did not return to Athens and was sentenced to death *in absentia*.[41]

In the *Wasps*, Aristophanes (894–1008) may allude to a prosecution of the general Laches by Cleon. To keep his father Philocleon away from the courts, Bdelycleon arranges a mock trial in which the dog Kyon tries the dog Labes for eating a Sicilian cheese (894–97). Several scholars have interpreted this as an allegory of a real prosecution of Laches, who served as general in Sicily from 427/6 to 426/5 (Th. 3.115.2, 6) by Cleon.[42] In the same play Philocleon asks whether Dracontides will be acquitted,[43] and it is possible to identify this man with the general of the same name who participated in the expedition to Corcyra in 433/2.[44] Bdelycleon refers to a trial of Thucydides, who is probably Thucydides, the son of Melesias, who was a prominent politician and an opponent of Pericles and was ostracized in 443.[45] This trial must have taken place in the years 432–426. Some scholars have noted that Thucydides (2.70) reports that the Athenians were angry with the generals Xenophon, Phanomachus, and Hestiodorus for negotiating the terms of surrender for Poteidaea without consulting the Assembly and have interpreted this to mean that they were put on trial.[46] But Thucydides' word may only indicate that they were harshly criticized.[47]

The pattern is unmistakable: between 480 and 433, almost fifty years, there is no solid evidence for a general or major politician being convicted and harshly punished by the courts. But between 431 and 421, only a decade, there is good evidence for convictions of six generals (Pericles, Phormio, Paches, Sophocles, Pythodorus, and Thucydides the historian), for one general not returning to Athens out from fear of being tried (Demosthenes),

41. Sentenced to death in absentia: Hansen (1975) 74. Hansen believes that the trial must have been an *eisangelia*, but his reasons are not compelling.

42. Ostwald (1986) 212 with note 59 argues that the trial of the dog was based on a real trial. Westlake (1975) 115–16 believes that Cleon only threatened to prosecute Laches, MacDowell (1971) 251 and Gomme (1945–56) I: 430–31 express doubts.

43. Ar. *V.* 157.

44. *IG* i^3 364, lines 20–21. Th. 1.51.4. For other possible identifications see MacDowell (1971) 153.

45. Ar. *V.* 946–49 with MacDowell (1971) 255. The trial is also mentioned at *Ach.* 703–12, performed at the Lenaea of 425. For the ostracism of Thucydides see Plu. *Per.* 16.3.

46. See Kagan (1974) 98, note 85; Pritchett (1991) 418.

47. See Hamel (1998a) 142.

and three possible allusions to trials of other generals or major politicians. The atmosphere had clearly changed.[48]

The man who was either primarily responsible for this change or the most accomplished practitioner of the new tactics was Cleon.[49] From Aristophanes' *Knights* we know that Cleon used the threat of prosecution to intimidate his political enemies and to win influence with the people.[50] When he enters, the Paphlagonian slave who is a parody of Cleon charges his two fellow slaves with treason and conspiracy (Ar. *Eq.* 235–39). He boasts to the judges in the courts that he keeps them busy with cases so they can receive their three obols a day (Ar. *Eq.* 255–57). The chorus says that he extorts money from officials who have not yet passed their audits, who are ripe for exploiting (Ar. *Eq.* 258–63). He makes one charge after another: an *endeixis* for smuggling equipment to the Spartans (Ar. *Eq.* 278–79: *endeiknumi*), a *phasis* before the *prytaneis* for failure to pay tax (Ar. *Eq.* 300–2),[51] a denunciation of plotting with the enemy to the Council (Ar. *Eq.* 475–79, 626–29), and attacks on officials during their audits (*euthynai*) (Ar. *Eq.* 825–6). Just as Cleon charges his opponents with bribery (Th. 3.38.2 [*kerdei epairomenos*]; 3.42.3; 43.1. Cf. Lys. 21.19 [*hypo kerdous eparthenai*] charge of bribery), the Paphlagonian threatens four charges of bribery, each with a penalty of a hundred talents (Ar. *Eq.* 442–43).[52] The chorus complains that he fills the courts with his criminal charges (*graphai*) (Ar. *Eq.* 304–10). In the *Wasps* Aristophanes portrays Cleon and his supporters in a similar way.[53] The chorus of wasps suspect treason in Thrace (Ar. *V.* 288–89, 475), conspiracy

48. Rhodes (1994a) 97–98 believes that the tactic of removing opponents through a lawsuit instead of ostracism began after the ostracism of Hyperbolus, which he dates to the spring of 415, but this evidence shows that it began in the 420s. Alcibiades and Nicias were traditional politicians, who were attempting to revive a tactic that had become outmoded after the rise of Cleon.

49. The scholia to Ar. *V.* 88 and 300 say that Cleon increased the pay of judges from two obols to three obols, but there is no contemporary evidence for Cleon's role in the increase. The information found in the scholia is probably only guesswork. Besides, in the *Wasps*, Aristophanes makes it clear that Cleon is popular with the judges not for increasing their pay, but for providing cases for them. Even if their pay were higher, the judges would not be paid much unless there was someone bringing frequent prosecutions.

50. Though Aristophanes obviously exaggerates the traits of Cleon's character and tactics, his parody must be based on his actual behavior. As Andrewes (1962) 81 observes, 'a successful comedy cannot be created out of nothing, and the real Kleon must have provided Aristophanes with usable materials.'

51. On the procedure of *phasis* see MacDowell (1991) and Wallace (2003).

52. I accept Göttling's supplement δωροδοκίας at 442.

53. For the chorus as supporters of Cleon see Ar. *V.* 242, 409, 596–97.

(Ar. *V.* 344–35), and tyranny (Ar. *V.* 417, 470, 474–76, 487. Cf. 488–502). The chorus says that Cleon has ordered them to report for service in the courts with three days' worth of rage, the emotion prosecutors try to arouse (Ar. *V.* 242–44), and they several times talk about their anger (Ar. *V.* 277–80, 403, 406, 424–5, 454–5). In the *Acharnians* (377–84) Dicaeopolis may allude to an attack on Aristophanes by Cleon in the Council.[54]

Thucydides and Aristophanes make it clear that the charges against generals and other officials were very unfair, if not completely false. How then did Cleon and those who followed his tactics succeed in manipulating the courts to intimidate their enemies? Here one needs to bear in mind that the Athenian courts had certain weaknesses, which made them vulnerable to abuse.[55]

1. In Athens there was nothing similar to jury selection as in modern British and American courts. For every trial there was a random selection of those serving as judges that year, but the litigants had no means of removing those who they believed were their enemies or the friends of their opponents. The Athenians were obsessed with preventing bribery by wealthy individuals (Arist. *Ath. Pol.* 41.3), but showed little concern for ensuring impartiality. This made it difficult for an unpopular general or politician to obtain a fair trial after a military defeat or a diplomatic setback. Even though the Judicial Oath required judges to vote without enmity or favor toward either litigant, it would have been very difficult to maintain impartiality in a charged political atmosphere where suspicions were running wild. In fact, Thucydides connects Cleon's success in getting the Athenians to believe his slanders with wartime conditions; in peacetime, when politics are conducted in a calmer atmosphere, Cleon would never have gotten away with abusing legal procedures (Th. 5.16.1).

2. In modern criminal trials in Britain and the United States, the prosecutor must obtain a unanimous verdict to convict a defendant on a criminal charge. In Athenian courts, by contrast, an accuser had to secure only a bare majority to win a conviction. Thus Socrates was convicted by Meletus only by a margin of thirty votes out of several hundred cast (Pl. *Ap.* 36a). This made it relatively easy for an accuser who brought a public charge in an Athenian court to secure a conviction.

54. See Olson (2002) xlvi–xlvii, l–li, 172–5.

55. This analysis of the weaknesses of the Athenian courts is taken from Harris (2005c) 21–22.

3. In a modern criminal trial, the prosecutor must prove guilt 'beyond a reasonable doubt,' a standard of proof that is higher than that followed in civil cases. The Athenians, by contrast, did not employ different standards of proof in public and private cases: the accuser in a public case was not held to a stricter standard of proof. Aeschines (1.90–91) distinguishes between those who are 'clearly' guilty and those who must be convicted on the basis of probability, but he takes it for granted that men could be condemned to death merely for their reputation and on the basis of mere likelihood.

4. These weaknesses were exacerbated by the fact that trials took place in a single day, not over a period of weeks. Judges therefore did not have a long time to reflect on arguments and to evaluate a case, but had to decide before they left the court that day. This made them more susceptible to hasty judgments. In Plato's *Apology* (37a–b), Socrates singles out this practice as harmful: he complains that he has only one day to disprove all the slanders that have accumulated against him over the years. If the Athenians had allowed him to speak over several days, as was permitted elsewhere in Greece, he might have convinced them to acquit him.

5. In cases where the court made a poor judgment in a public case, there was no system of appeals that could be used to reverse an unjust verdict.[56] Once the verdict against Socrates was rendered, there was no way to overturn it.

Another factor making it easier for prosecutors to obtain a conviction was the financial situation during the Peloponnesian War. Even though the Athenians started the war with plenty of money in their Treasury and reserves in sacred accounts (Th. 2.13.3–5), the war proved to be longer and more expensive than anticipated. In 428 the Athenians had to levy a property tax (Th. 3.19) and in 425 raised the tribute on their allies to pay for military expenses (*IG* i³ 68).[57] The strain on Athenian finances put pressure on the courts to convict wealthy men and to collect large fines or to confiscate their estates. One defendant complains about unscrupulous prosecutors who try to intimidate the judges into condemning innocent men by predicting there will be no money to pay them unless they confiscate the defendant's estate (Lys. 27.1). Another says that defendants receive

56. The Assembly might reverse a verdict, but this appears to have been rare. See Pecorella Longo (2004).

57. On the problems of Athenian finances during the Archidamian War see Samons (2000) 171–211.

a fair trial when there are sufficient funds for state business, but when there are not, the Council is forced to convict on baseless charges in order to balance the budget by seizing their assets (Lys. 30.22). Both of these speeches were delivered after 404, but the problem already existed during the Peloponnesian War: in the *Knights* of Aristophanes (1358–63) the sausage-seller urges the people to destroy advocates who tell the judges they will not receive their pay unless they convict. He associates this pernicious practice with Hyperbolus, one of Cleon's associates.[58]

There is no reason to believe that Cleon represented a new class of men who drew their wealth from industry and challenged a traditional ruling class that relied on agriculture.[59] As J. G. Kron has written, 'The most common interpretation of the literary evidence in terms of a conflict between landed aristocrats and an emerging commercial middle class is a modern and anachronistic interpretation of ancient attitudes in terms of patterns familiar from Medieval and early Modern social history, specifically the conflict with the upper-classes between the feudal aristocracy and the bourgeoisie.'[60] Many distinguished families in Athens during the late fifth century engaged in commercial activities. Andocides could trace his lineage back to the sixth century, yet he also made money in trade.[61] Callias came from an equally respectable family and drew revenues from mining.[62] Alcibiades also belonged to an old family, but he too relied on slaves working in crafts and other nonagricultural sources of income.[63] Cleon may not have been able to trace his family back many generations, but there is no reason to believe Aristophanes' slanders about his background. His father was wealthy enough to put on a chorus in 460/59.[64] There was thus no major social distance between Cleon and the men he

58. The problem continued into the fourth century. See Harris (2006a) 137.

59. For this view see above all Connor (1971) 151–63, followed by Rosenbloom (2004). For similar views see Mossé (1962) 28 and Ehrenberg (1962) 91. For the view that land owning was the preferred type of investment for the upper class see also Finley (1973) 44, 53–5, 58, 189.

60. Kron (1996) xii.

61. For his family see Davies (1971) note 828. For his activities in commerce see Lys. 6.19; And. 1.137; 2.20–21; Plu. *Vit. X Or.* 834e.

62. For references to his activities see Davies (1971) 258. For his lineage see Davies (1971) 254–56.

63. Davies (1971) 20 and Kron (1996) 172–74.

64. See *IG* ii^2 2318, line 34.

attacked in court.[65] What was different about Cleon was his tactics, which were associated with an aggressive personal style.

Having perfected his tactics in the courts, Cleon next tried to drag them into the Assembly.

III

In 428 BCE the city of Mytilene launched a revolt against the Athenians and invited the Spartans to send them assistance. The plans for the revolt were reported to the Athenians (Th. 3.2), who sent a force against the city (Th. 3.3). The Mytilenians asked for help from the Spartans (Th. 3.4, 8–15), but the fleet they sent arrived too late (3.26.4). The revolt appears to have been the initiative of the city's wealthier citizens: Thucydides (3.27–28) reports that heavy armor was not distributed to the people until Salaethus, the leader of the rebellion, realized that Spartan help would not arrive in time. Once the people received this armor, they refused to take orders from officials and held meetings, insisting that the government should distribute all available grain. If they did not, they threatened to negotiate on their own with the Athenians about surrender. The government was powerless to stop them and decided it was best to come to terms with the Athenians. It was agreed that the Athenians would have the power to act as they wished with the city and that the Mytilenians would have the right to send envoys to Athens to plead their case before the Assembly.

When the Athenians first met to decide about the fate of Mytilene, Cleon persuaded them to put the adult males to death and to enslave the women and children; a trireme was sent to inform Paches of the decision (Th. 3.36.2–3). On the next day, however, the Athenians changed their minds and found the decision to put everyone to death, not just the guilty, harsh and excessive (Th. 3.36.4). They therefore persuaded Athenian officials to hold another meeting to reconsider the decision (Th. 3.36.5). At this second meeting of the Assembly, Cleon defended his original proposal (Th. 3.37–40) and was opposed by a man named Diodotus (3.42–48).

65. See Kron (1996) 96: 'far from endorsing any inference that Cleon was of low social status, a careful reading of scattered remarks in Old Comedy will reveal that the poets recognize and acknowledge his actual privileged background, further cementing our interpretation of his portrayal as a slave tanner trading threats and insults with a sausage seller as a populist inversion of his actual place in society.'

Thucydides' version of the debate reflects a keen awareness of rhetorical practice and the implicit rules of different genres of oratory. The best evidence for these rules is found in Aristotle's *Rhetoric* and the *Rhetorica ad Alexandrum* attributed to Anaximenes.[66] These works drew on a long tradition of reflection on rhetorical practice reaching back to Corax and Tisias, contemporaries of Thucydides. Both Aristotle and the author of the *Rhetorica ad Alexandrum* (1.1.1421b1) divide oratory into three types: the judicial (*dikanikon*), the deliberative (*demegorikon* or *symbouleutikon*), and the epideictic (*epideiktikon*). Aristotle describes the basic characteristics of each speech in the first book of the *Rhetoric* (1.3.1–7.1358a–59b). A deliberative speech aims either to exhort or dissuade and concerns the future because the speaker discusses future events. The goal of this kind of speech is to show that a certain course of action is going to be either advantageous or harmful (*to sympheron kai to blaberon*). The audience for this kind of speech is the member of an assembly. A speaker may introduce considerations of justice, but they should be subordinate to the main issue of advantage. In the law court, there is either an accusation or a defense. This kind of speech concerns the past because the accusation and the defense examine what has been done. The goal of the speaker is to prove that an action is just or unjust. The audience for this speech is the judge. The aim of the epideictic speech is to praise or to blame. This kind of speech generally looks to the present and praises or blames existing qualities but may also glance at the past and future. The audience of the epideictic speech consists of spectators who are concerned with the speaker's ability (Arist. *Rh.* 1.3.2.1358b: *ho de peri tes dynameos ho theoros*).[67]

Aristotle did not invent these types of speeches; he codified existing practices.[68] The distinction between deliberative and judicial oratory was

---

66. On the authorship of this work see Chiron (2002) xl–cvii.

67. Quintilian (3.4.16) criticizes Aristotle's categories as too simplistic because 'all three genres to some extent rely on the mutual help of the others' (*stant enim quodam modo mutuis auxiliis omnia*), but follows the basic division. In fact, Diodotus does use an argument from justice even though he mainly appeals to expedience.

68. See Carey (2007) 236: 'Fourth century rhetoric codified but did not create the categories. The recognition that different modes of argument suit different spheres is already visible in Thucydides' account of the debate about the fate of the rebel city of Mytilene.' Carey further notes that in Pericles' Funeral Oration one can 'detect inherent principles of form and overt trends in content which are clearly understood by speaker and audience, if nowhere articulated—or perceived—as a set of rules.' Kennedy (1959) claims that rhetorical practice changed between the fifth and fourth centuries BCE, but see Heath (1990) who shows that there was a high degree of continuity.

rooted in the different constitutional functions of the Assembly and the courts. The role of the Assembly in both the fifth and the fourth centuries was to determine public policy and take decisions about matters affecting the community as a whole.[69] Aristotle (*Rh.* 1.4.7.1359b. Cf. *Rhetorica ad Alexandrum* 2.2.1423a20–26) says that the topics of deliberative speeches are finances, war and peace, national defense, imports and exports, and legislation, and the first three form the subject matter of addresses to the Assembly in Thucydides' speeches.[70] Speakers addressing the Assembly in Thucydides and Xenophon tend to base their arguments on the city's interest,[71] and the forensic speeches of Antiphon, Andocides, and Lysias already contain many of the arguments prescribed by Aristotle for courtroom speeches. As we saw in part II of this book, the different types of arguments used in the courts reflect their different function, which was to act as guardians of the laws and to punish those who broke the law (D. 24.36; Lycurg. *Leocr.* 4).

When Cleon attacks his opponents for reopening the debate about Mytilene, he claims that they are treating the issue as if it were a contest in epideictic oratory.[72] Instead of examining the merits of his opponents' arguments, Cleon accuses them of acting like sophists who revel in paradoxes (Th. 3.38.7). He claims that they seek to show that 'the wrongs done by the Mytilenians are to our advantage, and that our losses are harmful to our allies' and that 'what was completely decided has on the contrary not been decided' (Th. 3.38.1). Just as sophists speaking in an epideictic contest try to disprove what appears to be self-evident, Cleon's opponents are criticized for defying common sense.[73] These are the paradoxes to which Cleon says the Athenians are enslaved (Th. 3.38.5: *douloi ontes ton aiei atopon*). As a result, they have become suspicious of common sense (Th. 3.38.5: *hyperoptai . . . ton eiothoton*). Cleon blames his audience

69. Cf. D. 18.192: the role of the *symboulos* is to discuss the present and future.

70. Finances: Th. 2.13. War and peace: Th. 1.140–44. On the importance of financial considerations in Thucydides see Kallet-Marx (1993) and Kallet (2001). Speakers in Thucydides do not discuss imports and exports in speeches to the Assembly, but this is because during the empire they were less significant sources of revenue than tribute. On this topic see Bresson (2000) 109–30. The topic of legislation comes to the fore only during the events of 411.

71. See Heath (1990).

72. Cf. Macleod (1978) 71; Yunis (1996) 90–91.

73. These kinds of sophistic arguments would be out of place in a funeral oration, one type of epideictic oratory.

for holding these wicked contests (Th. 3.38.4: *kakos agonothetountes*), which are dangerous for the city, and acting like spectators (Th. 3.38.4 and 7: *theatai . . . theatais*) in a speaking competition rather than men deliberating about public matters (Th. 3.38.7). It is significant that Aristotle (*Rh.* 1.3.2.1358b) also calls the person who hears an epideictic speech a 'spectator' (*theoros*). Cleon also upbraids the Athenians for being 'very good at allowing themselves to be deceived' (Th. 3.38.5: *apatasthai aristoi*). This may be an allusion to the view of Gorgias that the art of speaking was a form of deceit (*apate*).[74] Those who speak in the Assembly should not be overcome by their own impressive talents (*deinoteti*) and this competition to show off one's intelligence (*xyneseos agoni*) (Th. 3.37.5).

After Cleon attacks his opponents for making the wrong kind of speech in the Assembly, one would expect him to make the right kind of speech and use the language and arguments found in deliberative oratory. Toward the end of the speech he does address the issue of public revenues (Th. 3.39.8: *prosodou*), which Aristotle (*Rh.* 1.4.7.1359b) says is one of the five topics that form the subject matter of deliberative oratory. He predicts that if the Athenians impose the same penalties on those who are forced to revolt by the enemy and those who do so willingly and do not impose harsh punishments on the latter, there will be no deterrent to prevent them from rebelling. Even if the Athenians succeed in putting down each revolt, they will lose a valuable source of revenue (Th. 3.39.8). In the rest of the speech, however, he approaches the debate as if he were a prosecutor in court rather than a speaker in the Assembly. He speaks of the injustices done by the Mytilenians to the Athenians (3.38.1: *adikias;* 3.39.1: *edikekotas*). He says that they are guilty (Th. 3.39.6: *he aitia*). He also uses the language of punishment, which is suitable for forensic oratory. He argues that punishment is most effective when retaliation follows as soon as possible after the crime (Th. 3.38.1). At the end of his speech, he urges the Athenians to pay the Mytilenians back with the same punishment (Th. 3.40.5: *zemia*) and to punish them as they deserve for their guilt (Th. 3.39.6: *kolasthenton . . . axios tes adikias;* Th. 3.40.7: *kolasate axios*). In this way they will demonstrate that revolt will be punished by death (Th. 3.40.7). Those making deliberative

74. See Gorgias *Helen* 8 (ὁ πείσας καὶ τὴν ψυχὴν ἀπατήσας) and 10 (ἀπατήματα δόξης) with Verdenius (1981). Is it a coincidence that the debate about Mytilene took place in the same year that Gorgias is reported to have come to Athens? See D. S. 12.53.1–2. But Cleon's charge that his opponents attempt to mislead the audience is a standard accusation in forensic oratory.

speeches in Thucydides tend to avoid this language; outside this pair of speeches the noun *zemia* and the related verb *zemioun* tend to occur only in narrative and in legal contexts.[75]

Scholars have often noted that Cleon uses the language of justice, wrongdoing, and punishment.[76] Less attention has been paid, however, to Cleon's use of many common themes and arguments found in forensic oratory and to his unusual political tactics.[77] Cleon strikes a legal tone very early in his speech when he declares 'the most terrible thing of all would be . . . for us not to realize that a city that abides by laws which are worse but remain unchanged is stronger than one that has good laws that are never enforced' (Th. 3.37.3). Here Cleon draws on several themes often found in court speeches. The first is that the laws should remain the same and that it is dangerous to have laws constantly changed.[78] To keep the laws stable, Solon is said to have made the Athenians swear that they

75. In legal contexts: Th. 2.24, 65.3; 3.70.4, 5; 4.65.3; 5.63.2, 4; 8.15.1, 21, 67.2, 73.6, 74.3. The other pair of speeches in which the terms are found is the 'trial' of the Plataeans (Th. 3.63.1, 67.2). The only other speaker to use the noun is Sthenelaidas, who accuses the Athenians of violating the Thirty Years Peace and uses the language of justice (Th. 1.86.1). The verb is also found in a pre-battle speech by Spartan generals who remind their troops about the penalties for cowardice (Th. 2.87.9).

76. See Macleod (1978) 71, 72, 77 (= Macleod [1983] 95, 96, 101). Winnington-Ingram (1965) believed that Cleon was drawing on ideas found in tragedy, but does not observe the echoes of judicial language. Hesk (2000) 248–53 discusses only Diodotus' statement that speakers in the Assembly must use deceit to convince the people but fails to note that Diodotus does not approve of this situation and considers it a symptom of dysfunction in Athenian institutions. The discussion of the Mytilene debate by Ober (1998) 94–104 is vulnerable to the same criticism. Both these authors miss Cleon's use of judicial rhetoric and do not see the main point of Diodotus' critique.

77. Gomme (1945–56) II: 297–318; Hornblower (1991) 420–38; Rhodes (1994b) 204–9; Andrewes (1962), and Yunis (1996) 87–92 do not notice the parallels between Cleon's speech and courtroom oratory. Connor (1984) 84–5, Macleod (1978), and Carey (2007) 236 note the forensic style of Cleon's speech but do not note all the specific parallels between Cleon's speech and forensic oratory.

78. Winnington-Ingram (1965) 72 thought that the idea of unchanging laws 'had a strong appeal for the Greeks and particularly for conservatives,' but the passages cited later in the chapter show that the idea appealed to all Athenians in general. Commentators have been puzzled because Cleon's measure about the Mytilenians was a decree, not a law. For brief discussion with references to earlier treatments see Hornblower (1991) 423–24. But the law in question may not be the decree passed at an earlier meeting of the Assembly, but the general rule that Athenian allies did not have the right to revolt and would be severely punished if they did as in the case of Naxos (Th. 1.98), Thasos (1.101), Euboea (1.114), and Samos (1.115–17). Note that Cleon alludes to these revolts and their suppression by Athens and argues that the Mytilenians should have learned from these examples (Th. 3.39.3). For the oaths of allegiance sworn by the allies see Meiggs (1972) 579–82.

would not alter them for either ten or a hundred years.[79] Antiphon (6.2) praises the laws about homicide because they have remained unchanged for a long time (cf. D. 20.153). Demosthenes (24.139–43) tells the court that the Locrians ordered that all those who proposed to introduce a new law did so with a noose around their neck. If the proposal did not pass, the noose was pulled tight and the proposer hanged. Demosthenes praises the Locrians because they have only passed one new law in many years. Earlier in the same speech, Demosthenes (24.24) commends the laws about legislation because they have been in effect for a long time and have often proved their worth. In his speech *Against Leptines*, Demosthenes (20.90–2) views frequent changes in the laws as a symptom of disorder. Already in the fifth century the Athenians often added entrenchment clauses to important measures to ensure that they would not be altered.[80]

The second theme is that the city owes its strength and power to obedience to the laws (Th. 3.37.3: *nomois akinetois xromene polis kreisson*). According to Aeschines (3.6), when the Athenians observe the laws, the democracy remains strong. By the same token, when judges are distracted by irrelevant matters, the laws are neglected and the democracy undermined (cf. Aeschin. 3.23; Lycurg. *Leocr.* 3–4; And. 1.9).

The third theme is the importance of enforcing the laws for them to have their full effect. Cleon contrasts laws that are followed with those that are not enforced (Th. 3.37.3: *akyrois*). In his speech *Against Meidias*, Demosthenes (21.224) asks: 'What makes the laws strong? Will they come running and be there to help someone if he is wronged and cries out? Of course, they cannot; the laws have force only if the court confirms them and makes them valid (*kyrious*) each time a victim asks for justice.' When prosecuting Neaera, Apollodorus tells the court that if they do not punish her, their laws about marriage and citizenship will not longer be valid (*akyroi*) ([D.] 59.112. Cf. Lys. 1.34). Aeschines (1.177) reminds the judges in the trial of Timarchus that if they punish wrongdoers, the laws will be excellent and valid, but if they let them go, the laws will be excellent but no longer valid (*kyrioi*) (cf. D. 50.1). Note, however, that Aeschines' contrast is slightly different from Cleon's. Aeschines contrasts laws that are enforced with those that are not, but in both cases he calls the laws of Athens good. Cleon's

79. Ten years: Hdt. 1.29. Hundred years: Arist. *Ath. Pol.* 7.2; Plu. *Solon* 25. For an analysis of the differences and similarities among these three passages see Rosivach (2010).

80. For entrenchment clauses see Lewis (1997) 136–49 and Harris (2006a) 24–5.

contrast goes one step beyond this when he claims that it is better consistently to follow laws that are not as good than to have laws that are good but are never enforced. Aeschines makes a general point about the importance of enforcing the law whereas Cleon argues that it is more important to follow the law than to enact good laws. Cleon therefore gives priority to obedience to the laws. Aeschines (1.6) would have disagreed, for he thinks that both aims are important: 'When we legislate, we must see to it that we enact laws that are good and beneficial to our constitution, but after we have legislated, we must obey the established laws and punish those who do not obey.' Cleon's argument (or Thucydides' version of it), though based on several traditional ideas about the law, distorts these views. No litigant addressing an Athenian court ever says that the city's laws are bad.[81]

In forensic oratory it was normal for the accuser to urge the judges to be angry with the defendant because he has broken the law.[82] At the same time, the accuser would argue that the judges should not feel pity for the defendant.[83] By contrast, defendants would claim that they deserved pity because they were innocent.[84] In one of the earliest preserved court speeches, a young man who is prosecuting his stepmother for killing his father tells the court that they should show no pity for her because she showed none for his father (Antiphon 1.26). When prosecuting Meidias on a charge of outrage (*hybris*), Demosthenes (21.46) tells the court: 'There is nothing, men of Athens, nothing at all that is more intolerable than outrage (*hybris*) nor anything that more deserves your anger (*orgizesthai*).' Meidias does not deserve pity because 'it is right to pity the victims of some injustice that they will not be able to endure, not those who are being punished for the terrible things that they have done' (D. 21.99). Later in the speech he predicts that Meidias will bring his children into court to make the judges feel sorry for him (D. 21.186). Addressing Meidias, Demosthenes (21.196) asserts that 'there is no way that pity is the appropriate response for you, not in any respect, but the opposite: hatred

81. See 107.

82. On appeals to anger in judicial oratory see Rubinstein (2004).

83. For this kind of argument (*ekbole eleou*) see Stevens (1944) 9–15.

84. There is no reason to believe that appeals to anger and pity are extra-legal arguments and attempts to subvert the law. See Konstan (2000), who shows that defendants argue that they deserve pity because they have not violated the law. No defendant in an extant forensic oration asks the court to pity him and ignore the law. By the same token, prosecutors say that the judges should be angry with defendants because they have broken the law.

and loathing and anger. These are the responses that your actions deserve.' An accuser in a case of military desertion reminds the judges of their duty to vote according to the established laws 'and not to pity those who do wrong, but rather to be angry with them' (Lys. 15.9). Another accuser tells the court that they should be angry with some metic grain dealers for trying to deceive the Athenians to help themselves (Lys. 22.3–9).

Like a prosecutor in court, Cleon argues that the Athenians should act on their feelings of anger. He says that they should not hesitate to punish the Mytilenians because when one delays, one's anger (*orge*) is less keen (Th. 3.38.1).[85] Diodotus recognizes that Cleon appeals to this emotion when he admits that his opponent's speech is more attractive to the Athenians because of their anger toward the people of Mytilene (Th. 3.44.4: *orge*). Cleon also warns the Assembly that there are three things most detrimental to those who hold power, and pity is one of them: only those who can reciprocate have a right to pity, not those who will never pity the Athenians in return and are by necessity their enemies (Th. 3.40.2–3). Earlier in his speech, he orders them 'not to give in to pity' (Th. 3.37.2: *oikto endote*).[86] It is significant that the words used for pity (*oiktos*; *eleos*) in this speech occur in no other deliberative speech in Thucydides; the only other pair of speeches in which they are found is the quasi-judicial debate about the Plataeans. The Plataeans, who defend their conduct, ask for pity (Th. 3.59.1), and the Thebans, who act as prosecutors, deny that they are entitled to pity (3.67.2, 4).[87] Some scholars argue that Cleon's approach is more emotional and contrast it with Diodotus' more rational and intellectual approach. This is not quite accurate because Cleon makes rational arguments to argue his points; his argument that it is necessary to punish the Mytilenians to discourage other allies from revolting is far from irrational. The reason why Cleon employs the language of anger and pity is that he approaches the debate like a prosecutor in court who seeks to make the judges so angry that they are willing to impose a harsh punishment. As we will see, Diodotus' main objection to this language is that it is inappropriate for debate in the Assembly.

---

85. The verb *epexerchetai* is the legal term for prosecuting a crime and bringing the case to court. See Antiphon 6.37; D. 21.103; 58.8–10 with Harris (2006a) 405–22. Gomme (1945–56) 302–3 and Hornblower (1991) 425 make no comment on Cleon's use of the term.

86. Cf. Macleod (1978) 72 (= Macleod [1983] 96).

87. Nicias uses the noun *oiktos* in his speech to the Athenian troops retreating from Syracuse, but here the context is very different: the general says the Athenians are more likely to receive pity than *phthonos* from the gods (Th. 7.77.4).

To prove that a defendant was guilty, the accuser had to show not only that he had violated the law but also that there were no extenuating circumstances.[88] As we saw in chapter 8, even though Athenian judges were strictly bound by oath to follow the law, they could take various factors like ignorance, duress, lack of intent, or pleas of necessity into account when reaching their decision and show forgiveness (*syngnome*). This was called fairness (*epieikeia*), to which Demosthenes (21.90) says that all defendants were entitled. Cleon, like other prosecutors, asserts that fairness does not apply in this case and that the defendants do not deserve forgiveness. In fact, he says that fairness (*epieikeia*), like pity, is against the interests of those in power (Th. 3.40.2). Only those who will be friendly to Athens in the future, not those who will remain their enemies, deserve fairness (Th. 3.40.3).[89] This denial of fairness is similar to an argument made by Agoratus' accuser, who says that if their crimes are very great, defendants should be punished even when they act against their will (Lys. 13.52).[90] The Mytilenians, however, have no excuse: they did not harm Athenian interests against their will (*akontes men gar ouk eblapsan*) but plotted against them in full knowledge (*eidotes de epebouleusan*) (Th. 3.40.1).[91] Only those actions done against one's will deserve forgiveness (*xyngnomon d'esti to akousion*).[92] Cleon admits that he has forgiveness (*xyngnomen*) for allies who revolt because the Athenians have oppressed them or because they are compelled (*anagkasthentes*) by the enemy (Th. 3.39.2). He then shows that the Mytilenians have not been oppressed and therefore do not have the first excuse: they have fortifications and triremes to protect them and enjoy autonomy and good treatment from the Athenians (Th. 3.39.2). It is important that the Athenians not impose the same punishment (*tas autas zemias*) on those who revolt when compelled by the enemy and on those

88. Macleod (1978) 69 believes that Cleon 'puts a case for summary and retaliatory, not legal justice' and claims that 'this contrasts strongly with his vaunted respect for the laws.' As the following analysis shows, however, Cleon follows generally accepted legal principles when justifying his punishment of the Mytilenians.

89. It is worth noting that the term *epieikeia* occurs only in this pair of speeches in Thucydides. The topic is not considered relevant in other deliberative speeches in Thucydides.

90. Cf. D. 19.103: one should not allow the excuse of ignorance for men in politics. Cf. Isoc. 18.34.

91. Compare the *Rhetorica ad Alexandrum* (4.6.1427a18–20), which says that accusers must deny their opponents any claim to forgiveness. Cf. Lys. 14.2; D. 56.48. For types of excuses see Arist. *Rh.* 1.15.3.1416a.

92. Compare D. 24.49 and Antiphon 1.27. Both these passages are from accusers' speeches.

who do so willingly (Th. 3.39.7). Aristotle (*Rh.* 1.13.16.1374a–b) gives this argument as an example of *epieikeia*, which he discusses in his analysis of forensic rhetoric (*to ta hamartemata kai ta adikemata me tou isou axioun*). Nor can the Mytilenians plead ignorance as an excuse: they knew that other rebellious allies had been punished (Th. 3.39.3).[93] Just as Demosthenes (21.38–41) tries to prove that Meidias acted with deliberate intent to humiliate when he punched him at the Dionysia and had no excuses, Cleon says that the Mytilenians committed an act of planned aggression, a deliberate choice to side with Athens' enemies (Th. 3.39.2: *epebouleusan*). Cleon makes a distinction between those who revolt (*apostasis*) because they have suffered some violence (Th. 3.39.2) and those who attack (*epanestesan*) and act with the intent to destroy the Athenians.[94] This argument is aimed at proving that the Mytilenians did not act in self-defense but with clear criminal intent, another standard feature of speeches made by accusers in court. After showing that there are no extenuating circumstances, Cleon asserts that the Mytilenians were motivated by *hybris*, which was brought on by their prosperity (Th. 3.39.3–5). It is significant that other speakers addressing the Athenian Assembly in Thucydides do not in general use this term, which they find inappropriate for a deliberative speech.[95]

Another commonplace from forensic oratory found in Cleon's speech is the warning against talented speakers who use their skill to undermine the law. Cleon charges that his opponents 'always wish to appear more clever (*sophoteroi*) than the laws and want to come out ahead in all public debates because they cannot express their opinions on other more important issues. With such behavior they often destroy their own communities' (Th. 3.37.4).[96] The best-known example of this *topos* occurs in the opening phrases of Socrates' speech at his trial (Pl. *Ap.* 17a–18a) in which

93. For ignorance as an excuse see D. 21.38 and [D.] 58.24.

94. Note that the author of the *Rhetorica ad Alexandrum* (4.3.1427a3–5) says that in accusations 'above all it must be demonstrated that he [i.e., the defendant] did wrong willingly and deliberately, not with ordinary intent but with the greatest possible preparation.'

95. The term *hybris* is found elsewhere in Thucydides only in narrative: Th. 2.65.9; 3.84; 4.98.5; 6.28. The only exception is the Corinthians who accuse the Corcyreans of *hybris* resulting from wealth (Th. 1.38.5).

96. King Archidamus praises the Spartans for not being so highly educated that they despise the laws and for having too much self-control to disobey them (Th. 1.84.3). Cleon's argument is not 'democratic' or 'oligarchic'—he is espousing the ideal of the rule of law common to all Greek city-states. See Harris (2006a) 14–25.

he reminds the judges how his opponents have warned them that Socrates is a clever speaker (*deinos legein*), who will attempt to mislead them.[97] One can find several other examples. For instance, Diodorus, when prosecuting Androtion for passing an illegal decree, makes a similar warning: 'When it comes to public speaking, this man is a skilled practitioner and has devoted his whole life to this subject. To make sure that you will not be misled and persuaded to cast a vote that violates your oath and to acquit this man, whom you should punish for many reasons, pay close attention to what I am going to say.' (D. 22.4. Cf. D. 52.2). The Judicial Oath obligated judges to follow the laws of Athens; Diodorus, like Cleon, claims that Androtion will use his skill in speaking to forget the oath and to ignore the laws. Demosthenes (29.13) makes a similar charge against Aphobus.

Closely related to this forensic tactic is the charge of accusing one's opponent of being a sophist. Cleon implicitly makes this accusation when he compares the Assembly to an audience listening to sophists (Th. 3.38.7: *sophiston theatais eoikotes*). Aeschines accuses Demosthenes of being a sophist, who will boast to his students that he distracted the judges from the charges against Timarchus (Aeschin. 1.173–76. Cf. 3.35). A speaker in a maritime case accuses his opponent Lacritus of being a sophist trained by Isocrates, who will attempt to use his cleverness to deny him justice (D. 35.39–40). In his speech against Ctesiphon, Aeschines (3.16, 202) warns the judges not once but twice that Demosthenes is a sophist who thinks that he can destroy the laws. Demosthenes (19.246) later flung the same charge back at Aeschines.[98] In his defense of Ctesiphon, Demosthenes (18.226–27) accuses Aeschines of acting like a sophist (*sophizetai*) and treating the trial like a speaking contest (*rhetoron agona*) in which the eloquence of the speeches are judged, not an examination of his political career. Just as litigants in court claim their opponents will try to distract the judges from the main issue, Cleon predicts that his opponents will try to mislead the Assembly with specious arguments (Th. 3.38.2: *paragein*).[99]

97. For the charge that one's opponent is *deinos legein* see also Isoc. 21.5.

98. There is no need to follow Connor (1971) 163–68 in seeing Cleon's attacks on sophists as anti-intellectual and aimed at currying favor with the masses. One needs to make a distinction between attitudes toward the traditional education, which was universally admired, and widespread suspicion of the sophists shared by upper and lower classes. See Harris (1995) 28 and 185.

99. For this charge in forensic oratory see D. 19.228; 20.98, 132; 22.4; 23.191, 215; 35.41; 45.87; [D.] 46.1. In all these passages one finds a form of the verb *paragein*.

Other litigants echo Cleon's argument by accusing their opponents of despising or looking down on the laws (Antiphon 6.47; D. 42.2; [D.] 59.66; Isoc. 16.2; 18.1; 20.22; Lys. 14.9; fr. 195 [Carey] [= Athenaeus 12.551b–552d]; Aeschin. 3.203), which implies that they consider themselves superior to the laws.[100] In Thucydides no other speaker in the Athenian Assembly uses these tactics.

In the concluding section of his speech (*epilogos*) the accuser often asks the court to punish the defendant and make an example out of him as a deterrent to crime. Toward the end of his speech against Meidias, Demosthenes (21.227) tells the court: 'you were chosen by lot to judge the case, and it is in your power to put an end to the matter with a single vote, will you now hesitate to help me, to bring joy to the people, to teach discipline to others, and to enable you yourselves to live in complete security for the future by making this man an example (*paradeigma*) for others?' Another accuser exhorts the court to make an example of Androtion: 'You should impose a penalty today for all his crimes and provide an example for others so they will show greater restraint' (D. 22.68). In a prosecution for treason during an embassy, Demosthenes (19.343) asks the court to punish Aeschines and make an example of him for the citizens and the other Greeks (cf. Lycurg. *Leocr.* 150). Other speakers stress the deterrent effect of harsh penalties (cf. D. 45.87).[101] An accuser in a case about bribery predicts that if the judges punish the defendant, their verdict will send a warning to those who steal public property and make them more virtuous (Lys. 30.23–24).[102] Apollodorus urges the court to condemn Neaera so that others will be more careful and respect the gods and the city ([D.] 59.77). At the end of his speech in a case of assault, Ariston says that if the court acquits Conon, there will be more violent crime; if they convict, there will be less (D. 54.43). In a similar fashion, Cleon emphasizes the deterrent effect of punishment and tells the Assembly to 'punish these men as they deserve and set a clear example (*paradeigma*) for your other allies that whoever rebels will be punished with death. If they understand this, you will spend less time fighting your

100. Cf. Carey (1996) 45.

101. Compare the *Rhetorica ad Alexandrum* (4.5–6.1427a10–18) for advice to accusers concerning arguments about punishment as a deterrent.

102. Cf. Lycurg. *Leocr.* 10; Lys. 14.12; 15.9–10; 22.19; 27.7; 28.11.

allies and neglecting your enemies' (Th. 3.40.7).[103] It is no coincidence that Cleon, like other accusers, places this argument in the concluding section of his speech.

In his reply to Cleon, Diodotus not only opposes his decree but rejects his entire approach to the debate. His attack is directed not only at Cleon's language but also at his political tactics. He signals his own attitude in the first sentence of his speech (Th. 3.42.1): he says that he neither accuses (*aitiomai*) those who have proposed another debate nor praises (*epaino*) those who blame those who criticize the practice of holding several discussions of important issues. When he says he does not 'accuse,' he indicates that he is not going to deliver a judicial speech; when he says he does not 'praise,' he hints that he is not about to give an epideictic speech. He continues by denouncing Cleon's attacks on his opponents as inappropriate behavior in the Assembly. These tactics may be acceptable in a law court, but in the Assembly attacks on character inhibit free discussion by discouraging speakers from expressing their actual views (Th. 3.42.1–3). The city does not gain from this approach, which deprives it of advisors by intimidation (Th. 3.42.4). Diodotus refuses to play by Cleon's rules, which are unsuitable for debate in the Assembly. He is not going to make an accusation (Th. 3.44.1: *kategoreson*) or discuss guilt or forgiveness (Th. 3.44.1–2: *adikias . . . xyngnomes*). This is because the Athenians are not engaged in litigation (*ou dikazometha*) but deliberating (*bouleuometha*) about how the people of Mytilene can serve their interests (*chresimos hexousin*) (Th.3.44.4).[104] He therefore looks to the future just as Aristotle says that a speaker should do when addressing the Assembly (Th. 3.44.3: *mellontos*). Those in the Assembly should likewise not act as judges (Th. 3.46.4: *ou dikastas*). His rejection of Cleon's judicial rhetoric and tactics could not be more explicit.[105] On the other hand, Diodotus does not object to putting the guilty on trial; he objects to trying them at a meeting of the Assembly (Th. 3.48.1: *krinai*). His overall argument is constitutional as well as rhetorical: the Athenians should deliberate about public policy in the Assembly and try individuals in the courts. By trying to conduct a trial in the Assembly, Cleon is urging the Athenians to make a serious political mistake.

---

103. The parallel with forensic oratory is noted by Navarre (1900), 305–6. Cf. Macleod (1978) 71 (= Macleod [1983] 95). Neither of these scholars notes that this argument tends to occur in the final section of a speech.

104. For the argument that an Assembly should not act like a court see also Th. 1.73.1.

105. Yunis (1996) 92–101 misses Diodotus' critique of Cleon's judicial rhetoric.

Diodotus also refuses to use the standard appeals to anger or pity found in judicial rhetoric. Anger is out of place in discussions before the Assembly because it inhibits proper deliberation by encouraging hasty and foolish decisions (Th. 3.42.1). He also states that the Athenians should not be influenced by pity or a sense of fairness just as Cleon does (Th. 3.48.1), but his reasons are different. Cleon argues that the Mytilenians do not deserve pity or fairness because they are clearly guilty; Diodotus rejects this language because it is not appropriate to debate in the Assembly. While Cleon champions the importance of enforcing the law and the deterrent value of punishment, Diodotus questions the power of the law to prevent revolts. Even though many laws have been passed with the death penalty, men will still commit crimes if they are confident of success; the same is true for states (Th. 3.45.1–2, 6–7). In an earlier period, punishments were less severe, but as time went on, they grew more and more harsh and included the death penalty, yet men still broke the law (Th. 3.45.3–4). Because the law is ineffective in preventing revolts, the Athenians should adopt a policy that makes it more likely that a rebellious city will surrender rather than fight to the end. In contrast to Cleon, who lays great stress on what the Mytilenians have done in the past, Diodotus looks to the future in the way one should in a deliberative speech. If it is possible for a rebellious city to come to terms and expect lenient treatment, it is more likely that the city will surrender rather than fight to the bitter end (Th. 3.46.1–2). This way the Athenians will not have to spend their resources on a lengthy siege and will regain the revenue from tribute they need to fight their war against Sparta (Th. 3.46.3). Diodotus does not just oppose Cleon's proposal; he questions his use of language and political tactics. All the important terms in Cleon's vocabulary—punishment, guilt, law, anger and pity, fairness, attacks on intelligence—are shown to be inappropriate when addressing the Assembly.[106] What Diodotus in effect criticizes Cleon for is dragging the tactics of the law courts into the Assembly.[107] Thucydides may have distorted some of Cleon's arguments and rendered the tone of his speech

106. Diodotus is not above some forensic mud-slinging when he insinuates that Cleon uses an aggressive style to cover up his own corruption (Th. 3.42.2).

107. Other scholars believe that Thucydides' criticism is directed mainly at Cleon's imperial policies. See for example Andrewes (1962) 85. But see Macleod (1978) 77 (= Macleod [1983] 101): 'Diodotus' speech overall makes a point hard to rebut—that what is needed is not a legal judgement inspired by anger, but a deliberation on matters of expediency governed by reason.' This however underestimates the rational character of many of Cleon's arguments.

more violent than it actually was, but there is no reason to doubt that Cleon would have used such tactics in the Assembly.

Unlike other politicians before him, Cleon exploited the weaknesses of the courts for political advantage. When he spoke in the Assembly, he used the same methods of intimidation he employed in the courts. This breakdown of the separation between the deliberative sphere (the Assembly) and the judicial sphere (the courts), which Thucydides has Diodotus so perceptively criticize, was a dangerous development in the history of Athenian democracy. Even though Cleon was defeated on this occasion, he appears to have continued using these tactics until his death in 422 when Thucydides (5.16.1) says that he was still notorious for his 'slanders.'

IV

Even though Cleon died in battle at Amphipolis in 422 BCE, his tactics lived on. His immediate successor in the courts was Hyperbolus. As early as 425, Aristophanes (*Ach.* 846–47) alludes to his constant prosecutions and in the *Clouds* (874–76) mentions his detailed knowledge of legal procedure. In the *Wasps* (1007) Bdelykleon denounces him for making fools of the judges with his lies. As mentioned earlier, Aristophanes in the *Knights* (1358–63) links him with the practice of encouraging the courts to convict wealthy men to make sure they receive their pay and Plutarch (*Alc.* 13.1) with sycophancy. After the death of Cleon, Hyperbolus used Cleon's tactics to establish himself as the leading politician in the Assembly (*Pax* 679–81).

His main competitors were Nicias, who negotiated the end of the war with Sparta in 421, and Alcibiades, who rose to prominence after 420. As we have seen, both of these men practiced politics in the traditional way by spending money and aspiring to lead Athens' armed forces. Despite their similar tactics, their views on foreign policy were at loggerheads. Nicias was in favor of recovering Athenian possessions in Northern Greece and maintaining peace with Sparta, while Alcibiades had tried to stir up trouble for Sparta in the Peloponnese and would argue for an invasion of Sicily in 415.[108] Hyperbolus was clearly pleased that his two rivals were fighting each other (Plu. *Nic.* 11.4; *Alc.* 13.3). On the other hand, he knew that they would not eliminate each other by a battle in the courts. After all,

108. For their differences in foreign policy see Rhodes (1994a) 94–6.

they were gentlemen, and gentlemen did not use the courts. The only way to encourage them to attack each other directly was to propose an ostracism, and that is precisely what Hyperbolus did in either 416 or 425 (Plu. *Alc.* 13.4).[109] But the plan backfired, and Hyperbolus was hoist on his own petard: Alcibiades and Nicias saw through his ruse and joined forces against him. When the ostracism was held, it was Hyperbolus who was ostracized (Plu. *Alc.* 13.4; *Nic.* 11.4). The traditional politicians used their own tactics to get rid of someone practicing the new style of politics. But the ostracism of Hyperbolus left a bad taste. As the comic poet Plato remarked (Plu. *Nic.* 11.6; *Alc.* 13.5),

> Indeed he suffered a worthy fate for men of old
> Albeit a fate too good for him and for his brands.
> For such as him the ostrakon was ne'er devised. (Trans. Perrin)

Ostracism was a tool designed to help gentlemen resolve their differences without getting their hands dirty by resorting to the courts, not for men like Hyperbolus. One should not assume that the comic poet's contempt was stirred by Hyperbolus' social origins. It was his methods which drew his disapproval in the same way that Cleon's had tactics offended Aristophanes and prompted him to cast aspersions on his origins.

Alcibiades' triumph over Hyperbolus was short-lived. The practitioners of the new style of politics soon struck back when Alcibiades and dozens of other men were accused during the hysteria following the mutilation of the Herms and the parody of the Mysteries in 415. Thucydides reports that just before the expedition to Sicily was supposed to depart, the Herms in the city were mutilated. The Athenians voted to investigate the crime and offered immunity to anyone, citizen, slave or foreigner, who provided testimony (Th. 6.27.1–2). Several metics and slaves did not give testimony about the Herms but reported about statues of gods being mutilated as a youthful, drunken prank.[110] They also charged Alcibiades and others with parodying the Mysteries in private houses (Th. 6.28.1–2). The people who supported these charges were the enemies of Alcibiades, who saw in him an obstacle to their ambitions. They exaggerated (*emegalunon*) the significance

109. For discussion of the date see Rhodes (1994a) 86–91. Ellis (1989) 45–9 thinks the initiative came from Alcibiades, but see Rhodes (1994) 96.

110. *Pace* Graf (2000) 123, followed by Hornblower (2008) 377, the word *agalmata* means statues of gods as opposed to *eikones*, statues of men.

of the crimes and claimed that they were part of a plot to overthrow the democracy. Apparently their only evidence for this charge was Alcibiades' behavior, his 'undemocratic lawlessness' (Th. 6.28.2). Thucydides makes a clear distinction between the charges of mutilating statues, which was said to be a drunken prank, and of performing the Mysteries in an insulting way (*eph' hybrin*) made by the informants, and the charge of overthrowing the democracy made by Alcibiades' enemies, who according to Thucydides 'were exaggerating.' Alcibiades denied the charges and offered to stand trial immediately (6.29.1–2). His enemies, however, did not want him to stand trial at this point out of fear that the people would go easy on him because he had convinced the Argives and some of the Mantineans to join the expedition to Sicily. They urged him to leave so that they could poison the atmosphere in his absence and have him recalled to stand trial after they were able to multiply their slanders (*ek meizonos diaboles*) against him (Th. 6.29.3).

After Alcibiades left, the Athenians continued to investigate the two crimes, but Thucydides makes it clear that the informers who came forward were not reliable (Th. 6.53.2: *poneron . . . ponerian*). Suspicions were further inflamed when one of those arrested decided to confess; this led to the execution of those in prison and death sentences for those who had fled (Th. 6.60). The confession also led the Athenians to believe that the parody of the Mysteries was part of a plot by Alcibiades to overthrow the democracy (Th. 6.61.1). The appearance of a Spartan force at the Isthmus seemed to confirm this suspicion (Th. 6.61.2). The *Salaminia* was sent to Sicily to arrest Alcibiades, who escaped at Thurii and went to the Peloponnese (Th. 6.61.4–7).

This is not the place to undertake a detailed analysis of the events of 415, but two points need to be made. First, there is no reason to view the two offenses 'as part of a climate . . . in which religious traditions, as well as democratic values, were becoming increasingly fragile.'[111] Thucydides (6.27.3) gives a very good explanation for the public reaction to the mutilation of the Herms: it was seen as a bad omen (*ekplou oionos*) for the departure of the expedition. The launching of an expedition was a time of great anxiety and uncertainty, as Thucydides (6.31.1) notes about the Sicilian expedition. To allay these fears, military leaders might go to great lengths to secure good omens or favorable oracles to assure success. Herodotus

111. Hornblower (2008) 372, following Graf (2000). For sensible doubts about the existence of a 'religious crisis' in the late fifth century see Parker (1996) 210–14.

describes at length Croesus' attempts to gain encouraging responses from Delphi and other sanctuaries before he set out to attack Cyrus the king of the Persians (Hdt. 1.46–56). Xenophon reports that the Spartan kings performed sacrifices before leading the army out of Spartan territory (*Lac. Pol.* 13.2–3. Cf. X. *HG* 5.1.33). If the omens from a sacrifice did not turn out well, defeat would be the result (X. *An.* 6.4.22–25).[112] When the Athenian fleet was about to leave for Sicily, everyone joined in prayers said by a herald, sang the paian, and poured libations (Th. 6.32). This was not the only way they calmed their fears. Thucydides (8.1.1) says that the Athenians took courage from the size of their expedition, but when describing the reaction of the Athenians to the news of the defeat in Sicily, he reveals that the Athenians had also gained confidence from *chresmologoi* and seers who had predicted victory. It was not the mutilation of the Herms by itself that caused alarm among the Athenians, but its juxtaposition with the departure of the fleet that made them panic. Any Greek in Sparta, Corinth, Argos, or countless other cities would have reacted the same way if a disturbing omen had been observed when the army was about to depart on a campaign. One does not, therefore, need to conjure up a religious crisis to explain the Athenian reaction to the mutilation of the Herms.

Second, the best way to understand the prosecutions of Alcibiades and others is to place these events in the context of the new political tactics pioneered by Cleon in the 420s. The charges made by Alcibiades' enemies were exactly the same as those made by Cleon against his opponents: conspiracy, aiming at tyranny, and treason (Th. 6.27.2; Ar. *V.* 417, 470, 474–76, 487. Cf. 488–502). Though the Athenians were concerned about the bad omen for the expedition, Thucydides says that it was the memory of the tyrants that caused their greatest fears (Th. 6.53.3; 60.1). This was the charge that caused them to recall Alcibiades from Sicily (Th. 6.61.1–3). Of course, the charges make no sense. First, Alcibiades may have had an extravagant lifestyle, but up to this point he had obeyed the law and had a distinguished career of public service.[113] Second, he had just been elected to lead a major expedition to Sicily and had no cause for resentment against the democracy. Third, there is no reason to question his piety, which he conspicuously demonstrated after his return to Athens (X. *HG* 1.4.20; Plu. *Alc.* 34). Fourth,

---

112. On sacrifice before battle see Jameson (1991). For similar anxiety about an omen when an expedition was about to depart see Plu. *Dion* 24.1–5.

113. For Alcibiades' public service see section I of this chapter.

Thucydides casts doubt on the charges by calling them slander (Th. 6.29.3: *diaboles*) and questioning the character of the informants. Andocides (1.47–66. Cf. Plu. *Alc.* 20.5) tells the story of one of the accusers, Diocleides, who claimed to have seen dozens of men meeting at night to conspire against the democracy. When asked how he was able to identify so many men in the dark, Diocleides said there was a full moon that night. His charges went unchallenged until someone pointed out that on the night in question there was no full moon. Diocleides was executed but had his false testimony not been discovered many innocent men would have been executed or sent into exile. There is no reason to believe that the evidence against the others convicted was any better. Fifth, Thucydides gives Alcibiades' enemies a convincing motive for their false charges: they wished to eliminate a powerful rival (Th. 6.28.2). According to Xenophon (*HG* 1.4.9–12) many Athenians by 407 BCE were certain that Alcibiades had been the innocent victim of a plot against him in 415. Alcibiades was not guilty of plotting against the democracy; he was the victim of enemies who had learned their tactics from Cleon. Alcibiades' distrust of the courts was justified. The help he gave to the Spartans may have been treason, but his decision to disobey the summons and flee was quite reasonable given the atmosphere in Athens.

It might be tempting to see a contrast between Cimon's behavior after his ostracism and that of Alcibiades during his exile and to see this as evidence for a moral decline in Athens, possibly brought about by the pernicious individualism of the Sophists. Before yielding to this temptation, however, one must recall that their situations were very different. Cimon had a strong incentive to remain loyal to Athens after his ostracism: he knew that his exile would end after ten years and that he could return to Athens and resume his political career, as in fact he did. On the other hand, there was also a powerful disincentive against collaborating with the enemy. Even though he was in exile, he retained his property in Athens. Were he to commit treason, he would lose his chance to return and his property as well. For Alcibiades there was no such incentive. Unlike Cimon, Alcibiades was sentenced to death in absentia. In 415 he had no idea that he would ever be able to return to Athens. One should not blame his conduct on his association with Socrates; it was those who attacked him in the courts who drove him into the hands of the Spartans.

Distrust of the courts was also responsible a few years later for transforming what might have been minor defeat into a complete disaster. When Nicias was deciding whether to lift the siege of Syracuse after it became obvious that they could not capture the city, his fear of the Athenian courts caused him to make a disastrous decision. If he had withdrawn immediately, he could have saved most of the Athenian and allied troops in the expedition. But Thucydides tells us that 'rather than be put to death on a disgraceful charge and by an unjust verdict of the Athenians, he preferred to take his chance, and if it must be, to meet his own death at the hands of the enemy' (Th. 7.48.3–4). His fear was not unreasonable; as noted, Sophocles, Pythodorus, and Eurymedon were convicted after their campaign in Sicily, and Demosthenes was afraid to return after his defeat in Acarnania. The decision may have saved Nicias' reputation, but it had devastating consequences for the expedition, which suffered terrible losses and was finally forced to surrender.

In the next few years, the Spartans began negotiations with the Persians and were able to obtain money to build a fleet and hire rowers. Despite some initial Spartan victories, the Athenians were able to recover many of their losses with the help of Alcibiades, who aided the fleet and army on Samos, then returned in triumph to Athens in 407. Many at the time of his return believed that his banishment had been unjust and the charges against him unfounded. In the following year, however, Alcibiades left the fleet at Notion under the command of a subordinate named Antiochus with orders not to join battle with the enemy (X. *HG* 1.5.11). When Antiochus disobeyed the order, the Spartan general Lysander won a victory (X. *HG* 1.5.12–14. Cf. Plu. *Alc.* 35.4–6).[114] Even though Alcibiades played no part in the battle, his enemies in Athens blamed him for the defeat (X. *HG* 1.5.16). Afraid of prosecution, Alcibiades withdrew into exile again, never to return (X. *HG*. 1.5.17).[115] Diodorus (13.73.3–74.4) gives a slightly different version of the events leading up to his exile from that found in Xenophon and adds that the people of Cyme brought complaints against him but says that Alcibiades decided not to return to Athens from fear of lawsuits (D. S. 13.74.2: *dikas*).

In the following year, 406, the tactic of using legal charges to destroy one's enemies was responsible for the condemnation and execution of six generals after the battle of Arginousai. This dealt a major blow to the Athenian military. One cannot argue that this trial in the Assembly was an aberration in the history of Athenian democracy. As we have seen, attacks on generals began

114. For discussion of the battle see Andrewes (1982), Kagan (1987) 301–322, and Bleckmann (1998) 162–82.

115. Cf. Lys. 14.38, which states that Alcibiades did not dare to submit to his *euthynai*. Lys. 21.7 might appear to indicate that Alcibiades was deposed, but see Hamel (1998a) 210–12.

in the 420s and continued in the next two decades. On the contrary, the debacle of 406 was the climax of a long development and was one of the causes for the disastrous defeat at Aegospotamoi the following year.

To set the trial in context, we need to recall the events leading up to it. In 406 the Spartans under Callicratidas captured Methymna on Lesbos and started to blockade Mytilene (X. *HG* 1.6.12–23). The Athenians sent a fleet of 110 ships from Athens, which joined other ships at Samos and the surrounding area, to lift the blockade. The Athenians met and defeated the Spartan fleet under Callicratidas at Arginousai off the coast of Lesbos. According to Xenophon (*HG* 1.6.35), after the battle the Athenian generals decided that the trierarchs Theramenes and Thrasybulus and some of the taxiarchs should take forty-seven ships and help the disabled triremes and recover the men on board. The generals were to sail to Mytilene and attack the Spartan fleet under Eteonicus, which was blockading the city. Neither group was able to carry out its part of the plan because a storm prevented them. According to Diodorus (13.100.1–2), after the battle there was a debate whether to recover the bodies of the dead or to sail to Mytilene and relieve the city. A storm intervened making it impossible to recover the dead. Both authors agree about the storm, but Xenophon says that the task of the trierarchs was to save living men while Diodorus says it was to recover corpses for burial.

Xenophon (*HG* 1.7.1–34) gives a very detailed account of the following events. He reports that the people deposed all the generals except Conon and elected Adeimantus and Philocles in their place. Out of the eight generals who participated in the battle, Protomachus and Aristogenes did not return home, but the six others did. Xenophon does not say why the people deposed the generals and does not report that the Assembly ordered them to return to Athens. Diodorus (13.101.1–5) supplies the explanation missing in Xenophon's account: the generals had sent a letter blaming Theramenes and Thrasybulus for the failure to recover the dead, but the two trierarchs, who had returned to Athens before the generals, struck back by turning the people's anger against the generals.[116] As a result, the Assembly summoned them to return to Athens for trial.

Once the generals returned, Archedemus brought a charge of bribery and misconduct against Erasinides, and the court voted that he be placed in prison (X. *HG* 1.7.2). The other generals reported to the Council. At this

116. By omitting the charges made in their letter, Xenophon (*HG* 1.7.4) makes the generals look like innocent victims and places Theramenes in a worse light. See Andrewes (1974a) for the different portrayals of Theramenes in Diodorus and Xenophon.

meeting Timocrates passed a motion to imprison the generals and to place them on trial in the Assembly (X. *HG*. 1.7.3).[117] When the Assembly met, Theramenes demanded that the generals explain why they had not picked up the shipwrecked sailors and read out a letter from the generals placing the blame on the storm (X. *HG* 1.7.4). The generals then replied that they sailed against the enemy and entrusted the task of rescuing the sailors to Theramenes and Thrasybulus, but blamed the death of the sailors on the storm and exonerated their opponents (X. *HG* 1.7.5–6). They provided several witnesses to support their account of events. At this point they were persuading the Assembly, but it was getting late, and a decision was postponed to a subsequent meeting. In the meantime, the Assembly instructed the Council to submit a proposal about the procedure to be followed for the trial of the generals (X. *HG* 1.7.7).

Theramenes and his allies met with the relatives of the men lost at sea at the Apaturia and persuaded them to attend the next meeting of the Assembly in mourning (X. *HG* 1.7.8. Cf. D. S. 13.101.6). At this meeting, Callixeinus, who (Xenophon alleges) was bribed, introduced a motion calling for an immediate vote by secret ballot about the guilt of the generals with death as the penalty for conviction (X. *HG* 1.7.9–10). Euryptolemus and several others then charged Callixeinus with making an illegal motion and presented him with a summons, which would have suspended the motion until the case was heard. Another speaker named Lyciscus proposed that unless they withdrew the summons, they too would be tried by the same vote. This succeeded in forcing Euryptolemus to back down (X. *HG* 1.7.12–13). Next the board of *prytaneis* who were presiding over the meeting refused to put the motion to a vote, but Callixeinus made the same threat against them and intimidated them into backing down. The only member of the board who refused was Socrates, who said that he would do nothing against the law (X. *HG* 1.7.14–15).[118]

---

117. Hansen (1975) 84–5 believes that the procedure against the generals was an *eisangelia*, but the charges against them do not resemble the offenses listed in the law about *eisangelia*. The trial was more likely to have been an ad hoc procedure created by a decree. X. *HG* 1.7.7 makes it clear that the Assembly was not following any prescribed rules when he says that the Council was ordered to determine who should conduct the trial. This would not have been necessary if the Assembly had been following an established procedure. MacDowell (1978) 186–7 rightly doubts that the procedure was *eisangelia*. A new study of *eisangelia* is a desideratum.

118. For Socrates' refusal see also Pl. *Ap*. 32b; X. *Mem*. 1.1.18.

What law did the decree of Callixeinus violate? Xenophon and Diodorus do not say. Plato in the *Apology of Socrates* (32b) and Xenophon in the *Memorabilia* (1.1.18) imply that it was illegal to judge the six generals all at once but do not indicate which law this procedure violated. In fact, there is no evidence for such a law.[119] Xenophon (*HG* 1.7.5) states that the generals were not given the legally allotted amount of time to speak,[120] and Diodorus (13.101.6) reports that those who wished to defend the generals were not allowed to speak. This would indicate that what was illegal about Callixeinus' motion was that it violated the law that no one should be put to death without a trial,[121] which is what Euryptolemus actually says in his speech to the Assembly (X. *HG* 1.7.25: *apolluntes akritous para ton nomon*).[122] Had Euryptolemus been able to bring Callixeinus to trial, he would have argued that the generals had not been given a chance to defend themselves so that Callixeinus' proposal to vote about their sentence was an attempt to put them to death without a proper trial. In his speech to the Assembly, Euryptolemus proposes to try the generals under the decree of Cannonus, which would allow them to address the Assembly in chains, or under the law about traitors and temple-robbers, which would have given them the right to speak once about their guilt and once about the penalty to be imposed (X. *HG* 1.7.20–23). The proposal to vote about them collectively would have violated their right to defend themselves.

Euryptolemus offered a motion that each of the men be tried separately under the law of Cannonus. The Assembly passed this motion instead of

119. See MacDowell (1978) 189. Bleckmann (1998) 523–32 goes so far as to claim that the Assembly had the power to hold the six generals collectively responsible and claims that the condemnation of Sophocles, Pythodorus, and Eurymedon proves this. But these generals were given different penalties, which implies separate trials.

120. The translation of X. *HG* 1.7.5 by Ostwald (1986) 438, 'For in conformity with the law no opportunity was given them to make a speech (or perhaps give an accounting)' is inconsistent with the tenor of Xenophon's account, which stresses the illegality of the proceedings against the generals.

121. Illegal to execute someone without trial: Lys. 22.2. Cf. And. 4.3, and *IG* i³ 40, line 9 (Athenians pledge not to put Chalcidians to death without a trial). See Carawan (1984).

122. *Pace* Bleckmann (1998) 522: 'Hält man sich an die Darstellung Xenophons, war die gegen die Strategen erhobene Anklage keineswegs abwegig oder normenwidrig.' MacDowell (1978) 189 misses the reference to the law forbidding the execution of anyone without trial at X. *Hell.* 1.7.25 ('it is noticeable that Euryptolemus, in the speech attributed to him by Xenophon, does not quote or refer to any written law on the point . . . there is no good reason to suppose that there was any legal impropriety in the procedure followed in the case.').

Callixeinus' motion until Menecles brought an accusation against Euryptolemus. A second vote was then taken endorsing Callixeinus' motion. The Assembly then condemned all eight generals to death, and the six remaining in Athens were put to death (X. *HG* 1.7.34). Very soon afterward, the Athenians realized that they had made a serious mistake. According to Xenophon (*HG* 1.7.35), Callixeinus and others were charged and placed in prison but escaped before trial. According to Diodorus (13.103.1–2), Callixeinus was brought to trial in chains, not allowed to speak, then thrown into prison but later escaped and joined the enemy at Deceleia. In Plato's *Apology* (32b), Socrates, speaking before an Athenian court, states that everyone later regretted the executions.[123]

The consequences of the trial were readily apparent. In the next year, 405, the Spartan general Lysander sailed to the Hellespont to stop the supply of grain coming from the Black Sea regions from reaching Athens (X. *HG* 2.1.17). The Athenian fleet followed him and moored at Aegospotamoi, an exposed beach without a nearby city to provide supplies (X. *HG* 2.1.20–21; D. S. 13.105.1–2). Alcibiades happened to be nearby and advised the Athenian generals to move their base to Sestos, where there was a safe harbor and a market (X. *HG* 2.1.25).[124] They ignored his advice, and their military blunders led to the worst defeat in Athenian history (X. *HG* 2.1.27–28). This was no chance event, a mere accident not caused by Athenian actions. Thucydides (2.65) firmly contradicts this view and states that Athenians brought about their downfall by their mistakes and their *stasis*, internal strife. In particular, he points to the *diabolas*, a word that covers false charges made in court. It was the weaknesses of the Athenian courts that failed to keep political competition within safe limits and to protect generals from the unfair attacks that caused their death or exile. These flaws deprived Athens of the military talent it needed to defeat Sparta. This is not to say that military factors and diplomacy did not play a role in Sparta's victory and Athens' defeat. Sparta's decision to build a navy and to seek money from the Persian king obviously made a difference. But these factors only help to explain Sparta's victory; they do not fully explain Athens' defeat. Even

---

123. The attempt of Bleckmann (1998) 510–14 to explain away 'die angebliche Reue des Demos' is unconvincing.

124. According to Diodorus (13.105.3–4), Alcibiades offered to bring Thracian troops to help the Athenians, but the Athenian generals refused the offer.

after the Spartans increased their fleet and obtained Persian money, the Athenians still managed to win victories and hold their own against the Spartans. As Thucydides' says, however, it was Athenian mistakes that finally tipped the balance against them.

One cannot therefore claim that the accounts of Thucydides and Xenophon are tainted by oligarchic bias and thereby dismiss them; the harshest critics of this miscarriage of justice were the Athenians themselves. After the defeat of Athens, the Thirty who seized power and overthrew the democracy arrested the sycophants (*apo sykophantias zontas*), those men who made a career of bringing charges against officials, and had them put to death.[125] Although the Thirty later turned their violence against ordinary citizens, this initial action won the approval of the people. This is reported in three independent sources: Xenophon (*HG* 2.3.12), Aristotle's *Constitution of the Athenians* (35.3), and Diodorus (14.4.2). And a client of Lysias (25.19), when speaking before a democratic court, states that if the Thirty had eliminated only those who stole public funds, took bribes, and were sycophants who brought malicious charges, they would have been accounted good men. If this was an unpopular or heterodox view, why did Lysias dare to express it when attempting to convince hundreds of Athenian citizens?[126]

125. Osborne (1990) tries to argue that the sycophants played a positive role in supporting the democracy, but this passage shows that they were considered one of the main reasons for Athens' defeat.

126. The attempt of Finley (1962) to whitewash the demagogues pays no attention to the prosecutions of politicians like Cleon and their deleterious effect on the military.

Epilogue

MANY RECENT STUDIES of Athenian law take a static approach to the subject and assume that attitudes toward litigation did not change over time.[1] Even though there was considerable continuity in basic convictions about the rule of law and in the form of legal procedures, there was a major shift in the use of litigation in the 420s when some politicians started to use the courts to attack enemies. This development did not occur in a political vacuum; it was made possible by the harsh circumstances of the Peloponnesian War when it was easier to arouse suspicions and to put pressure on the courts. Once the change occurred, the new practices, which were considered disreputable in the fifth century, became standard practice in the fourth century. Many politicians including Callistratus, Conon, Archinus, Eubulus, Leodamas, Apollodorus, Androtion, Demosthenes, Aeschines, Chares, Aristophon, Hyperides, and Lycurgus, a descendant of one of the most distinguished families in Athens, prosecuted their political enemies. In fact, Demosthenes (4.47) thought that prosecutions of generals were so frequent that they interfered with the war against Philip.

But the change would never have come about unless there were weaknesses in Athenian legal institutions waiting to be exposed. In parts I and II, we saw how they Athenians carefully constructed a legal system aimed at implementing the rule of law. In Chapter 1 we saw how the system placed the use of force primarily in the hands of officials and restricted the use of violence by individuals to promote peace and to protect the average citizen from the powerful. Chapter 2 showed that the system also discouraged the use of the courts for feuding by instituting measures against frivolous prosecutions. Chapter 3 demonstrated that the Judicial Oath sought to

1. For synchronic approaches see Ober (1989), Cohen (1995), Christ (1998a), Rubinstein (2000), and Lanni (2006). Allen (2000a) claims that attitudes toward punishment evolved, but her arguments are unconvincing.

ensure fairness and to place all on a level of equality before the law. Chapter 4 studied the contents of Athenian statutes and discovered that they were mostly concerned with formulating substantive rules, which shaped the conduct and behavior of all citizens and other residents of Attica. Chapters 5 and 6 revealed how the Judicial Oath and the plaint compelled litigants to pay close attention to the substantive rules contained in statutes when bringing their cases to court. Yet at the same time, the legal system allowed litigants to explore law's open texture. Chapters 6 and 7 showed how the courts tended to keep to the standard meaning of key terms in statutes when deciding cases and therefore attempted to apply the law with some consistency. On the other hand, as we saw in chapter 8, the courts did not apply the laws rigidly without consideration for extenuating circumstances. The Athenians made a sincere attempt to create the rule of law. For this the Athenians deserve our admiration.

But the Athenians were also obsessed with preventing the abuse of power by officials. This aim went back to the laws of Solon, who provided a range of procedures to prevent the accumulation of power in the hands of one man or group. He divided functions among many officials, assigned power to boards of magistrates, imposed term limits on offices, and allowed citizens to appeal against the decisions of magistrates.[2] He also made officials accountable for their actions. The ultimate weapon against tyrants was, of course, ostracism, which was created after the overthrow of the tyranny and the reforms of Cleisthenes, a method to be used if all else failed. But in their fear of tyranny, the Athenians made it too easy to convict powerful men on public charges. As we saw in chapter 9, the Athenians did not create adequate safeguards to protect the rights of individuals accused of major crimes. And when they realized that certain verdicts were unfair, they tended to blame the accuser and not the courts or the shape of the procedures they followed. It was much easier to find a scapegoat than to take a critical view of one's own institutions. Some scholars have seen the continuity of Athenian institutions as evidence of stability and success.[3] A better way to explain this continuity would be to see it as an example of what New Institutionalism has called 'path dependence.'[4] Athenian democracy suffered too many disasters to be considered a

2. For the aims of Solon's laws see Harris (2006a) 3–28.

3. Most notably Ober (1989).

4. I hope to explore the 'path dependence' of Athenian democracy in the future.

success. As Demosthenes saw, in times of war the courts could be dysfunctional. And as we have seen, the flaws in the legal system had much to answer for in the defeats that led to Athens' surrender in 404. Despite their attempts to create democracy and the rule of law, the Athenians did not completely succeed in their aims. But then again, no community has ever fully implemented the rule of law. The pursuit of equality before the law, the attempt to ensure procedural fairness, the campaign to abolish torture and slavery, the promotion of consistency in adjudication, the effort to make the law accessible, and the task of keeping officials accountable are all ongoing projects. The Athenians and the citizens of the other Greek city-states made important steps in establishing democracy and the rule of law. It is our duty to continue their work and to extend the protections they created for their citizens (and in some cases for free non-citizens) to all people on earth.

APPENDIX I

Hunter on Citizens Enforcing the Law

None of the passages discussed by Hunter show that very often arguments were settled, violence quelled, and miscreants apprehended without the intervention of the authorities at all.[1] The first passage is the narrative from Lysias' speech *Against Simon*, where two incidents involving violence are described. The defendant has been charged with intentional wounding (*trauma ek pronoias*). In his narrative of events, the defendant tells the court how he desired Theodotus, a boy from Plataea, and brought him to his house (Lysias 3.5). Simon too was in love with the boy and broke into the defendant's house and entered the women's quarters in an attempt to find him (6). Simon next asked the defendant to step outside the room where he was dining and, once outside, began to strike him (7). After the defendant pushed him away, Simon started to throw stones at him. He missed the defendant but hit one of his own comrades names Aristocritus (8). Instead of seizing Simon or bringing an action against him, the defendant decided to live abroad (9–10). It is difficult to see any attempt to enforce the law in this incident. Despite Simon's alleged violation of his rights, the defendant does not seize him or denounce him to a magistrate. Aside from pushing him away, the defendant does not use force against Simon.

In the second incident, Simon and some friends attacked the defendant and Theodotus in the Piraeus as they were leaving the house of Lysimachus (12). With the help of some friends, they tried to seize Theodotus, who succeeded in running away (12). Once again the defendant did not use force against Simon. In fact, he avoided him by turning down another street (13). Next Simon and his comrades dragged Theodotus out of the fuller's shop where he was hiding and started to beat him (15–16). When the defendant pulled Theodotus away, they began to strike him too (17). This developed into a brawl with both sides hitting each other, and everyone ended up with their heads battered (18). Once more one could not describe this

1. Hunter (1994) 120–24.

melee as 'law enforcement': no one is arrested, and no official is summoned. There is no 'violence quelled' or 'miscreant apprehended': the incident ends when the two sides stop throwing punches.

For her second example of self-help, Hunter cites Nicomedes' arrest of Pancleon in Lysias' speech *Against Pancleon* (23.9–11), but this passage is not relevant to her point. Pancleon is thought to be a slave, and Nicomedes is simply enforcing his rights of ownership in seizing him (Νικομήδους, ὃς ἐμαρτύρησεν αὐτοῦ δεσπότης εἶναι). This is not a case of a citizen using force against another citizen or foreigner who is breaking the law. In similar fashion Hunter claims that Phrynion's abduction of Neaera is another example of a private citizen enforcing the law ([D.] 59.37–40), but Phrynion too claims that Neaera is his slave. In Classical Athens, as in all slave societies, masters had the power to recover slaves who ran away. In this regard they were acting no differently from a farmer who led back an animal who had wandered off his property.

For her final example, Hunter claims that the trierarch who tried to recover naval equipment from Theophemus resorted to self-help ([D.] 47.18–38).[2] This incident hardly qualifies as a case of self-help or enforcement of the law by a private citizen. A trierarch was a magistrate and required to render accounts after his term of office (Aeschin. 3.13–15) and acting under the orders of the Council. He was also a supervisor of his symmory, an official post ([D.] 47.21). Finally, he was not acting on his own initiative but on the orders of a decree passed in the Council by Chaeredemus and by the terms of Periander's law about symmories ([D.] 47.20–21). This example actually contradicts Hunter's thesis, for here we encounter an official who is enforcing the law on the instructions of the Council.

In short, none of the evidence provided by Hunter proves her point about the role played by ordinary citizens in policing Athens.

2. Hunter (1994) 123–24.

APPENDIX 2

Magistrates Enforcing Laws and Decrees in the Fifth Century BCE

IG i^3 1 (510–500), lines 7–8 (fine on those who lease their land in Salamis levied by archon)

IG i^3 4 (before 485/4), lines B6–16 (treasurers have power to impose fines for lighting fires, throwing dung, dwelling, baking, etc. on the Acropolis)

IG i^3 45 (c. 445), lines 3–6 (regulation concerning runaway slaves and thieves [*lopodytai*]; three archers from the tribe holding the prytany are to act as guards)

IG i^3 58B (c. 430), lines 16–19 (archons or architects instructed to place guards to prevent illegal access at Eleusis)

IG i^3 65 (c. 427/6), lines 11–17 (generals, Council, and prytaneis are to keep precinct of Zeus safe)

IG i^3 78 (422?), lines 8–10, 57–9 (demarchs are to collect first-fruits and give to the *hieropoioi*; provisions to be enforced by the *basileus* who brings matter before Council)

IG i^3 82 (421/0), lines 24–28 (*hieropoioi* responsible for keeping order at Hephaestaea and have power to impose fines. If fine is higher than fifty drachmas, they must take case to court)

IG i^3 98 (411), lines 19–26 (Pythophanes is granted protection against harm and *asylia*; the generals and Council are responsible for his safety)

IG i^3 101 (410/09), lines 51–55 (generals to protect people of Neapolis against harm from public officials and private individuals)

IG i^3 102 (410/09), lines 32–34, 39–47 (Thrasybulus of Calydon is given *enktesis*; the Council and the *prytaneis* are responsible for protecting him; Council instructed to conduct investigation about those bribed to pass a decree and to punish them and/or bring them to court as well as to report its findings)

IG i^3 107 (c. 409), lines 3–5 (*prytaneis*, Council, and generals are ordered to see that no harm is done to an unknown honorand)

IG i³ 110 (408/7), lines 15–20 (Council, generals, and official in Sciathus responsible for protecting Oeniades of Palaeosciathus)

IG i³ 138 (before 434), lines 15–18 (two treasurers and priest are to oversee shrine of Apollo)

IG i³ 153 (440–25), lines 16–19 (fine of one thousand drachmas on captains and trierarchs. Dock supervisors enforce)

IG i³ 156 (440–425), lines 1–9 (*prytaneis* and Council to protect the *proxenos* Leonidas of Halicarnassus in Athens, officials in other cities when he is abroad)

IG i³ 159 (c. 430), lines 17–20 (the generals and the Council [?] are ordered to see that no harm is done to an unknown honorand, probably a *proxenos*)

IG i³ 167 (430–415), lines 12–7 (Council and *prytaneis* responsible for protecting an unknown *proxenos*)

IG i³ 170 (430–405) (generals [?] and Council are ordered to see that no harm is done to an unknown honorand)

IG i³ 178 (420–405), lines 4–6 (Council is ordered to see that no harm is done Dorcis, his wife, and probably his descendants)

IG i³ 181 (c. 410), lines 7–9 (Council is ordered to see that no harm is done to an unknown *proxenos* and possibly his children.)

A similar phrase is plausibly restored in *IG* i³ 183 (after 445), lines 4–6.

The identity of the archers in *IG* i³ 45 is discussed by Wernicke (1891) 60–75. He believes that they are citizens and compares the archers mentioned in *IG* i² 60, line 17. He argues that their functions are police were later taken over by the Scythians mentioned at [And.] 3.7. But see now Couvenhes (2012).

One could perhaps add *IG* i³ 61 (426/5), lines 36–38, where it is clear that the Hellespontine guards have the power to control traffic through the Hellespont.

A *lex sacra* from Paeania grants *hieropoioi* the right to carry a rod or staff (*rhabdos*) (*IG* i³ 250 [450–430], lines 9–11). This clause may give them the power to keep order at festivals. For officials using a rod to enforce rules see Herodotus 8.59; Thucydides 5.50. For metaphorical usage see Aristophanes *Peace* 734–35; Plato *Protagoras* 338a.

By contrast, the phrase *ho boulomenos* (voluntary prosecutor) is found in fifth-century Attic inscriptions only at *IG* i³ 34, line 34 and is plausibly restored at *IG* i³ 68, line 46. The phrase is also found at *IG* i³ 14, line 8; 34, line 34; 41, line 61, but all these inscriptions are fragmentary, and not enough remains of the stone to determine whether these decrees allow for voluntary prosecution.

APPENDIX 3

Quotations or Allusions to Judicial Oath in Attic Orators

Aeschin. 1.154—vote about charges in the indictment
Aeschin. 1.170—vote about charges in the indictment
Aeschin. 2.1—listen to both sides
Aeschin. 2.7—listen to both sides
Aeschin. 3.6—vote according to the laws
Aeschin. 3.8—vote according to the laws
Aeschin. 3.31—vote according to the laws
Aeschin. 3.57—listen to both sides
Aeschin. 3.198—vote according to the laws
Aeschin. 3.233—general
Aeschin. 3.257—vote according to the laws
And. 1.2—vote according to the laws
And. 1.9—listen to both sides
And. 1.31—general
And. 1.91—respect the amnesty and vote according to the laws
Antiphon 5.8—general
Antiphon 5.85—vote according to the laws
Antiphon 5.96—general
D. 18.2—listen to both sides
D. 18.6–7—listen to both sides
D. 18.121—vote according to the laws
D. 18.217—general
D. 18.249—general
D. 19.1—vote according to the laws
D. 19.132—general
D. 19.134—general

D. 19.179—vote according to the laws
D. 19.219–20—vote according to the laws
D. 19.239–40—general
D. 19.284—general
D. 19.297—vote according to the laws
D. 20.93—general
D. 20.101—vote according to the laws
D. 20.118–9—vote according to the laws, most just judgment.
D. 20.159—general
D. 20.167—general
D. 21.4—general
D. 21.24—general
D. 21.34—vote according to the laws
D. 21.42—vote according to the laws
D. 21.177—vote according to the laws
D. 21.188—vote according to the laws
D. 21.211–12—vote according to the laws
D. 22.4—vote about charges in the indictment
D. 22.20—vote according to the laws
D. 22.39—general
D. 22.43—vote about charges in the indictment
D. 22.45—vote according to the laws
D. 22.45—vote about charges in the indictment, according to the laws
D. 23.19—listen to both sides
D. 23.96—vote according to most just judgment
D. 23.101—vote according to the laws
D. 23.194—general
D. 24.2—general
D. 24.35–6—vote according to the laws
D. 24.58—general
D. 24.78—general
D. 24.90—general
D. 24.148, 151—general (the oath does not contain the words 'I shall not imprison any Athenian citizen')
D. 24.175—general
D. 24.189—vote about charges in indictment
D. 24.191—general
D. 27.3—listen to both sides
D. 27.68—vote according to the laws
D. 29.53—general
D. 30.9—vote about charges in the indictment
D. 32.13—vote about charges in the indictment

D. 33.38—vote according to the laws
D. 34.45 (cf. 52)—vote according to the laws
D. 36.26—vote according to the laws
D. 36.61—general
D. 37.17—vote about charges in the indictment
D. 38—Judicial Oath not mentioned
D. 39.37—general
D. 39.38—general
D. 39.40—vote according to most just judgment
D. 39.41—vote according to the laws; vote according to most just judgment
D. 40.60—vote about charges in the indictment
D. 41—Judicial Oath not mentioned
D. 42.10—general
D. 43.84—vote according to the laws
D. 44.14—vote about charges in the indictment
D. 45.50—vote about charges in the indictment
D. 45.87—vote according to the laws
D. 45.88—general
[D.] 46.27—vote according to the laws
D. 48.17—general
[D.] 52—vote according to the laws
D. 55.35—general
D. 57.1—listen to both sides
D. 57.63—vote with most just judgment
D. 57.69—general
D. 57.70—general
[D.] 58.17—general
[D.] 58.25—vote according to the laws
[D.] 58.36—vote according to the laws
[D.] 58.41—vote according to the laws
[D.] 58.61—vote according to the laws
[D.] 58.62—vote according to the laws
[D.] 59.115—vote according to the laws
Din. 1.14—general
Din. 1.17—vote according to the laws
Din. 1.84—vote according to the laws
Din. 1.86—general
Din. 2.20—general
Din. 3.17—general
Hyp. *Lycurg.* fr. 1—listen to both sides
Hyp. *Phil.* 5—vote according to the laws
Hyp. *Eux.* 40—vote according to the laws

Hyp. *D.* 1—vote according to the laws
Hyp. *D.* 39—vote according to the laws
Is. 2.47—vote according to the laws
Is. 4.31—vote according to the laws.
Is. 6.2—listen to both sides
Is. 6.51–52—vote on charges in the indictment.
Is. 6.65—vote according to the laws
Is. 8.46—vote according to the laws.
Is. 10—vote on charges in the indictment
Is. 11.6—vote according to the laws
Is. 12.18—general
Isoc. *Antidosis* 18—general
Isoc. *Antidosis* 21—listen to both sides
Isoc. *Antidosis* 173—general (laws)
Isoc. *Against Callimachus* 34—general
Lycurg. *Leocr.* 11–13—vote on charges in the indictment
Lycurg. *Leocr.* 79—general
Lycurg. *Leocr.* 128—general
Lycurg. *Leocr.* 143—vote according to the laws
Lys. 10.32—general
Lys. 14.22—vote according to the laws.
Lys. 14.40—vote according to the laws.
Lys. 14.47—vote justly
Lys. 15.1—listen to both sides
Lys. 15.9–10—listen to both sides, vote according to the laws
Lys. 18.13—general (?—another oath?)
Lys. 19.11—listen to both sides
Lys. 22.7—vote according to the laws

APPENDIX 4

Organization of the Gortyn Law Code

FROM GAGARIN (1982) 131

(1) 1.2–2.2: Seizure of Persons (57 lines)
(2) 2.2–10: Rape (8 lines)
(3) 2.11–16: Forcible Intercourse with a Slave (5 lines)
(4) 2.16–20: Adultery (25 lines)
(5) 2.20–45: Seduction (25 lines)
(6) 2.45–3.16: Divorce (26 lines)
(7) 3.17–37: Separation of Spouses (21 lines)
(8) 3.37–40: Special Payments to a Spouse (3 lines)
(9) 3.40–44: Separation of Slaves (4 lines)
(10) 3.44–4.8: Children of Divorced Women (19 lines)
(11) 4.8–17: Exposure of Children (9 lines)
(12) 4.18–23: Unwed Slave Mothers (5 lines)
(13) 4.23–5.1: Distribution of Property Among Women (32 lines)
(14) 5.1–9: Nonretroactivity of Law on Gifts to Women (8 lines)
(15) 5.9–54: Inheritance and Division of the Estate (45 lines)
(16) 6.1–2: Gifts to a Daughter (1 line)
(17) 6.2–46: Sale and Mortgage of Property (44 lines)
(18) 6.46–56: Ransom of Prisoners (10 lines)
(19) 6.56 (?)–7.10: Marriage of Slave Men and Free Women (10 lines)
(20) 7.10–15: Liability of a Master for his Slave (5 lines)
(21) 7.15–8.30: Marriage or Remarriage of the Heiress (70 lines)
(22) 8.30–9.1: Further Provisions Concerning Heiresses (26 lines)
(23) 9.1–24: Sale or Mortgage of Heiresses' Property (23 lines)

(24) 9.24–40: Liability of Heirs (16 lines)
(25) 9.40–43: The Son as Surety (3 lines)
(26) 9.43–10.?: Business Contracts (11+ lines)
(27) 10.?—25: Gifts of Males to Females (10+ lines)
(28) 10.25–32: Restrictions on the Sale of Slaves (7 lines)
(29) 10.33–11.23: Adoption (43 lines)
(30) 11.24–25: Amendment to Section 1 (1 line)
(31) 11.26–31: The Duty of Judges (5 lines)
(32) 11.31–45: Amendment to Section 24 (14 lines)
(33) 11.46–55: Amendment to Section 6 (9 lines)
(34) 12.1–5: Amendment to Section 27 (4 lines)
(35) 12.6–19: Amendment to Section 22 (13 lines)

APPENDIX 5

Laws in the Attic Orators

Antiphon

Antiphon 1—No laws cited.

Antiphon 5.9–10 (cf. 85)—Law about *kakourgoi* includes thieves and clothes-snatchers and provides for a *timesis*—substantive and procedural.

Antiphon 5.11—Law requires that cases for homicide be tried in the open air—procedural.

Antiphon 5.13—Law on homicide allows the defendant to leave Attica after his first speech—procedural.

Antiphon 5.17—Law allows the person who provides three sureties to be released from prison before trial—procedural.

Antiphon 5.47—Law does not permit allied cities to execute people without the approval of the Athenians—procedural.

Antiphon 5.48—Law orders that the slave who has killed his master must be handed over to public officials and cannot be put to death by the victim's relatives—substantive (no procedure is mentioned to enforce the law).

Antiphon 6.4—Law banishes murderers from the city—punishment.

Antiphon 6.5—Law orders that prosecutors speak only about the charge they have brought—procedural.

Antiphon 6.36—Law bans the person accused of homicide from the Agora, etc. as soon as the charge is registered—procedural.

Antiphon 6.41–45—Law orders the *basileus* to hold three hearings (*prodikasias*) during the three months after a charge of murder is registered and to bring the case to court in the fourth month—procedural.

Lysias

Lys. 1.30–33—Law grants the right to kill a man caught with his wife or concubine kept for the purpose of free children and forbidding Areopagus to convict in such cases—substantive and procedural.

Lys. 1.49—Law grants the right to do whatever one wishes to a seducer whom he has caught—substantive (no mention of legal procedure).

Lys. 2—This is a funeral oration, not a forensic speech.

Lys. 3.42—Law about deliberate wounding (no details given other than the charge).

Lys. 3.46—Law requires that litigants stick to the issue (i.e., raised in the indictment)—procedural.

Lys. 6.52—Law bars those convicted of impiety from entering temples—substantive (denies a right).

Lys. 9.6, 9–10—Law forbids insult of an official in the *synedrion*—substantive (mention of a fine, but nothing about legal procedure).

Lys. 10.6–14—Law about slander forbids the use of the word 'murderer' (*androphonos*) and to say that someone has thrown away his shield—substantive (no mention of procedure, though the action is a *dike kakegorias*).

Lys. 10.16—Law permits the court to order confinement in the stocks as an additional punishment—procedure and punishment.

Lys. 10.17—Law commands someone to swear an oath and pledge surety or to go into exile—procedural (this is one clause from a law whose nature is unclear).

Lys. 10.18—Law permits loans of money at any rate of interest—substantive (no mention of procedure).

Lys. 10.19—Law about prostitution (only a brief excerpt given).

Lys. 10.19—Law orders double compensation—penalty.

Lys. 11—This is a summary of the preceding speech.

Lys. 12—There are no laws cited or mentioned in this speech.

Lys. 13—There are no laws cited or mentioned in this speech.

Lys. 14.5–6—Law provides that soldiers judge the case of someone who leaves his position and retreats during battle and one who does not report for duty—mainly substantive with brief mention of procedure.

Lys. 14.8—Law requires that the person who serves in the cavalry without passing a scrutiny to lose his citizen rights—substantive and penalty (no mention of procedure).

Lys. 15.11—Law states that neither a general nor a hipparch nor any other official is to have more authority than the laws—substantive (no mention of procedure).

Lys. 16—There are no laws cited or mentioned in this speech.

Lys. 17—There are no laws cited or mentioned in this speech.

Lys. 18—There are no laws cited or mentioned in this speech.

Lys. 19—There are no laws cited or mentioned in this speech.

Lys. 20—There are no laws cited or mentioned in this speech.

Lys. 21—There are no laws cited or mentioned in this speech.

Lys. 22.5–6—Law limits the joint purchase of wheat to fifty *phormoi*—substantive (no mention of procedure).

Lys. 23—There are no laws cited or mentioned in this speech.

Lys. 24—There are no laws cited or mentioned in this speech.

Lys. 25—There are no laws cited or mentioned in this speech.

Lys. 26.6—Law forbids the courts to meet on the last day of the year—procedural.

Lys. 27—There are no laws cited or mentioned in this speech.

Lys. 28—There are no laws cited or mentioned in this speech.

Lys. 29—There are no laws cited or mentioned in this speech.

Lys. 30.11–14—The litigant accuses Nicomachus of providing a law to the enemies of Cleophon requiring the Council to join in judging a case of conspiracy but implies the law was not genuine.

Lys. 31—There are no laws cited or mentioned in this speech.

Lys. 32.23—Law allows guardians to lease the estate of orphans—substantive (no procedure mentioned).

Lys. 33—This is an oration composed for delivery at Olympia.

Lys. 34—This oration appears not to have been composed for a trial in court.

Lys. fr. 97 (Carey) (cf. fr. 19)—Law provides for penalty of one thousand drachmas and a form of *atimia* for those who do not gain one-fifth of the votes in *graphe*—procedural and penalty.

Lys. fr. 178 (Carey)—Law permits the death penalty in cases of *hybris*—penalty.

Lys. fr. 228 (Carey)—Statute of limitations—procedural.

Lys. fr. 246 (Carey)—Law orders that if anyone does not look after his parent, he is to lose his rights—substantive and penalty (no mention of procedure though a *graphe kakoseos goneon* could be brought).

Lys. fr. 428 (Carey)—Law orders guardians to provide land as property for orphans—substantive (no mention of procedure).

Several fragments of Lysias, especially those found in *Lexicon* of Harpocration, name various procedures. For example, Lys. frs. 35 (Carey), 37 (Carey), 38 (Carey), 40b (Carey), 80 (Carey), 127 (Carey), 150 (Carey), 262 (Carey), 270 (Carey), 301 (Carey), 302 (Carey), 482 (Carey). One cannot, however, know from the fragment whether the passage contained a paraphrase or summary of a law or just named the procedure.

Andocides

And. 1.20—Law grants immunity to informer if his information is true, but puts him to death if false—substantive and procedural.

And. 1.33—Law imposes penalty of *atimia* on accuser who does not get one-fifth of votes and forbids entering sanctuary of Demeter and Kore—substantive and procedural.

And. 1.43–4—Law of Scamandrius forbidding torture of citizens—substantive and procedural.

And. 1.71—Decree of Isotimides forbidding those who have committed impiety and admitted their guilt to enter temples—substantive (no mention of procedure).

And. 1.73—Decree of Patrocleides—substantive.

And. 1.82—Decree ordering scrutiny of the laws—substantive.

And. 1.86—Law forbidding officials to enforce an unwritten law—procedural.

And. 1.88—Law ordering that all decisions in private suits and by arbitrators under the democracy are binding—procedural.

And. 1.88—Law orders that the laws should be enforced starting with the archonship of Eucleides—procedural.

And. 1.89—Law orders that no decree, either of the Council or Assembly, is to override a law—substantive (this was enforced by the *graphe paranomon*, but the procedure is not mentioned in the text of the statute).

And. 1.89—Law orders that no law can be directed at an individual (this would be enforced by the procedure against an inexpedient law, but the procedure is not mentioned here).

And. 1.93—Law allows Council to place defaulting tax farmer in prison—procedural.

And. 1.94—Law holds person who plans a crime and person who commits is it subject to the same procedures (mainly procedural—specifies how to proceed against offender).

And. 1.95 (cf. 101)—Law of Solon about tyranny (substantive and procedural—grants right to kill person overthrowing democracy, which implies no accusation in court).

And. 1.107—Law ordering that exiles should be restored and that disfranchised citizens should regain their rights (this law is not read out and may be an ad hoc invention to provide a precedent for Patrocleides' decree).

And. 1.111—Law of Solon orders the Council to meet in the Eleusinion on the day after the Mysteries (substantive—no mention of procedure).

And. 1.116—Law forbids anyone to place a suppliant branch in the Eleusinion during the Eleusinian Mysteries and imposes a fine of one thousand drachmas—substantive (no mention of procedure but And. 1.110 shows that it was enforced by *endeixis*).

Isocrates

Isoc. 16—No laws are cited or mentioned in this speech.

Isoc. 17—No laws are cited or mentioned in this speech.

Isoc. 18.2—Law of Archinus grants defendants a *paragraphe* when the accuser's charge violates the amnesty (procedural—bars accuser's action).

Isoc. 19—This speech was delivered before a court on Aegina.

Isoc. 20.3—Law about slander imposes a fine of five hundred drachmas—punishment (no mention of procedure).

Isaeus

Is. 1.4. Cf. 46—Laws give the right of succession to relatives—substantive.

Is. 2.13. Cf. 16, 45—Laws give the testator the right to dispose of his property as he wishes if he has no legitimate male sons—substantive.

Is. 3.35–8—Law denies a man the right to demand the return of any portion of a dowry whose value was not assessed—substantive.

Is. 3.42—Law orders man with no male children to marry daughters to his designated heirs—substantive.

Is. 3.46–7. Cf. 53—Law does not impose penalties on those who bring *eisangelia* for an heiress and do not gain one-fifth of votes—procedural.

Is. 3.58—Law orders claim for inheritance must be made five years after death of last heir—procedural.

Is. 3.64—Law requires that heiress pass into control of her next-of-kin after her father dies—substantive.

Is. 3.68—Same as 3.42.

Is. 3.76—Laws required that legitimate daughter be introduced to phratry—substantive.

Is. 4.14. Cf. 17.—Law orders that for a will to be valid the testator must be in his right mind—substantive.

Is. 6.3—Law requires posthumously adopted son to make formal claim in court—procedural.

Is. 6.3—Law allows any Athenian to lay claim to an inheritance—substantive and procedural.

Is. 6.9—Same as 4.14.

Is. 6.25—Law gives equal share to all legitimate sons—substantive.

Is. 6.44—Law does not allow adopted son to return to his natural family unless he leaves a son in the house of his adoptive father—substantive.

Is. 6.47—Laws orders that no *nothos* or *nothe* have rights to cult or property of their family—substantive.

Is. 6.63—Law orders that if someone has a natural son after adopting one, both are to inherit equally—substantive.

Is. 7.19—Law provides that if a brother by the same father dies without issue, his estate is shared by surviving sister and any nephew born from another sister—substantive.

Is. 7.20—Law grants rights of inheritance to males and children of males descended from same persons even though their relationship to the deceased is more remote—substantive.

Is. 7.22—Law grants right of inheritance to relatives on the mother's side specifying the order of succession in absence of cousins or their children on the father's side—substantive.

Is. 8.31—Same as 10.12—substantive.

Is. 8.32. Cf. 34—Law orders children to support parents—substantive.

Is. 10.2—Law grants the right to dispose of property as one wishes—substantive.

Is. 10.10—Laws forbids child or woman to make contract for more than a *medimnos* of barley—substantive.

Is. 10.12—Law orders sons to obtain possession of estate of *epikleros* two years after reaching maturity—substantive.

Is. 10.13—Same as 3.42.

Is. 11.1–3. Cf. 4, 11—Law of inheritance grants rights to relatives in a fixed order—substantive (no mention of procedure).

Is. 11.23–25—Law about adjudicating claims to inherit—procedural.
Is. 11.27–28—Laws about suits against guardians—vague.
Is. 11.46—Law requires that if there is a conviction for perjury, the entire case must be heard again—procedural.

Aeschines

Aeschines 1.3—Laws forbid a man who has led a shameful life to speak before the people—substantive (no mention of procedure).
Aeschines 1.9—Law prescribes when free boys can go to school—substantive (no mention of procedure).
Aeschines 1.9—Law provides official to supervise children in school and to regulate slave attendants—substantive (no mention of procedure).
Aeschines 1.10—Law forbids teachers to open schools and athletic instructors to open gymnasia before sunrise and orders them to close before sunset—substantive (no mention of procedure).
Aeschines 1.10—Law regulates Mouseia and Hermaia—substantive (no mention of procedure).
Aeschines 1.10—Law regulates meetings of boys and cyclic choruses—substantive (no mention of procedure).
Aeschines 1.11—Law prescribes age of *choregoi*—substantive (no mention of procedure).
Aeschines 1.13–14—Law provides for *graphe* if a boy is let out for hire—substantive and procedural.
Aeschines 1.13–14—Law frees son who has been prostituted by his father from the duty to support him in old age but still requires him to bury him and perform rites—substantive (no mention of procedure).
Aeschines 1.14—Law provides heavy penalties for someone who panders for a free boy or woman—substantive and penalties (no mention of procedure).
Aeschines 1.15—Law provides *graphe* and *timema* if anyone commits *hybris* against man or woman, free person, or slave—substantive and procedural.
Aeschines 1.18–20. Cf. 40, 72—Law forbids anyone who has been a prostitute from becoming an archon, priest, *synegoros*, and from holding any office, be it elective or filled by lot, serving as ambassador or herald, and from addressing the Council and Assembly and provides *graphe hetaireseos*—mainly substantive with procedure and penalties mentioned very briefly.
Aeschines 1.23—Law orders *proedroi* to hold discussion of religious matters, heralds, embassies, and secular business after the sacrifice and prayers, then to invite 'whoever wishes to speak.'—substantive (no mention of procedure though a *graphe proedrike* could be brought).
Aeschines 1.28–32. Cf. 154—Law orders that if anyone speaks in the Assembly after beating his father or mother, failing to provide them support, not performing military service, throwing away his shield, acting as prostitute, or squandering

patrimony, anyone can bring a *dokimasia*—primarily substantive with brief mention of procedure.

Aeschines 1.33–4—Law orders one tribe to keep order at meetings of Assembly—substantive (no mention of procedure).

Aeschines 1.79—Law prescribes type of ballots to be used in court—procedural.

Aeschines 1.87—Law punishes those who give or receive bribes with death—penalty.

Aeschines 1.113—Law about thieves—punishment alone given.

Aeschines 1.138—Law forbids slaves to exercise in *palaistra* and allows free men to do so—substantive (no mention of procedure).

Aeschines 1.139—Law forbids slaves to be lovers (*erastai*) of free boys; those who do so will suffer fifty lashes—substantive and penalty (no mention of procedure).

Aeschines 1.158—Law orders archon to protect orphans—substantive (no mention of procedure).

Aeschines 1.160—*Graphe hetaireseos*. See above.

Aeschines 1.183—Law forbids women who have been seduced to wear fine clothes or attend sacrifices and grants men right to strip clothes from women who do either—substantive (no mention of procedure).

Aeschines 1.184—Law orders that procurers be prosecuted on public charge and if convicted put to death—substantive, procedural, penalty.

Aeschines 1.188—Law forbids those 'of impure body' to hold priesthood selected by lot—substantive (no procedure mentioned).

Aeschines 2.87—Law requires that the successful litigant in cases of unwilling homicide must swear an oath that the judges decided truly and justly and that he said nothing false and if he did not, that he and his household be cursed—procedural.

Aeschines 2.95—Law does not permit those elected by the Assembly to resign from office in the Council—substantive (no mention of procedure).

Aeschines 3.2—Law requires the oldest to speak first in the Assembly—substantive (no mention of procedure).

Aeschines 3.11 (cf. 31, 36)—Law forbids the award of crowns to officials who have not yet passed their *euthynai*—substantive (no mention of procedure though a *graphe paranomon* could be brought against a decree proposing such honors).

Aeschines 3.13–22. Cf. 29—Law orders officials to serve after passing scrutiny (*dokimasia*) and to submit accounts—substantive and procedural.

Aeschines 3.32–5. Cf. 205—Law permits proclamation of crowns in Council and Assembly and nowhere else—substantive (no mention of procedure).

Aeschines 3.34–6. Cf. 47. Law about the Dionysia allows proclamation of crowns in the theater if the Assembly so votes—substantive (no mention of procedure).

Aeschines 3.38—Law orders Thesmothetai to inspect the laws for contradictions and to submit laws contradicting each other to the Assembly—substantive (no mention of procedure).

Aeschines 3.44—Law forbids the announcement of manumissions in the theater, penalty of *atimia* for heralds—substantive (no mention of procedure).

Aeschines 3.46—Law requires that crowns announced in the theater be dedicated to Athena—substantive (no mention of procedure).

Aeschines 3.50—Law forbids false statements in decrees—substantive (no mention of procedure though a *graphe paranomon* could be brought against a decree containing false statements).

Aeschines 3.158—Law forbids those who have overturned boat through negligence in strait near Salamis to be ferrymen—substantive (no mention of procedure).

Aeschines 3.175–76—Law of Solon assigns same penalties to the person who does not report for duty, deserts his post or is a coward and provides public actions—substantive, procedural, penalties.

Aeschines 3.249—Law orders assurance of title for all sales—substantive (no mention of procedure).

Lycurgus

Lycurg. *Leocr.* 27—Law imposes severe penalties on those who transport grain to ports other than Athens—substantive and penalty.

Lycurg. *Leocr.* 102—Law orders rhapsodes to recite Homer at the Panathenaea—substantive (no mention of procedure).

Lycurg. *Leocr.* 120–21—Gives the terms of a decree passed during the Peloponnesian War (413–404) imposing the death penalty on those who moved to Decelea and gave citizens the right to arrest any Athenian caught returning from the city. This would probably have been a *nomos* if it was passed after 403—substantive and procedural.

Hyperides

Hyp. *Lyc.* fr. 3—Law about *synegoroi* in court—procedural.

Hyp. *Phil.* 3—Law forbids defamation or insulting songs about Harmodius and Aristogeiton—substantive (no mention of procedure).

Hyp. *Phil.* 4—Law about *Proedroi*—no details.

Hyp. *Ath.* 13—Law makes unjust agreements nonbinding—substantive.

Hyp. *Ath.* 14—Law forbids false statements in the Agora—substantive.

Hyp. *Ath.* 15—Law requires seller of slaves to declare physical defect—substantive.

Hyp. *Ath.* 16—Law declaring children of betrothed woman are legitimate—substantive.

Hyp. *Ath.* 17—Law allows men to make wills except when affected by old age, sickness, or insanity, or under influence of women, or held in prison, or under constraint—substantive (no mention of procedure).

Hyp. *Ath.* 22—Law makes master liable for damage caused by slaves—substantive.

Hyp. *Ath.* 29, 33—Law forbids metics to leave Attica in wartime—procedural (mentions *endeixis* and *apagoge*) and substantive.

Hyp. *Eux.* 7–8—Law provides the procedure of *eisangelia* against those who subvert the democracy, meet anywhere for the purpose of subverting the democracy, forms a political club, or betrays a city, ship, land or naval force, or as a politician (*rhetor*) does not give the best advice because he has accepted gifts—mostly substantive; procedure only named.

Hyp. *D.* 24—Laws set penalties for those taking bribes—penalty.

Hyp. *Epit.*—This is a funeral oration, not a forensic speech.

Hyperides *Against Diondas* p. 8, lines 3–5 (Carey et al.)—Law forbids anyone to serve in court before the age of thirty—procedural.

Hyp. *Against Timandrus* 138r, lines 3–11 (Tchernetska et al.)—Law forbids guardians to lease property (or orphans) for their own benefit and orders them to register the property with the archon—substantive (no mention of procedure though a *graphe orphanon kakoseos* could be brought)

Hyp. *Against Timandrus* 138v, lines 17–21 (Tchernetska et al.)—The speaker states that the law requires that orphans who are siblings be brought up together and in the place where they would best be raised. The first phrase may, however, only be the speaker's interpretation of the second phrase, which was a general provision in the law (see Rubinstein [2009])—substantive (no mention of procedure though a *graphe orphanon kakoseos* could be brought).

Demosthenic Corpus—Public Speeches

D. 18.102–4—Law of Demosthenes compels rich to pay their fair share, stops oppression of the poor, and ends payment by contributors—substantive (no mention of procedure).

D. 18.121—Law allows awards made by the Assembly to be announced in the Theater of Dionysus—substantive (no mention of procedure).

D. 18.170—Law orders the herald to ask who wishes to speak in the Assembly—substantive (no mention of procedure).

D. 18.224—Law does not allow the same charge to be brought twice about the same facts—procedural.

D. 19.70—Law orders the herald to pronounce the curse at meetings of the Council and Assembly—substantive (no mention of procedure).

D. 19.126—Law imposes the death penalty for going on an embassy after resigning—substantive and penalty.

D. 19.286—A decree of Timarchus imposes the death penalty on those who transport arms or naval equipment to Philip—substantive and penalty.

D. 20.8—Law grants an exemption from liturgies every other year—substantive (no mention of procedure).

D. 20.9—Law prohibits false statements in the marketplace—substantive (no mention of procedure).

D. 20.18, 27–8—Laws do not allow for any exemptions from the trierarchy and *eisphora*—substantive (no mention of procedure).

D. 20.89, 93—Law grants a public action against an inexpedient law and requires that one must rescind the old law before proposing a new law on the same subject—substantive and procedural.

D. 20.94—Law about enacting new legislation—substantive (no mention of procedure).

D. 20.96—Law makes all awards granted by the people valid—substantive.

D. 20.100, 135—Law imposes harsh penalties on those who make a promise to the Assembly and do not fulfill it—substantive and penalty (no mention of procedure).

D. 20.102—Law of Solon grants the right to give one's property to anyone provided that he does not have legitimate sons—substantive (no mention of procedure).

D. 20.104—Law of Solon prohibits slander of the dead—substantive (no mention of procedure).

D. 20.147—Law does not allow one to bring the same charge twice—procedural.

D. 20.152—Law does not allow one to serve as a public advocate more than once—procedural.

D. 20.155—Law forbids a court from imposing more than one punishment for a single offense—procedural.

D. 20.157–58—Law forbids those accused of murder from religious ceremonies and the Agora—procedural or penalty.

D. 20.158—Law grants the right to kill in certain circumstances and makes the killer free from ritual pollution—substantive (no mention of procedure).

D. 20.159—Decree of Demophantus gives same rewards to someone who kills a tyrant as were given to Harmodius and Aristogeiton—substantive (no mention of procedure).

D. 20.167—Law imposes the death penalty on those who debases the currency—substantive and penalty (no mention of procedure).

The speech was delivered in a case brought against the law of Leptines, which is quoted and discussed in several passages. The main provision of the law bans exemptions from liturgies (2, 55, 160) but makes an exception for the descendants of Harmodius and Aristogeiton (128, 160). Anyone who asks for an exemption is to be punished with loss of rights and confiscation of property (156). The procedures of *endeixis* and *apagoge* can be used against those convicted of this crime (156). The law contains both substantive and procedural features.

D. 21.9—Law orders a meeting of the Assembly after the Dionysia about the administration of the Archon and about offenses committed in regard to the festival—mostly procedural.

D. 21.10–11. Cf. 35.—Law forbids anyone to use force against debtors in default or others during the Dionysia and grants the right to bring *probolai*—substantive and procedural.

D. 21.43 (cf. 35)—Law imposes a simple penalty for damage done against one's will, double penalty for damage done willingly—substantive and penalty.

D. 21.43—Laws about homicide impose death or permanent exile and confiscation of property for deliberate homicide, but provide for the possibility of pardon for homicide against one's will—penalties.

D. 21.44—Law about the private suit for ejectment imposes an additional fine paid to the Treasury—penalty.

D. 21.44—Law imposes an additional fine paid to the penalty for theft with violence—penalty.

D. 21.45–6, 48—Law allows public actions for *hybris*—substance and procedure.

D. 21.56–7—Law forbids chorus leaders to issue summons to dancers or to order them to sit down during a festival—substantive and penalty.

D. 21.93–94—Law about arbitrators—procedural.

D. 21.107, 113—Law about gifts (the law is not summarized or paraphrased).

D. 21.175—Law allows for *probolai* against those who seize defaulting debtors during the Mysteries—substantive and procedural.

D. 22.5—Law allows the Assembly to vote honors for the Council—substantive (no mention of procedure).

D. 22.8–12—Law forbids honors for the Council when it has not had triremes constructed—substantive (no mention of procedure though a *graphe paranomon* could be brought against such a proposal).

D. 22.21, 30—Law forbids male prostitutes to speak and move proposals (i.e., in the Council and Assembly)—substantive (no procedure mentioned though the *dokimasia rhetoron* could be used).

D. 22.33—Law forbids the person who owes money to the Treasury to speak and move proposals—substantive (no procedure mentioned though a *graphe paranomon* could be brought against the proposer).

D. 22.73—Law prohibits prostitutes from entering sanctuaries—substantive (no procedure mentioned).

D. 23.24 (cf. 215)—Law provides that the Areopagus Council judge cases of homicide, deliberate wounding, arson, and poisoning—mainly concerned with jurisdiction of the Areopagus with no mention of procedures.

D. 23.31—Law gives the Thesmothetai the power to execute those who have gone into exile after a conviction for murder and return to Attica—jurisdiction of Thesmothetai and procedure.

D. 23.33 (cf. 216)—Law forbids mistreatment or accepting blood money from man accused of murder—substantive (no procedure mentioned).

D. 23.37–43—Law forbids the killing of a convicted murderer in exile and imposes the same penalty as for an Athenian citizen; the Ephetai judge—substantive, jurisdiction, and procedural.

D. 23.44–49—Law forbids anyone from pursuing or arresting a man in exile on a charge of unwilling homicide and punishes those who violate this with the same penalty as if he had done this in Athenian territory—substantive and penalty (no procedure mentioned).

D. 23.51—Law forbids private suits against those who denounce an exile who has returned (i.e., to Attica)—substantive and procedural.

D. 23.53–61—Law allows killing in certain circumstances (in an athletic contest, in battle in ignorance, catching someone on top of his wife or female relative, when robbing goods, etc.)—substantive (no mention of procedure).

D. 23.62—Law forbids anyone to repeal or alter homicide laws under penalty of loss of rights and confiscation of property—substantive and penalty (no mention of procedure).

D. 23.67–68—Law requires that those who bring a charge of homicide before the Areopagus swear an oath of destruction on themselves and their families and perform a sacrifice—procedural.

D. 23.69—Law requires that officials carry out the punishment of those convicted of homicide—procedural.

D. 23.69—Law allows the defendant in a case of homicide to leave Attica and go into exile after the first speech—procedural.

D. 23.72 (cf. 37.59)—Law orders men convicted of involuntary homicide to remain in exile until one of the victim's relatives grants pardon and a purificatory sacrifice is performed—penalty and procedural.

D. 23.76—Law allows for proceedings against inanimate objects before the Prytaneum in cases of murder—mainly procedural.

D. 23.77–78—Law allows for trial at Phreatto of those in exile on a charge of involuntary homicide when charged with another murder—procedural.

D. 23.80—Law permits *apagoge* to prison against murderers—procedural.

D. 23.82–3—Law allows kin to take up to three hostages in cases of homicide until they are tried or surrender the guilty person—procedural.

D. 23.86 (cf. 218)—Law forbids the enactment of a law aimed at one person. Same as the laws at D. 24.59 and And. 1.86—substantive.

D. 23.87 (cf. 219)—Law requires that no decree be more valid than a law. Same as the laws at D. 24.30 and And. 1.89—substantive.

D. 23.92—Law provides that decrees of the Council are to remain in effect for one year only—substantive.

D. 24. 17–19, 24–25—Law prescribes the method of legislation (mostly substantive, but the possibility of bringing a public action against those who violate the provisions is mentioned at 18).

D. 24.18—Law orders that all proposals for new legislation be placed in front of the Eponymous Heroes for anyone to see, then orders that the same law apply to all citizens equally, and in addition to repeal any laws contrary to it—substantive (no procedure mentioned, although there was a procedure for repealing laws).

D. 24.29—Law about festivals (no details—probably the same as the law at D. 21.10–11).

D. 24.30—Law orders that no decree is superior to a law. Same laws at D. 23.87 and And. 1.89—substantive.

D. 24.32–34—Law forbids anyone to propose a law in conflict with existing laws unless the opposing law is first rescinded—substantive (although there is a procedure for rescinding laws).

D. 24.40—Law orders that all laws are effective from the day they are enacted unless a specific provision states they are to go into effect later—substantive (no mention of procedure).

D. 24.46—Law forbids anyone to make proposals or the *proedroi* to hold a discussion about the disenfranchised or debtors to the Treasury unless six thousand vote—substantive (no mention of procedure).

D. 24.52—Law forbids anyone to supplicate the Council or Assembly about a court decision—procedural.

D. 24.55—Law forbids anyone to bring the same charge against the same person twice—procedural. Same as the law at D. 20.147; 38.16.

D. 24.56–7—Law declares invalid all judgments rendered under the Thirty. Same as the law at And. 1.88—procedural.

D. 24.59—Law forbids legislation aimed at a single individual. Same as the laws at And. 1.89 and D. 23.86—substantive (no mention of procedure, although a *graphe* against an inexpedient law could be used in this case).

D. 24.64—Law of Timocrates that those convicted should remain in prison until they pay their fines—procedural.

D. 24.65—Laws order that *kakourgoi* who confess their crimes are punished without trial. Same as law at Antiphon 5.9–10—procedural, although another part of the law concerns substance.

D. 24.83—Different laws call for fines to be doubled or increased tenfold—punishment.

D. 24.113—Law of Solon allows the arrest of a thief caught stealing more than fifty drachmas during daytime and to kill a thief caught at night—substantive.

D. 24.114—Law of Solon enacts death penalty for theft of items worth more than ten drachmas from Lyceum, Academy, Cynosarges or gymnasia, or harbors—substantive and punishment (no mention of procedure).

D. 24.212—Law prescribes death penalty for those who debase currency. Same as law at D. 20.167—substantive and punishment (no mention of procedure).

[D]. 53.2—Law grants three-quarters of property reported in *apographe* to accuser—procedural.

[D.] 53.11—Law makes the person who has not repaid loan for ransom the property of the lender until he pays—substantive (no mention of procedure).

[D.] 53.15—Law provides action for false summons—procedural.

[D.] 53.27—Law orders the confiscation of property of person who guarantees payment to the state and does not make this payment—substantive and penalty (no mention of procedure though the *apographe* could be used).

D. 57.4—Law forbids hearsay evidence—procedural.

D. 57.30—Law forbids anyone to slander working in the Agora (or for working in the Agora—substantive (no procedure mentioned, although possibly a *dike kakegorias* could be brought).

D. 57.31—Law forbids foreigners to do business in the Agora—substantive (no mention of procedure).

D. 57.32—Law of Aristophon; probably the law requiring candidates for citizenship to have two citizen parents—substantive.

D. 57.32—Law about idleness—too vague.

D. 57.61—Law requires demesmen to take an oath before casting votes for review of citizenship rolls—this could be considered substantive or procedural depending on how one views the vote.

[D.] 58.5–6. Cf. 20—Law forbids illegal out-of-courts settlements in public cases—procedural.

[D.] 58.10–11—Law forbids forbidding malicious prosecutions against merchants and shipowners and provides procedures of *apagoge* and *endeixis*—procedural.

[D.] 58.14–5—Law allows *endeixis* against those in debt to state, Athena, other gods or Eponymous Heroes—procedural.

[D.] 58.15—Law forbids public debtors to exercise public rights—procedural.

[D.] 58.17—Law orders that descendants inherit liability for debts owed to the state—substantive (no procedure mentioned though *apographe* could be used).

[D.] 58.19–20—Law imposes penalty of half sum assessed for damages to be paid to the Treasury for falsely asserting freedom of a slave—penalty.

[D.] 58.21–2 (cf. 49, 50)—Law requires that one is a public debtor from the day he incurs the fine whether he has been inscribed or not—substantive (no mention of procedure).

[D.] 58.50—Law orders that whatever portion of a public debt has been paid should be erased from the public record—substantive.

[D.] 58.51—Law requires that public actions for nonregistration against those who have not paid their debts and have their names erased—procedural.

[D.] 59.4—Law allows the excess in the budget to be devoted to military purposes during wartime—substantive.

[D.] 59.17—Law forbids marriage between Athenian citizens and foreigners or for foreigners to have children with Athenians, provides for a *graphe* in such cases and establishes penalty of enslavement for those convicted on this charge—substantive, procedural, and penalty.

[D.] 59.26–27—Law forbids those who have lost citizen rights to testify—procedural.

[D.] 59.27—Law exempts those who have bought the contract to collect the 2% tax from military service—substantive (no mention of procedure).

[D.] 59.40—Law allows anyone to protect a free person who is being seized as a slave—substantive and procedural.

[D.] 59.52—Law requires that a man who divorces his wife, he must return her dowry or pay interest of 1.5% a month and allows her guardian to bring an action at the Odeum—substantive and procedural.

[D.] 59.52—Law provides for a *graphe* against the person who gives a foreign woman in marriage to an Athenian citizen—substantive and procedural.

[D.] 59.66—Law allows the person who has been falsely imprisoned as a *moichos* to bring a public charge. If the court determines that he was a *moichos*, the person who caught him can inflict punishment without a knife—substantive, procedural, and punishment.

[D.] 59.67—Law does not permit the arrest of someone as a *moichos* when he has sexual relations with a prostitute—substantive and procedural.

[D.] 59.75—Law requires that the wife of the *basileus* be a virgin at her marriage—substantive (no mention of procedure).

[D.] 59.85–7—Law forbids a woman who has been seduced to participate in public sacrifices and allows anyone to administer physical punishment (except death) to those who do—substantive and punishment (no mention of procedure).

[D.] 59.89—Law allows *graphe paranomon* to be brought against grants of citizenship—procedural.

[D.] 59.89–90—Law does not permit the Assembly to grant citizenship to anyone who has not performed services for Athens—substantive (no mention of procedure).

[D.] 59.90—Law requires that citizenship be granted only when six thousand vote by secret ballot. Rules about method of conducting vote substantive (no procedure mentioned).

[D.] 59.92—Law forbids those who become citizens by decree to be one of the nine archons or to become a priest but allows their legitimate descendants to hold these offices—substantive (no procedure mentioned).

[D.] 59.113—Law provides for dowries—very general and vague.

Demosthenic corpus—Private Speeches

D. 27.17—Law orders that the person who does not return a dowry must pay interest of nine obols a month—substantive (no mention of procedure).

D. 27.58—Law permits guardians to lease the property of orphans—substantive (no mention of procedure).

D. 28—No laws are cited or mentioned in this speech.

D. 29.36—Law makes the person who helped someone to embezzle funds liable for theft even if he does not have the stolen funds in his possession—substantive (no procedure mentioned though the *dike klopes* would probably apply).

D. 29.57—Same as law at D. 27.58.

D. 30—No laws are cited or discussed in this speech.

D. 31—No laws are cited or discussed in this speech.

D. 32.1 (cf. 23)—Law provides actions before maritime courts in cases concerning shipments to and from Athens for shipowners and merchants (procedural).

D. 33.1—Same as law at 32.1 but adding the clause about imprisonment until judgment paid—procedural.

D. 33.2—Law provides an action for *paragraphe*—procedural.

[D.] 33.27—Law states that contracts of personal security are valid only for a year—substantive (no procedure mentioned).

[D.] 34.4 (cf. 42)—Law allows for *paragraphe* when there is no contract for commerce in Athens or to Athens—procedural.

[D.] 34.37—Law provides for severe penalties if anyone resident at Athens transports grain to somewhere other than Athens—substantive and penalty (no procedure mentioned).

D. 35.50–51—Same as law at 34.37 but adds that those who lend are also subject to penalties—penalty (no procedure mentioned).

D. 36.23–5—Law does not allow anyone to bring an action in a case where a release has been granted—procedural.

D. 36.26–7—Law does not allow an action to be brought more than five years after the offense—procedural.

D. 37.1—Law grants an action for *paragraphe* when a release has been granted. Same as law at D. 36.23–25—procedural.

D. 37.18, 21—Law does not allow another suit to be brought on the same charge after the court makes a decision—procedural.

D. 37.33—Law grants an action for *paragraphe* when the case is brought before the wrong magistrate—procedural.

D. 37.35–6—Law provides an action if anyone ejects someone from his work area, makes an armed attack or makes a cutting inside the boundaries—mainly substantive (brief mention of procedure without details).

D. 37.58–59—Law does not allow further prosecution in a case of homicide once pardon has been granted—procedural.

D. 38.1—Law allows for a *paragraphe* in a case where a release has been granted. Same as law at D. 36.23–5 and D. 37.1—procedural.

D. 38.16—Law requires that only one action can be brought against a single person for the same offense. Same as law at D. 37.18, 21—procedural.

D. 38.16 (cf. 27)—Law requires that suits regarding orphans be brought within five years (possibly the same as law at D. 36.26–7)—procedural.

D. 39.39—Law gives parents the right to disinherit children—substantive (no procedure mentioned).

D. 40.19—Law grants legitimate sons the right to their mother's dowry—substantive (no procedure mentioned).

D. 40.50—Law forbids anyone to speak ill of the dead—substantive (no procedure mentioned).

D. 41.7, 10–11—Law denies an action to those who have pledged property as security and their heirs—substantive and procedural.

D. 42.1. Cf. 7, 26, 28—Law orders that person involved in *antidosis* present inventory three days after taking oath—legal procedure in *antidosis*.

D. 42.4. Cf. 5, 28—Laws allow *antidosis* every year—procedural.

D. 42.18, 23—Law makes mines exempt from inventory in *antidosis*—substantive and procedural.

D. 42.27—Law makes son the owner of his mother's dowry after her husband's death—substantive.

D. 42.30—Law provides that private agreements are binding. Same as law at 56.2—substantive.

D. 43.7 (cf. 17)—Law requires summons given to party in possession of estate—procedural.

D. 43.10—Law about number of ballot boxes at trial for inheritance—procedural.

D. 43.19—Laws about marriage—vague.

D. 43.27 (cf. 50, 78)—Law about succession and heirs (probably same as law at D. 44.12)—substantive.

D. 43.41—Laws about adoption—vague.

D. 43.59—Law about duties of relatives—vague.

D. 43.63–65—Law orders relatives to perform funerals—substantive.

D. 43.72—Law forbids anyone to dig up sacred olive trees—substantive.

D. 44.12 (cf. 2, 14)—Law grants right of succession to nearest kin in the male line when there are no children—substantive (no mention of procedure).

D. 44.49—Law states that the children born of a woman who has been betrothed by her father, brother, or grandfather are legitimate—substantive (no mention of procedure).

D. 44.55—Law does not allow hearsay evidence—procedural.

D. 44.64 (cf. 67)—Law forbids the person who is adopted to adopt a son—substantive.

D. 44.68—Law states that all those who had not been adopted when Solon became archon have the right to bequeath property as they wish—substantive (no mention of procedure).

D. 45.44—Law requires that all testimony be given in writing—procedural.

[D.] 46.7—Law does not allow hearsay evidence from a man who is alive but only from one who is dead. Same as law at D. 44.55 with an additional clause—procedural.

[D]. 46.7—Law allows hearsay evidence in written form from one who is sick or abroad; the absent person and the person submitting testimony are both liable to the private action for false testimony—procedural.

[D.] 46.9–10—Law forbids giving evidence on one's own behalf—procedural.

[D.] 46.10—Law provides an action for false testimony against those who do not testify according to the laws—procedural.

[D.] 46.12—Law forbids passing a law about an individual. Same laws as at And. 1.86, D. 23.86 and D. 24.59—substantive.

[D.] 46.15—Law forbidding disposing of property by will if one has legitimate children—substantive.

[D.] 46.16—Law forbids anyone who is not of sound mind to dispose of his property (this is the same law as that at Is. 2.13)—substantive.

[D.] 46.18—Law about marriage—very vague.

[D.] 46.19–20—Law indicates who can act as guardians—substantive.

[D.] 46.22—Law requires that there be *epidikasia* about citizen heiresses before the archon and about metic heiresses before the polemarch—procedural.

[D.] 46.25–6—Law makes a will valid if the children die before reaching the age of manhood—substantive.

[D.] 46.26—Law provides an action against those who subvert the legal system—procedural.

[D.] 47.1—Law allows suits for false testimony. Same as law at D. 46.10—procedural.

[D.] 47.1—Law allows suits for suborning perjury—procedural.

[D.] 47.8—Law orders that testimony must be made in writing. Same as the law at D. 45.44—procedural.

[D.] 47.21–22—Law of Periander creating symmories orders trierarchs to receive list of equipment owed to the state—substantive.

[D.] 47.21—Law commands trierarchs to collect equipment belonging to the state from those who hold it—substantive.

[D.] 47.70, 72—Law permits only relatives and masters of slaves to bring an action for homicide—procedural.

D. 48.11—Law about agreements—no details are given; this may be same law as at D. 56.2.

D. 48.31—Law about the summons made for counter-claims in inheritance—procedural.

D. 48.56—Law makes the acts of a man acting under the influence of a woman invalid—Same as law at D. 46.16.

[D.] 49.56—Law allows suits for suborning perjury. Same as law at D. 47.1—procedural.

[D.] 49.67—Law provides *eisangelia* against those who do not fulfill a promise made to the people—substantive and procedural.

[D.] 50.9 (cf. D. 20)—Law providing exemption for trierarchs from other liturgies—substantive (no mention of procedure).

[D.] 50.48–9—Law forbids anyone to harbor exiles condemned in Athenian courts—substantive (no mention of procedure).

[D.] 50.57—Law imposes penalty on trierarch who does not take up his duty on time—substantive and penalty (no mention of procedure).

D. 51—No laws cited or discussed in this speech.

[D.] 52.17—Law requires that an heir who is sued in court on a charge brought against his father must swear an oath—procedural.

D. 54—Several types of actions are mentioned in this speech (17–19), but no laws cited or discussed.

D. 55—No laws are cited or discussed in this speech.

D. 56.2—Law orders that all agreements willingly made are binding—substantive.

D. 56.3 and 10—Law requiring that shipowners and supercargoes sail to the ports to which they have agreed to sail—substantive (no mention of procedure).

Dinarchus

Din. 1.42—Law about trierarchs—content not discussed.

Din. 1.44—Laws forbidding traitors to enter Attica—penalty (no mention of procedure).

Din. 1.60—Laws impose double damages for suits involving money, penalty of ten times the amount for bribes—penalty.

Din. 1.71—Law orders public speakers and generals to have children according to the laws, to own land in Attica, swear standard oaths—substantive (no procedure mentioned, although might be enforced through the *dokimasia* procedure).

Din. 1.71—Laws about oaths at trial—procedural.

Din. 2.13—Laws about punishment of public debtors—penalty.

Din. 2.14—Law ordering herald to make prayers at the start of Assembly meetings—substantive (no mention of procedure).

Din. 2.17—Same as law at 1.60.

Din. 3.4—Law states that any one who breaks an agreement with another citizen is subject to legal action—substantive and procedural.

APPENDIX 6

Categories of Atimoi *Listed in the Decree of Patrocleides (And. 1.73–76)*

A. State-debtors: (1) those owing money for *euthynai*, (2) those owing money for ejectment suits, (3) public actions, or (4) fines, (5) those who did not make payments on public contracts, (6) those who were sureties to the state and did not make payment before the ninth prytany.

B. Those who lost civic rights, but retained property: (1) those convicted of theft, (2) those convicted of bribes, [military offenses] (3) those who left their position in battle, (4) were convicted of desertion, (5) cowardice, (6) desertion from the fleet, or (7) throwing away their shield, (8) those convicted three times for false testimony, (9) or falsely witnessing a summons, or (10) guilty of mistreating their parents.

C. Those who lost some but not all civic rights: (1) soldiers who remained in Athens under the Four Hundred (loss of right to speak in Assembly or serve in Council), (2) those who lost right to bring public case or an indictment, (3) those forbidden to sail to the Hellespont, or (4) to Ionia or (5) to enter the Agora.

APPENDIX 7

Issues in the Orators

Aeschines

Aeschin. 1—fact (Did Timarchus violate the law about the scrutiny of public speakers by (1) being a male prostitute, (2) squandering his inheritance and (3) accepting bribes?)

Aeschin. 2—fact (Did Aeschines betray his duty as ambassador by giving bad advice, making false reports and accepting gifts from Philip?)

Aeschin. 3—fact and law (Did Ctesiphon pass an illegal decree? The decree violates three laws, the first about awarding crowns to officials who have not undergone their *euthynai,* the second about announcing crowns in the theater of Dionysus, and the third forbidding false statements in decrees. There are legal issues involved in the first and second charges).

Andocides

And. 1—fact (Did Andocides participate in the mutilation of the Herms and the parody of the Mysteries?) and law (Was Andocides covered by the Amnesty of 403?).

And. 2—Petition to the Council.

And. 3—Speech is a post-Classical forgery—see Harris (2000b).

And. 4—Speech is a post-Classical forgery.

Antiphon

Antiphon 1—fact (Did the accuser's stepmother kill Philoneos?)

Antiphon 2—fact (Did the defendant kill the victim?)

Antiphon 3—law (The fact that the defendant's javelin caused the victim's death is not disputed. The issue is whether he or the victim is responsible).

Antiphon 4—law (The fact that the defendant's blow caused the death of the victim is not disputed. The issue is whether the victim's provocation is exculpatory).

Antiphon 5—fact (Did Euxitheus kill Herodes?)

Antiphon 6—fact (Was the defendant responsible for the death of the chorister?)

Demosthenes—Private Speeches

D. 27—fact (Did Aphobus embezzle ten talents from Demosthenes' estate?)

D. 28—fact (Did Gylon owe money to the Treasury?)

D. 29—fact (Did Phano give false testimony?)

D. 30—fact (Did Aphobus divorce the sister of Onetor?)

D. 31—fact (Did Onetor give Aphobus a dowry for the marriage of his sister?)

D. 32—(paragraphe) fact (Was there an obligation between Demo and Zenothemis? The charge in the suit of Zenothemis is that Demo has the cargo belonging to Hegestratus, to whom Zenothemis lent money.)

D. 33—(paragraphe) fact (Is there an obligation of the speaker to Apaturius? Charge in the suit of Apaturius is that the speaker was surety for Parmeno and owes him money for the judgment in his lawsuit.)

D. 34—(paragraphe) fact (Did Phormio pay money to Lampis? A legal issue about the circumstances in which a *paragraphe* can be brought is discussed at 3–4.)

D. 35—(paragraphe) fact (Does an obligation exist between Androcles and Lacritus? Charge in the suit of Androcles is that Lacritus owes him money because he inherited Artemo's estate and Artemo owed him money.)

D. 36—(paragraphe) fact (Did Apollodorus give Phormio a release for the bank and did he bring the charge after the statute of limitations had expired? Charge in the suit of Apollodorus is that Phormio embezzled money from Pasion's bank, which Apollodorus inherited.)

[D.] 37 (paragraphe) fact (Did Pantaenetus grant Nicobulus a release? Charge in the suit of Pantaenetus is that Nicobulus caused damage by seizing his mining works.)

D. 38—(paragraphe) fact (Did Nausimachus grant Aristaechmus a release and was the suit brought after the statute of limitations expired? Charge in the suit of Nausimachus is that the heirs of Aristaechmus owe Nausimachus money he collected from the state and did not turn over to the heirs.)

D. 39—fact (Does Boeotus cause damage to Mantitheus by using his name? There may be a legal issue about the applicability of the statute about damage).

D. 40—fact (Should Mantitheus receive the portion of his father's estate which was received as his mother's dowry?)

D. 41—fact (Does Spoudias owe the plaintiff several sums of money from the estate of Polyeuctus?)

D. 42—fact (Does the property of Phaenippus exceed in value the estate of the plaintiff?)
D. 43—fact and law (Who is entitled to inherit the estate of Hagnias?)
D. 44—fact (Does the estate of Archiades belong to Aristodemus?)
D. 45—fact (Did Stephanus give false testimony that Apollodorus refused to open the original copy of Pasion's will?)
[D.] 46—Same as D. 45
[D.] 47—fact (Did Evergus and Mnesibulus give false testimony about the altercation between the trierarch and Theophemus?)
D. 48—fact (Does Olympiodorus owe money to Callistratus from the estate of Comon?)
[D.] 49—fact (Does Timotheus owe money to Pasion's bank?)
[D.] 50—fact (Does Polycles owe Apollodorus money for failing to take over his duties as trierarch?)
D. 51—Speech delivered before the Council and concerns the award of a crown.
[D.] 52—fact (Does Callippus have a right to the money left by Lycon in Pasion's bank?)
[D.] 53—fact (Did the slaves reported by Apollodorus belong to Arethusius?)
D. 54—fact (Did Conon and his son strike the first blow in their assault of Ariston?)
D. 55—fact (Did the defendant do damage to Callicles' property?)
D. 56—law (Did Dionysodorus and his partner violate their contract with Dareius and Parmeno? There is a legal issue about the interpretation of the phrase 'if the ship returns safely.')

Demosthenes—Public Speeches

D. 18—law and fact (Is Ctesiphon's decree of praise for Demosthenes illegal? There are two legal issues concerning the law about crowning officials and the law about announcing crowns at the Dionysia.)
D. 19—fact (Did Aeschines take gifts from Philip in return for betraying his duties as ambassador? There is a legal issue about the duties of ambassadors.)
D. 20—fact and law (Is the law of Leptines' inexpedient? There are two types of legal issues in the speech: (1) does the law violate any Athenian statutes? (2) did Leptines' follow the correct procedure in passing his law?)
D. 21—fact (Did Meidias commit *hybris* against Demosthenes? The fact of the assault is beyond dispute; the case concerns the nature of Meidias' intent.)
D. 22—law and fact (Did Androtion pass an illegal decree? There are several issues about the interpretation of specific statutes.)
D. 23—law and fact (Did Aristocrates pass an illegal decree? There is a legal issue about the meaning of the term *agogimos* in Aristocrates' decree for Charidemus.)
D. 24—law (Did Timocrates propose an inexpedient law?)
D. 25 and 26—Post-Classical forgeries.

D. 57—fact (Is Eubulides a member of the deme and an Athenian citizen?)
[D.] 58—fact (Does Theocrines owe money to the state?)
[D.] 59—fact (Did Neaera attempt to exercise the rights of a citizen?)

Dinarchus

The three speeches of Dinarchus were delivered at trials arising from the Harpalus affair. Since the fact of the defendant's guilt was determined by the report of the Areopagus, the accusers concentrate mainly on justifying a harsh penalty.

Hyperides

Against Lycophron—fact and law (Did Lycophron seduce the sister of Dioxippus? and was his seduction covered by the law about *eisangelia*?)
Against Philippides—law (Was the decree of Philippides illegal?)
Against Athenogenes—law (Is the contract between Athenogenes and Epicrates valid?)
For Euxenippus—law (Was Euxenippus' speech in the Assembly covered by the law about *eisangelia*?)
Against Demosthenes—This speech was delivered at a trial arising from the Harpalus affair. See under Dinarchus.

Isaeus

Isaeus 1—fact and law (Is the will of Cleonymus valid? There is a potential legal issue about the meaning of the term 'in his right mind' in the law about wills).
Isaeus 2—fact (Did Menecles legally adopt a son?)
Isaeus 3—fact (Is Phile the legitimate daughter of Pyrrhus?)
Isaeus 4—fact (Did Nicostratus adopt Chariades?)
Isaeus 5—fact (Does Leochares as surety have an obligation to hand over property?)
Isaeus 6—fact (Did Philoctemon adopt Chaerestratus? Are Antidorus and his brother legitimate?)
Isaeus 7—fact and law (Is Thrasyllus the legitimate heir of Apollodorus? There may have been a legal issue about the formal requirements for an adoption—was it necessary to be enrolled in the deme of the adopter?)
Isaeus 8—fact and law (Is the speaker the legitimate son of the daughter of Ciron and is his mother his legitimate daughter?—there may be a question about the law of succession.)
Isaeus 9—fact (Did Astyphilus adopt the opponent, did Astyphilus leave a will, did Astyphilus give his property to anyone, does the speaker have the right to inherit? That is, is he the closest relative?)

Isaeus 10—fact (Was Aristarchus II legitimately adopted by Aristarchus I?)
Isaeus 11—fact (Does Theopompus have the right to inherit the estate of Hagnias?)
Isaeus 12—fact (Is Euphiletus a member of the deme of Erchia?)

Note that the ancient hypotheses to most of these speeches state that the issue was one of fact (*stochastikon* 2, *stochasmos* 3, 4, 5, 6, 7, 9, and *pragmatike* in the case of 10 and 11).

Isocrates

Isoc. 16—fact (Did Alcibiades rob Teisias of a team of horses?)
Isoc. 17—fact (Does Pasion hold a deposit belonging to the plaintiff?)
Isoc. 18—(paragraphe) fact (Has the action been brought in violation of the Amnesty?)
Isoc. 19—fact (Does the speaker have the right to the estate of Thrasylochus?)
Isoc. 20—fact (The initial part of the speech is missing, but the main issue appears to have been, did Lochites strike the defendant?)
Isoc. 21—fact (Did Euthynus fail to return the full amount of a deposit left by Nicias?)

Lycurgus

Against Leocrates—law—The fact that Leocrates left Athens after the battle of Chaeronea is not in dispute. The issue is whether his voyage to Rhodes qualifies as treason.

Lysias

Lysias 1—fact (Did Euphiletus attempt to entrap Eratosthenes?)
Lysias 2—Epideictic speech (not relevant).
Lysias 3—The issue is mainly one of fact (did the defendant initiate violence?), but see 40–43 where the defendant discusses the meaning of the phrase deliberate wounding and appeals to previous cases tried by the Areopagus at 43.
Lysias 4—fact (Did the defendant deliberately wound the accuser?)
Lysias 5—Only a fragment of the speech remains, but the issue appears to have been one of fact and concerns with the reliability of denunciations made by slaves.
Lysias 6—fact (Did Andocides commit impiety?)
Lysias 7—fact (Did the defendant dig up the olive stump?)
Lysias 8—It is not even certain whether this speech was delivered in court.
Lysias 9—There appears to have been a legal issue involved concerning the meaning of the statute that forbids uttering slander about magistrates. The defendant appeals to the decision made by the treasurers in support of his interpretation of the law (7).

Lysias 10—This case concerns the interpretation of the law about slander. The accuser does not appear to have any precedents on his side but argues mainly from his interpretation of other statutes.

Lysias 11—Summary of the previous speech.

Lysias 12—fact (Did Eratosthenes act under compulsion when he arrested Polemarchus? And did he object to his execution?)

Lysias 13—This case mainly examines issues of fact (Under what circumstances did Agoratus denounce Dionysodorus and others?) But a legal issue is discussed in 85–87.

Lysias 14—law (Does the law about desertion and leaving one's post apply to Alcibiades?) Here the accuser admits that he is asking the court to act as lawgivers by applying the law to a new category of offenders (4).

Lysias 15—Speech written for the same case as 14.

Lysias 16—fact (Did Mantitheus serve in the cavalry under the Thirty?)

Lysias 17—fact (Did the plaintiff have a lien on the property of Erasistratus for the unpaid debt of his dead father Eraton?)

Lysias 18—Only the peroration remains, but the defendant at 13–14 cites a previous case similar to the present one where the accuser lost. This case appears, however, to be cited in support of the defendant's version of the facts.

Lysias 19—fact (Does the defendant hold property belonging to Aristophanes?)

Lysias 20—fact (What did Polystratus do during the regime of the Four Hundred?)

Lysias 21—Only the peroration remains, but the issue appears to have concerned the facts (Did the defendant receive bribes?)

Lysias 22—fact (Did the magistrates grant the grain-dealers permission to buy more than the legal amount of grain?)

Lysias 23—fact (Is Pancleon a Plataean?)

Lysias 24—fact (Is the defendant disabled?)

Lysias 25—fact (Did the defendant support the oligarchy?)

Lysias 26—fact (What did Evander do under the Thirty?)

Lysias 27—fact (Did Epicrates and his fellow envoys take bribes?)

Lysias 28—fact (Did Ergocles commit extortion?)

Lysias 29—fact (Does Philocrates have Ergocles' money in his possession?)

Lysias 30—fact (How did Nicomachus conduct himself in office?)

Lysias 31—This case is a *dokimasia* and concerns Philon's activities during the Thirty and the way he treated his mother. There may, however, have been a legal issue since the speaker says the defendant will claim that no existing law condemns what he did under the Thirty (27). The speaker asks the members of the Council to compare their own cases (34). In other words, he invites them to consider their own cases and apply the same standard that was used when their own qualifications were examined.

Lysias 32—fact (Did Diogeiton mismanage the orphans' estate?)

APPENDIX 8

Mentions of Public Service in the Attic Orators

All mentions of public service in the orators have been classified into the following categories:

1. Relevant—directly relevant to the legal charges in the plaint.
2. Character—public service is cited as evidence of good character to show that the defendant is unlikely to have committed the offenses with which he has been charged in the plaint.
3. Wealth—public service is mentioned to prove that someone is wealthy.
4. Explanation—public service is mentioned to explain some aspect of the narrative.
5. Goodwill—public service is mentioned to obtain the goodwill of the judges.

The list of public services mentioned in the orators in Hunt (2010) 279–82 is incomplete and unreliable. More seriously, Hunt does not indicate how public service is relevant to the legal charge in the speech.

Antiphon

Antiphon 1—No mention of public service.

Antiphon 2.2.12—The defendant mentions his public service to prove his good character and obedience to the law ('That's the way I am.')—character.

Antiphon 2.3.8—The accuser says that public service is not proof of innocence but of wealth and that his wealth makes him likely to have committed murder. Cf. 2.4.9—wealth.

Antiphon 3—No mention of public service.

Antiphon 4—No mention of public service.

Antiphon 5.77—The speaker's father has produced choruses and paid the *eisphora*. The speaker cites his father's public service to refute the charge that he is disloyal to Athens because he participated in the revolt of Mytilene—character.

Antiphon 6.11–15—The defendant was appointed *choregos* for the Thargelia. Because the defendant is accused of causing the death of one of the boys in his chorus, his public service is directly relevant to the legal charge—relevant.

Andocides

And. 1.132—My opponents have nominated me for public office. Andocides mentions this to prove that his opponents do not really think that he is guilty of impiety—relevant.

And. 1.141, 147–9—Andocides mentions his ancestors' service to win the court's sympathy—goodwill.

And. 1.144–45—Andocides says that he will perform services if acquitted. Andocides mentions this to provide an incentive to the court to acquit him—goodwill.

And. 2—This speech was delivered when making a request to the Council and not at a trial before a court.

Lysias

Lys. 1—No mention of public service.

Lys. 2—Funeral Oration.

Lys. 3—No mention of public service.

Lys. 4—No mention of public service.

Lys. 5—No mention of public service.

Lys. 6.46–7—The defendant Andocides should not be acquitted for his public services because he has performed none—goodwill.

Lys. 7.31—The defendant has served as a trierarch, contributed to the *eisphora*, and performed liturgies. His generosity is used to demonstrate that he has not committed the offense with which he has been charged—character.

Lys. 7.41—I have fought in many battles. It would therefore be unjust for me to lose my citizenship—this does not fit easily into any category, but emphasizes the injustice of an unfair verdict.

Lys. 8—No mention of public service.

Lys. 9—The defendant has been charged with insulting generals who enrolled him for military service. Military service is directly relevant to the legal charge—relevant.

Lys. 10.1—Lysitheides accused Theomnestus of throwing away his shield. This charge about public service is mentioned as background to the speaker's case—explanation.

Lys. 10.21—It is worse to be accused of killing one's father than of throwing away one's shield—compares two kinds of offenses.

Lys. 10.22–3—The speaker saved his shield while Theomnestus was accused of throwing his away—character.

Lys. 10.27—The speaker's father served as general many times and was never accused at his *euthynai* but was killed by the Thirty. The speaker mentions this to explain why he is bringing his charge of slander—explanation.

Lys. 11—Summary of the previous speech.

Lys. 12—The charge is against Eratosthenes for bringing about the death of Polemarchus. The service of Eratosthenes as a member of the Thirty is directly relevant to the legal charges—relevant.

Lys. 13.62–65—Agoratus' denunciations deprived Athens of men who had served as generals and performed liturgies. The public service of Agoratus' victims is mentioned to show their good character and innocence and to make his crimes appear worse—character.

Lys. 13.65—Agoratus' brother was caught sending signals to the enemy and executed by Lamachus. The brother's public service is mentioned to show that treason runs in Agoratus' family—character.

Lys. 13.70–76—Agoratus claims to have killed Phrynichus. Agoratus mentions this public service to show that he was loyal to the democracy and thus unlikely to have collaborated with the Thirty in killing Dionysodorus—character.

Lys. 13.77–79—Agoratus claims to have joined the men of Phyle who fought against the Thirty. Same reason for citing public service as in 13.70–76—character.

Lys. 14—The defendant is charged with desertion. Military service is directly relevant to the legal charge—relevant.

Lys. 15—The defendant is charged with desertion. Military service is directly relevant to the legal charge—relevant.

Lys. 16.5–8—Mantitheus says that he did not serve in the cavalry under the Thirty. His service is directly relevant to the main issue at his *dokimasia*, his qualifications for office—relevant.

Lys. 16.13—At Haliartus, Mantitheus had himself transferred from the infantry to the cavalry so that he could face danger. His service is directly relevant to the main issue at his *dokimasia*, his qualifications for office—relevant.

Lys. 16.15—Mantitheus recalls his military service in the Corinthian War, which is directly relevant to the main issue at his *dokimasia*—relevant.

Lys. 17—No mention of public service.

Lys. 18—The case concerns the confiscation of property, but the speech does not indicate why the defendant's property was subject to confiscation. If the defendant had been charged with treason, the mention of his family's public service (3–4, 21, 24) is relevant to the legal charge—relevant (?).

Lys. 19—The defendant's father was charged with holding the property of Aristophanes, who had been executed and his property seized by the state. The defendant mentions Aristophanes' public service to show that he did not have much money because he spent it all on the state (42–44)—wealth.

Lys. 19.57–59, 62–3—The defendant's father spent much money on liturgies to show that he was not the sort of person who would withhold money from the state and was thus unlikely to have committed the offense with which he was charged—character.

Lys. 20—The defendant's father has been charged with crimes associated with the regime of the Four Hundred. His public service is therefore directly relevant to the legal charges—relevant.

Lys. 20.6—The defendant's father committed no crime during his magistracy at Oropus. Public service is mentioned to show his father's good character—character.

Lys. 20.13–17—When the defendant's father was appointed to register members of the Five Thousand, he appointed over nine thousand. Public service is mentioned to show that he tried to undermine the work of the Four Hundred, which is relevant to the legal charge—relevant.

Lys. 21.1–11—The defendant provides a long list of his public services but says that they should not acquit him because of these. The speech is not complete and appears to belong to the exordium. The defendant appears to have been charged with theft of public funds (16) and bribery (21). He mentions his public service to show his good character and that therefore he did not commit the crimes with which he is charged (19–21)—character.

Lys. 22—No mention of public service.

Lys. 23—No mention of public service.

Lys. 24—No mention of public service.

Lys. 25—The charge is subverting the democracy. The defendant cites his public service to demonstrate his patriotism and thereby refute the legal charge—relevant.

Lys. 26.3–4—The accuser says that Euandrus will discuss the public service of his family in an attempt to distract the court from the charges in the *dokimasia*. The speaker says the family used public service to gain the confidence of the people in order to overthrow the democracy. The mention of public service is relevant to the legal charge—relevant.

Lys. 26.10—Euandrus served in the cavalry under the Thirty. The mention of public service is directly relevant to the legal charge—relevant.

Lys. 26.20—Those who restored the democracy have been elected as cavalry commanders, generals, and ambassadors. The point is mentioned to show that the courts take loyalty to the democracy into account at the *dokimasia*—relevant.

Lys. 27.10—Men like Epicrates were poor during the peace but now have enough money to pay the *eisphora*, perform dramas, and live in big houses. Public service is mentioned as evidence of wealth—wealth.

Lys. 28.3—When you are oppressed by the *eisphora*, you should not be indulgent to those who embezzle public funds. The speech is delivered at a trial for embezzlement so the public service of Ergocles is relevant to the charges—relevant.

Lys. 29.3—Ergocles chose Philocrates as his treasurer to help him embezzle public funds—explanation.

Lys. 29.7—Philocrates would not have volunteered to perform a trierarchy under Ergocles if he were his enemy. The mention of public service is directly relevant to the legal charge—relevant.

Lys. 30—The defendant Nicomachus is accused of abusing his powers when serving as *anagrapheus*. The defendant's public service is directly relevant to the legal charges—relevant.

Lys. 30.1—Some men who have appeared to be guilty have been acquitted by mentioning their ancestors' achievements and virtues. The speaker implies that this practice is dangerous.

Lys. 31.8–19—The speaker says that Philon's failure to join the democrats in overthrowing the Thirty disqualifies him at his *dokimasia*. At 27 he says that Philon will say that he violated no law by staying away from Athens. The speaker claims that Philon's failure to help the democracy is relevant to his case—relevant.

Lys. 32.5—When Diodotus was enrolled as a hoplite, he made a will and gave it to his family. Public service is mentioned to explain why he made out a will—explanation.

Lys. 32.24, 26—Diogeiton equipped a trireme with Alexis, the son of Aristodicus, but charged his wards for the money. The public service is mentioned to explain how Diogeiton illegally took money from his wards and is directly relevant to the legal charges—relevant.

Isocrates

Isoc. 17.4—The speaker says that when he was registered as a foreigner to pay the *eisphora*, he was given the largest contribution. He pleaded with the registrars because Pasion had his money. The speaker mentions the *eisphora* to show that his money was on deposit in Pasion's bank, which is directly relevant to the legal issue—wealth, relevant.

Isoc. 18.59–67—The speaker served as trierarch and returned with his ship to the Piraeus after the defeat at Aegospotamoi. The speaker is careful to say that he mentions his public service to show his good character (66) and not to gain what he does not deserve to have (67)—character.

Isoc. 19.36–7—This speech was delivered by a man from Siphnos before a court on Aegina. The speaker claims that Thrasyllus adopted him by will and is married to his sister. His opponent claims that he was not worthy to be adopted, but he cites the public service of his ancestors to show that he did deserve Thrasyllus' respect—explanation.

Isoc. 20—No mention of public service.

Isoc. 21—No mention of public service.

Isaeus

Is. 1—No mention of public service.

Is. 2.6—The speaker served with Iphicrates in Thrace. The public service is mentioned to explain how the speaker earned money after giving dowries to his sister—explanation.

Is. 2.42—The speaker served as gymnasiarch in the deme of his adoptive father. The public service is mentioned to defend his claim to his Menecles' estate—explanation.

Is. 3—No mention of public service.

Is. 4.27–31—Hagnon and Hagnotheus have been good citizens and obey the law. Their opponent Chariades has embezzled public funds. The speaker cites public service to show that Hagnon and Hagnotheus have good character and their claims are therefore more likely to be truthful. Their behavior is contrasted with that of Chariades who has been caught stealing, which shows that he has a tendency to take property belonging to others—character.

Is. 5.35–8—Dicaeogenes has no claim to pity for his misfortune or to favor because he has performed services. He undertook few public services and only under compulsion. He did not pay *eisphora*, and when he promised money in the Assembly, he did not pay it—character and goodwill.

Is. 5.40–42—The speaker's ancestors performed many public services. The speaker mentions this fact to show that the estate Dicaeogenes inherited was large and that his opponent has squandered it (43)—wealth.

Is. 5.46—Dicaeogenes never served in the war in which the Olynthians and islanders fought—explanation.

Is. 6.1—The speaker served with Chaerestratus in Sicily, and both were captured. The speaker mentions this to explain his relationship with Chaerestratus and his role as *synegoros* in the case—explanation.

Is. 6.5—Philoctemon was serving in the cavalry. The speaker mentions the fact to explain why Philoctemon made a will—explanation.

Is. 7.32—My opponents have allowed an estate to die out which was capable of supporting a trierarchy. Public service is mentioned to indicate the size of the estate—wealth.

Is. 7.35—I had acted honestly as a *thesmothete*. This fact is mentioned as one of several to show that the Apollodorus knew the speaker's good character when he adopted him, which indicated that he was of sound mind when he made his will—character.

Is. 7.37–41—Apollodorus performed services to the state. For this reason the court should honor his wishes—goodwill.

Is. 7.41–42—We have done public service and therefore you should help us to gain the property to which we are legally entitled—goodwill.

Is. 8—No mention of public service.

Is. 9—No mention of public service.

Is. 10—No mention of public service.

Is. 11.50—I allowed my son to be adopted into the family of Macartetus not with the intention of avoiding public services. This fact is mentioned to show that the adoption was not undertaken for dishonest reasons—character.

Aeschines

Aeschin. 1.56—Hegesander was treasurer for the general Timomachus in the Hellespont. Aeschines mentions this to explain where Hegesander got his money—explanation.

Aeschin. 1.107–13—Timarchus' public service is mentioned to show how he has been dishonest in public life. This is loosely relevant to the charge that Timarchus does not have the moral character to be a public speaker—character, relevant.

Aeschin. 2—Demosthenes has charged Aeschines with treason at his *euthynai*. Aeschines' public service is directly relevant to the legal charge—relevant.

Aeschin. 3—Aeschines indicts Ctesiphon's decree of praise for Demosthenes on the grounds that it contains a false statement, namely, that Demosthenes' words and actions have constantly benefited the state (49–50). Demosthenes' public service is thus directly relevant to one of the main charges in the case—

Demosthenes

D. 18—Demosthenes defends Ctesiphon against Aeschines' charge that he proposed an illegal decree. Because Aeschines charges that Ctesiphon's decree contains false statements about Demosthenes' political career, public service is directly relevant to the legal charge—relevant.

D. 19—Demosthenes charges that Aeschines committed treason as ambassador to Philip in 346. Aeschines' public service as ambassador is directly relevant to the legal charge—relevant.

D. 20—The speech was delivered in support of Apsephion's charge that the law of Leptines was inexpedient. Because the law concerned exemptions from liturgies, public service is directly relevant to the legal issue—relevant.

D. 21—Demosthenes charged Meidias with punching him while he was chorus producer at the Dionysia. Demosthenes' status as an official is relevant to the legal charge (1, 13–19). Demosthenes mentions Euctemon's charge of desertion as an example of Meidias' hostility (103). Toward the send of the speech, Demosthenes predicts that Meidias will discuss his public service during the *timesis* phase of the trial. Demosthenes shows that the public service of Meidias is not all that impressive (143–74)—relevant.

D. 22—The speech was delivered by Diodorus in support of Euctemon's charge that Androtion had passed an illegal decree of praise for the Council. The failure of the members of the Council to have triremes built is directly relevant to the legal issue (8–20). Diodorus also anticipates that Androtion will claim that the prosecution was motivated by anger about his collection of arrears of the *eisphora* and his supervision of the gods' treasures on the Acropolis (42–78). Androtion's public service here is relevant to his defense against the charges—relevant.

D. 23.110–186—The public service of Charidemus is mentioned because it is relevant to the decree granting him protection. The speaker argues that Charidemus has repeatedly acted against Athenian interests in Northern Greece—relevant.

D. 24—Diodorus charged Timocrates with passing an inexpedient law granting public debtors who have been sentenced to prison the right to name sureties (see 46, 64, 77, 79, 83, 87, 93, 103). Diodorus criticizes the public service of Androtion and Timocrates as a way of undermining their credibility (170–86)—character.

[D.] 25—Speech is a post-Classical forgery.

[D.] 26—Speech is a post-Classical forgery.

D. 27.7–9 (cf. 64)—Demosthenes' guardians made contributions (*eisphora*) of five hundred drachmas for each twenty-five minas to the symmory. Demosthenes mentions these financial contributions to prove the value of his father's estate and to show how much his guardians embezzled, which is directly relevant to the legal charge—character, relevant, and wealth.

D. 27.14—Aphobus sailed to Corcyra as a trierarch and gave Therippides a receipt for the sums he had received. Aphobus' public service is mentioned to explain why he gave Therippides the receipt—explanation.

D. 27.64—The estates of orphans have been leased and as a result increased so much in value that they were eligible for liturgies. Demothenes' mentions liturgies here to show how his father's estate lost money through his guardians' mismanagement—wealth.

D. 27.66—The city is asking him to pay *eisphora*. Demosthenes mentions this to describe the difficult position he finds himself in as a result of his guardians' embezzlement—wealth.

D. 28.3—Demochares is a chorus producer and trierarch and performs liturgies. Demosthenes mentions his public service as part of his attempt to show that Gylon was not a public debtor, which is directly relevant to the legal charge—relevant.

D. 28.7–8—Demosthenes' guardians assessed his property for *eisphora*—wealth. See D. 27.7–9.

D. 28.17—Thrasylochus challenged me to an exchange of property. I declined the exchange, but the court ordered me to perform the liturgy. Demosthenes mentions the challenge to illustrate how his guardians are trying to steal his property, which is relevant to the legal charge—relevant.

D. 28.24—If I regain my property, I will willingly perform liturgies, but if Aphobus retains it, he will attempt to conceal it and avoid performing liturgies. This is a brief attempt to win the court's goodwill at the end of the speech—goodwill.

D. 29.24—Aphobus claims that Demosthenes' witnesses are lying, but one cannot say it was because of poverty because they perform liturgies. Public service is mentioned to demonstrate the wealth of the witnesses—wealth.

D. 29.60—Aphobus assessed Demosthenes' estate at a value high enough to qualify for paying the *eisphora* but gave me only twenty minas. Demosthenes uses the payment of *eisphora* to show the value of the estate and the amount of his guardians' theft—wealth.

D. 30—No mention of public service.

D. 31—No mention of public service.

D. 32—No mention of public service.

D. 33—No mention of public service.

D. 34.38–9—The speaker sold grain at a reduced price when there was a shortage. The public service is mentioned to show that the speaker has a good reputation, which he would not have jeopardized by bringing a malicious lawsuit against Phormio—character.

D. 35—No mention of public service.

D. 36.39–42—Apollodorus claims that he does not have much money because he has spent it on liturgies. The speaker denies that he has performed much public service, then argues that even if he did, this would be no reason to support his unjust claims against Phormio—public service not relevant to verdict.

D. 36.56–7—The speaker mentions Phormio's public service as evidence of his good character to show that he is not the sort of person who would harm Apollodorus and thus is unlikely to have committed the offense with which he is charged—character.

D. 37—No mention of public service.

D. 38.25–26—Nausimachus and Xenopeithes will mention their liturgies and argue that you should out of gratitude give them what they do not deserve. The speaker replies that gratitude should only be given to those who perform liturgies and do not bring false charges. In other words, public service by itself is not a reason to vote for a plaintiff—public service is not relevant to verdict.

D. 39.7–9—The plaintiff Mantitheus says that it will be difficult to assign public services if he and his half-brother share the same name. The point is directly relevant to the legal charge—relevant.

D. 39.16–17—Mantitheus asks the court to imagine what would have happened if Boeotus was charged with desertion and they shared the same name. The point is directly relevant to the legal charge—relevant.

D. 40.25—Mantitheus' mother was married to Cleomedon, whose father, Cleon, captured many Spartans at Pylos. Mantitheus recalls Cleon's victory in support of his argument that Cleomedon must have received a dowry, which would have been returned to his mother's brothers Menexenus and Bathyllus after Cleomedon's death and that her brothers would have given a dowry to Mantitheus' father. The argument is directly relevant to Mantitheus' claim to his mother's dowry—relevant.

D. 40.36–37—Boeotus charges that when Mantitheus was at Mytilene as a soldier he collected a debt owed to his father by the city. Mantitheus mentions that he spent money on mercenaries fighting for Athens. Military service is mentioned only to indicate the circumstances in which the debt was collected and to prove that he collected money from other sources, not from his father's debtors—relevant and explanation.

D. 41—No mention of public service.

D. 42—The case concerns an *antidosis* brought by the speaker who was a member of the Three Hundred. Public service is directly relevant to the main legal issue—relevant.

D. 43—No mention of public service.

D. 44.9—Archippus dies while trierarch at Methymna. Public service is mentioned only in regard to the circumstances of Archippus' death—explanation.

D. 45.66—Stephanus has never performed public duties and conceals his wealth to make profits. The failure to perform public service is mentioned to show Stephanus' greed, which led him to commit perjury—character.

D. 45.85—Apollodorus' father donated a thousand shields and served five times as trierarch. Apollodorus says that this does not place the judges in his debt. He only wishes to make them aware so that he does not receive unjust treatment—goodwill.

[D.] 46.20—Apollodorus was abroad on military service as a trierarch when Phormio married his mother. Public service is mentioned to explain Apollodorus' absence from Athens and why he did not try to prevent the marriage—explanation.

[D.] 47—The speaker is a trierarch who was ordered by the Council to recover naval equipment held by Theophemus. The speaker's public service is therefore directly relevant to the main legal issue in the case—relevant.

D. 48—No mention of public service.

[D.] 49.8—Timotheus was a general when he borrowed his first loan from Pasion. Timotheus' public service is mentioned as background to the loan—explanation.

[D.] 49.9—Timotheus is deposed and tried in the Assembly. Apollodorus mentions the trial to explain why his father did not ask for immediate repayment of the loan—explanation.

[D.] 49.11–14—Timotheus as general pledges his property as security to Boeotian trierarchs to pay their crews (cf. 48–54). Timotheus' public service is mentioned to explain the background to his second loan—explanation.

[D.] 50—The plaintiff Apollodorus brings an action against Polycles for not taking up his responsibilities as trierarch. Public service is directly relevant to the legal charge in the case—explanation.

D. 51—The case is about the award for a crown for performing the duties of a trierarch. Public service is directly relevant to the legal issue in the case—relevant.

[D.] 52.26—Apollodorus' father paid *eisphora*, performed liturgies, and made gifts to the city. His father's public service is adduced as evidence of his good character and to show that he would not have cheated Calippus—character.

[D.] 53.4–5—Nicostratus used to manage Apollodorus' affairs when I was abroad as trierarch. Public service is mentioned to explain why Apollodorus let Nicostratus manage his affairs—explanation.

D. 54.3–6—Ariston was on military service at Panacton when Ctesias and his friends first attacked him. Military service is mentioned in a description of the circumstances surrounding Ctesias' attack—explanation.

D. 54.44—Ariston says that he has much to say about public services, but they are not relevant. Even if he had performed no public services, he still should not have been mistreated—public service not relevant to verdict.

D. 55—No mention of public service.

D. 56—No mention of public service.

D. 57.8—Eubulides was a member of the Council. Euxitheus mentions his public service to explain how he controlled the procedure for reviewing deme register of citizens—explanation.

D. 57.25—The father of Euxitheus was selected by lot for offices and passed his *dokimasia*. Euxitheus mentions this to prove his father was a citizen, which is directly relevant to the legal issue—relevant.

D. 57.37–8—Euxitheus' maternal uncle Amytheon was killed during the campaign on Sicily. His cousin Ctesibius was killed serving under Thrasybulus at Abydos. Both facts are relevant to Euxitheus' attempt to prove his citizenship—relevant.

D. 57.42—The father of Euxitheus served under Thrasybulus. Euxitheus mentions this to explain why his mother had to work as a wet nurse—explanation.

D. 57.46–7 (cf. 62)—I was nominated to be a priest of Heracles and passed the *dokimasia* for the offices I held. This is directly relevant to Euxitheus' attempt to prove his citizenship—relevant.

D. 57.63–4—I collected debts while demarch of Halimous. Euxitheus mentions this to explain why there was a conspiracy against him—explanation.

[D.] 58.29—When he died, the brother of Theocrines held the office of *hieropoios*, which Theocrines illegally assumed. The accuser uses this as evidence of Theocrines' bad character—character.

[D.] 59.2—Pasion received Athenian citizenship for his services to the city. Pasion's public service is mentioned to explain how he obtained citizenship—explanation.

[D.] 59.3–4—Apollodorus was a member of the Council when he made a proposal to transfer the budget surplus to the Military Fund. This provides background for the narrative—explanation.

[D.] 59.72—Theogenes was Basileus when he married Neaera's daughter. This is background and explains why he divorced her—explanation.

Lycurgus

Against Leocrates—The speech was delivered in a case charging Leocrates with treason for deserting Athens and failing to protect Athenian territory. Military service is therefore relevant to the legal charge. The achievements of Athenian soldiers at Salamis (68–74) and Marathon (104) are used to contrast their bravery with his cowardice—relevant.

Lycurg. *Leocr.* 139–40—No one who has performed public service can ask the court to acquit a traitor as a favor to himself—public service does not affect the verdict.

Even though Lycurgus was one of the most powerful politicians in Athens at the time, he never mentions his own public service.

Hyperides

For Lycophron 16–18—Lycophron says that he has been crowned by the cavalry and his colleagues in office when he was Phylarch and commander on Lemnos for three years. He was also praised by the citizens of Hephaisteia. Lycophron cites his public service as evidence of good character—character.

Against Philippides—The speech is delivered in a prosecution of Philippides for proposing an illegal decree of praise for the *prytaneis*. The public service of the *prytaneis* is relevant to the charge—relevant.

Against Athenogenes—No mention of public service.

For Euxenippus—No mention of public service.

Against Demosthenes—Demosthenes' political activity is discussed, but there is no mention of his liturgies, payment of *eisphorai*, or his trierarchies—special type of speech. See 135–36.

Dinarchus

For the relevance of public service in these speeches see 000–00.

Din. 1.12–3—Demosthenes will say that he concluded the alliance with Thebes and brought the Greeks to Chaeronea.

Din. 1.16—Demosthenes will boast about his embassy to Chaeronea.

Din. 1.20–21—Demosthenes did not give the ten talents he received from the Great King to the Arcadians so that they would join the Greeks.

Din. 1.28—Demosthenes summoned the Macedonian embassy from Thebes and helped to conclude the Peace of Philocrates.

Din. 1.42—Demosthenes accepted bribes for changing the law about the trierarchy.

Din. 1.69—Even though he has ten talents, Demosthenes contributed only fifty drachmas for the last *eisphora*.

Din. 1.82–83—Demosthenes ran away at Chaeronea but went on a sacred embassy to Olympia.

Din. 1.96—Demosthenes has accomplished nothing during his public career.

Din. 2.8—Supporters of Aristogeiton will say that he should be spared because of his many public services.

Din. 2.10—Aristogeiton was selected by lot to be supervisor of the port but was rejected at his *dokimasia*.

Din. 2.13—Aristogeiton was one of the Prytaneis while a public debtor.

Din. 3.12—Philocles was cavalry commander and general over ten times, but now deserves punishment for betraying the city.

Din. 3.15—Philocles was rejected for the office of supervising the ephebes.

Din. 3.17—You convicted Timotheus for bribery despite his many public services.

APPENDIX 9

The Authenticity of the Speeches in the Demosthenic Corpus

The authenticity of several speeches in the demosthenic corpus remains a vexed issue. In this appendix, I give my own tentative views; I hope to return to this issue in the future, especially the authenticity of *Against Aristogeiton* I. For earlier scholarship on this issue see Schaefer (1858) and Blass (1887–98). For more recent views see McCabe (1981), Trevett (1992), and MacDowell (2009), and the works cited in those works. I have divided the speeches into four categories: (1) authentic speeches of Demosthenes; (2) speeches of Apollodorus, the son of Pasion; (3) speeches not written by Demosthenes but composed during the fourth century BCE; and (4) speeches composed after the Classical period. When referring to these speeches in this book, I use brackets [D.] only for the speeches that can be placed in categories 2–4 with some certainty.

D. 1–5 (authentic speeches of Demosthenes), [D.] 6 (contemporary speech, probably by Hegesippus), D. 8–10 (authentic speeches of Demosthenes), D. 11 (either an authentic speech of Demosthenes or a speech composed after the Classical period), [D.] 12 (either a genuine letter of Philip or a letter composed by Anaximenes), D. 13 (either an authentic speech of Demosthenes or a speech composed after the Classical period), D. 14–16 (authentic speeches of Demosthenes), [D.] 17 (either a speech not written by Demosthenes but composed during the fourth century BCE or a speech composed after the Classical period), D. 18–24 (authentic speeches of Demosthenes), [D.] 25–26 (speeches composed after the Classical period), D. 27–31 (authentic speeches of Demosthenes), D. 32–35 (either authentic speeches of Demosthenes or speeches not written by Demosthenes but composed during the fourth century BCE), D. 36–39 (authentic speeches of Demosthenes), D. 40 (either an authentic speech of Demosthenes or a speech not written by Demosthenes but composed during the fourth century BCE), D. 41–44 (authentic speeches of Demosthenes), D. 45 (either an authentic speech of Demosthenes or a speech of Apollodorus), [D.] 46–47 (either speeches of Apollodorus or speeches not written by Demosthenes but composed during the fourth century BCE), D. 48 (either an authentic speech of Demosthenes or a speech not written by Demosthenes but composed during the fourth century BCE), [D.] 49–50 (speeches of Apollodorus), D. 51 (an authentic speech of Demosthenes or a speech not written by Demosthenes but composed during the fourth century BCE), [D.] 52–3 (speeches of Apollodorus), D. 54–55 (authentic speeches of Demosthenes), D. 56 (either an authentic speech of Demosthenes or a speech not written by Demosthenes but composed during the fourth century BCE), D. 57 (authentic speech of Demosthenes), [D.] 58 (speech not written by Demosthenes but composed during the fourth century BCE), [D.] 59 (speech of Apollodorus), D. 60 (either an authentic speech of Demosthenes or a speech not written by Demosthenes but composed during the fourth century BCE).

Bibliography

The names of periodicals have been abbreviated according to the system followed in *L'Année philologique*.

Allen, D. (2000a). *The World of Prometheus: The Politics of Punishing in Democratic Athens*. Princeton.

Allen, D. S. (2000b). 'Changing the Authoritative Voice: Lycurgus' *Against Leocrates*.' *ClAnt* 19.1:5–33.

Amyx, D. (1958). 'The Attic Stelai: Part III.' *Hesperia* 27:163–310.

Andrewes, A. (1962). 'The Mytilene Debate: Thucydides 3.36–49.' *Phoenix* 16:64–85.

Andrewes, A. (1974a). 'The Arginousai Trial.' *Phoenix* 28:112–22.

Andrewes, A. (1974b). 'The Survival of Solon's *Axones*.' In Bradeen and MacGregor (1974): 21–8.

Andrewes, A. (1982). 'Notion and Kyzikos: The Sources Compared.' *JHS* 102:15–25.

Arnaoutoglou, I. N. (2003). *Thusias heneka kai synousias: Private Religious Associations in Hellenistic Athens*. Athens.

Badian, E. (1970). 'Police.' In *Oxford Classical Dictionary*, ed. N. G. L. Hammond, and H. H. Scullard. Oxford (1970): 851.

Badian, E. (1993). *From Plataea to Potidaea: Studies in the History and Historiography of the Pentekontaetia*. Baltimore.

Beauchet, L. (1897). *Histoire du droit privé de la république athénienne*. Paris.

Berent, M. (1996). 'Hobbes and the Greek Tongues.' *History of Political Thought* 17:36–59.

Berent, M. (2000). 'Anthropology and the Classics: War, Violence, and the Stateless Polis.' *CQ* 50:257–89.

Bertrand, J.-M. (2001). 'Platon et les lois sur la discipline militaire.' *Quaderni del dipartimento di filologia linguistica e tradizione classica* Augusto Rostagni 2001:9–27.

Bertrand, J.-M. (2002). 'À propos de la Rhetorique d'Aristote (I 1373b1–1374b23), analyse du processus judiciaire,' *Dike* 5, 161–85.

Bertrand, J.-M., ed. (2005). *La violence dans le mondes grec et romain*. Paris.

Bianchi, E. (2002). 'Ancora su Eschine 3.252.' *Dike* 5:83–94.

Bingham, T. (2010). *The Rule of Law*. London.

Biscardi, A. (1999). *Scritti di diritto Greco*. Milan.

Blackwell, C. W. (1999). *In the Absence of Alexander*. New York.

Blass, F. (1887–98). *Die attische Beredsamkeit*. Leipzig.

Bleckmann, B. (1998). *Athens Weg in die Niederlage: Die letzten Jahre des Peloponnesischen Kriegs*. Stuttgart and Leipzig.

Blundell, M. W. (1989). *Helping Friends and Harming Enemies*. Cambridge.

Bolmarcich, S. (2007). 'The Afterlife of a Treaty.' *CQ* 57:477–89.

Bonner, R. J., and G. Smith. (1930–38). *The Administration of Justice from Homer to Aristotle*. Chicago.

Bradeen, D. W., and M. F. MacGregor, eds. (1974). *ΦΟΡΟΣ: Tribute to Benjamin Dean Meritt*. Locust Valley, NY.

de Brauw, M. (2001–2). '"Listen to the Laws Themselves": Citation of Laws and Portrayal of Character in Attic Oratory.' *CJ* 97:161–76.

Brélaz, C., and P. Ducrey, eds. (2007). *Sécurité collective et ordre public dans les sociétés anciennes* (= *Entretiens de la Fondation Hardt Tome LIV*). Vandœuvres and Geneva.

Brenne, S. (2001). *Ostrakismos und Prominenz in Athen*. Vienna.

Bresson, A. (2000). *La cité marchande*. Paris and Bordeaux.

Broadbent, M. (1968). *Studies in Greek Genealogy*. Leiden.

Bruce, I. A. F. (1966). 'Athenian Embassies in the Early Fourth Century.' *Historia* 15:272–81.

Brüggenbrock, C. (2006). *Die Ehre in den Zeiten der Demokratie: Das Verhältnis von athenischer Polis und Ehre in klassischer Zeit*. Göttingen.

Brunschwig, J. (1996). 'Rule and Exception: On the Aristotelian Theory of Equity.' In Frede and Striker (1996): 115–55.

de Bruyn, O. (1995). *La compétence de l'Aréopage en matière de procès publics*. Stuttgart.

Buckland, W. W. (1908). *The Roman Law of Slavery*. Cambridge.

Buckland, W. W. (1963). *A Text-Book of Roman Law from Augustus to Justinian*. 3rd edition. Revised by P. Stein. Cambridge.

Bultrighini, U., ed. (2005). *Democrazia e antidemocrazia nel mondo greco: atti del Convegno internazionale di Studi Chieti, 9–11 aprile 2003*. Alessandria.

Burckhardt, L., and J. von Ungern-Sternberg, eds. (2000). *Grosse Prozesse im antiken Athen*. Munich.

Burnett, A. P. (1998). *Revenge in Attic and Later Tragedy*. Berkeley and Los Angeles.

Burtt, J. O. (1954). *Minor Attic Orators II: Lycurgus, Dinarchus, Demades, Hyperides*. Cambridge, MA.

Bushala, E. (1968). 'Torture of Non-Citizens in Homicide Investigations.' *GRBS* 9:61–68.

Cairns, D. L. (1996). '*Hybris*, Dishonour, and Thinking Big.' *JHS* 116:1–32.

Canevaro, M. (2010). 'The Naturalisation Decree for the Plataeans' (Ps.-D. 59.104), *GRBS* 50:337–69.

Canevaro, M. (forthcoming). 'The Sources for *Nomothesia* in Athenian Law.' *CQ*.

Canevaro, M., and E. M. Harris. (2012). 'The Documents in Andocides' *On the Mysteries*.' *CQ* 62.1:98–129.

Cantarella, E., ed. (2007). *Symposion 2005: Vorträge zur griechischen und hellenistischen Rechtsgeschichte*. Vienna.

Carawan, E. (1984). '*Akriton Apokteinein*: Execution Without Trial in Fourth-Century Athens.' *GRBS* 25:111–21.

Carawan, E. (1998). *Rhetoric and the Law of Draco*. Oxford.

Carawan, E., ed. (2007). *Oxford Readings in the Attic Orators*. Oxford.

Carey, C. (1989). *Lysias: Selected Speeches*. Cambridge.

Carey, C. (1992). *Apollodoros: Against Neaera [Demosthenes 59]*. Warminster.

Carey, C. 1995. 'Rape and Adultery in Athenian Law.' *CQ* 45:407–17.

Carey, C. (1996). '*Nomos* in Attic Rhetoric and Oratory.' *JHS* 116:33–46.

Carey, C. (1998). 'The Shape of Athenian Laws.' *CQ* 48:93–109.

Carey, C. (2000). *Aeschines*. Austin, TX.

Carey, C. (2004). 'Offence and Procedure in Athenian Law.' In Harris and Rubinstein (2004): 111–56.

Carey, C. (2007). 'Epideictic Oratory.' In Worthington (2007): 236–52.

Carey, C. et al. (2008). 'Fragments of Hypereides' *Against Diondas* from the Archimedes' Palimpsest.' *ZPE* 165:1–19.

Carey, C., and R. A. Reid. (1985). *Selected Private Speeches*. Cambridge.

Cartledge, P. (1999). Review of Nielsen (1997), Hansen (1997), and Hansen (1998). *Classical Review* 49:465–69.

Cartledge, P., P. Millett, and S. von Reden. (1998). *Kosmos. Essays in Order, Conflict and Community in Classical Athens*. Cambridge 1998.

Cartledge, P., P. Millett, and S. C. Todd. (1990). *Nomos: Essays in Athenian Law, Politics, and Society*. Cambridge.

Cavanaugh, M. B. (1996). *Eleusis and Athens. Documents in Finance, Religion and Politics in the Fifth Century* B.C. (= American Classical Studies 35). Atlanta.

Charles, J. F. (1938). *Statutes of Limitations at Athens*. Chicago.

Chiron, P. (2002). *Ps.-Aristote, Rhétorique à Alexandre*. Paris.

Christ, M. (1998a). *The Litigious Athenian*. Baltimore and London.

Christ, M. (1998b). 'Legal Self-Help on Private Property in Classical Athens.' *AJP* 119:521–45.

Christ, M. R. (2005). 'Response to Edward Harris.' In Wallace and Gagarin (2005): 143–46.

Clinton, K. (1980). 'A Law in the City Eleusinion Concerning the Mysteries.' *Hesperia* 49:258–88.

Clinton, K. (2005). *Eleusis: The Inscriptions on Stone*. Vol. 1A: *Text*. Athens.

Clinton, K. (2008). *Eleusis: The Inscriptions on Stone. Documents of the Sanctuary of the Two Goddesses and Public Documents of the Deme*. Vol. 2: *Commentary*. Athens.

Cohen, D. (1984). 'The Athenian Law of Adultery.' *RIDA* 31:147–65.

Cohen, D. (1991). *Law, Sexuality and Community: The Enforcement of Morals in Classical Athens*. Cambridge.

Cohen, D. (1995). *Law, Violence, and Community in Classical Athens*. Cambridge.

Cohen, D. (1997). 'Democracy and Individual Rights in Athens.' *ZRG* 114:27–44.

Connor, W. R. (1971). *The New Politicians of Fifth-Century Athens*. Princeton.

Connor, W. R. (1984). *Thucydides*. Princeton.

Cooper, C., ed. (2007). *The Politics of Orality (= Orality Ancient Greece and Literacy in Ancient Greece 6. Mnemosyne* Suppl. 280). Leiden.

Coss, P., ed. (2000). *The Moral World of the Law*. Cambridge.

Couvenhes, J.-C. (1999). 'La réponse athénienne à la violence territoriale.' *Cahiers du Centre Gustave Glotz* 10:189–207.

Couvenhes, J.-C. (2005). '*De disciplina graecorum*: les relations de violence entre les chefs militaires grecs et leurs soldats.' In Bertrand (2005): 431–54.

Couvenhes, J.-C. (2007). 'La fourniture d'armes aux citoyens athéniens du IVe au IIIe siècle avant J.-C.' In Sauzeau and von Compernolle (2007): 521–40.

Couvenhes, J.-C. (2012). 'L'introduction des archers scythes, esclaves publics, à Athènes; la date et l'agent d'un transfert culturel.' In Legras (2012): 99–118.

Crook, J. A. (1967). *Law and Life of Rome, 90 B.C.–A.D. 212*. Ithaca.

Daverio Rocchi, G. (1988). *Frontiera e confini nella Grecia antica*. Rome.

Davies, J. K. (1971). *Athenian Propertied Families, 600–300 BC*. Oxford.

Davies, J. K. (1981). *Wealth and the Power of Wealth in Classical Athens*. New York.

Davis, G. (2011). '*Axones* and *Kurbeis*: A New Answer to an Old Problem.' *Historia* 60:1–35.

Debnar, P. (2001). *Speaking the Same Language*. Michigan.

Develin, R. (1989). *Athenian Officials 684–321 B.C.* Cambridge.

Dicey, A. (1885). *An Introduction to the Study of the Law of the Constitution*. London.

Dillon, M. (2006). 'Was Cleisthenes or Pleisthenes Archon at Athens in 525 *BC*?' *ZPE* 155:91–107.

Dorjahn, A. P. (1928). 'Legal Precedent in Athenian Courts.' *Philological Quarterly* 7:375–89.

Dorjahn, A. P. (1935). 'Anticipation of Arguments in Athenian Courts,' *TAPA* 65: 274–95.

Dover, K. J. (1974). *Greek Popular Morality*. Oxford.

Dreher, M. (1994). 'Diskussionsbeitrag zum Referat von Douglas MacDowell.' In Thür (1994): 165–68.

Drerup, E. (1898). 'Über die bei den attischen Rednern eingelegten Urkunden.' *Jahrbuch für classische Philologie* Supplementband 24:221–366.

Dworkin, R. (1986). *Law's Empire*. Cambridge, MA.

Eder, W., ed. (1995). *Die Demokratie im 4. Jahrhundert v. Chr.: Vollendung oder Verfall einer Verfassungsform?* Stuttgart.

Edwards, M. (1995). *Greek Orators IV: Andocides*. Warminster.

Ehrenberg, V. (1962). *The People of Aristophanes: A Sociology of Old Comedy*. New York.

Ellis, W. M. (1989). *Alcibiades*. London.

Engels, J. (1993). *Studien zur politischen Biographie des Hypereides: Athen in der Epoche der lykurgische Reformen und des makedonischen Universalreiches*. Munich.

Engels, J. (2008). *Lykurg: Rede gegen Leokrates*. Darmstadt.

Faraguna, M. (1992). *Atene nell'età di Alessandro: problemi politici, economici, finanziari*. Rome.

Faraguna, M. (2006). 'Alcibiade, Cratero e gli archivi guidiziari ad Atene.' In Faraguna and Vedaldi Iasbez (2006): 197–207.

Faraguna, M. (2007). 'Risposta a Eva Jakab.' In Cantarella (2007): 123–30.

Faraguna, M., and V. Vedaldi Iasbez, eds. (2006). *Δύνασθαι διδάσκειν: Studi in onore di Filippo Cassola*. Trieste.

Feyel, C. (2009). *Dokimasia: la place et le rôle de l'examen préliminaire dans les institutions des cités grecques*. Nancy.

Finley, M. I. (1962). 'The Athenian Demagogues.' *Past and Present* 21:3–24.

Finley, M. I. (1973). *The Ancient Economy*. Berkeley and Los Angeles.

Finley, M. I. (1983). *Politics in the Ancient World*. Cambridge.

Fisher, N. R. E. (1992). *Hybris: A Study in the Values of Honour and Shame in Ancient Greece*. Warminster.

Fisher, N. R. E. (1998). 'Violence, Masculinity and the Law in Classical Athens.' In Foxhall and Salmon (1998): 68–97.

Fisher, N. R. E. (2001). *Aeschines: Against Timarchos*. Oxford.

Fisher, N. R. E. (2003). '"Let Envy Be Absent": Envy, Liturgies, and Reciprocity in Athens.' In Konstan and Rutter (2003): 181–215.

Fisher, N. R. E., and H. van Wees, eds. (1998). *Archaic Greece: New Approaches and New Evidence*. London.

Flensted-Jensen, P., T. H. Nielsen, and L. Rubinstein, eds. (2000). *Polis and Politics: Studies in Ancient Greek History*. Copenhagen.

Fletcher, G. (1978). *Rethinking Criminal Law*. Boston and Toronto.

Forsdyke, S. (2008). 'Street Justice and Popular Justice in Ancient Greece: Shaming, Stoning, and Starving Offenders Inside and Outside the Courts.' *Past and Present* 201:3–50.

Foxhall, L., and A. D. E. Lewis, eds. (1996a). *Greek Law in Its Political Setting*. Oxford.

Foxhall, L. and Lewis, A. D. E., eds. (1996b). 'Introduction.' In Lewis and Foxhall (1996a): 1–8.

Foxhall, L., and J. Salmon, eds. (1998). *When Men Were Men: Masculinity, Power and Identity in Classical Antiquity*. London.

Fraenkel, M. (1878). 'Der attische Heliasteneid.' *Hermes* 13:452–66.

Frede, M., and G. Striker, eds. (1996). *Rationality in Greek Thought*. Oxford.

Fröhlich, P. (2004). *Les cités grecques et le contrôle des magistrats (IVe–I[e] siècle avant J.-C.)*. Geneva.

Frost, F. (1980). *Plutarch's Themistocles: A Historical Commentary*. Princeton.

Fuhrman, C. (2012). *Policing the Roman Empire*. New York and Oxford.

Fuller, L. L. (1964). *The Morality of Law*. New Haven.

Furley, W. D. (1996). *Andokides and the Herms: A Study of Crisis in Fifth-Century Religion*. London.

Gabrielsen, V. (1994). *Financing the Athenian Fleet: Public Taxation and Social Relations*. Baltimore and London.

Gadbery, L. (1992). 'The Sanctuary of the Twelve Gods in the Athenian Agora: A Revised View.' *Hesperia* 61:447–89.

Gagarin, M. (1978). 'Self-Defense in Athenian Homicide Law.' *GRBS* 19:111–20.

Gagarin, M. (1981). *Drakon and Early Athenian Homicide Law*. New Haven and London.

Gagarin, M. (1982). 'The Organization of the Gortyn Lawcode.' *GRBS* 23:129–46.

Gagarin, M. (1986). *Early Greek Law*. Berkeley and Los Angeles.

Gagarin, M. (1990). '*Bouleusis* in Athenian Homicide Law.' In Nenci and Thür (1990): 81–99.

Gagarin, M., ed. (1991). *Symposion 1990: Vorträge zur griechischen und hellenistischen Rechtsgeschichte*. Cologne, Weimar, and Vienna.

Gagarin, M. (1996). 'The Torture of Slaves in Athenian Law.' *CP* 91:1–18.

Gagarin, M. (1997). *Antiphon: The Speeches*. Cambridge.

Gagarin, M. (2008). *Writing Greek Law*. Cambridge.

Gagarin, M., and D. Cohen, eds. (2005). *The Cambridge Companion to Ancient Greek Law*. Cambridge.

Gagarin, M., and D. M. MacDowell. (1998). *Antiphon and Andocides*. Austin, TX.

Gauthier, P. (1972). *Symbola: Les étrangers et la justice dans les cités grecques*. Paris.

Gauthier, P. (1981). 'De Lysias à Aristote (*Ath. Pol.* 51.4): le commerce du grain à Athènes et les fonctions des sitophylaques.' *RHDFE* 59:5–28.

Gauthier, P., and M. B. Hatzopoulos. (1993). *La loi gymnasiarque de Beroia*. Athens.

Gentili, B., and F. Perusino, eds. (2002). *Le orse di Brauron: Un rituale di iniziazione femminile nel santuario di Artemide*. Pisa.

Georgiadis, C. (1987). 'Equitable and Equity in Aristotle.' In Panagiotou (1987): 159–72.

Ghiggia, P. C. (1995). *[Andocide] Contro Alcibiade. Introduzione, testo critico, traduzione e commento (= Studi e testi di storia antica* 4). Pisa.

Ghiggia, P. C. (1999). *Adozione ad Atene in epoca classica*. Alessandria.

Gomme, A. W. (1945–56). *A Historical Commentary on Thucydides* I–III. Oxford.

Gomme, A. W., A. Andrewes, and K. J. Dover. (1970). *A Historical Commentary on Thucydides IV: Books V 25–VII*. Oxford.

Graf, F. (2000). 'Der Mysterienprozess.' In Burckhardt and von Ungern-Sternberg (2000): 114–27.

Gwatkin, W. E. (1957). 'The Legal Arguments in Aeschines' *Against Ktesiphon* and Demosthenes' *On the Crown*.' *Hesperia* 26:129–41.

Habicht Chr. (1961). 'Falsche Urkunden zur Geschichte Athens im Zeitalter der Perserkriege.' *Hermes* 89:1–35.

Hall, E. M. (1989). 'The Archer Scene in Aristophanes' *Thesmophoriazusae*.' *Philologus* 133:38–54.

Hamel, D. (1998a). *Athenian Generals: Military Authority in the Classical Period*. (= *Mnemosyne* Suppl. 182). Leiden.

Hamel, D. (1998b). 'Coming to Terms with *lipotaxion*.' *GRBS* 39:361–405.

Hamilton, C. D. (1979). *Sparta's Bitter Victories*. Ithaca.

Hammond, N. G. L., and H. H. Scullard, eds. (1970). *The Oxford Classical Dictionary*. Oxford.

Hansen, M. H. (1975). *Eisangelia: The Sovereignty of the People's Court in Athens in the Fourth Century* B.C. *and the Impeachment of Generals and Politicians* (= *Odense University Classical Studies* 6). Odense.

Hansen, M. H. (1976a). *Apagoge, Endeixis, and Ephegesis against Kakourgoi, Atimoi, and Pheugontes* (= *Odense University Classical Studies* 8). Odense.

Hansen, M.H. (1976b). 'The Theoric Fund and the *graphe paranomon* Against Apollodoros.' *GRBS* 17:235–46.

Hansen, M. H. (1978). '*Nomos* and *Psephisma* in Fourth-Century Athens.' *GRBS* 19:315–30.

Hansen, M. H. (1979). 'Did the Athenian Assembly Legislate after 403/2 B.C.?' *GRBS* 20:27–53.

Hansen, M. H. (1980a). 'Seven Hundred *Archai* in Classical Athens.' *GRBS* 21:151–73.

Hansen, M. H. (1980b). '*Eisangelia*: A Reply.' *JHS* 100: 89–95.

Hansen, M. H. (1981–82). '*IG* ii^2 412. A Fragment of a Fourth-Century Athenian Law.' *Classica et Mediaevalia* 33:119–23.

Hansen, M. H. (1983). 'The Athenian Politicians, 403–322 B.C.' *GRBS* 24: 33–55.

Hansen, M. H. (1991). *The Athenian Democracy in the Age of Demosthenes*. Oxford.

Hansen, M. H., ed. (1997). *The Polis as an Urban Centre and as a Political Community* (= *Acts of the Copenhagen Polis Centre*). Copenhagen.

Hansen, M. H. (1998). *Polis and City-State. An Ancient Concept and its Modern Equivalent*. (= *Acts of the Copenhagen Polis Centre* vol. 5). Copenhagen.

Hansen, M. H. (2002). 'Was the *Polis* a State or a Stateless Society?' In Nielsen (2002): 17–48.

Hansen, M. H. (2009). 'A Note on Agyrrhios' Grain-Tax Law of 374/3.' In Mitchell and Rubinstein (2009): 145–54.

Hanson, V. D., ed. (1991). *Hoplites: The Classical Greek Battle Experience*. London and New York.

Harris, E. M. (1988). 'The Date of Aeschines' Birth.' *Classical Philology* 83:211–14.

Harris, E. M. (1989). 'Demosthenes' Speech Against Meidias.' *Harvard Studies in Classical Philology* 92:117–36.

Harris, E. M. (1990). 'Did the Athenians Regard Seduction as a Worse Crime than Rape?' *CQ* 40:370–77.

Harris, E. M. (1991). 'Response to Trevor Saunders.' In Gagarin (1991): 133–38.

Harris, E. M. (1992). Review of MacDowell (1990). *Classical Philology* 87:71–80.

Harris, E. M. (1994a). '"In the Act" or "Red-Handed"? *Furtum Manifestum* and *Apagoge* to the Eleven.' In *Symposion 1993: Vorträge zur griechischen und hellenistischen Rechtsgeschichte*, ed G. Thür. Cologne, Weimar, and Vienna (1994): 169–84.

Harris, E. M. (1994b). 'Law and Oratory.' In Worthington (1994): 130–50.

Harris, E. M. (1995). *Aeschines and Athenian Politics*. New York.

Harris, E. M. (1997). Review of de Bruyn (1995). *CR* 47.2:351–53.

Harris, E. M. (1999a). 'The Penalties for Frivolous Prosecution in Athenian Law.' *Dike* 2:123–42.

Harris, E. M. (1999b). 'Notes on the New Grain Tax Law.' *ZPE* 128:269–72.

Harris, E. M. (2000a). 'Open Texture in Athenian Law.' *Dike* 3:27–79.

Harris, E. M. (2000b). 'The Authenticity of Andocides' *De Pace*: A Subversive Essay.' In Flensted-Jensen, Nielsen, and Rubinstein (2000): 479–505.

Harris, E. M. (2004a). 'Le rôle de l'*epieikeia* dans les tribunaux athéniens.' *Revue historique de droit français et étranger* 82:1–13.

Harris, E. M. (2004b). 'More Thoughts on Open Texture in Athenian Law.' In Leão, Rosetti, and Fialho (2004): 241–63.

Harris, E. M. (2005a). 'Feuding or the Rule of Law? The Nature of Litigation in Classical Athens: An Essay in Legal Sociology.' In *Symposion 2001: Vorträge zur griechischen und hellenistischen Rechtsgeschichte*, ed. R. W. Wallace and M. Gagarin (2005): 125–41.

Harris, E. M. (2005b). Review of Yunis (2001). *CJ* 101.2:215–17.

Harris, E. M. (2005c). 'Was All Criticism of Athenian Democracy Anti-Democratic?' In Bultrighini (2005): 11–23.

Harris, E. M. (2006a). *Democracy and the Rule of Law in Classical Athens: Essays on Law, Society and Politics*. Cambridge and New York.

Harris, E. M. (2006b). 'The Rule of Law in Athenian Democracy: Reflections on the Judicial Oath.' *Dike* 9:157–81.

Harris, E. M. (2006c). 'Reply to Robert Wallace.' In Rupprecht (2006): 67–71.

Harris, E. M. (2007a). 'Did the Athenian Courts Attempt to Achieve Consistency? Oral Tradition and Written Records in the Athenian Administration of Justice.' In *The Politics of Orality*, ed. C. Cooper. Leiden (2007): 343–70.

Harris, E. M. (2007b). 'Who Enforced the Law in Classical Athens?' In Cantarella (2007): 159–76.

Harris, E. M. (2008). *Demosthenes: Speeches 20–22*. Austin, TX.

Harris, E. M. (2009/10a). 'What Are the Laws of Athens About? Substance and Procedure in Athenian Statutes.' *Dike* 12/13:5–67.

Harris, E. M. (2009/10b). Review of Lanni (2006). *Dike* 12/13:323–31.

Harris, E. M. (2010). 'Is Oedipus Guilty? Sophocles and Athenian Homicide Law.' In Harris, Leão, and Rhodes (2010): 122–46.

Harris, E. M. (2012). '*Hypotheca* in Roman Law and *ὑποθήκη* in Greek Law.' In Legras (2012): 433–41.

Harris, E. M (forthcoming a). 'How Strictly Did the Athenian Courts Apply the Law? The Role of *Epieikeia*.' *BICS*.

Harris, E. M. (forthcoming b). 'The Plaint in Athenian Law and Legal Procedure.' In *Legal Documents in Ancient Societies*, ed. M. Faraguna. Trieste.

Harris, E. M. (forthcoming c). 'How to Address the Athenian Assembly' *CQ*.

Harris, E. M., D. Leão, and P. J. Rhodes, eds. (2010). *Law and Drama in Ancient Greece*. London.

Harris, E. M., and L. Rubinstein. (2004). *The Law and the Courts in Ancient Greece*. London.

Harris, E. M., and G. Thür, eds. (2008). *Symposion 2007: Akten der Gesellschaft für griechische und hellenistische Rechtsgeschichte*. Vienna.

Harris, W. V. (1997). 'Lysias III and Athenian Beliefs about Revenge.' *CQ* 91:363–66.

Harrison, A. R. W. (1968). *The Law of Athens: Family and Property*. Oxford.

Harrison, A. R. W. (1971). *The Law of Athens: Procedure*. Oxford.

Hart, H. L. A. (1961). *The Concept of Law*. Oxford.

Harvey, D. (1990). 'The Sycophant and Sycophancy: Vexatious Redefinition?' In Cartledge, Millett, and Todd (1990): 103–21.

Haussoullier, B. (1884). *La vie municipale en Attique: Essai sur l'organisation des dèmes au quatrième siècle*. Paris.

Heath, M. (1990). 'Justice in Thucydides' Athenian Speeches.' *Historia* 39:385–400.

Herman, G. (1994). 'How Violent was Athenian Society?' In Osborne and Hornblower (1994): 99–117.

Herman, G. (1995). 'Honour, Revenge and the State in Fourth-Century Athens.' In Eder (1995): 43–66.

Herman, G. (2000). 'Athenian Beliefs about Revenge: Problems and Methods.' *PCPS* 46:7–27.

Herman, G. (2006). *Morality and Behaviour in Democratic Athens: A Social History*. Cambridge.

Hesk, J. (2000). *Deception and Democracy in Classical Athens*. Cambridge.

Heusler, A. (1911). *Das Strafrecht der Isländersagas*. Leipzig.

Hewitt, J. W. (1910). 'The Necessity of Ritual Purification after Justifiable Homicide.' *TAPA* 41:99–113.

Hillgruber, M. (1988). *Die zehnte Rede des Lysias: Einleitung, Text, und Kommentar mit einem Anhang über di Gesetzinterpretationen bei den attischen Rednern* (= *Untersuchungen zur antiken Literatur und Geschichte* 29). Berlin.

Hornblower, S. (1991). *A Commentary on Thucydides*. Vol. 1. Oxford.

Hornblower, S. (2008). *A Commentary on Thucydides*. Vol. III: *Books 5.25–8.109*. Oxford.

Humphreys, S. C. (2007). 'Social Relations on Stage: Witnesses in Classical Athens.' In Carawan (2007): 140–213.

Hunt, P. (2010). *War, Peace and Alliance in Demosthenes' Athens*. Cambridge.

Hunter, V. (1994). *Policing Athens: Social Control in the Attic Lawsuits, 420–320 B.C.* Princeton.

Hunter, V. (1997). 'The Prison of Athens: A Comparative Perspective.' *Phoenix* 51:296–326.

Hunter, V. (2000). 'Policing Public Debtors in Classical Athens.' *Phoenix* 54:21–38.

Hunter, V., and J. Edmondson, eds. (2000). *Law and Social Status in Classical Athens.* Oxford.

Ismard, P. (2010). *La cité des réseaux: Athènes et ses associations, VIer à Ier siècle avant J.-C.* Paris.

Jacob, O. (1979). *Les esclaves publics à Athènes.* New York.

Jakab, E. (2007). '*SEG* XLVIII 96: Steuergesetz oder Frachtvertrag?' In Cantarella (2007): 105–21.

Jameson, M. H. (1991). 'Sacrifice Before Battle.' In Hanson (1991): 197–227.

Johnstone, S. (1999). *Disputes and Democracy: The Consequences of Litigation in Ancient Athens.* Austin, TX.

Jones, J. W. (1956). *The Law and Legal Theory of the Greeks.* Oxford.

Kafka, F. (2008). *The Trial.* Translated with an introduction by J. Williams. Ware.

Kagan, D. (1974). *The Archidamian War.* Ithaca and London.

Kagan, D. (1987). *The Fall of the Athenian Empire.* Ithaca and London.

Kallet, L. (2001). *Money and the Corrosion of Power in Thucydides: The Sicilian Expedition and its Aftermath.* Berkeley.

Kallet-Marx, L. (1993). *Money, Expense, and Naval Power in Thucydides' History 1–5.24.* Berkeley.

Kapparis, K. A. (1999). *Apollodorus Against Neaera.* Berlin and New York.

Kästle, D. J. (2012). '*Νόμος μεγίστη βοήθεια*: Zue Gesetzargumentation in der attischen Gerichtsrede.' *ZRG* 129:161–205.

Katz, L. (1987). *Bad Acts and Guilty Minds.* Chicago.

Keen, A. G. (1995). 'A "Confused" Passage of Philochorus (F 149A) and the Peace of 392/1.' *Historia* 44:1–10.

Kennedy, G. (1959). 'Focusing of Arguments in Greek Deliberative Oratory.' *TAPA* 90:131–8.

Kerferd, G. B., ed. (1981). *The Sophists and their Legacy* (= *Hermes Einzelschriften* 44). Wiesbaden.

Klaffenbach, G. (1954). *Die Astynomeninschrift von Pergamon.* Berlin.

Knoepfler, D. (1993). 'Les *kryptoi* du stratège Epicharès à Rhamnonte et le début de la guerre de Chrémonidès.' *BCH* 118:327–341.

Konstan, D. (2000). 'Pity and the Law in Greek Theory and Practice.' *Dike* 4:125–45.

Konstan, D., and K. Rutter, eds. (2003). *Envy, Spite and Jealousy: The Rivalrous Emotions in Ancient Greece.* Edinburgh.

Kristensen, K. R. (2004). 'Codification, Tradition, and Innovation in the Law Code of Gortyn.' *Dike* 7:135–68.

Kron, J. G. (1996). *Landed and Commercial Wealth at Classical Athens 500–300 B.C.* Diss. Toronto.

Kurihara, A. (2003). 'Personal Enmity as a Motivation in Forensic Speeches.' *CQ* 53:464–77.

Lambert, S. (2005). 'Athenian State Law and Decrees, 352/51–332/1: II Religious Regulations.' *ZPE* 154:125–159.

Lanni, A. (2004). 'Arguing from Precedent: Modern Perspectives on Athenian Practice.' In Harris and Rubinstein (2004): 159–71.

Lanni, A. (2006). *Law and Justice in the Courts of Classical Athens.* New York and Cambridge.

Leão, D., D. Rossetti, and M. Fialho, eds. (2004). *Nomos—estudos sobre direito antigo.* Coimbra.

Legras, B. ed. (2012). *Transferts culturels et droits dans le monde grec et hellénistique.* Paris.

Lewis, D. M. (1959). 'Law on the Lesser Panathenaia.' *Hesperia* 28:239–47.

Lewis, D. M. (1990). 'Public Property in the City.' In Murray and Price (1990): 245–63.

Lewis, D. M. (1997). *Selected Papers in Greek and Near Eastern History.* Ed. P. J. Rhodes. Cambridge.

Liddel, H. G., and R. Scott. (1996). *A Greek-English Lexicon.* Oxford.

Liddel, P. (2003). 'The Places of Publication of Athenian State Decrees from the 5th Century BC to the 3rd Century AD,' *ZPE* 143:79–93.

Liddel, P. (2007). *Civic Obligation and Individual Liberties in Ancient Athens.* Oxford.

Lintott, A. (1982). *Violence, Civil Strife and Revolution in the Classical City: 750–330 B.C.* London and Canberra.

Lipsius, J. H. (1905–15). *Das attische Recht und Rechtsverfahren.* 3 vols. Leipzig.

Lisi, F. L., ed. (2001). *Plato's Laws and Its Historical Significance.* Sankt Augustin.

Lonis, R., ed. (1988a). *L'Étranger dans le monde grec. Actes du colloque organisé par l'Institut d'Études anciennes, Nancy mai 1987.* Nancy.

Lonis, R. (1988b). 'Extradition et prise de corps des refugiés politiques.' In Lonis (1988a): 69–88.

Loomis, W. T. (1972). 'The Nature of Premeditation in Athenian Homicide Law.' *JHS* 92:86–95.

Loomis, W. T. (1998). *Wages, Welfare Costs, and Inflation in Classical Athens.* Ann Arbor.

MacDowell, D. M. (1963). *Athenian Homicide Law in the Age of the Orators.* Manchester. Reprint 1999.

MacDowell, D. M. (1971). *Aristophanes: Wasps.* Oxford.

MacDowell, D. M. (1976). '*Hybris* in Athens.' *G&R* 23: 14–31.

MacDowell, D. M. (1978). *The Law in Classical Athens.* London.

MacDowell, D. M. (1990). *Demosthenes: Against Meidias.* Oxford.

MacDowell, D. M. (1991). 'The Athenian Procedure of *Phasis.*' In Gagarin (1991): 187–98.

MacDowell, D. M. (1994). 'The Case of the Rude Soldier (Lysias 9).' In Thür (1994): 153–64.

MacDowell, D. M. (1995). *Aristophanes and Athens*. Oxford.

MacDowell, D. M. (1997). 'Prosecution for Homicide.' *CR* 47:384–385.

MacDowell, D. M. (2000). *Demosthenes: On the False Embassy (Oration 19)*. Oxford.

MacDowell, D. M. (2005). 'The Athenian Procedure of *Dokimasia* of Orators.' In Wallace and Gagarin (2005): 79–87.

MacDowell, D. M. (2008). 'The Athenian Penalty of *Epobelia*.' In Harris and Thür (2008): 87–94.

MacDowell, D. M. (2009). *Demosthenes the Orator*. Oxford.

Macleod, C. (1977). 'Thucydides' Plataean Debate.' *GRBS* 18:227–246.

Macleod, C. (1978). 'Reason and Necessity: Thucydides III 9–14, 37–48.' *JHS* 98:64–78.

Macleod, C. (1983). *Collected Essays*. Oxford.

Maffi, A. (2008). 'Economia e diritto nell' Atene del IV secolo.' In Harris and Thür (2008): 203–22.

Maffi, A. (2009/10). 'Recensioni.' *Dike* 12/13:332–71.

Mann, C. (2007). *Die Demagogen und das Volk: Zur politisichen Kommunikation im Athen des 5. Jahrhunderts v. Chr.* Berlin.

Manville, P. B. (1994). 'Toward a New Paradigm of Athenian Citizenship.' In Boegehold and Scafuro (1994): 21–33.

March, J. G., and J. P. Olsen (1989). *Rediscovering Institutions: The Organizational Basis of Politics*. New York.

Mattingly, H. B. (1961). 'The Athenian Coinage Decree.' *Historia* 10:148–88.

McCabe, D. F. (1981). *The Prose-Rhythm of Demosthenes*. New York.

Meiggs, R. (1972). *The Athenian Empire*. Oxford.

Meiggs, R., and D. Lewis. (1969). *A Selection of Greek Historical Inscriptions*. Oxford.

Meinecke, J. (1971). 'Gesetzinterpretation und Gesetzanwendung im attischen Zivilprozess.' *RIDA*[3] 18:275–360.

Meyer-Laurin, H. (1965). *Gesetz und Billigkeit im attischen Prozess*. Weimar.

Migeotte, L. (1992). *Les souscriptions publiques dans les cités grecques*. Geneva and Quebec.

Migeotte, L. (2005). 'Les pouvoirs des agoranomes dans les cités grecques.' In Wallace and Gagarin (2005): 287–301.

Miles, J. C. (1950). 'The Attic Law of Intestate Succession (Demosthenes, *Contra Macart.* 51).' *Hermathena* 75:69–77.

Miller, F. D. (1995). *Nature, Justice and Rights in Aristotle's* Politics. Oxford.

Miller, W. I. (1990). *Bloodtaking and Peacemaking: Feud, Law, and Society in Saga Iceland*. Chicago.

Mirhady, D. (1990). 'Aristotle on the Rhetoric of Law,' *GRBS* 31 (1990): 393–410.

Mirhady, D. (2000). 'The Athenian Rationale for Torture.' In Hunter and Edmondson (2000): 53–74.

Mirhady, D. (2007). 'The Dikast's Oath and the Question of Fact.' In Sommerstein and Fletcher (2007): 48–59, 228–33.

Mitchell, L., and L. Rubinstein, eds. (2009). *Greek History and Epigraphy: Essays in Honour of P. J. Rhodes*. Swansea.

Moreno, A. (2007). *Feeding the Democracy: The Athenian Grain Supply in the Fifth and Fourth Centuries* B.C. Oxford.

Morrow, G. (1960). *Plato's Cretan City: A Historical Interpretation of the* Laws. Princeton.

Mossé, C. (1962). *La fin de la démocratie athénienne: aspects sociaux et politiques du déclin de la cité grecque au IVme siècle avant J.-C.* Paris.

Murray, O., and S. Price. (1990). *The Greek City from Homer to Alexander*. Oxford.

Naiden, F. S. (2004). 'Supplication and the Law.' In Harris and Rubinstein (2004): 71–91.

Naiden, F. S. (2006). *Ancient Supplication*. New York and Oxford.

Navarre, O. (1900). *La rhétorique grecque avant Aristote*. Paris.

Nenci, G., and G. Thür, eds. (1990). *Symposion 1988: Vorträge zur griechischen und hellenistischen Rechtsgeschichte*. Cologne and Vienna.

Nicholas, B. (1962). *An Introduction to Roman Law*. Oxford.

Nielsen, T. H., ed. (1997). *Yet More Studies in the Ancient Greek* Polis. (*Papers of the Copenhagen Polis Centre* 4 = *Historia* Einzelschriften 117). Stuttgart.

Nielsen, T. H., ed. (2002). *Even More Studies in the Ancient Greek* Polis. Stuttgart.

Ober, J. (1989). *Mass and Elite in Democratic Athens*. Princeton.

Ober, J. (1998). *Political Dissent in Democratic Athens: Intellectual Critics of Popular Rule*. Princeton.

Ober, J. (2000). 'Living Freely as a Slave of the Law. Notes on Why Sokrates Lives in Athens.' In Flensted-Jensen, Nielsen, and Rubinstein (2000): 541–552.

Ober, J., and C. Hedrick, eds. (1996). *Demokratia. A Conversation on Democracies, Ancient and Modern*. Princeton.

Oliver, J. H. (1935). 'Greek Inscriptions.' *Hesperia* 4:1–70.

Oliver, J. H. (1970). *Marcus Aurelius: Aspects of Civic and Cultural Policy in the East* (= *Hesperia* Suppl. 13). Princeton.

Olson, S. D. (2002). *Aristophanes Acharnians*. Oxford.

Osborne, R. (1985a). *Demos: The Discovery of Classical Attika*. Cambridge.

Osborne, R. (1985b). 'Law in Action in Classical Athens.' *JHS* 105:40–58.

Osborne, R. (1990). 'Vexatious Litigation in Classical Athens: Sykophancy and the Sykophant.' In Cartledge, Millett, and Todd (1990): 83–102.

Osborne, R. (2000). 'Religion, Imperial Politics, and the Offering of Freedom to Slaves.' In Hunter and Edmondson (2000): 75–92.

Osborne, R., and S. Hornblower, eds. (1994). *Ritual, Finance, Politics: Athenian Democratic Accounts Presented to David Lewis*. Oxford.

Ostwald, M. (1986). *From Popular Sovereignty to the Rule of Law: Law, Society and Politics in Fifth Century Athens*. Berkeley and Los Angeles.

Panagiotou, S. ed. (1987). *Justice, Law and Method in Plato and Aristotle*. Edmonton.

Paoli, U. E. (1933). *Studi sul processo attico*. Padua.

Parker, R. (1996). *Athenian Religion: A History*. Oxford.

Patterson, C. (2000). 'The Hospitality of Athenian Justice: The Metic in Court.' In Hunter and Edmondson (2000): 93–112.

Paulsen, T. (1999). *Die Parapresbeia-Reden des Demosthenes und Aischines. Die Parapresbeia-Reden des Demosthenes und des Aischines: Kommentar und Interpretationen zu Demosthenes, or. XIX, und Aischines, or. II* (= *Bochumer altertumwissenschaftliches Colloquium* 40). Trier.

Peçirka, J. (1966). *The Formula for the Grant of Enktesis in Attic Inscriptions*. Prague.

Pecorella Longo, C. (2004). 'Il condono della pena in Atene in età classica.' *Dike* 7:85–111.

Pelloso, C. (2008). 'Influenze greche nel regime Romano della hypotheca?' *Teoria et Storia del Diritto Privato* 1:1–106.

Pelloso, C. (2009/10). '"Astreintes" e regime probatorio nel processo gortinio: considerazioni in margine a *IC* IV 72 I, 15–35.' *Dike* 12/13:91–170.

Pelloso, C. (2012). 'Riflessioni intorno all'elemento soggettivo dell' omicidio doloso in diritto draconiano.' *Rivista di Diritto Ellenico* 2:183–252.

Pepe, L. (2009/10). 'Osservazioni sulla *pronoia* in tema di omicidio.' *Dike* 12/13:69–90.

Petrakos, B. Ch. (1999). *Ο δήμος του Ραμνούντος: σύνοψη των ανασκαφών και των ερευνών, 1813–1998*. Athens.

Phillips, D. D. (2007). '*Trauma ek pronoias* in Athenian Law.' *JHS* 127:74–105.

Phillips, D. D. (2008). *Avengers of Blood: Homicide in Athenian Law and Custom from Draco to Demosthenes*. Stuttgart.

Phillips, D. D. (2009). 'Hypereides 3 and the Athenian Law of Contracts.' *TAPA* 139:89–122.

Piérart, M. (2008). *Platon et la cité grecque: théorie et realité dans la constitution de Lois*. 2nd ed. Paris.

Posner, R. (1990). *The Problems of Jurisprudence*. Cambridge, MA.

Pringsheim, F. (1950). *The Greek Law of Sale*. Weimar.

Pritchett, W. K. (1991). *The Greek State at War*. Vol. 5. Berkeley and Los Angeles.

Rawls, J. (1971). *A Theory of Justice*. Cambridge, MA.

Raz, J. (1977). 'The Rule of Law and Its Virtue.' *The Law Quarterly Review* 93:195–211.

Reinmuth, O. (1971). *The Ephebic Inscriptions of the Fourth Century* B.C. (= *Mnemosyne* Suppl. 14). Leiden.

Rhodes, P. J. (1972). *The Athenian Boule*. Oxford.

Rhodes, P. J. (1979). 'Εἰσαγγελία in Athens.' *JHS* 99:103–14.

Rhodes, P. J. (1981). *A Commentary on the Aristotelian Athenaion Politeia*. Oxford.

Rhodes, P. J. (1984). '*Nomothesia* in Fourth-Century Athens.' *CQ* 35:55–60.

Rhodes, P. J. (1988). *Thucydides: History II*. Warminster.

Rhodes, P. J. (1994a). 'The Ostracism of Hyperbolus.' In Osborne and Hornblower (1994): 85–98.

Rhodes, P. J. (1994b). *Thucydides: History III*. Warminster.

Rhodes, P. J. (1995). 'Judicial Procedures in Fourth-Century Athens: Improvement or Simply Change?' In Eder (1995): 303–19.

Rhodes, P. J. (1998). 'Enmity in Fourth-Century Athens.' In Cartledge, Millett, and von Reden (1998): 144–161.

Rhodes, P. J. (2004). 'Keeping to the Point.' In Harris and Rubinstein (2004): 137–58.

Rhodes, P. J. (2008a). 'After the Three-Bar *Sigma* Controversy: the History of Athenian Imperialism Reassessed.' *CQ* 58:500–6.

Rhodes, P. J. (2008b). 'Response to David Whitehead.' In Harris and Thür (2008): 37–40.

Rhodes, P. J., and R. Osborne. (2003). *Greek Historical Inscriptions 404–323 BC*. Oxford.

Rickert, G. (1989). *HEKON and AKON in Early Greek Thought*. Atlanta.

Riess, W. (2007). 'Private Violence and State Control. The Prosecution of Homicide and Its Symbolic Meanings in Fourth-Century BC Athens.' In C. Brélaz and P. Ducrey (2007): 49–101.

Rizzo, R., and O. Vox. (1978). 'διαβολή.' *QS* 8:307–21.

Roberts, J. T. (1982). *Accountability in Athenian Government*. Madison, WI.

Roisman, J. (2005). *The Rhetoric of Manhood: Masculinity in the Attic Orators*. Berkeley and Los Angeles.

de Romilly, J. (1947). *Thucydide et l'impérialisme athénien: La pensée de l'historien et la genèse de l'oeuvre*. Paris.

de Romilly, J. (1979). *La douceur dans la pensée grecque*. Paris.

Rosenbloom, D. (2004). '*Ponêroi* vs. *Chrêstoi*: The Ostracism of Hyperbolos and the Struggle for Hegemony in Athens After the Death of Pericles.' *TAPA* 134:55–105, 323–58.

Rosivach, V. (1987). 'Execution by Stoning in Athens.' *ClAnt* 6:232–48.

Rosivach, V. (2010). 'The Oaths of the Athenians at the Ratification of Solon's Reforms.' *Phoenix* 64:223–37.

Rousset, D. (1994). 'Les frontières des cités grecques. Premières reflections à partir du recueil des documents épigraphiques.' *Cahiers du Centre Gustave Glotz* 5:97–126.

Rowe, G. O. (1995). 'The Charge Against Meidias.' *Hermes* 122:55–63.

Rowe, G. (2000). 'Anti-Isocratean Sentiments in Demosthenes' *Against Androtion*.' *Historia* 49:278–392.

Rubel, A. (2009). 'Die ökonomische und politische Bedeutung von Bosporos und Hellespont in der Antike.' *Historia* 58:336–55.

Rubinstein, L. (1993). *Adoption in IV Century Athens*. Copenhagen.

Rubinstein, L. (1998). 'The Athenian Perception of the *idiotes*.' In Cartledge, Millett, and von Reden (1998): 25–43.

Rubinstein, L. (2000). *Litigation and Cooperation: Supporting Speakers in the Courts of Classical Athens*. Stuttgart.

Rubinstein, L. (2003). 'Volunteer Prosecutors in the Greek World.' *Dike* 6:87–113.

Rubinstein, L. (2004). 'Stirring up Dicastic Anger.' In Cairns and Knox (2004): 187–203.

Rubinstein, L. (2005). 'Main Litigants and Witnesses in the Athenian Courts.' In Wallace and Gagarin (2005): 99–120.

Rubinstein, L. (2007). 'Arguments from Precedent in Attic Oratory.' In Carawan (2007): 359–71.

Rubinstein, L. (2009). 'Legal Argumentation in Hypereides' *Against Timandros.*' *BICS* 52:149–59.

Rubinstein, L. (2010). 'Praxis: the Enforcement of Penalties in the Greek Cities in the Late Classical and Early Hellenistic Periods.' In Thür (2010): 193–216.

Rudhardt, J. (1960). 'La définition du délit d'impiété.' *MH* 17:87–105.

Rupprecht, H.-A. ed. (2006). *Symposion 2003: Vorträge zur griechischen und hellenistischen Rechtsgeschichte.* Cologne and Vienna.

Ruschenbusch, E. (1957). 'ΔΙΚΑΣΤΗΡΙΟΝ ΠΑΝΤΩΝ ΚΥΡΙΟΝ.' *Historia* 6:257–74.

Ruschenbusch, E. (1966). *ΣΟΛΩΝΟΣ ΝΟΜΟΙ: Die Fragmente des Solonischen Gesetzeswerkes mit einer Text- und Überlieferungsgeschichte.* Wiesbaden.

Rusten, J. (1989). *Thucydides: The Peloponnesian War Book II.* Cambridge.

Salmond, J. W. (1913). *Jurisprudence.* 4th ed. London.

Samons, L. J. (2000). *Empire of the Owl: Athenian Imperial Finance.* Stuttgart.

Saunders, T. (1991a). *Plato's Penal Code: Tradition, Controversy, and Reform in Greek Penology.* Oxford.

Saunders, T. (1991b). 'Penal Law and Family Law in Plato's Magnesia.' In Gagarin (1991): 115–32.

Saunders, T. J. (2001). 'Epieikeia: Plato and the Controversial Virtue of the Greeks' in Lisi (2001): 65–93.

Sauzeau, P., and T. von Compernolle, eds. (2007). *Les armes dans l'Antiquité: De la technique à l'imaginaire.* Montpellier.

Scafuro, A. (1997). *The Forensic Stage: Settling Disputes in Graeco-Roman New Comedy.* Cambridge.

Scafuro, A. (2004). 'The Role of the Prosecutor and Athenian Legal Procedure.' *Dike* 7:113–33.

Schaefer, A. (1858). *Demosthenes und seine Zeit. Beilagen.* Leipzig.

Schaefer, A. (1885–87). *Demosthenes und seine Zeit.* 2nd ed. 3 vols. Leipzig.

Schläpfer, P. L. (1939). *Untersuchungen zu den attischen Staatsurkunden und denAmphiktionenbeschlüssen der demosthenischen Kranzrede.* Paderborn.

Schmitz, W. (2004). *Nachbarschaft und Dorfgemeinschaft im archaischen und klassischen Griechenland.* Berlin.

Schönhammer, M. (1995). *Coinage and Empire: The Athenian Standards Decree of the Fifth Century* B.C. Diss. City University of New York.

Schwenk, C. (1985). *Athens in the Age of Alexander the Great: The Dated Laws and Decrees of the Lykourgan Era, 338–322* BC. Chicago.

Sealey, B. R. I. (1960). 'Regionalism in Archaic Athens.' *Historia* 9:155–80.

Sealey, R. (1982). 'On the Athenian Conception of Law.' *CJ* 77:289–302.

Sealey, R. (1984). 'The *Tetralogies* Attributed to Antiphon.' *TAPA* 114:71–85.

Sealey, R. (1993). *Demosthenes and His Time. A Study in Defeat.* New York and Oxford.

Shear, T. L. (1978). *Kallias of Sphettos and the Revolt of Athens in 286 B.C.* (= *Hesperia* Suppl. 17). Princeton.

Shiner, R. A. (1987). 'Aristotle's Theory of Equity.' In Panagiotou (1987): 173–91.

Sickinger, J. P. (1999). *Public Records and Archives in Classical Athens.* Chapel Hill.

Sickinger, J. (2004). "The Laws of Athens: Publication, Preservation and Consultation," in Harris and Rubinstein (2004): 93–111.

Sickinger, J. P. (2008). 'Indeterminacy in Greek Law: Statutory Gaps and Conflicts.' In Harris and Thür (2008): 99–112.

Siewert, P., ed. (2002). *Ostrakismos-Testimonien* I. Stuttgart.

Sommerstein, A. H., and J. Fletcher, eds. (2007). *Horkos: The Oath in Greek Society.* Exeter.

Stadter, P. A. (1989). *A Commentary on Plutarch's* Pericles. Chapel Hill and London.

Stanley, P. V. (1976). *Ancient Greek Market Regulations and Controls.* Diss. Berkeley.

Steinwenter, A. (1925). *Die Streitbeendigung durch Urteil, Schiedsspruch, und Vergleich nach griechischem Recht.* Munich.

Sternberg, R. H. (2006). *Tragedy Offstage: Suffering and Sympathy in Ancient Athens.* Austin, TX.

Stevens, E. B. (1944). 'Some Attic Commonplaces of Pity.' *AJP* 65:1–25.

Stroud, R. S. (1968). *Drakon's Law on Homicide.* Berkeley and Los Angeles.

Stroud, R. S. (1974). 'An Athenian Law on Silver Coinage.' *Hesperia* 43:157–88.

Stroud, R. S. (1979). *The Axones and Kyrbeis of Drakon and Solon.* Berkeley.

Stroud, R. S. (1998). *The Athenian Grain-Tax Law of 374/3 B.C.* (= *Hesperia* Suppl. 29). Princeton.

Stumpf, G. (1988). 'Prozessrechtliches in der Mysterieninschrift SEG XXX 61.' *Tyche* 3:223–28.

Sullivan, J. (2002). 'Second Thoughts on Aeschines 3.252.' *G&R* 49.1: 1–7.

Talamanca, M. (2008). 'Risposta a Alberto Maffi.' In Harris and Thür (2008): 223–28.

Tchernetska, N., E. W. Handley, C. Austin, and L. Horváth. (2007). 'New Readings in the Fragment of Hyperides' *Against Tiimandros* from the Archimedes Palimpsest.' *ZPE* 162:1–4.

Themelis, P. (2002). 'Contribution to the Topography of the Sanctuary at Brauron.' In Gentili and Perusino (2002): 103–16.

Thompson, H. A. (1952). 'The Altar of Pity in the Athenian Agora.' *Hesperia* 21:47–82.

Thompson, W. E. (1976). *De Hagniae Hereditate: An Athenian Inheritance Case.* Leiden.

Thür, G. (1977). *Beweisführung vor die Schwurgerichtshofen Athens: Die Prosklesis zur Basanos.* Vienna.

Thür, G. (1991). 'The Jurisdiction of the Areopagus in Homicide Cases.' In Gagarin (1991): 53–72.

Thür, ed. (1994). *Symposion 1993: Vorträge zur griechischen und hellenistischen Rechtsgeschichte.* Vienna.

Thür, G. (2007). 'Das Prinzip der Fairness im attischen Prozess.' In Cantarella (2007): 131–50.

Thür, G. ed. (2010). *Symposion 2009: Akten der Gesellschaft für griechische und hellenistische Rechtsgeschichte*. Vienna.

Thür, G., and F. J. F. Nieto, eds. (2003). *Symposion 1999: Vorträge zur griechischen und hellenistischen Rechtsgeschichte*. Cologne and Vienna.

Todd, S. C. (1990). 'The Purpose of Evidence in Athenian Courts.' In Cartledge, Millett, and Todd (1990): 19–39.

Todd, S. C. (1993). *The Shape of Athenian Law*. Oxford.

Todd, S. C. (1996). 'Lysias Against Nikomachos: The Fate of the Expert in Athenian Law.' In Foxhall and Lewis (1996): 101–32.

Todd, S. C. (2000a). 'How to Execute People in Fourth-Century Athens.' In Edmondson and Hunter (2000): 31–51.

Todd, S. C. (2000b). 'The Language of Law in Classical Athens.' In Coss (2000): 17–36.

Todd, S. C. (2007). *A Commentary on Lysias, Speeches 1–11*. Oxford.

Todd, S. C. (2008). 'Response to Michael J. Edwards.' In Harris and Thür (2008): 55–62.

Todd, S. C., and P. C. Millett (1990). 'Law, Society, and Athens.' In Cartledge, Millett, and Todd (1990): 1–18.

Too, Y. L. (2008). *A Commentary on Isocrates'* Antidosis. Oxford.

Traill, J. S. (1975). *The Political Organization of Attica* (= *Hesperia* Suppl. 14). Princeton.

Trevett, J. (1991). 'The Date of [Demosthenes] 49: A Re-Examination.' *Phoenix* 45:21–27.

Trevett, J. (1992). *Apollodorus the Son of Pasion*. Oxford.

van Wees, H. (1998). 'Greeks Bearing Arms: The State, the Leisure Class, and the Display of Weapons in Archaic Greece.' In Fisher and van Wees (1998): 333–78.

Verdenius, W. J. (1981). 'Gorgias' Doctrine of Deception.' In Kerferd (1981): 116–28.

Vérilhac, A.-M., and C. Vial. (1998). *Le marriage grec: du VIe siècle av. J.-C. à l'époque d'Auguste*. Athens.

Vinogradoff, P. (1922). *The Outlines of Historical Jurisprudence*. Vol. II: *The Jurisprudence of the Greek City*. Oxford.

Walbank, M. B. (1982). 'The Confiscation and Sale by the *Poletai* in 402/1 B.C. of the Property of the Thirty Tyrants.' *Hesperia* 51:74–98.

Wallace, R. W. (1989). *The Areopagus Council, to 307 B.C.* Baltimore and London.

Wallace, R. W. (2000). '"Investigations and Reports" by the Areopagus Council and Demosthenes' Areopagus Decree.' In Flensted-Jensen, Nielsen, and Rubinstein (2000): 581–96.

Wallace, R. W. (2003). '*Phainein* Athenian Laws and Legal Procedures.' In Thür and Nieto (2003): 167–81.

Wallace, R. W. (2006). 'Withdrawing *Graphai* in Ancient Athens: A Case Study in "Sycophancy" and Legal Idiosyncrasies.' In Rupprecht (2006): 57–66.

Wallace, R. W. (2008). 'Response to Douglas MacDowell.' In Harris and Thür (2008): 95–98.

Wallace, R. W., and M. Gagarin (2005). *Symposion 2001: Akten der Gesellschaft für griechische und hellenistische Rechtsgeschichte*. Vienna.

Wallace-Hadrill, J. M. (1962). *The Long-Haired Kings*. London.

Wankel, H. (1976). *Rede für Ktesiphon über den Kranz*. Heidelberg.

Weber, M. (1972). *Wirtschaft und Gesellschaft*. Tübingen.

Weiss, E. (1923). *Griechisches Privatrecht auf rechtsvergleichender Grundlage*. Leipzig.

Wernicke, K. (1891). 'Die Polizeiwache auf der Burg von Athens.' *Hermes* 26:51–75.

Westlake, H. D. (1975). 'Paches.' *Phoenix* 29:107–16.

Whitehead, D. (1977). *The Ideology of the Athenian Metic* (= *Proceedings of the Cambridge Philological Society* Suppl. vol. 4). Cambridge.

Whitehead, D. (1986). *The Demes of Attica 508/7 to ca. 250 B.C: A Political and Social Study*. Princeton.

Whitehead, D. (2000). *Hypereides: The Forensic Speeches. Introduction, Translation and Commentary*. Oxford.

Whitehead, D. (2002). 'Athenian Laws and Lawsuits in the Late Fifth Century B.C.' *MH* 59:71–96.

Whitehead, D. (2006). 'Absentee Athenians: Lysias *Against Philon* and Lycurgus *Against Leocrates*,' *MH* 63:132–51.

Whitehead, D. (2008). 'Athenian Juries in Military *Graphai*.' In Harris and Thür (2008): 23–36.

Whitehead, D. (2009). 'Hypereides' *Timandros*: Observations and Suggestions.' *BICS* 52:135–48.

Wilamowitz-Moellendorf, U. von (1893). *Aristoteles und Athen*. 2 vols. Berlin.

Winnington-Ingram, R. P. (1965). 'TA ΔEONTA EIΠEIN: Cleon and Diodotus.' *BICS* 12:70–82.

Wohl, V. (2010). *Law's Kosmos*. Cambridge.

Wolf, E. (1956). *Griechisches Rechtsdenken*. III/2. Weimar.

Wolff, H.-J. (1963). 'Verjährung von Ansprüchen nach attischem Recht.' In *Eranion in Honorem G. S. Maridakis*. Vol 1. *Historia Iuris*. Athens: 87–109.

Wolff, H.-J. (1966). *Die attische Paragraphe*. Weimar.

Wolff, H.-J. (1968). *Demosthenes als Advokat*. Berlin.

Wood, E. M. (1996). 'Demos Versus "We the People": Freedom and Democracy Ancient and Modern.' In Ober and Hedrick (1996): 121–37.

Worthington, I. (1992). *A Historical Commentary on Dinarchus*. Ann Arbor.

Worthington, I. ed. (1994). *Persuasion: Greek Rhetoric in Action*. London and New York.

Worthington, I. ed. (2007). *A Companion to Greek Rhetoric*. Malden, MA.

Worthington, I., C. R. Cooper and E. M. Harris (2001). *Dinarchus, Hyperides, Lycurgus*. Austin, TX.

Wyse, W. (1904). *The Speeches of Isaeus*. Cambridge.

Yunis, H. (1996). *Taming Democracy: Models of Political Rhetoric in Classical Athens*. Ithaca and London.

Yunis, H. (2001). *Demosthenes: On the Crown*. Cambridge.

Yunis, H. (2005). 'The Rhetoric of Law in Fourth-Century Athens.' In Gagarin and Cohen (2005): 191–208.

Subject Index

Index Locorum

ANCIENT GREEK AUTHORS

Aeschines

This index was prepared by Vassia Psilakakou.

Athenaeus

Isaeus